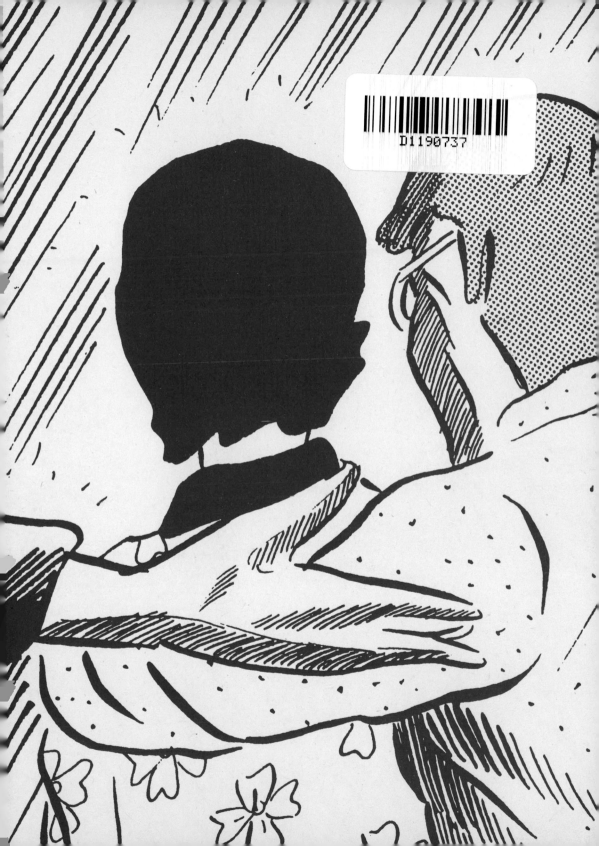

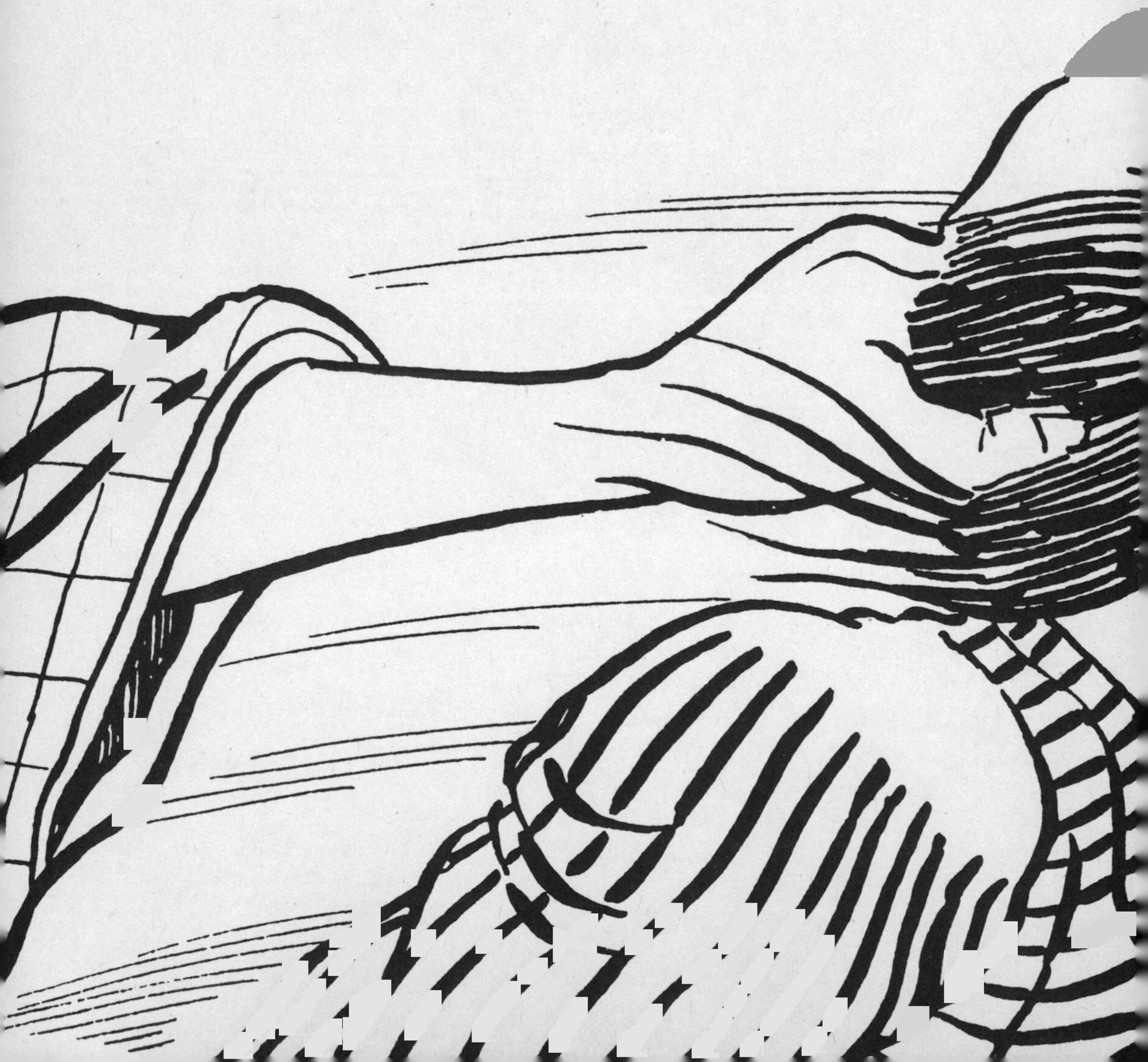

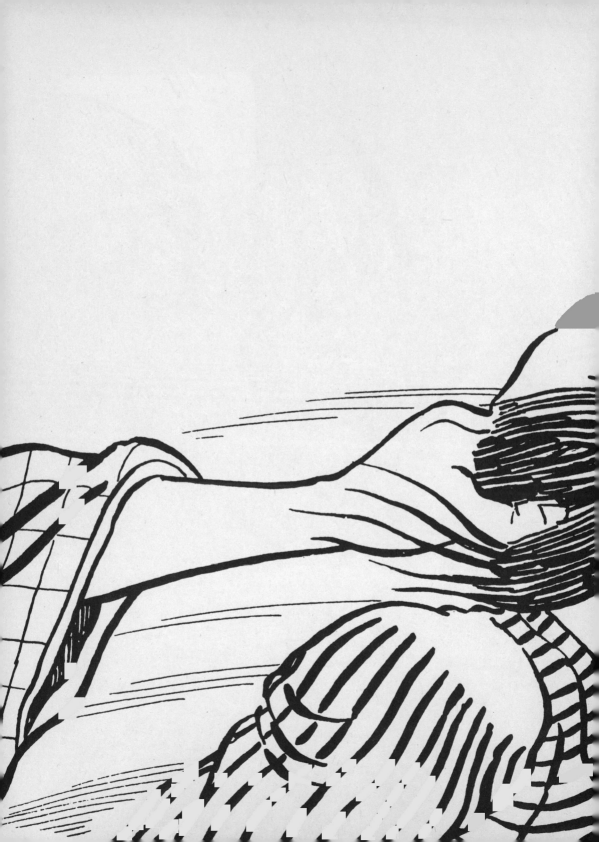

TRASH MARKET

TADAO TSUGE

EDITED & TRANSLATED BY
RYAN HOLMBERG

DRAWN & QUARTERLY

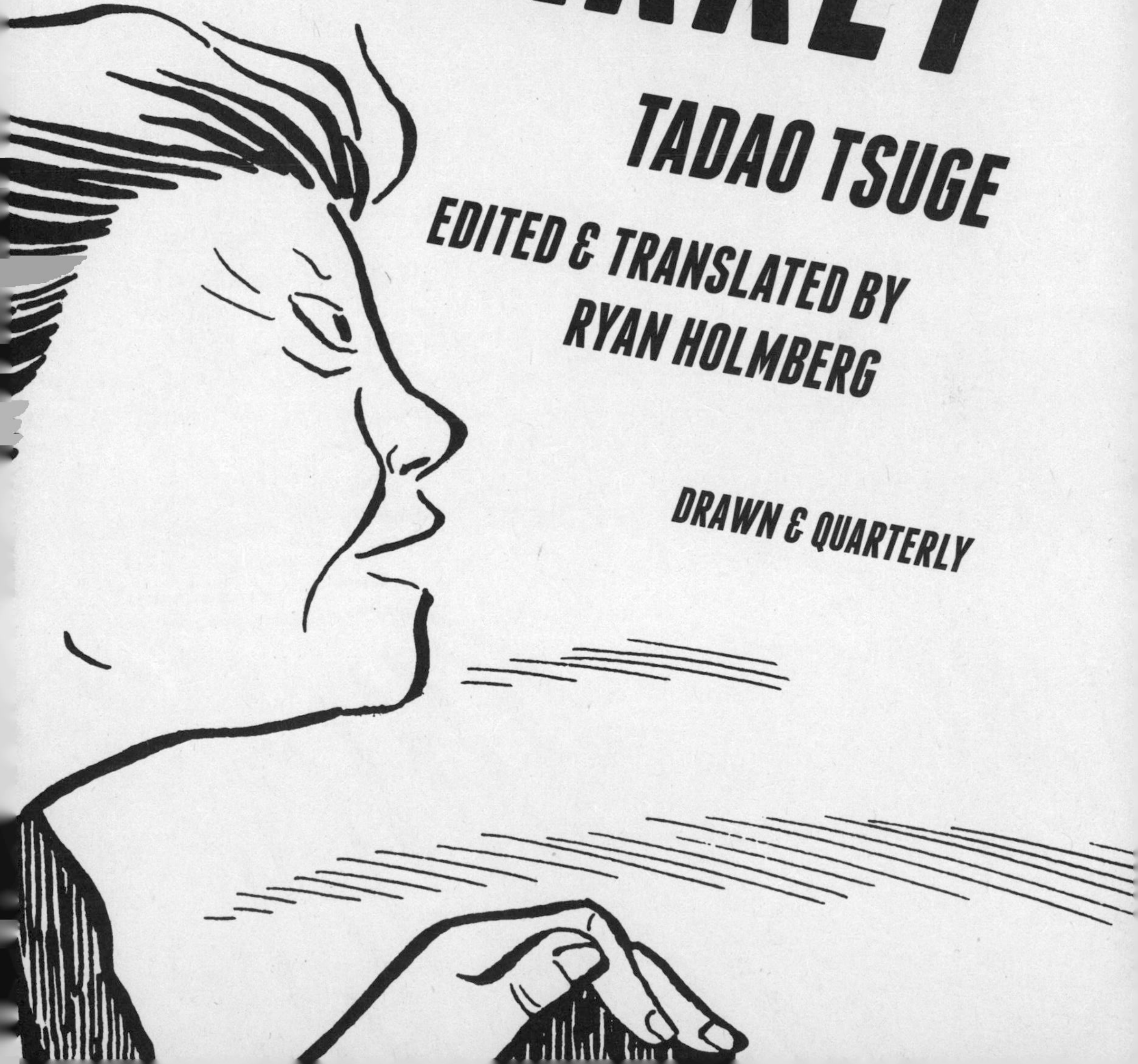

UP ON THE HILLTOP,
VINCENT VAN GOGH...

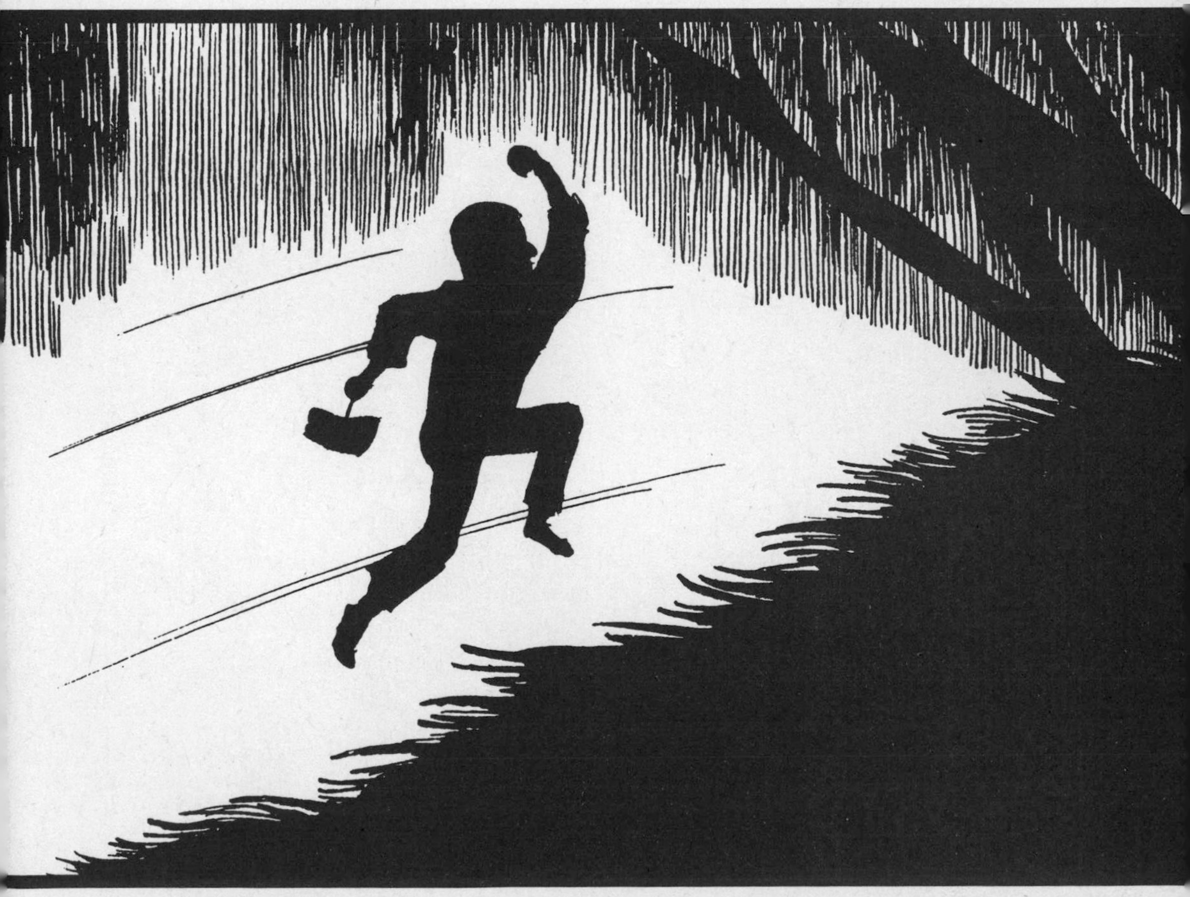

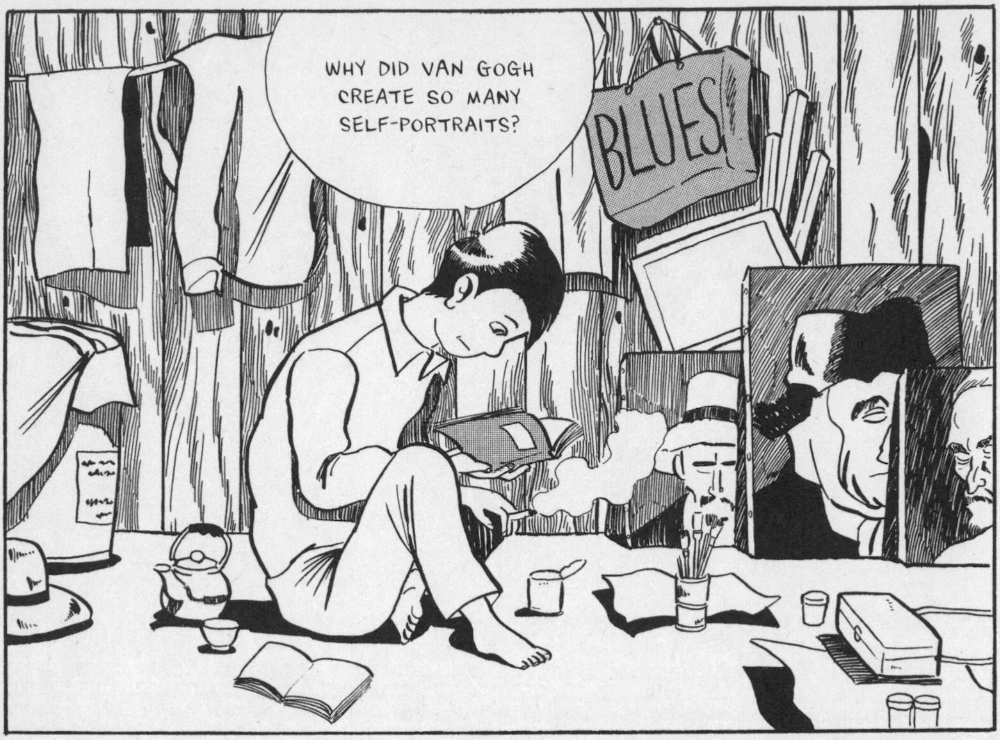
WHY DID VAN GOGH CREATE SO MANY SELF-PORTRAITS?
BLUES

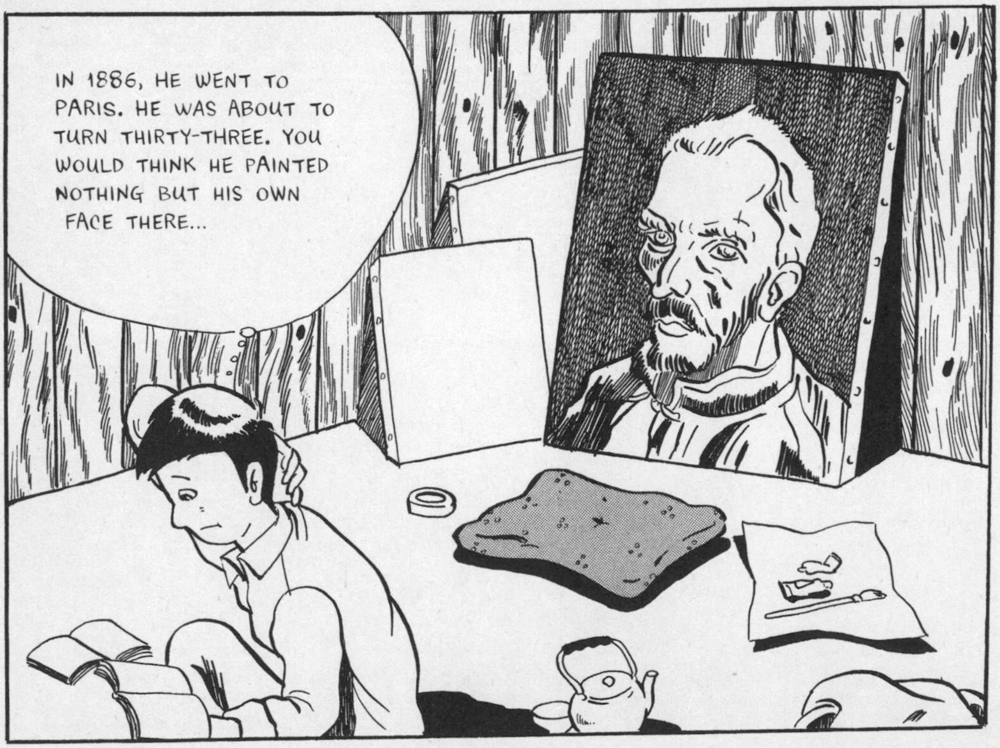
IN 1886, HE WENT TO PARIS. HE WAS ABOUT TO TURN THIRTY-THREE. YOU WOULD THINK HE PAINTED NOTHING BUT HIS OWN FACE THERE...

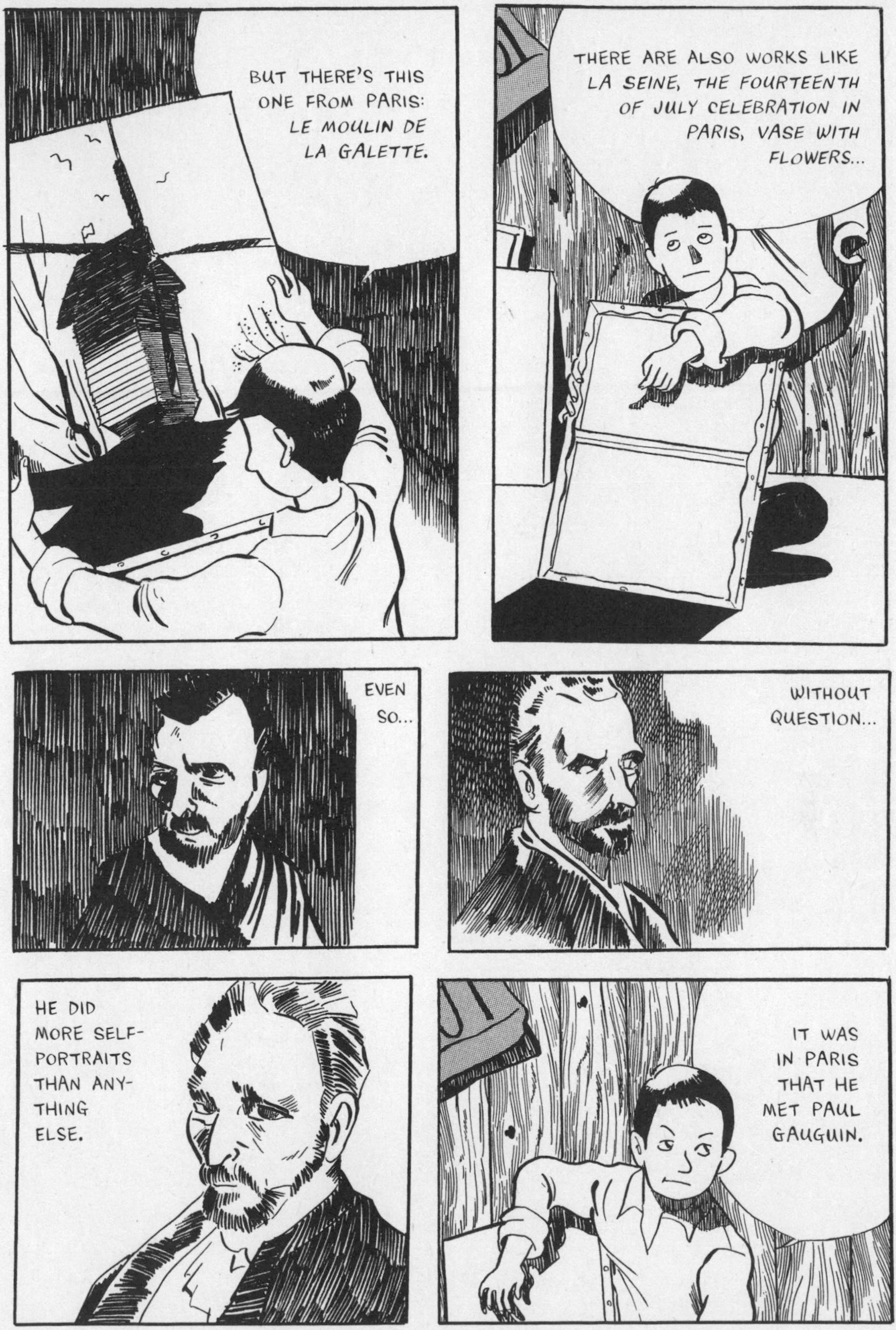
BUT THERE'S THIS ONE FROM PARIS: LE MOULIN DE LA GALETTE.
THERE ARE ALSO WORKS LIKE LA SEINE, THE FOURTEENTH OF JULY CELEBRATION IN PARIS, VASE WITH FLOWERS...
EVEN SO...
WITHOUT QUESTION...
HE DID MORE SELF-PORTRAITS THAN ANYTHING ELSE.
IT WAS IN PARIS THAT HE MET PAUL GAUGUIN.

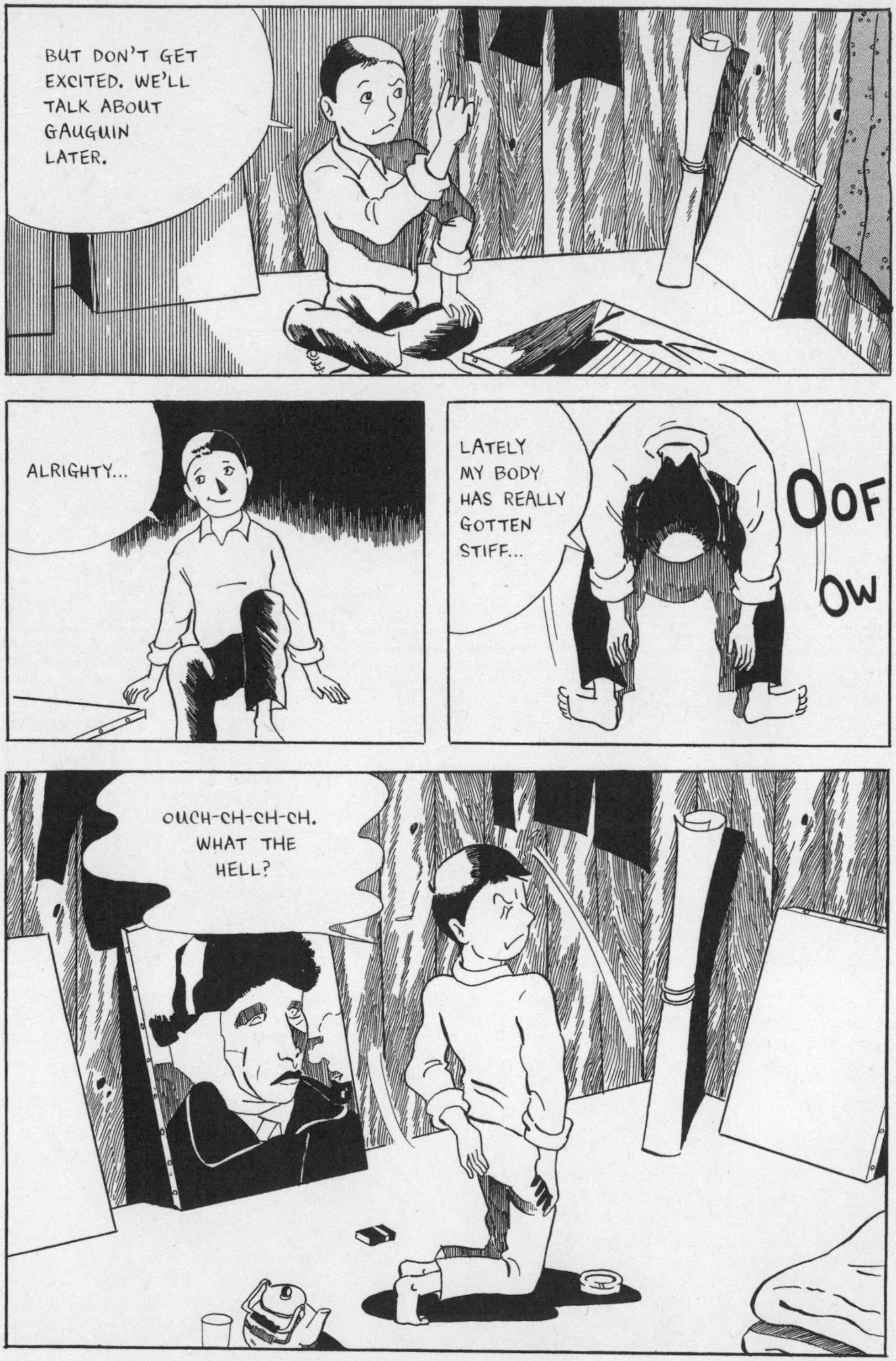
BUT DON'T GET EXCITED. WE'LL TALK ABOUT GAUGUIN LATER.
ALRIGHTY...
LATELY MY BODY HAS REALLY GOTTEN STIFF...
OOF
OW
OUCH-CH-CH-CH. WHAT THE HELL?

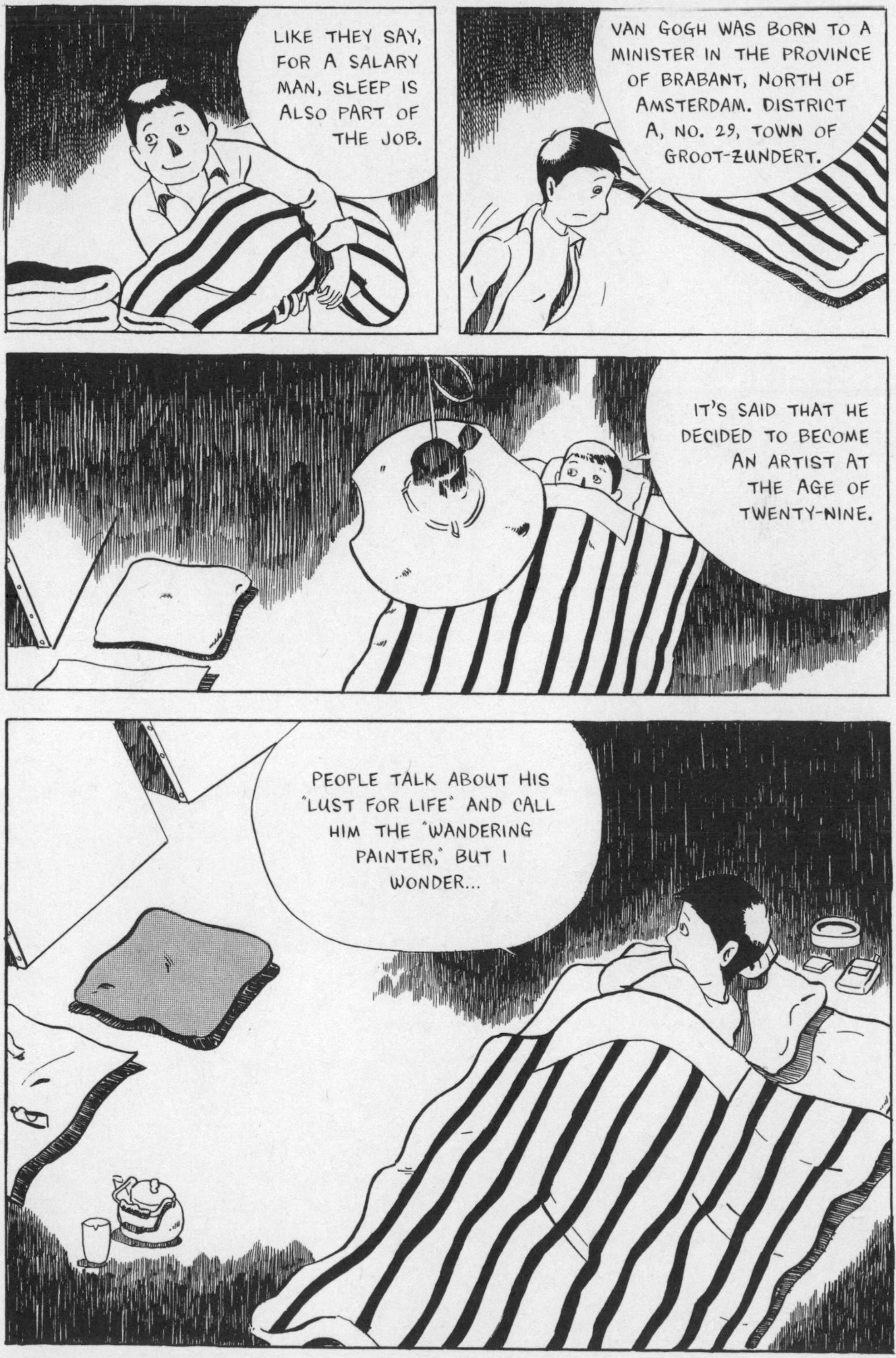
LIKE THEY SAY, FOR A SALARY MAN, SLEEP IS ALSO PART OF THE JOB.
VAN GOGH WAS BORN TO A MINISTER IN THE PROVINCE OF BRABANT, NORTH OF AMSTERDAM. DISTRICT A, NO. 29, TOWN OF GROOT-ZUNDERT.
IT'S SAID THAT HE DECIDED TO BECOME AN ARTIST AT THE AGE OF TWENTY-NINE.
PEOPLE TALK ABOUT HIS "LUST FOR LIFE" AND CALL HIM THE "WANDERING PAINTER," BUT I WONDER...

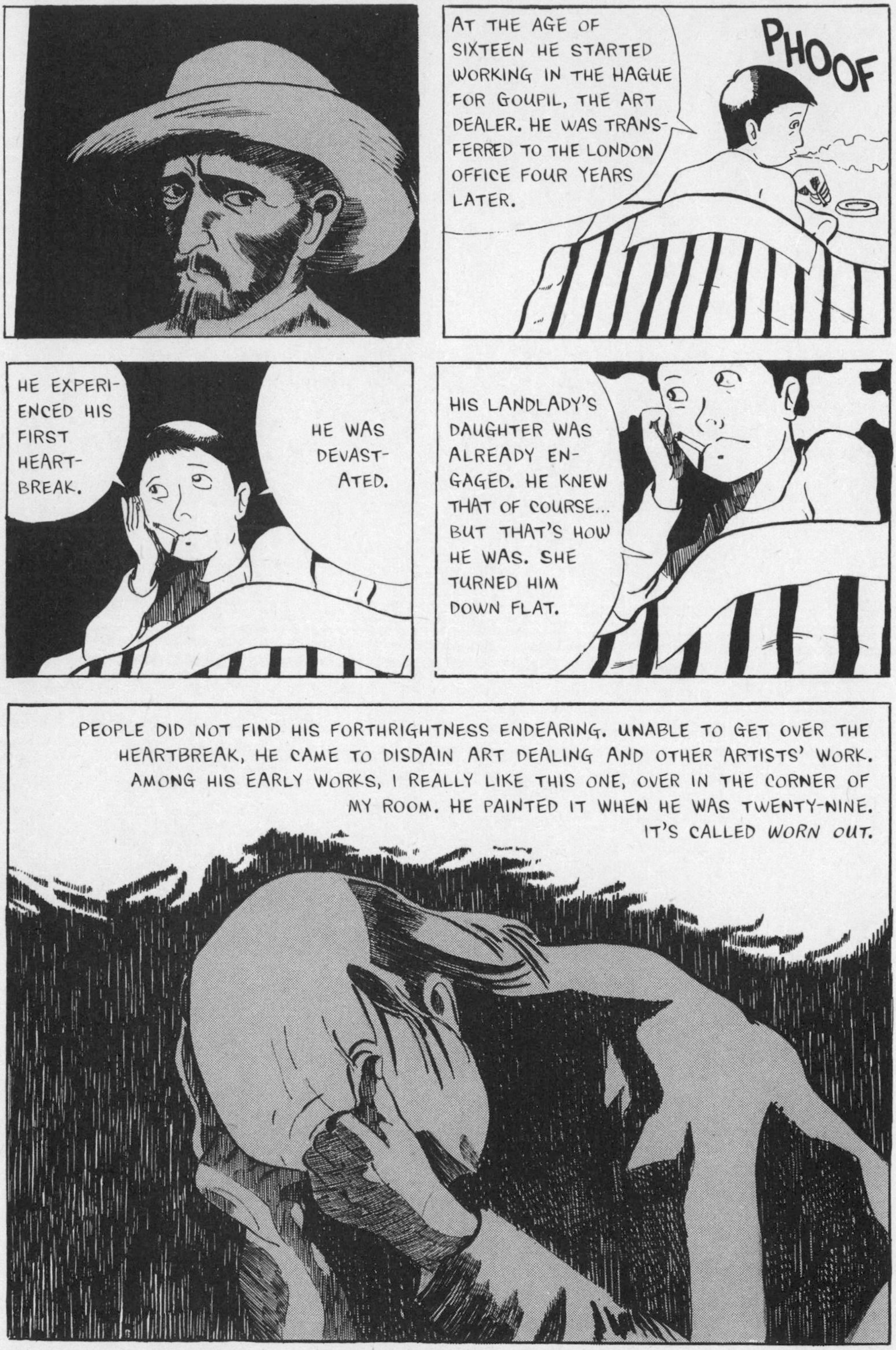
AT THE AGE OF SIXTEEN HE STARTED WORKING IN THE HAGUE FOR GOUPIL, THE ART DEALER. HE WAS TRANSFERRED TO THE LONDON OFFICE FOUR YEARS LATER.
PHOOF
HE EXPERIENCED HIS FIRST HEARTBREAK.
HE WAS DEVASTATED.
HIS LANDLADY'S DAUGHTER WAS ALREADY ENGAGED. HE KNEW THAT OF COURSE... BUT THAT'S HOW HE WAS. SHE TURNED HIM DOWN FLAT.
PEOPLE DID NOT FIND HIS FORTHRIGHTNESS ENDEARING. UNABLE TO GET OVER THE HEARTBREAK, HE CAME TO DISDAIN ART DEALING AND OTHER ARTISTS' WORK. AMONG HIS EARLY WORKS, I REALLY LIKE THIS ONE, OVER IN THE CORNER OF MY ROOM. HE PAINTED IT WHEN HE WAS TWENTY-NINE. IT'S CALLED *WORN OUT*.

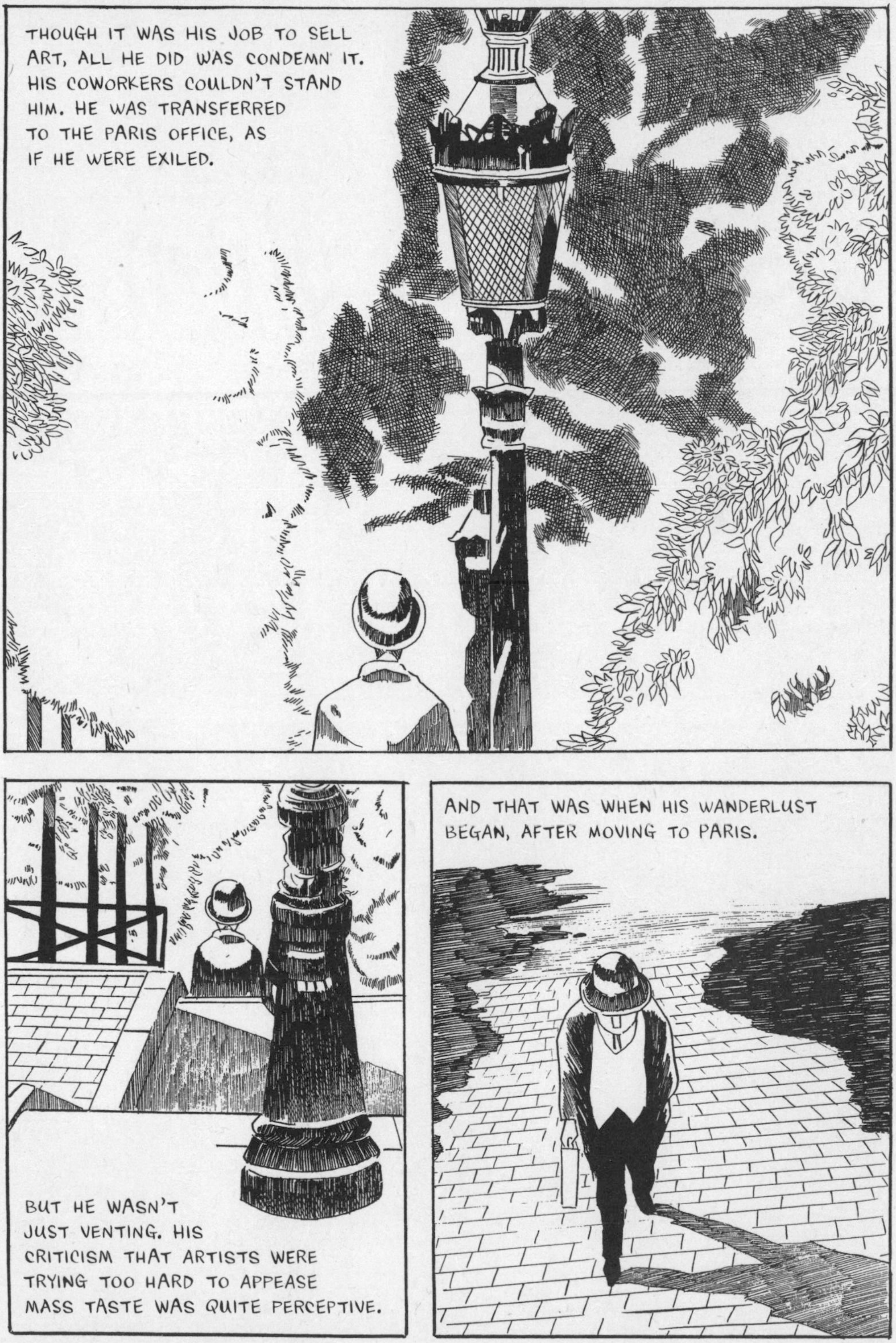
THOUGH IT WAS HIS JOB TO SELL ART, ALL HE DID WAS CONDEMN IT. HIS COWORKERS COULDN'T STAND HIM. HE WAS TRANSFERRED TO THE PARIS OFFICE, AS IF HE WERE EXILED.
BUT HE WASN'T JUST VENTING. HIS CRITICISM THAT ARTISTS WERE TRYING TOO HARD TO APPEASE MASS TASTE WAS QUITE PERCEPTIVE.
AND THAT WAS WHEN HIS WANDERLUST BEGAN, AFTER MOVING TO PARIS.

AT TWENTY-THREE, HE LOST HIS JOB. SO WHAT THEN? WELL...HE STARTED TEACHING FRENCH.

HE CHANGED JOBS FIVE TIMES BEFORE REACHING TWENTY-FIVE.

A MINISTER...

A BOOKSELLER.

THEN AGAIN A MINISTER.

HE ENROLLED IN A SHORT-TERM MISSIONARY COURSE IN BRUSSELS. THREE MONTHS LATER, HE WAS SENT TO A COAL-MINING TOWN IN BELGIUM. HE LIVED THE CHRISTIAN LIFE TO THE LETTER—DRESSED IN RAGS, SLEEPING ON THE GROUND, WITH NOTHING BUT BREAD AND WATER. BUT OTHER CLERGY THOUGHT IT UNSIGHTLY, SO HE WAS REMOVED FROM HIS POSITION.

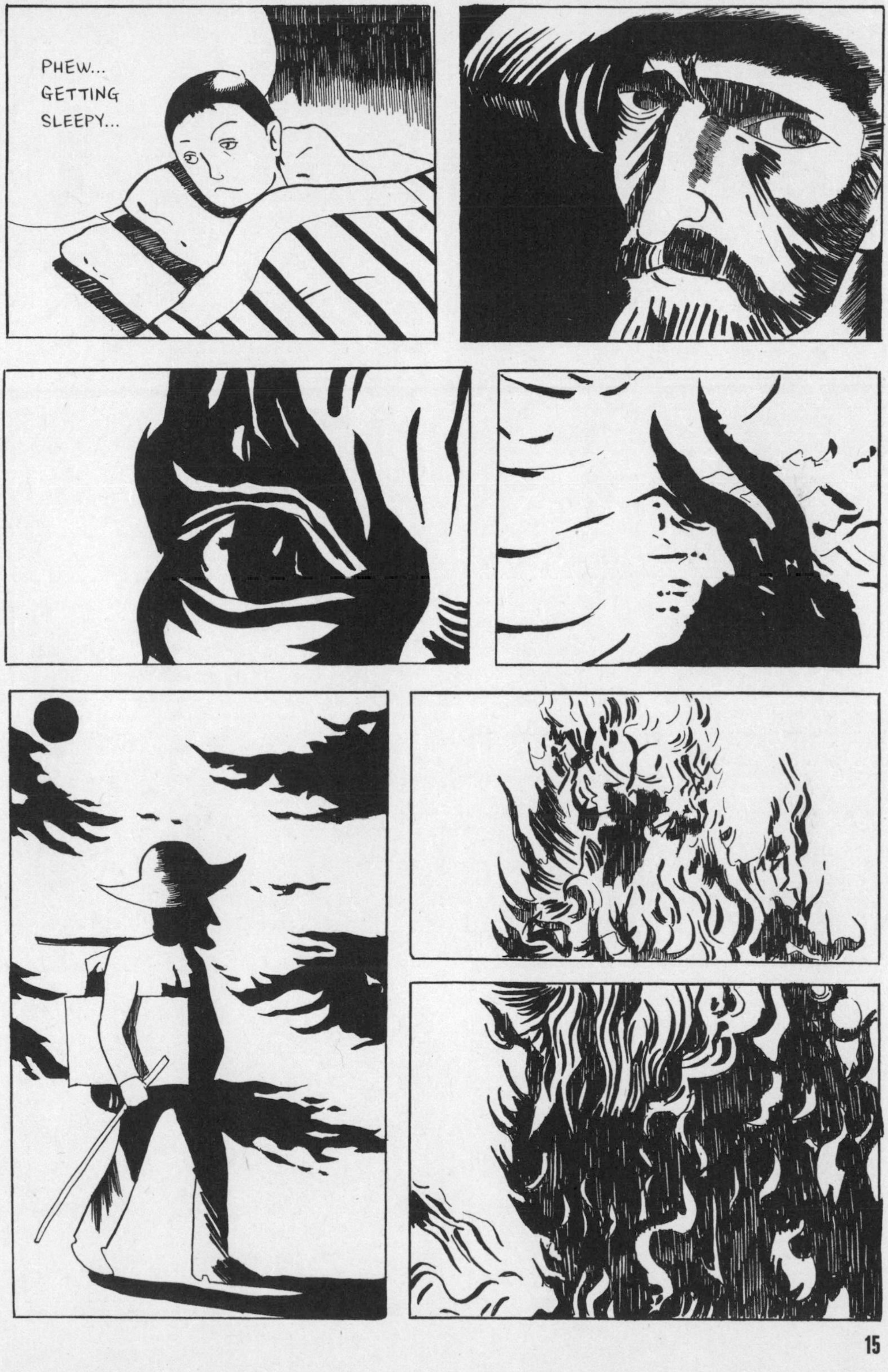
PHEW... GETTING SLEEPY...

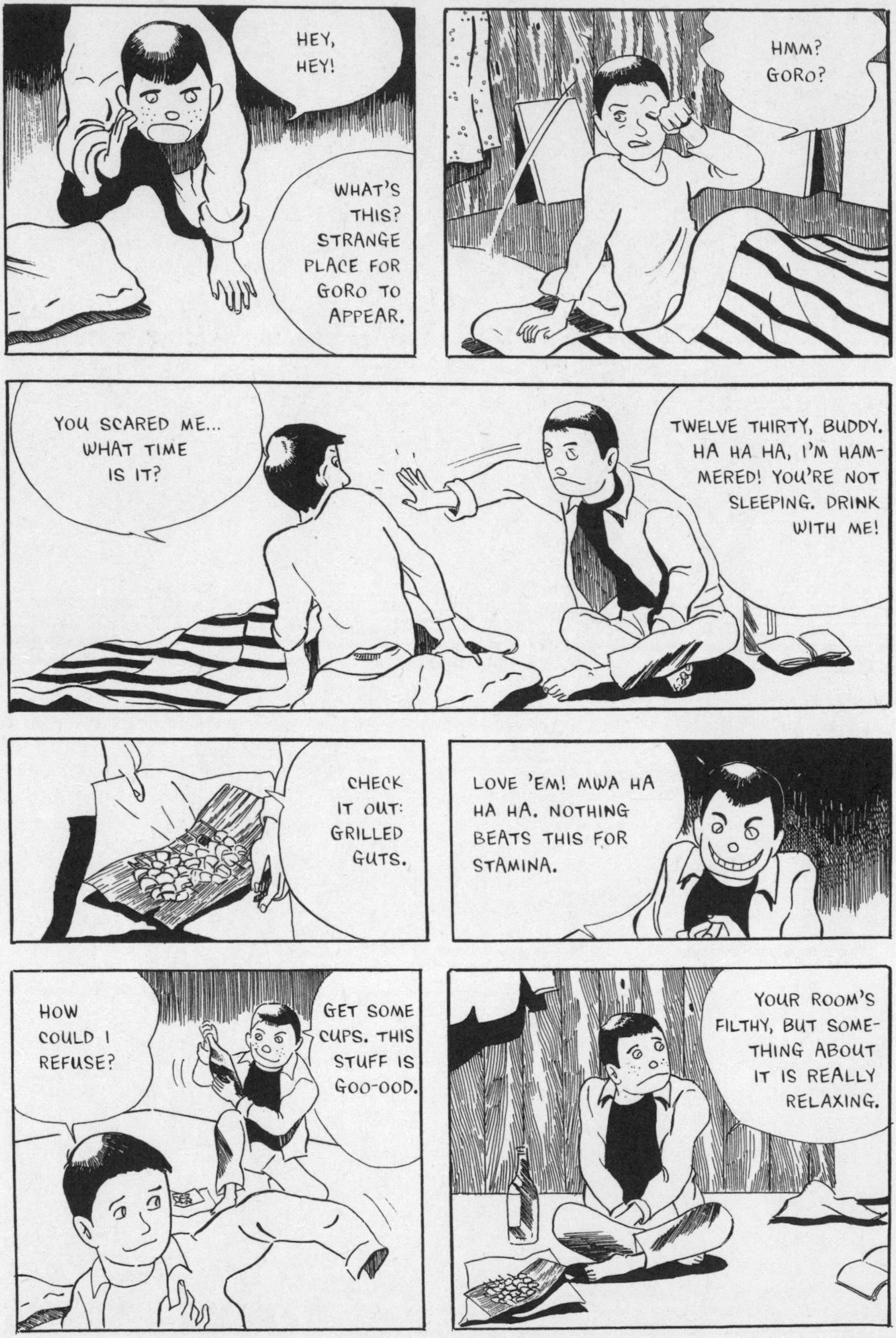
HEY, HEY!
WHAT'S THIS? STRANGE PLACE FOR GORO TO APPEAR.
HMM? GORO?
YOU SCARED ME... WHAT TIME IS IT?
TWELVE THIRTY, BUDDY. HA HA HA, I'M HAMMERED! YOU'RE NOT SLEEPING. DRINK WITH ME!
CHECK IT OUT: GRILLED GUTS.
LOVE 'EM! MWA HA HA HA. NOTHING BEATS THIS FOR STAMINA.
HOW COULD I REFUSE?
GET SOME CUPS. THIS STUFF IS GOO-OOD.
YOUR ROOM'S FILTHY, BUT SOMETHING ABOUT IT IS REALLY RELAXING.

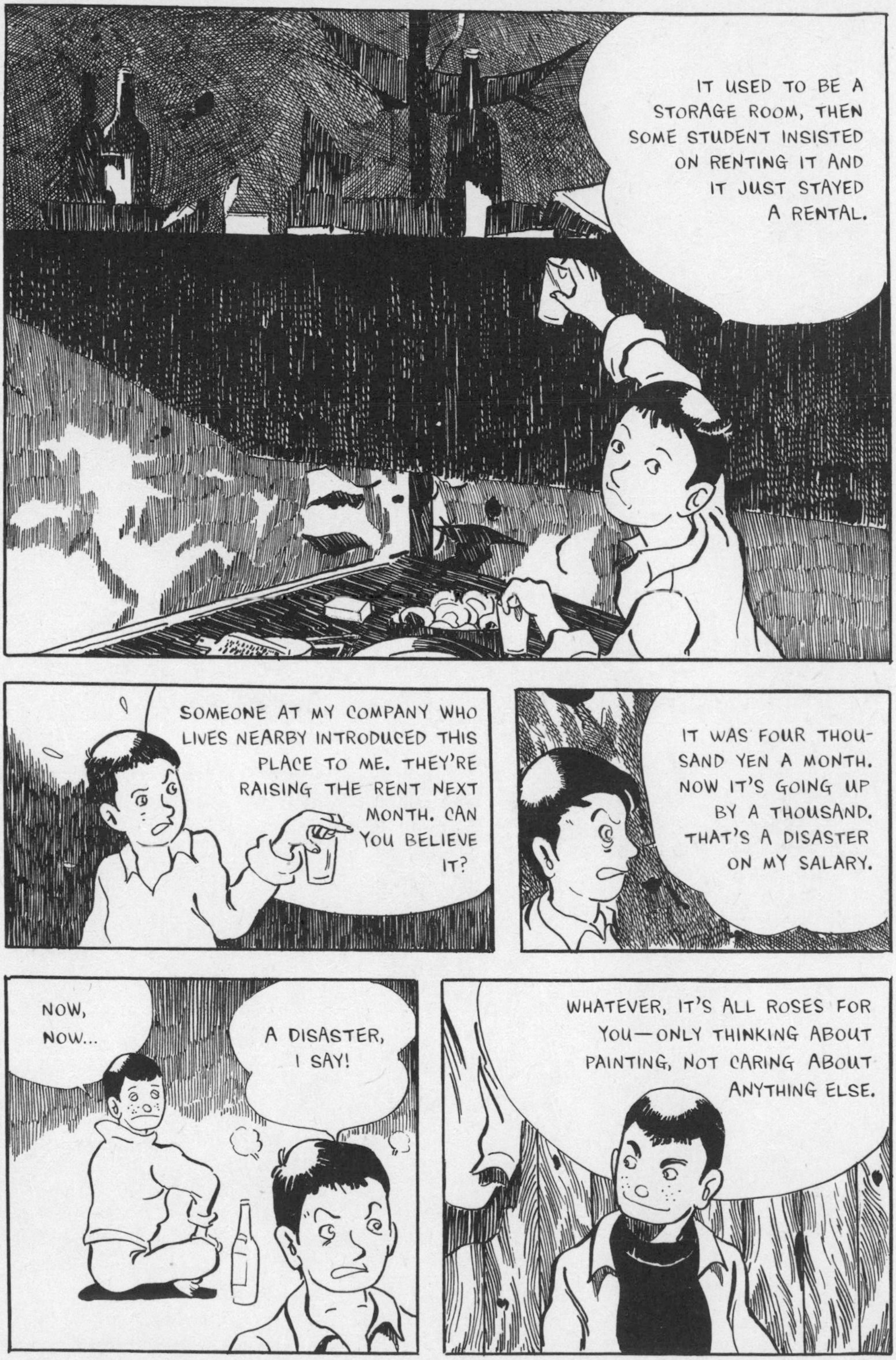
IT USED TO BE A STORAGE ROOM, THEN SOME STUDENT INSISTED ON RENTING IT AND IT JUST STAYED A RENTAL.
SOMEONE AT MY COMPANY WHO LIVES NEARBY INTRODUCED THIS PLACE TO ME. THEY'RE RAISING THE RENT NEXT MONTH. CAN YOU BELIEVE IT?
IT WAS FOUR THOU-SAND YEN A MONTH. NOW IT'S GOING UP BY A THOUSAND. THAT'S A DISASTER ON MY SALARY.
NOW, NOW...
A DISASTER, I SAY!
WHATEVER, IT'S ALL ROSES FOR YOU—ONLY THINKING ABOUT PAINTING, NOT CARING ABOUT ANYTHING ELSE.

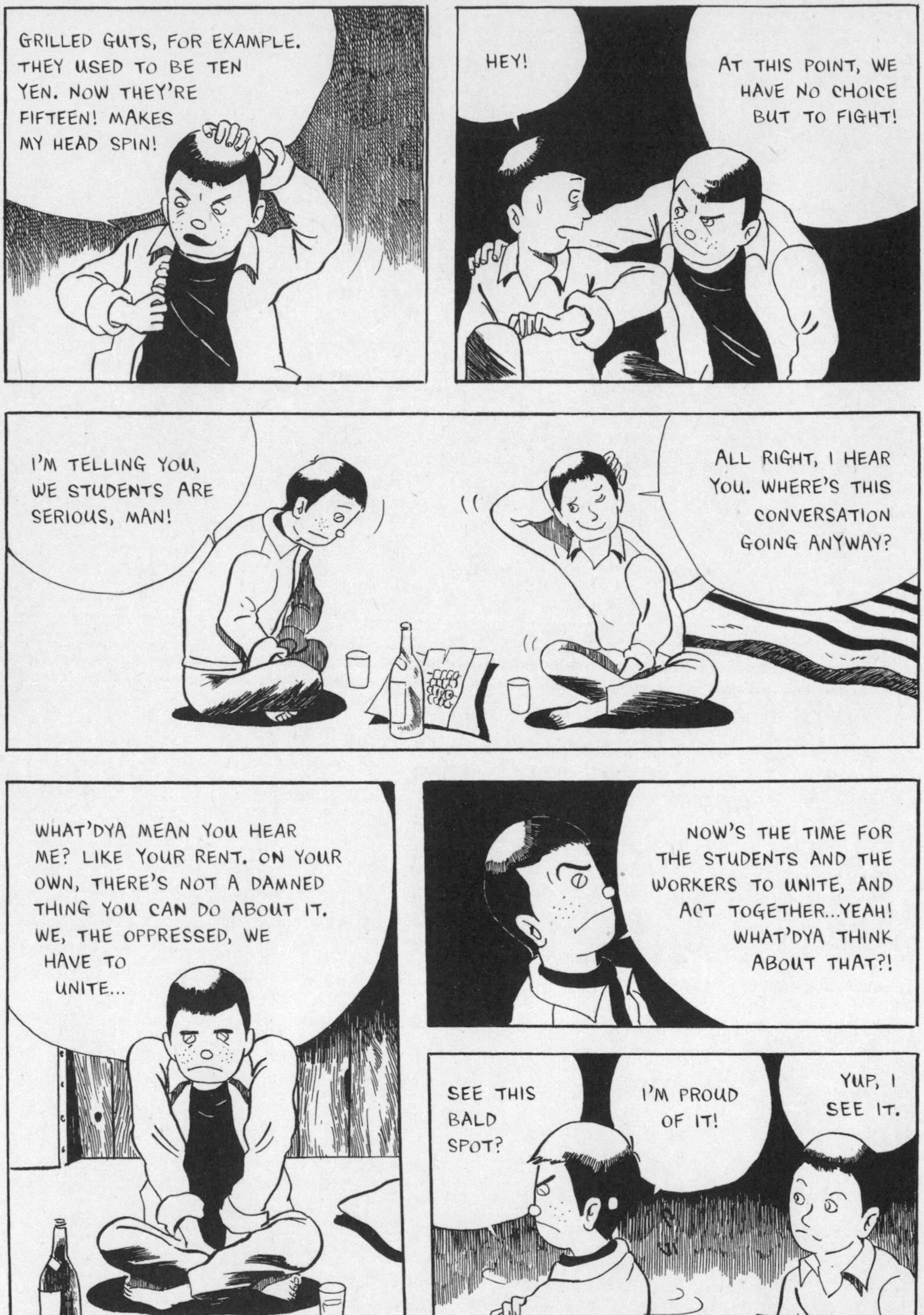
GRILLED GUTS, FOR EXAMPLE. THEY USED TO BE TEN YEN. NOW THEY'RE FIFTEEN! MAKES MY HEAD SPIN!
HEY!
AT THIS POINT, WE HAVE NO CHOICE BUT TO FIGHT!
I'M TELLING YOU, WE STUDENTS ARE SERIOUS, MAN!
ALL RIGHT, I HEAR YOU. WHERE'S THIS CONVERSATION GOING ANYWAY?
WHAT'DYA MEAN YOU HEAR ME? LIKE YOUR RENT. ON YOUR OWN, THERE'S NOT A DAMNED THING YOU CAN DO ABOUT IT. WE, THE OPPRESSED, WE HAVE TO UNITE...
NOW'S THE TIME FOR THE STUDENTS AND THE WORKERS TO UNITE, AND ACT TOGETHER...YEAH! WHAT'DYA THINK ABOUT THAT?!
SEE THIS BALD SPOT?
I'M PROUD OF IT!
YUP, I SEE IT.

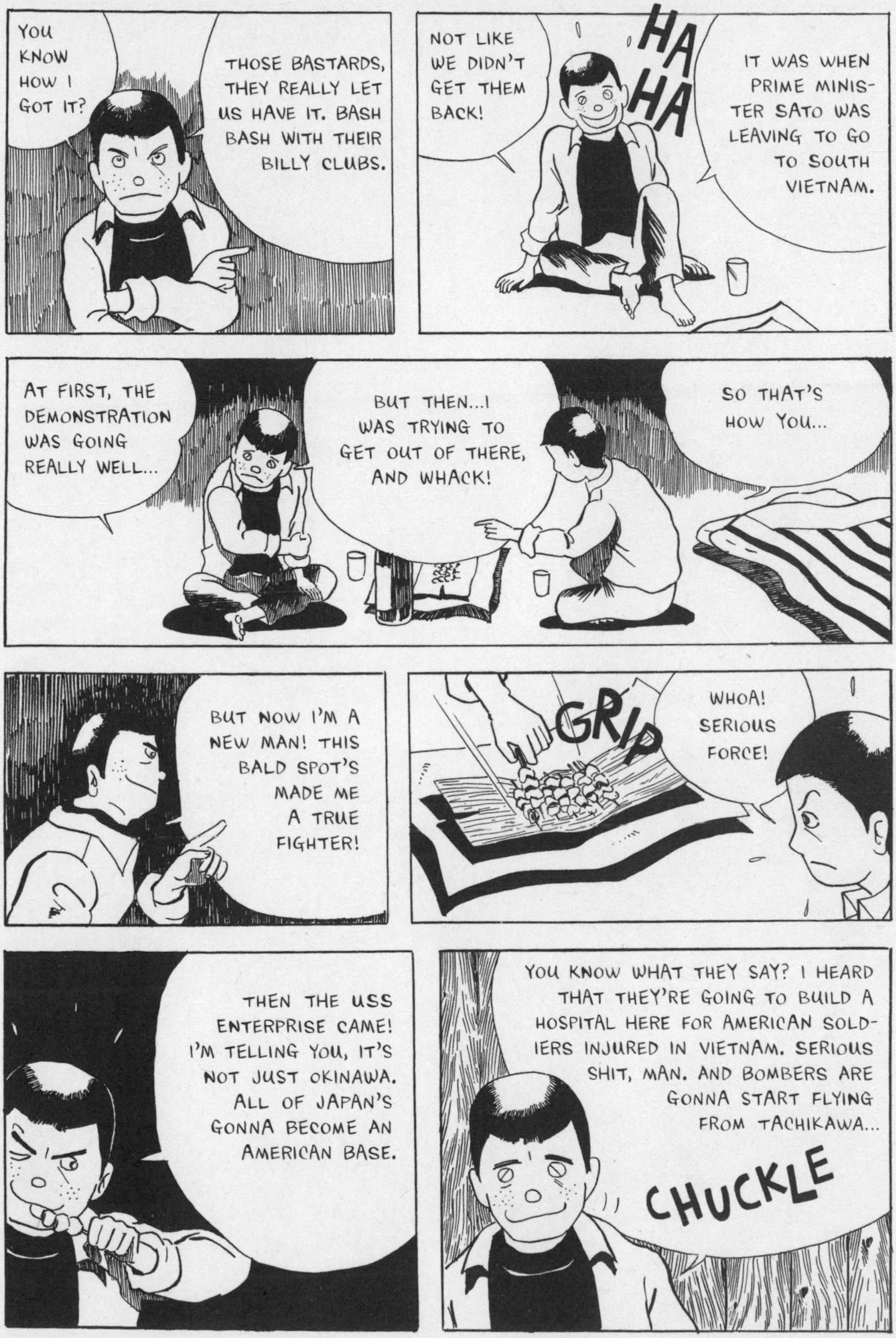
YOU KNOW HOW I GOT IT?
THOSE BASTARDS, THEY REALLY LET US HAVE IT. BASH BASH WITH THEIR BILLY CLUBS.
NOT LIKE WE DIDN'T GET THEM BACK!
HA HA
IT WAS WHEN PRIME MINISTER SATO WAS LEAVING TO GO TO SOUTH VIETNAM.
AT FIRST, THE DEMONSTRATION WAS GOING REALLY WELL...
BUT THEN...I WAS TRYING TO GET OUT OF THERE, AND WHACK!
SO THAT'S HOW YOU...
BUT NOW I'M A NEW MAN! THIS BALD SPOT'S MADE ME A TRUE FIGHTER!
GRIP
WHOA! SERIOUS FORCE!
THEN THE USS ENTERPRISE CAME! I'M TELLING YOU, IT'S NOT JUST OKINAWA. ALL OF JAPAN'S GONNA BECOME AN AMERICAN BASE.
YOU KNOW WHAT THEY SAY? I HEARD THAT THEY'RE GOING TO BUILD A HOSPITAL HERE FOR AMERICAN SOLDIERS INJURED IN VIETNAM. SERIOUS SHIT, MAN. AND BOMBERS ARE GONNA START FLYING FROM TACHIKAWA...
CHUCKLE

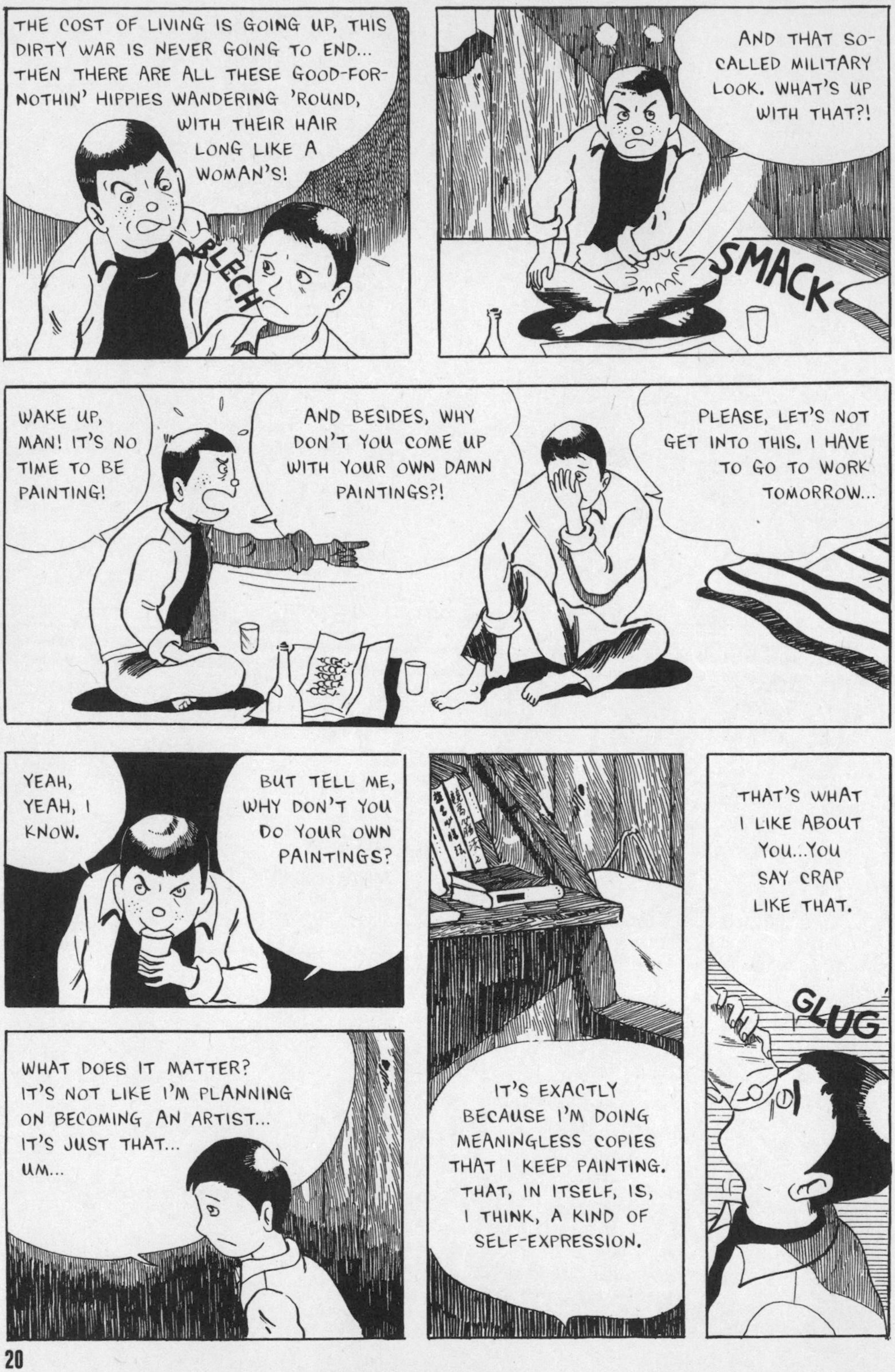
THE COST OF LIVING IS GOING UP, THIS DIRTY WAR IS NEVER GOING TO END... THEN THERE ARE ALL THESE GOOD-FOR-NOTHIN' HIPPIES WANDERING 'ROUND, WITH THEIR HAIR LONG LIKE A WOMAN'S!
BLECH
AND THAT SO-CALLED MILITARY LOOK. WHAT'S UP WITH THAT?!
SMACK
WAKE UP, MAN! IT'S NO TIME TO BE PAINTING!
AND BESIDES, WHY DON'T YOU COME UP WITH YOUR OWN DAMN PAINTINGS?!
PLEASE, LET'S NOT GET INTO THIS. I HAVE TO GO TO WORK TOMORROW...
YEAH, YEAH, I KNOW.
BUT TELL ME, WHY DON'T YOU DO YOUR OWN PAINTINGS?
WHAT DOES IT MATTER? IT'S NOT LIKE I'M PLANNING ON BECOMING AN ARTIST... IT'S JUST THAT... UM...
IT'S EXACTLY BECAUSE I'M DOING MEANINGLESS COPIES THAT I KEEP PAINTING. THAT, IN ITSELF, IS, I THINK, A KIND OF SELF-EXPRESSION.
THAT'S WHAT I LIKE ABOUT YOU...YOU SAY CRAP LIKE THAT.
GLUG

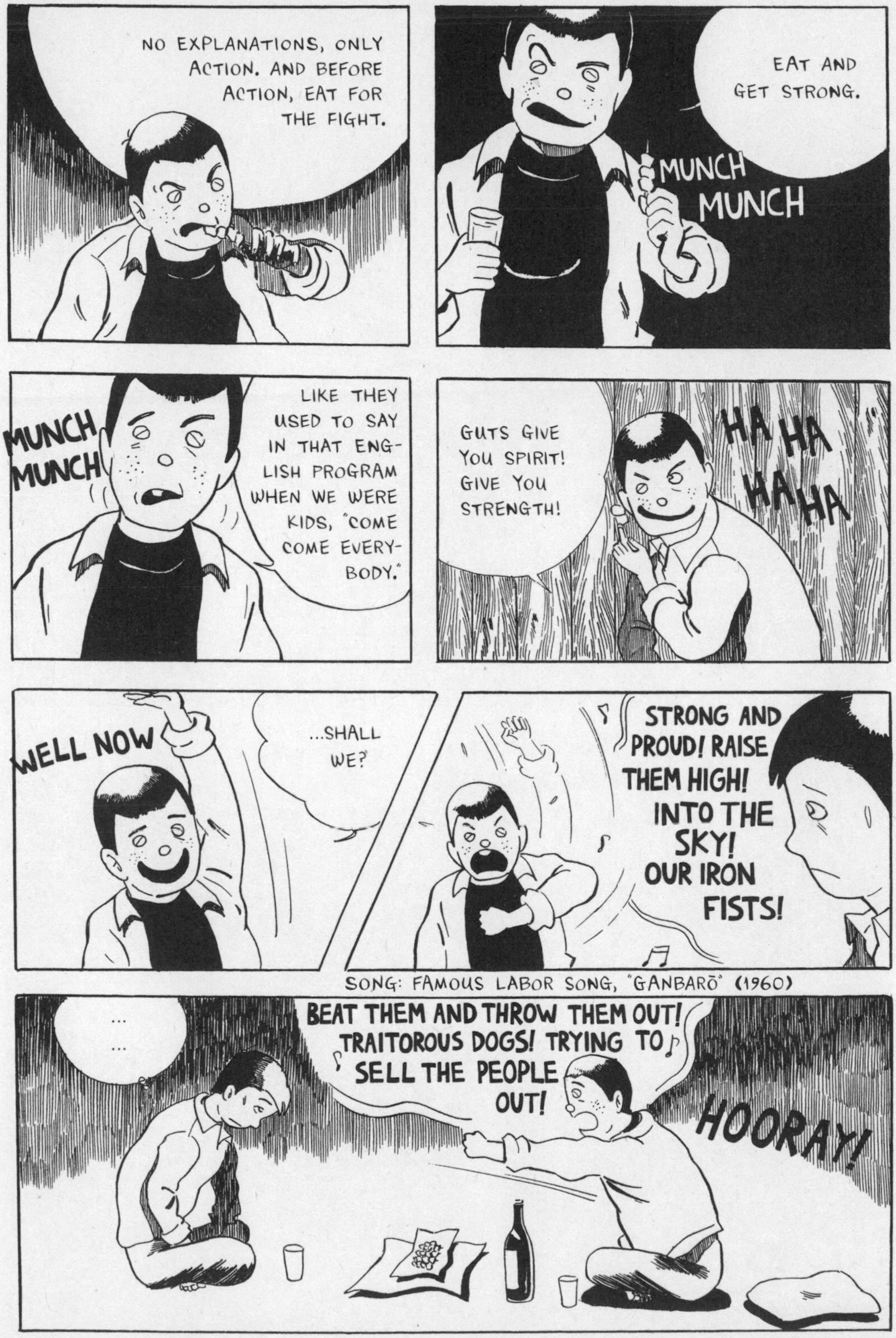
NO EXPLANATIONS, ONLY ACTION. AND BEFORE ACTION, EAT FOR THE FIGHT.
EAT AND GET STRONG.
MUNCH MUNCH
MUNCH MUNCH
LIKE THEY USED TO SAY IN THAT ENGLISH PROGRAM WHEN WE WERE KIDS, "COME COME EVERYBODY."
GUTS GIVE YOU SPIRIT! GIVE YOU STRENGTH!
HA HA HA HA
WELL NOW
...SHALL WE?
STRONG AND PROUD! RAISE THEM HIGH! INTO THE SKY! OUR IRON FISTS!
SONG: FAMOUS LABOR SONG, "GANBARŌ" (1960)
...
...
BEAT THEM AND THROW THEM OUT! TRAITOROUS DOGS! TRYING TO SELL THE PEOPLE OUT!
HOORAY!

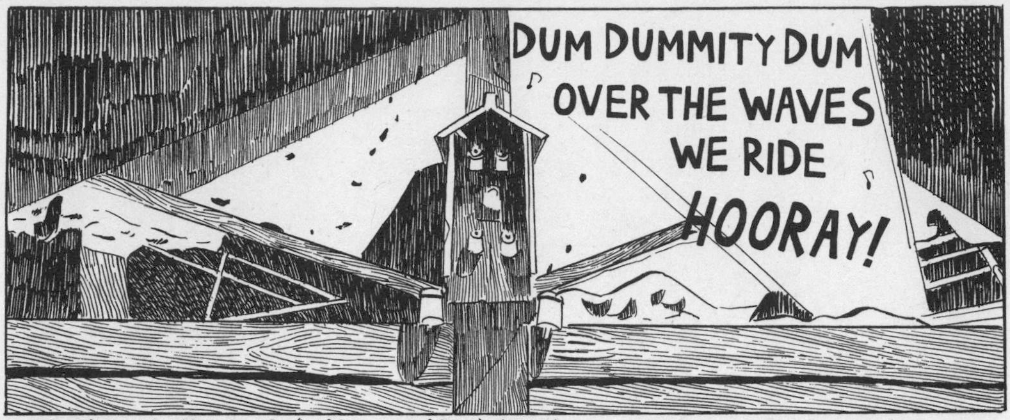
DUM DUMMITY DUM
OVER THE WAVES
WE RIDE
HOORAY!

SONG: FAMOUS WAR SONG, "WARSHIP MARCH" (1900)

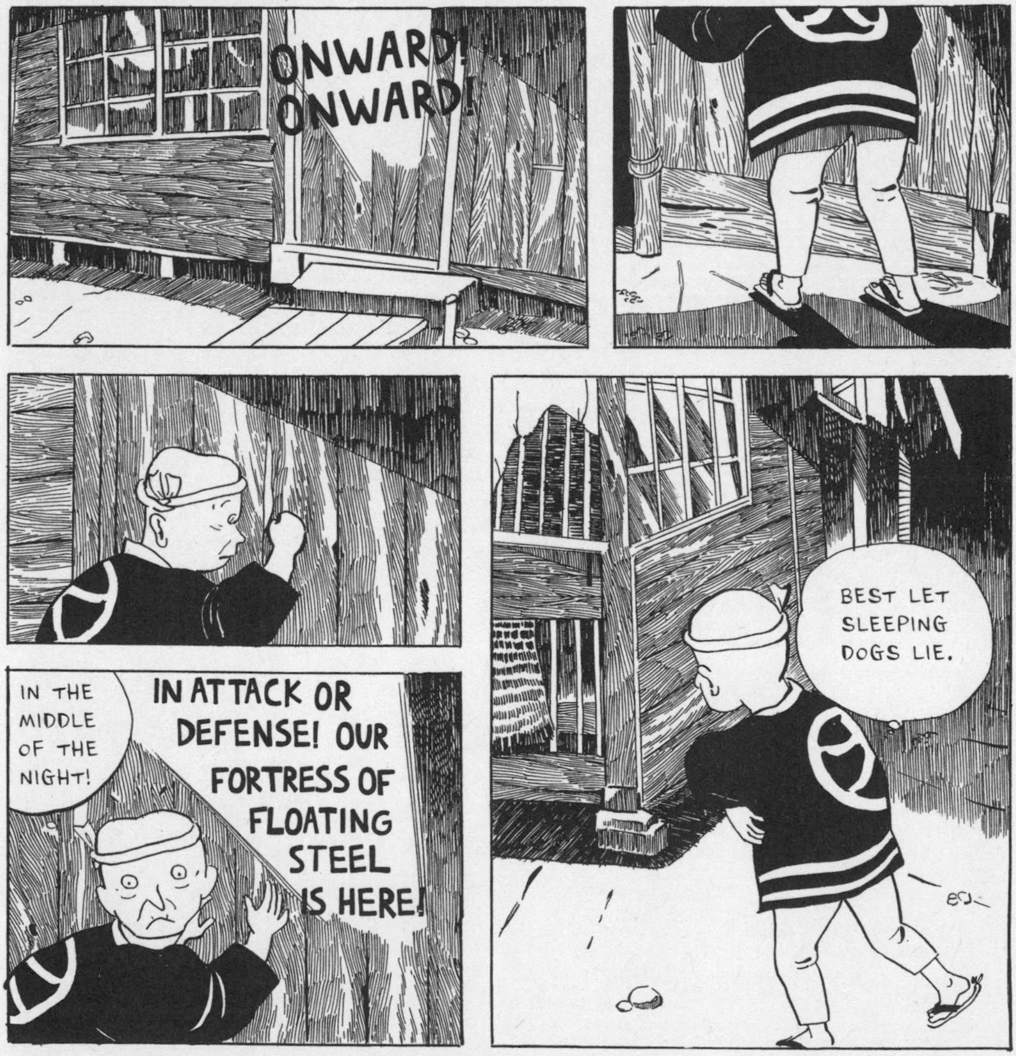
ONWARD! ONWARD!
IN THE MIDDLE OF THE NIGHT!
IN ATTACK OR DEFENSE! OUR FORTRESS OF FLOATING STEEL IS HERE!
BEST LET SLEEPING DOGS LIE.

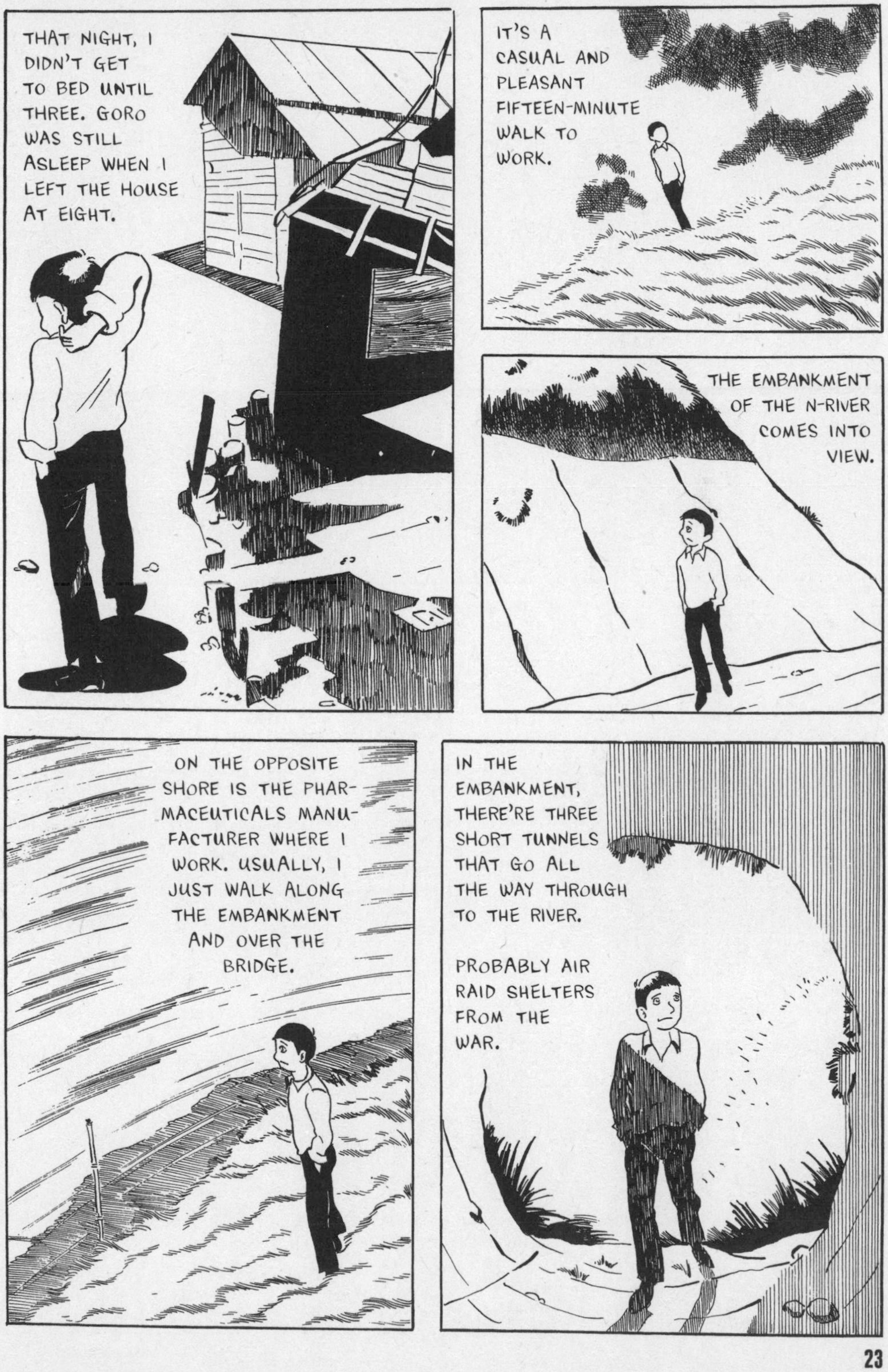
THAT NIGHT, I DIDN'T GET TO BED UNTIL THREE. GORO WAS STILL ASLEEP WHEN I LEFT THE HOUSE AT EIGHT.
IT'S A CASUAL AND PLEASANT FIFTEEN-MINUTE WALK TO WORK.
THE EMBANKMENT OF THE N-RIVER COMES INTO VIEW.
ON THE OPPOSITE SHORE IS THE PHARMACEUTICALS MANUFACTURER WHERE I WORK. USUALLY, I JUST WALK ALONG THE EMBANKMENT AND OVER THE BRIDGE.
IN THE EMBANKMENT, THERE'RE THREE SHORT TUNNELS THAT GO ALL THE WAY THROUGH TO THE RIVER.
PROBABLY AIR RAID SHELTERS FROM THE WAR.

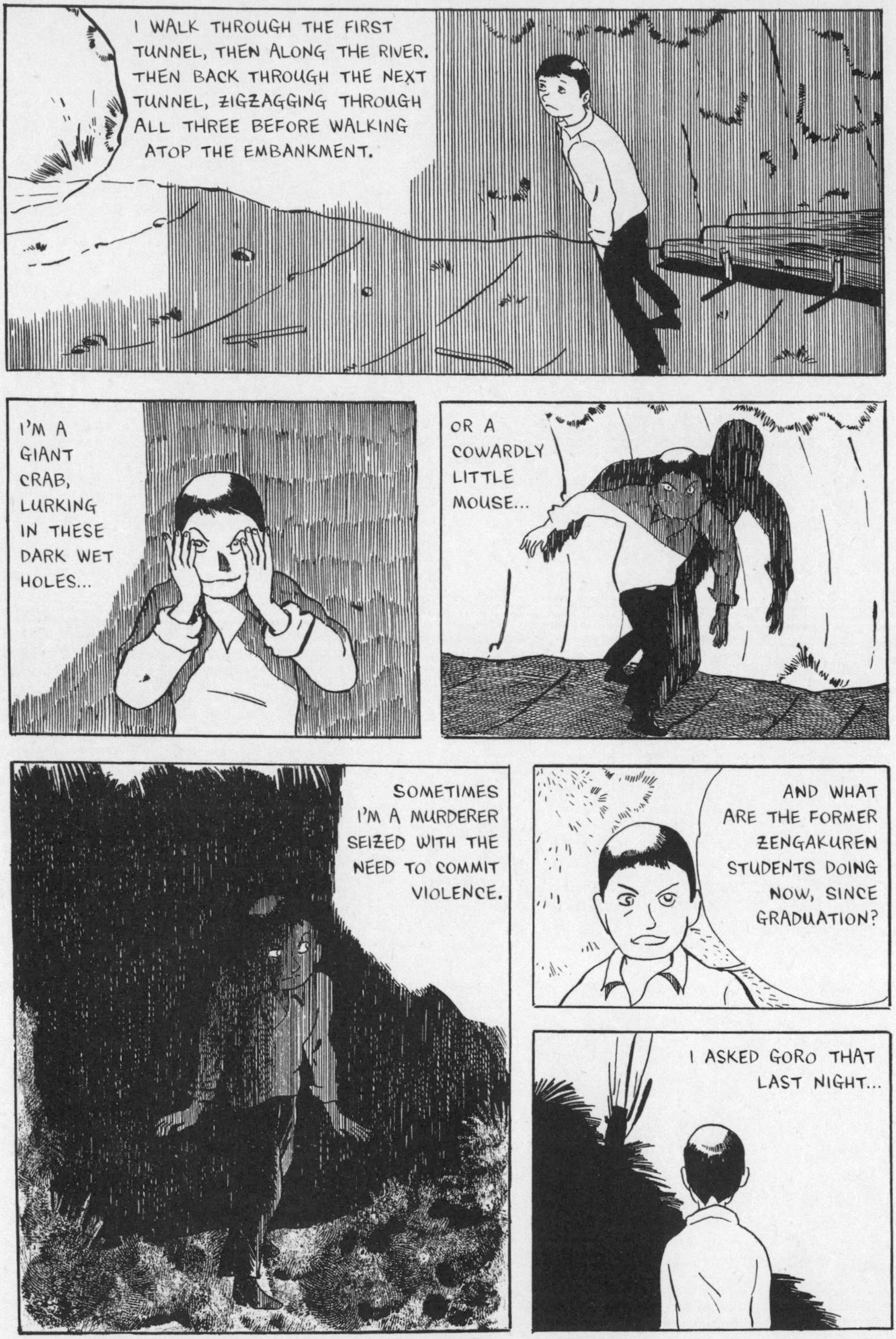
I WALK THROUGH THE FIRST TUNNEL, THEN ALONG THE RIVER. THEN BACK THROUGH THE NEXT TUNNEL, ZIGZAGGING THROUGH ALL THREE BEFORE WALKING ATOP THE EMBANKMENT.
I'M A GIANT CRAB, LURKING IN THESE DARK WET HOLES...
OR A COWARDLY LITTLE MOUSE...
SOMETIMES I'M A MURDERER SEIZED WITH THE NEED TO COMMIT VIOLENCE.
AND WHAT ARE THE FORMER ZENGAKUREN STUDENTS DOING NOW, SINCE GRADUATION?
I ASKED GORO THAT LAST NIGHT...

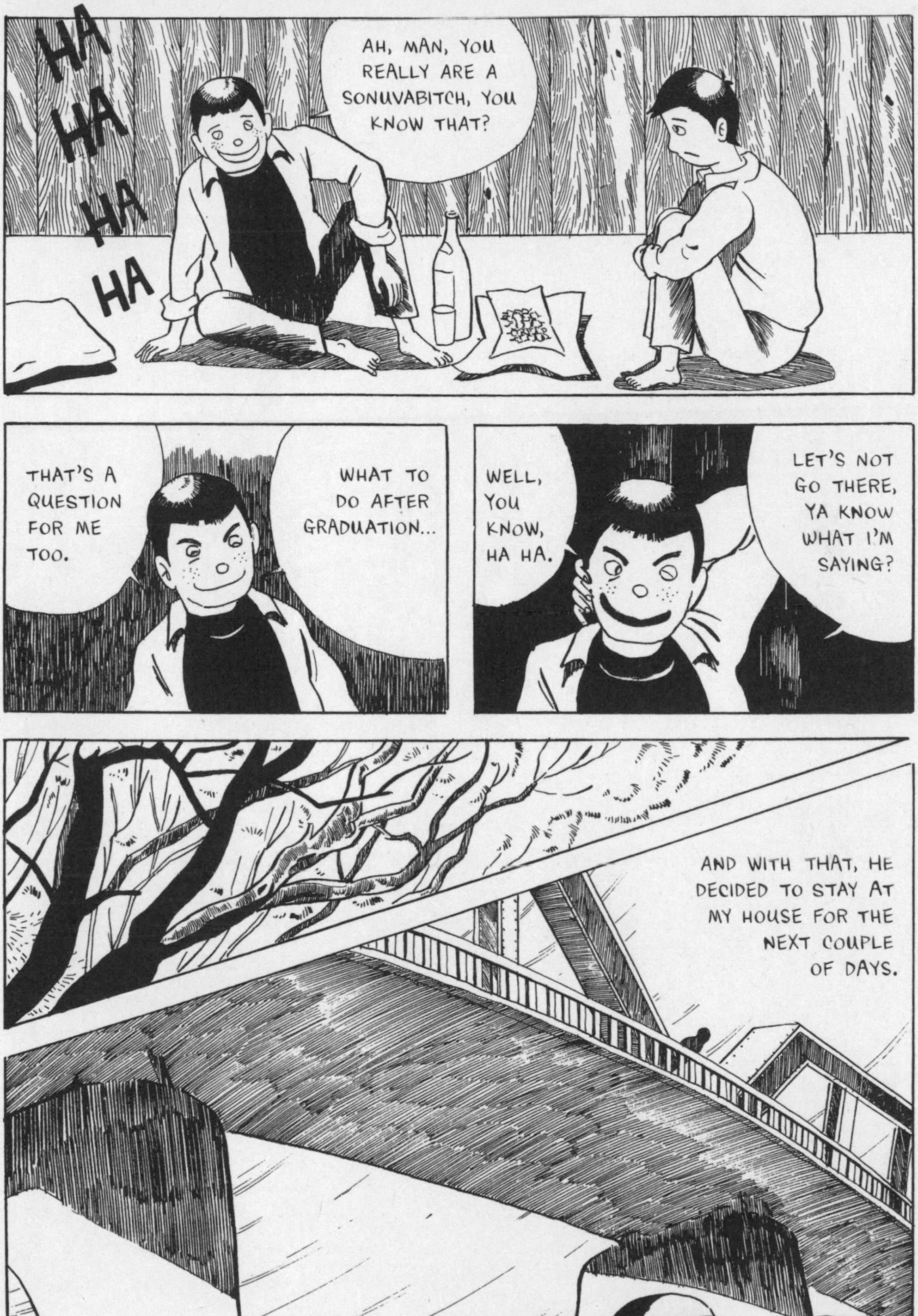
HA HA HA HA
AH, MAN, YOU REALLY ARE A SONUVABITCH, YOU KNOW THAT?
THAT'S A QUESTION FOR ME TOO.
WHAT TO DO AFTER GRADUATION...
WELL, YOU KNOW, HA HA.
LET'S NOT GO THERE, YA KNOW WHAT I'M SAYING?
AND WITH THAT, HE DECIDED TO STAY AT MY HOUSE FOR THE NEXT COUPLE OF DAYS.

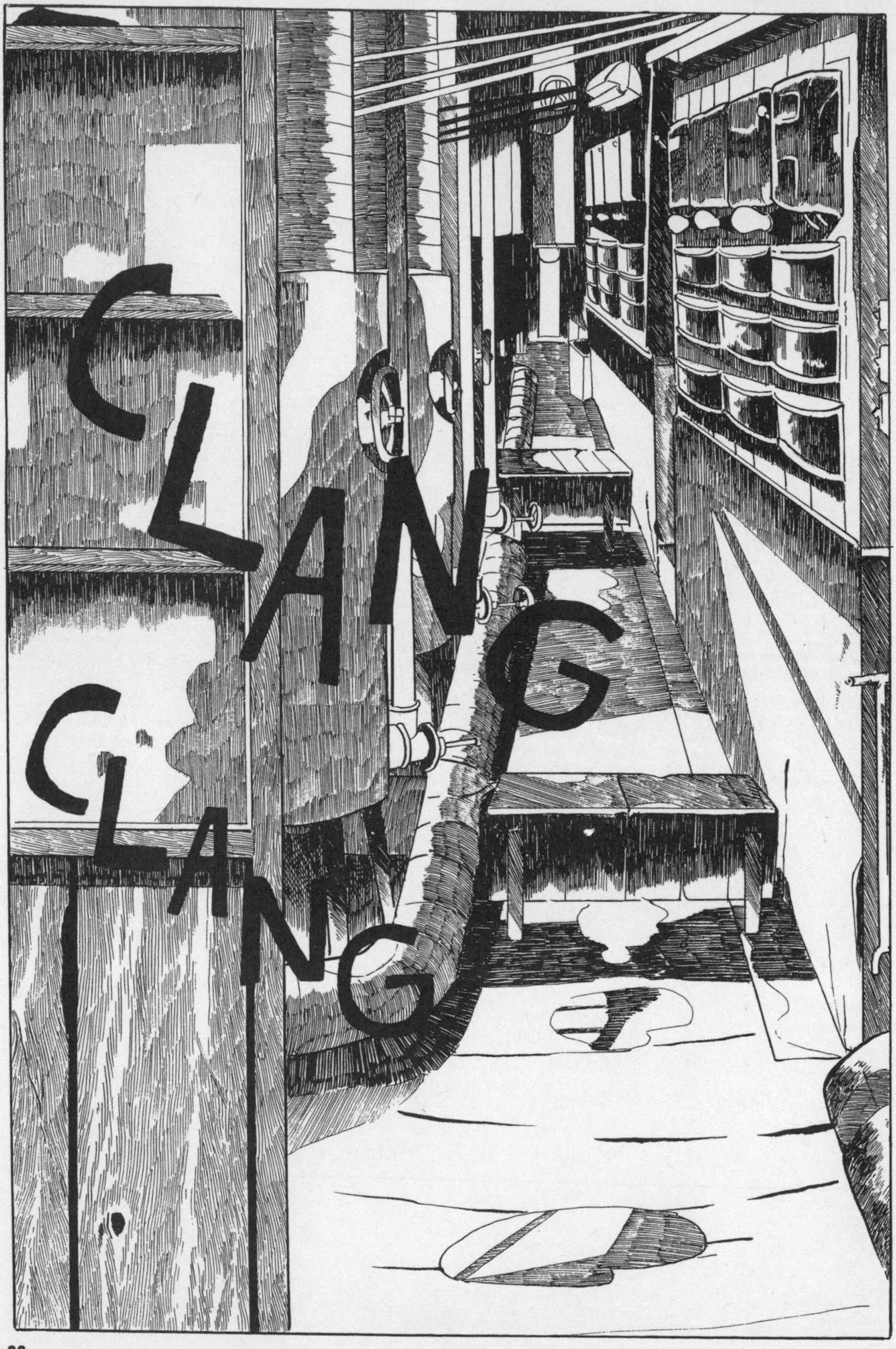
CLANG
CLANG

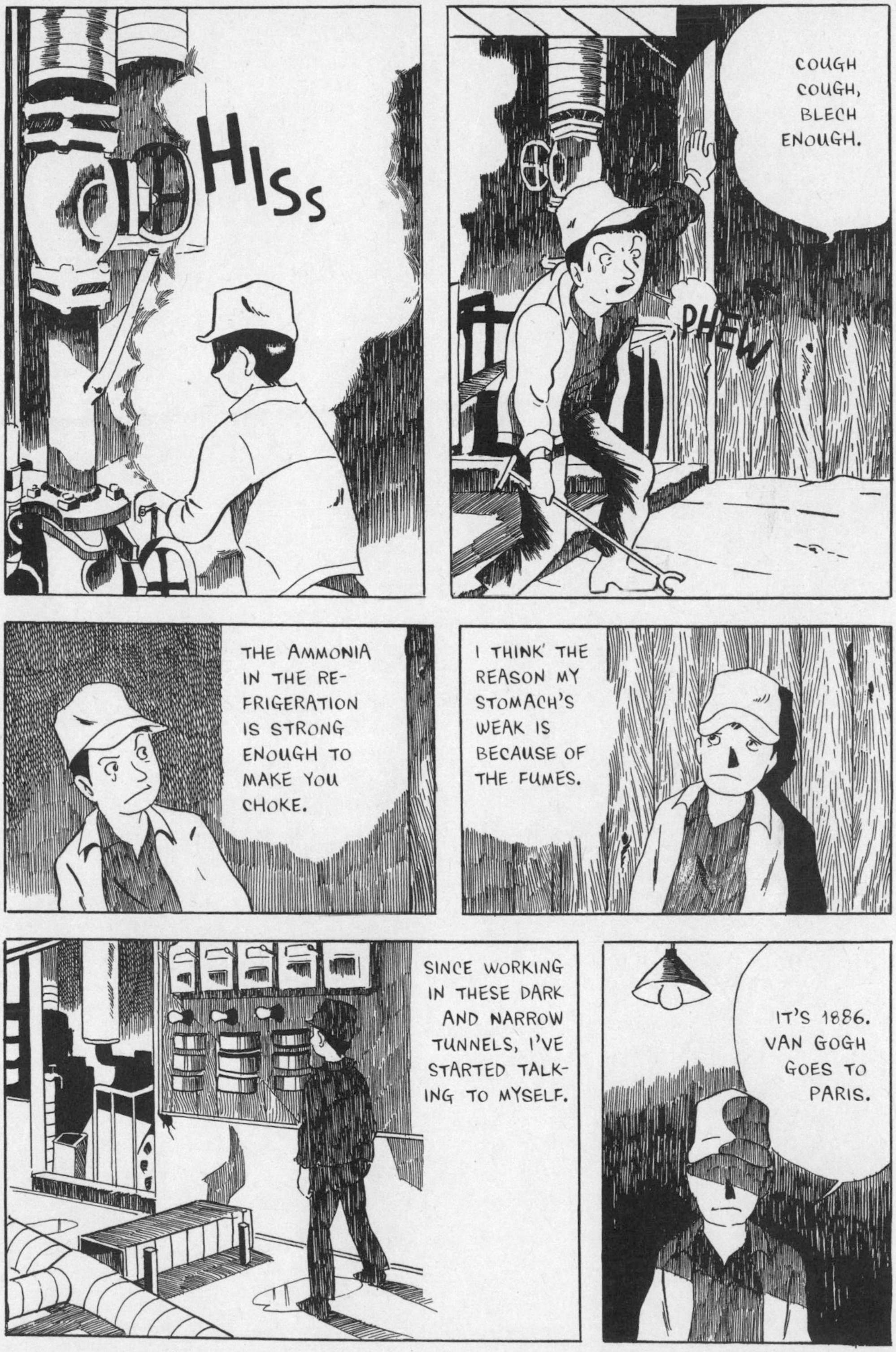
HISS
COUGH COUGH, BLECH ENOUGH.
PHEW
THE AMMONIA IN THE RE-FRIGERATION IS STRONG ENOUGH TO MAKE YOU CHOKE.
I THINK THE REASON MY STOMACH'S WEAK IS BECAUSE OF THE FUMES.
SINCE WORKING IN THESE DARK AND NARROW TUNNELS, I'VE STARTED TALK-ING TO MYSELF.
IT'S 1886. VAN GOGH GOES TO PARIS.

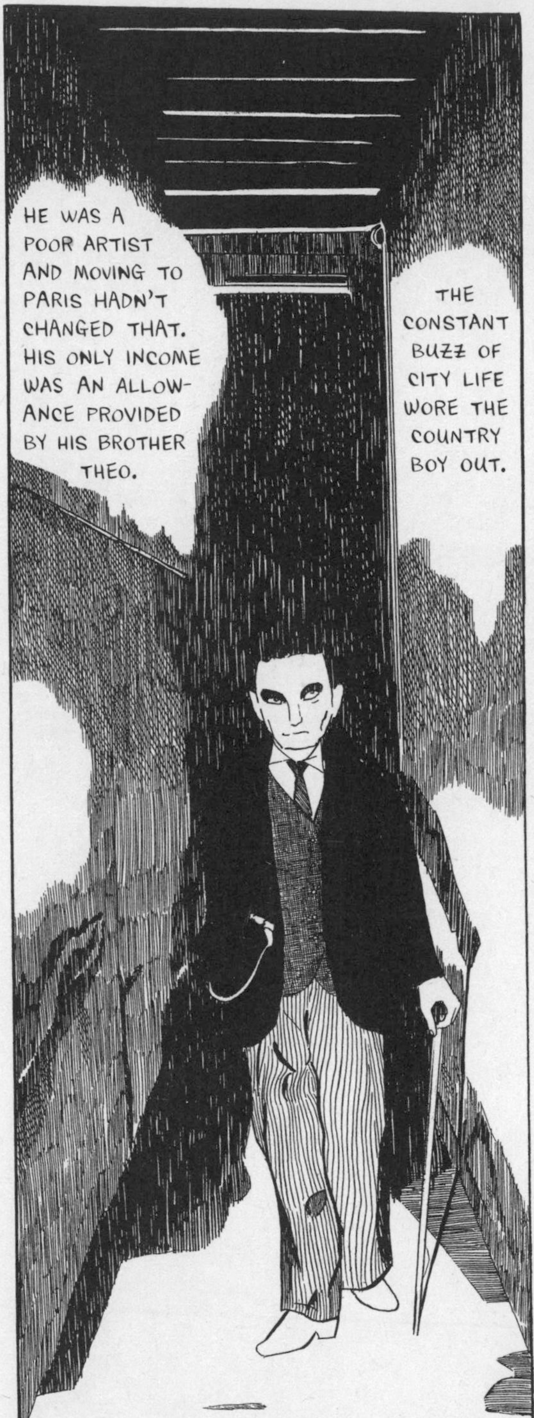
HE WAS A POOR ARTIST AND MOVING TO PARIS HADN'T CHANGED THAT. HIS ONLY INCOME WAS AN ALLOW-ANCE PROVIDED BY HIS BROTHER THEO.
THE CONSTANT BUZZ OF CITY LIFE WORE THE COUNTRY BOY OUT.

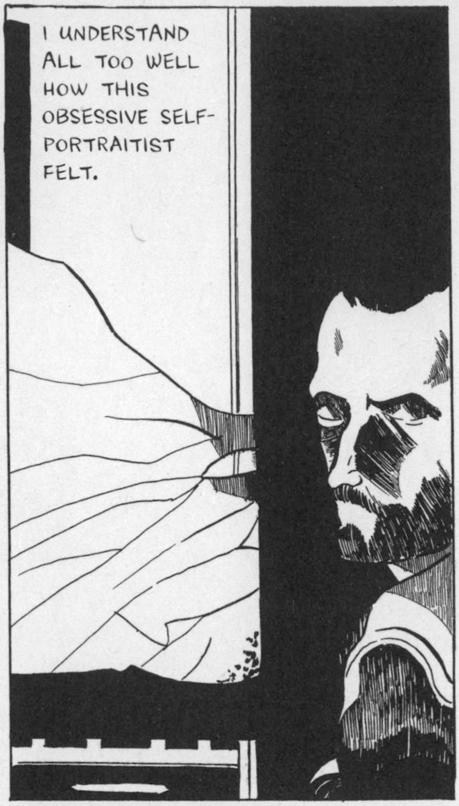
I UNDERSTAND ALL TOO WELL HOW THIS OBSESSIVE SELF-PORTRAITIST FELT.

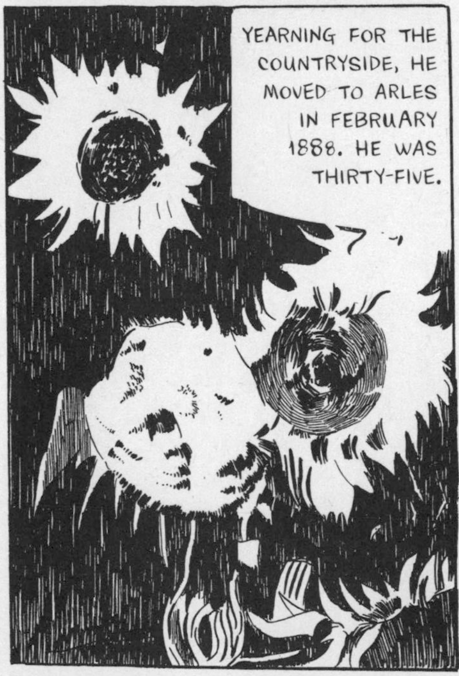
YEARNING FOR THE COUNTRYSIDE, HE MOVED TO ARLES IN FEBRUARY 1888. HE WAS THIRTY-FIVE.

"HE FOUND THE VIVIDNESS OF THE SOUTHERN FRENCH LANDSCAPE SIMPLY RAPTUROUS. IN JUNE, HE TOOK A SHORT TRIP TO SAINT-MARIES, RETURNING AFTER A MARVELOUS STRETCH OF PAINTING. THAT SUMMER WAS THE MOST PRODUCTIVE OF VAN GOGH'S ENTIRE CAREER."

FROM *THE LIFE OF VAN GOGH*, BY SHIKIBA RYUZABURO

SELF-PORTRAIT DEDICATED TO PAUL GAUGUIN (OCTOBER 1888, AGE THIRTY-FIVE)

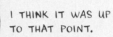

I THINK IT WAS UP TO THAT POINT.

IT WAS UP TO THAT POINT THAT VINCENT VAN GOGH HELD HIMSELF TOGETHER.

OCTOBER, SAME YEAR: ON VAN GOGH'S INVITATION, GAUGUIN HEADS FOR ARLES. THEY WERE TO BEGIN LIVING TOGETHER.

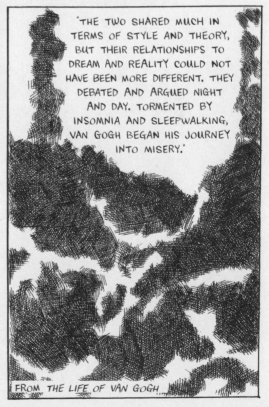

"THE TWO SHARED MUCH IN TERMS OF STYLE AND THEORY, BUT THEIR RELATIONSHIPS TO DREAM AND REALITY COULD NOT HAVE BEEN MORE DIFFERENT. THEY DEBATED AND ARGUED NIGHT AND DAY. TORMENTED BY INSOMNIA AND SLEEPWALKING, VAN GOGH BEGAN HIS JOURNEY INTO MISERY."

FROM *THE LIFE OF VAN GOGH*

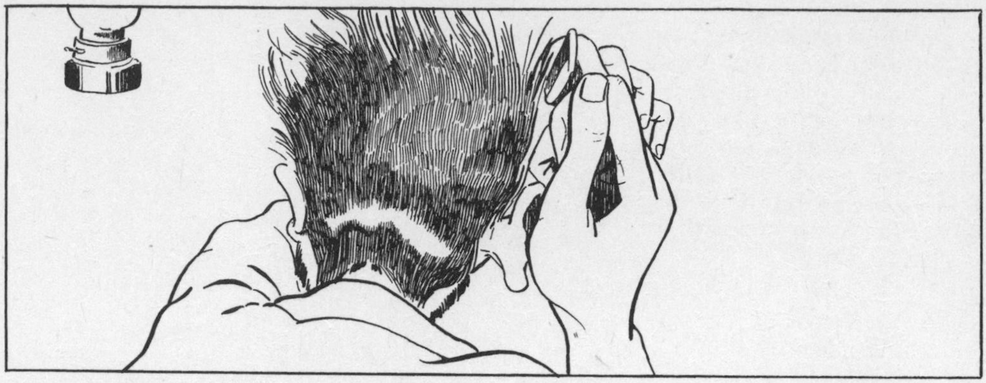

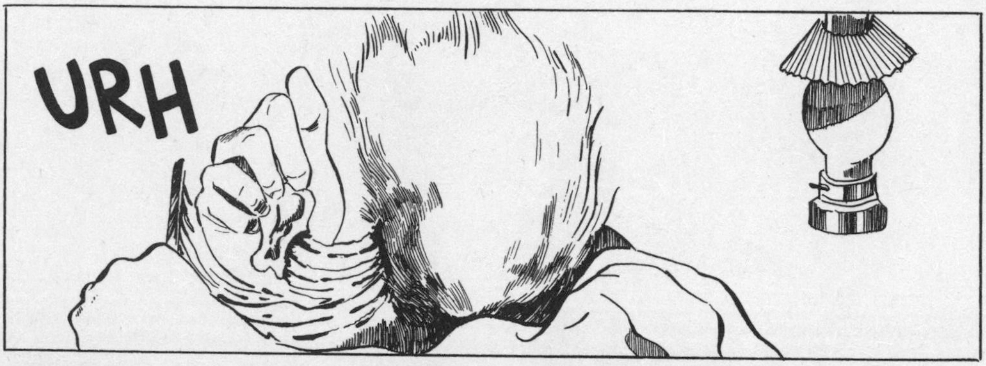
URH

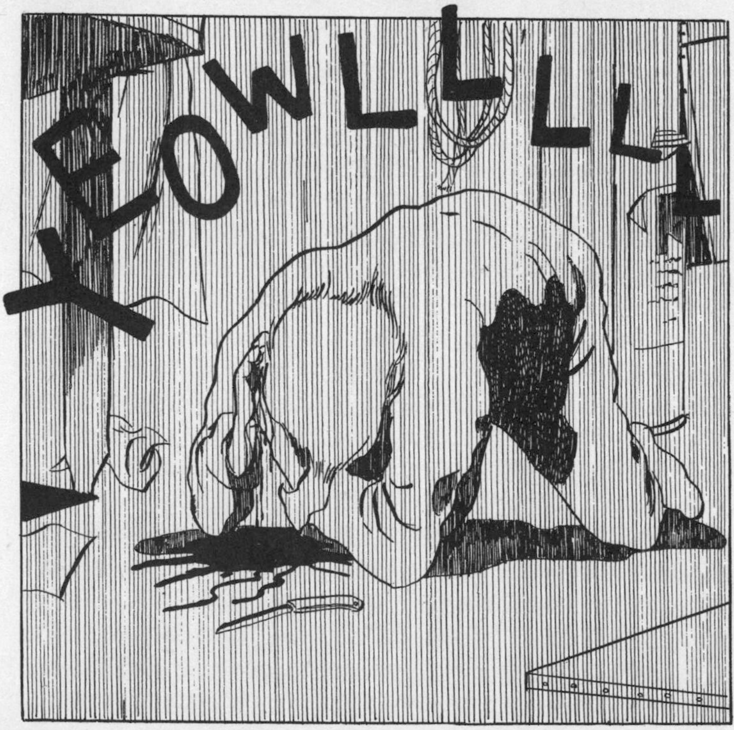
YEOWLLLLL

IT WAS THE NIGHT OF DECEMBER 22. WHILE EATING WITH GAUGUIN AT A RESTAURANT, VAN GOGH SUDDENLY SMASHED HIS GLASS OF ABSINTHE. TWO DAYS LATER, POSSESSED BY SOME TERRIFIC EXCITEMENT, HE TOOK A RAZOR BLADE AND SEVERED HIS LEFT EAR. HE FELL INTO A COMA AND WAS SENT TO THE HOSPITAL. HE REMAINED UNCONSCIOUS FOR THREE DAYS.

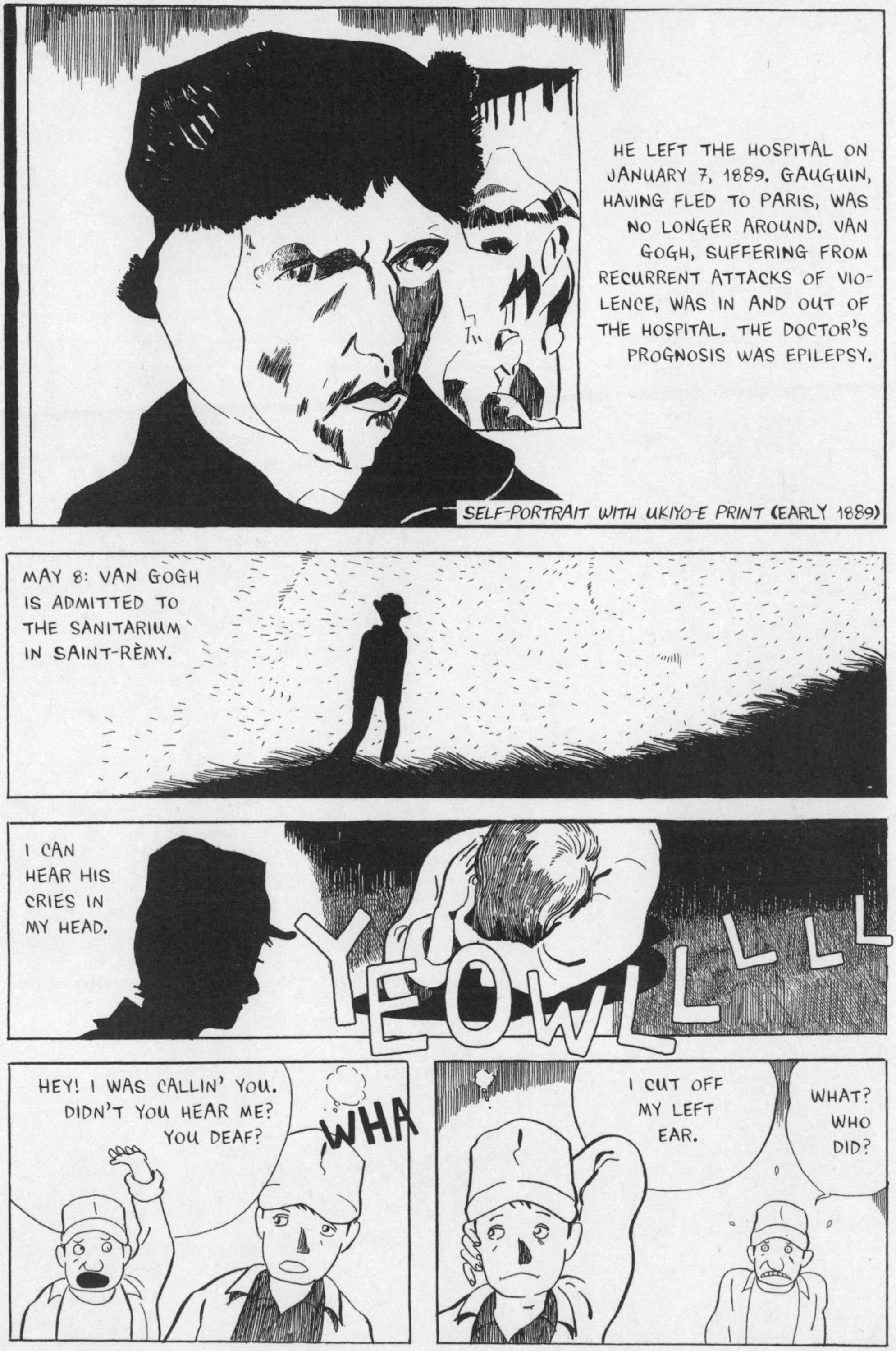

HE LEFT THE HOSPITAL ON JANUARY 7, 1889. GAUGUIN, HAVING FLED TO PARIS, WAS NO LONGER AROUND. VAN GOGH, SUFFERING FROM RECURRENT ATTACKS OF VIOLENCE, WAS IN AND OUT OF THE HOSPITAL. THE DOCTOR'S PROGNOSIS WAS EPILEPSY.
SELF-PORTRAIT WITH UKIYO-E PRINT (EARLY 1889)
MAY 8: VAN GOGH IS ADMITTED TO THE SANITARIUM IN SAINT-RÈMY.
I CAN HEAR HIS CRIES IN MY HEAD.
YEOWLLLLL
HEY! I WAS CALLIN' YOU. DIDN'T YOU HEAR ME? YOU DEAF?
WHA
I CUT OFF MY LEFT EAR.
WHAT? WHO DID?

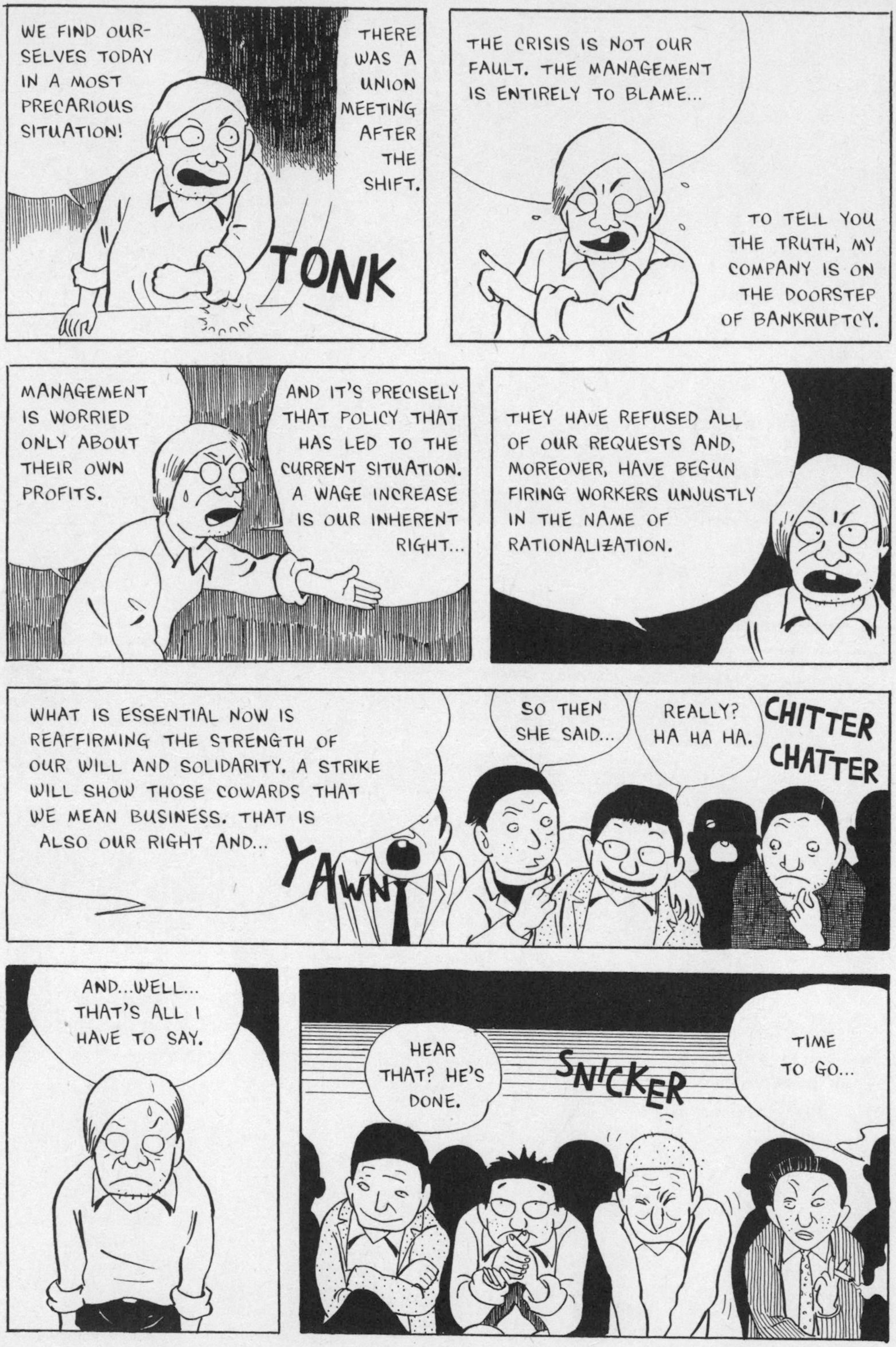
WE FIND OURSELVES TODAY IN A MOST PRECARIOUS SITUATION!
THERE WAS A UNION MEETING AFTER THE SHIFT.
TONK
THE CRISIS IS NOT OUR FAULT. THE MANAGEMENT IS ENTIRELY TO BLAME...
TO TELL YOU THE TRUTH, MY COMPANY IS ON THE DOORSTEP OF BANKRUPTCY.
MANAGEMENT IS WORRIED ONLY ABOUT THEIR OWN PROFITS.
AND IT'S PRECISELY THAT POLICY THAT HAS LED TO THE CURRENT SITUATION. A WAGE INCREASE IS OUR INHERENT RIGHT...
THEY HAVE REFUSED ALL OF OUR REQUESTS AND, MOREOVER, HAVE BEGUN FIRING WORKERS UNJUSTLY IN THE NAME OF RATIONALIZATION.
WHAT IS ESSENTIAL NOW IS REAFFIRMING THE STRENGTH OF OUR WILL AND SOLIDARITY. A STRIKE WILL SHOW THOSE COWARDS THAT WE MEAN BUSINESS. THAT IS ALSO OUR RIGHT AND...
YAWN
SO THEN SHE SAID...
REALLY? HA HA HA.
CHITTER CHATTER
AND...WELL... THAT'S ALL I HAVE TO SAY.
HEAR THAT? HE'S DONE.
SNICKER
TIME TO GO...

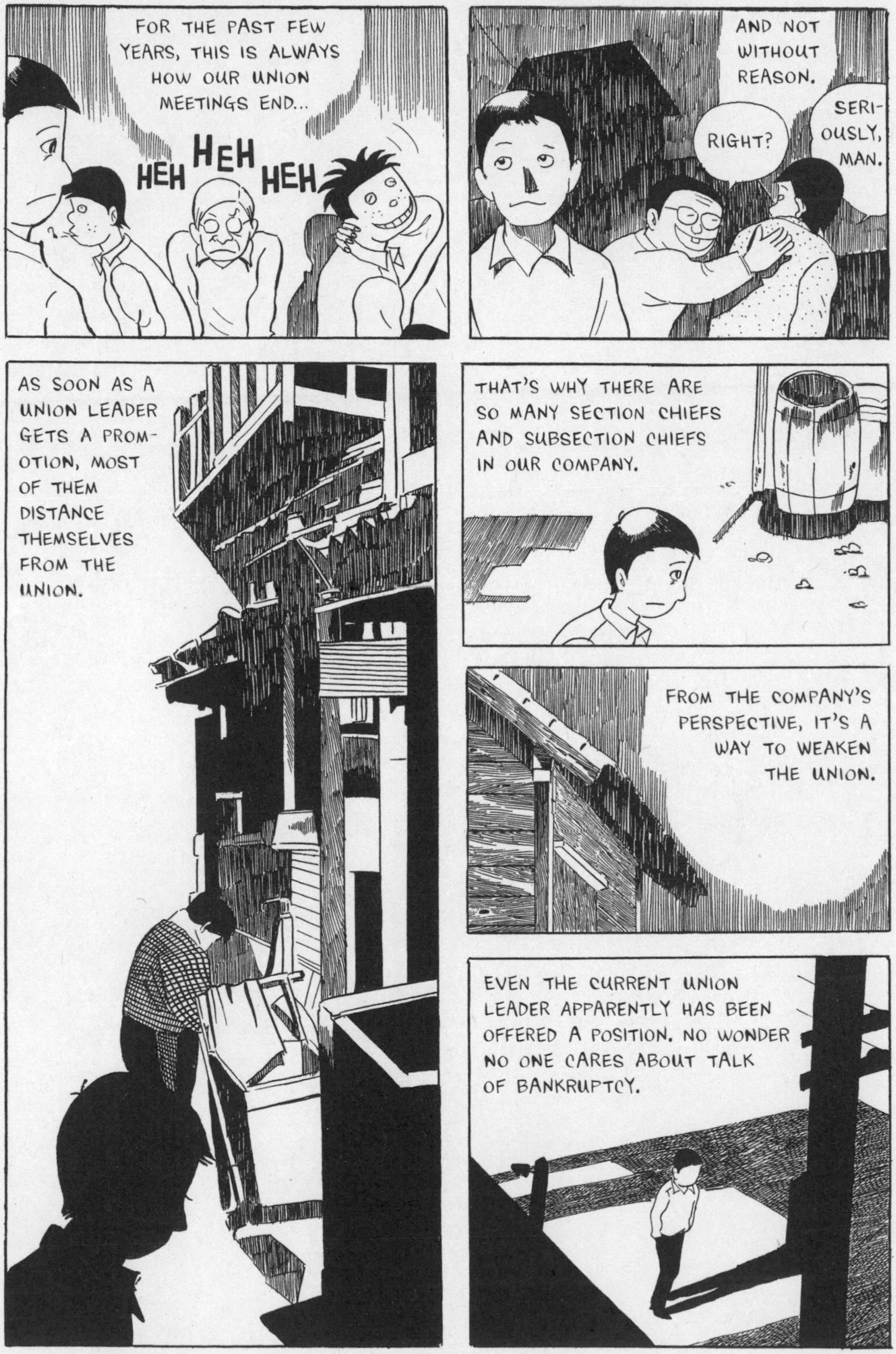
FOR THE PAST FEW YEARS, THIS IS ALWAYS HOW OUR UNION MEETINGS END...
HEH HEH HEH HEH
AND NOT WITHOUT REASON.
RIGHT?
SERI-OUSLY, MAN.
AS SOON AS A UNION LEADER GETS A PROM-OTION, MOST OF THEM DISTANCE THEMSELVES FROM THE UNION.
THAT'S WHY THERE ARE SO MANY SECTION CHIEFS AND SUBSECTION CHIEFS IN OUR COMPANY.
FROM THE COMPANY'S PERSPECTIVE, IT'S A WAY TO WEAKEN THE UNION.
EVEN THE CURRENT UNION LEADER APPARENTLY HAS BEEN OFFERED A POSITION. NO WONDER NO ONE CARES ABOUT TALK OF BANKRUPTCY.

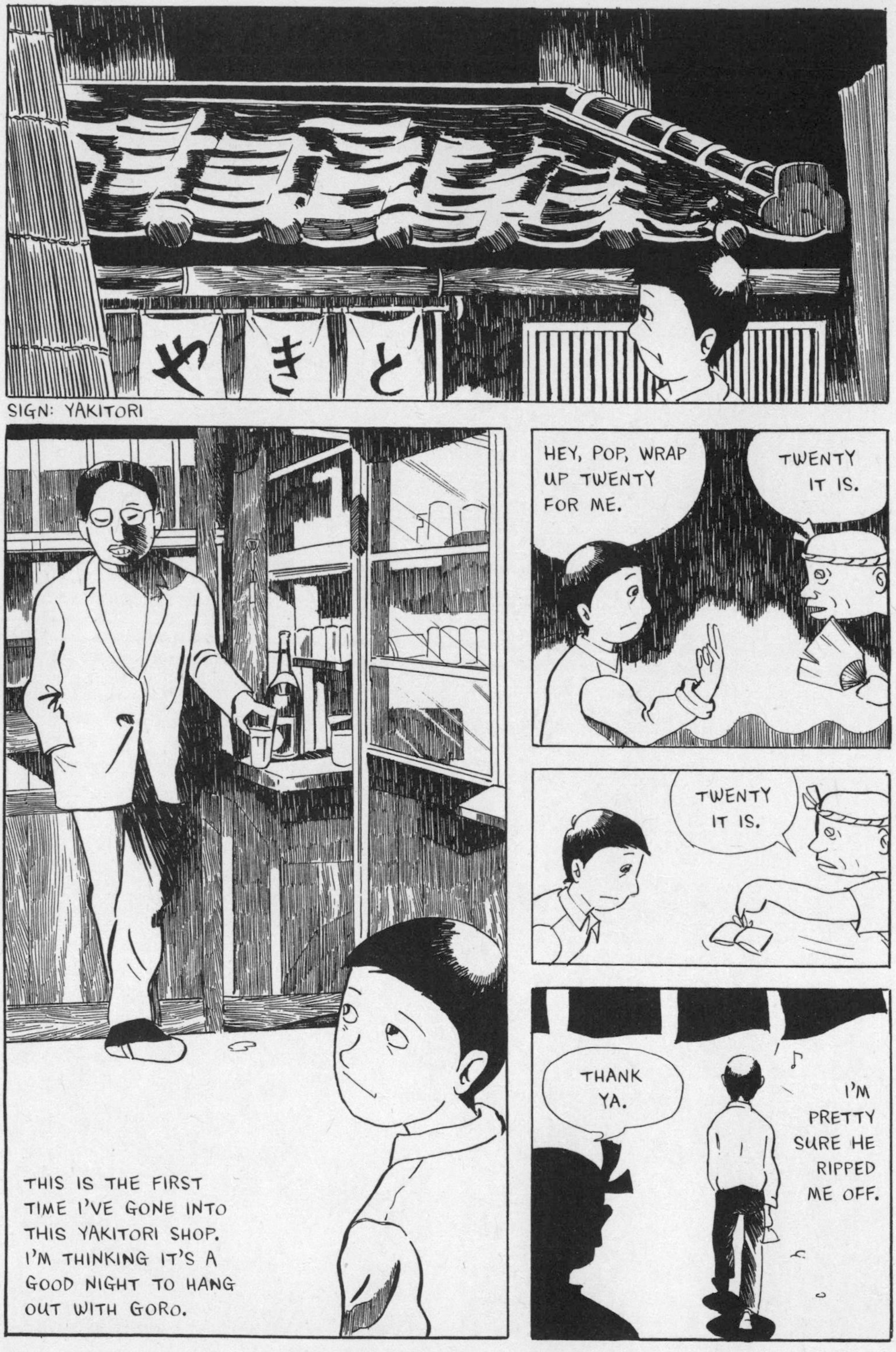
やきと
SIGN: YAKITORI
THIS IS THE FIRST TIME I'VE GONE INTO THIS YAKITORI SHOP. I'M THINKING IT'S A GOOD NIGHT TO HANG OUT WITH GORO.
HEY, POP, WRAP UP TWENTY FOR ME.
TWENTY IT IS.
TWENTY IT IS.
THANK YA.
♪
I'M PRETTY SURE HE RIPPED ME OFF.

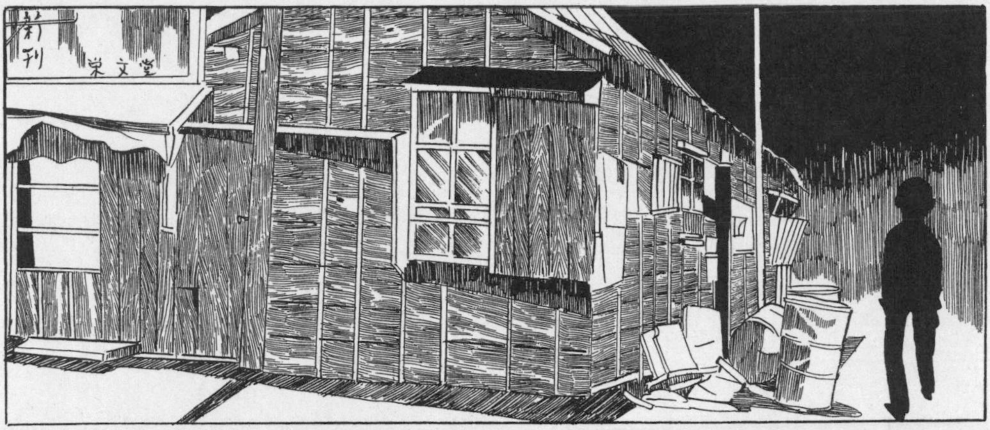
新刊
栄文堂

SIGN: EIBUNDO BOOKS

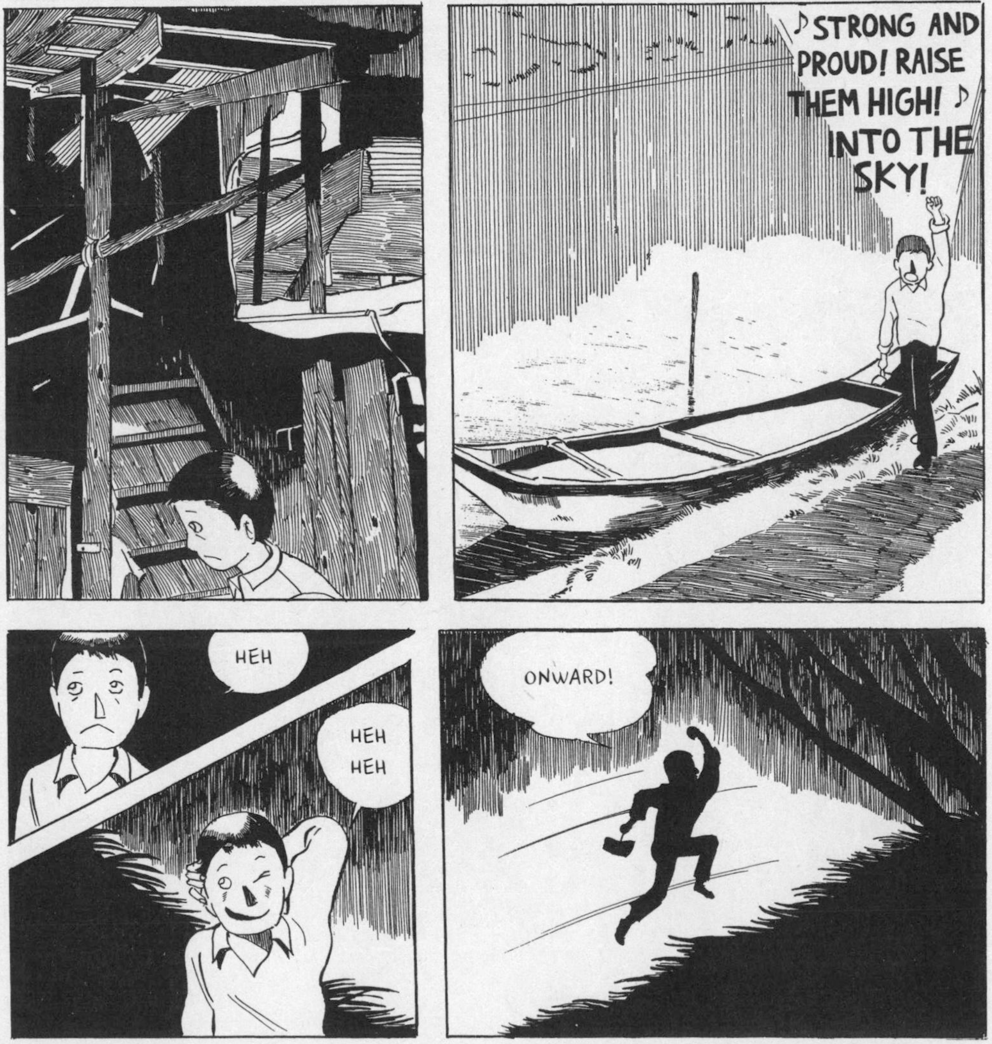
♪ STRONG AND PROUD! RAISE THEM HIGH! ♪ INTO THE SKY!
HEH
HEH HEH
ONWARD!

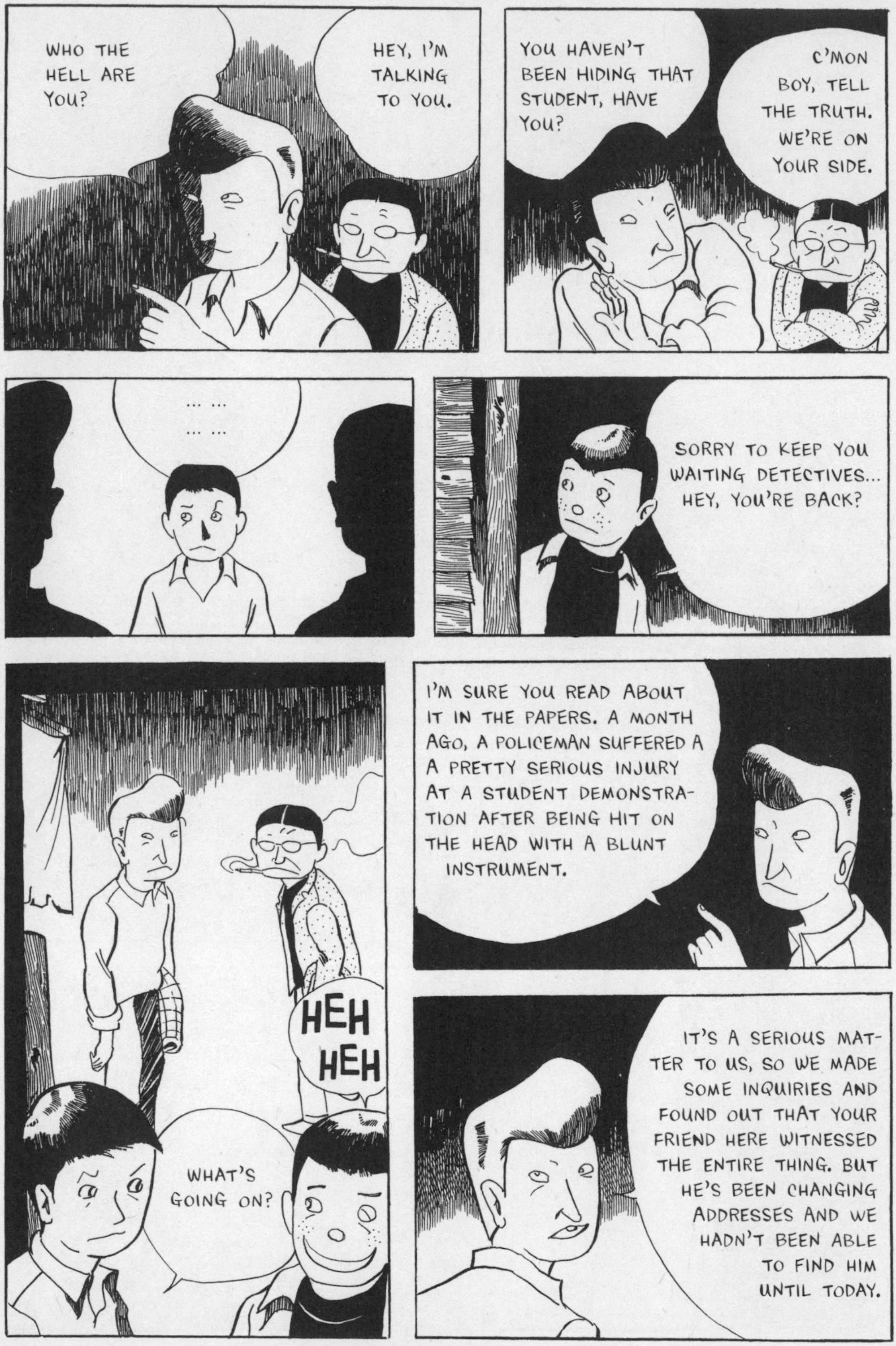
WHO THE HELL ARE YOU?
HEY, I'M TALKING TO YOU.
YOU HAVEN'T BEEN HIDING THAT STUDENT, HAVE YOU?
C'MON BOY, TELL THE TRUTH. WE'RE ON YOUR SIDE.
... ...
... ...
SORRY TO KEEP YOU WAITING DETECTIVES... HEY, YOU'RE BACK?
HEH HEH
WHAT'S GOING ON?
I'M SURE YOU READ ABOUT IT IN THE PAPERS. A MONTH AGO, A POLICEMAN SUFFERED A A PRETTY SERIOUS INJURY AT A STUDENT DEMONSTRATION AFTER BEING HIT ON THE HEAD WITH A BLUNT INSTRUMENT.
IT'S A SERIOUS MATTER TO US, SO WE MADE SOME INQUIRIES AND FOUND OUT THAT YOUR FRIEND HERE WITNESSED THE ENTIRE THING. BUT HE'S BEEN CHANGING ADDRESSES AND WE HADN'T BEEN ABLE TO FIND HIM UNTIL TODAY.

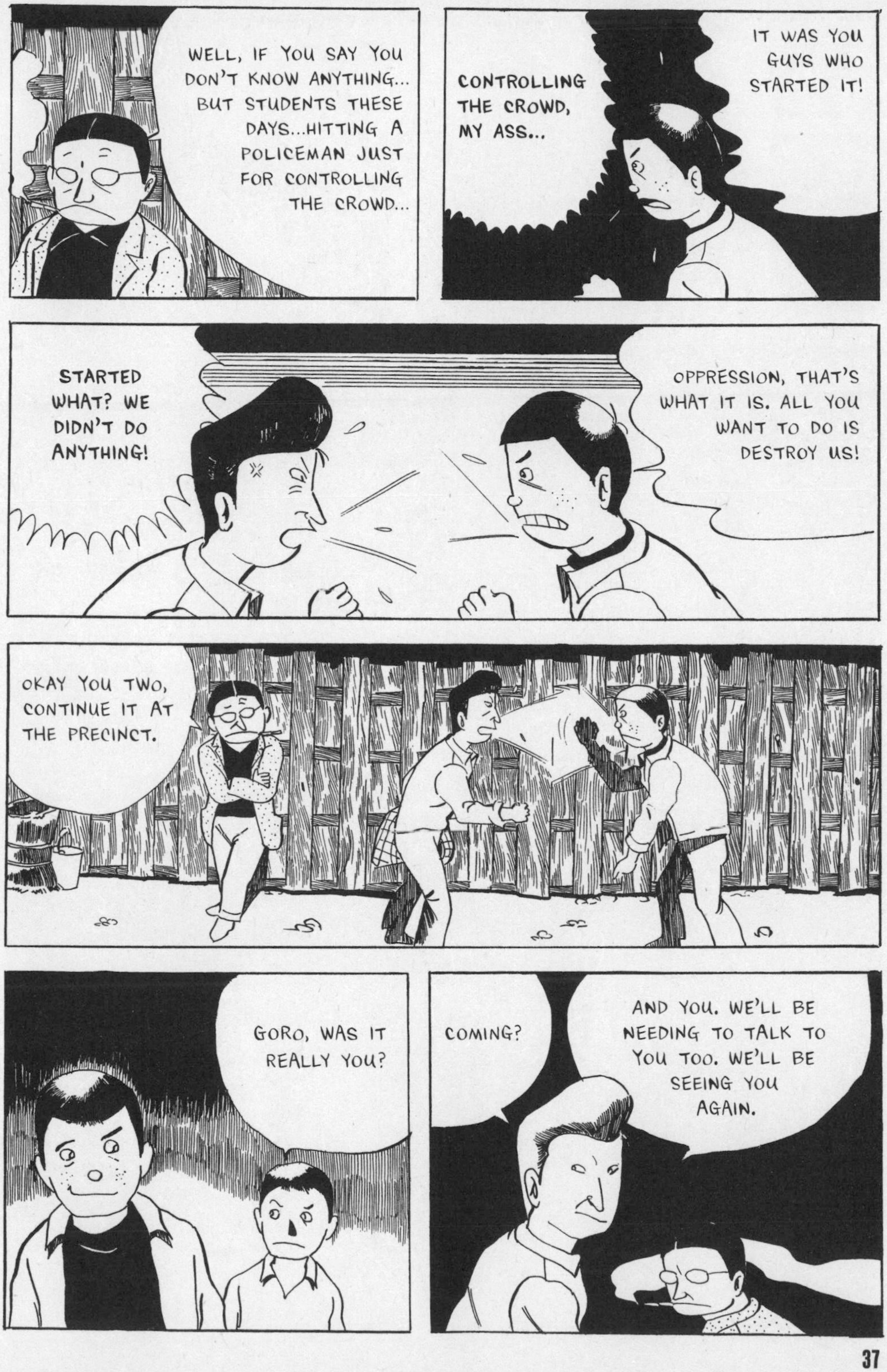

WELL, IF YOU SAY YOU DON'T KNOW ANYTHING... BUT STUDENTS THESE DAYS...HITTING A POLICEMAN JUST FOR CONTROLLING THE CROWD...
CONTROLLING THE CROWD, MY ASS...
IT WAS YOU GUYS WHO STARTED IT!
STARTED WHAT? WE DIDN'T DO ANYTHING!
OPPRESSION, THAT'S WHAT IT IS. ALL YOU WANT TO DO IS DESTROY US!
OKAY YOU TWO, CONTINUE IT AT THE PRECINCT.
GORO, WAS IT REALLY YOU?
COMING?
AND YOU. WE'LL BE NEEDING TO TALK TO YOU TOO. WE'LL BE SEEING YOU AGAIN.

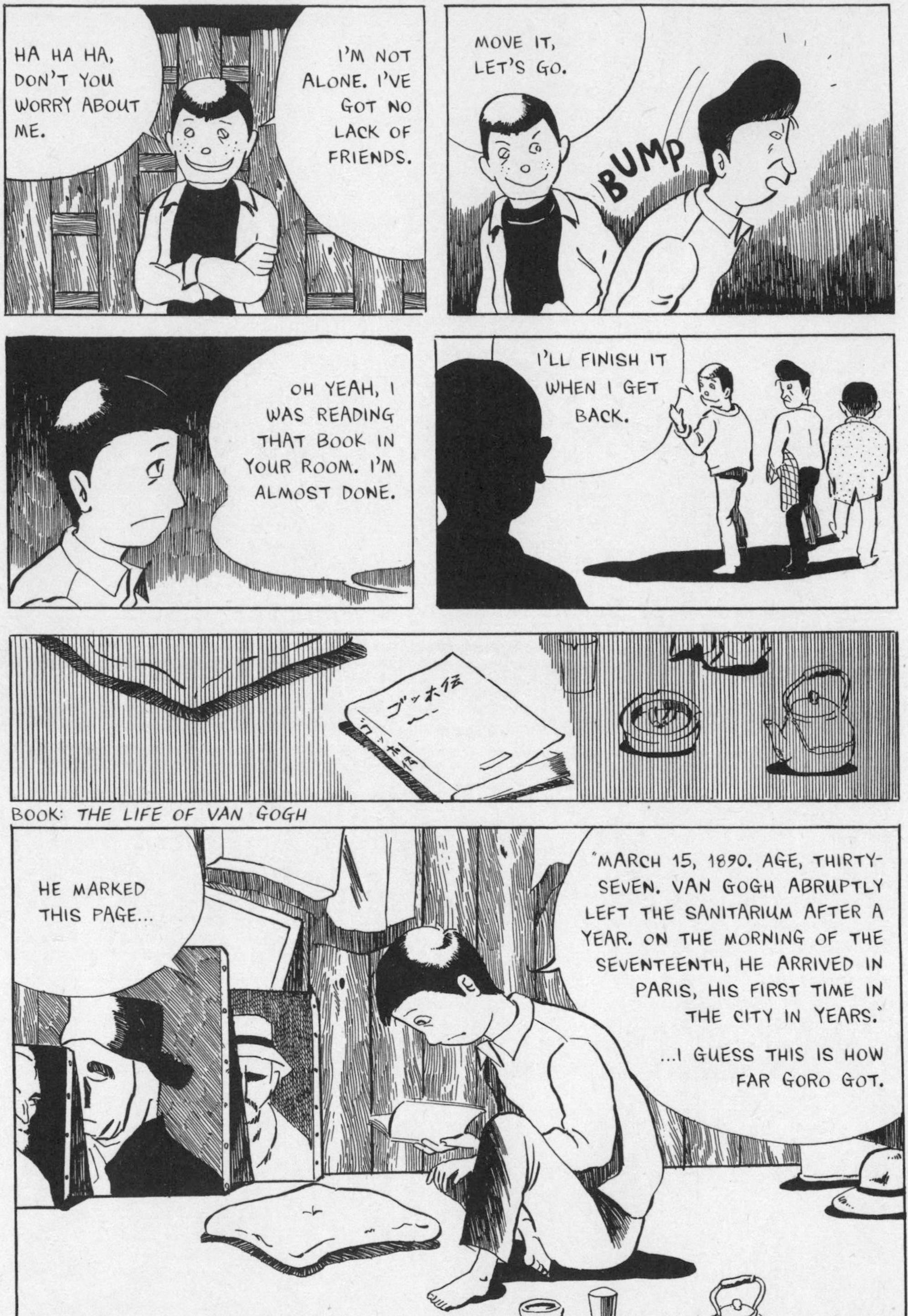
HA HA HA, DON'T YOU WORRY ABOUT ME.
I'M NOT ALONE. I'VE GOT NO LACK OF FRIENDS.
MOVE IT, LET'S GO.
BUMP
OH YEAH, I WAS READING THAT BOOK IN YOUR ROOM. I'M ALMOST DONE.
I'LL FINISH IT WHEN I GET BACK.
BOOK: THE LIFE OF VAN GOGH
HE MARKED THIS PAGE...
"MARCH 15, 1890. AGE, THIRTY-SEVEN. VAN GOGH ABRUPTLY LEFT THE SANITARIUM AFTER A YEAR. ON THE MORNING OF THE SEVENTEENTH, HE ARRIVED IN PARIS, HIS FIRST TIME IN THE CITY IN YEARS."
...I GUESS THIS IS HOW FAR GORO GOT.

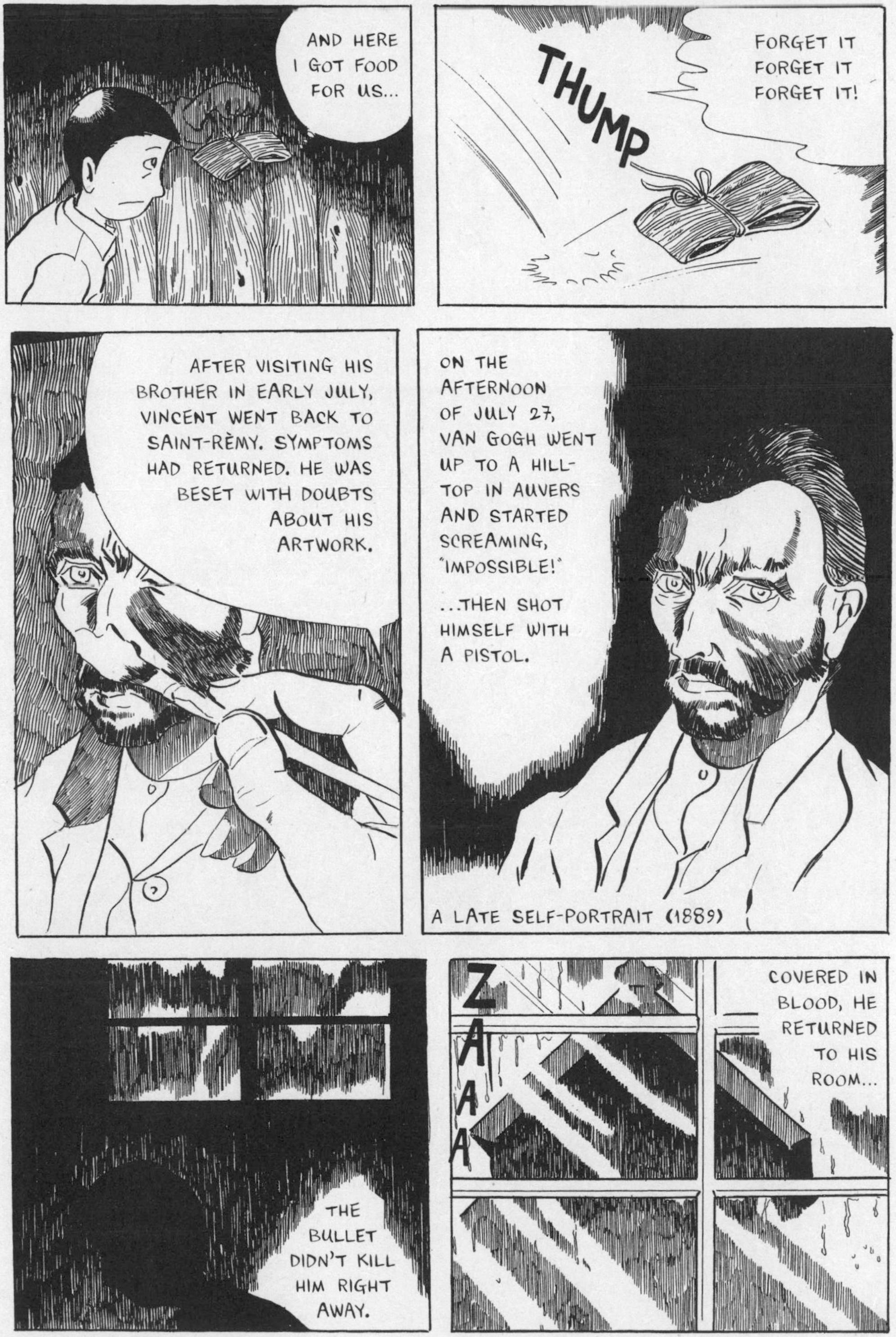
AND HERE I GOT FOOD FOR US...
THUMP
FORGET IT FORGET IT FORGET IT!
AFTER VISITING HIS BROTHER IN EARLY JULY, VINCENT WENT BACK TO SAINT-RÈMY. SYMPTOMS HAD RETURNED. HE WAS BESET WITH DOUBTS ABOUT HIS ARTWORK.
ON THE AFTERNOON OF JULY 27, VAN GOGH WENT UP TO A HILLTOP IN AUVERS AND STARTED SCREAMING, "IMPOSSIBLE!"
...THEN SHOT HIMSELF WITH A PISTOL.
A LATE SELF-PORTRAIT (1889)
THE BULLET DIDN'T KILL HIM RIGHT AWAY.
ZAAAA
COVERED IN BLOOD, HE RETURNED TO HIS ROOM...

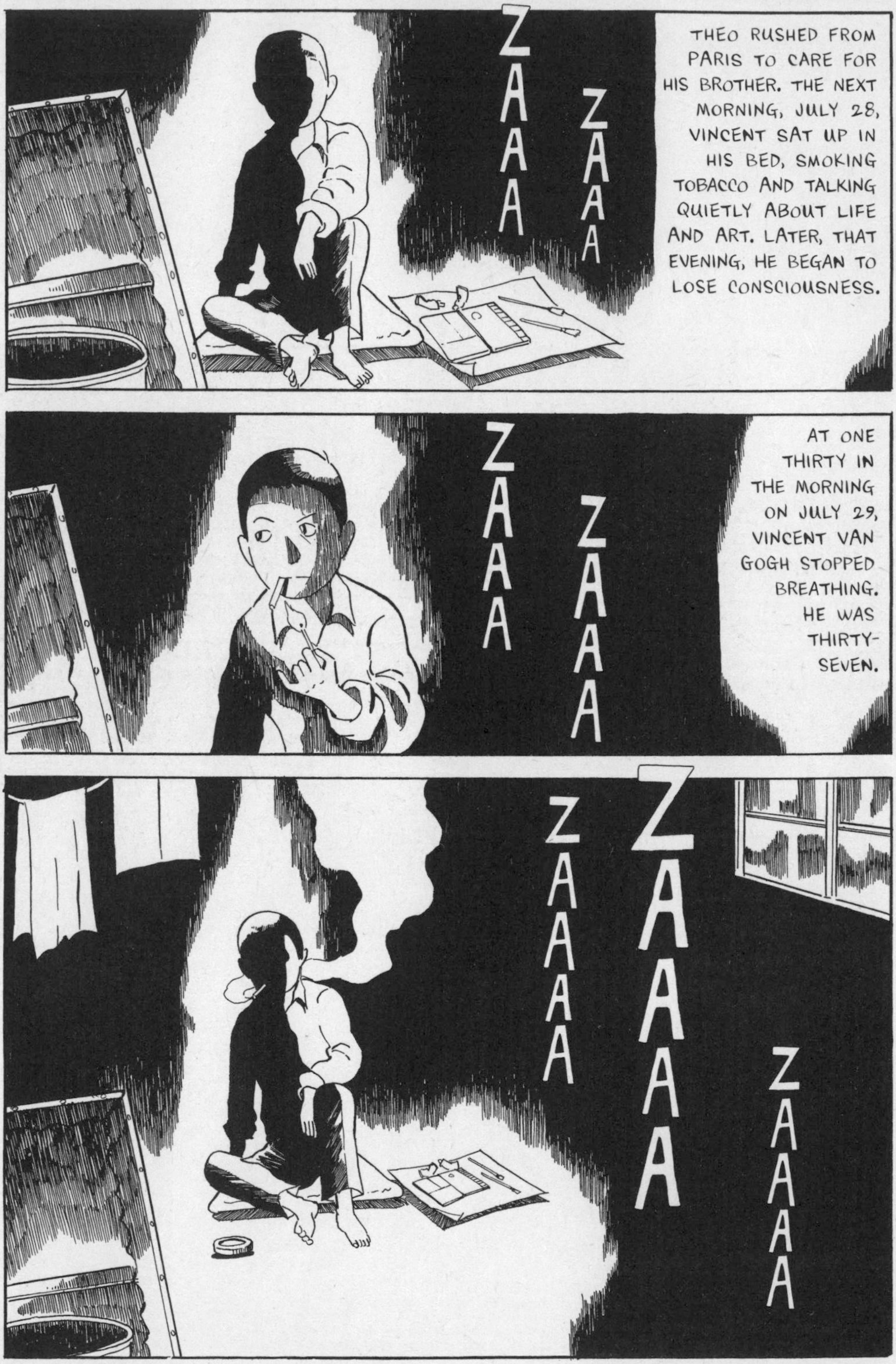
ZAAA
ZAAA
THEO RUSHED FROM PARIS TO CARE FOR HIS BROTHER. THE NEXT MORNING, JULY 28, VINCENT SAT UP IN HIS BED, SMOKING TOBACCO AND TALKING QUIETLY ABOUT LIFE AND ART. LATER, THAT EVENING, HE BEGAN TO LOSE CONSCIOUSNESS.
ZAAA
ZAAAA
AT ONE THIRTY IN THE MORNING ON JULY 29, VINCENT VAN GOGH STOPPED BREATHING. HE WAS THIRTY-SEVEN.
ZAAAA
ZAAAA
ZAAAA

SONG OF SHOWA

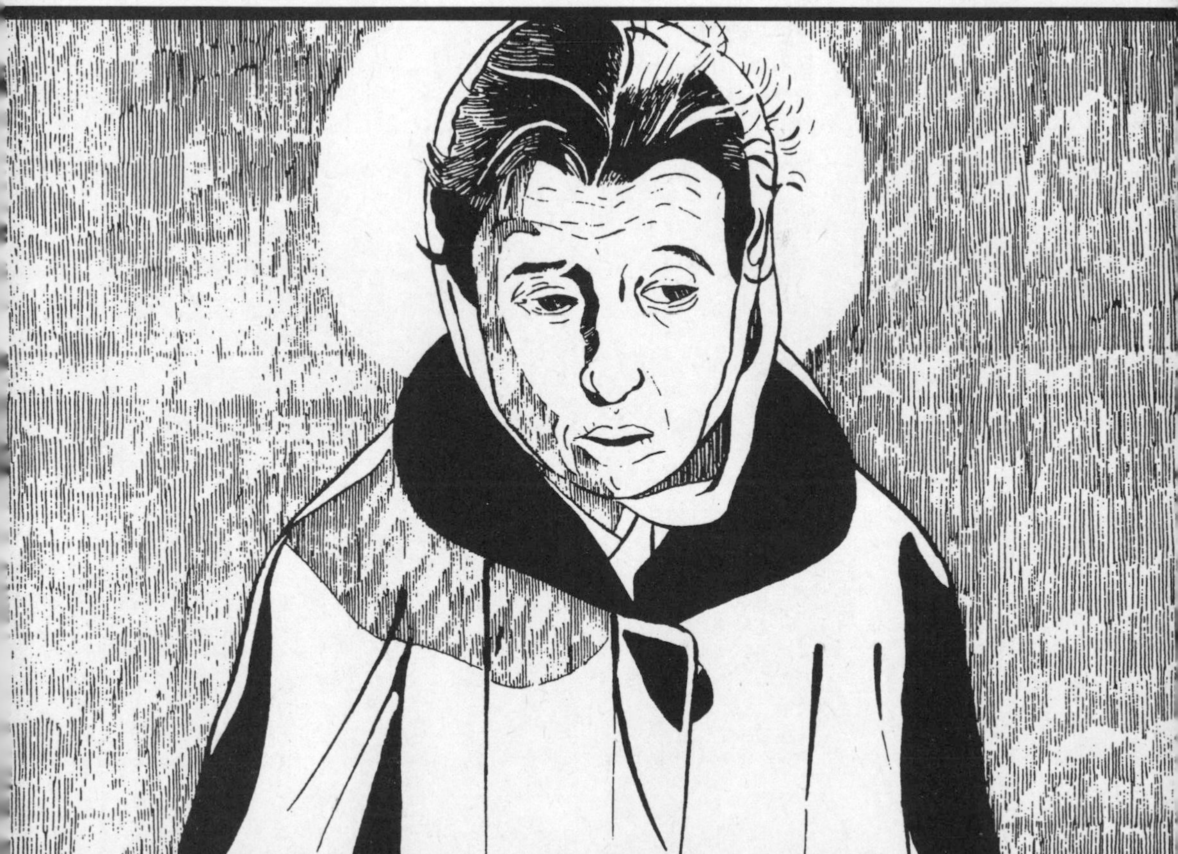

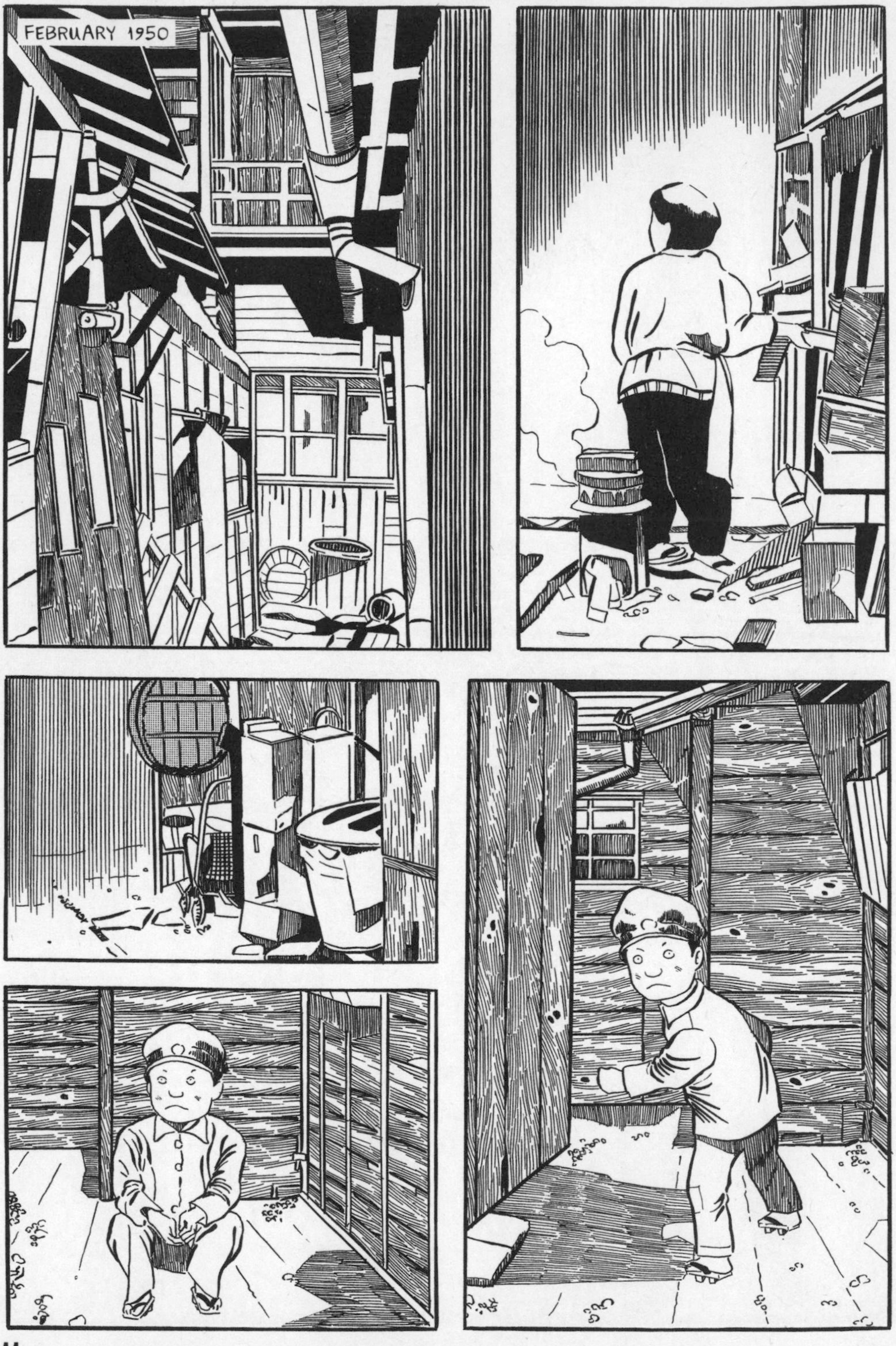
FEBRUARY 1950

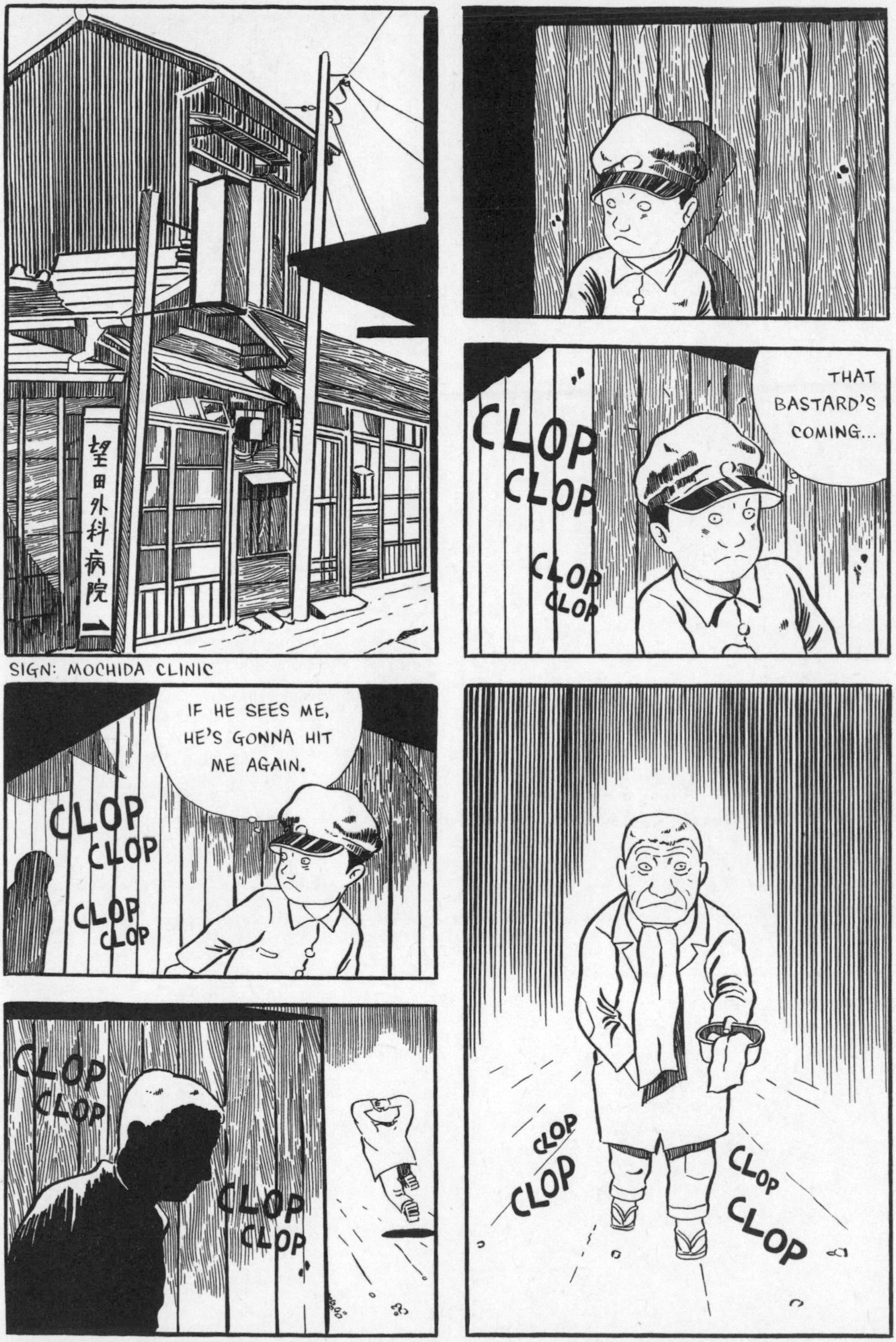
望田外科病院
SIGN: MOCHIDA CLINIC
CLOP CLOP CLOP CLOP
THAT BASTARD'S COMING...
IF HE SEES ME, HE'S GONNA HIT ME AGAIN.
CLOP CLOP CLOP CLOP
CLOP CLOP CLOP CLOP
CLOP CLOP CLOP CLOP

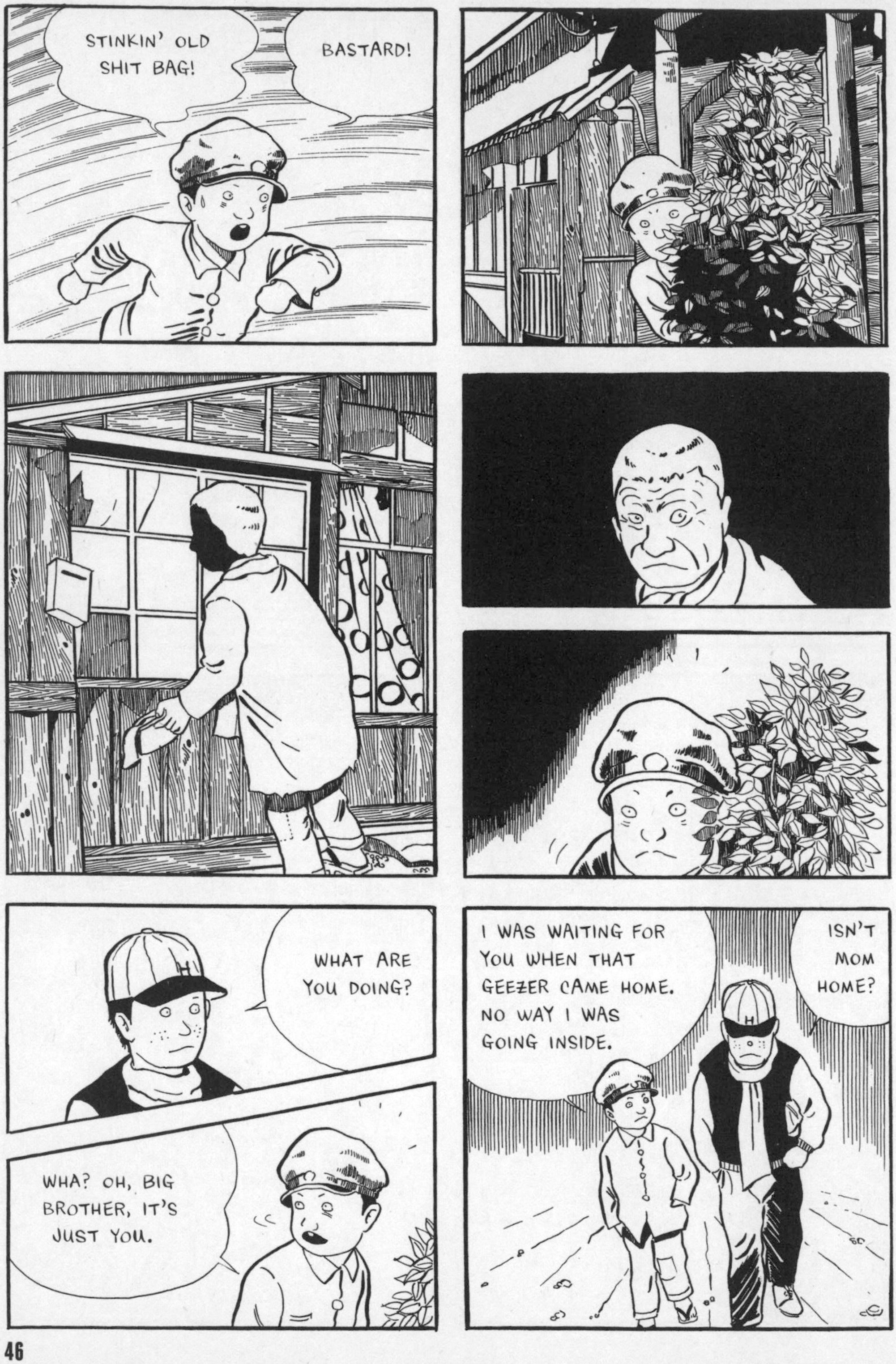
STINKIN' OLD SHIT BAG!
BASTARD!
WHAT ARE YOU DOING?
WHA? OH, BIG BROTHER, IT'S JUST YOU.
I WAS WAITING FOR YOU WHEN THAT GEEZER CAME HOME. NO WAY I WAS GOING INSIDE.
ISN'T MOM HOME?

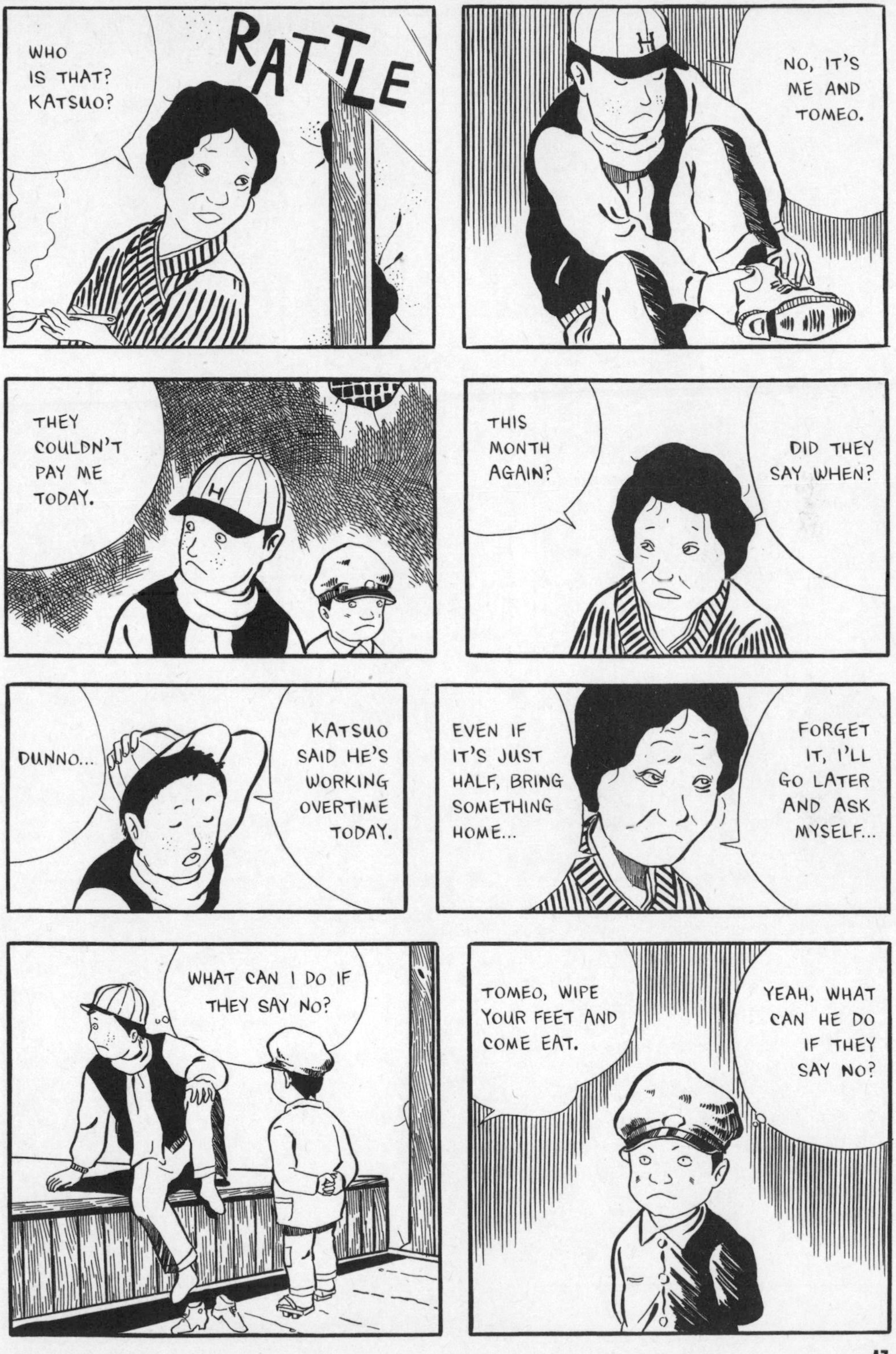
WHO IS THAT? KATSUO?
RATTLE
NO, IT'S ME AND TOMEO.
THEY COULDN'T PAY ME TODAY.
THIS MONTH AGAIN?
DID THEY SAY WHEN?
DUNNO...
KATSUO SAID HE'S WORKING OVERTIME TODAY.
EVEN IF IT'S JUST HALF, BRING SOMETHING HOME...
FORGET IT, I'LL GO LATER AND ASK MYSELF...
WHAT CAN I DO IF THEY SAY NO?
TOMEO, WIPE YOUR FEET AND COME EAT.
YEAH, WHAT CAN HE DO IF THEY SAY NO?

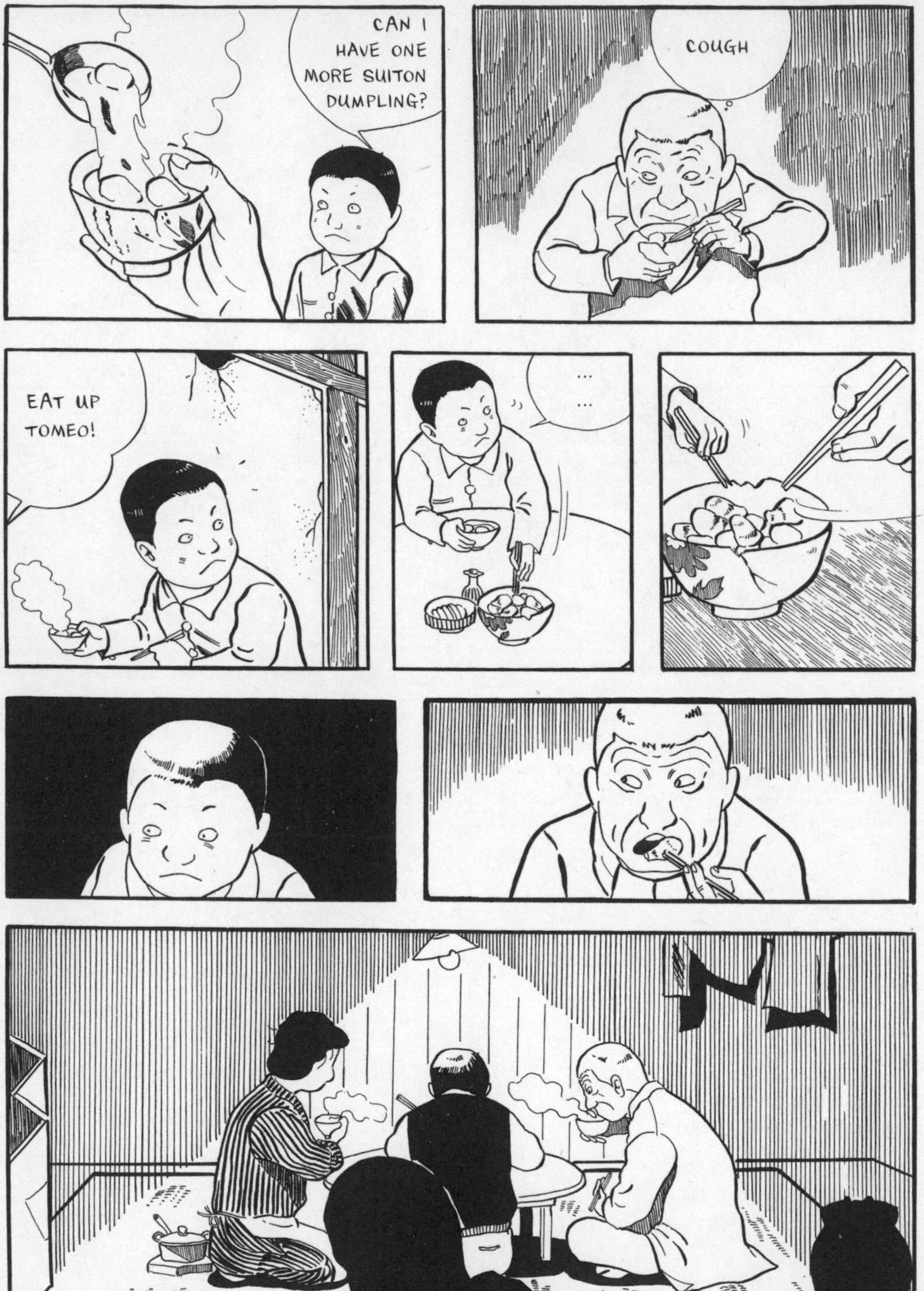

CAN I HAVE ONE MORE SUITON DUMPLING?
COUGH
EAT UP TOMEO!
...
...

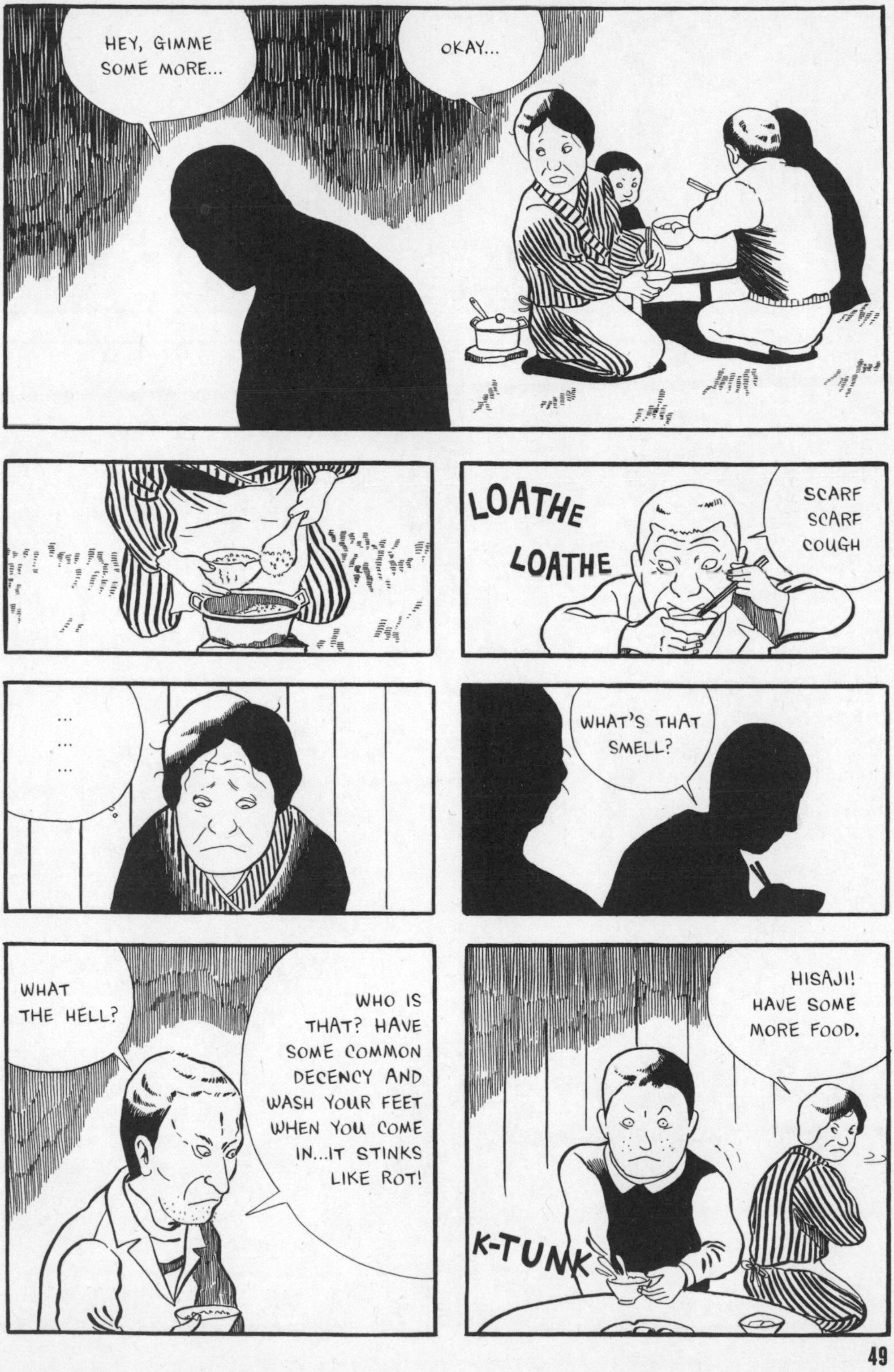
HEY, GIMME SOME MORE...
OKAY...
LOATHE
LOATHE
SCARF SCARF COUGH
...
...
...
WHAT'S THAT SMELL?
WHAT THE HELL?
WHO IS THAT? HAVE SOME COMMON DECENCY AND WASH YOUR FEET WHEN YOU COME IN...IT STINKS LIKE ROT!
HISAJI! HAVE SOME MORE FOOD.
K-TUNK

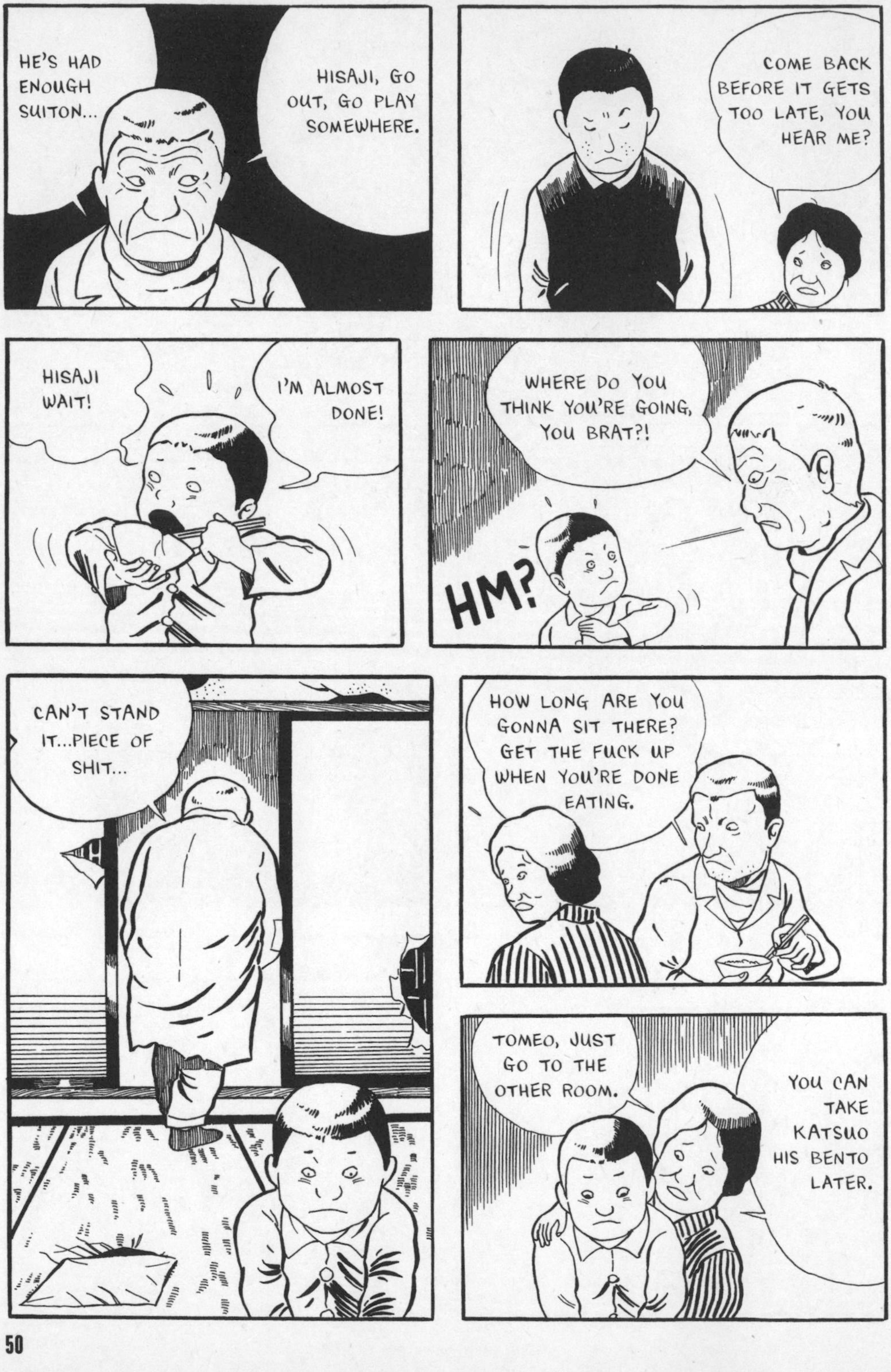

HE'S HAD ENOUGH SUITON...
HISAJI, GO OUT, GO PLAY SOMEWHERE.
COME BACK BEFORE IT GETS TOO LATE, YOU HEAR ME?
HISAJI WAIT!
I'M ALMOST DONE!
WHERE DO YOU THINK YOU'RE GOING, YOU BRAT?!
HM?
CAN'T STAND IT...PIECE OF SHIT...
HOW LONG ARE YOU GONNA SIT THERE? GET THE FUCK UP WHEN YOU'RE DONE EATING.
TOMEO, JUST GO TO THE OTHER ROOM.
YOU CAN TAKE KATSUO HIS BENTO LATER.

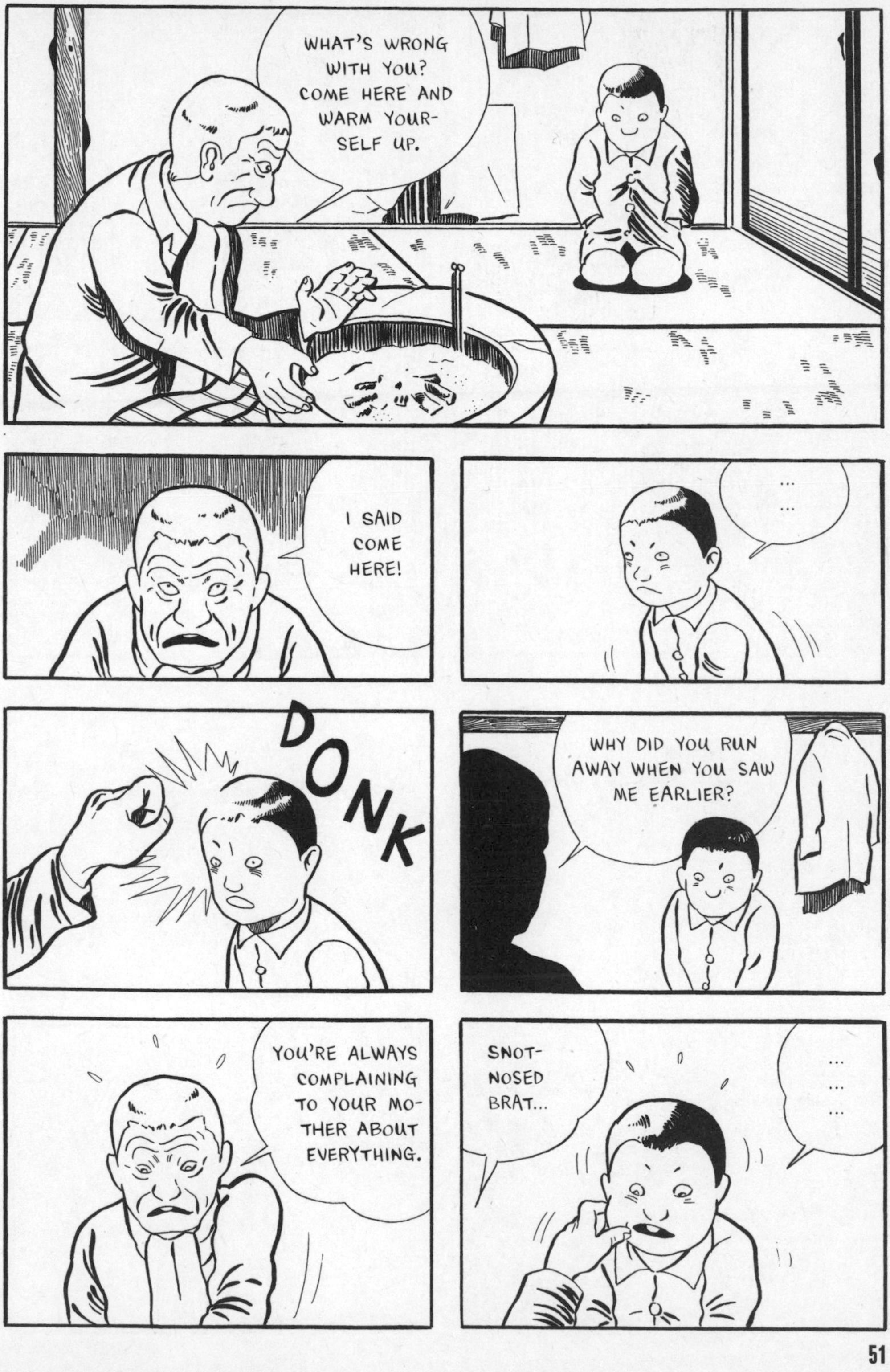
WHAT'S WRONG WITH YOU? COME HERE AND WARM YOUR-SELF UP.
I SAID COME HERE!
... ...
DONK
WHY DID YOU RUN AWAY WHEN YOU SAW ME EARLIER?
YOU'RE ALWAYS COMPLAINING TO YOUR MO-THER ABOUT EVERYTHING.
SNOT-NOSED BRAT...
... ...

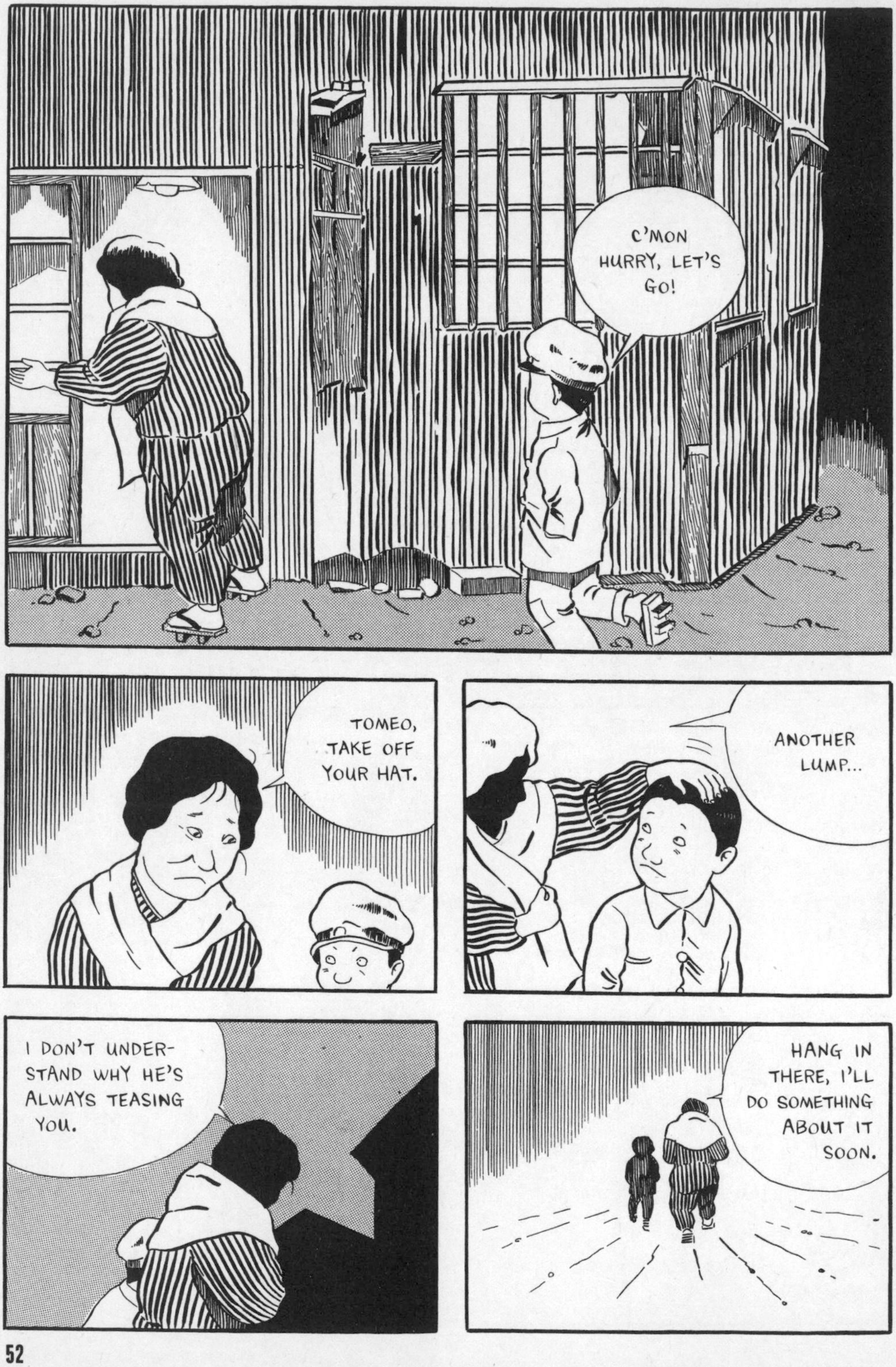
C'MON HURRY, LET'S GO!
TOMEO, TAKE OFF YOUR HAT.
ANOTHER LUMP...
I DON'T UNDER-STAND WHY HE'S ALWAYS TEASING YOU.
HANG IN THERE, I'LL DO SOMETHING ABOUT IT SOON.

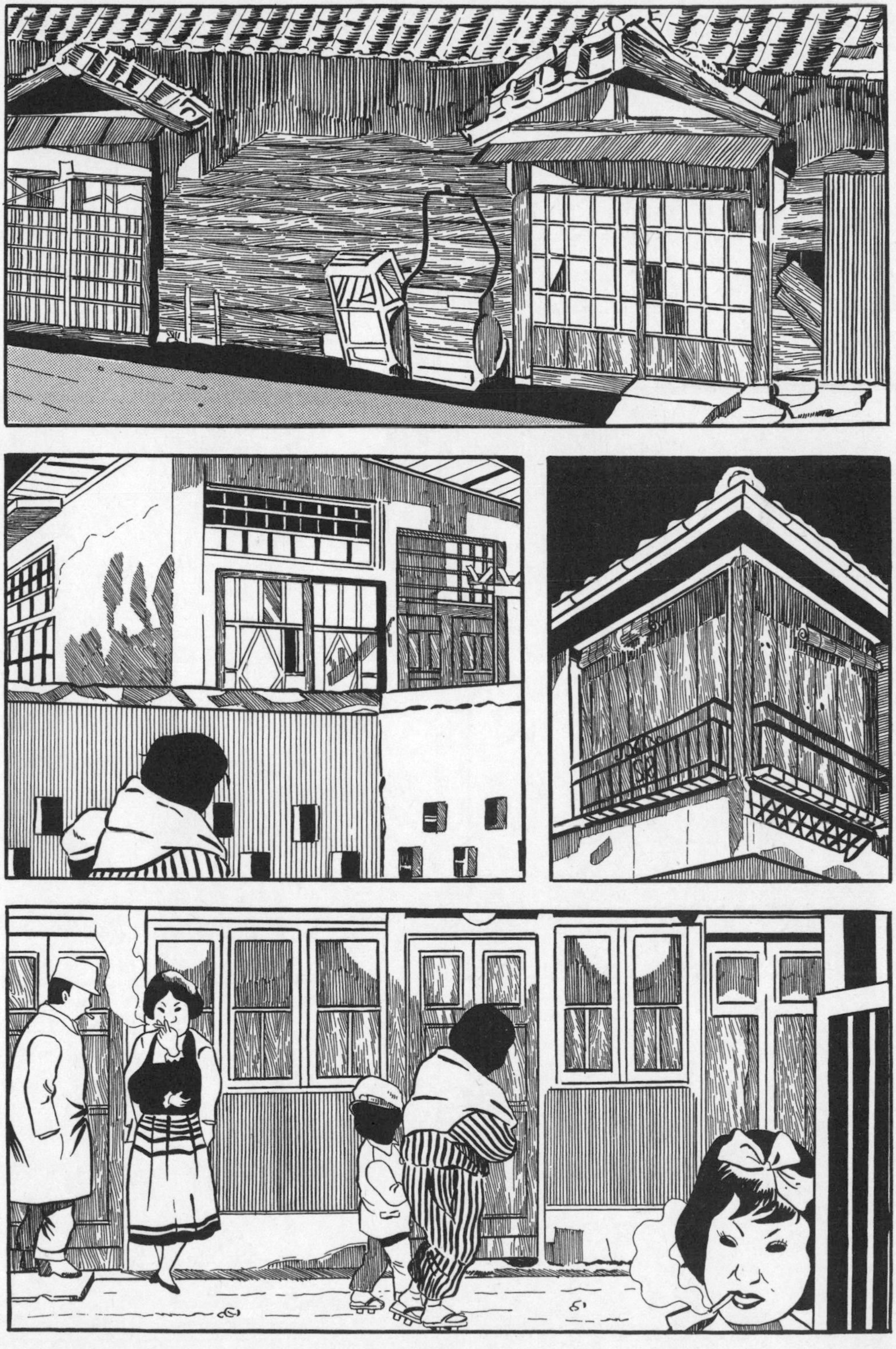

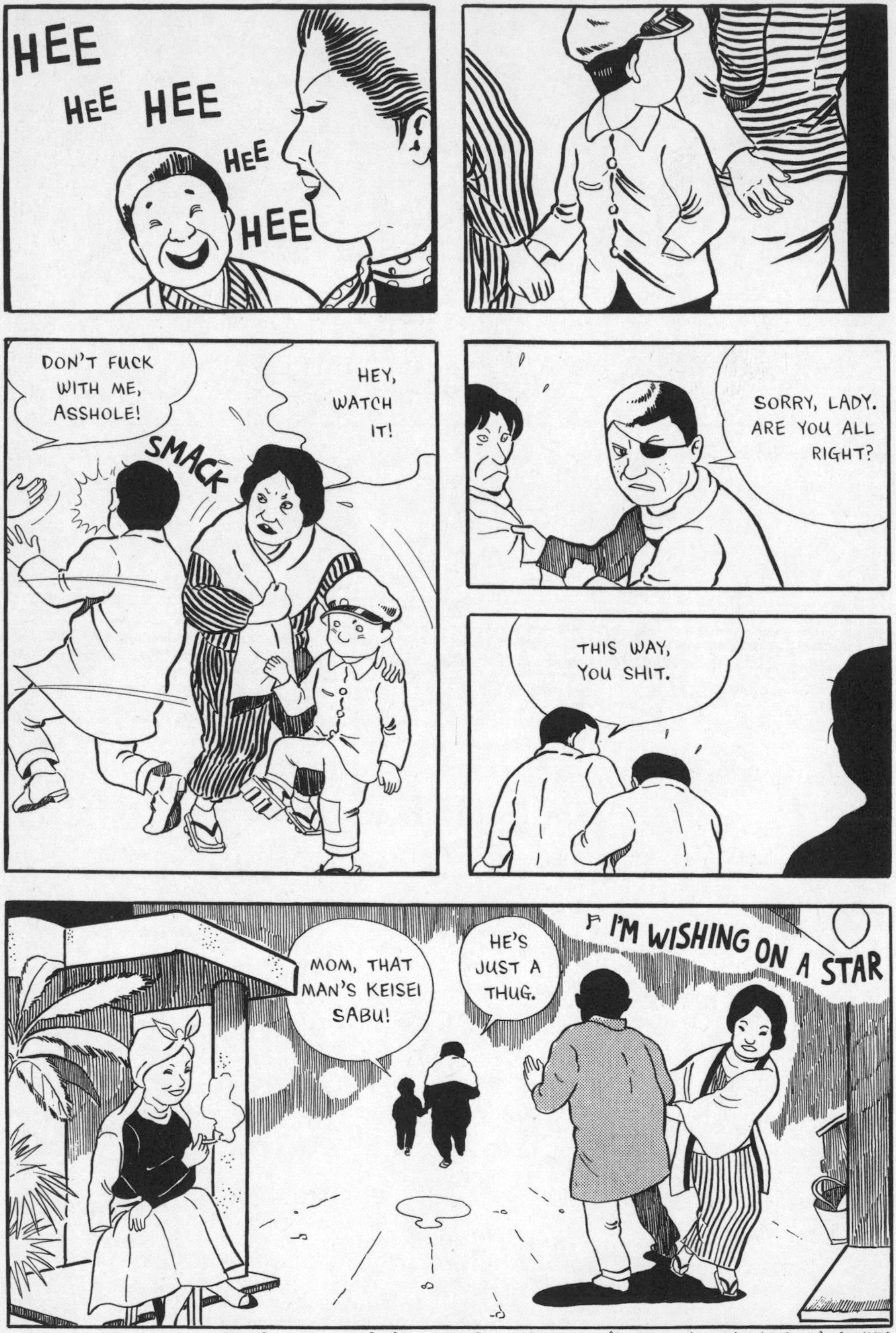
HEE
HEE HEE
HEE
HEE
DON'T FUCK WITH ME, ASSHOLE!
SMACK
HEY, WATCH IT!
SORRY, LADY. ARE YOU ALL RIGHT?
THIS WAY, YOU SHIT.
MOM, THAT MAN'S KEISEI SABU!
HE'S JUST A THUG.
♪ I'M WISHING ON A STAR

SONG: POP SONG ABOUT PROSTITUTION, "HOSHI NO NAGARE NI" (1947)

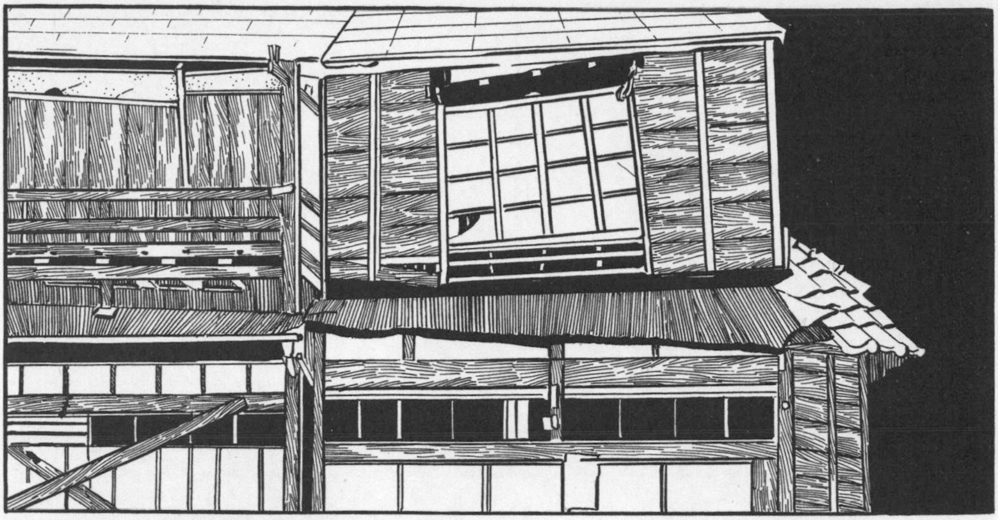

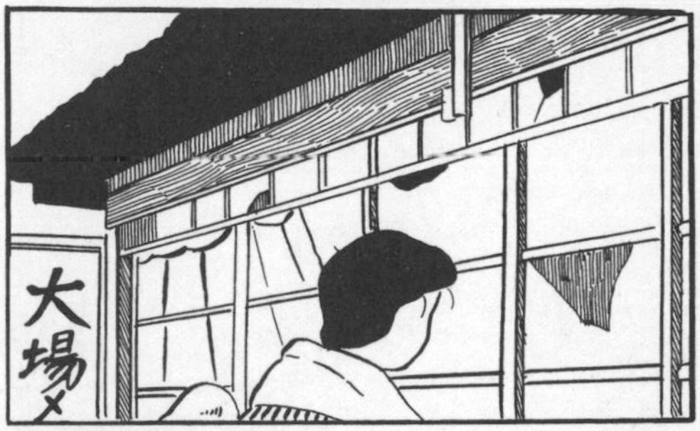
大場

SIGN: OBA

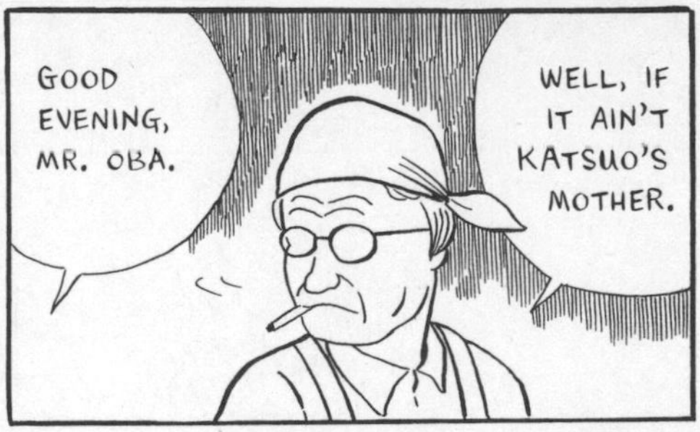
GOOD EVENING, MR. OBA.
WELL, IF IT AIN'T KATSUO'S MOTHER.

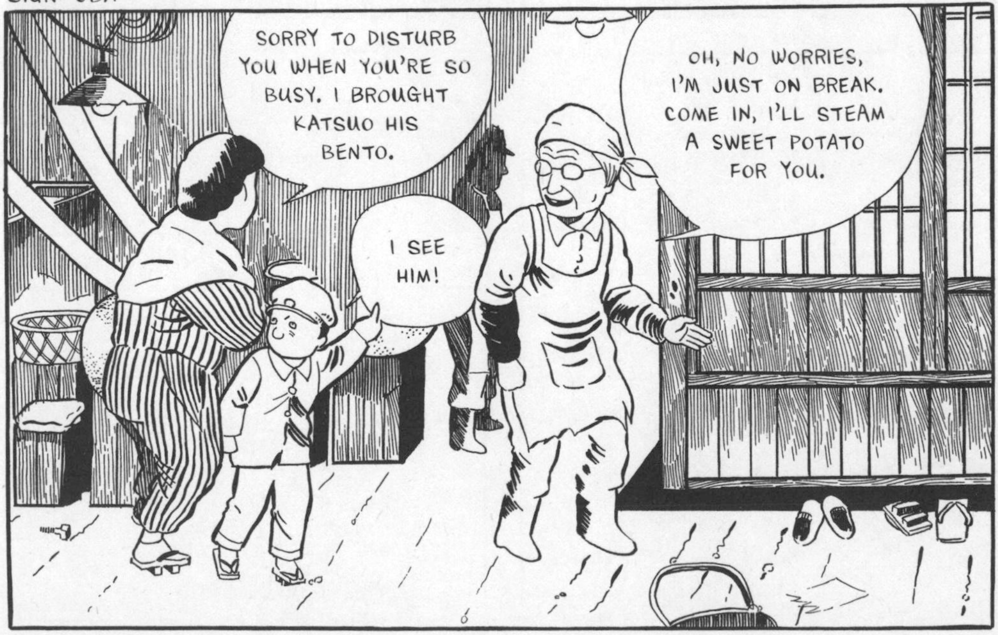
SORRY TO DISTURB YOU WHEN YOU'RE SO BUSY. I BROUGHT KATSUO HIS BENTO.
I SEE HIM!
OH, NO WORRIES, I'M JUST ON BREAK. COME IN, I'LL STEAM A SWEET POTATO FOR YOU.

SORRY TO SPRING THIS ON YOU, BUT CAN'T YOU SPARE AT LEAST HALF HIS PAY?

WELL, THAT'S JUST THE THING...

FRANKLY, THINGS ARE REALLY TIGHT RIGHT NOW. I CAN'T EVEN AFFORD RICE.

TOMEO, TAKE THIS TO YOUR BROTHER. TELL HIM THE BUNS ARE BUTTERED.

MOMMY HAS TO TALK TO MR. OBA.

SUBCON- TRACTORS LIKE ME ARE ALL HAVING A HARD TIME.

I EVEN ASKED THE CONTRACTORS, BUT THEY SAID NO MONEY UNTIL THE GOODS ARE DELIVERED.

BESIDES, IT'S HARD TO ASK FOR AN ADVANCE FROM THEM WHEN YOU'RE ALREADY BEHIND SCHEDULE. WORSE WOULD BE IF THEY GAVE THE WORK TO SOMEONE ELSE, THEN I'D BE FINISHED.

...
...

THAT'S WHY I'M ASKING YOU TO GIVE ME TWO DAYS. TWO DAYS ARE ALL I NEED.

I GUESS IT'S TOUGH FOR EVERY- ONE...

...WELL... WHAT TO DO...

KATSUO, YOUR MOM'S LEAVING.

WAIT A SEC.

KATSUO, I'M GOING.

SO, DID HE GIVE YOU THE MONEY?

HE SAID NO.

HMMM. YOU DON'T HAVE ANYTHING FOR TOMORROW, RIGHT?

DON'T WORRY ABOUT THAT. JUST COME HOME AS SOON AS YOU CAN.

SINCE I'M NOT IN THE SAME ROOM AS TOMEO, WHEN YOU'RE NOT HOME...POOR CHILD...

HE DOESN'T DARE TOUCH TOMEO IN FRONT OF HISAJI OR ME.

YOUR FATHER HAS SUCH A SHORT TEMPER. I CAN'T HAVE TOMEO IN OUR ROOM...

THERE'S NOWHERE FOR HIM TO GO.

WHEN HE DOESN'T OBEY YOUR FATHER, WHO KNOWS WHAT'LL HAPPEN? AND GRANDDAD CONSTANTLY PICKS ON HIM...

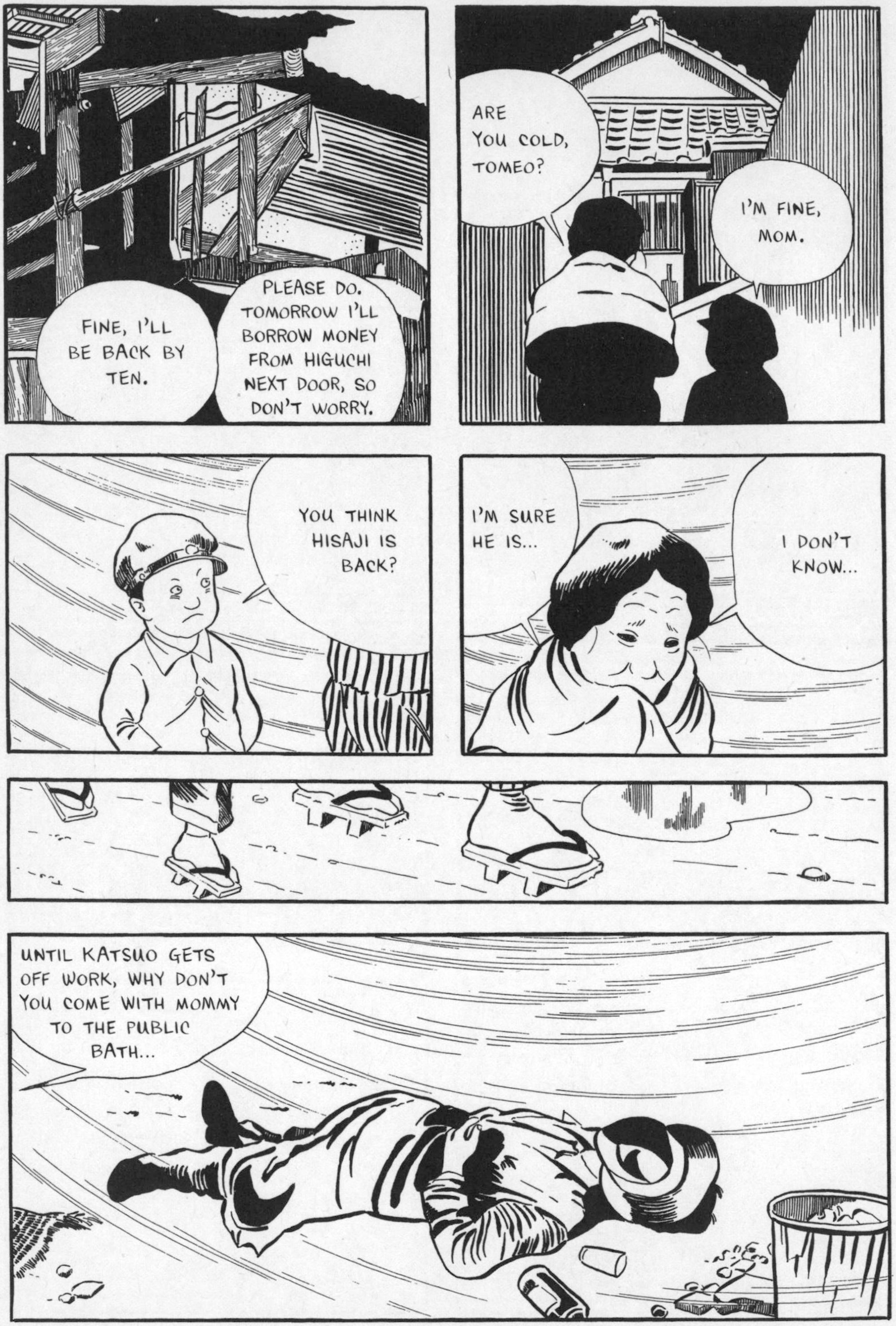
FINE, I'LL BE BACK BY TEN.
PLEASE DO. TOMORROW I'LL BORROW MONEY FROM HIGUCHI NEXT DOOR, SO DON'T WORRY.
ARE YOU COLD, TOMEO?
I'M FINE, MOM.
YOU THINK HISAJI IS BACK?
I'M SURE HE IS...
I DON'T KNOW...
UNTIL KATSUO GETS OFF WORK, WHY DON'T YOU COME WITH MOMMY TO THE PUBLIC BATH...

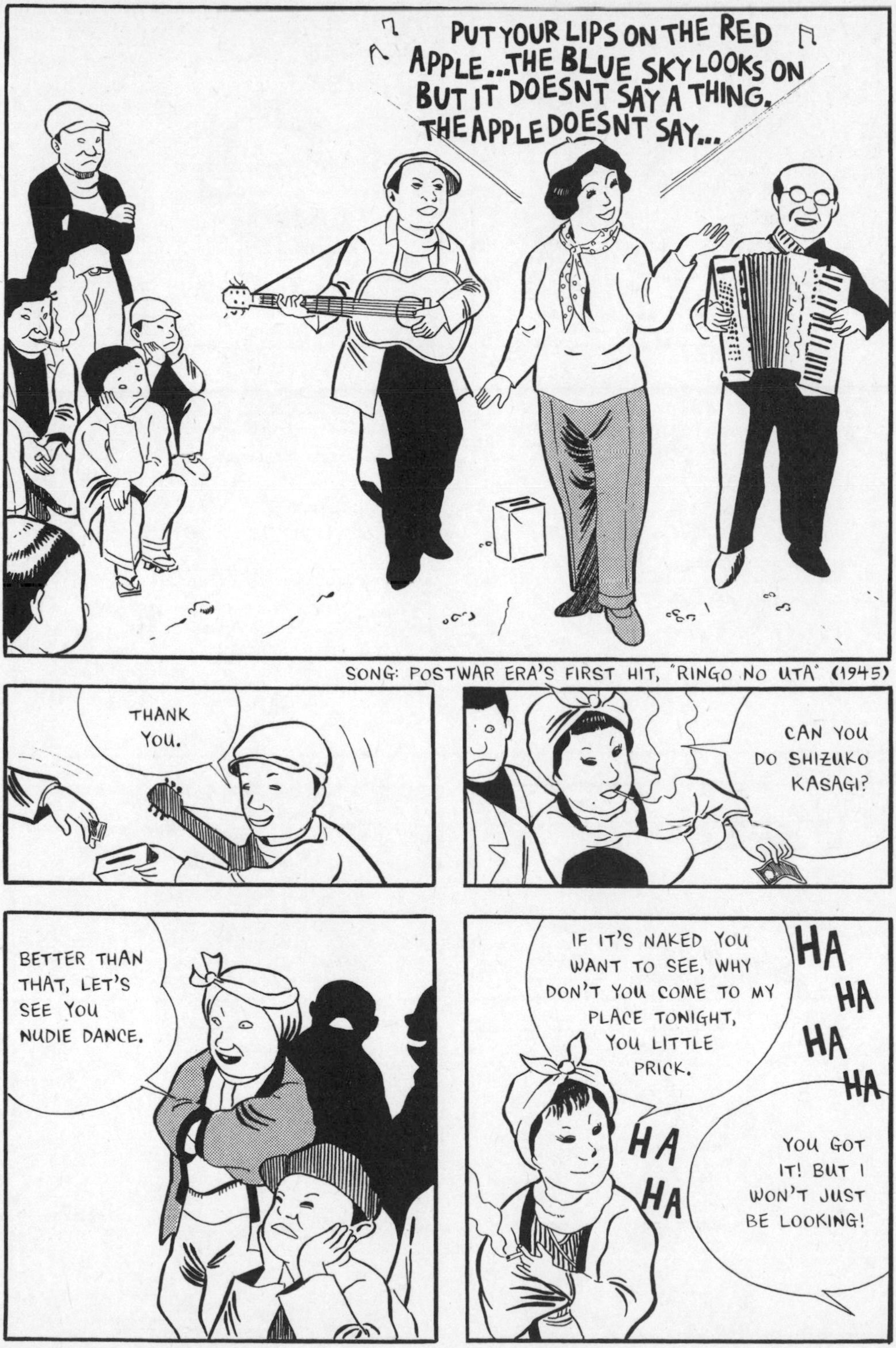
PUT YOUR LIPS ON THE RED APPLE...THE BLUE SKY LOOKS ON BUT IT DOESNT SAY A THING. THE APPLE DOESNT SAY...
SONG: POSTWAR ERA'S FIRST HIT, "RINGO NO UTA" (1945)
THANK YOU.
CAN YOU DO SHIZUKO KASAGI?
BETTER THAN THAT, LET'S SEE YOU NUDIE DANCE.
IF IT'S NAKED YOU WANT TO SEE, WHY DON'T YOU COME TO MY PLACE TONIGHT, YOU LITTLE PRICK.
HA HA HA HA
HA HA
YOU GOT IT! BUT I WON'T JUST BE LOOKING!

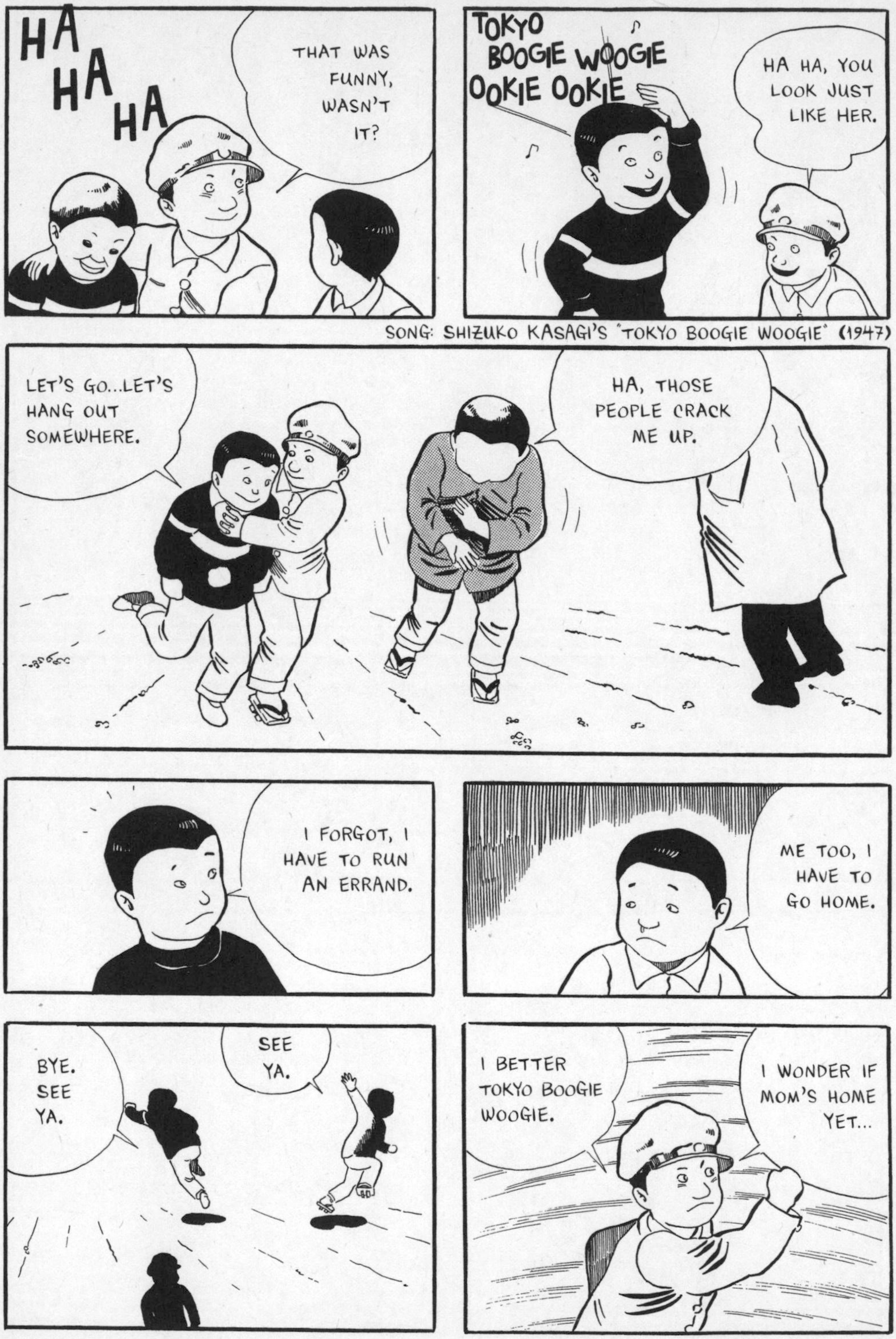
HA HA HA
THAT WAS FUNNY, WASN'T IT?
TOKYO BOOGIE WOOGIE OOKIE OOKIE
HA HA, YOU LOOK JUST LIKE HER.
SONG: SHIZUKO KASAGI'S "TOKYO BOOGIE WOOGIE" (1947)
LET'S GO...LET'S HANG OUT SOMEWHERE.
HA, THOSE PEOPLE CRACK ME UP.
I FORGOT, I HAVE TO RUN AN ERRAND.
ME TOO, I HAVE TO GO HOME.
BYE. SEE YA.
SEE YA.
I BETTER TOKYO BOOGIE WOOGIE.
I WONDER IF MOM'S HOME YET...

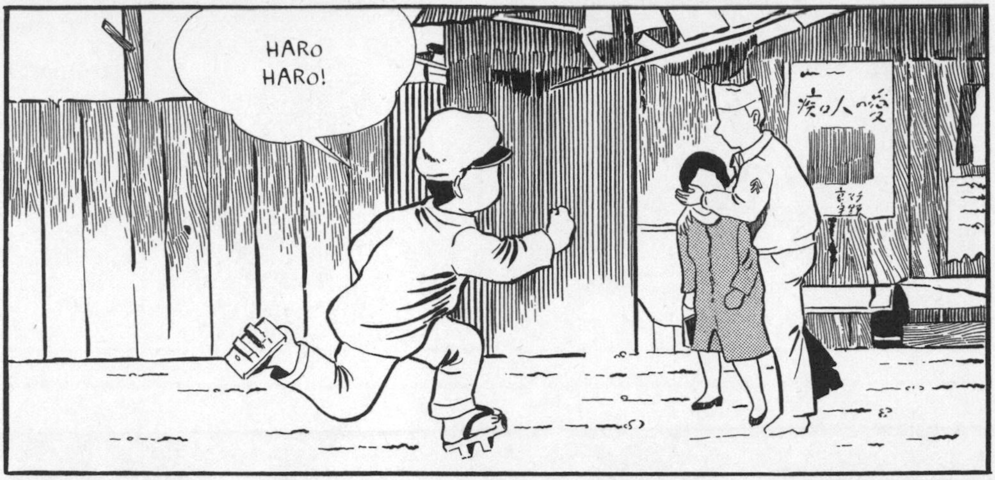
HARO
HARO!

SIGN: *A FOOL'S LOVE* (MOVIE POSTER)

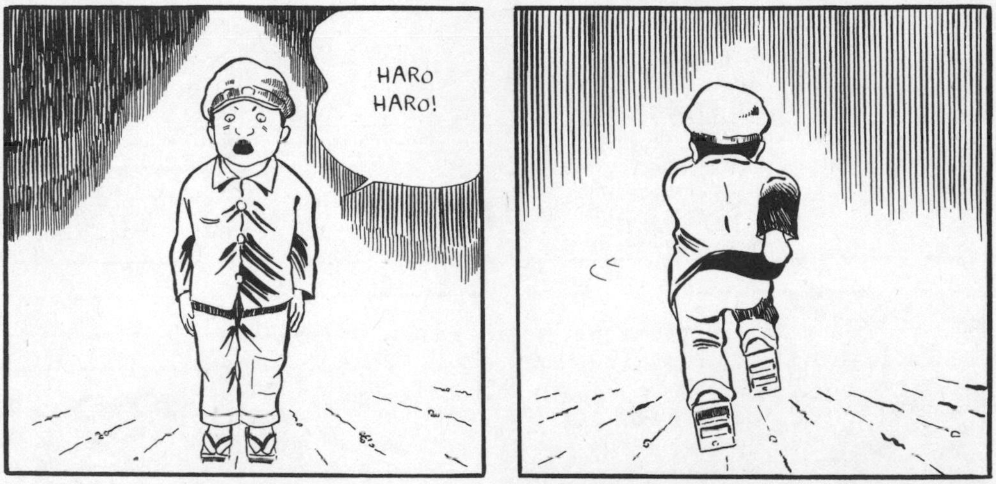
HARO
HARO!

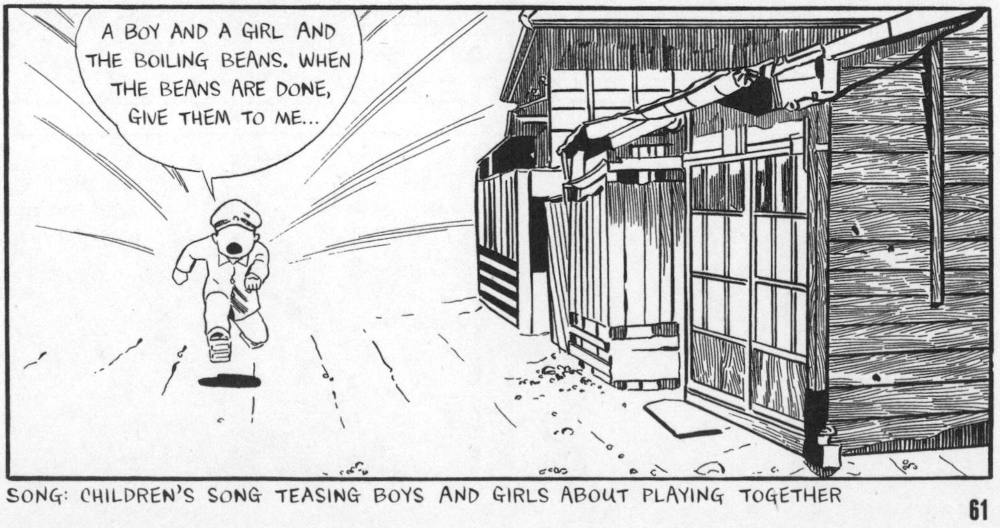
A BOY AND A GIRL AND THE BOILING BEANS. WHEN THE BEANS ARE DONE, GIVE THEM TO ME...

SONG: CHILDREN'S SONG TEASING BOYS AND GIRLS ABOUT PLAYING TOGETHER

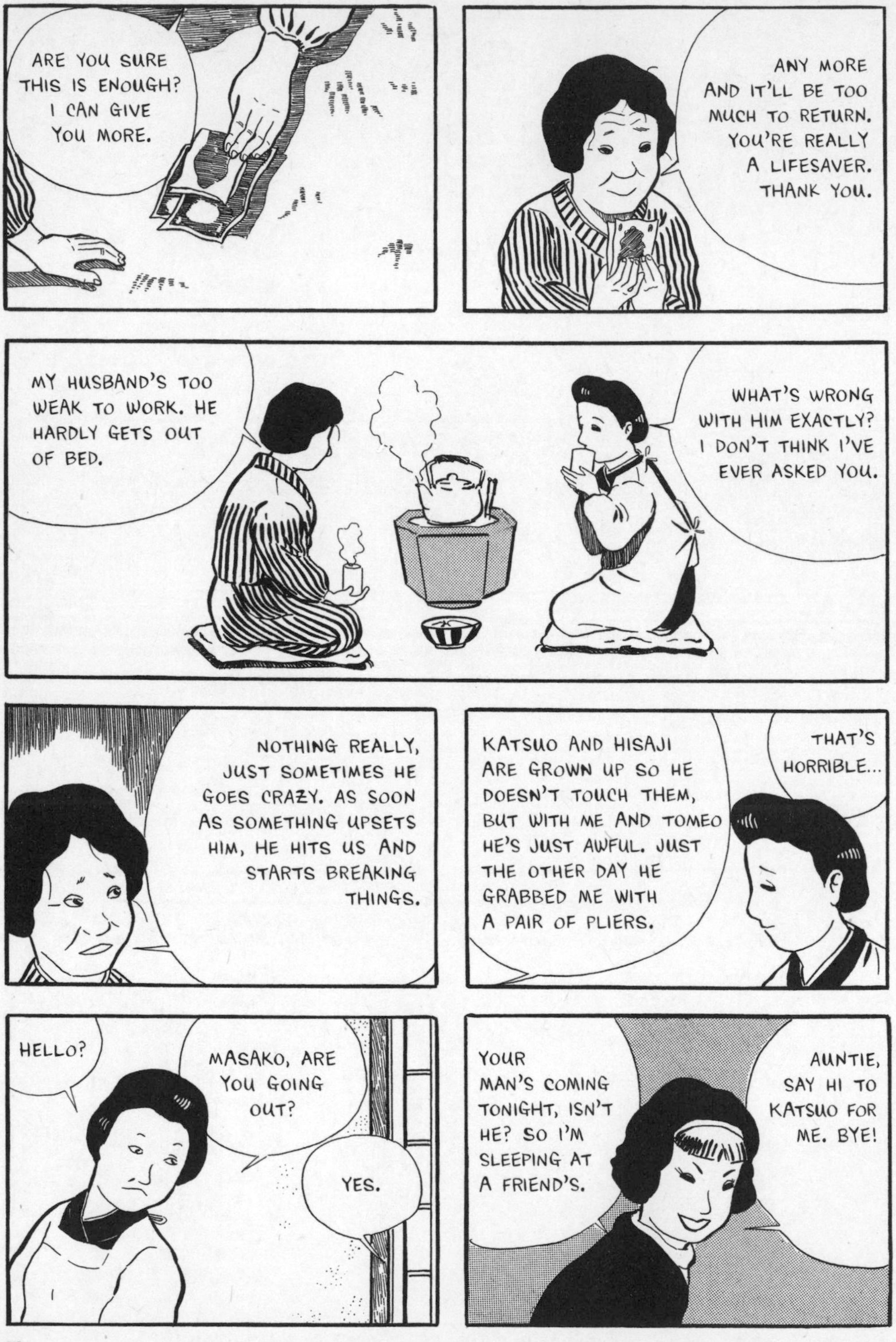
ARE YOU SURE THIS IS ENOUGH? I CAN GIVE YOU MORE.
ANY MORE AND IT'LL BE TOO MUCH TO RETURN. YOU'RE REALLY A LIFESAVER. THANK YOU.
MY HUSBAND'S TOO WEAK TO WORK. HE HARDLY GETS OUT OF BED.
WHAT'S WRONG WITH HIM EXACTLY? I DON'T THINK I'VE EVER ASKED YOU.
NOTHING REALLY, JUST SOMETIMES HE GOES CRAZY. AS SOON AS SOMETHING UPSETS HIM, HE HITS US AND STARTS BREAKING THINGS.
KATSUO AND HISAJI ARE GROWN UP SO HE DOESN'T TOUCH THEM, BUT WITH ME AND TOMEO HE'S JUST AWFUL. JUST THE OTHER DAY HE GRABBED ME WITH A PAIR OF PLIERS.
THAT'S HORRIBLE...
HELLO?
MASAKO, ARE YOU GOING OUT?
YES.
YOUR MAN'S COMING TONIGHT, ISN'T HE? SO I'M SLEEPING AT A FRIEND'S.
AUNTIE, SAY HI TO KATSUO FOR ME. BYE!

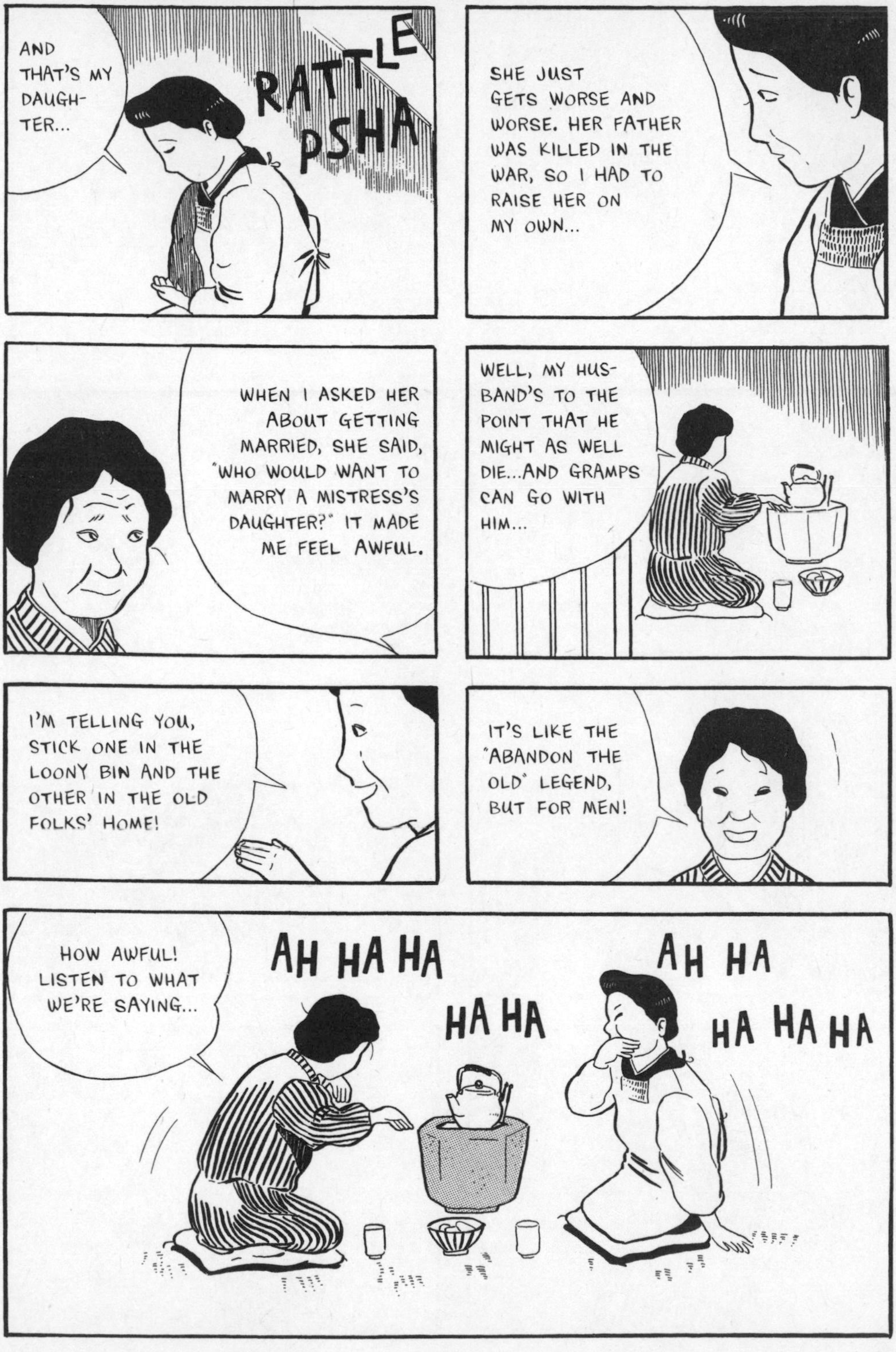
AND THAT'S MY DAUGHTER...
RATTLE
PSHA
SHE JUST GETS WORSE AND WORSE. HER FATHER WAS KILLED IN THE WAR, SO I HAD TO RAISE HER ON MY OWN...
WHEN I ASKED HER ABOUT GETTING MARRIED, SHE SAID, "WHO WOULD WANT TO MARRY A MISTRESS'S DAUGHTER?" IT MADE ME FEEL AWFUL.
WELL, MY HUSBAND'S TO THE POINT THAT HE MIGHT AS WELL DIE...AND GRAMPS CAN GO WITH HIM...
I'M TELLING YOU, STICK ONE IN THE LOONY BIN AND THE OTHER IN THE OLD FOLKS' HOME!
IT'S LIKE THE "ABANDON THE OLD" LEGEND, BUT FOR MEN!
HOW AWFUL! LISTEN TO WHAT WE'RE SAYING...
AH HA HA
HA HA
AH HA
HA HA HA

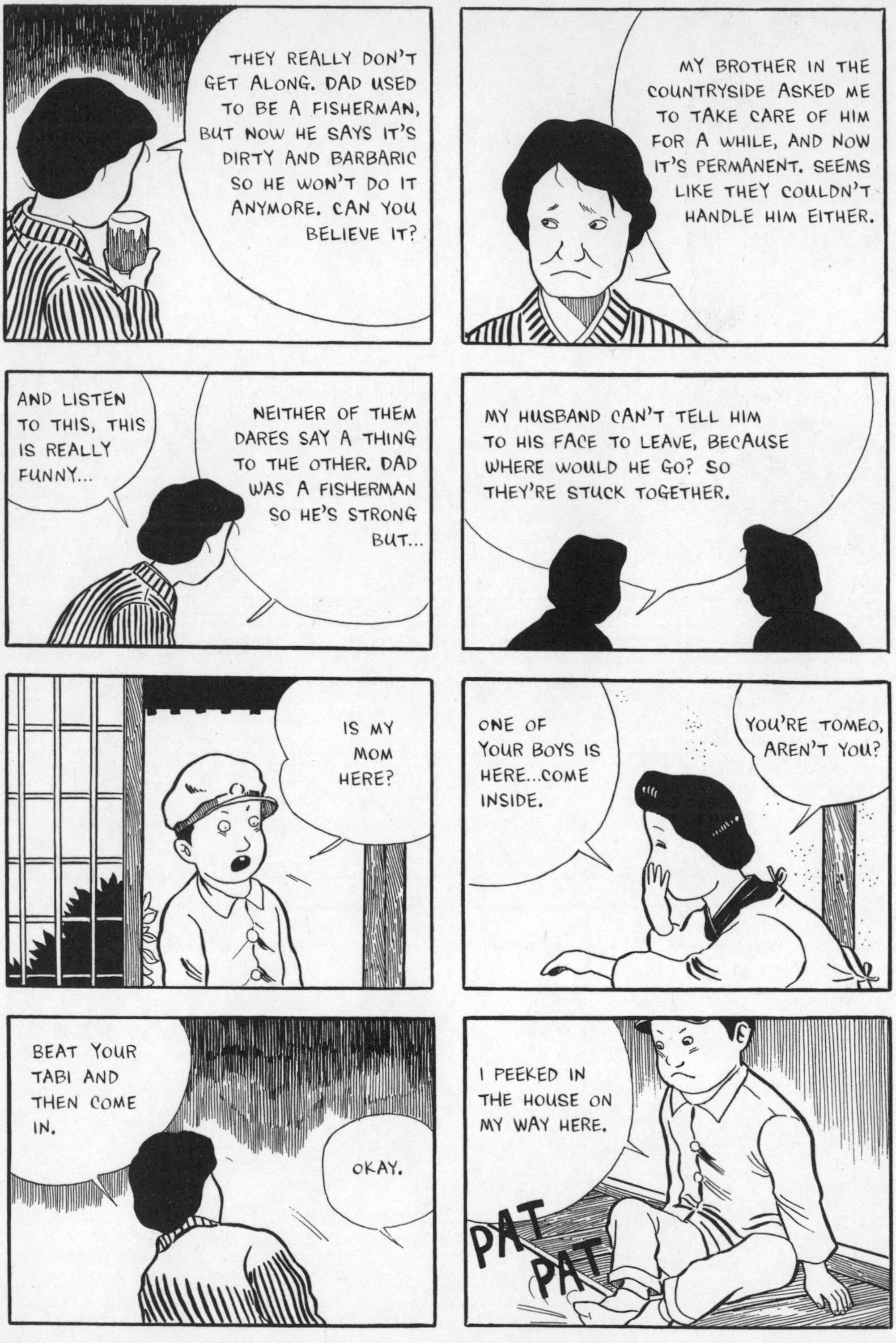
THEY REALLY DON'T GET ALONG. DAD USED TO BE A FISHERMAN, BUT NOW HE SAYS IT'S DIRTY AND BARBARIC SO HE WON'T DO IT ANYMORE. CAN YOU BELIEVE IT?
MY BROTHER IN THE COUNTRYSIDE ASKED ME TO TAKE CARE OF HIM FOR A WHILE, AND NOW IT'S PERMANENT. SEEMS LIKE THEY COULDN'T HANDLE HIM EITHER.
AND LISTEN TO THIS, THIS IS REALLY FUNNY...
NEITHER OF THEM DARES SAY A THING TO THE OTHER. DAD WAS A FISHERMAN SO HE'S STRONG BUT...
MY HUSBAND CAN'T TELL HIM TO HIS FACE TO LEAVE, BECAUSE WHERE WOULD HE GO? SO THEY'RE STUCK TOGETHER.
IS MY MOM HERE?
ONE OF YOUR BOYS IS HERE...COME INSIDE.
YOU'RE TOMEO, AREN'T YOU?
BEAT YOUR TABI AND THEN COME IN.
OKAY.
I PEEKED IN THE HOUSE ON MY WAY HERE.
PAT
PAT

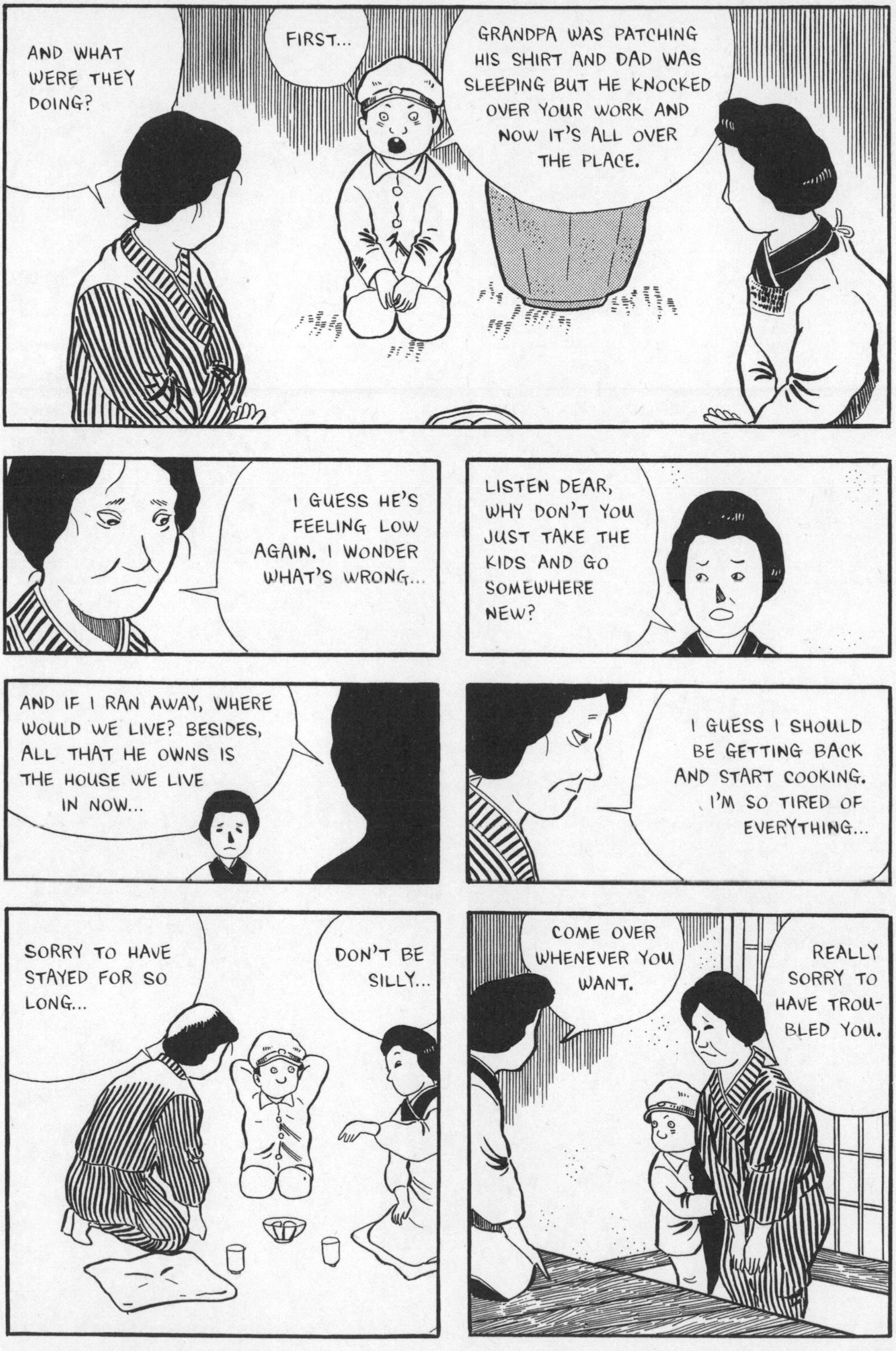
AND WHAT WERE THEY DOING?
FIRST...
GRANDPA WAS PATCHING HIS SHIRT AND DAD WAS SLEEPING BUT HE KNOCKED OVER YOUR WORK AND NOW IT'S ALL OVER THE PLACE.
I GUESS HE'S FEELING LOW AGAIN. I WONDER WHAT'S WRONG...
LISTEN DEAR, WHY DON'T YOU JUST TAKE THE KIDS AND GO SOMEWHERE NEW?
AND IF I RAN AWAY, WHERE WOULD WE LIVE? BESIDES, ALL THAT HE OWNS IS THE HOUSE WE LIVE IN NOW...
I GUESS I SHOULD BE GETTING BACK AND START COOKING. I'M SO TIRED OF EVERYTHING...
SORRY TO HAVE STAYED FOR SO LONG...
DON'T BE SILLY...
COME OVER WHENEVER YOU WANT.
REALLY SORRY TO HAVE TROU-BLED YOU.

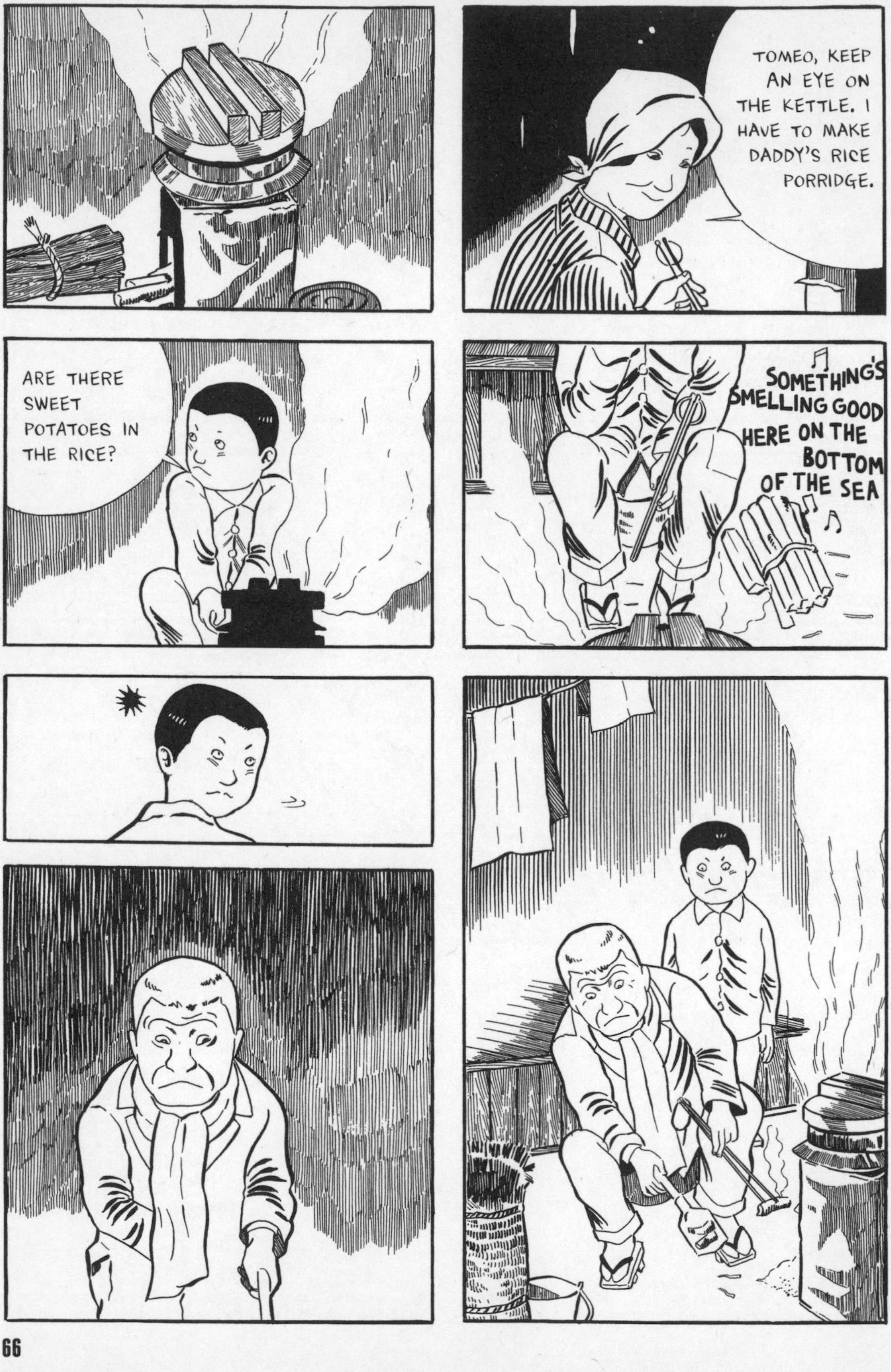
TOMEO, KEEP AN EYE ON THE KETTLE. I HAVE TO MAKE DADDY'S RICE PORRIDGE.
ARE THERE SWEET POTATOES IN THE RICE?
SOMETHING'S SMELLING GOOD HERE ON THE BOTTOM OF THE SEA

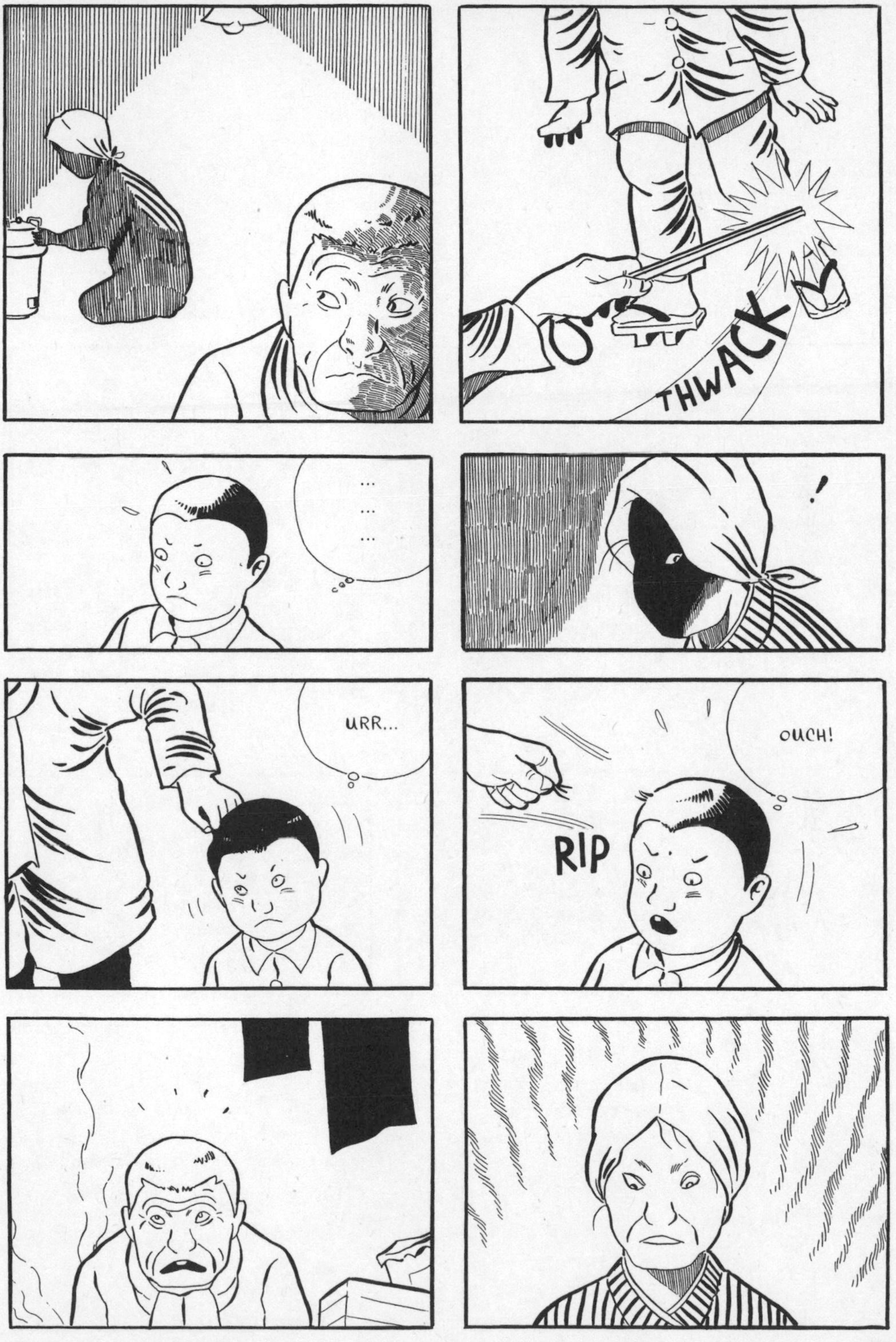
THWACK
...
...
...
URR...
OUCH!
RIP

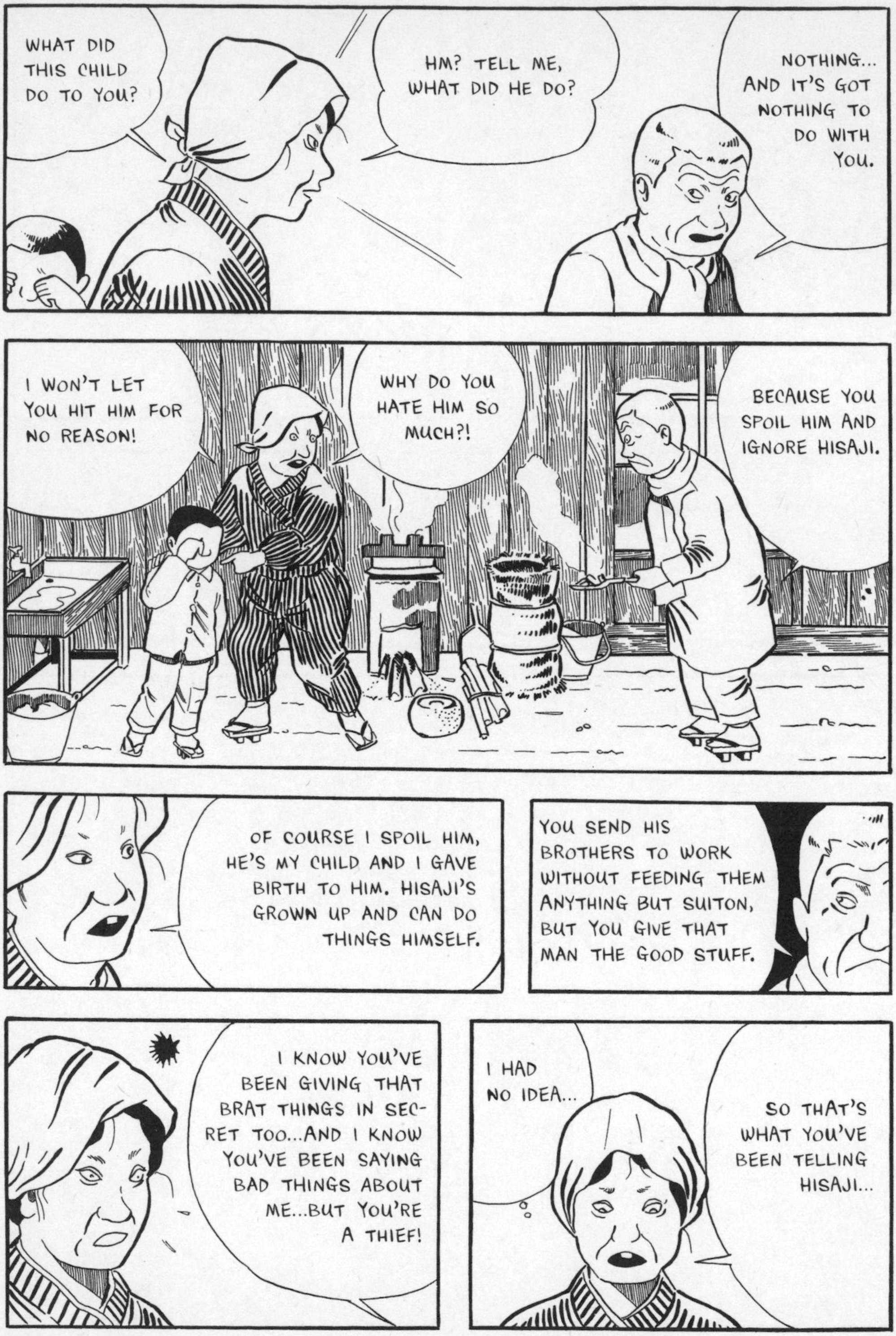

WHAT DID THIS CHILD DO TO YOU?
HM? TELL ME, WHAT DID HE DO?
NOTHING... AND IT'S GOT NOTHING TO DO WITH YOU.
I WON'T LET YOU HIT HIM FOR NO REASON!
WHY DO YOU HATE HIM SO MUCH?!
BECAUSE YOU SPOIL HIM AND IGNORE HISAJI.
OF COURSE I SPOIL HIM, HE'S MY CHILD AND I GAVE BIRTH TO HIM. HISAJI'S GROWN UP AND CAN DO THINGS HIMSELF.
YOU SEND HIS BROTHERS TO WORK WITHOUT FEEDING THEM ANYTHING BUT SUITON, BUT YOU GIVE THAT MAN THE GOOD STUFF.
I KNOW YOU'VE BEEN GIVING THAT BRAT THINGS IN SECRET TOO...AND I KNOW YOU'VE BEEN SAYING BAD THINGS ABOUT ME...BUT YOU'RE A THIEF!
I HAD NO IDEA...
SO THAT'S WHAT YOU'VE BEEN TELLING HISAJI...

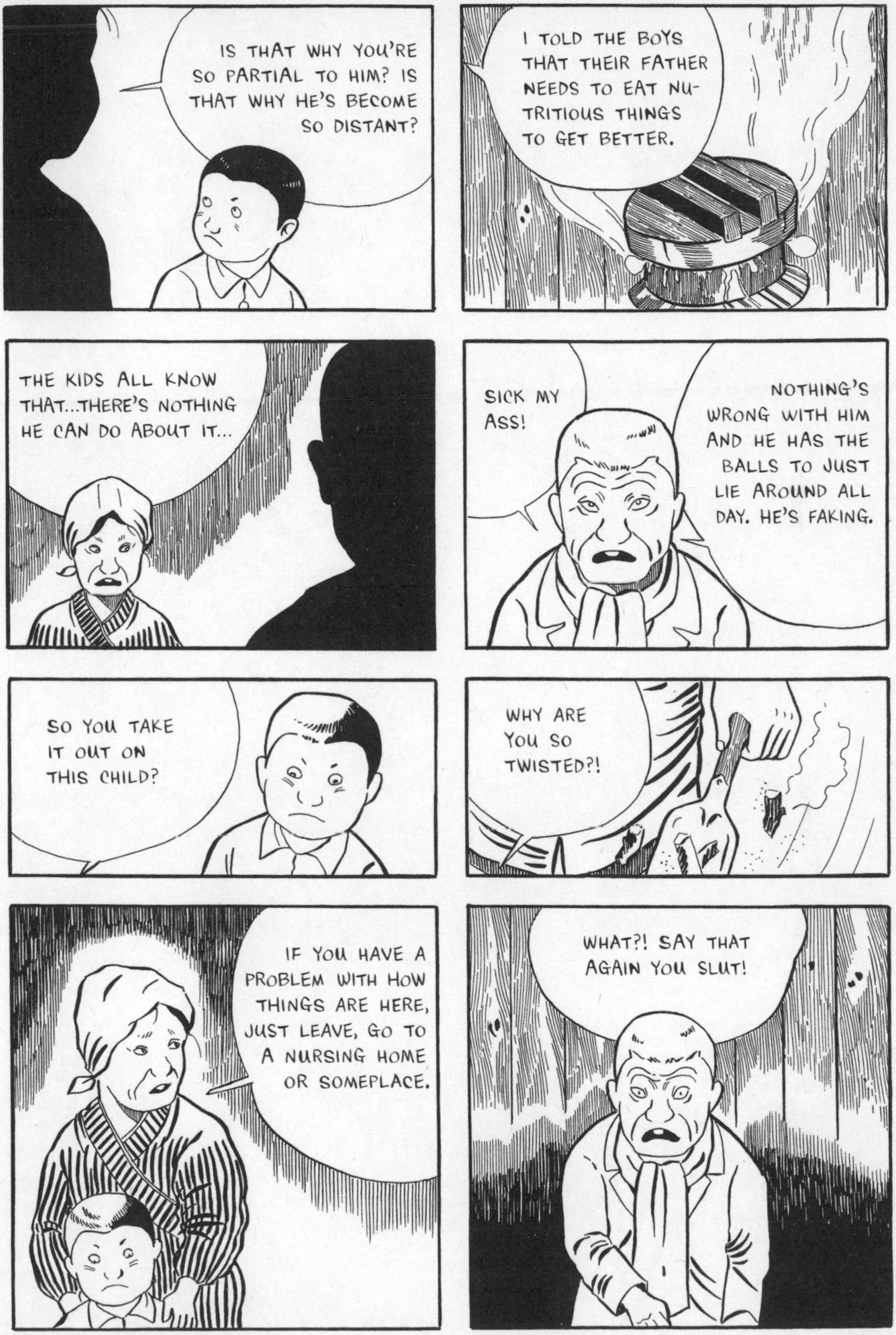
IS THAT WHY YOU'RE SO PARTIAL TO HIM? IS THAT WHY HE'S BECOME SO DISTANT?
I TOLD THE BOYS THAT THEIR FATHER NEEDS TO EAT NU-TRITIOUS THINGS TO GET BETTER.
THE KIDS ALL KNOW THAT...THERE'S NOTHING HE CAN DO ABOUT IT...
SICK MY ASS!
NOTHING'S WRONG WITH HIM AND HE HAS THE BALLS TO JUST LIE AROUND ALL DAY. HE'S FAKING.
SO YOU TAKE IT OUT ON THIS CHILD?
WHY ARE YOU SO TWISTED?!
IF YOU HAVE A PROBLEM WITH HOW THINGS ARE HERE, JUST LEAVE, GO TO A NURSING HOME OR SOMEPLACE.
WHAT?! SAY THAT AGAIN YOU SLUT!

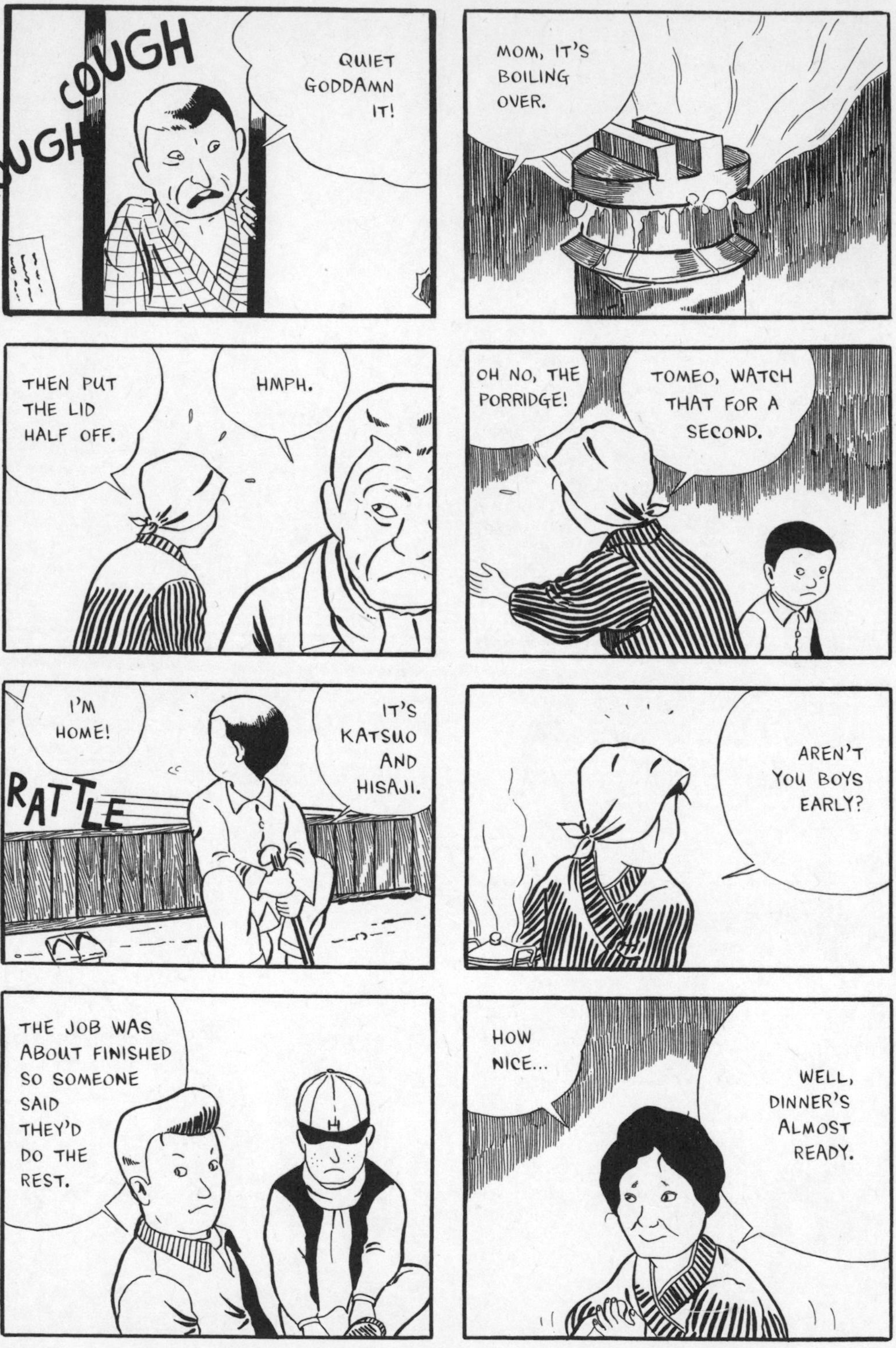
COUGH
COUGH
QUIET GODDAMN IT!
MOM, IT'S BOILING OVER.
THEN PUT THE LID HALF OFF.
HMPH.
OH NO, THE PORRIDGE!
TOMEO, WATCH THAT FOR A SECOND.
I'M HOME!
RATTLE
IT'S KATSUO AND HISAJI.
AREN'T YOU BOYS EARLY?
THE JOB WAS ABOUT FINISHED SO SOMEONE SAID THEY'D DO THE REST.
HOW NICE...
WELL, DINNER'S ALMOST READY.

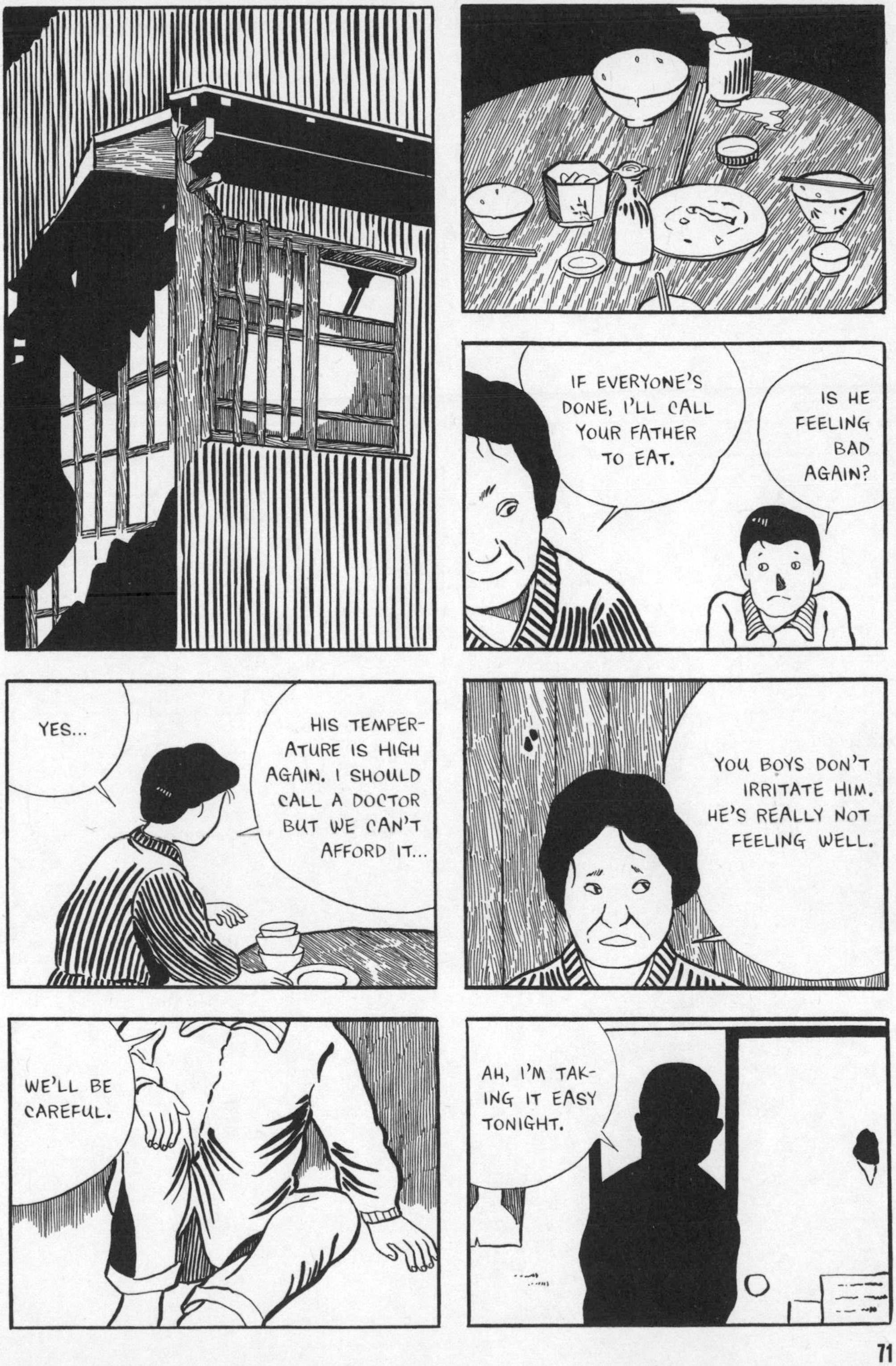
IF EVERYONE'S DONE, I'LL CALL YOUR FATHER TO EAT.
IS HE FEELING BAD AGAIN?
YES...
HIS TEMPERATURE IS HIGH AGAIN. I SHOULD CALL A DOCTOR BUT WE CAN'T AFFORD IT...
YOU BOYS DON'T IRRITATE HIM. HE'S REALLY NOT FEELING WELL.
WE'LL BE CAREFUL.
AH, I'M TAKING IT EASY TONIGHT.

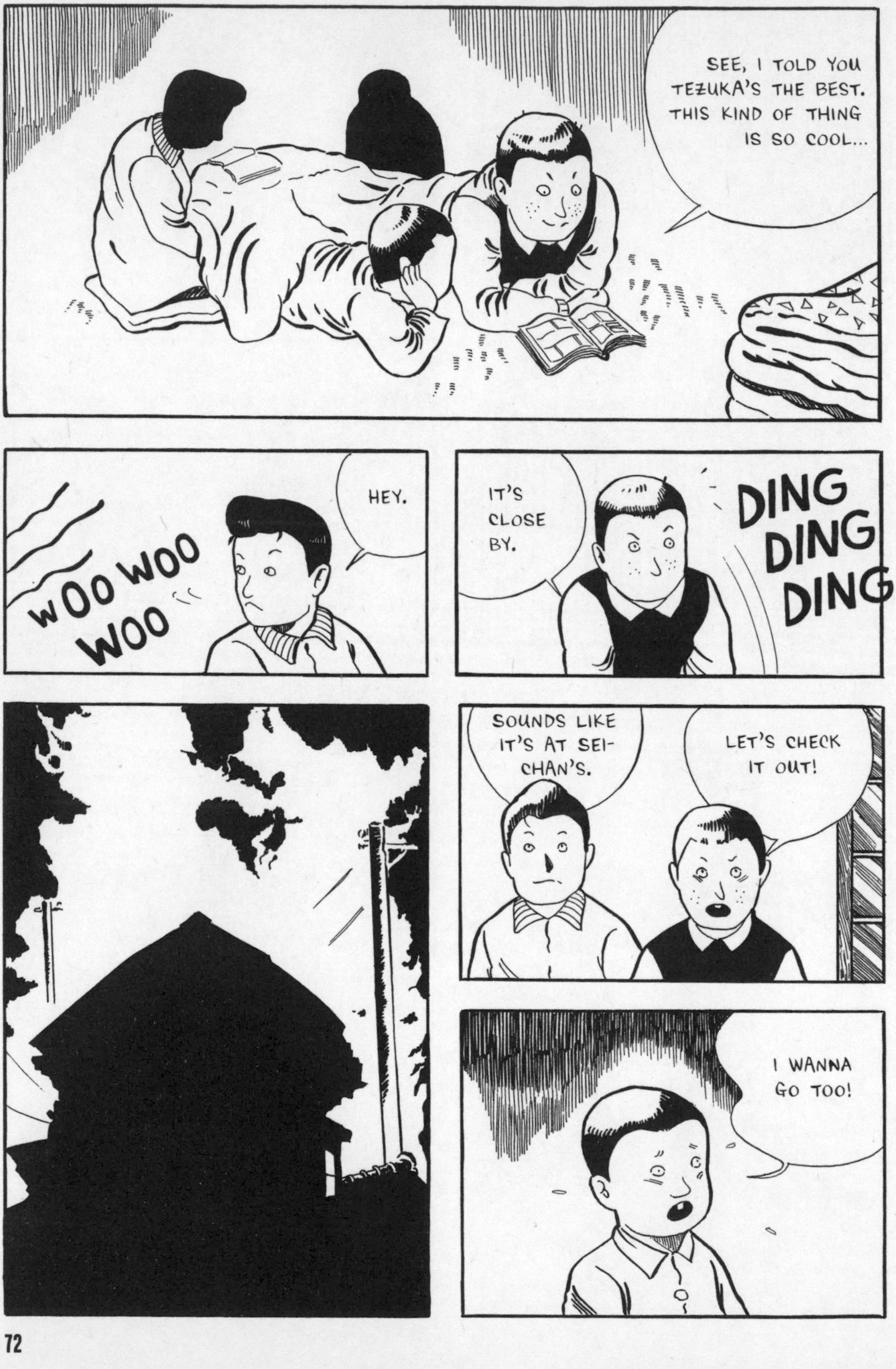
SEE, I TOLD YOU TEZUKA'S THE BEST. THIS KIND OF THING IS SO COOL...
WOO WOO WOO
HEY.
IT'S CLOSE BY.
DING DING DING
SOUNDS LIKE IT'S AT SEI-CHAN'S.
LET'S CHECK IT OUT!
I WANNA GO TOO!

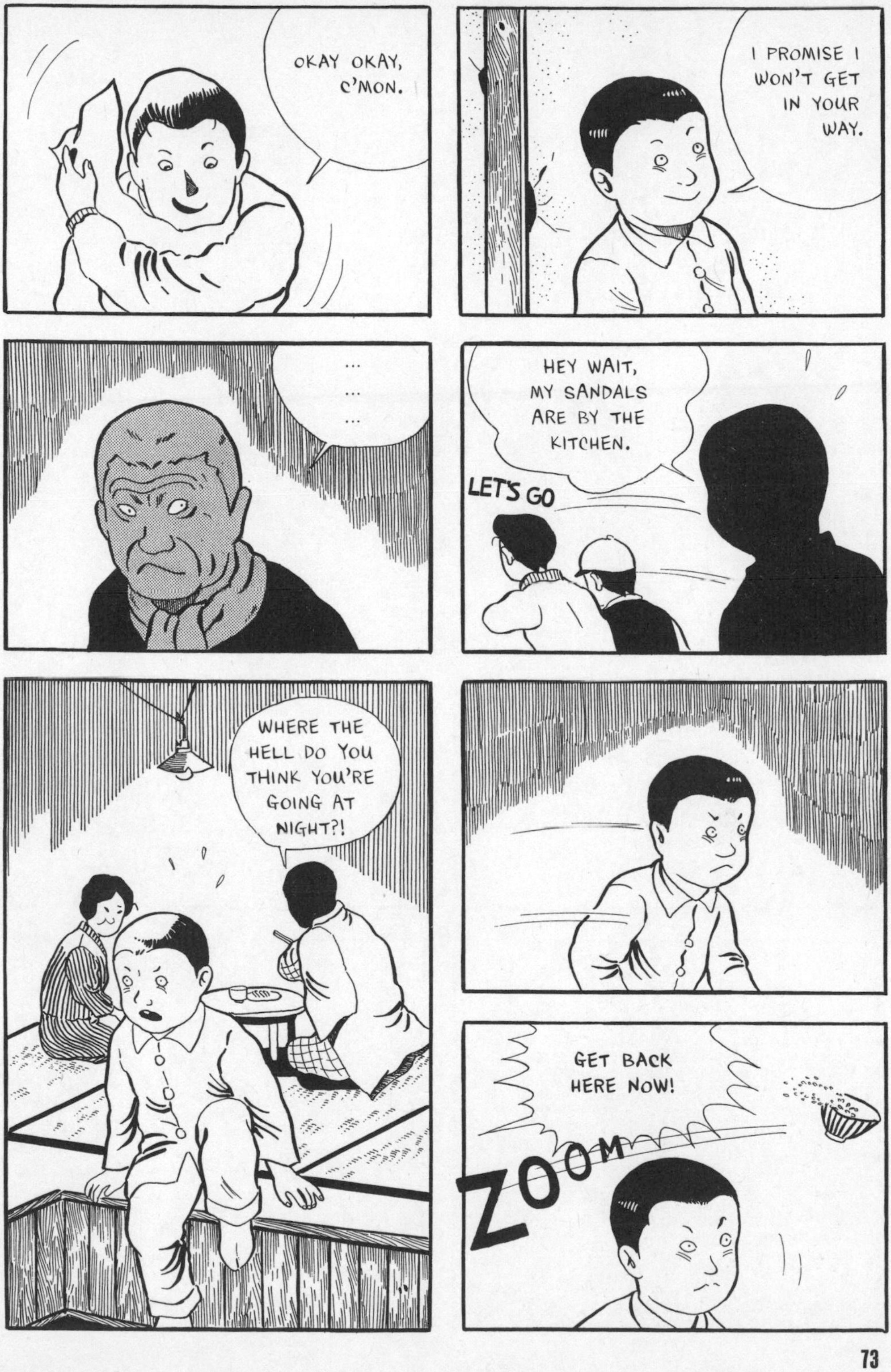
OKAY OKAY, C'MON.
I PROMISE I WON'T GET IN YOUR WAY.
...
...
...
HEY WAIT, MY SANDALS ARE BY THE KITCHEN.
LET'S GO
WHERE THE HELL DO YOU THINK YOU'RE GOING AT NIGHT?!
GET BACK HERE NOW!
ZOOM

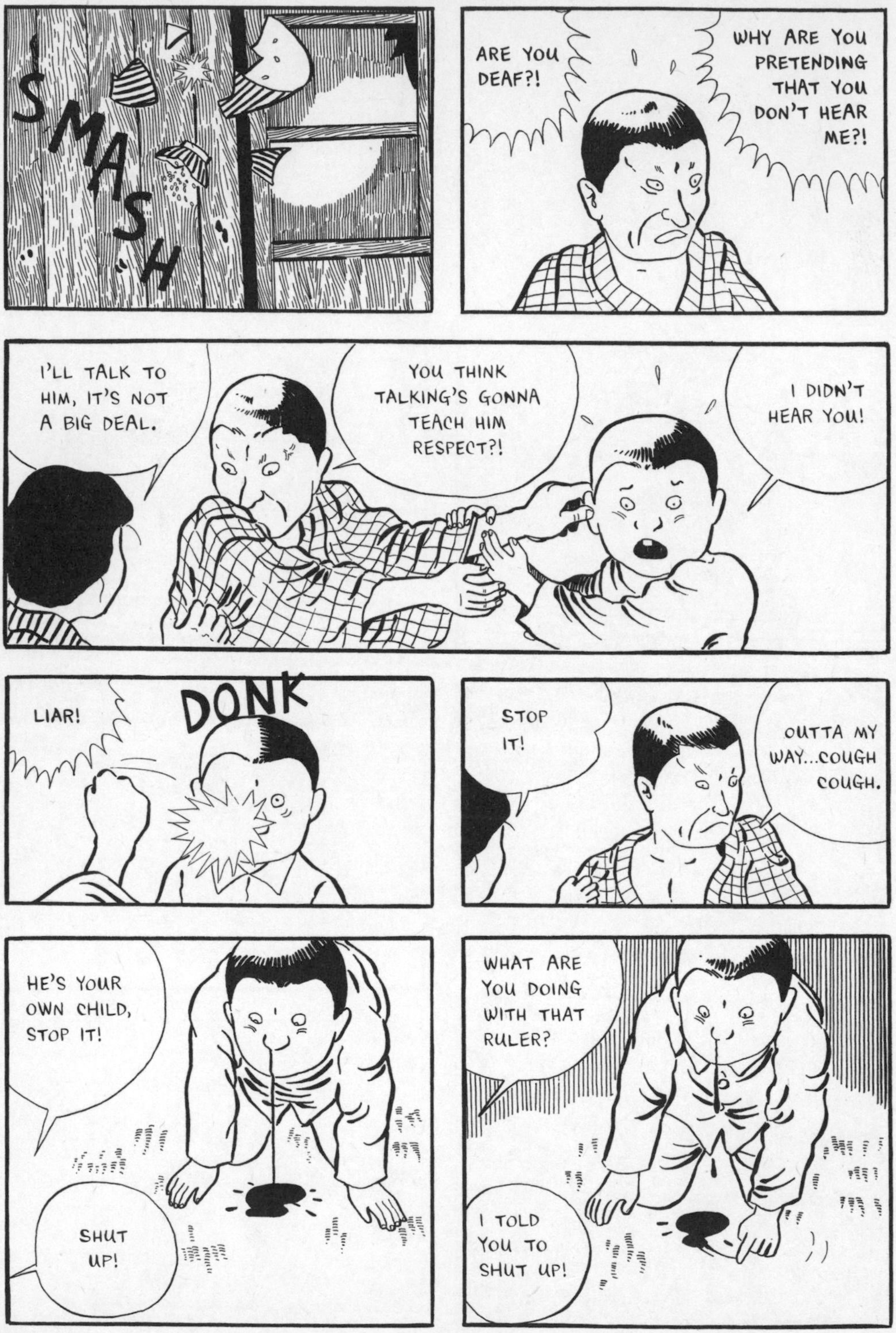
SMASH
ARE YOU DEAF?!
WHY ARE YOU PRETENDING THAT YOU DON'T HEAR ME?!
I'LL TALK TO HIM, IT'S NOT A BIG DEAL.
YOU THINK TALKING'S GONNA TEACH HIM RESPECT?!
I DIDN'T HEAR YOU!
LIAR!
DONK
STOP IT!
OUTTA MY WAY...COUGH COUGH.
HE'S YOUR OWN CHILD, STOP IT!
SHUT UP!
WHAT ARE YOU DOING WITH THAT RULER?
I TOLD YOU TO SHUT UP!

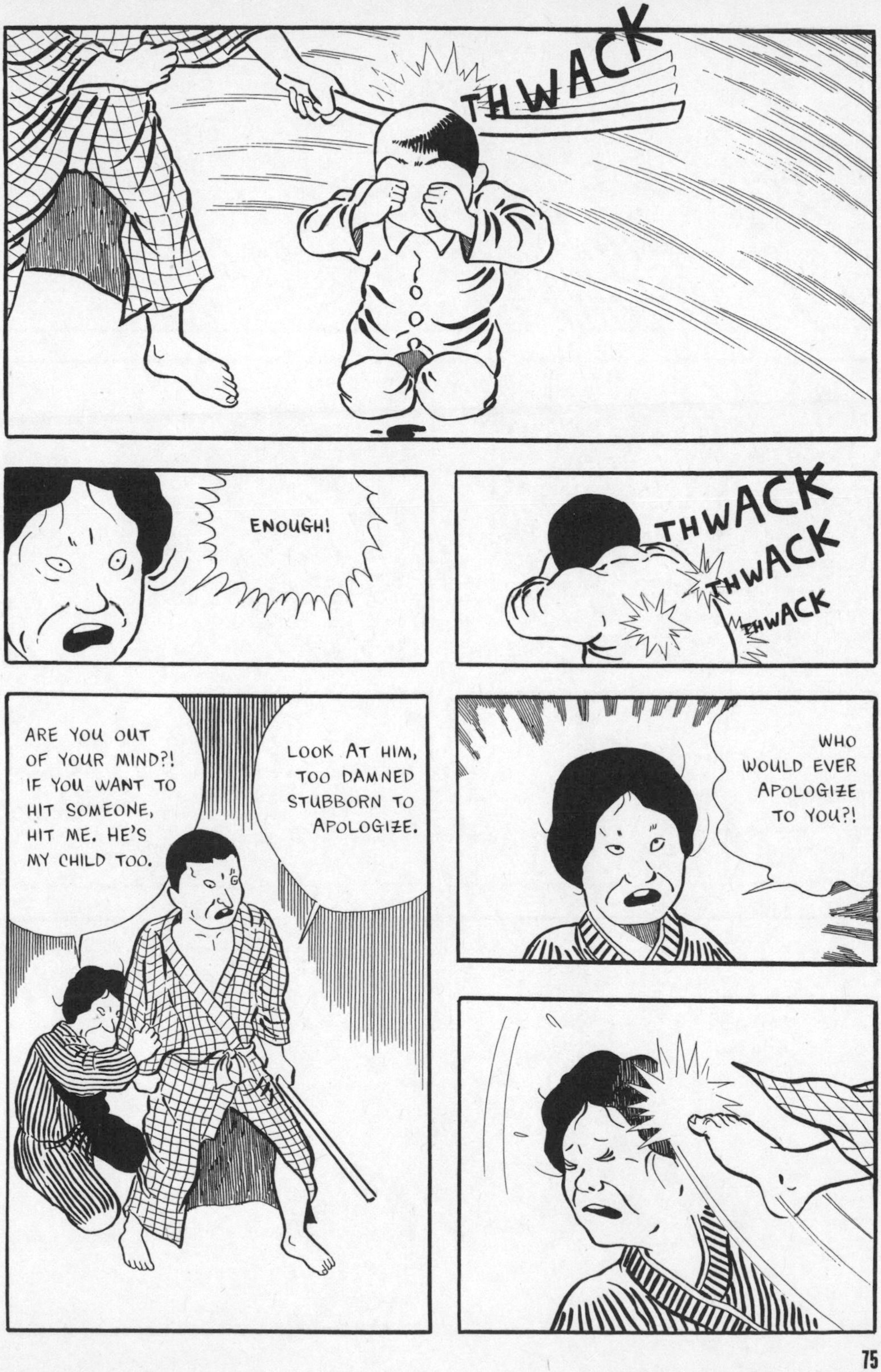
THWACK
ENOUGH!
THWACK
THWACK
THWACK
ARE YOU OUT OF YOUR MIND?! IF YOU WANT TO HIT SOMEONE, HIT ME. HE'S MY CHILD TOO.
LOOK AT HIM, TOO DAMNED STUBBORN TO APOLOGIZE.
WHO WOULD EVER APOLOGIZE TO YOU?!

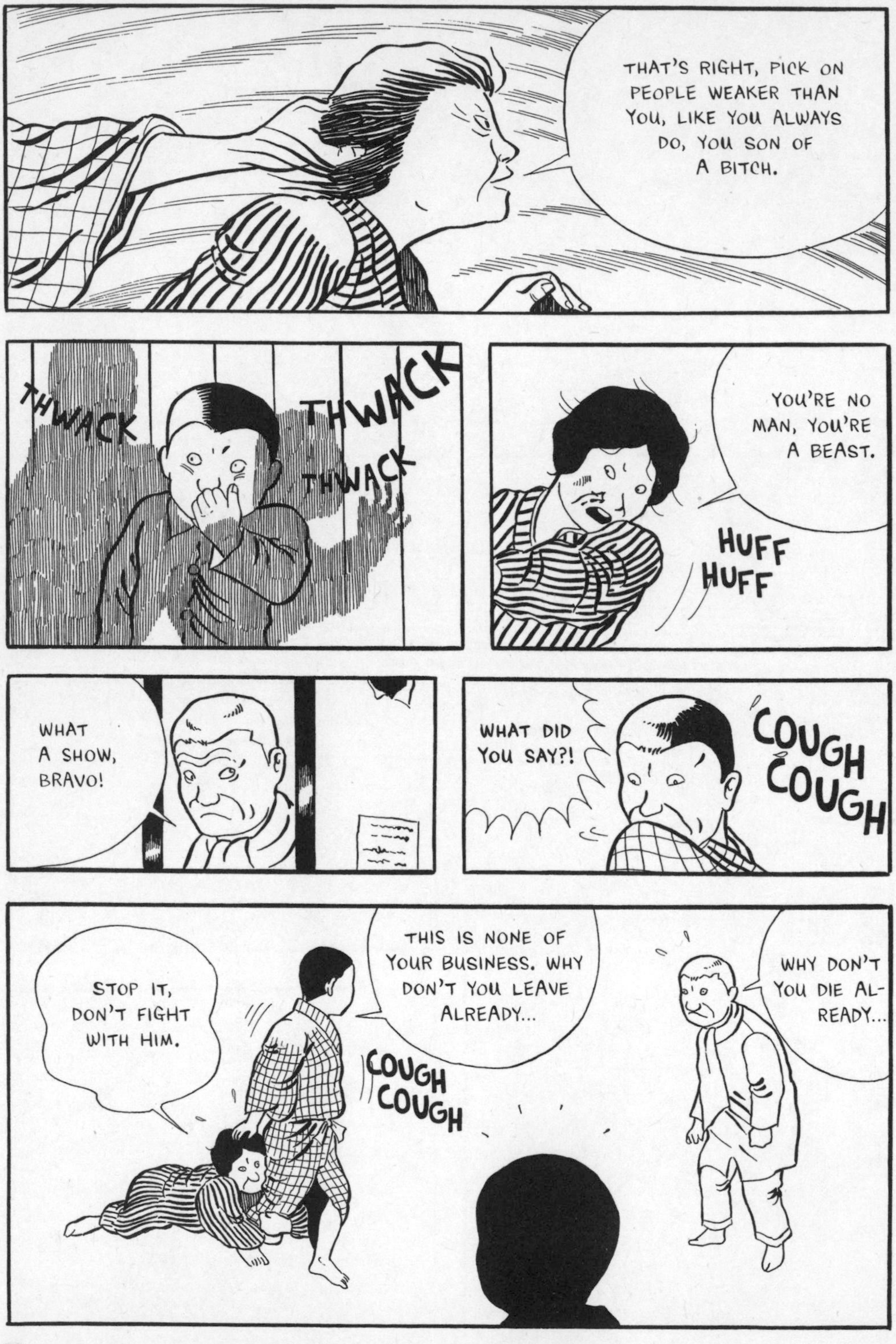
THAT'S RIGHT, PICK ON PEOPLE WEAKER THAN YOU, LIKE YOU ALWAYS DO, YOU SON OF A BITCH.
THWACK
THWACK
THWACK
YOU'RE NO MAN, YOU'RE A BEAST.
HUFF HUFF
WHAT A SHOW, BRAVO!
WHAT DID YOU SAY?!
COUGH COUGH
STOP IT, DON'T FIGHT WITH HIM.
THIS IS NONE OF YOUR BUSINESS. WHY DON'T YOU LEAVE ALREADY...
COUGH COUGH
WHY DON'T YOU DIE AL-READY...

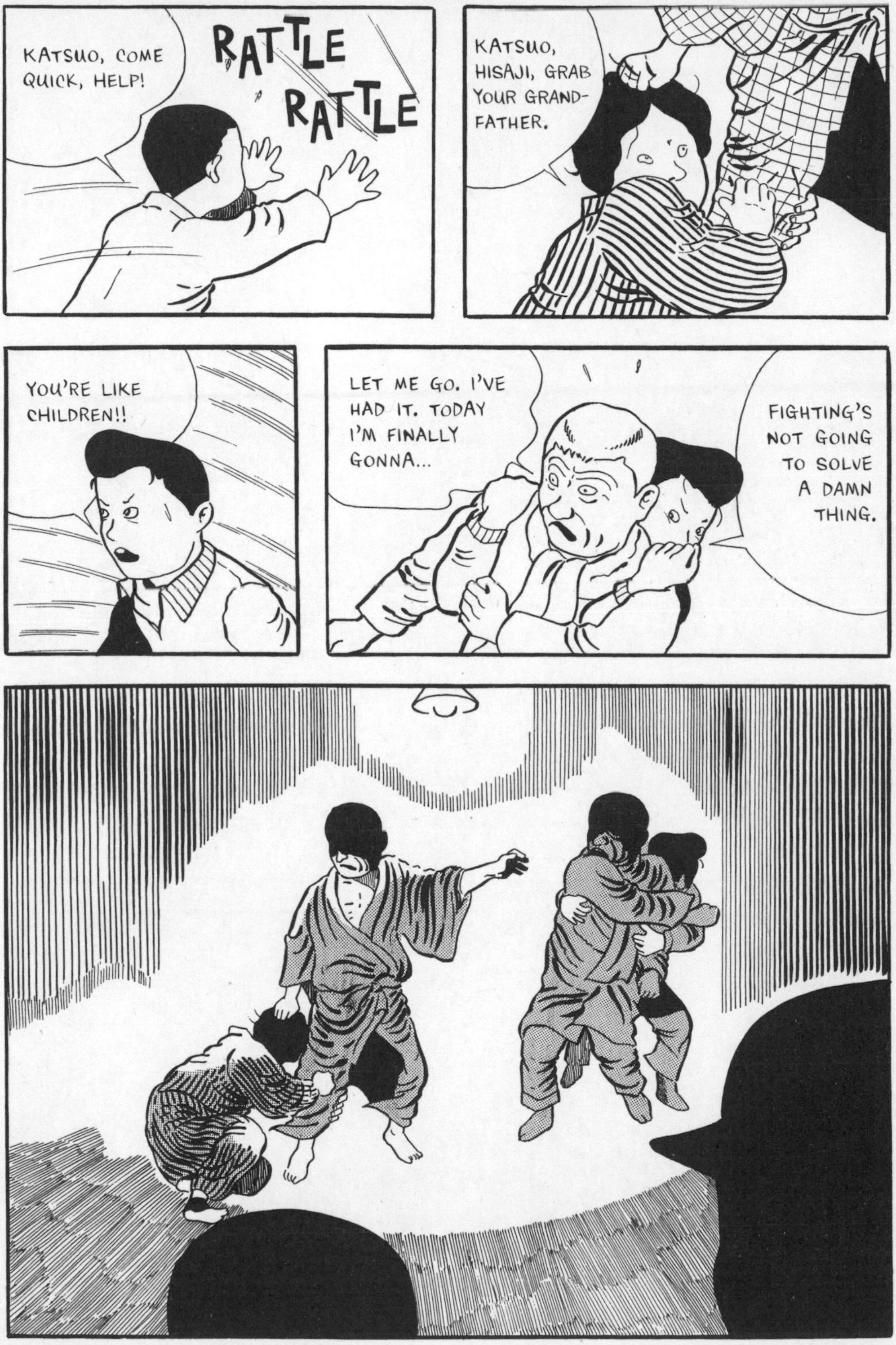
KATSUO, COME QUICK, HELP!
RATTLE RATTLE
KATSUO, HISAJI, GRAB YOUR GRAND-FATHER.
YOU'RE LIKE CHILDREN!!
LET ME GO. I'VE HAD IT. TODAY I'M FINALLY GONNA...
FIGHTING'S NOT GOING TO SOLVE A DAMN THING.

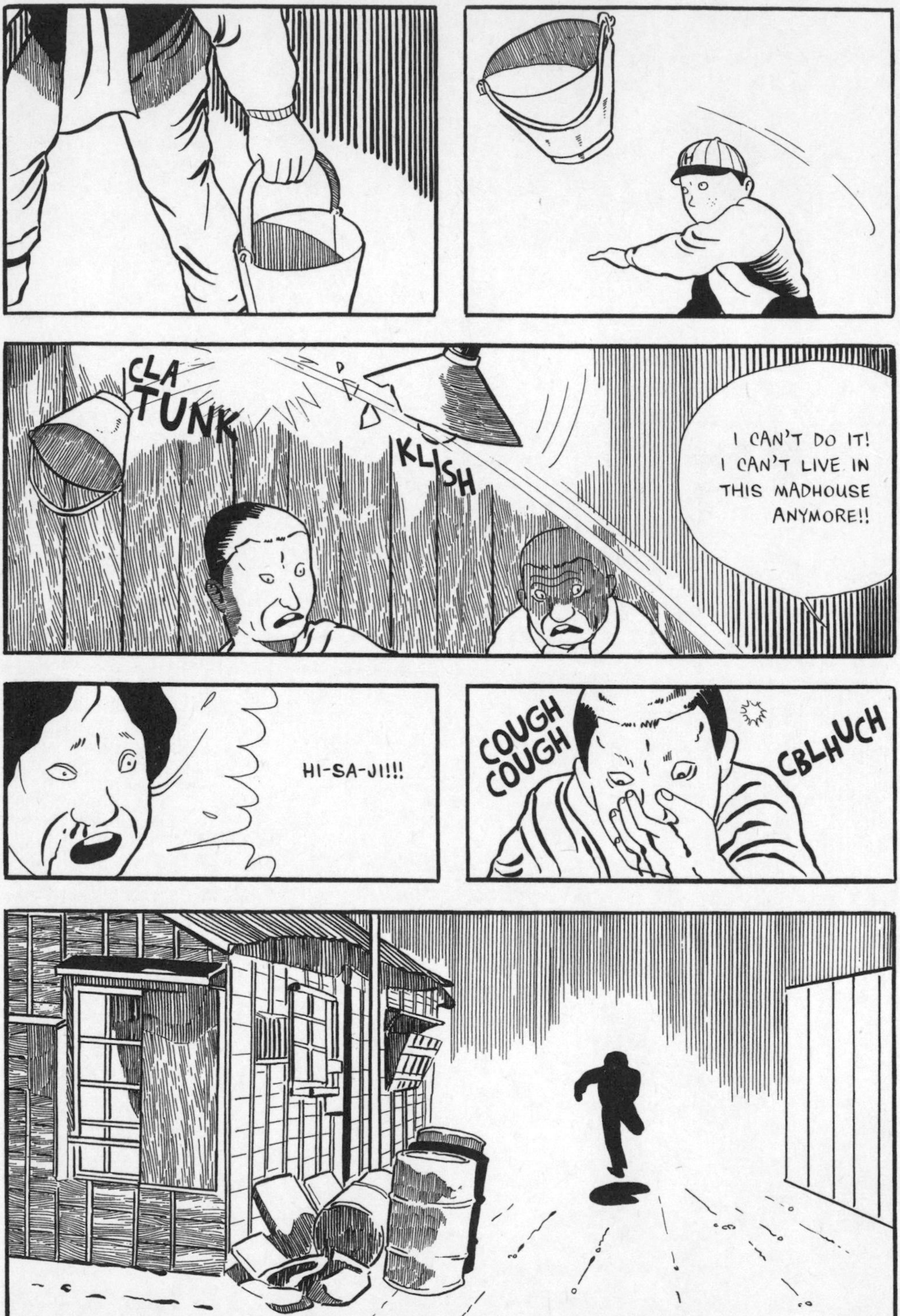
CLA
TUNK
KLISH
I CAN'T DO IT! I CAN'T LIVE IN THIS MADHOUSE ANYMORE!!
HI-SA-JI!!!
COUGH COUGH
CBLHUCH

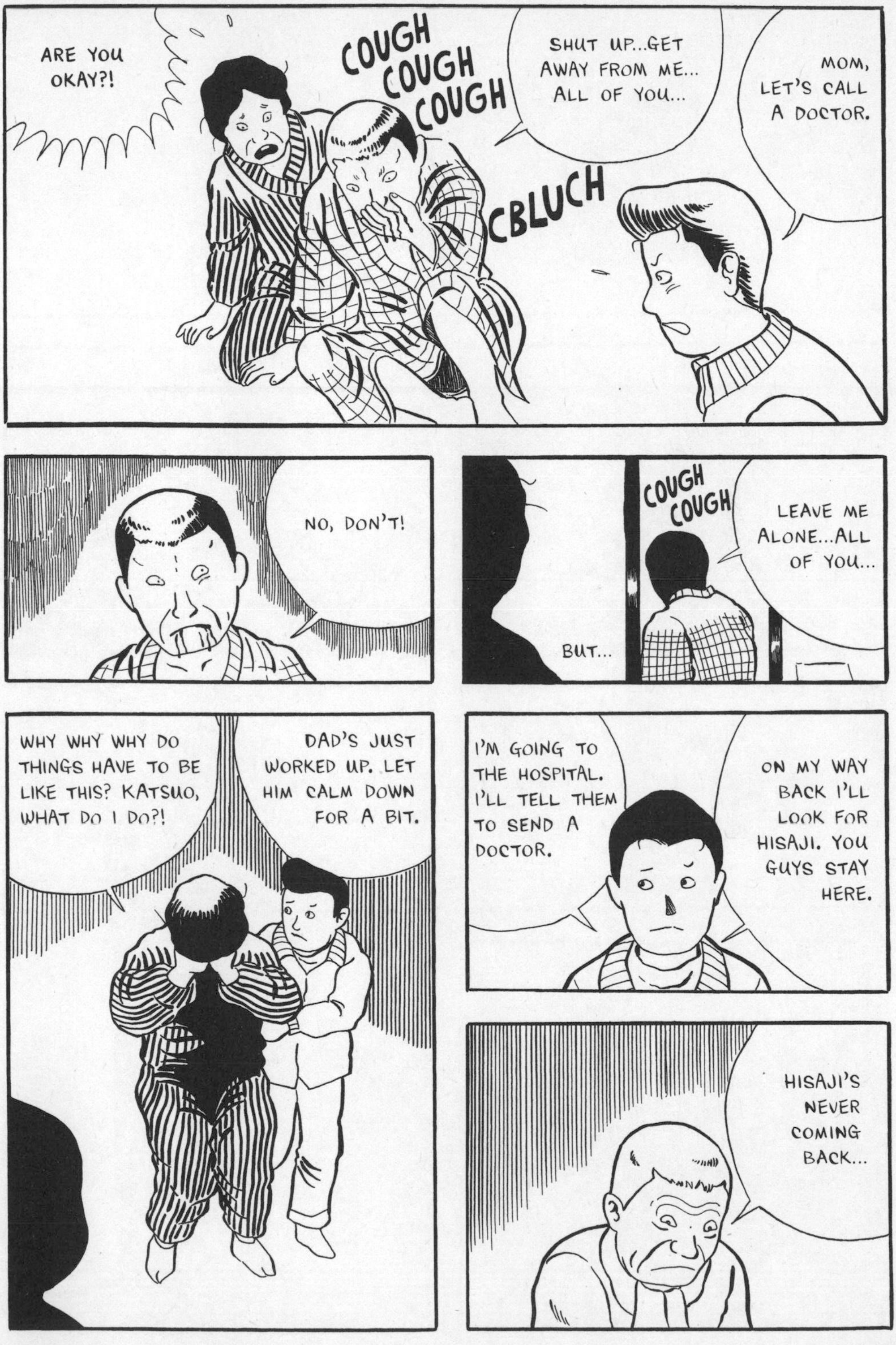
ARE YOU OKAY?!
COUGH COUGH COUGH
SHUT UP...GET AWAY FROM ME... ALL OF YOU...
MOM, LET'S CALL A DOCTOR.
CBLUCH
NO, DON'T!
COUGH COUGH
LEAVE ME ALONE...ALL OF YOU...
BUT...
WHY WHY WHY DO THINGS HAVE TO BE LIKE THIS? KATSUO, WHAT DO I DO?!
DAD'S JUST WORKED UP. LET HIM CALM DOWN FOR A BIT.
I'M GOING TO THE HOSPITAL. I'LL TELL THEM TO SEND A DOCTOR.
ON MY WAY BACK I'LL LOOK FOR HISAJI. YOU GUYS STAY HERE.
HISAJI'S NEVER COMING BACK...

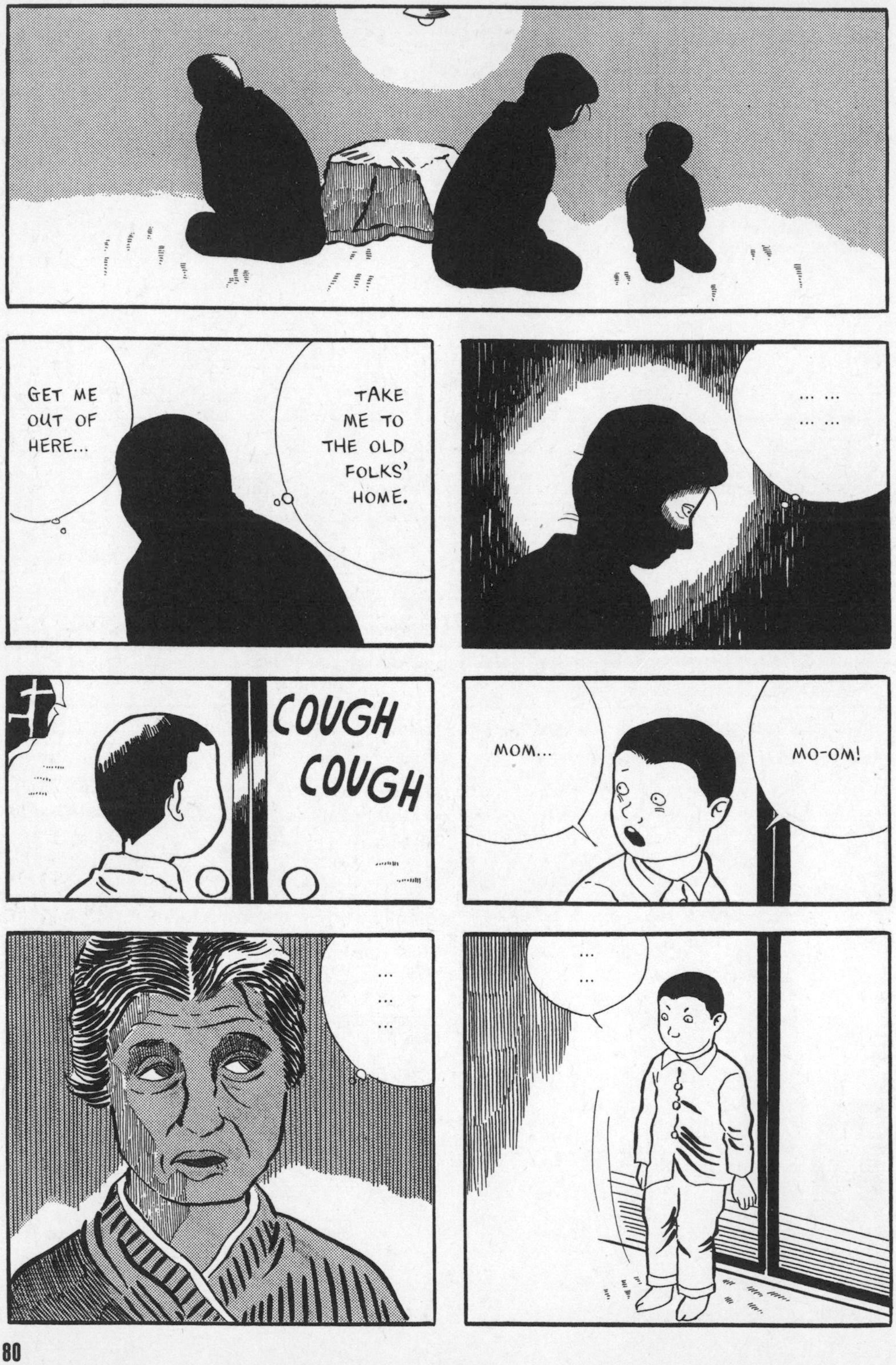
GET ME OUT OF HERE...
TAKE ME TO THE OLD FOLKS' HOME.
... ...
... ...
COUGH
COUGH
MOM...
MO-OM!
...
...
...
...
...

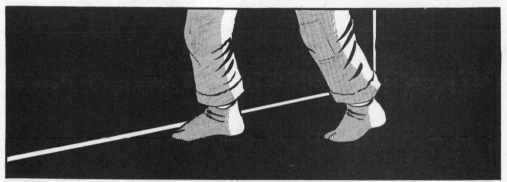

AH HA HA HA

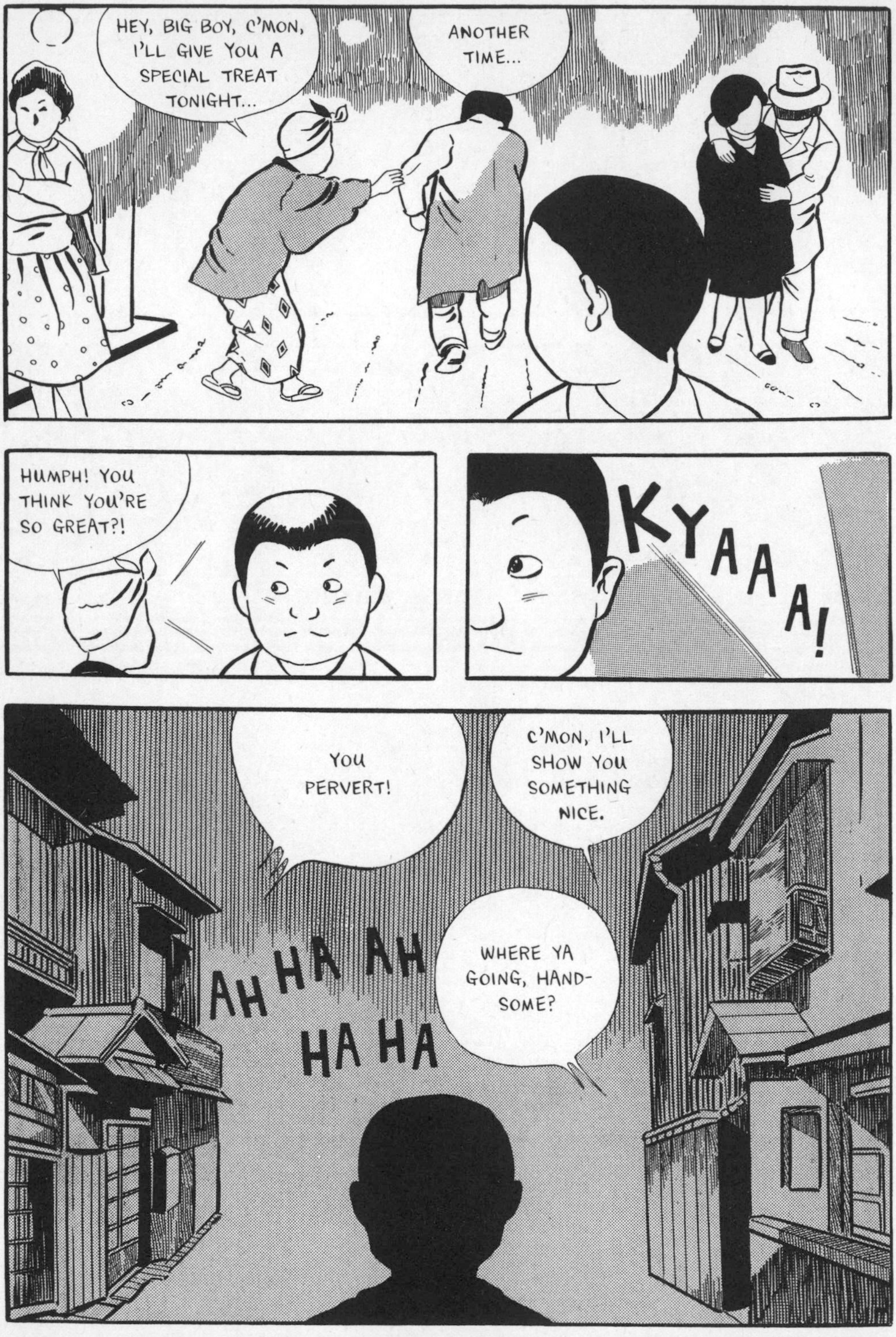
HEY, BIG BOY, C'MON, I'LL GIVE YOU A SPECIAL TREAT TONIGHT...
ANOTHER TIME...
HUMPH! YOU THINK YOU'RE SO GREAT?!
KYAAAA!
YOU PERVERT!
C'MON, I'LL SHOW YOU SOMETHING NICE.
AH HA AH HA HA
WHERE YA GOING, HAND-SOME?

MANHUNT

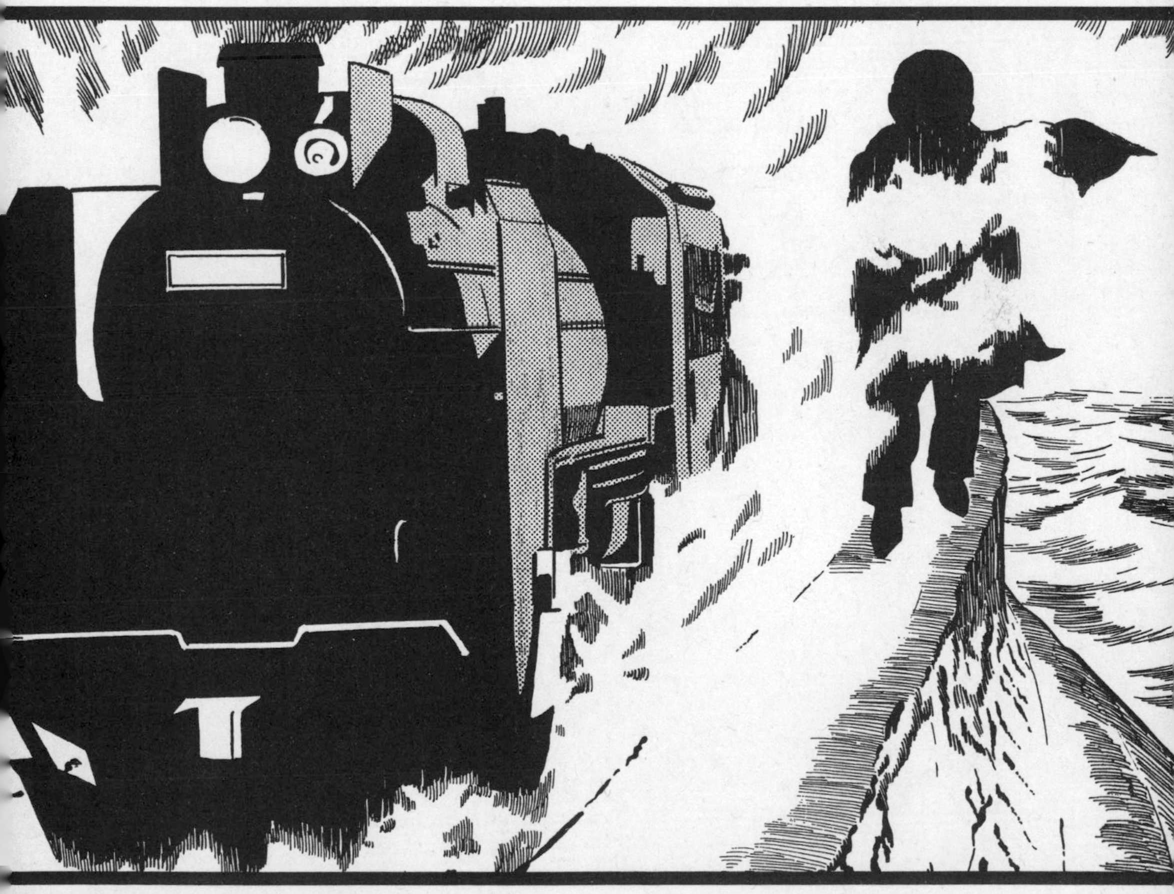

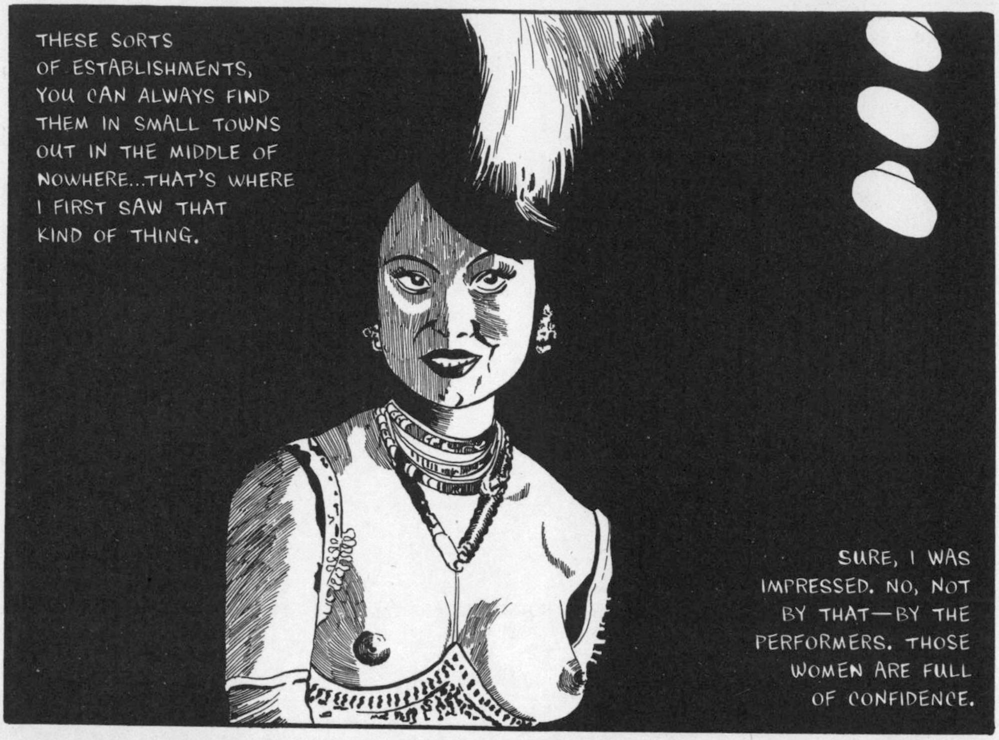
THESE SORTS OF ESTABLISHMENTS, YOU CAN ALWAYS FIND THEM IN SMALL TOWNS OUT IN THE MIDDLE OF NOWHERE...THAT'S WHERE I FIRST SAW THAT KIND OF THING.
SURE, I WAS IMPRESSED. NO, NOT BY THAT—BY THE PERFORMERS. THOSE WOMEN ARE FULL OF CONFIDENCE.
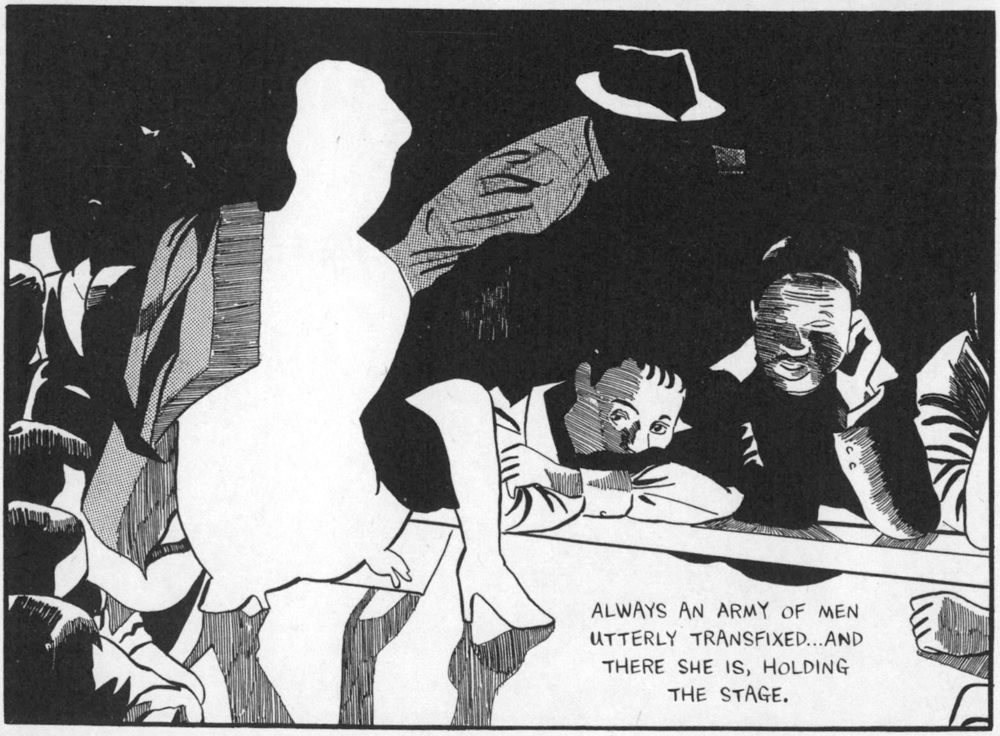
ALWAYS AN ARMY OF MEN UTTERLY TRANSFIXED...AND THERE SHE IS, HOLDING THE STAGE.

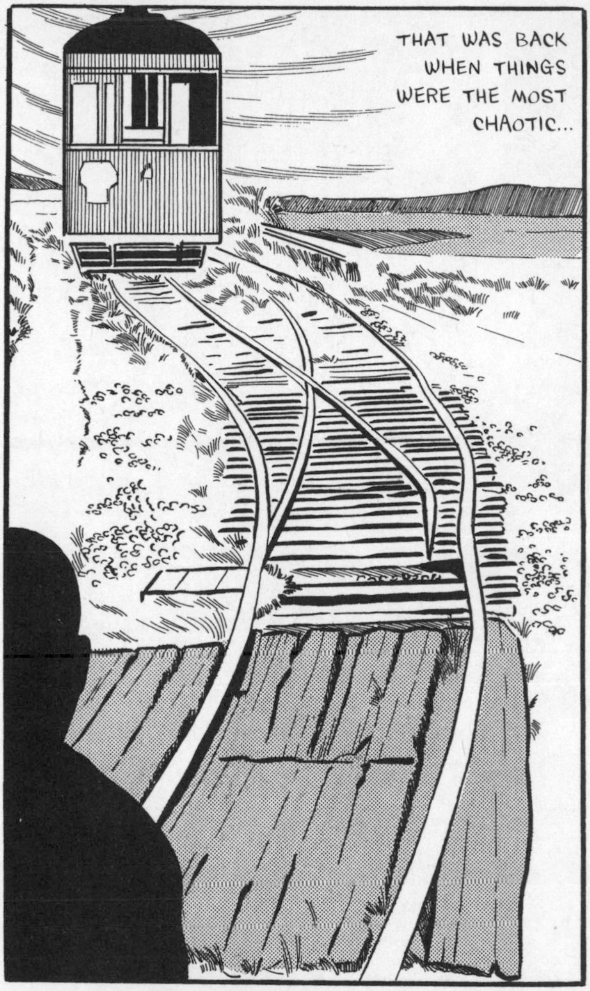
THAT WAS BACK WHEN THINGS WERE THE MOST CHAOTIC...

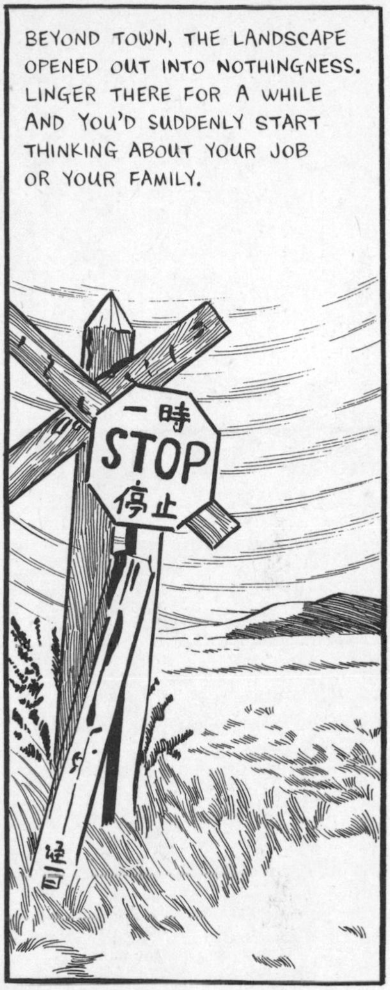
BEYOND TOWN, THE LANDSCAPE OPENED OUT INTO NOTHINGNESS. LINGER THERE FOR A WHILE AND YOU'D SUDDENLY START THINKING ABOUT YOUR JOB OR YOUR FAMILY.
一時
STOP
停止

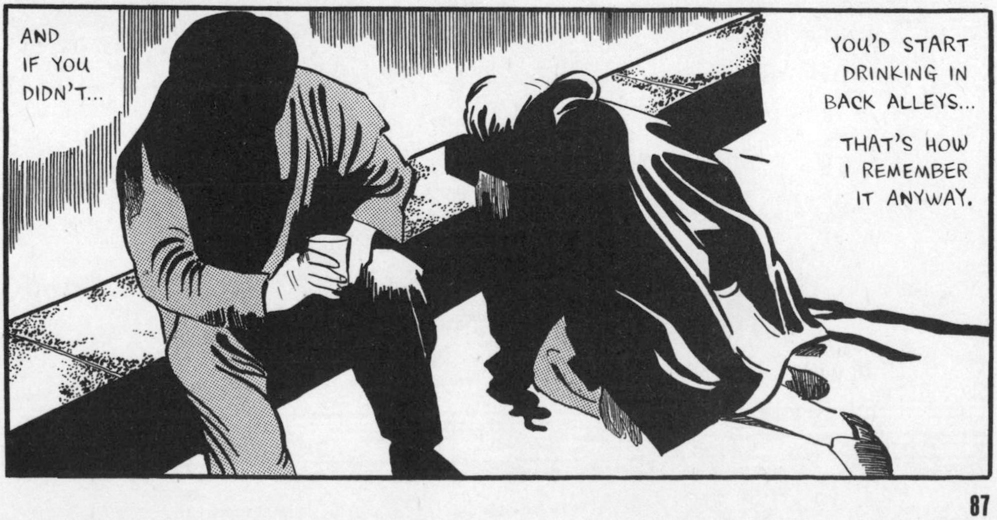
AND IF YOU DIDN'T...
YOU'D START DRINKING IN BACK ALLEYS...
THAT'S HOW I REMEMBER IT ANYWAY.

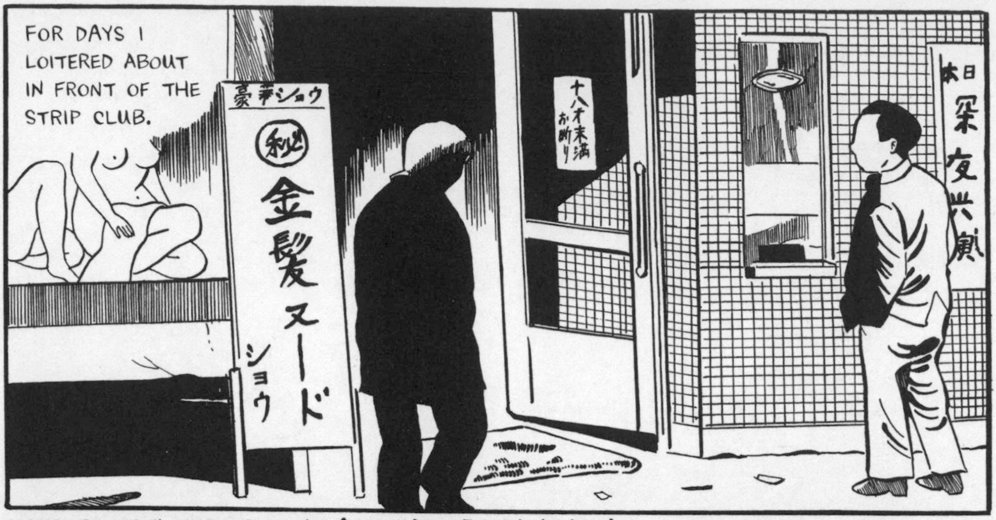
FOR DAYS I LOITERED ABOUT IN FRONT OF THE STRIP CLUB.
豪華ショウ
秘
金髪ヌードショウ
十八才未満お断り
本日深夜興行
SIGNS: BLONDE! NUDE SHOW! LATE NIGHT EXTRAVAGANZA.

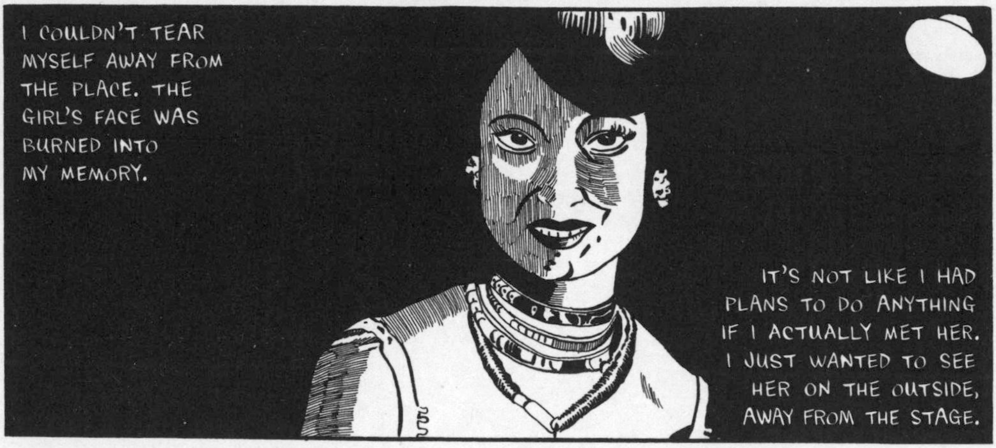
I COULDN'T TEAR MYSELF AWAY FROM THE PLACE. THE GIRL'S FACE WAS BURNED INTO MY MEMORY.
IT'S NOT LIKE I HAD PLANS TO DO ANYTHING IF I ACTUALLY MET HER. I JUST WANTED TO SEE HER ON THE OUTSIDE, AWAY FROM THE STAGE.

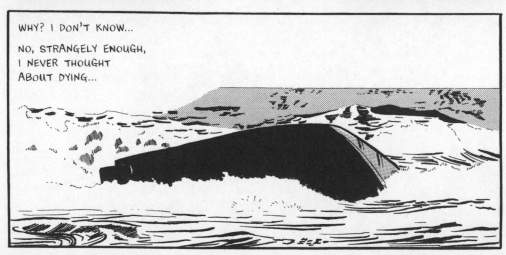

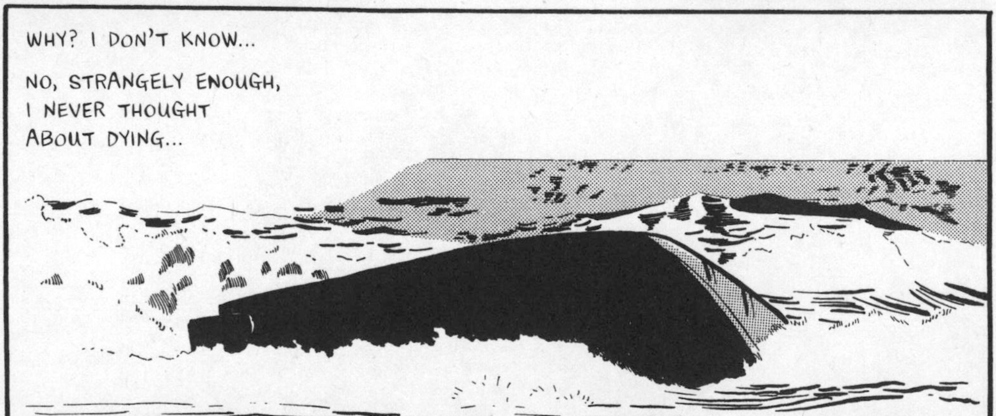
WHY? I DON'T KNOW...
NO, STRANGELY ENOUGH, I NEVER THOUGHT ABOUT DYING...

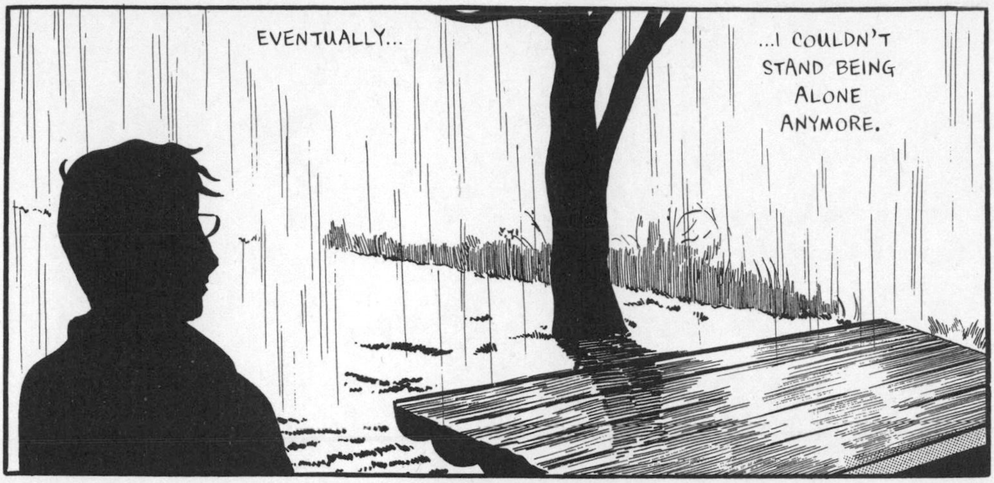
EVENTUALLY...
...I COULDN'T STAND BEING ALONE ANYMORE.

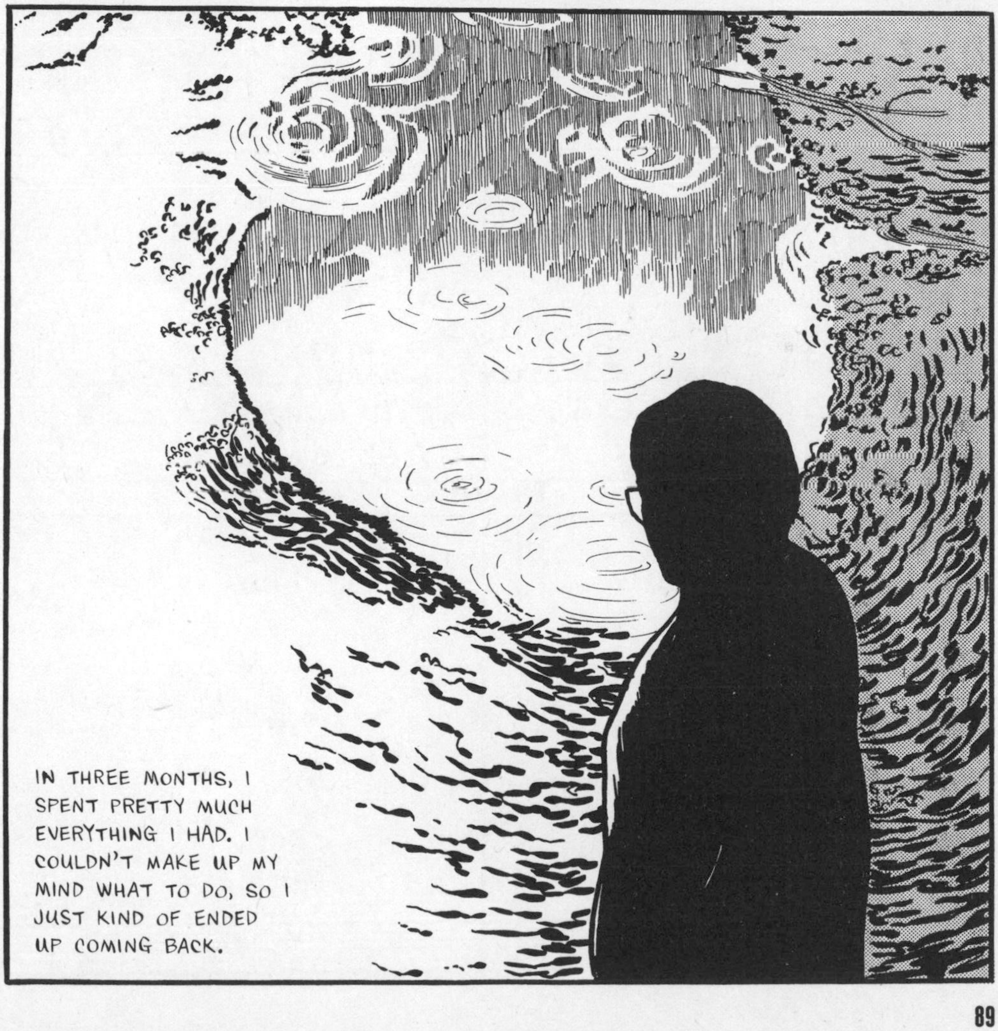
IN THREE MONTHS, I SPENT PRETTY MUCH EVERYTHING I HAD. I COULDN'T MAKE UP MY MIND WHAT TO DO, SO I JUST KIND OF ENDED UP COMING BACK.

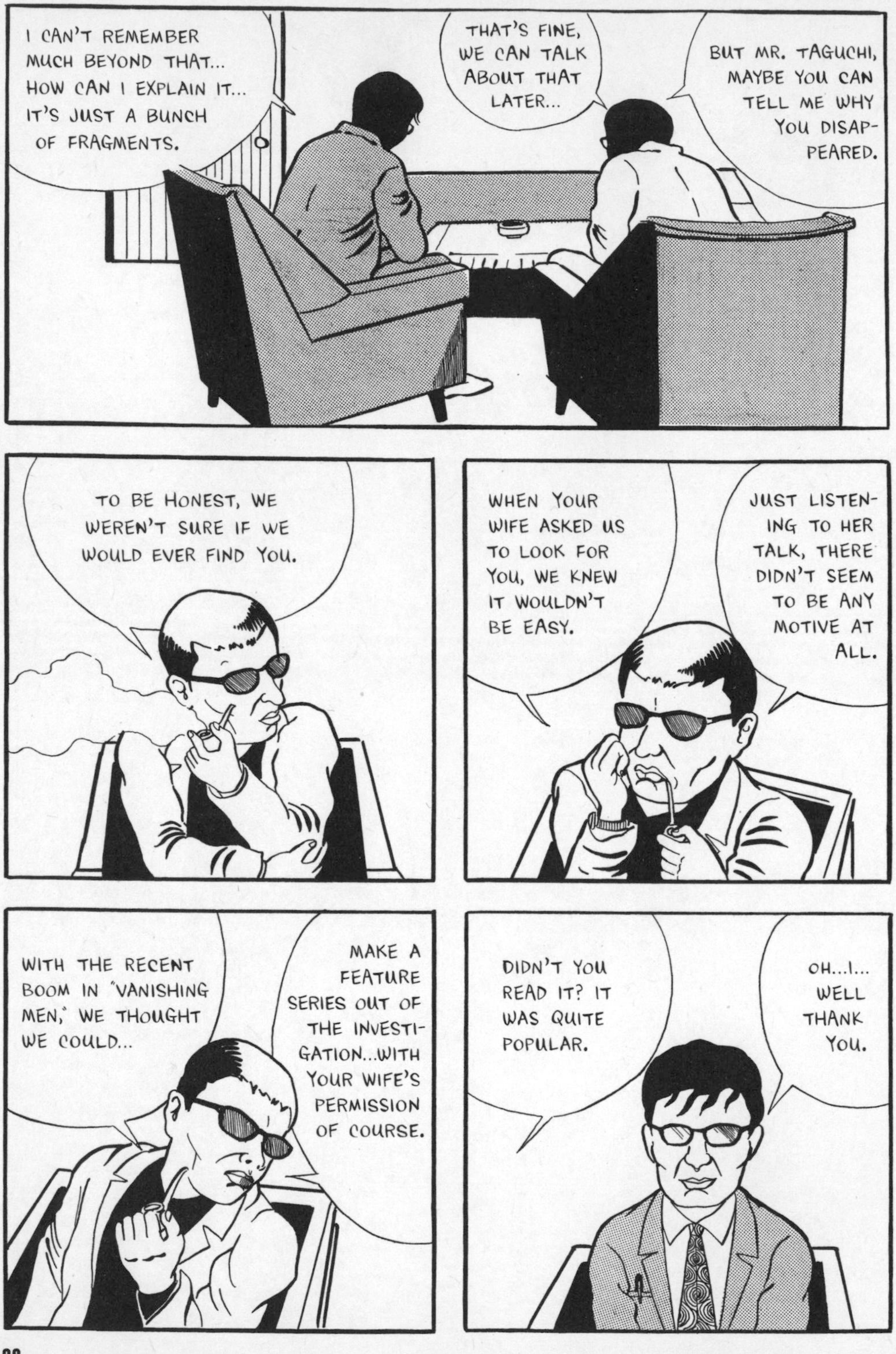
I CAN'T REMEMBER MUCH BEYOND THAT... HOW CAN I EXPLAIN IT... IT'S JUST A BUNCH OF FRAGMENTS.
THAT'S FINE, WE CAN TALK ABOUT THAT LATER...
BUT MR. TAGUCHI, MAYBE YOU CAN TELL ME WHY YOU DISAPPEARED.
TO BE HONEST, WE WEREN'T SURE IF WE WOULD EVER FIND YOU.
WHEN YOUR WIFE ASKED US TO LOOK FOR YOU, WE KNEW IT WOULDN'T BE EASY.
JUST LISTENING TO HER TALK, THERE DIDN'T SEEM TO BE ANY MOTIVE AT ALL.
WITH THE RECENT BOOM IN "VANISHING MEN," WE THOUGHT WE COULD...
MAKE A FEATURE SERIES OUT OF THE INVESTIGATION...WITH YOUR WIFE'S PERMISSION OF COURSE.
DIDN'T YOU READ IT? IT WAS QUITE POPULAR.
OH...I... WELL THANK YOU.

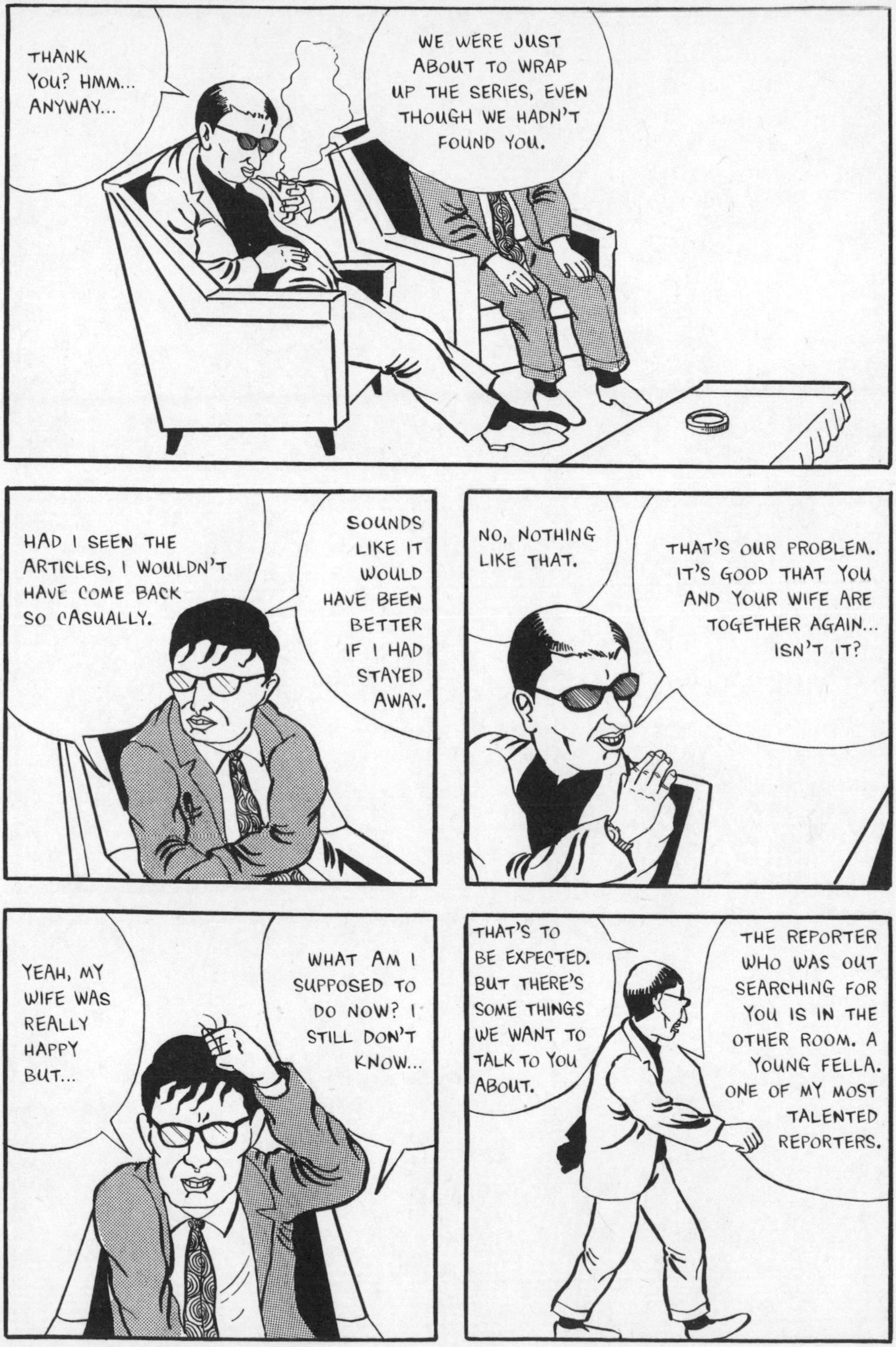
THANK YOU? HMM... ANYWAY...
WE WERE JUST ABOUT TO WRAP UP THE SERIES, EVEN THOUGH WE HADN'T FOUND YOU.
HAD I SEEN THE ARTICLES, I WOULDN'T HAVE COME BACK SO CASUALLY.
SOUNDS LIKE IT WOULD HAVE BEEN BETTER IF I HAD STAYED AWAY.
NO, NOTHING LIKE THAT.
THAT'S OUR PROBLEM. IT'S GOOD THAT YOU AND YOUR WIFE ARE TOGETHER AGAIN... ISN'T IT?
YEAH, MY WIFE WAS REALLY HAPPY BUT...
WHAT AM I SUPPOSED TO DO NOW? I STILL DON'T KNOW...
THAT'S TO BE EXPECTED. BUT THERE'S SOME THINGS WE WANT TO TALK TO YOU ABOUT.
THE REPORTER WHO WAS OUT SEARCHING FOR YOU IS IN THE OTHER ROOM. A YOUNG FELLA. ONE OF MY MOST TALENTED REPORTERS.

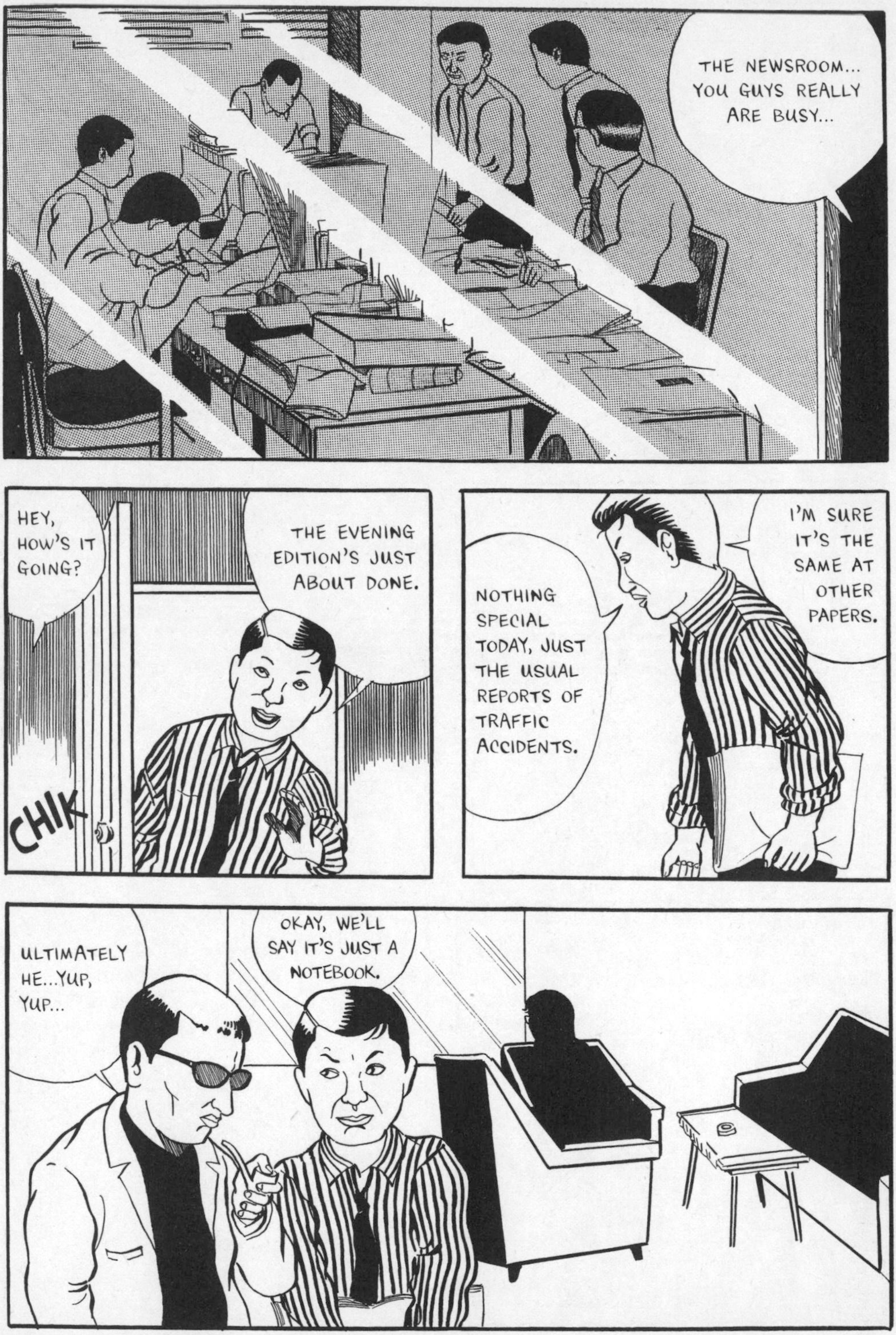
THE NEWSROOM... YOU GUYS REALLY ARE BUSY...
HEY, HOW'S IT GOING?
THE EVENING EDITION'S JUST ABOUT DONE.
CHIK
NOTHING SPECIAL TODAY, JUST THE USUAL REPORTS OF TRAFFIC ACCIDENTS.
I'M SURE IT'S THE SAME AT OTHER PAPERS.
ULTIMATELY HE...YUP, YUP...
OKAY, WE'LL SAY IT'S JUST A NOTEBOOK.

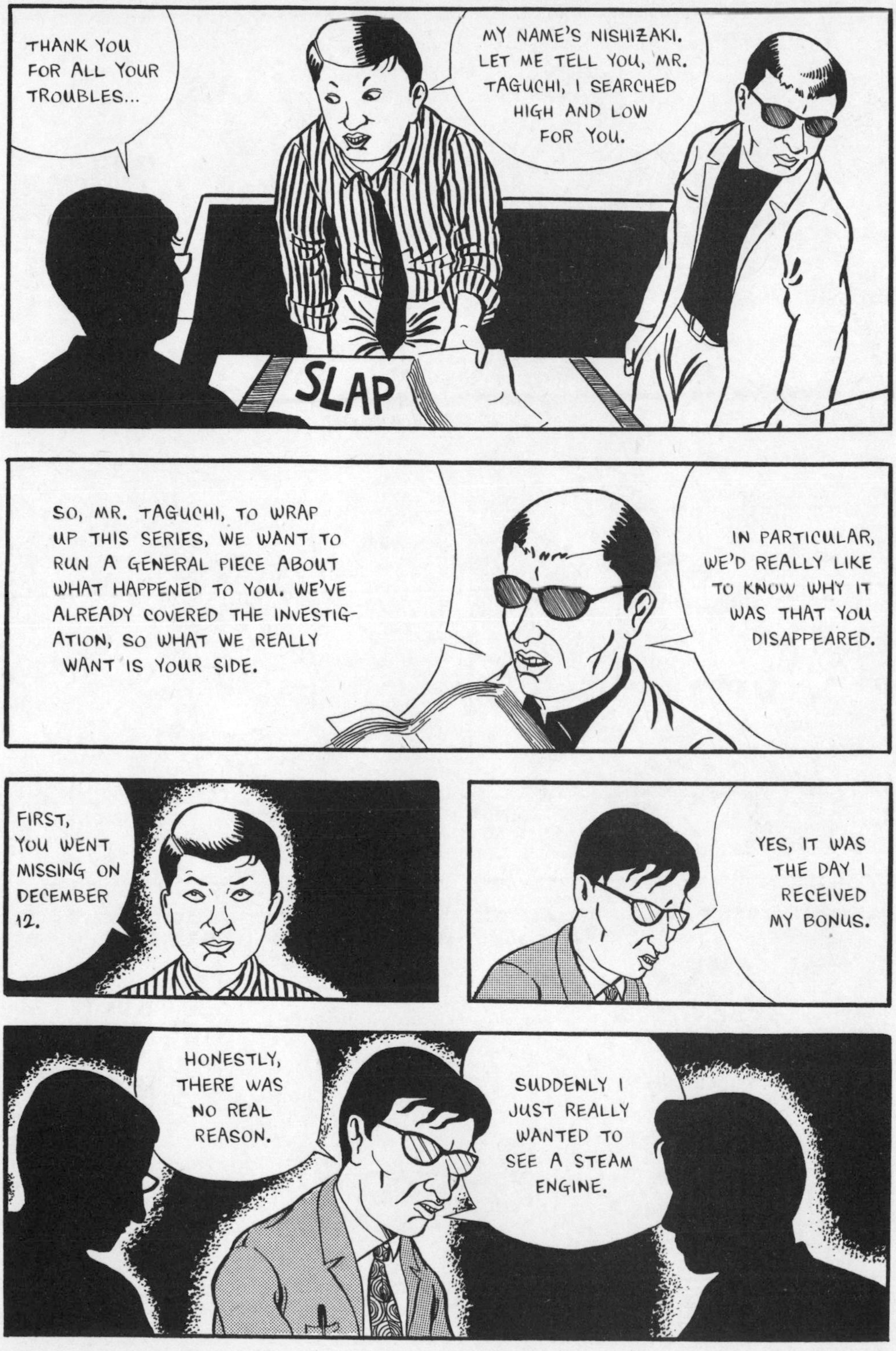
THANK YOU FOR ALL YOUR TROUBLES...
MY NAME'S NISHIZAKI. LET ME TELL YOU, MR. TAGUCHI, I SEARCHED HIGH AND LOW FOR YOU.
SLAP
SO, MR. TAGUCHI, TO WRAP UP THIS SERIES, WE WANT TO RUN A GENERAL PIECE ABOUT WHAT HAPPENED TO YOU. WE'VE ALREADY COVERED THE INVESTIG-ATION, SO WHAT WE REALLY WANT IS YOUR SIDE.
IN PARTICULAR, WE'D REALLY LIKE TO KNOW WHY IT WAS THAT YOU DISAPPEARED.
FIRST, YOU WENT MISSING ON DECEMBER 12.
YES, IT WAS THE DAY I RECEIVED MY BONUS.
HONESTLY, THERE WAS NO REAL REASON.
SUDDENLY I JUST REALLY WANTED TO SEE A STEAM ENGINE.

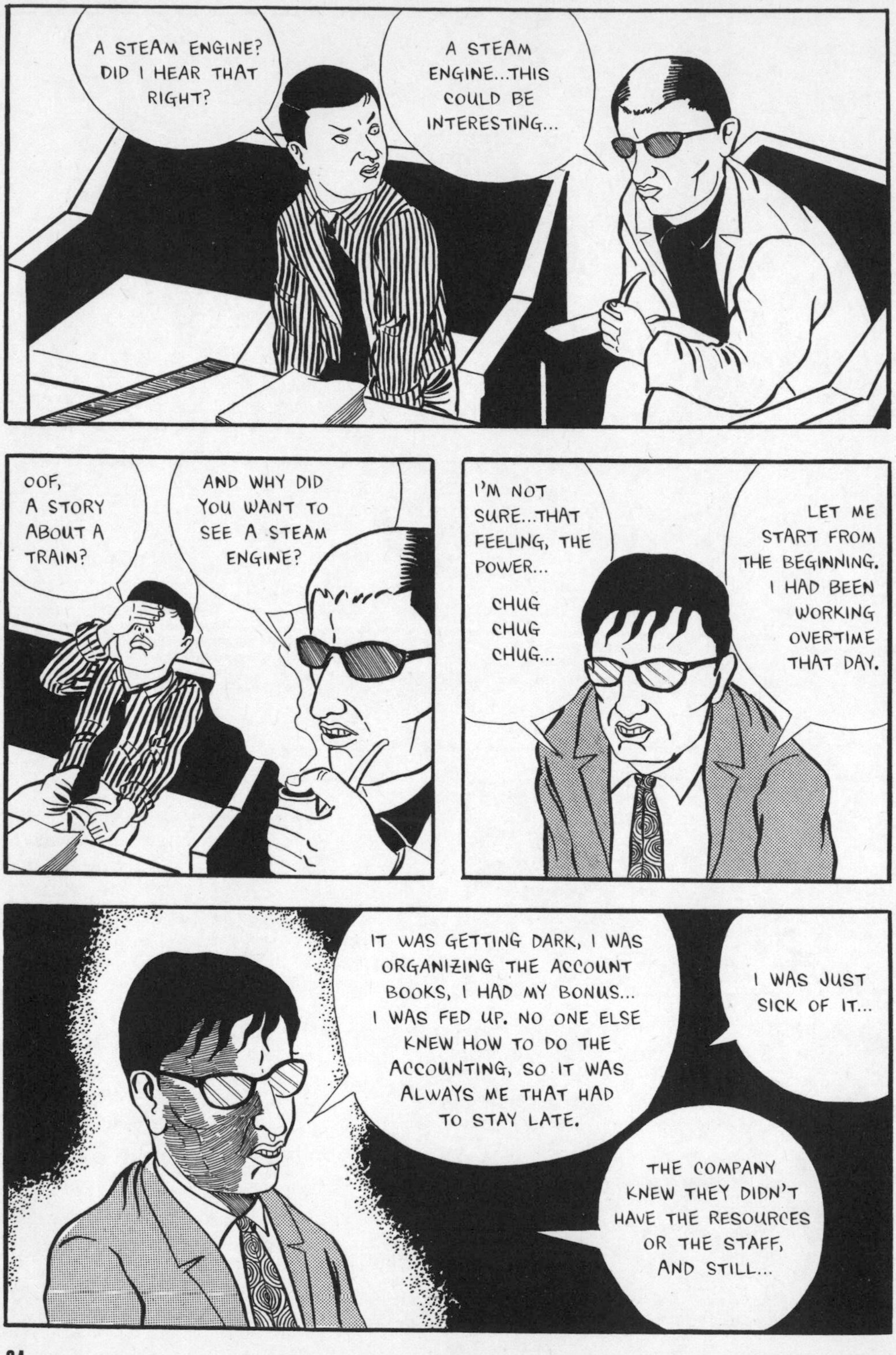
A STEAM ENGINE? DID I HEAR THAT RIGHT?
A STEAM ENGINE...THIS COULD BE INTERESTING...
OOF, A STORY ABOUT A TRAIN?
AND WHY DID YOU WANT TO SEE A STEAM ENGINE?
I'M NOT SURE...THAT FEELING, THE POWER...
CHUG CHUG CHUG...
LET ME START FROM THE BEGINNING. I HAD BEEN WORKING OVERTIME THAT DAY.
IT WAS GETTING DARK, I WAS ORGANIZING THE ACCOUNT BOOKS, I HAD MY BONUS... I WAS FED UP. NO ONE ELSE KNEW HOW TO DO THE ACCOUNTING, SO IT WAS ALWAYS ME THAT HAD TO STAY LATE.
I WAS JUST SICK OF IT...
THE COMPANY KNEW THEY DIDN'T HAVE THE RESOURCES OR THE STAFF, AND STILL...

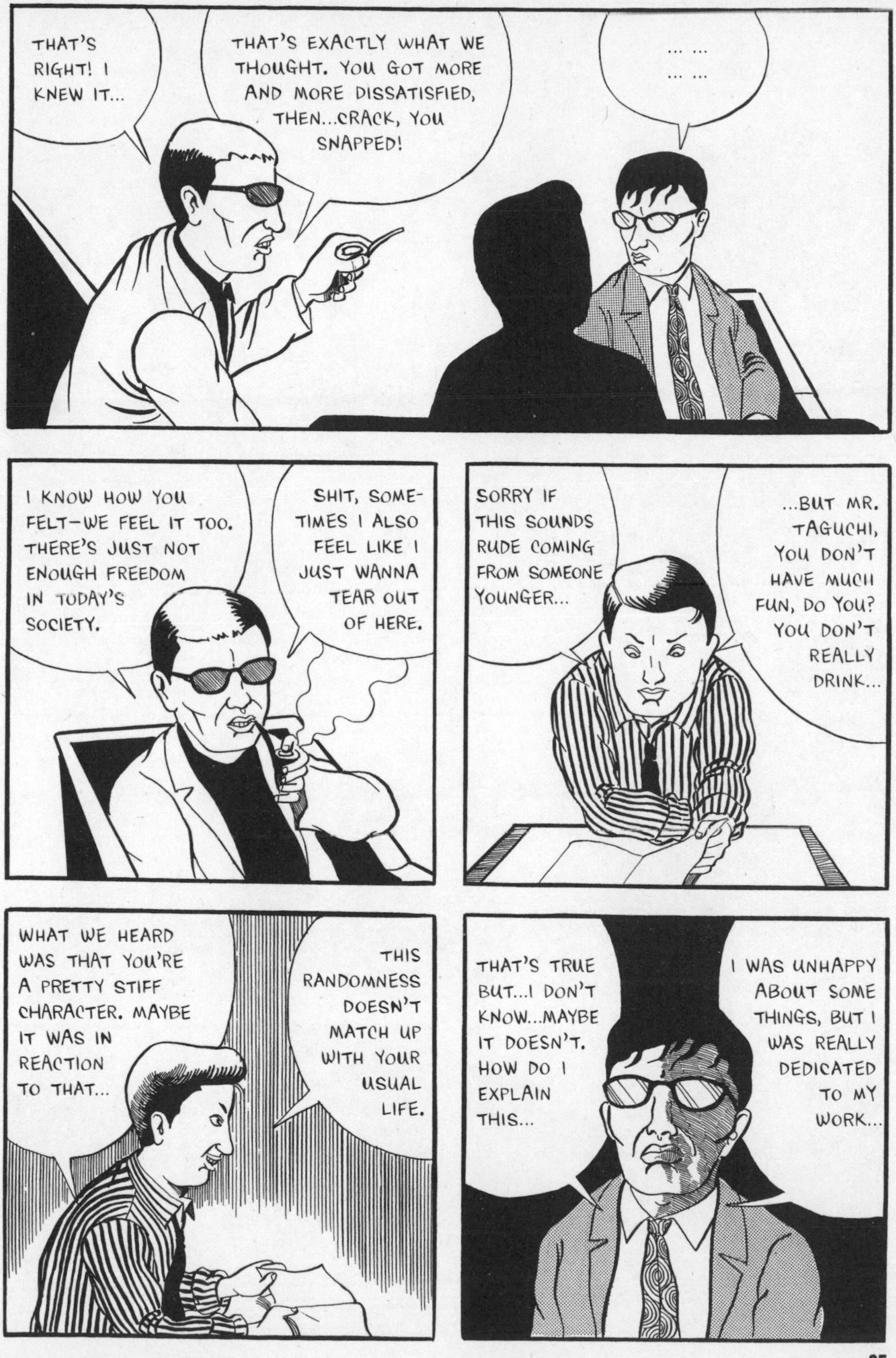
THAT'S RIGHT! I KNEW IT...
THAT'S EXACTLY WHAT WE THOUGHT. YOU GOT MORE AND MORE DISSATISFIED, THEN...CRACK, YOU SNAPPED!
... ...
I KNOW HOW YOU FELT—WE FEEL IT TOO. THERE'S JUST NOT ENOUGH FREEDOM IN TODAY'S SOCIETY.
SHIT, SOMETIMES I ALSO FEEL LIKE I JUST WANNA TEAR OUT OF HERE.
SORRY IF THIS SOUNDS RUDE COMING FROM SOMEONE YOUNGER...
...BUT MR. TAGUCHI, YOU DON'T HAVE MUCH FUN, DO YOU? YOU DON'T REALLY DRINK...
WHAT WE HEARD WAS THAT YOU'RE A PRETTY STIFF CHARACTER. MAYBE IT WAS IN REACTION TO THAT...
THIS RANDOMNESS DOESN'T MATCH UP WITH YOUR USUAL LIFE.
THAT'S TRUE BUT...I DON'T KNOW...MAYBE IT DOESN'T. HOW DO I EXPLAIN THIS...
I WAS UNHAPPY ABOUT SOME THINGS, BUT I WAS REALLY DEDICATED TO MY WORK...

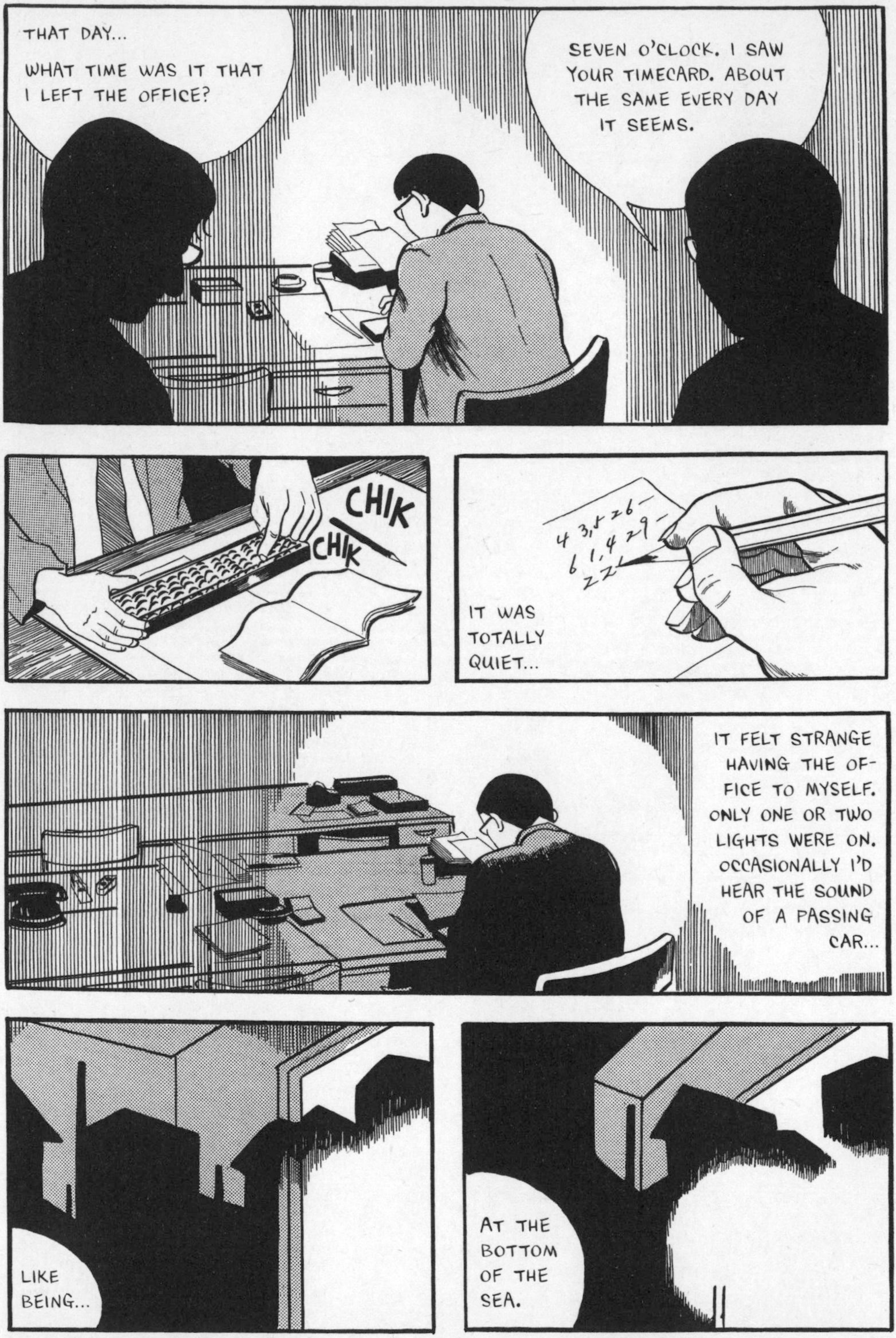
THAT DAY...
WHAT TIME WAS IT THAT I LEFT THE OFFICE?
SEVEN O'CLOCK. I SAW YOUR TIMECARD. ABOUT THE SAME EVERY DAY IT SEEMS.
CHIK
CHIK
IT WAS TOTALLY QUIET...
IT FELT STRANGE HAVING THE OF-FICE TO MYSELF. ONLY ONE OR TWO LIGHTS WERE ON. OCCASIONALLY I'D HEAR THE SOUND OF A PASSING CAR...
LIKE BEING...
AT THE BOTTOM OF THE SEA.

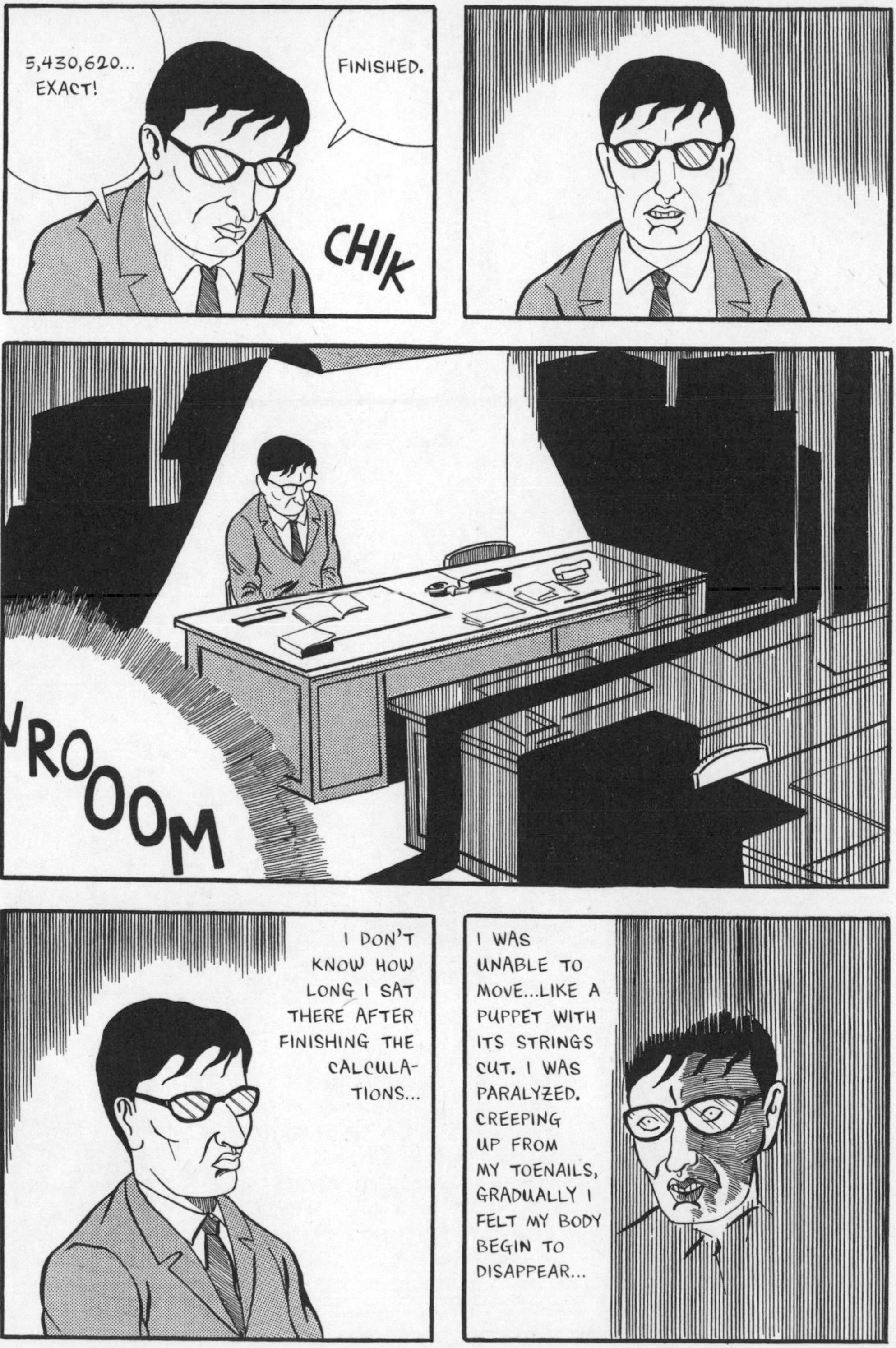
5,430,620... EXACT!
FINISHED.
CHIK
VROOOM
I DON'T KNOW HOW LONG I SAT THERE AFTER FINISHING THE CALCULATIONS...
I WAS UNABLE TO MOVE...LIKE A PUPPET WITH ITS STRINGS CUT. I WAS PARALYZED. CREEPING UP FROM MY TOENAILS, GRADUALLY I FELT MY BODY BEGIN TO DISAPPEAR...

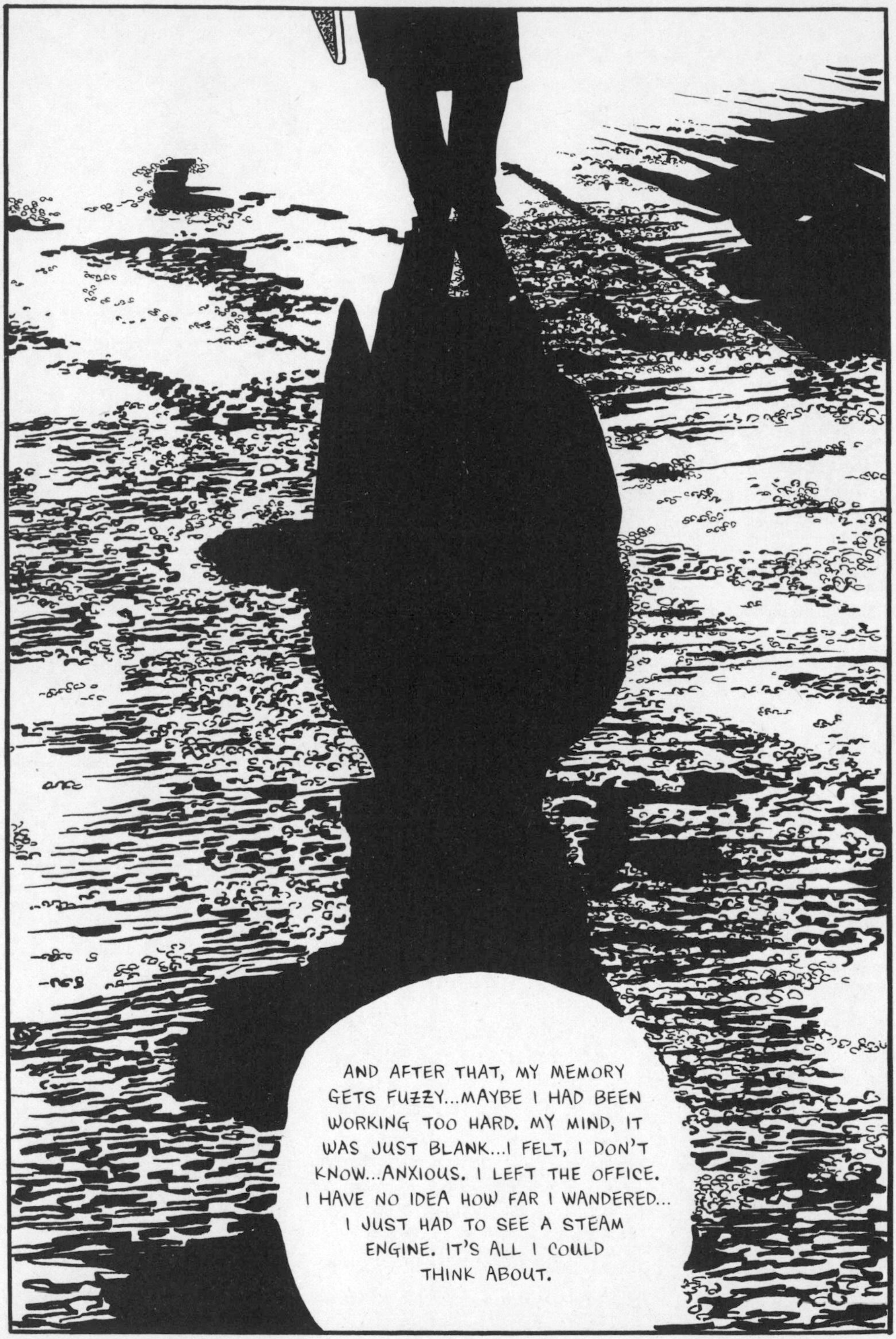
AND AFTER THAT, MY MEMORY GETS FUZZY...MAYBE I HAD BEEN WORKING TOO HARD. MY MIND, IT WAS JUST BLANK...I FELT, I DON'T KNOW...ANXIOUS. I LEFT THE OFFICE. I HAVE NO IDEA HOW FAR I WANDERED... I JUST HAD TO SEE A STEAM ENGINE. IT'S ALL I COULD THINK ABOUT.

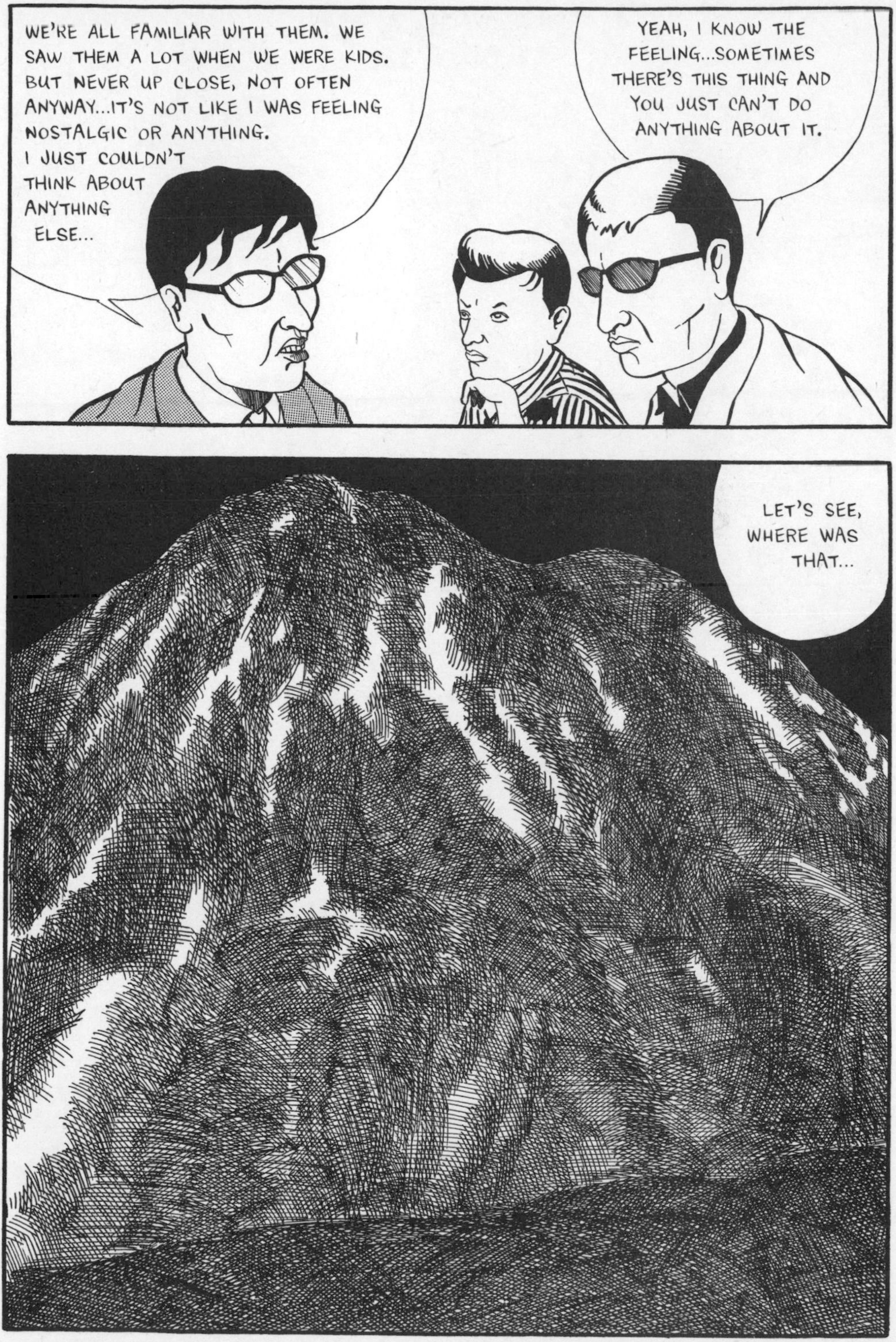
WE'RE ALL FAMILIAR WITH THEM. WE SAW THEM A LOT WHEN WE WERE KIDS. BUT NEVER UP CLOSE, NOT OFTEN ANYWAY...IT'S NOT LIKE I WAS FEELING NOSTALGIC OR ANYTHING. I JUST COULDN'T THINK ABOUT ANYTHING ELSE...
YEAH, I KNOW THE FEELING...SOMETIMES THERE'S THIS THING AND YOU JUST CAN'T DO ANYTHING ABOUT IT.
LET'S SEE, WHERE WAS THAT...

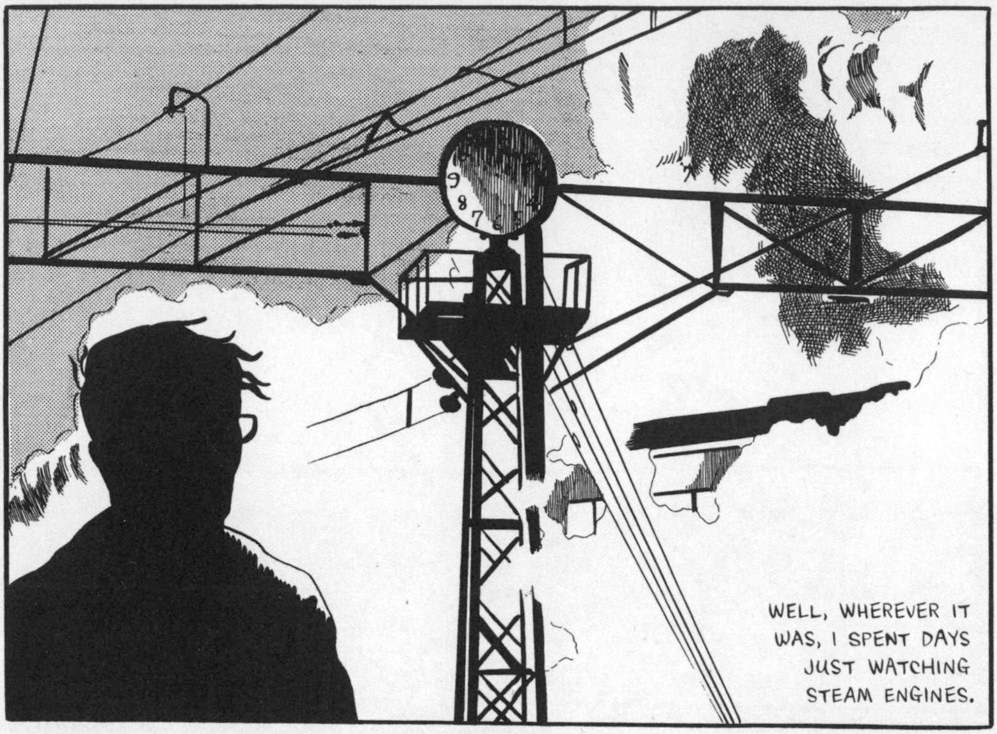
WELL, WHEREVER IT WAS, I SPENT DAYS JUST WATCHING STEAM ENGINES.

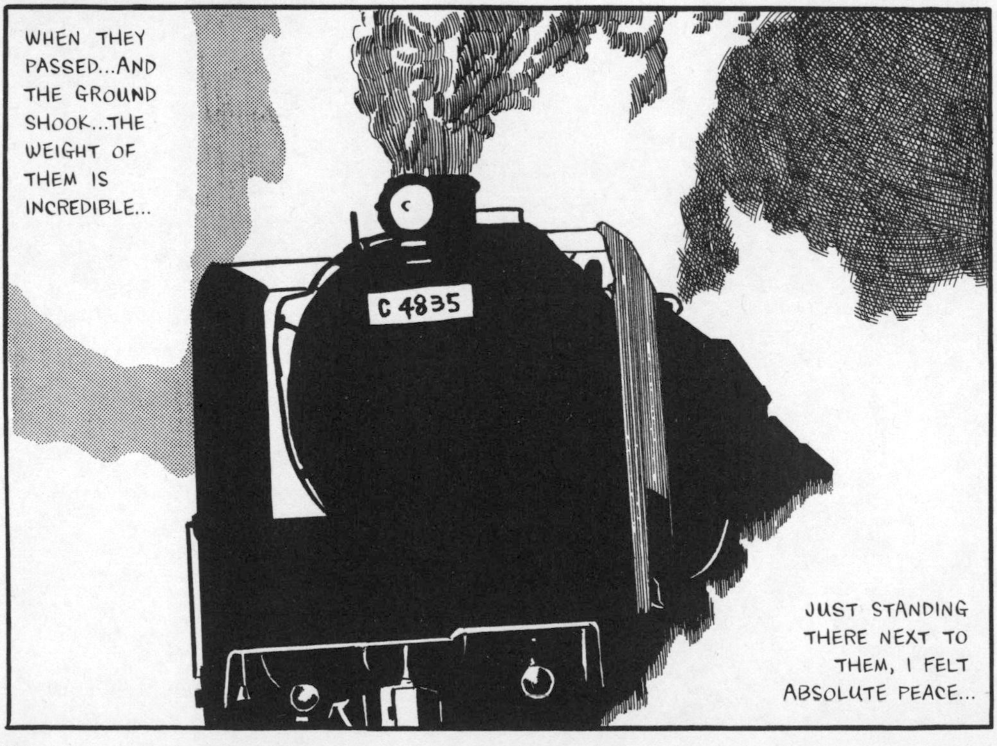
WHEN THEY PASSED...AND THE GROUND SHOOK...THE WEIGHT OF THEM IS INCREDIBLE...
C 4835
JUST STANDING THERE NEXT TO THEM, I FELT ABSOLUTE PEACE...

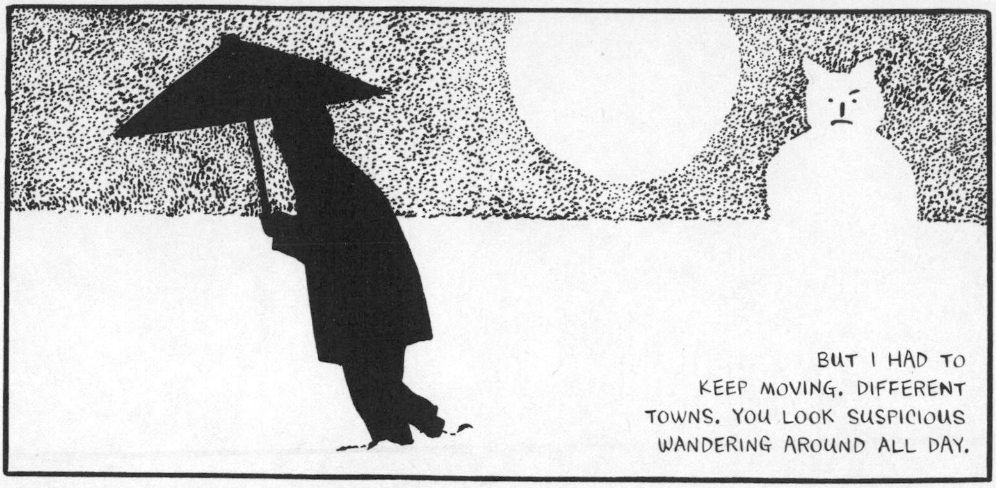
BUT I HAD TO KEEP MOVING. DIFFERENT TOWNS. YOU LOOK SUSPICIOUS WANDERING AROUND ALL DAY.
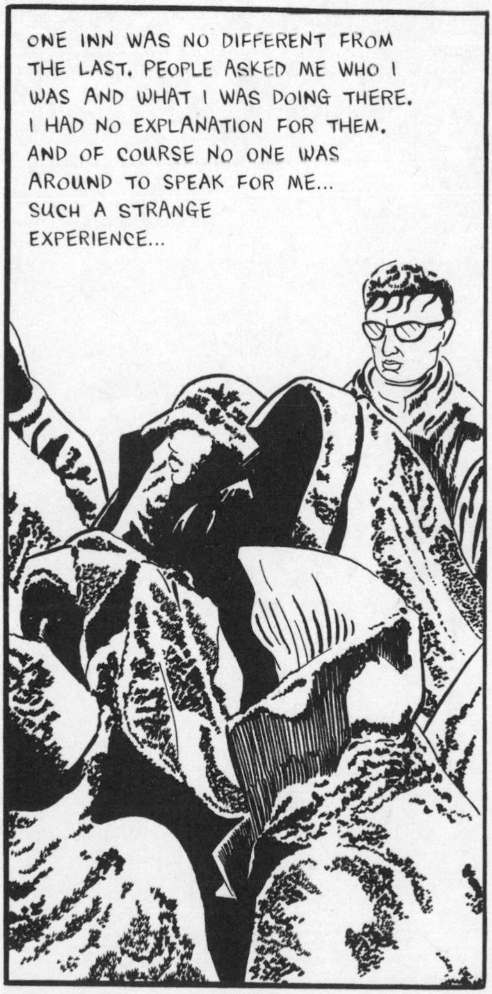
ONE INN WAS NO DIFFERENT FROM THE LAST. PEOPLE ASKED ME WHO I WAS AND WHAT I WAS DOING THERE. I HAD NO EXPLANATION FOR THEM. AND OF COURSE NO ONE WAS AROUND TO SPEAK FOR ME... SUCH A STRANGE EXPERIENCE...
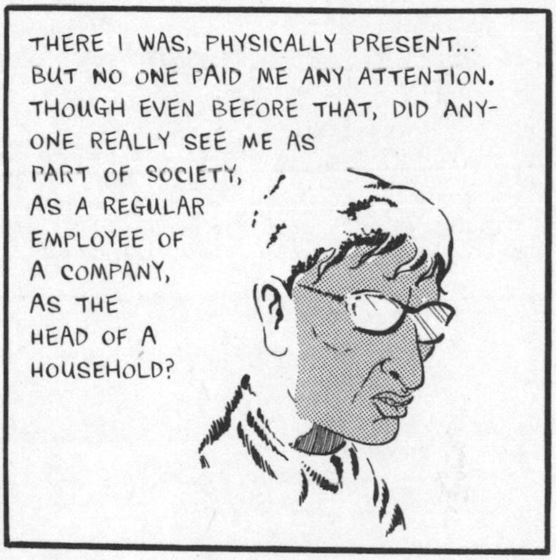
THERE I WAS, PHYSICALLY PRESENT... BUT NO ONE PAID ME ANY ATTENTION. THOUGH EVEN BEFORE THAT, DID ANY-ONE REALLY SEE ME AS PART OF SOCIETY, AS A REGULAR EMPLOYEE OF A COMPANY, AS THE HEAD OF A HOUSEHOLD?
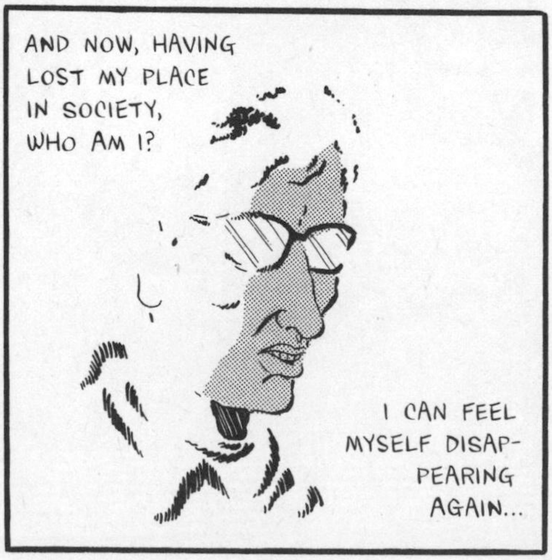
AND NOW, HAVING LOST MY PLACE IN SOCIETY, WHO AM I?
I CAN FEEL MYSELF DISAP-PEARING AGAIN...

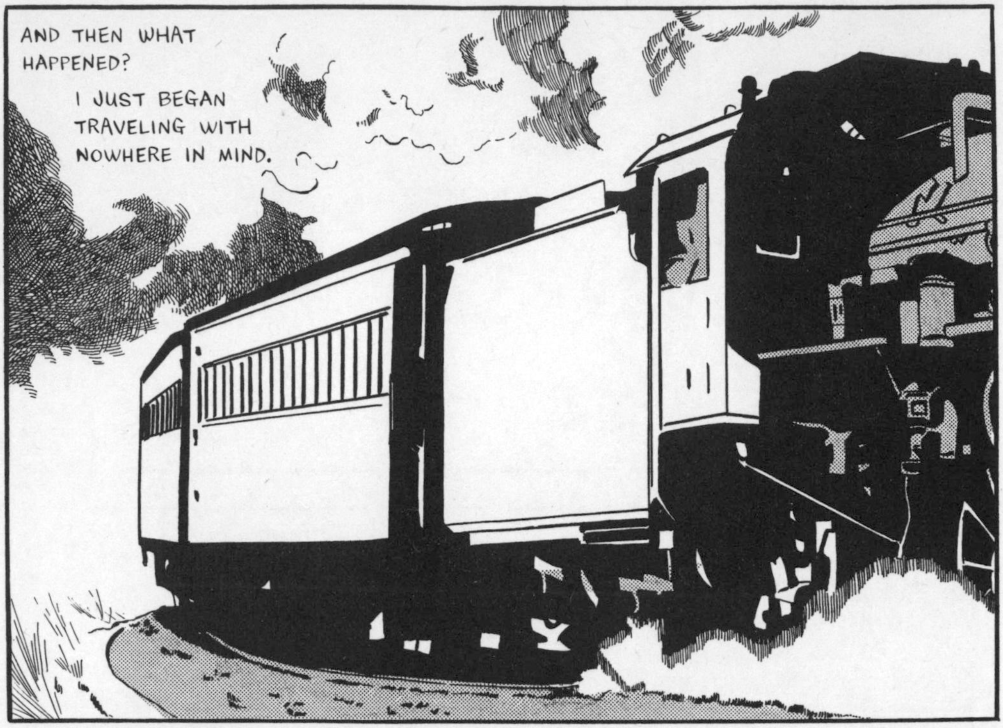
AND THEN WHAT HAPPENED?
I JUST BEGAN TRAVELING WITH NOWHERE IN MIND.

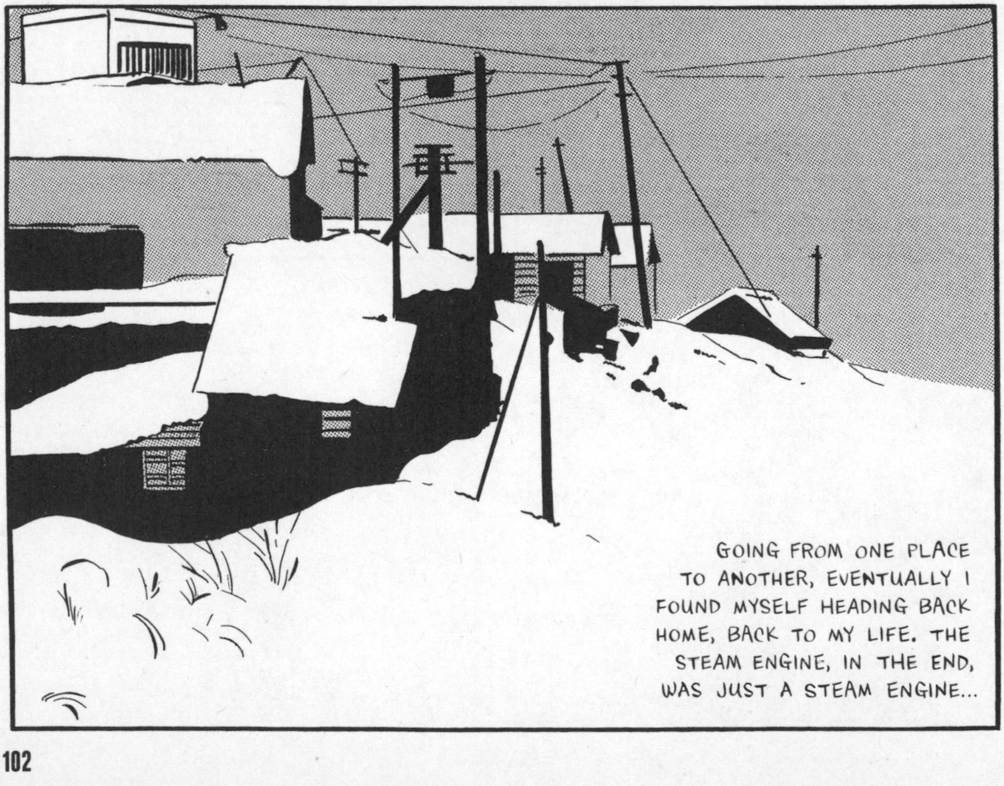
GOING FROM ONE PLACE TO ANOTHER, EVENTUALLY I FOUND MYSELF HEADING BACK HOME, BACK TO MY LIFE. THE STEAM ENGINE, IN THE END, WAS JUST A STEAM ENGINE...

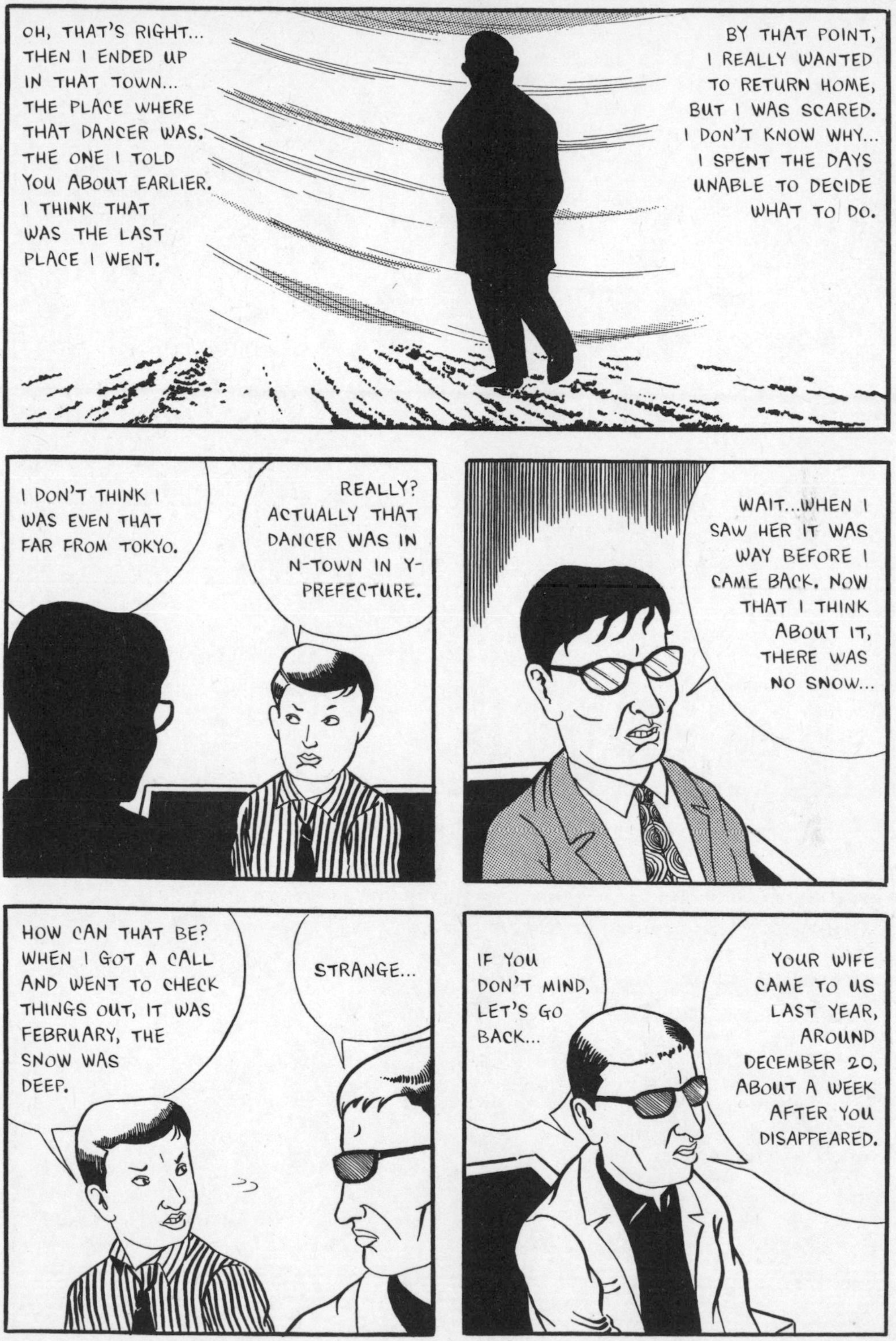
OH, THAT'S RIGHT... THEN I ENDED UP IN THAT TOWN... THE PLACE WHERE THAT DANCER WAS. THE ONE I TOLD YOU ABOUT EARLIER. I THINK THAT WAS THE LAST PLACE I WENT.
BY THAT POINT, I REALLY WANTED TO RETURN HOME, BUT I WAS SCARED. I DON'T KNOW WHY... I SPENT THE DAYS UNABLE TO DECIDE WHAT TO DO.
I DON'T THINK I WAS EVEN THAT FAR FROM TOKYO.
REALLY? ACTUALLY THAT DANCER WAS IN N-TOWN IN Y-PREFECTURE.
WAIT...WHEN I SAW HER IT WAS WAY BEFORE I CAME BACK. NOW THAT I THINK ABOUT IT, THERE WAS NO SNOW...
HOW CAN THAT BE? WHEN I GOT A CALL AND WENT TO CHECK THINGS OUT, IT WAS FEBRUARY, THE SNOW WAS DEEP.
STRANGE...
IF YOU DON'T MIND, LET'S GO BACK...
YOUR WIFE CAME TO US LAST YEAR, AROUND DECEMBER 20, ABOUT A WEEK AFTER YOU DISAPPEARED.

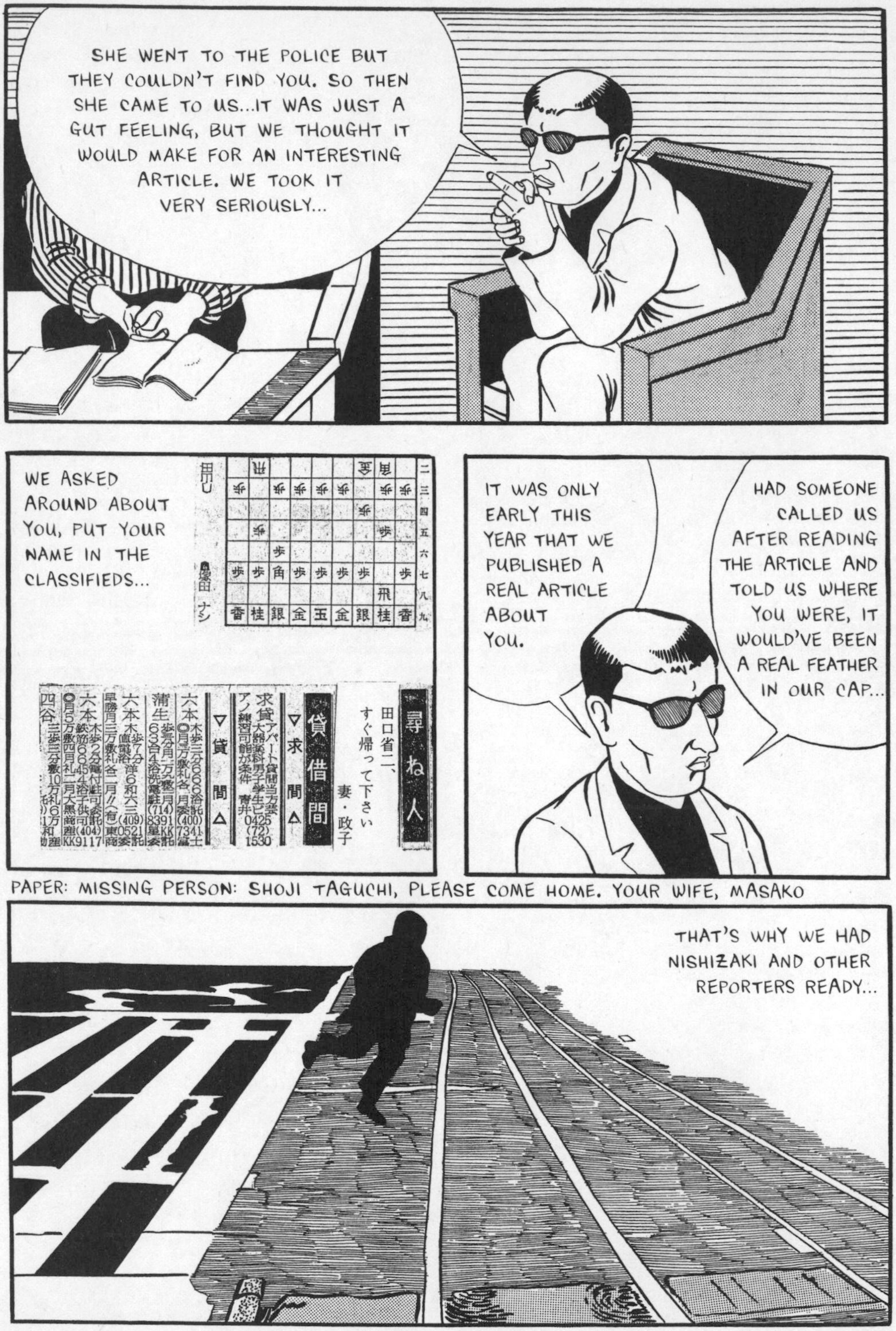
SHE WENT TO THE POLICE BUT THEY COULDN'T FIND YOU. SO THEN SHE CAME TO US...IT WAS JUST A GUT FEELING, BUT WE THOUGHT IT WOULD MAKE FOR AN INTERESTING ARTICLE. WE TOOK IT VERY SERIOUSLY...
WE ASKED AROUND ABOUT YOU, PUT YOUR NAME IN THE CLASSIFIEDS...
尋ね人
田口省二、すぐ帰って下さい 妻・政子
貸借間
IT WAS ONLY EARLY THIS YEAR THAT WE PUBLISHED A REAL ARTICLE ABOUT YOU.
HAD SOMEONE CALLED US AFTER READING THE ARTICLE AND TOLD US WHERE YOU WERE, IT WOULD'VE BEEN A REAL FEATHER IN OUR CAP...
PAPER: MISSING PERSON: SHOJI TAGUCHI, PLEASE COME HOME. YOUR WIFE, MASAKO
THAT'S WHY WE HAD NISHIZAKI AND OTHER REPORTERS READY...

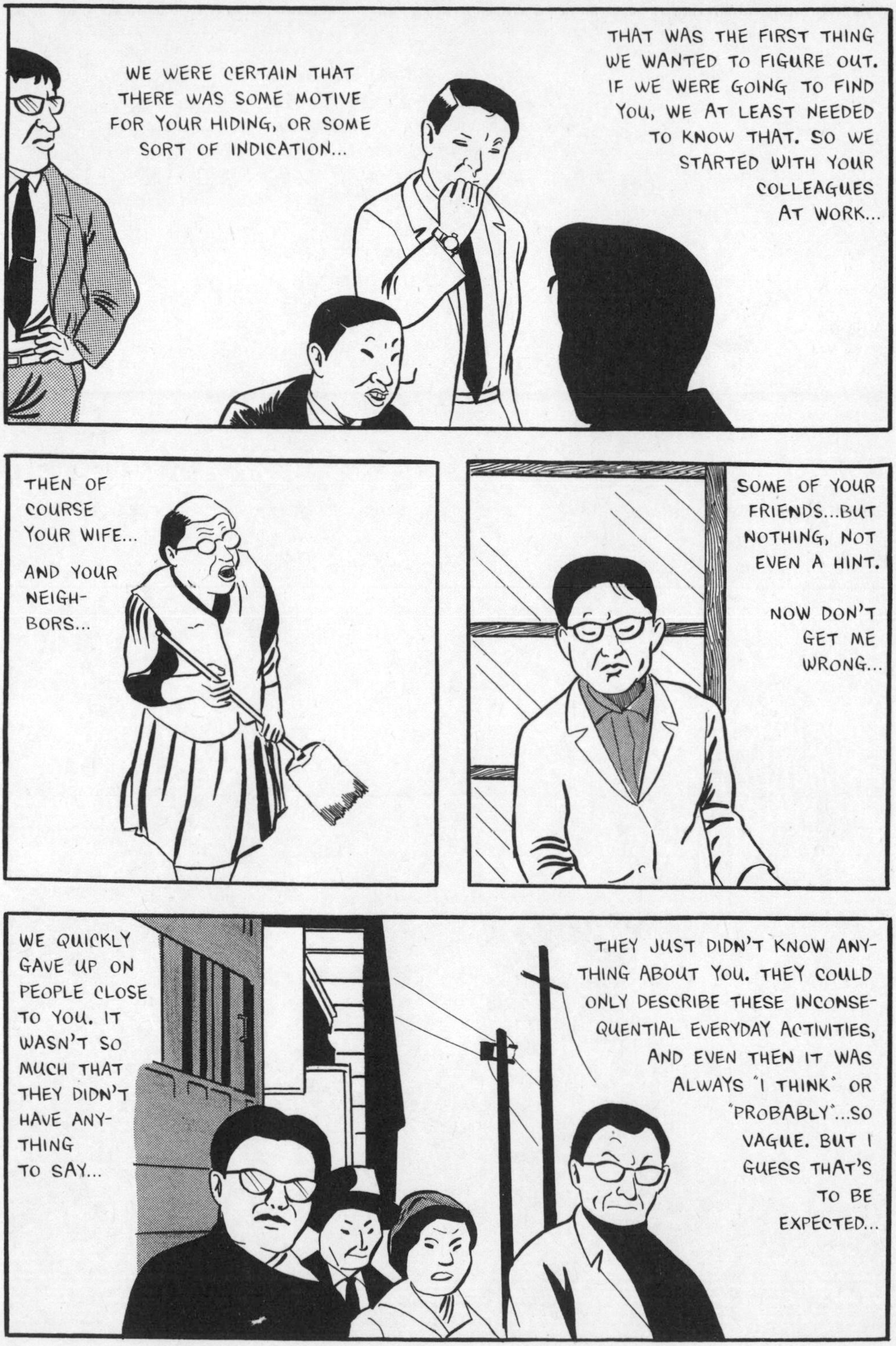
WE WERE CERTAIN THAT THERE WAS SOME MOTIVE FOR YOUR HIDING, OR SOME SORT OF INDICATION...
THAT WAS THE FIRST THING WE WANTED TO FIGURE OUT. IF WE WERE GOING TO FIND YOU, WE AT LEAST NEEDED TO KNOW THAT. SO WE STARTED WITH YOUR COLLEAGUES AT WORK...
THEN OF COURSE YOUR WIFE...
AND YOUR NEIGHBORS...
SOME OF YOUR FRIENDS...BUT NOTHING, NOT EVEN A HINT.
NOW DON'T GET ME WRONG...
WE QUICKLY GAVE UP ON PEOPLE CLOSE TO YOU. IT WASN'T SO MUCH THAT THEY DIDN'T HAVE ANYTHING TO SAY...
THEY JUST DIDN'T KNOW ANYTHING ABOUT YOU. THEY COULD ONLY DESCRIBE THESE INCONSEQUENTIAL EVERYDAY ACTIVITIES, AND EVEN THEN IT WAS ALWAYS "I THINK" OR "PROBABLY"...SO VAGUE. BUT I GUESS THAT'S TO BE EXPECTED...

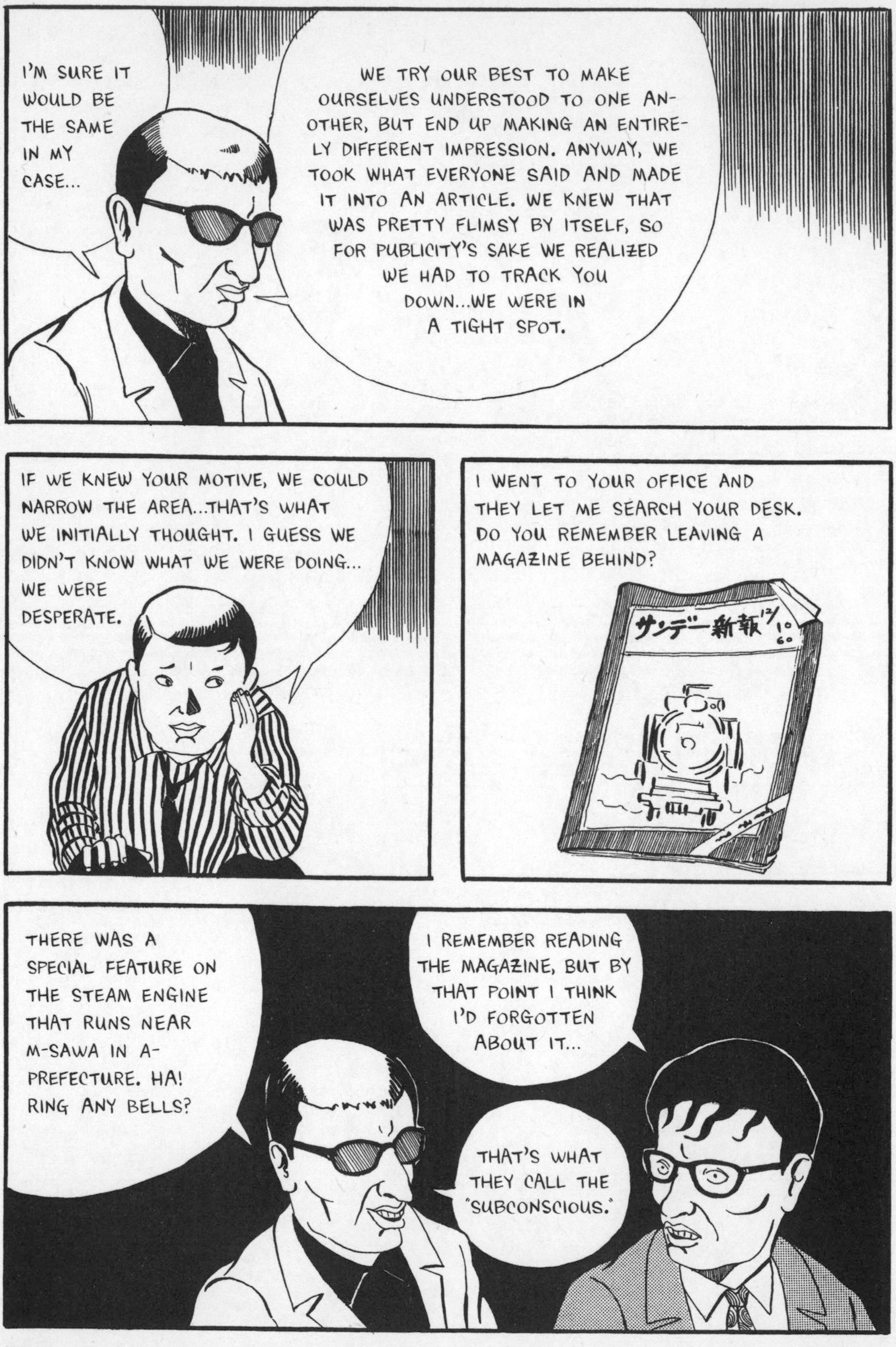

I'M SURE IT WOULD BE THE SAME IN MY CASE...
WE TRY OUR BEST TO MAKE OURSELVES UNDERSTOOD TO ONE ANOTHER, BUT END UP MAKING AN ENTIRELY DIFFERENT IMPRESSION. ANYWAY, WE TOOK WHAT EVERYONE SAID AND MADE IT INTO AN ARTICLE. WE KNEW THAT WAS PRETTY FLIMSY BY ITSELF, SO FOR PUBLICITY'S SAKE WE REALIZED WE HAD TO TRACK YOU DOWN...WE WERE IN A TIGHT SPOT.
IF WE KNEW YOUR MOTIVE, WE COULD NARROW THE AREA...THAT'S WHAT WE INITIALLY THOUGHT. I GUESS WE DIDN'T KNOW WHAT WE WERE DOING... WE WERE DESPERATE.
I WENT TO YOUR OFFICE AND THEY LET ME SEARCH YOUR DESK. DO YOU REMEMBER LEAVING A MAGAZINE BEHIND?
サンデー新報 12/10 60
THERE WAS A SPECIAL FEATURE ON THE STEAM ENGINE THAT RUNS NEAR M-SAWA IN A-PREFECTURE. HA! RING ANY BELLS?
I REMEMBER READING THE MAGAZINE, BUT BY THAT POINT I THINK I'D FORGOTTEN ABOUT IT...
THAT'S WHAT THEY CALL THE "SUBCONSCIOUS."

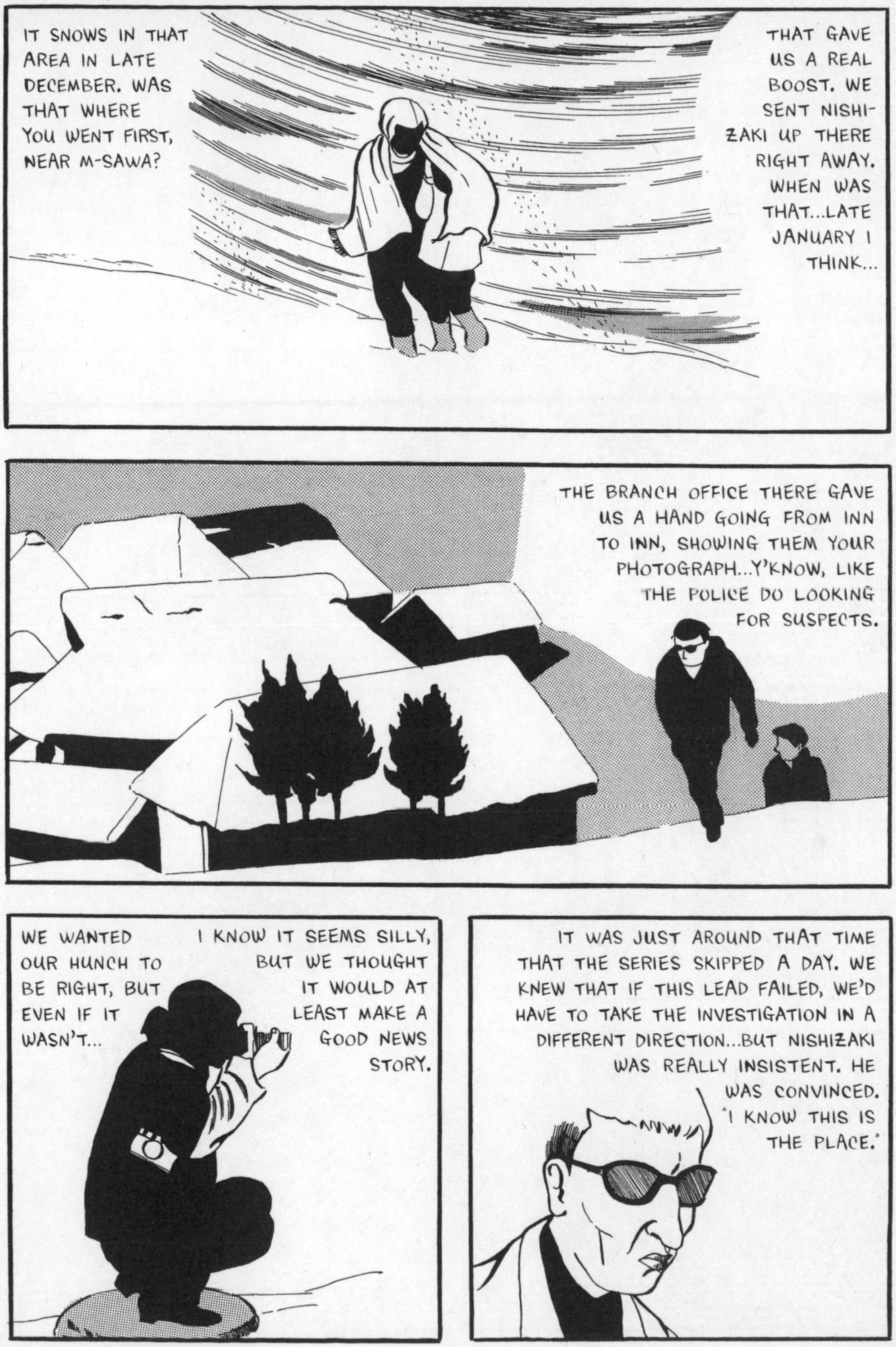
IT SNOWS IN THAT AREA IN LATE DECEMBER. WAS THAT WHERE YOU WENT FIRST, NEAR M-SAWA?
THAT GAVE US A REAL BOOST. WE SENT NISHI-ZAKI UP THERE RIGHT AWAY. WHEN WAS THAT...LATE JANUARY I THINK...
THE BRANCH OFFICE THERE GAVE US A HAND GOING FROM INN TO INN, SHOWING THEM YOUR PHOTOGRAPH...Y'KNOW, LIKE THE POLICE DO LOOKING FOR SUSPECTS.
WE WANTED OUR HUNCH TO BE RIGHT, BUT EVEN IF IT WASN'T...
I KNOW IT SEEMS SILLY, BUT WE THOUGHT IT WOULD AT LEAST MAKE A GOOD NEWS STORY.
IT WAS JUST AROUND THAT TIME THAT THE SERIES SKIPPED A DAY. WE KNEW THAT IF THIS LEAD FAILED, WE'D HAVE TO TAKE THE INVESTIGATION IN A DIFFERENT DIRECTION...BUT NISHIZAKI WAS REALLY INSISTENT. HE WAS CONVINCED. "I KNOW THIS IS THE PLACE."

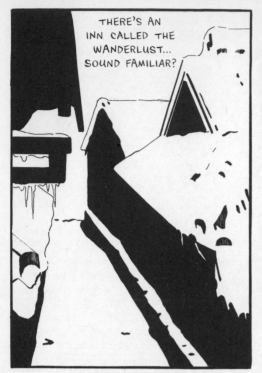

THERE'S AN INN CALLED THE WANDERLUST... SOUND FAMILIAR?

IT WAS A SMALL PLACE. YOU STAYED THERE UNTIL EARLY JANUARY. THEY RECOGNIZED YOUR PHOTO IMMEDIATELY.

THEY REMEMBERED HOW STRANGELY YOU ACTED...

SQUEAK

SQUEAK

YOU WENT OUT IN THE AFTERNOON...

SQUEAK

SQUEAK

FINE, BUT AT NIGHT YOU PACED ABOUT INSIDE THE INN.

SQUEAK

SQUEAK

MR. TAGUCHI...WHAT EXACTLY WERE YOU DOING? DID IT MEAN SOMETHING?

SQUEAK

SQUEAK

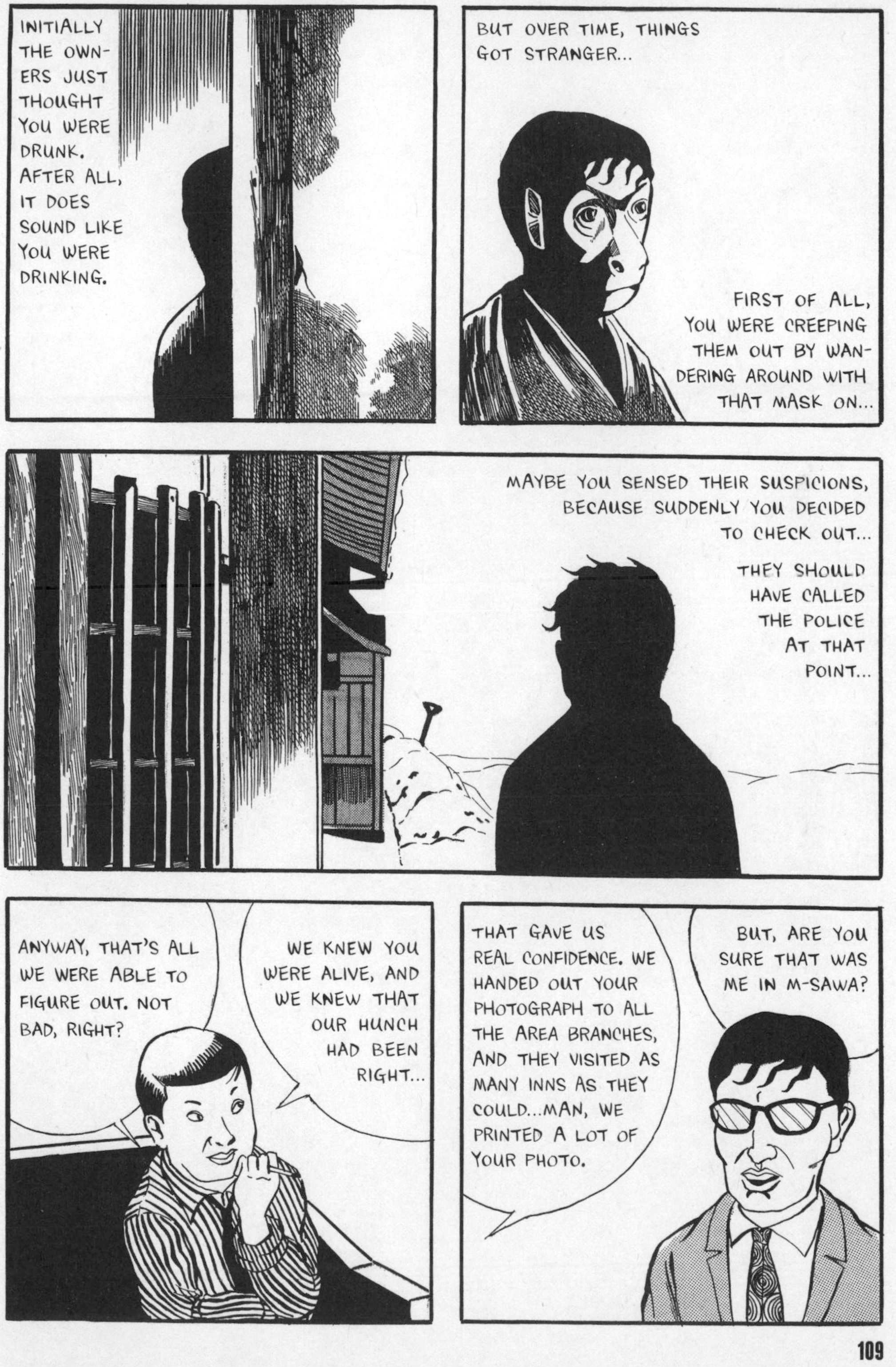

INITIALLY THE OWNERS JUST THOUGHT YOU WERE DRUNK. AFTER ALL, IT DOES SOUND LIKE YOU WERE DRINKING.
BUT OVER TIME, THINGS GOT STRANGER...
FIRST OF ALL, YOU WERE CREEPING THEM OUT BY WANDERING AROUND WITH THAT MASK ON...
MAYBE YOU SENSED THEIR SUSPICIONS, BECAUSE SUDDENLY YOU DECIDED TO CHECK OUT...
THEY SHOULD HAVE CALLED THE POLICE AT THAT POINT...
ANYWAY, THAT'S ALL WE WERE ABLE TO FIGURE OUT. NOT BAD, RIGHT?
WE KNEW YOU WERE ALIVE, AND WE KNEW THAT OUR HUNCH HAD BEEN RIGHT...
THAT GAVE US REAL CONFIDENCE. WE HANDED OUT YOUR PHOTOGRAPH TO ALL THE AREA BRANCHES, AND THEY VISITED AS MANY INNS AS THEY COULD...MAN, WE PRINTED A LOT OF YOUR PHOTO.
BUT, ARE YOU SURE THAT WAS ME IN M-SAWA?

HA HA HA, THERE'S NO NEED TO BE SO...

WHAT DO YOU MEAN, MR. TAGUCHI?

IF THAT REALLY WAS ME, I THINK I WOULD REMEMBER SOMETHING...BUT I DON'T REMEMBER ANYTHING AT ALL.

BESIDES, I DIDN'T SPEND THAT LONG AT ANY INN. ONLY THREE OR FOUR DAYS AT EACH ONE...

SIR, THEY IDENTIFIED YOU FROM THE PHOTOGRAPH.

I THINK YOU'VE JUST FORGOTTEN... YOU SAID YOURSELF THAT YOUR MEMORY IS HAZY. PARDON MY BLUNTNESS, BUT YOU WERE NOT IN YOUR RIGHT MIND.

THAT'S SO STRANGE...

WALKING AROUND AT NIGHT WITH A MASK ON, MR. TAGUCHI, IS NOT NORMAL.

ANYWAY, THAT WASN'T ALL. THEN YOU TURNED UP IN N-TOWN IN Y-PREFECTURE.

WE TRIED YOUR PHOTO AGAIN. ONE OF THE INNS CALLED THE LOCAL OFFICE.

SO WE SENT NISHIZAKI OUT AGAIN...THIS WAS MID-FEBRUARY...

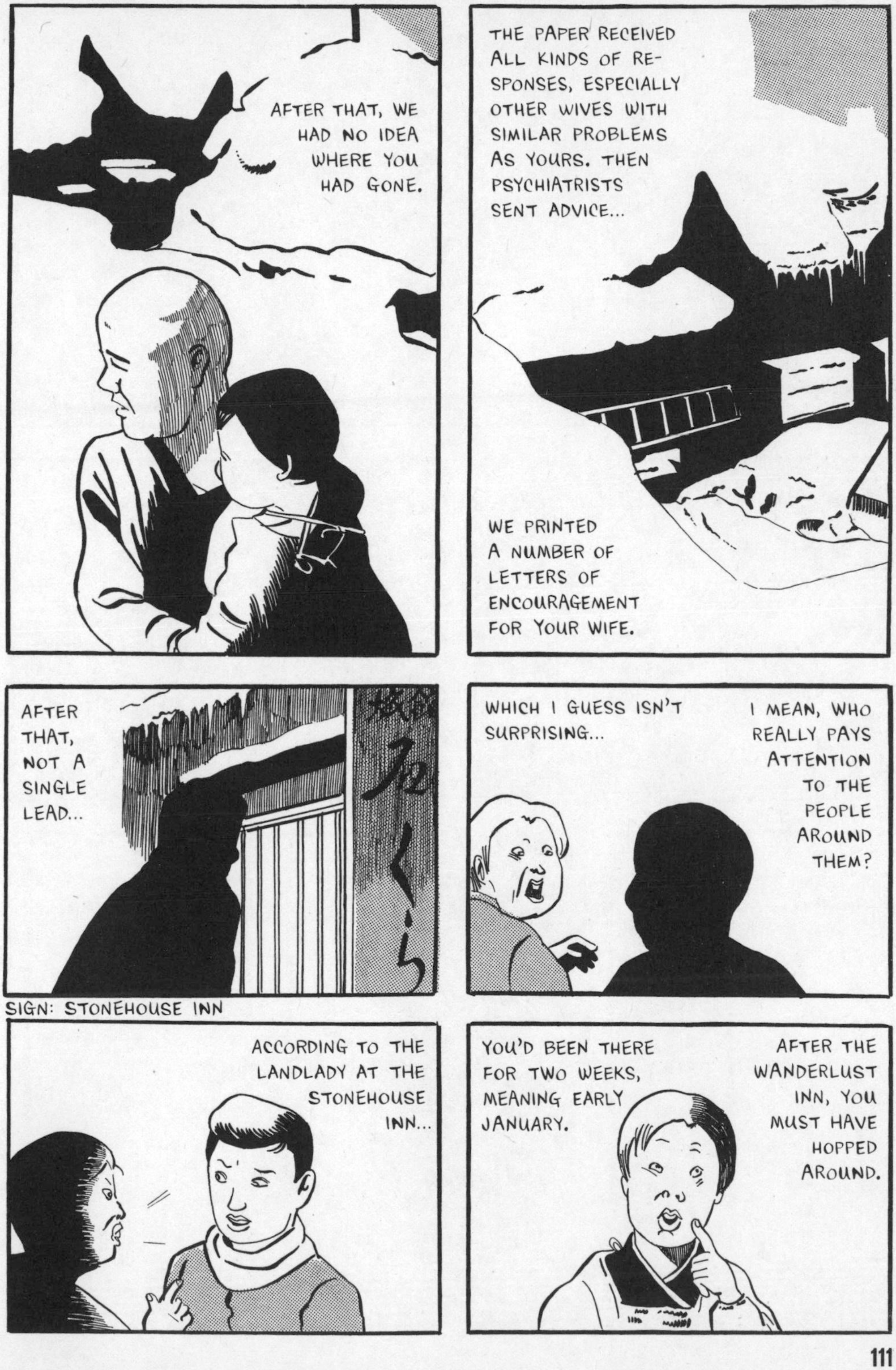
AFTER THAT, WE HAD NO IDEA WHERE YOU HAD GONE.
THE PAPER RECEIVED ALL KINDS OF RE-SPONSES, ESPECIALLY OTHER WIVES WITH SIMILAR PROBLEMS AS YOURS. THEN PSYCHIATRISTS SENT ADVICE...
WE PRINTED A NUMBER OF LETTERS OF ENCOURAGEMENT FOR YOUR WIFE.
AFTER THAT, NOT A SINGLE LEAD...
SIGN: STONEHOUSE INN
WHICH I GUESS ISN'T SURPRISING...
I MEAN, WHO REALLY PAYS ATTENTION TO THE PEOPLE AROUND THEM?
ACCORDING TO THE LANDLADY AT THE STONEHOUSE INN...
YOU'D BEEN THERE FOR TWO WEEKS, MEANING EARLY JANUARY.
AFTER THE WANDERLUST INN, YOU MUST HAVE HOPPED AROUND.

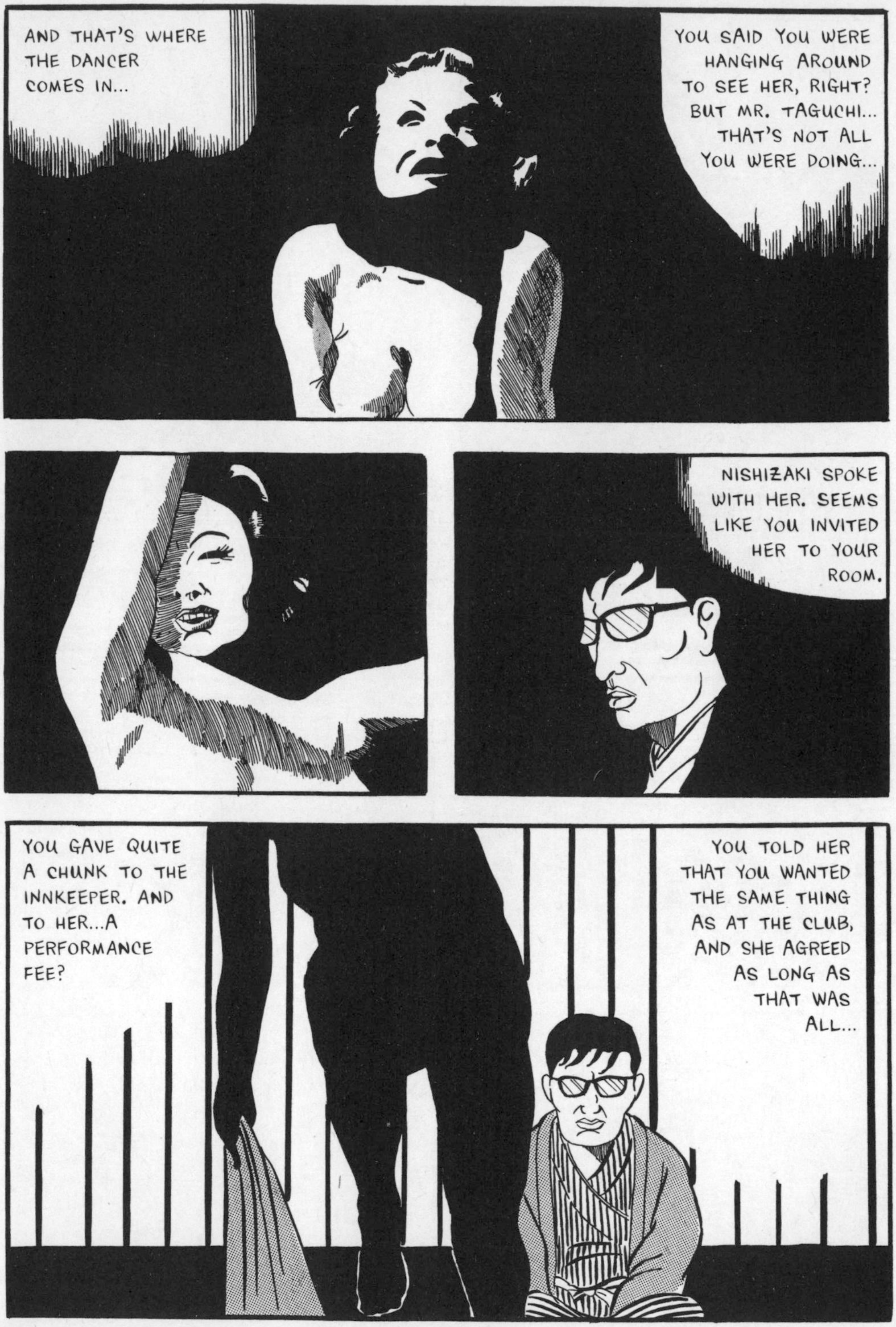
AND THAT'S WHERE THE DANCER COMES IN...
YOU SAID YOU WERE HANGING AROUND TO SEE HER, RIGHT? BUT MR. TAGUCHI... THAT'S NOT ALL YOU WERE DOING...
NISHIZAKI SPOKE WITH HER. SEEMS LIKE YOU INVITED HER TO YOUR ROOM.
YOU GAVE QUITE A CHUNK TO THE INNKEEPER. AND TO HER...A PERFORMANCE FEE?
YOU TOLD HER THAT YOU WANTED THE SAME THING AS AT THE CLUB, AND SHE AGREED AS LONG AS THAT WAS ALL...

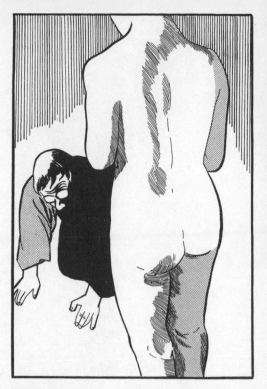

AT FIRST, SHE FOUND IT
CREEPY. BUT AFTER SEEING
THE SERIOUS LOOK ON YOUR
FACE, SHE BURST OUT LAUGH-
ING...SOUNDS LIKE YOU INVITED
HER TWO OR THREE TIMES FOR
A TWENTY-MINUTE SHOW...

POOR NISHIZAKI,
OUT ON A WILD GOOSE
CHASE. HE TOTALLY LOST
IT AFTER HE GOT BACK,
SAYING HE FELT LIKE
SOMEONE WAS
PLAYING HIM
FOR A FOOL.

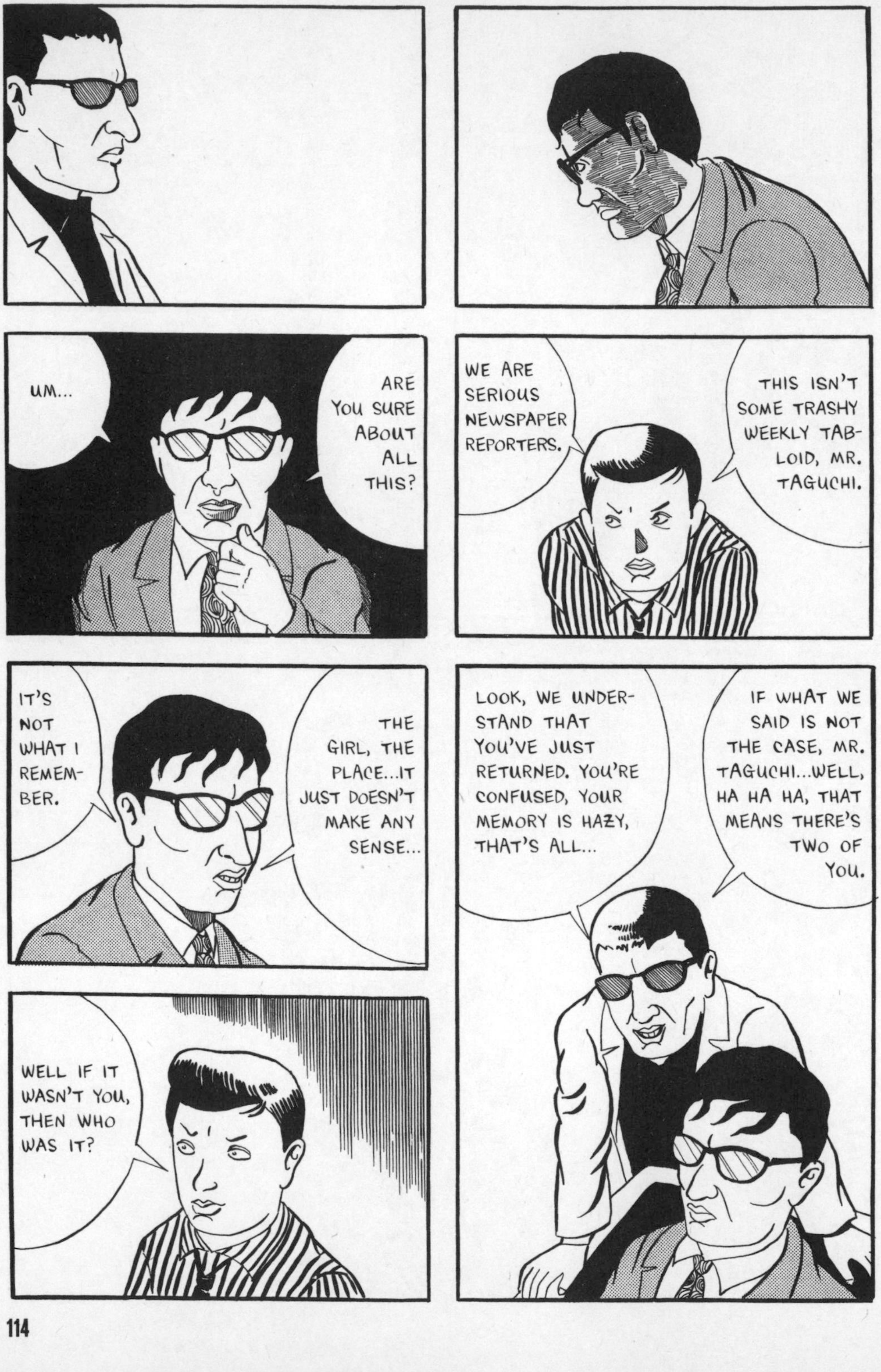

UM...
ARE YOU SURE ABOUT ALL THIS?
WE ARE SERIOUS NEWSPAPER REPORTERS.
THIS ISN'T SOME TRASHY WEEKLY TABLOID, MR. TAGUCHI.
IT'S NOT WHAT I REMEMBER.
THE GIRL, THE PLACE...IT JUST DOESN'T MAKE ANY SENSE...
WELL IF IT WASN'T YOU, THEN WHO WAS IT?
LOOK, WE UNDERSTAND THAT YOU'VE JUST RETURNED. YOU'RE CONFUSED, YOUR MEMORY IS HAZY, THAT'S ALL...
IF WHAT WE SAID IS NOT THE CASE, MR. TAGUCHI...WELL, HA HA HA, THAT MEANS THERE'S TWO OF YOU.

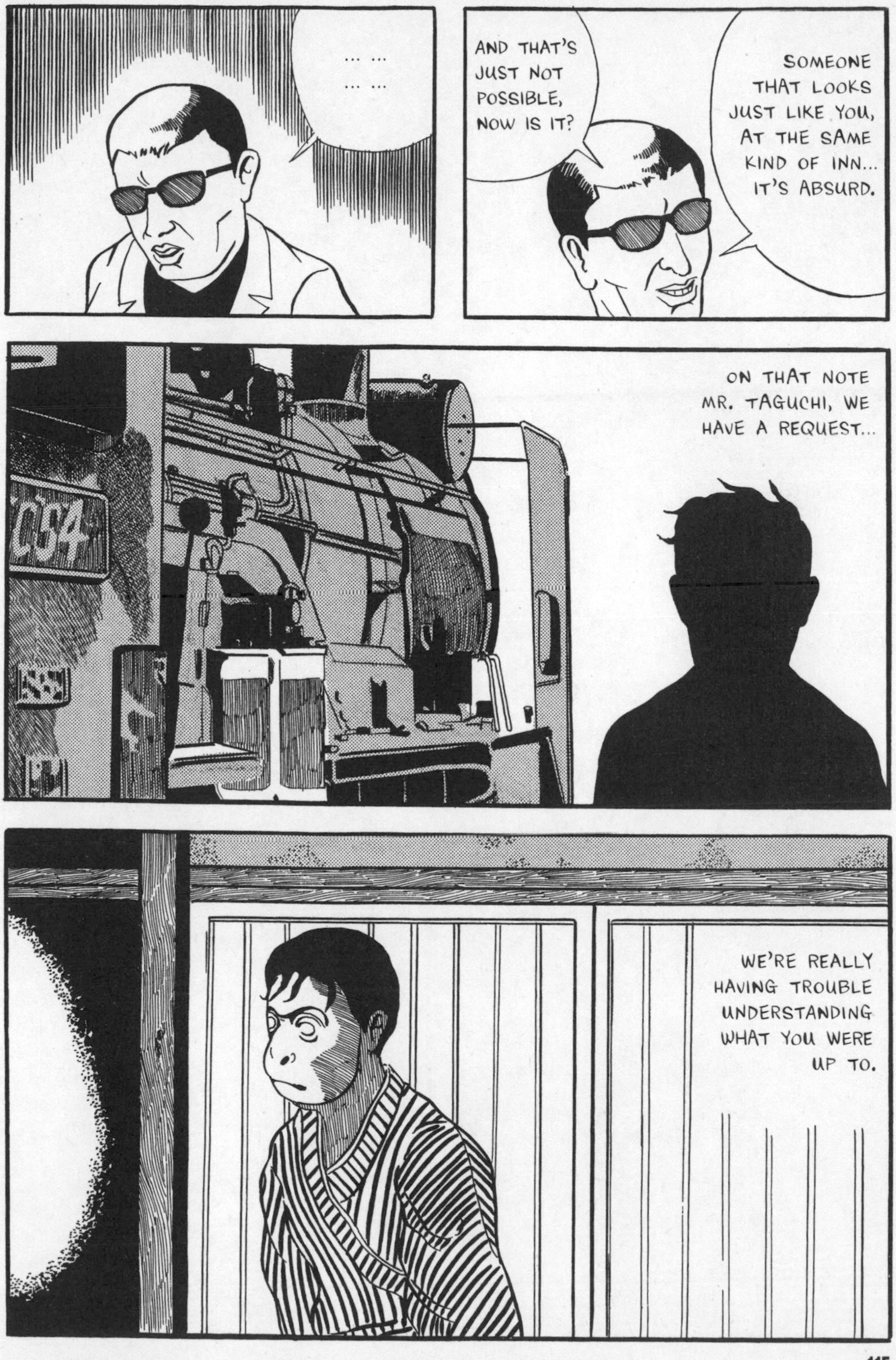
... ...
... ...
AND THAT'S JUST NOT POSSIBLE, NOW IS IT?
SOMEONE THAT LOOKS JUST LIKE YOU, AT THE SAME KIND OF INN... IT'S ABSURD.
ON THAT NOTE MR. TAGUCHI, WE HAVE A REQUEST...
WE'RE REALLY HAVING TROUBLE UNDERSTANDING WHAT YOU WERE UP TO.

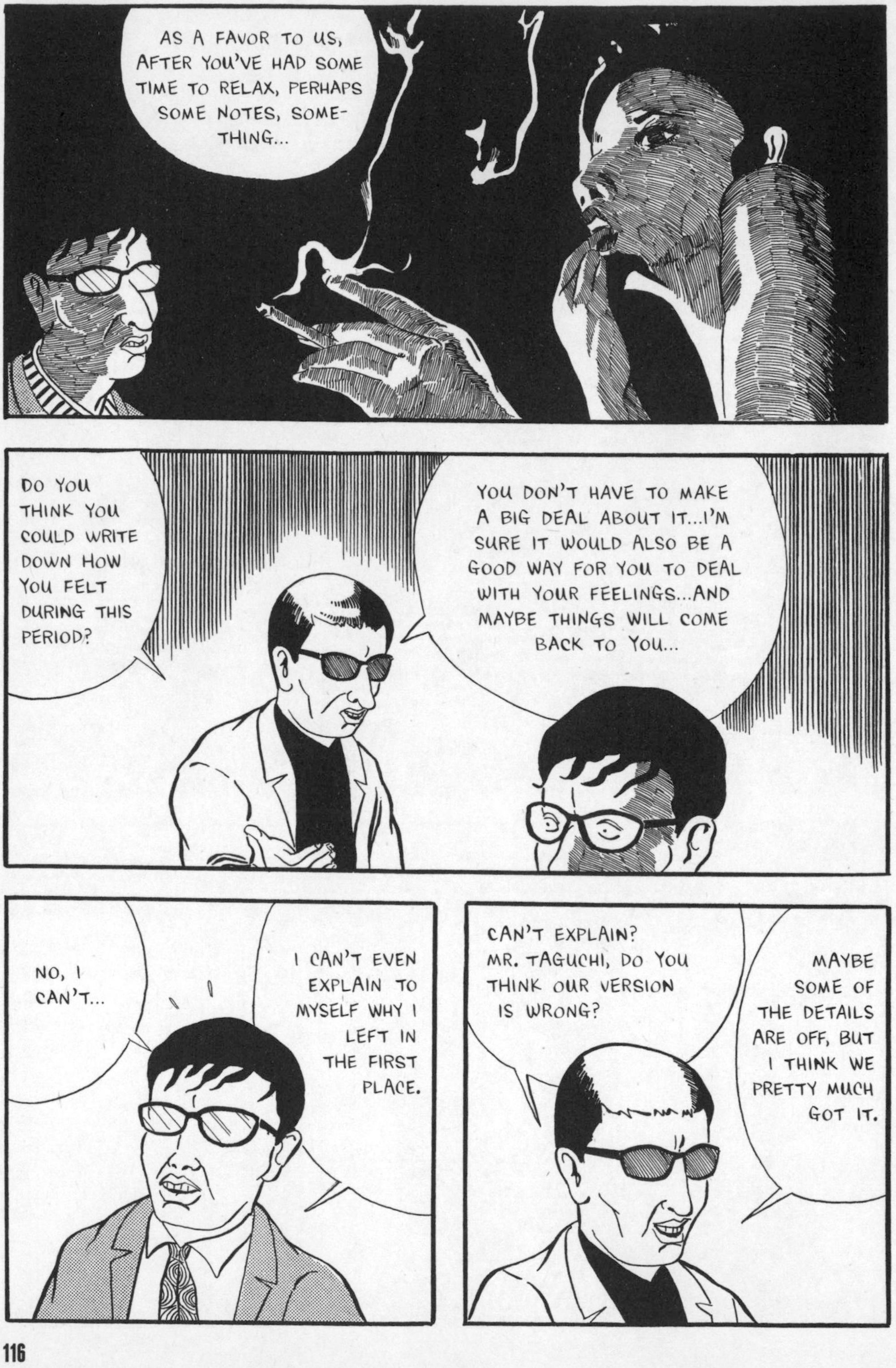
AS A FAVOR TO US, AFTER YOU'VE HAD SOME TIME TO RELAX, PERHAPS SOME NOTES, SOME-THING...
DO YOU THINK YOU COULD WRITE DOWN HOW YOU FELT DURING THIS PERIOD?
YOU DON'T HAVE TO MAKE A BIG DEAL ABOUT IT...I'M SURE IT WOULD ALSO BE A GOOD WAY FOR YOU TO DEAL WITH YOUR FEELINGS...AND MAYBE THINGS WILL COME BACK TO YOU...
NO, I CAN'T...
I CAN'T EVEN EXPLAIN TO MYSELF WHY I LEFT IN THE FIRST PLACE.
CAN'T EXPLAIN? MR. TAGUCHI, DO YOU THINK OUR VERSION IS WRONG?
MAYBE SOME OF THE DETAILS ARE OFF, BUT I THINK WE PRETTY MUCH GOT IT.

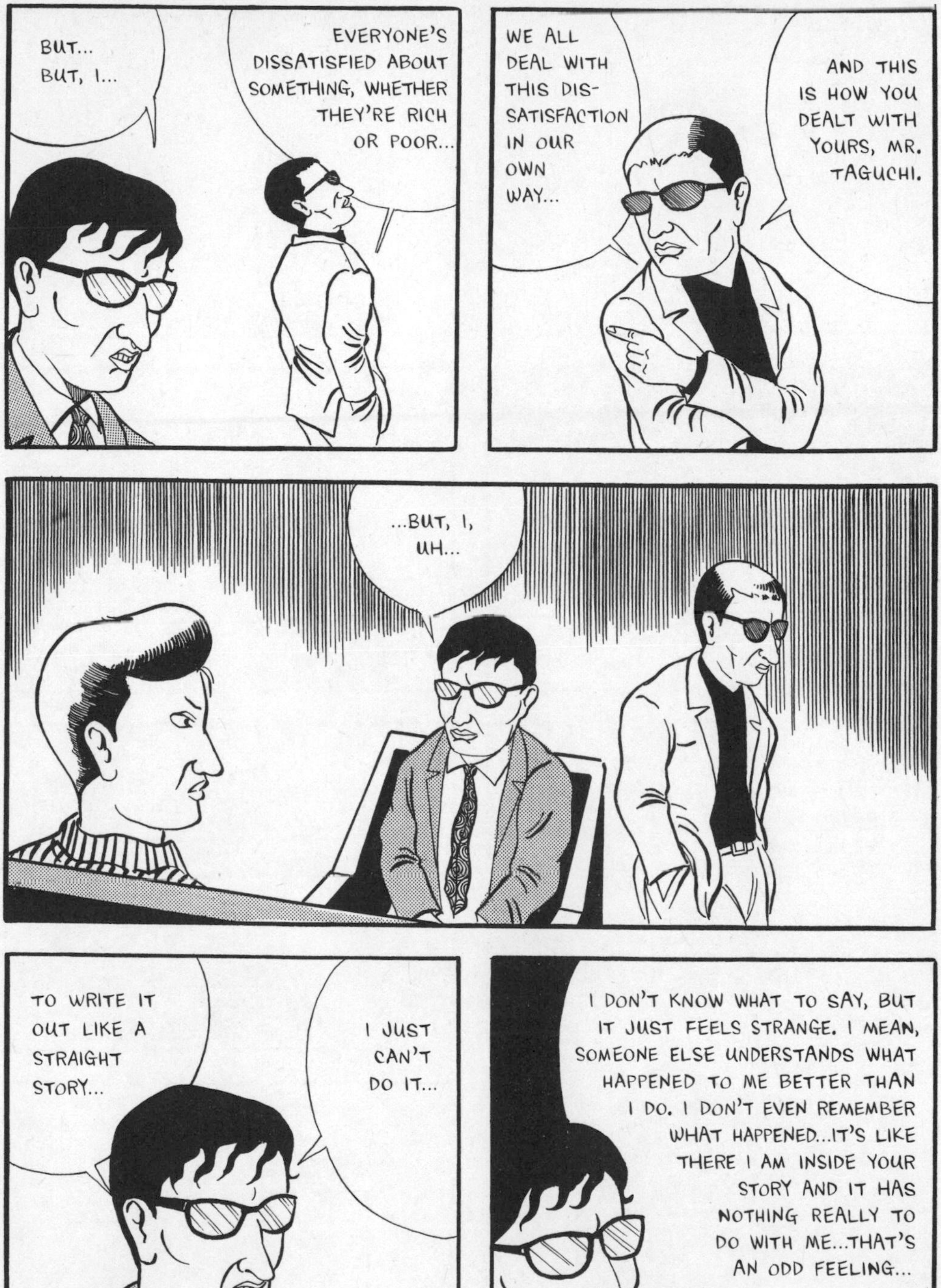
BUT... BUT, I...
EVERYONE'S DISSATISFIED ABOUT SOMETHING, WHETHER THEY'RE RICH OR POOR...
WE ALL DEAL WITH THIS DIS-SATISFACTION IN OUR OWN WAY...
AND THIS IS HOW YOU DEALT WITH YOURS, MR. TAGUCHI.
...BUT, I, UH...
TO WRITE IT OUT LIKE A STRAIGHT STORY...
I JUST CAN'T DO IT...
I DON'T KNOW WHAT TO SAY, BUT IT JUST FEELS STRANGE. I MEAN, SOMEONE ELSE UNDERSTANDS WHAT HAPPENED TO ME BETTER THAN I DO. I DON'T EVEN REMEMBER WHAT HAPPENED...IT'S LIKE THERE I AM INSIDE YOUR STORY AND IT HAS NOTHING REALLY TO DO WITH ME...THAT'S AN ODD FEELING...

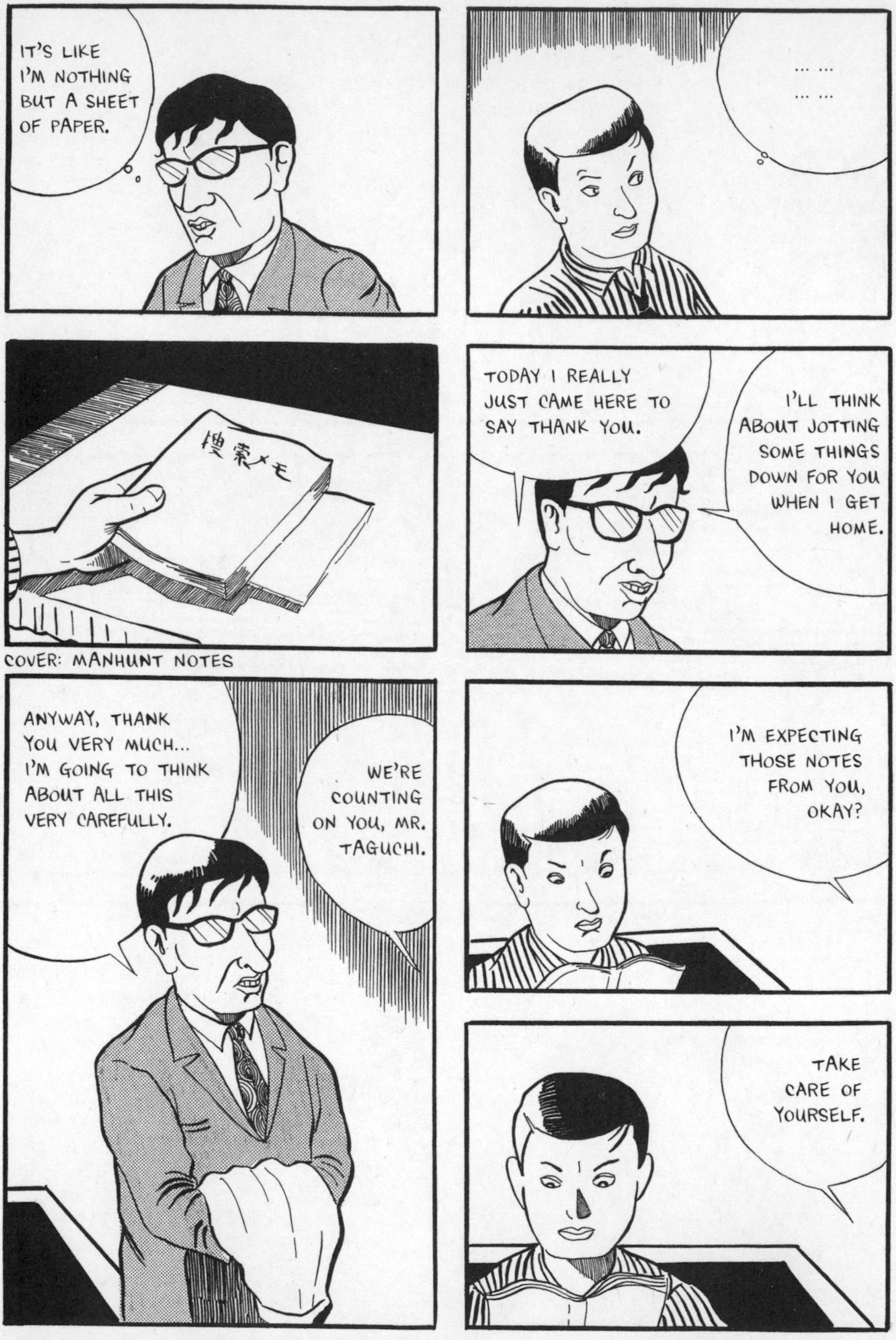
IT'S LIKE I'M NOTHING BUT A SHEET OF PAPER.
… …
… …
捜索メモ
COVER: MANHUNT NOTES
TODAY I REALLY JUST CAME HERE TO SAY THANK YOU.
I'LL THINK ABOUT JOTTING SOME THINGS DOWN FOR YOU WHEN I GET HOME.
ANYWAY, THANK YOU VERY MUCH… I'M GOING TO THINK ABOUT ALL THIS VERY CAREFULLY.
WE'RE COUNTING ON YOU, MR. TAGUCHI.
I'M EXPECTING THOSE NOTES FROM YOU, OKAY?
TAKE CARE OF YOURSELF.

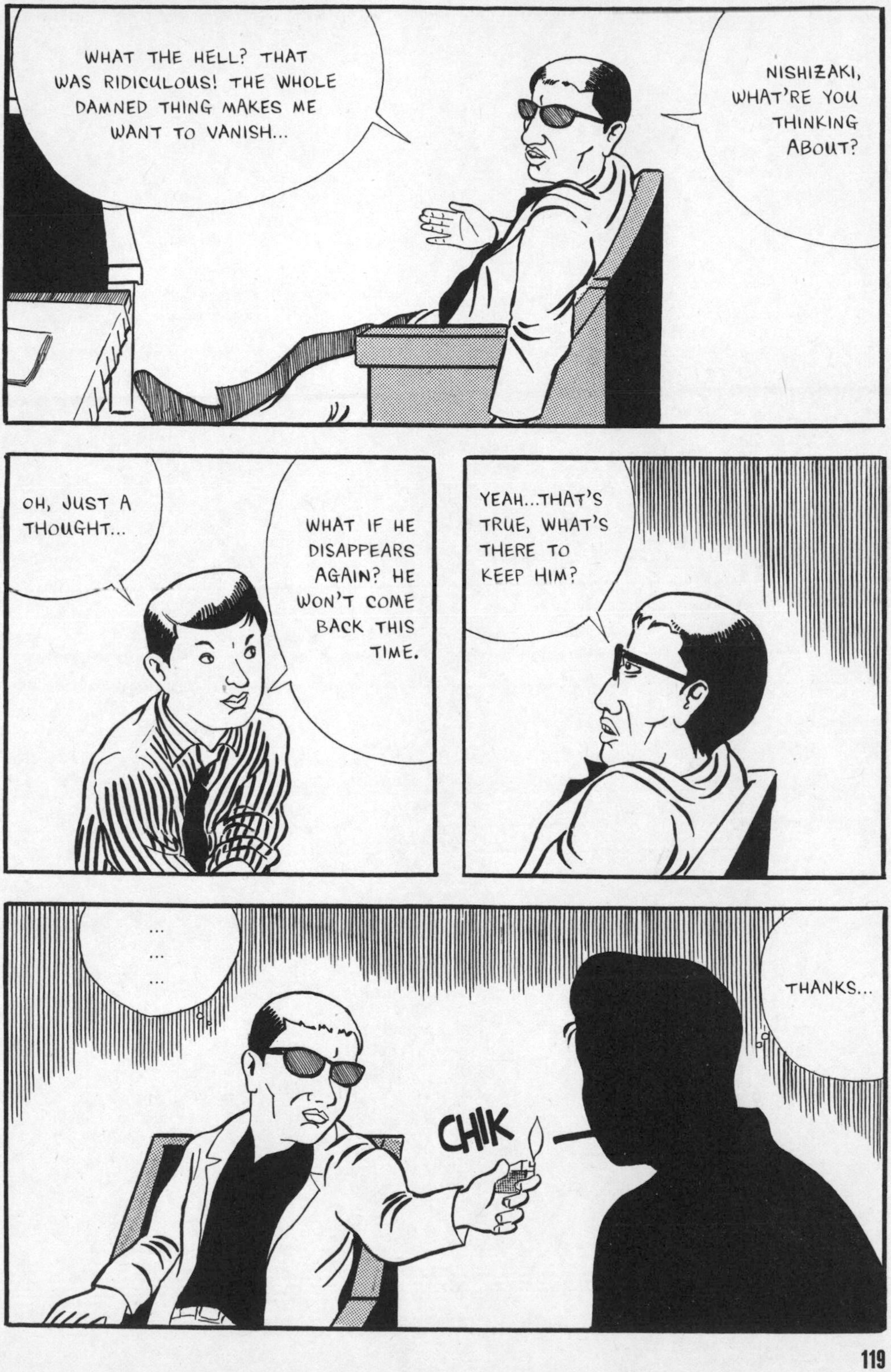
WHAT THE HELL? THAT WAS RIDICULOUS! THE WHOLE DAMNED THING MAKES ME WANT TO VANISH...
NISHIZAKI, WHAT'RE YOU THINKING ABOUT?
OH, JUST A THOUGHT...
WHAT IF HE DISAPPEARS AGAIN? HE WON'T COME BACK THIS TIME.
YEAH...THAT'S TRUE, WHAT'S THERE TO KEEP HIM?
...
...
...
THANKS...
CHIK

GENTLY GOES THE NIGHT

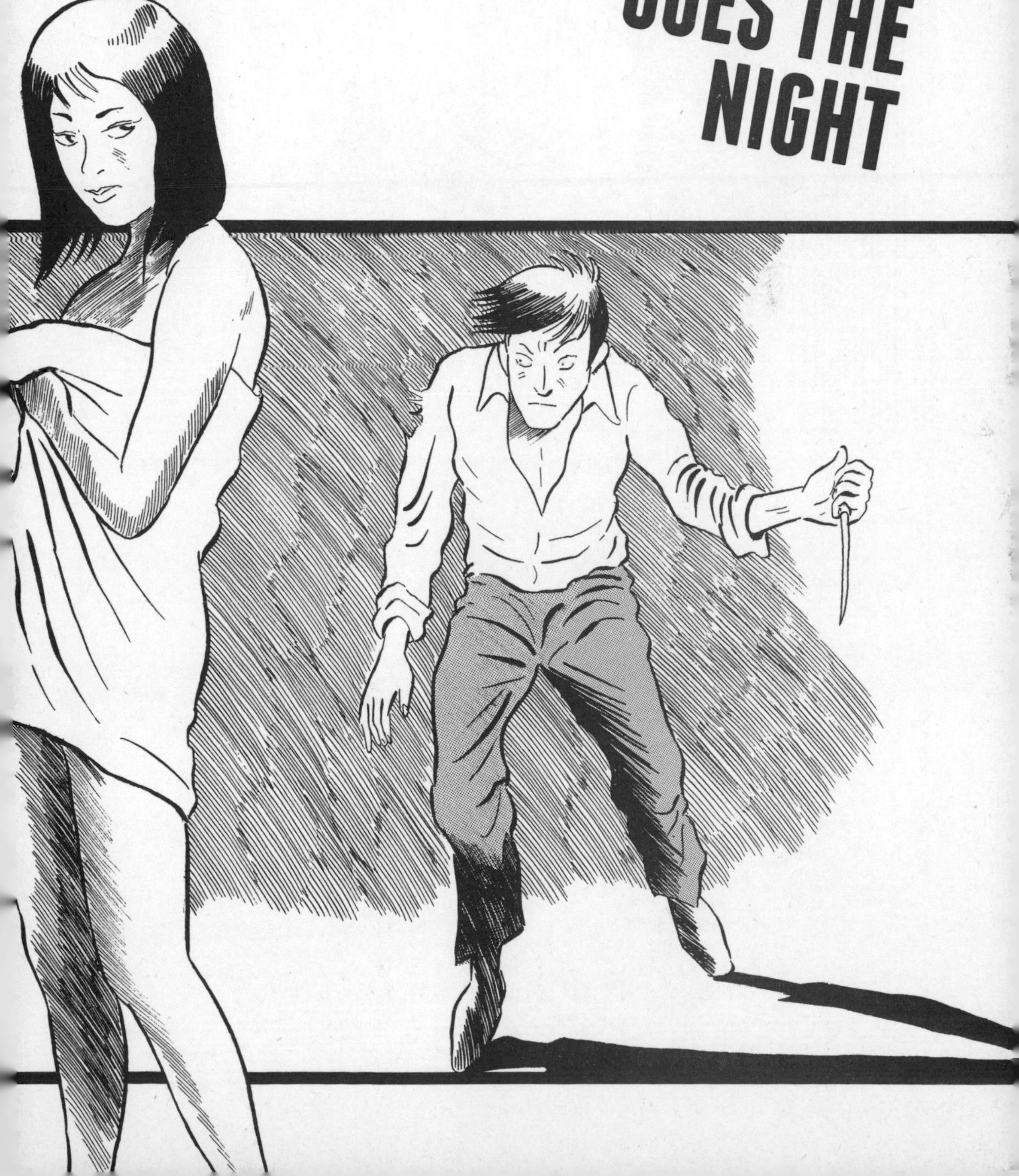

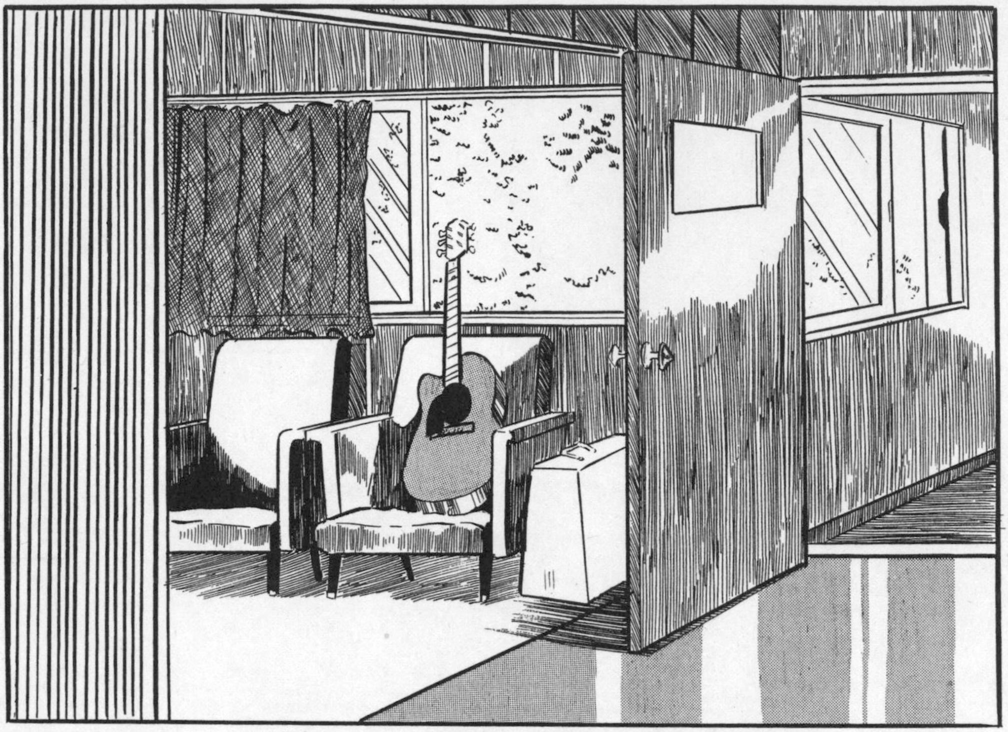

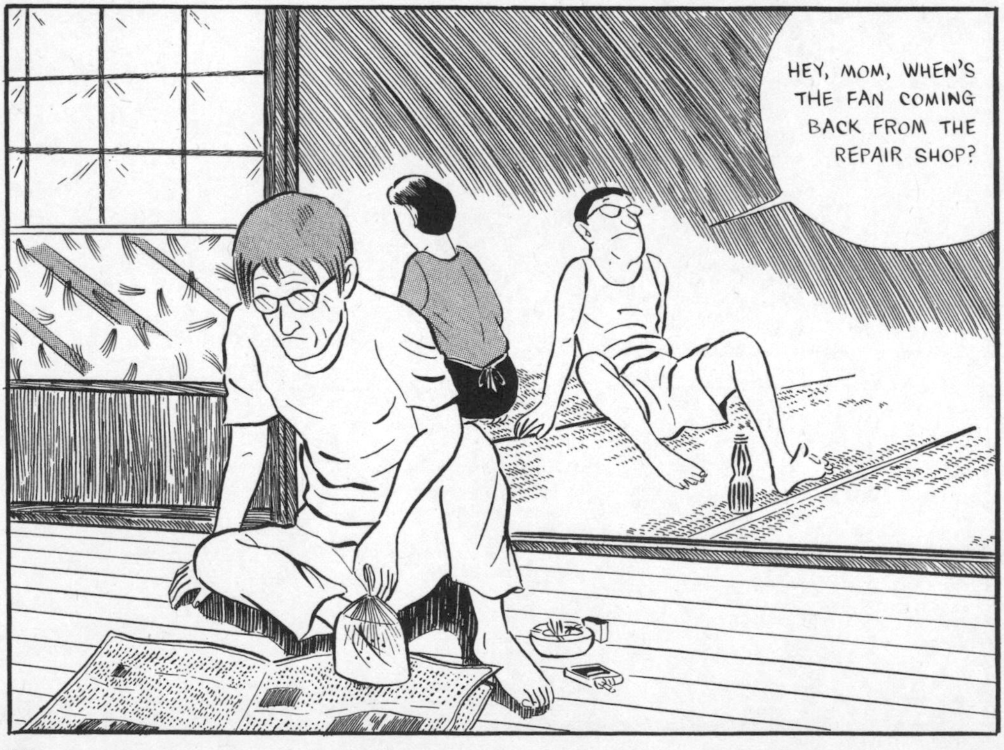
HEY, MOM, WHEN'S THE FAN COMING BACK FROM THE REPAIR SHOP?

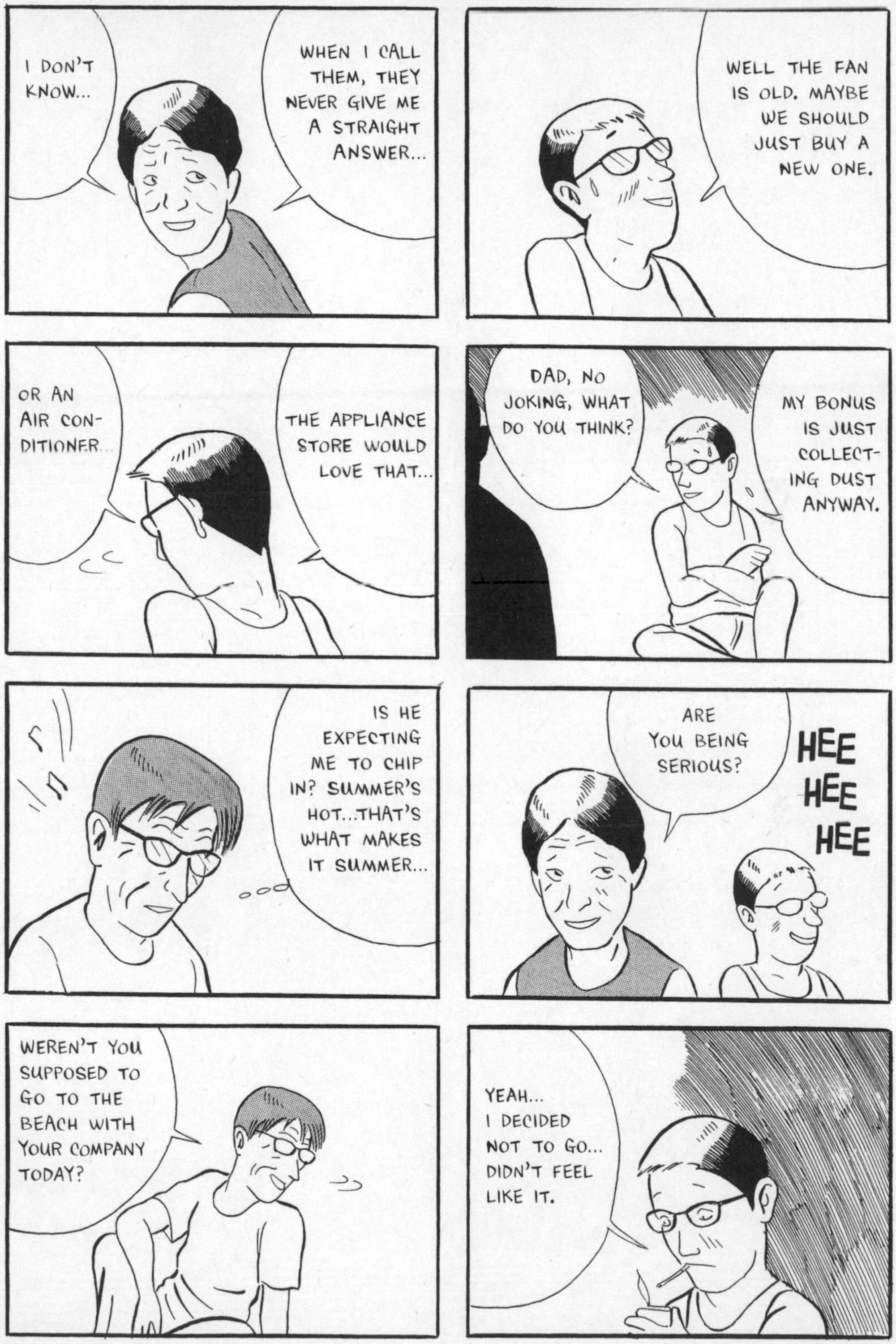
I DON'T KNOW...
WHEN I CALL THEM, THEY NEVER GIVE ME A STRAIGHT ANSWER...
WELL THE FAN IS OLD. MAYBE WE SHOULD JUST BUY A NEW ONE.
OR AN AIR CON-DITIONER...
THE APPLIANCE STORE WOULD LOVE THAT...
DAD, NO JOKING, WHAT DO YOU THINK?
MY BONUS IS JUST COLLECT-ING DUST ANYWAY.
IS HE EXPECTING ME TO CHIP IN? SUMMER'S HOT...THAT'S WHAT MAKES IT SUMMER...
ARE YOU BEING SERIOUS?
HEE HEE HEE
WEREN'T YOU SUPPOSED TO GO TO THE BEACH WITH YOUR COMPANY TODAY?
YEAH... I DECIDED NOT TO GO... DIDN'T FEEL LIKE IT.

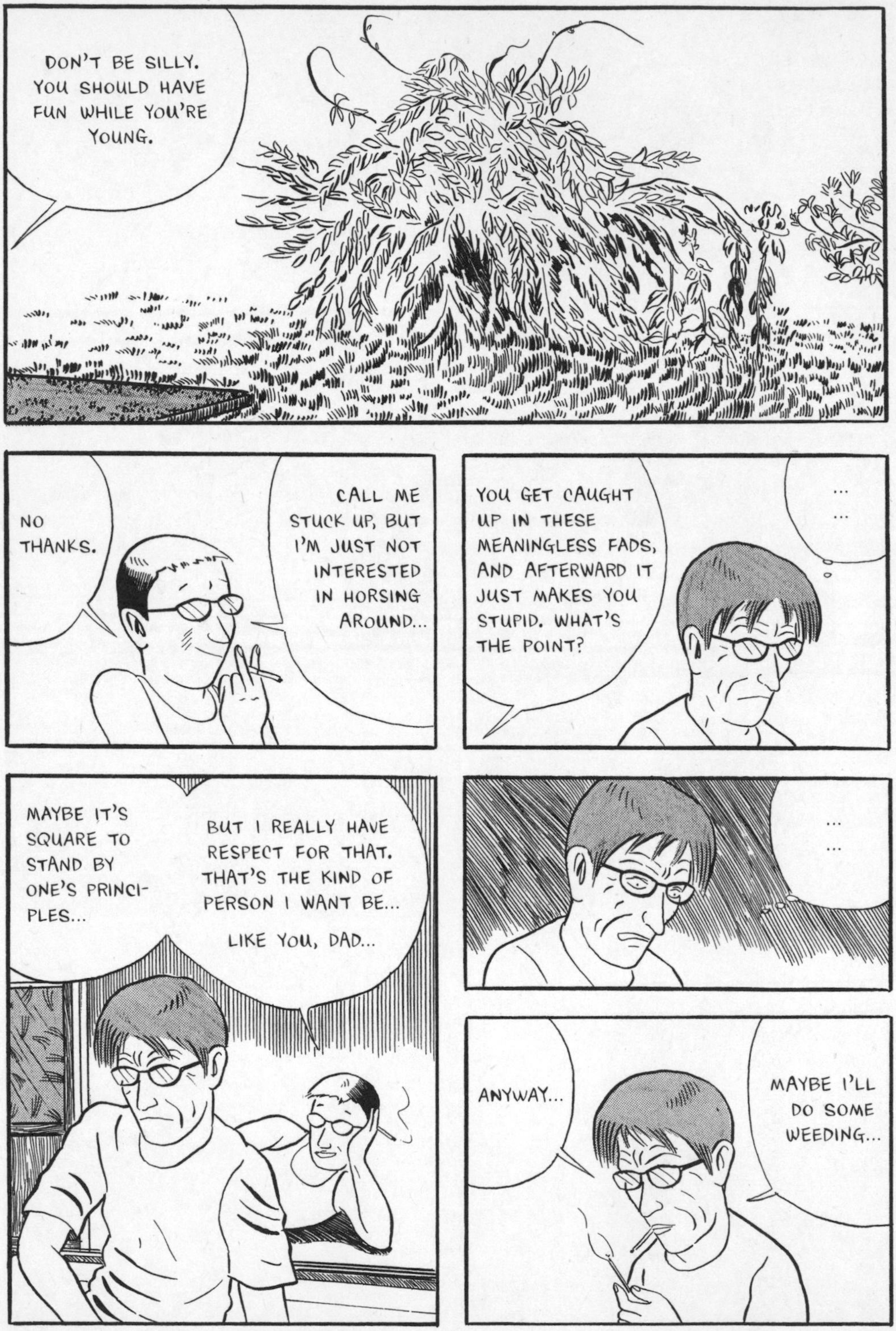
DON'T BE SILLY. YOU SHOULD HAVE FUN WHILE YOU'RE YOUNG.
NO THANKS.
CALL ME STUCK UP, BUT I'M JUST NOT INTERESTED IN HORSING AROUND...
YOU GET CAUGHT UP IN THESE MEANINGLESS FADS, AND AFTERWARD IT JUST MAKES YOU STUPID. WHAT'S THE POINT?
...
...
MAYBE IT'S SQUARE TO STAND BY ONE'S PRINCI-PLES...
BUT I REALLY HAVE RESPECT FOR THAT. THAT'S THE KIND OF PERSON I WANT BE...
LIKE YOU, DAD...
...
...
ANYWAY...
MAYBE I'LL DO SOME WEEDING...

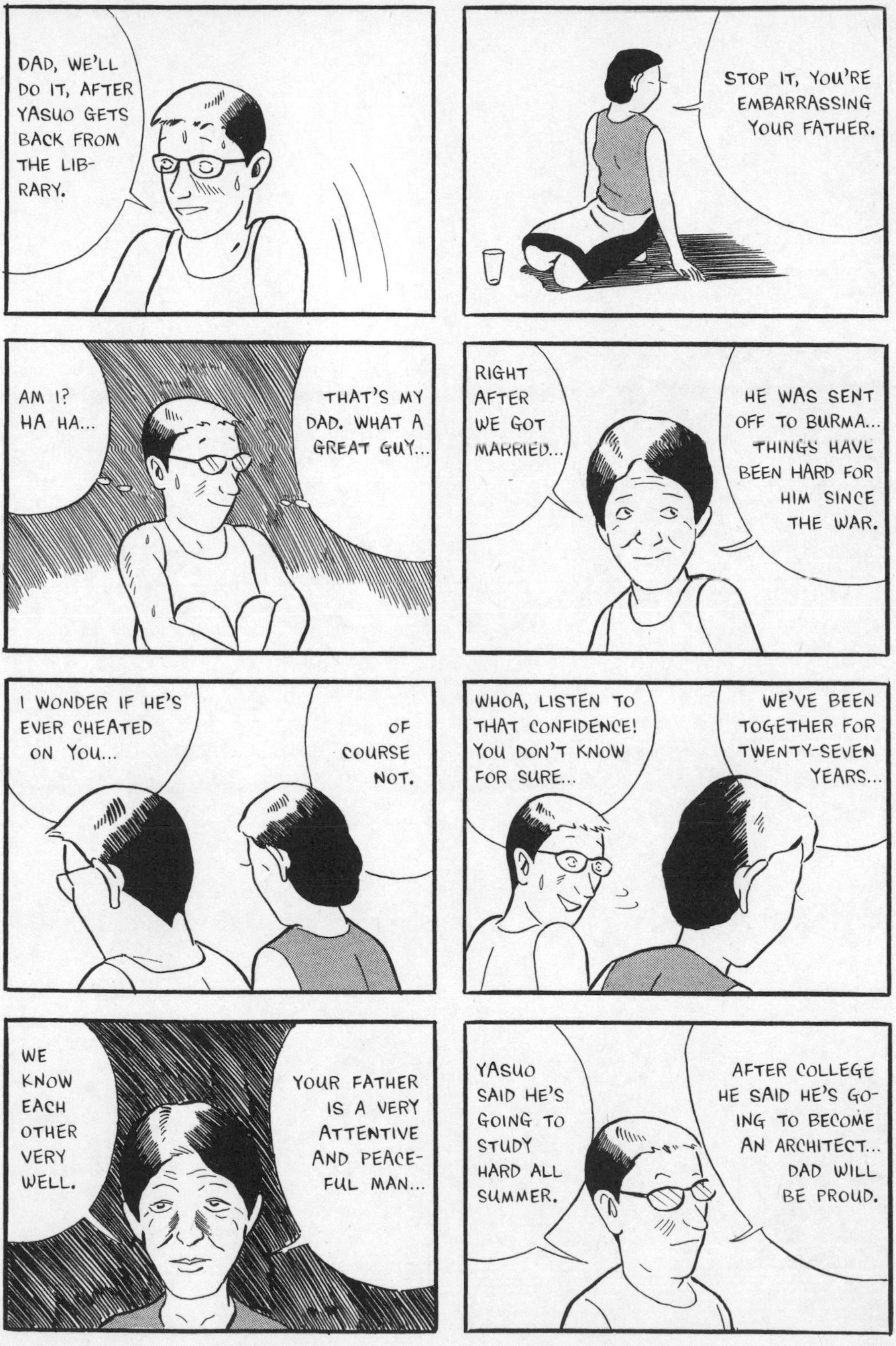
DAD, WE'LL DO IT, AFTER YASUO GETS BACK FROM THE LIB-RARY.
STOP IT, YOU'RE EMBARRASSING YOUR FATHER.
AM I? HA HA...
THAT'S MY DAD. WHAT A GREAT GUY...
RIGHT AFTER WE GOT MARRIED...
HE WAS SENT OFF TO BURMA... THINGS HAVE BEEN HARD FOR HIM SINCE THE WAR.
I WONDER IF HE'S EVER CHEATED ON YOU...
OF COURSE NOT.
WHOA, LISTEN TO THAT CONFIDENCE! YOU DON'T KNOW FOR SURE...
WE'VE BEEN TOGETHER FOR TWENTY-SEVEN YEARS...
WE KNOW EACH OTHER VERY WELL.
YOUR FATHER IS A VERY ATTENTIVE AND PEACE-FUL MAN...
YASUO SAID HE'S GOING TO STUDY HARD ALL SUMMER.
AFTER COLLEGE HE SAID HE'S GO-ING TO BECOME AN ARCHITECT... DAD WILL BE PROUD.

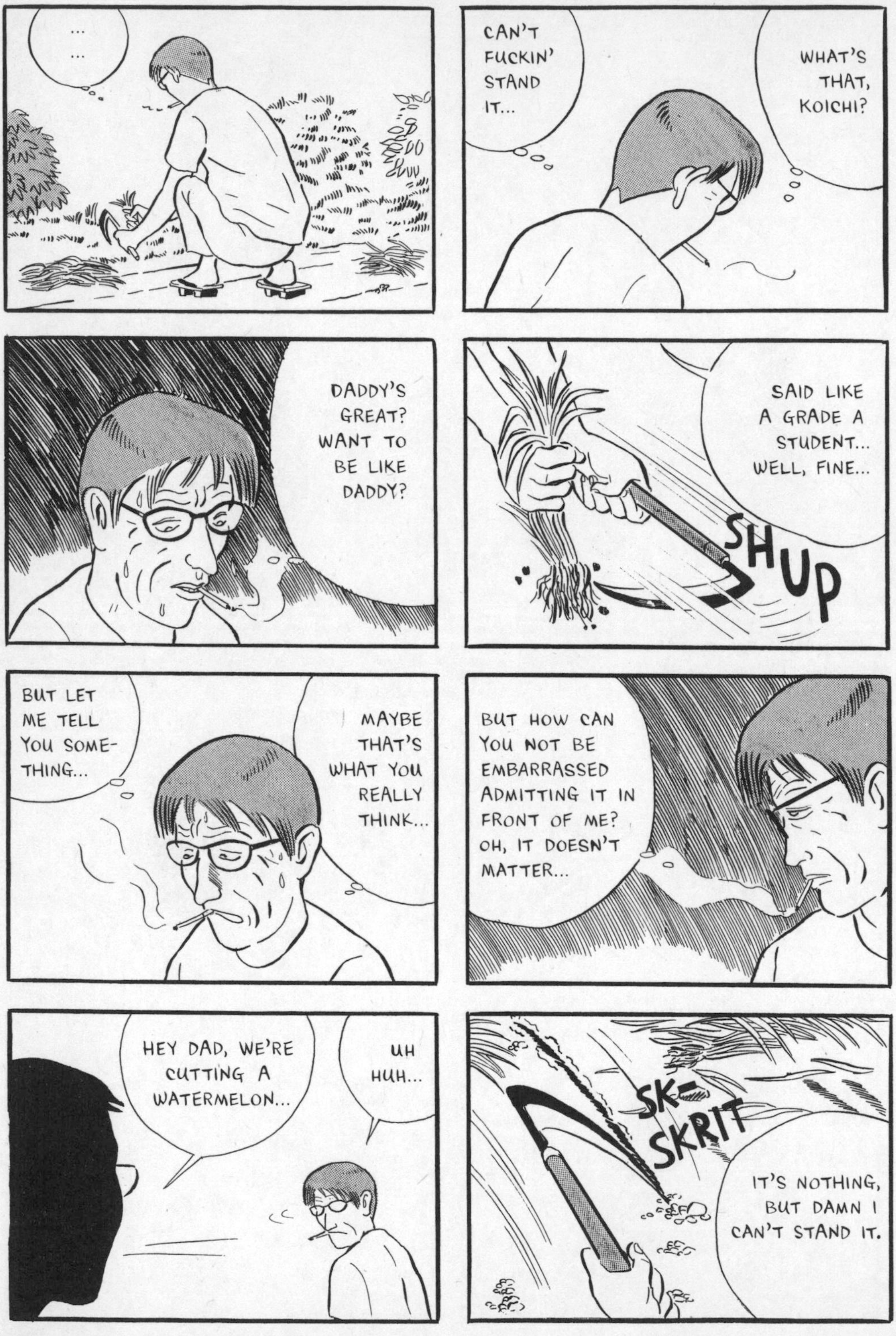
...
...
CAN'T FUCKIN' STAND IT...
WHAT'S THAT, KOICHI?
DADDY'S GREAT? WANT TO BE LIKE DADDY?
SAID LIKE A GRADE A STUDENT... WELL, FINE...
SHUP
BUT LET ME TELL YOU SOME-THING...
MAYBE THAT'S WHAT YOU REALLY THINK...
BUT HOW CAN YOU NOT BE EMBARRASSED ADMITTING IT IN FRONT OF ME? OH, IT DOESN'T MATTER...
HEY DAD, WE'RE CUTTING A WATERMELON...
UH HUH...
SK-SKRIT
IT'S NOTHING, BUT DAMN I CAN'T STAND IT.

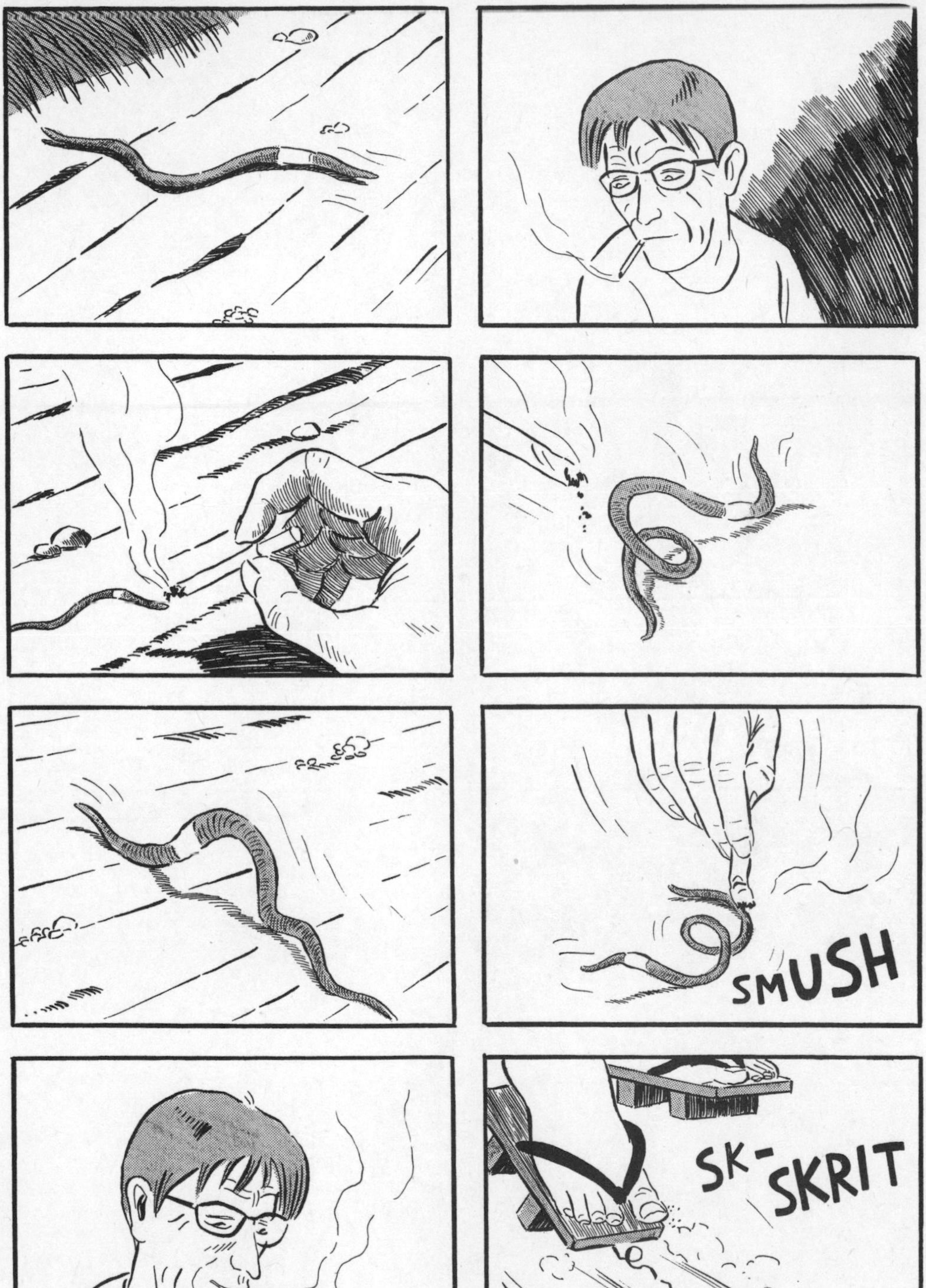
SMUSH
SK-SKRIT

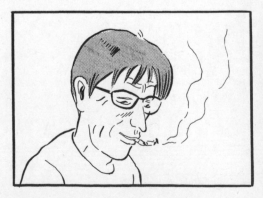

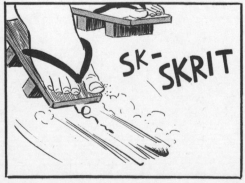

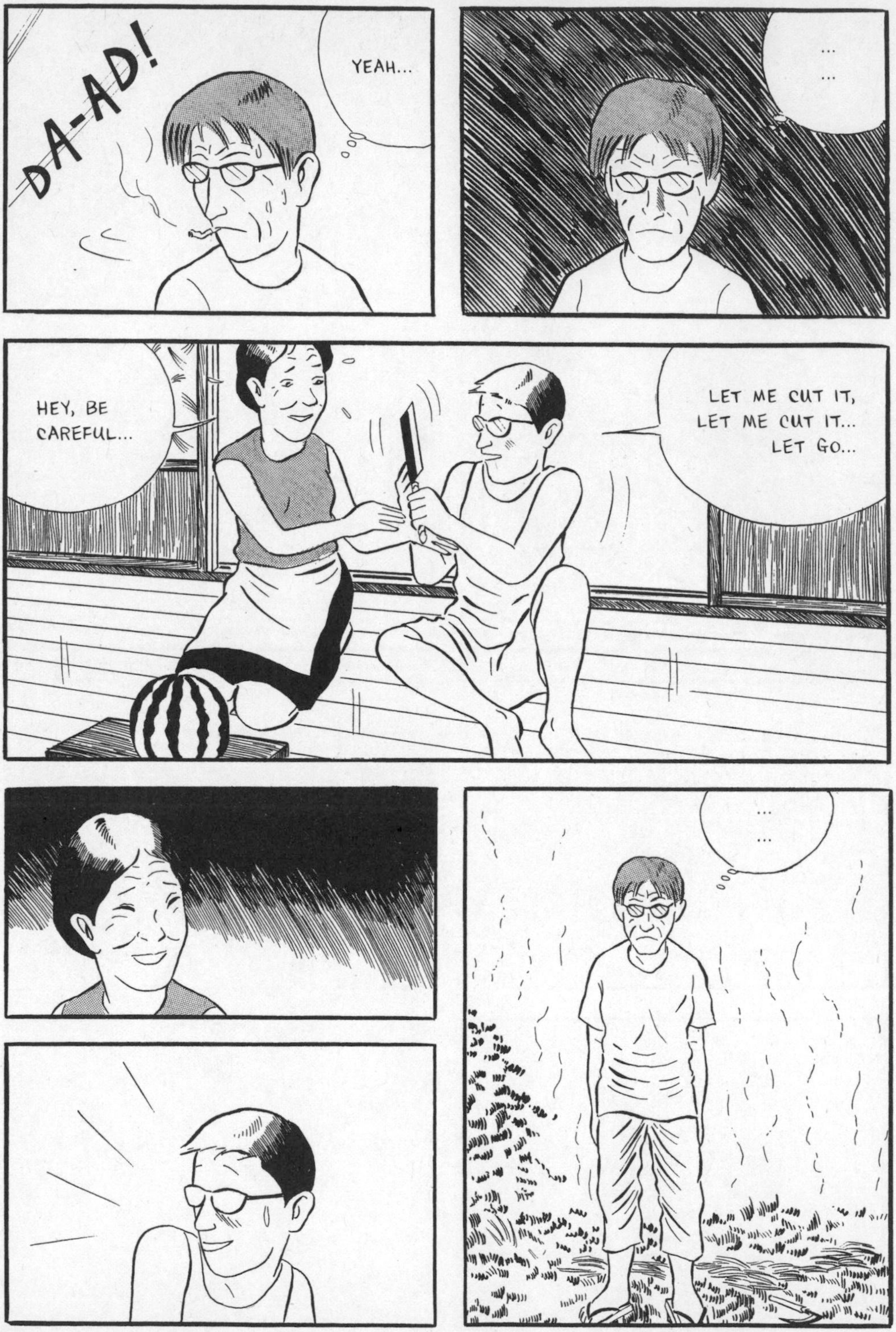
DA-AD!
YEAH...
...
...
HEY, BE CAREFUL...
LET ME CUT IT, LET ME CUT IT... LET GO...
...
...

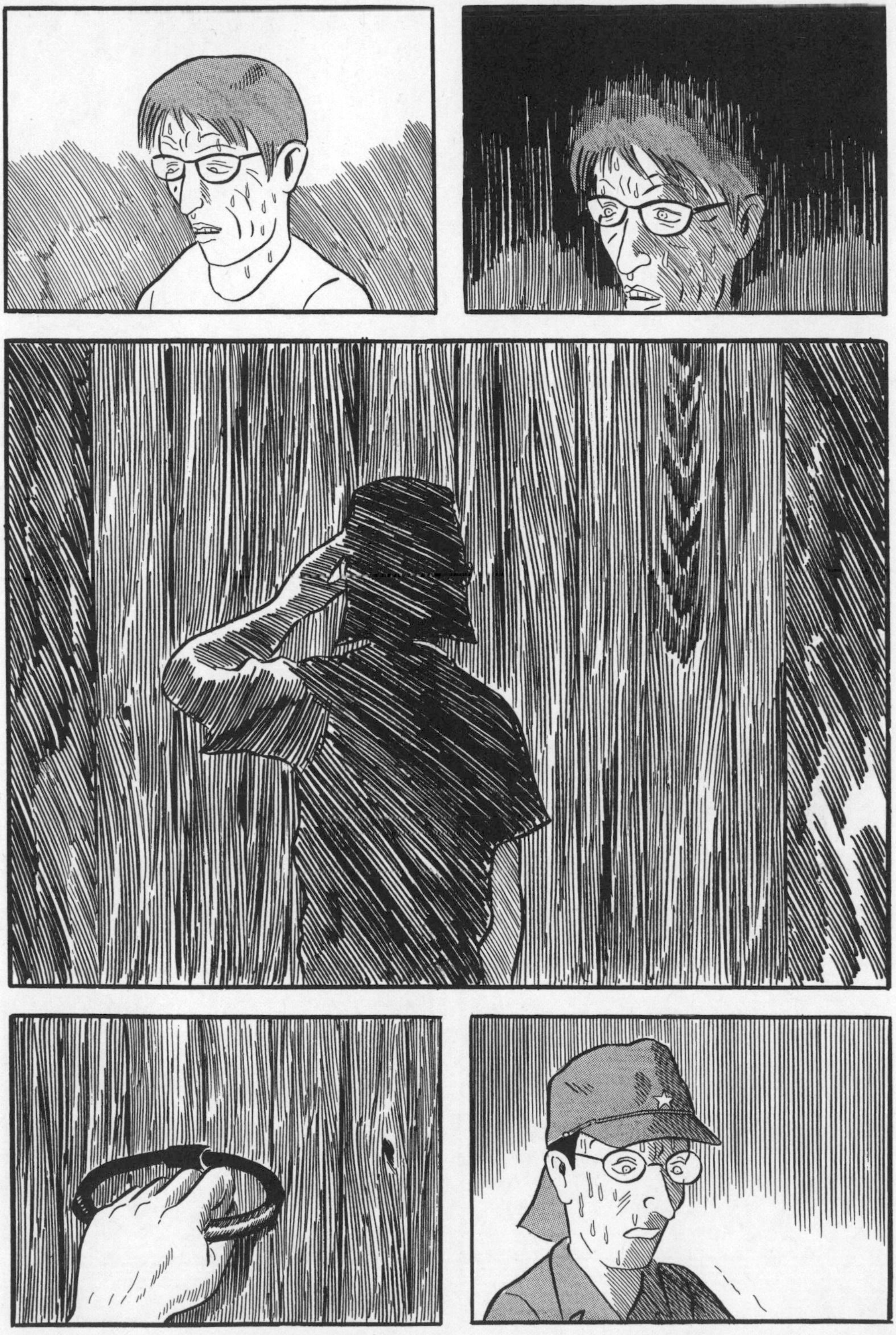

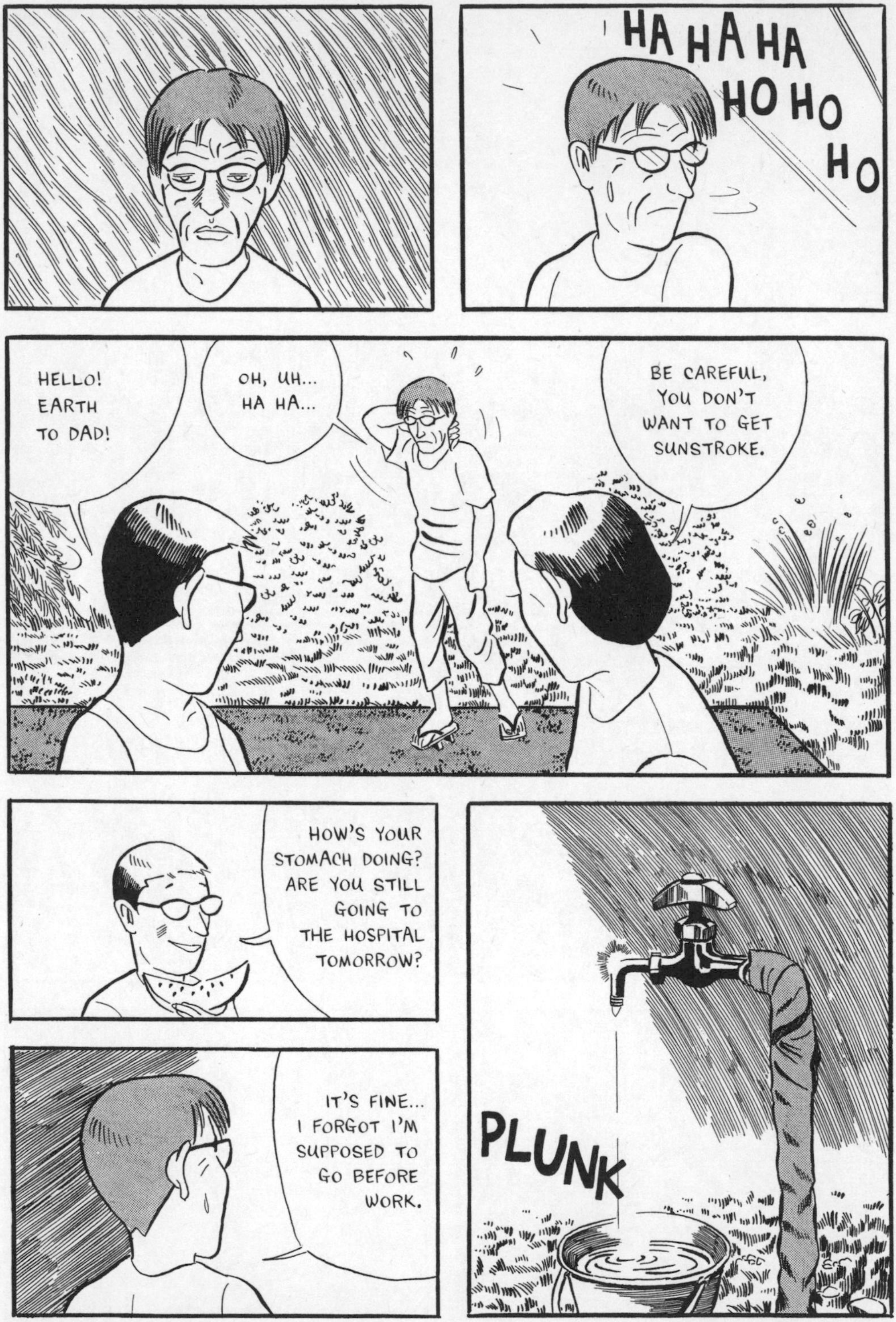
HA HA HA HA
HO HO HO HO
HELLO! EARTH TO DAD!
OH, UH... HA HA...
BE CAREFUL, YOU DON'T WANT TO GET SUNSTROKE.
HOW'S YOUR STOMACH DOING? ARE YOU STILL GOING TO THE HOSPITAL TOMORROW?
IT'S FINE... I FORGOT I'M SUPPOSED TO GO BEFORE WORK.
PLUNK

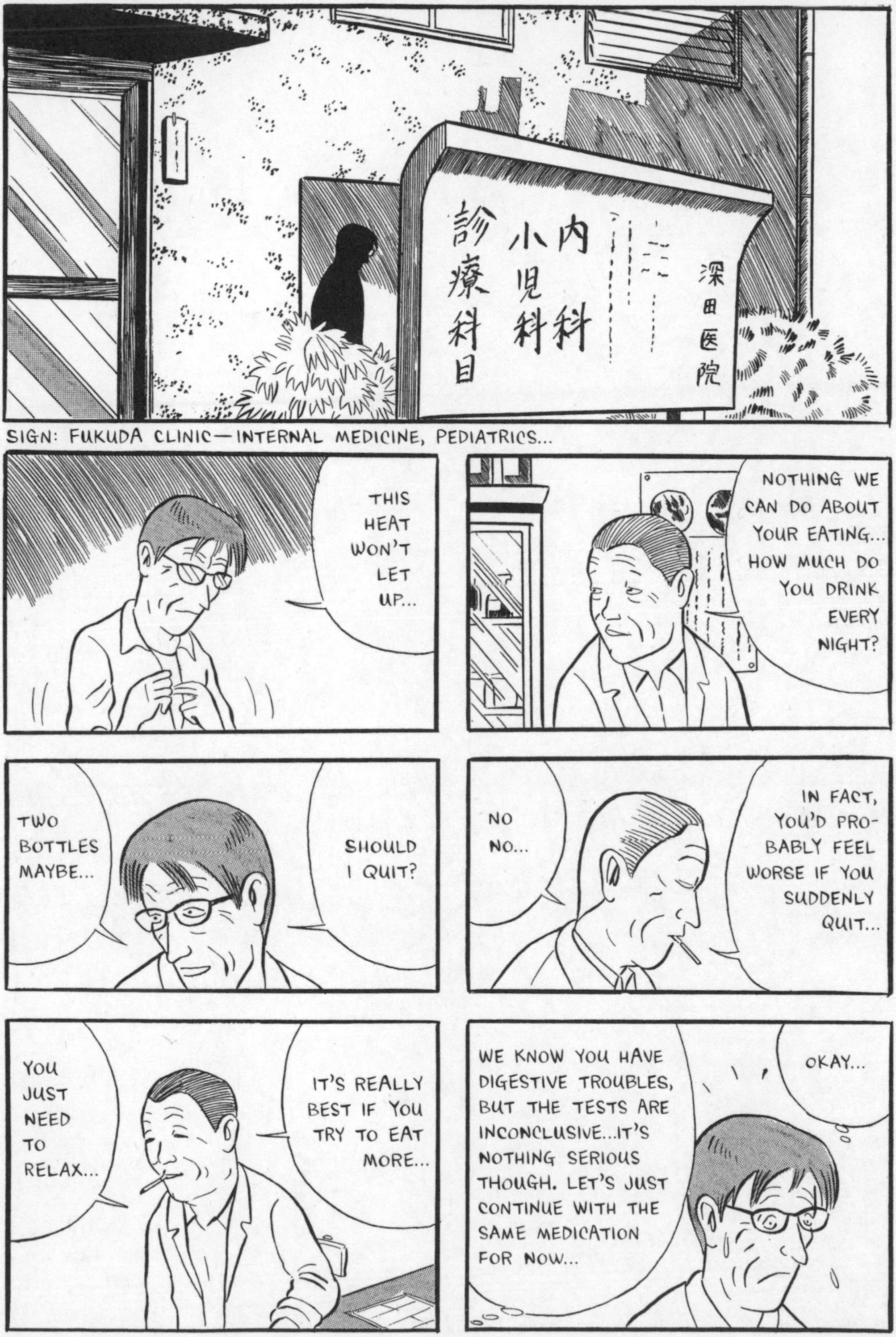
深田医院
内科
小児科
診療科目
SIGN: FUKUDA CLINIC—INTERNAL MEDICINE, PEDIATRICS...
THIS HEAT WON'T LET UP...
NOTHING WE CAN DO ABOUT YOUR EATING... HOW MUCH DO YOU DRINK EVERY NIGHT?
TWO BOTTLES MAYBE...
SHOULD I QUIT?
NO NO...
IN FACT, YOU'D PROBABLY FEEL WORSE IF YOU SUDDENLY QUIT...
YOU JUST NEED TO RELAX...
IT'S REALLY BEST IF YOU TRY TO EAT MORE...
WE KNOW YOU HAVE DIGESTIVE TROUBLES, BUT THE TESTS ARE INCONCLUSIVE...IT'S NOTHING SERIOUS THOUGH. LET'S JUST CONTINUE WITH THE SAME MEDICATION FOR NOW...
OKAY...

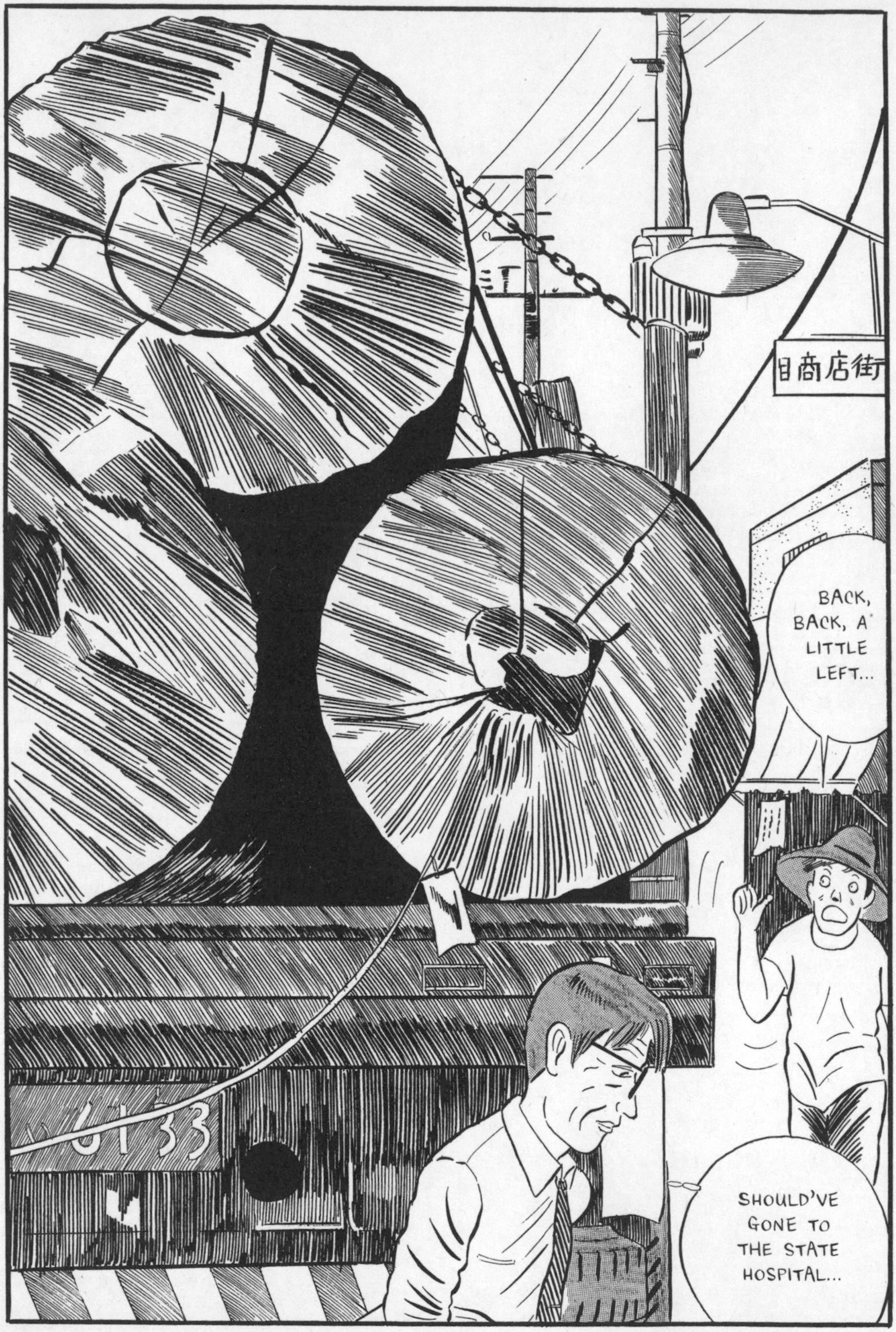

日商店街
BACK, BACK, A LITTLE LEFT...
SHOULD'VE GONE TO THE STATE HOSPITAL...

SIGN: TAKITA RUBBER INDUSTRIES

LOOK AT THE TIME...

YO.

HEY.

JUST GETTING IN?

LOOK AT THIS. IT'S SO SLOW WE'RE CHECKING FIRE EXTINGUISHERS!

DON'T COMPLAIN...IT'S TOO HOT TO WORK ANYWAY.

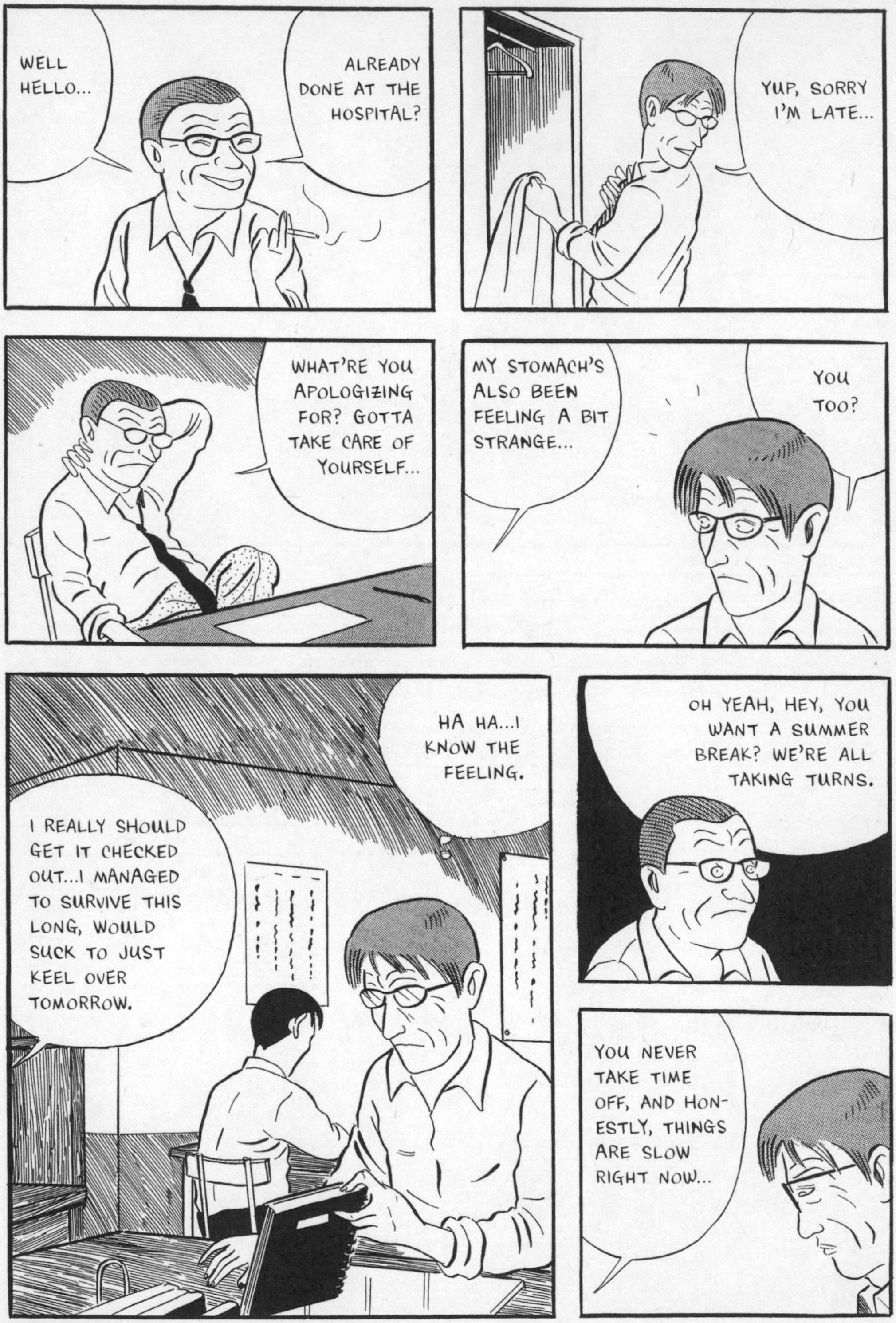
WELL HELLO...
ALREADY DONE AT THE HOSPITAL?
YUP, SORRY I'M LATE...
WHAT'RE YOU APOLOGIZING FOR? GOTTA TAKE CARE OF YOURSELF...
MY STOMACH'S ALSO BEEN FEELING A BIT STRANGE...
YOU TOO?
HA HA...I KNOW THE FEELING.
I REALLY SHOULD GET IT CHECKED OUT...I MANAGED TO SURVIVE THIS LONG, WOULD SUCK TO JUST KEEL OVER TOMORROW.
OH YEAH, HEY, YOU WANT A SUMMER BREAK? WE'RE ALL TAKING TURNS.
YOU NEVER TAKE TIME OFF, AND HON-ESTLY, THINGS ARE SLOW RIGHT NOW...

BUT UH...

LOOK, I DON'T KNOW HOW THE FACTORY WOULD RUN WITHOUT YOU...

BUT NOR DO I THINK IT'S FAIR THAT EVERYONE RELIES ON YOU SO HEAVILY.

YOU MIGHT THINK, WHY NOW? AFTER ALL THESE YEARS? BUT ANYWAY, HOW ABOUT IT? NOTHING TOO LONG, JUST TWO OR THREE DAYS...

DO IT, SECTION CHIEF!

IT'S A GREAT IDEA!

MAN, YOU'RE POPULAR...

OF COURSE HE IS!

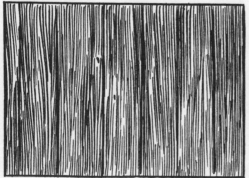

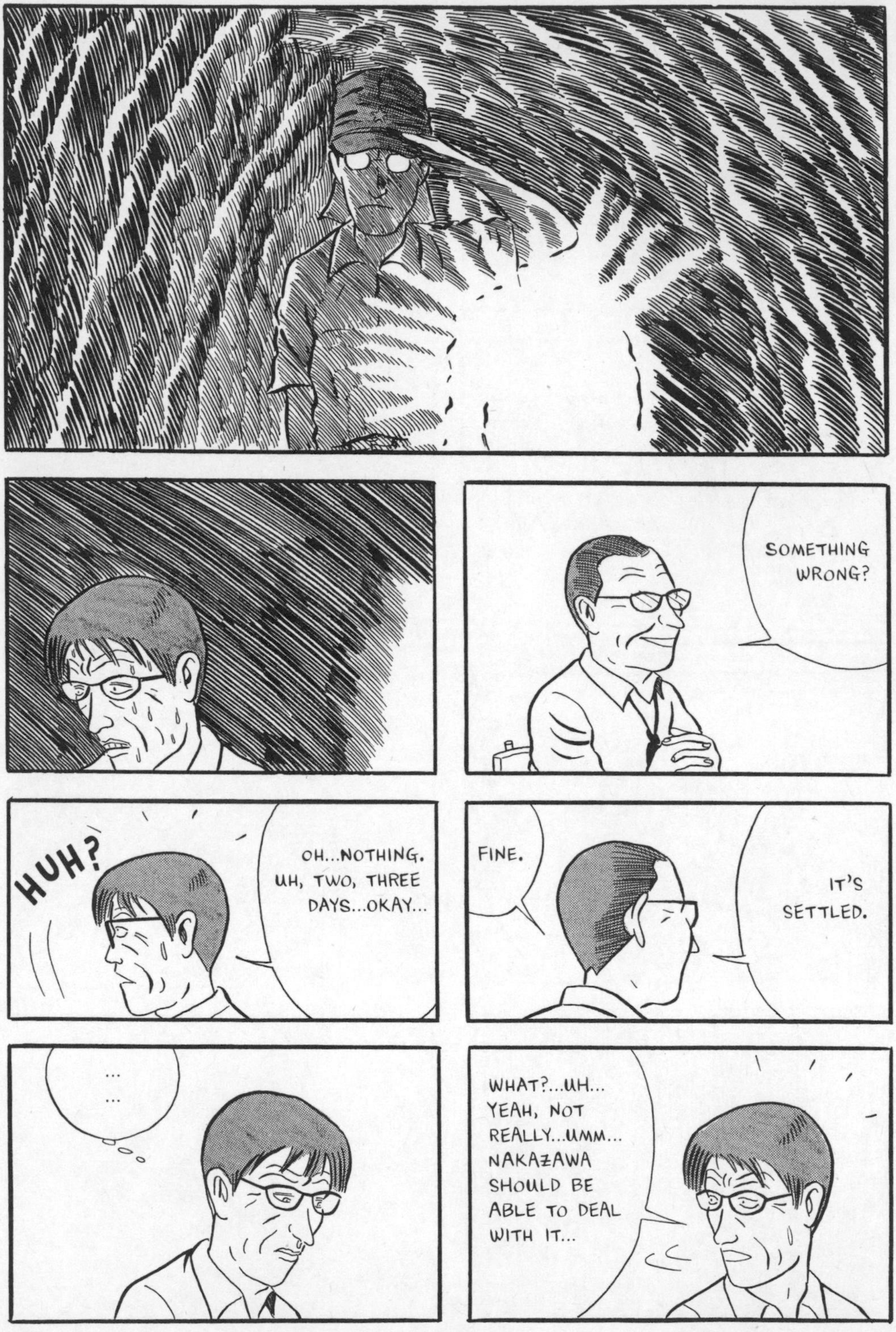
SOMETHING WRONG?
HUH?
OH...NOTHING. UH, TWO, THREE DAYS...OKAY...
FINE.
IT'S SETTLED.
...
...
WHAT?...UH... YEAH, NOT REALLY...UMM... NAKAZAWA SHOULD BE ABLE TO DEAL WITH IT...

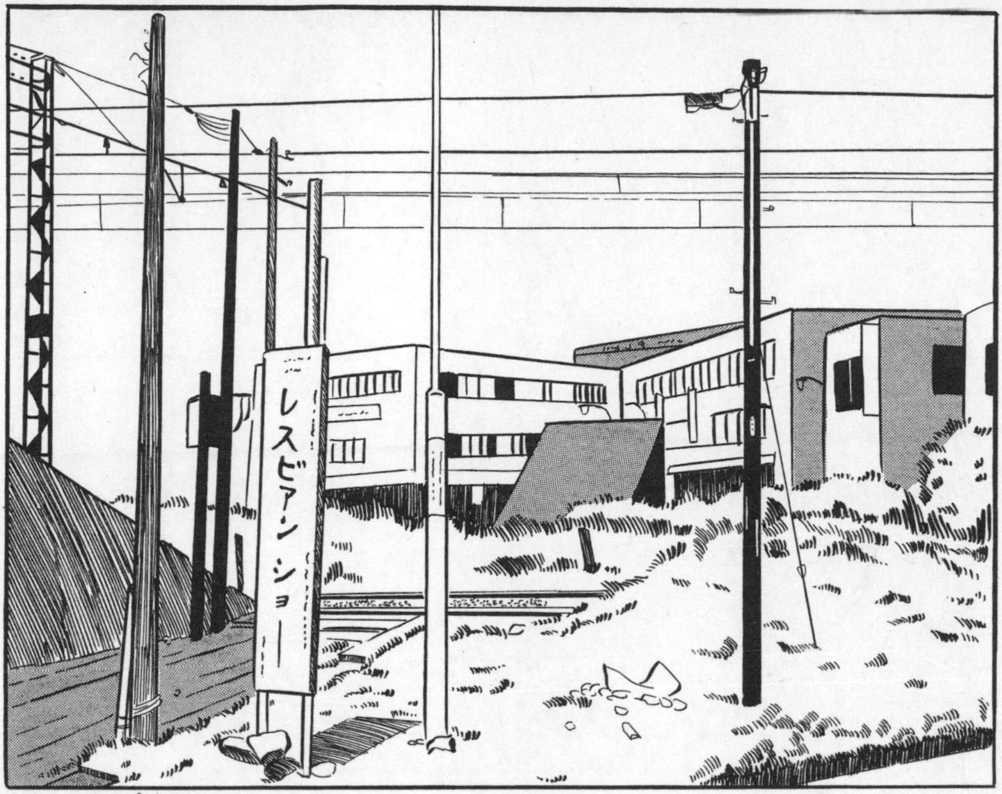
レスビアン ショー

SIGN: LESBIAN SHOW

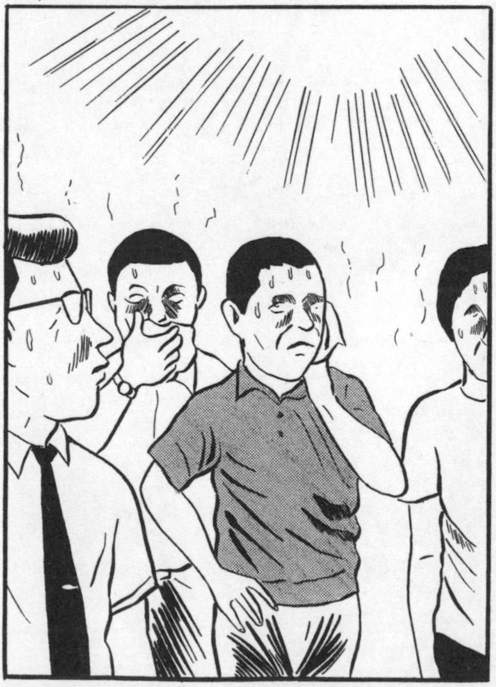

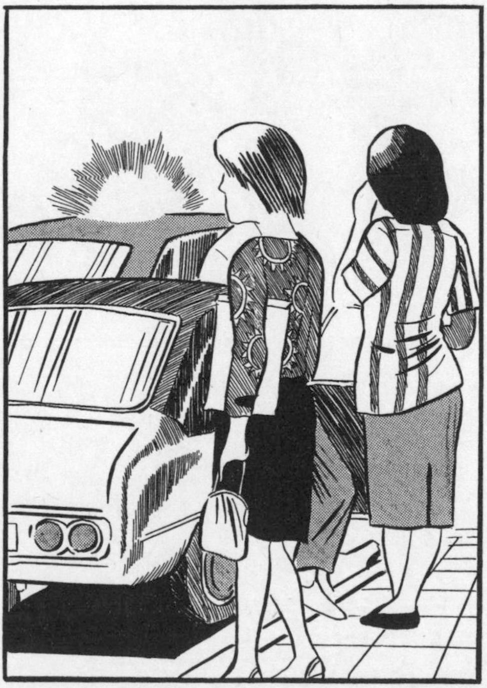

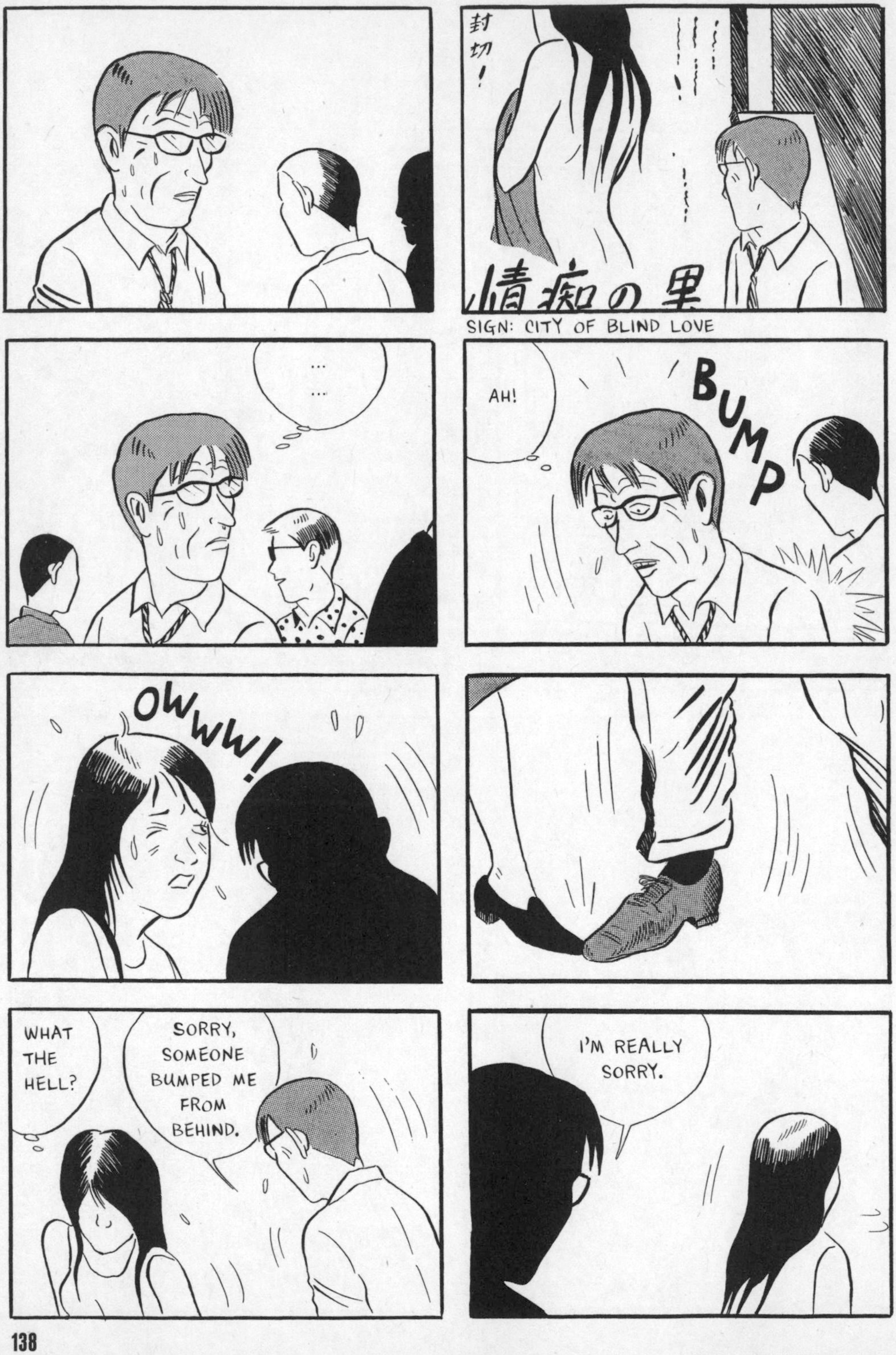
封切!
情痴の里
SIGN: CITY OF BLIND LOVE
...
...
AH!
BUMP
OWWW!
WHAT THE HELL?
SORRY, SOMEONE BUMPED ME FROM BEHIND.
I'M REALLY SORRY.

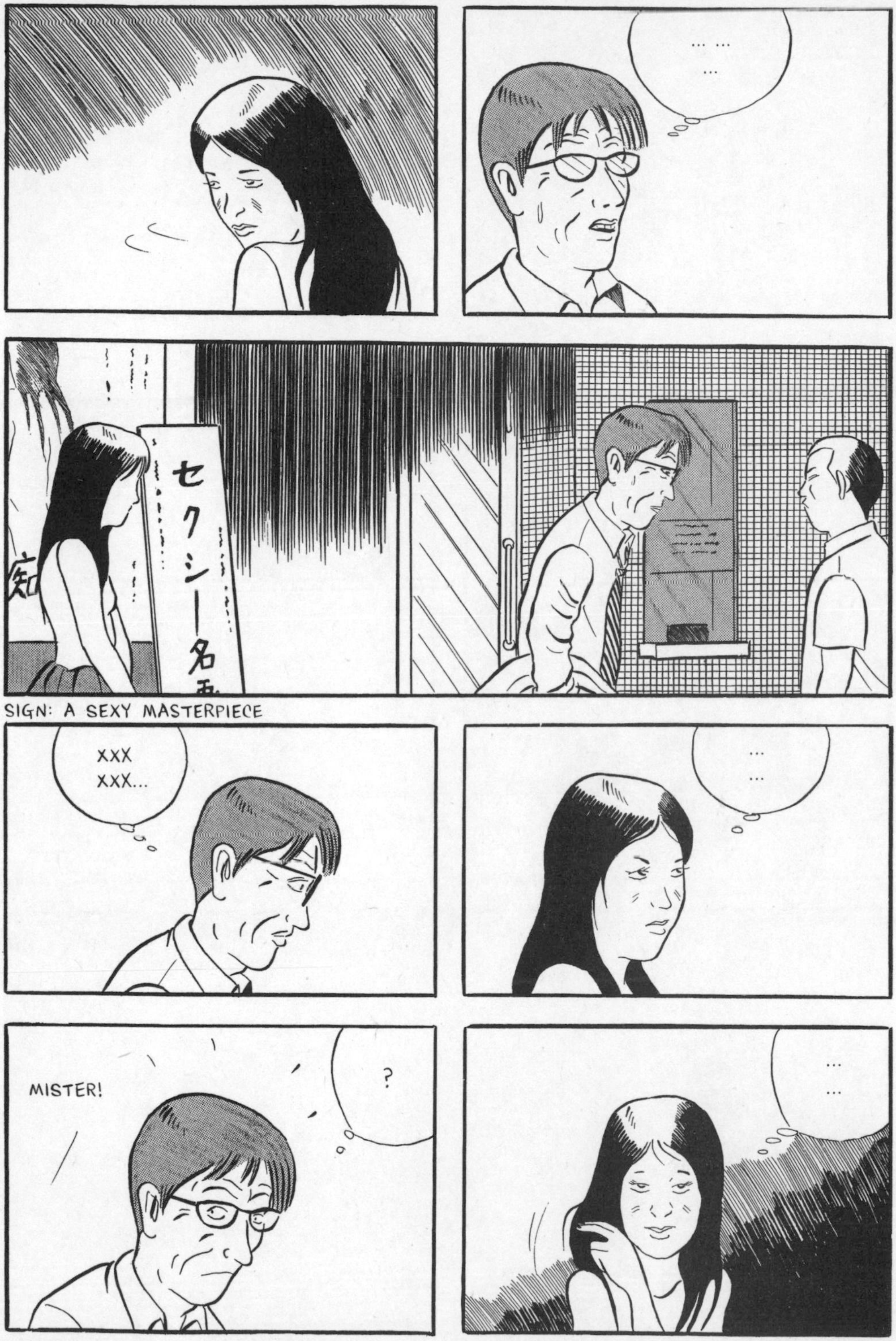
... ...
...
セクシー名
SIGN: A SEXY MASTERPIECE
XXX
XXX...
...
...
MISTER!
?
...
...

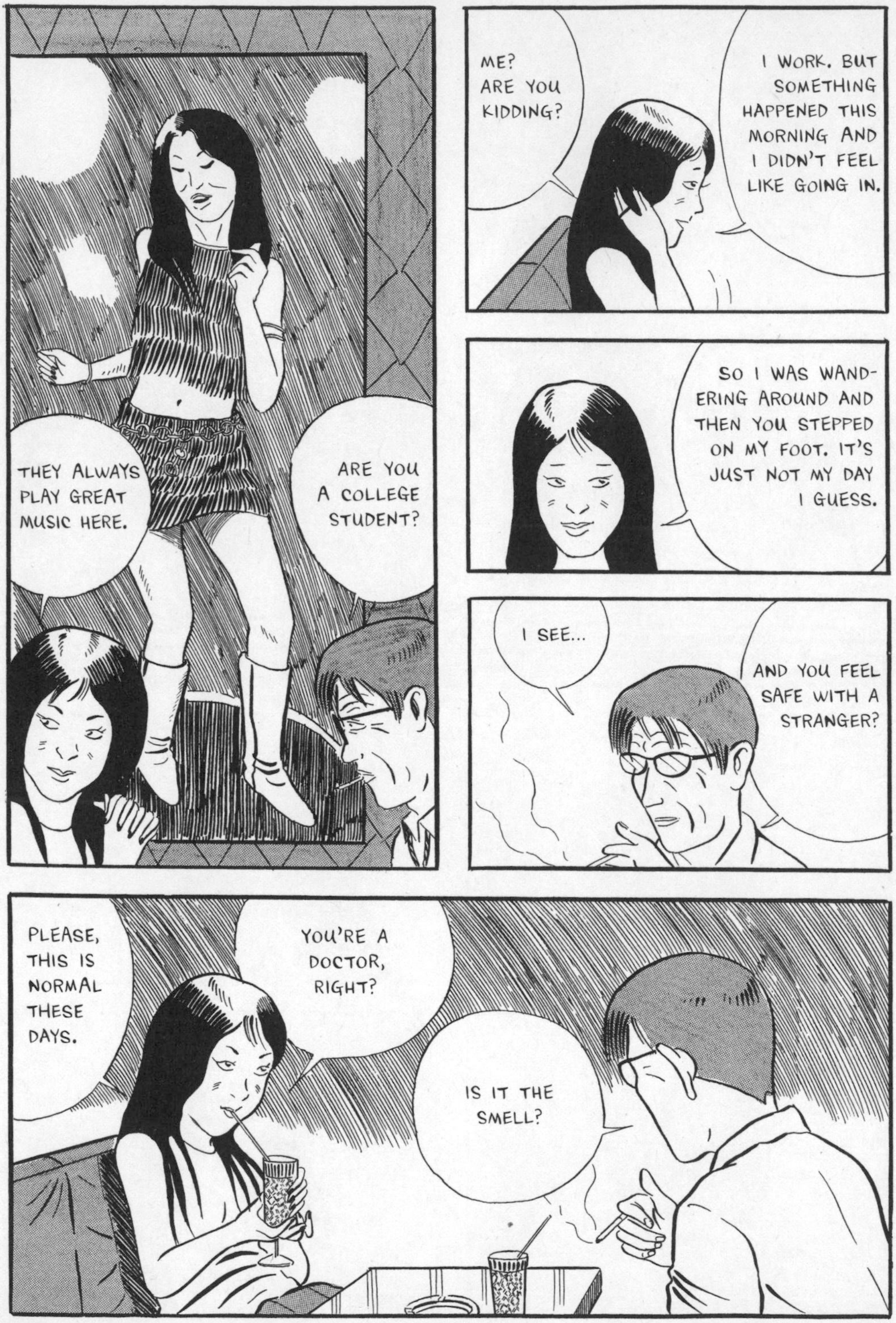
THEY ALWAYS PLAY GREAT MUSIC HERE.
ARE YOU A COLLEGE STUDENT?
ME? ARE YOU KIDDING?
I WORK. BUT SOMETHING HAPPENED THIS MORNING AND I DIDN'T FEEL LIKE GOING IN.
SO I WAS WANDERING AROUND AND THEN YOU STEPPED ON MY FOOT. IT'S JUST NOT MY DAY I GUESS.
I SEE...
AND YOU FEEL SAFE WITH A STRANGER?
PLEASE, THIS IS NORMAL THESE DAYS.
YOU'RE A DOCTOR, RIGHT?
IS IT THE SMELL?

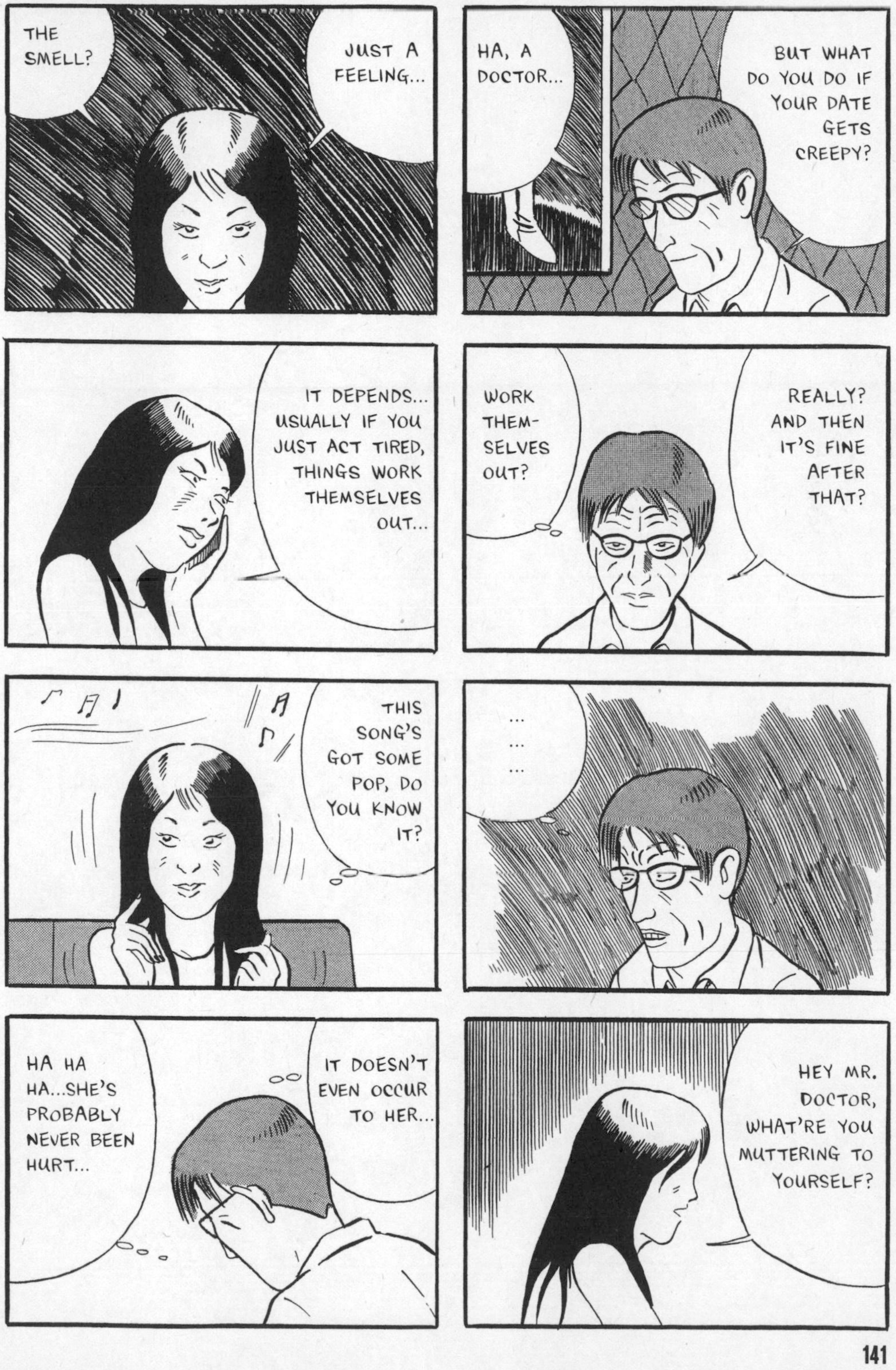
THE SMELL?
JUST A FEELING...
HA, A DOCTOR...
BUT WHAT DO YOU DO IF YOUR DATE GETS CREEPY?
IT DEPENDS... USUALLY IF YOU JUST ACT TIRED, THINGS WORK THEMSELVES OUT...
WORK THEM-SELVES OUT?
REALLY? AND THEN IT'S FINE AFTER THAT?
THIS SONG'S GOT SOME POP, DO YOU KNOW IT?
...
...
...
HA HA HA...SHE'S PROBABLY NEVER BEEN HURT...
IT DOESN'T EVEN OCCUR TO HER...
HEY MR. DOCTOR, WHAT'RE YOU MUTTERING TO YOURSELF?

OH, UH... NOTHING.

YOU KNOW, I'M AN OBSTETRICIAN...

...

...

GIGGLE

IF THERE'S SOMETHING WRONG, I CAN LOOK AT IT FOR YOU...

NOTHING'S WRONG WITH ME...WHY DO MEN ALWAYS GET THESE FUNNY IDEAS?

HA HA HA

I WAS JOKING ABOUT THE DOCTOR THING, BUT I WAS JUST AT THE HOSPITAL.

I WAS ON MY WAY BACK.

I KNEW SOMETHING WAS FISHY...

THE DOCTOR WON'T COME OUT AND SAY IT, BUT I THINK I HAVE INTESTINAL CANCER.

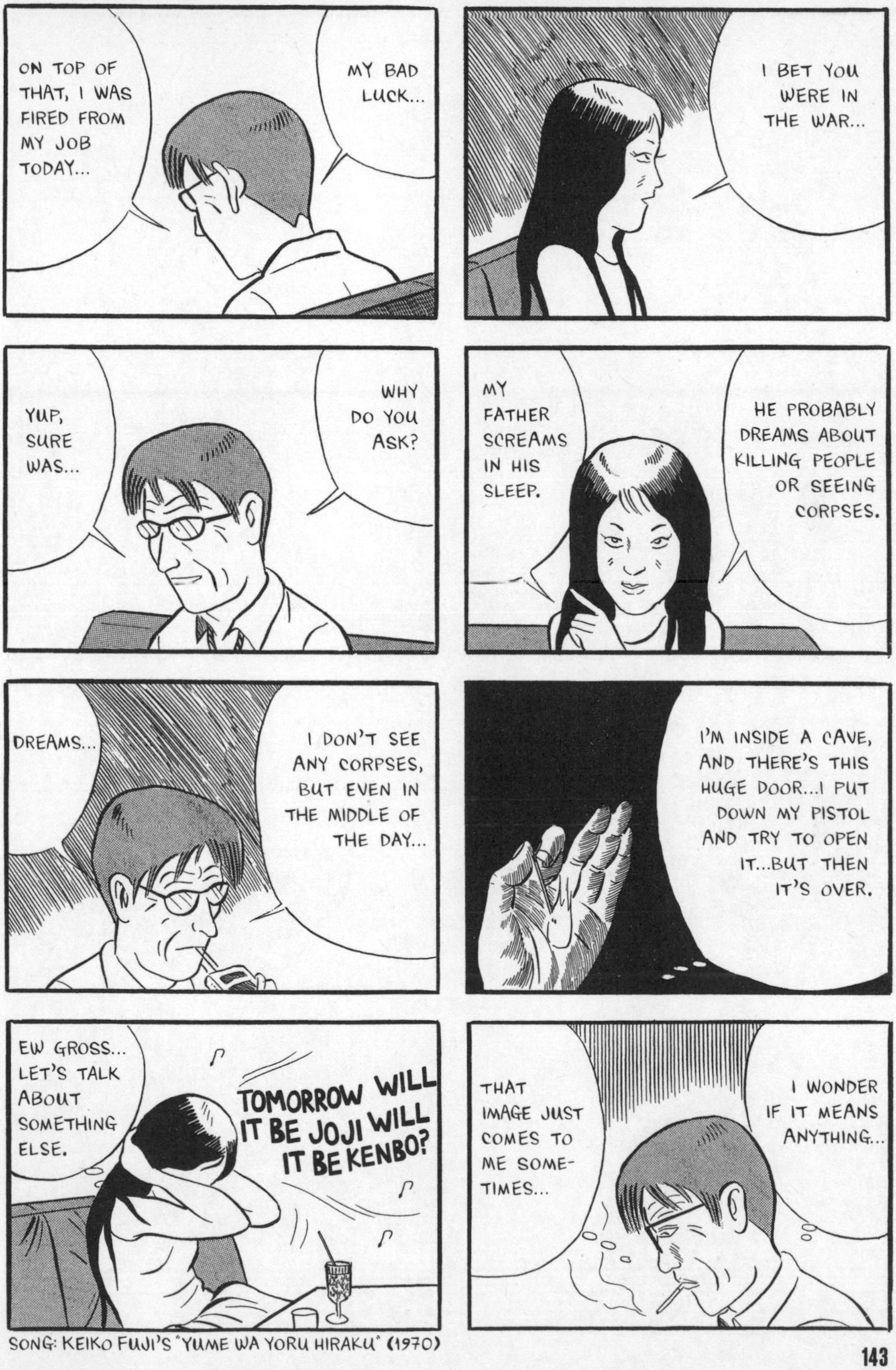
ON TOP OF THAT, I WAS FIRED FROM MY JOB TODAY...
MY BAD LUCK...
I BET YOU WERE IN THE WAR...
YUP, SURE WAS...
WHY DO YOU ASK?
MY FATHER SCREAMS IN HIS SLEEP.
HE PROBABLY DREAMS ABOUT KILLING PEOPLE OR SEEING CORPSES.
DREAMS...
I DON'T SEE ANY CORPSES, BUT EVEN IN THE MIDDLE OF THE DAY...
I'M INSIDE A CAVE, AND THERE'S THIS HUGE DOOR...I PUT DOWN MY PISTOL AND TRY TO OPEN IT...BUT THEN IT'S OVER.
EW GROSS... LET'S TALK ABOUT SOMETHING ELSE.
TOMORROW WILL IT BE JOJI WILL IT BE KENBO?
THAT IMAGE JUST COMES TO ME SOME-TIMES...
I WONDER IF IT MEANS ANYTHING...
SONG: KEIKO FUJI'S "YUME WA YORU HIRAKU" (1970)

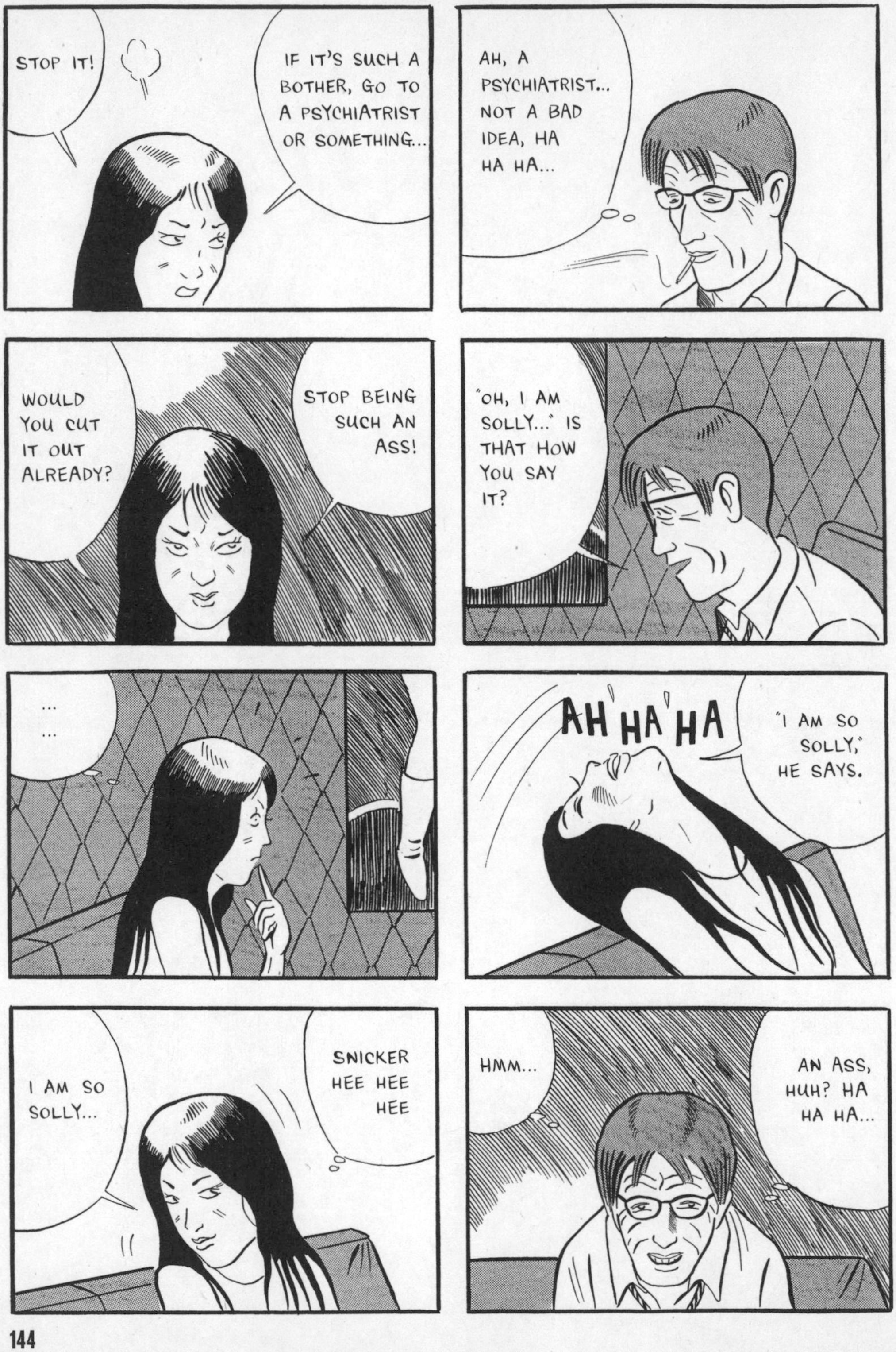
STOP IT!
IF IT'S SUCH A BOTHER, GO TO A PSYCHIATRIST OR SOMETHING...
AH, A PSYCHIATRIST... NOT A BAD IDEA, HA HA HA...
WOULD YOU CUT IT OUT ALREADY?
STOP BEING SUCH AN ASS!
"OH, I AM SOLLY..." IS THAT HOW YOU SAY IT?
...
...
AH HA HA
"I AM SO SOLLY," HE SAYS.
I AM SO SOLLY...
SNICKER HEE HEE HEE
HMM...
AN ASS, HUH? HA HA HA...

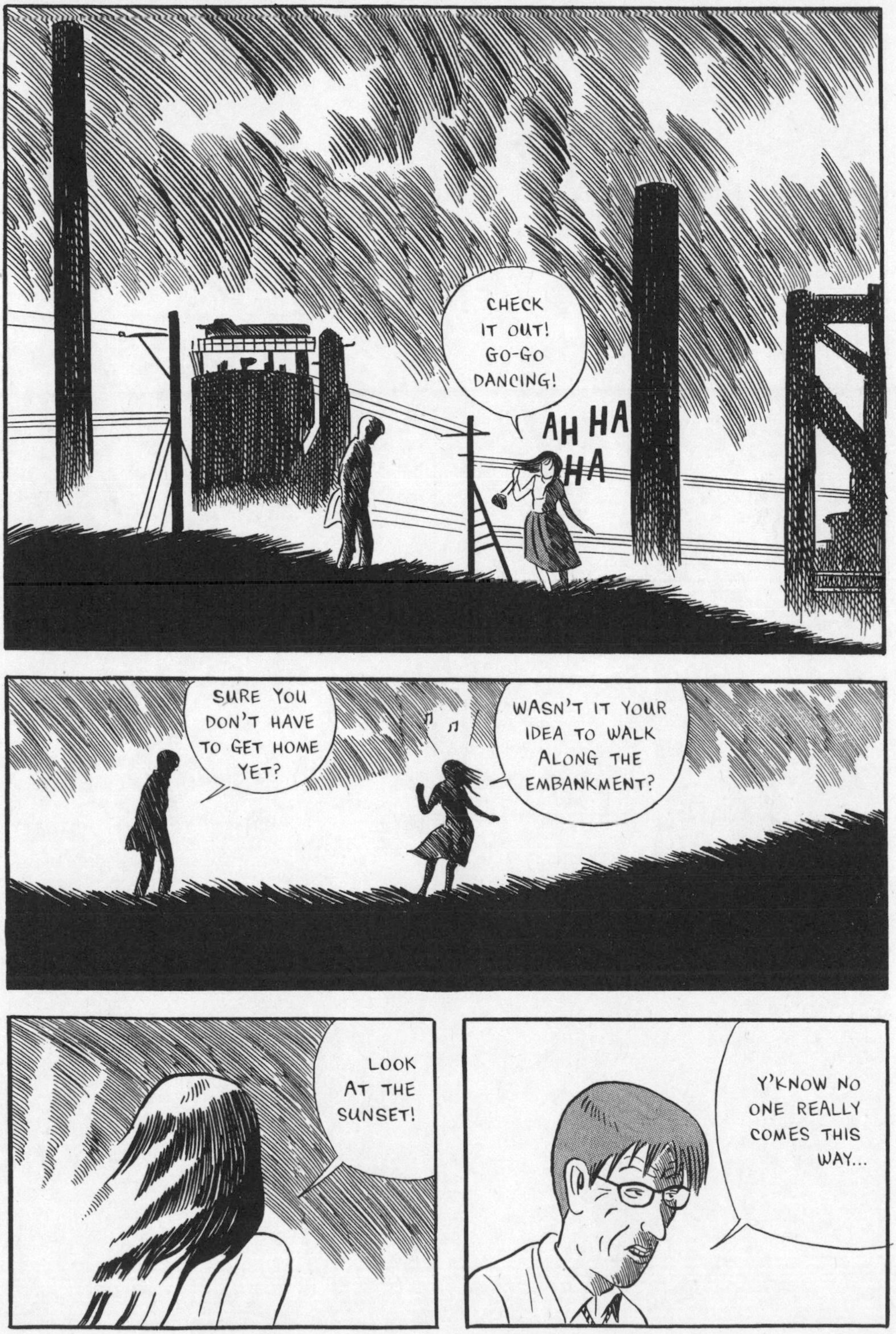
CHECK IT OUT! GO-GO DANCING!
AH HA HA
SURE YOU DON'T HAVE TO GET HOME YET?
WASN'T IT YOUR IDEA TO WALK ALONG THE EMBANKMENT?
LOOK AT THE SUNSET!
Y'KNOW NO ONE REALLY COMES THIS WAY...

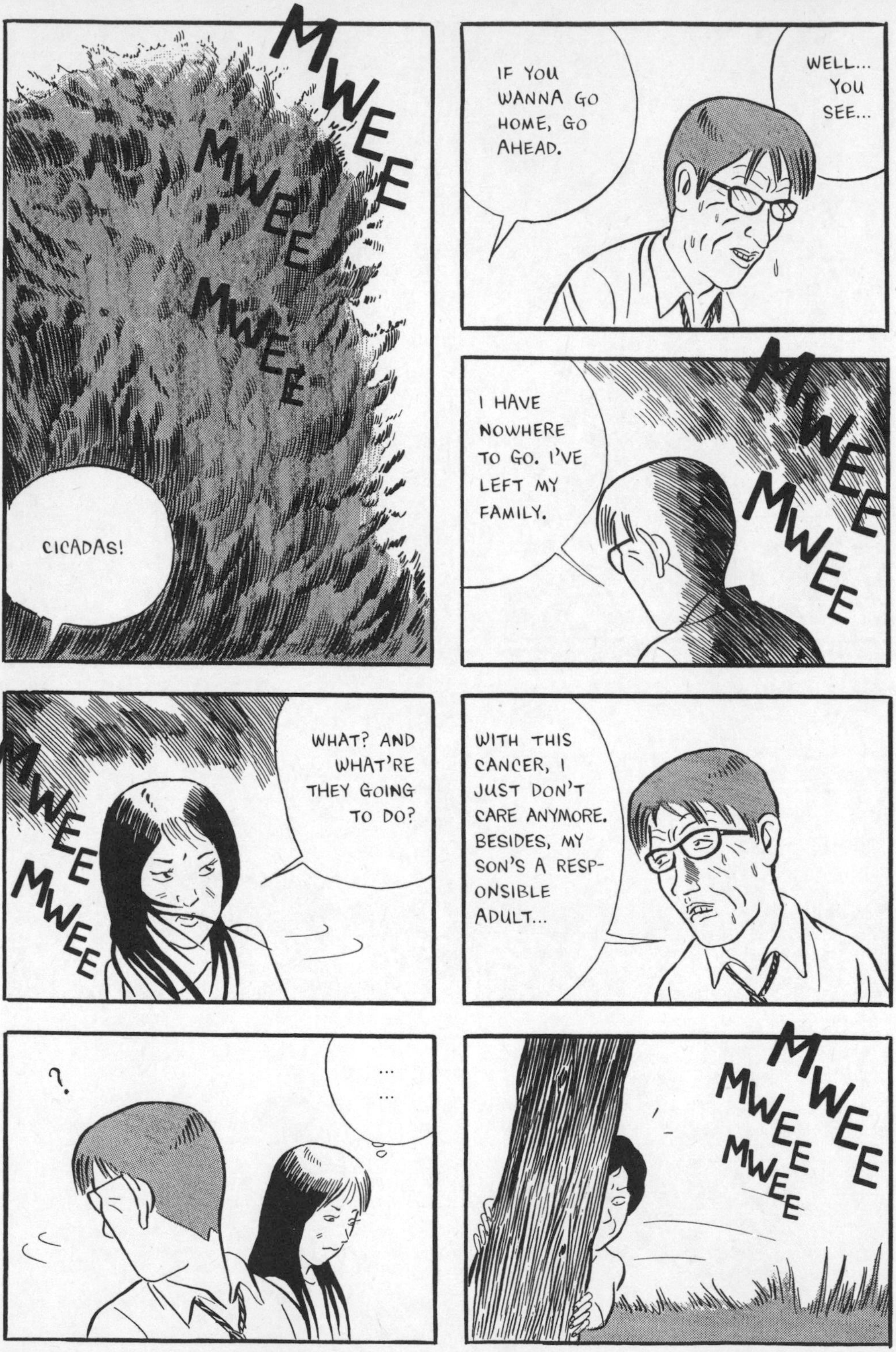
MWEE
MWEE
MWEE
MWEE
CICADAS!
IF YOU WANNA GO HOME, GO AHEAD.
WELL... YOU SEE...
I HAVE NOWHERE TO GO. I'VE LEFT MY FAMILY.
MWEE
MWEE
MWEE
MWEE
MWEE
WHAT? AND WHAT'RE THEY GOING TO DO?
WITH THIS CANCER, I JUST DON'T CARE ANYMORE. BESIDES, MY SON'S A RESPONSIBLE ADULT...
?
... ...
MWEE
MWEE
MWEE

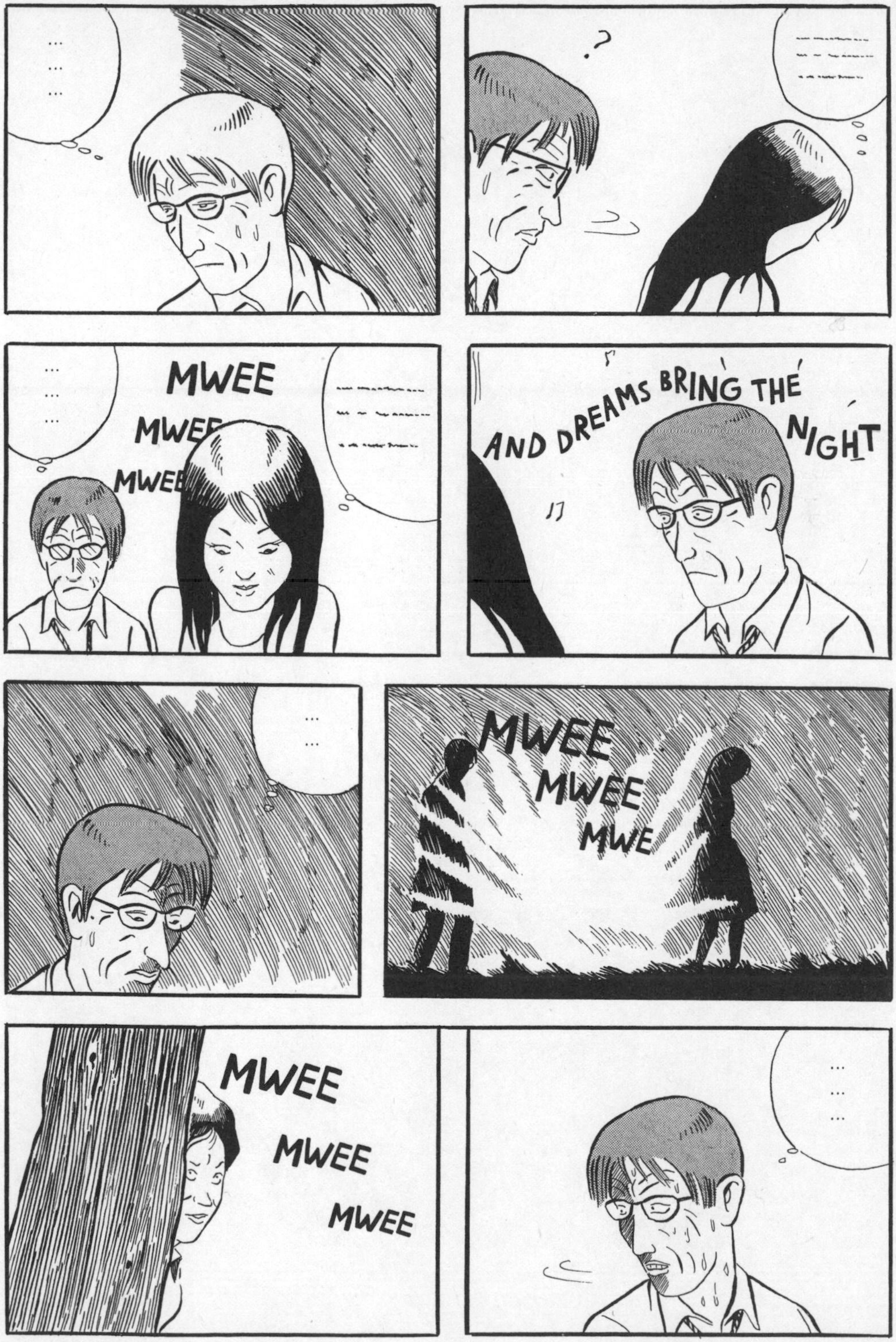
...
...
...
?
MWEE
MWEE
MWEE
...
...
...
AND DREAMS BRING THE NIGHT
...
...
MWEE
MWEE
MWE
MWEE
MWEE
MWEE
...
...
...

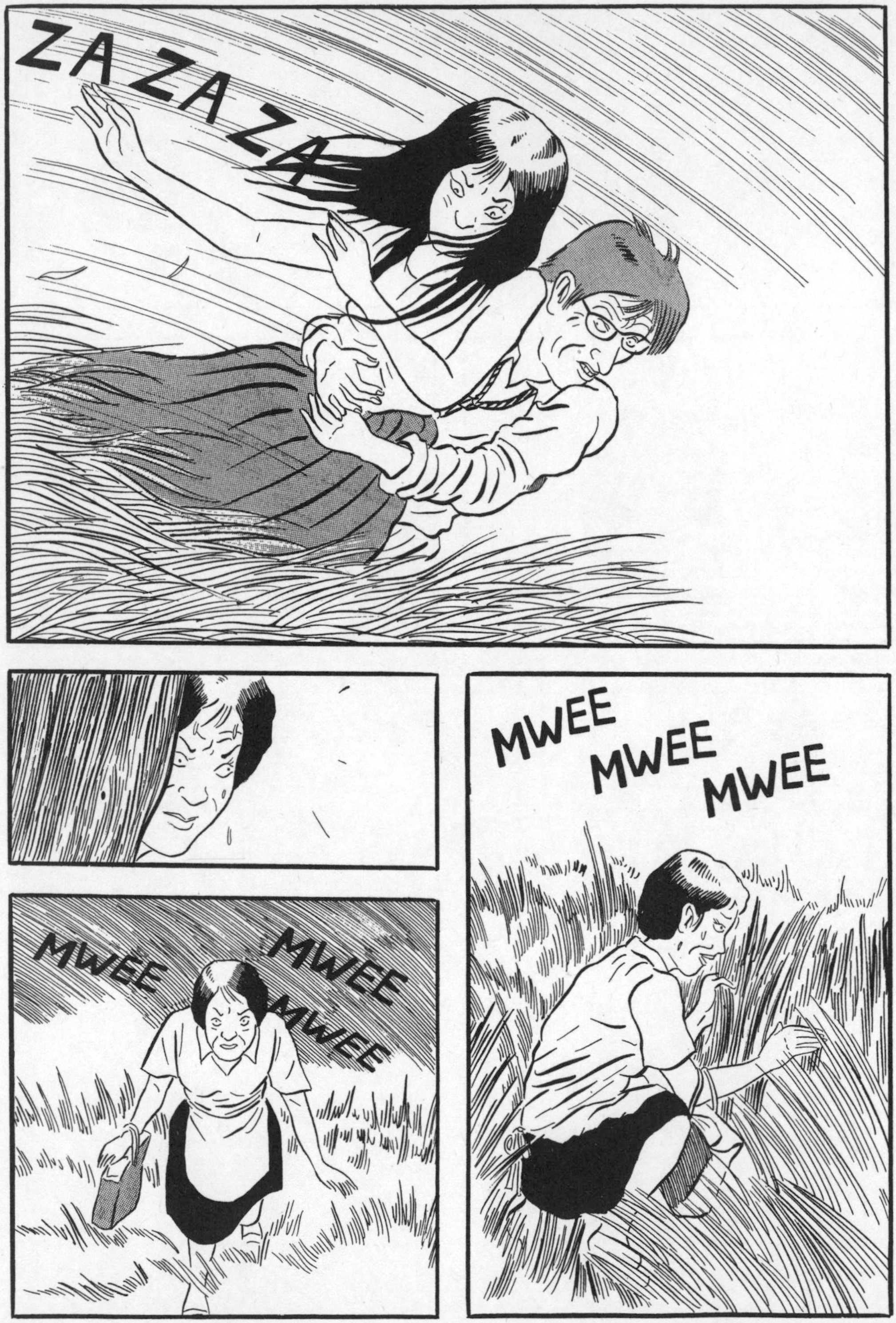
ZA ZA ZA ZA
MWEE
MWEE
MWEE
MWEE
MWEE
MWEE

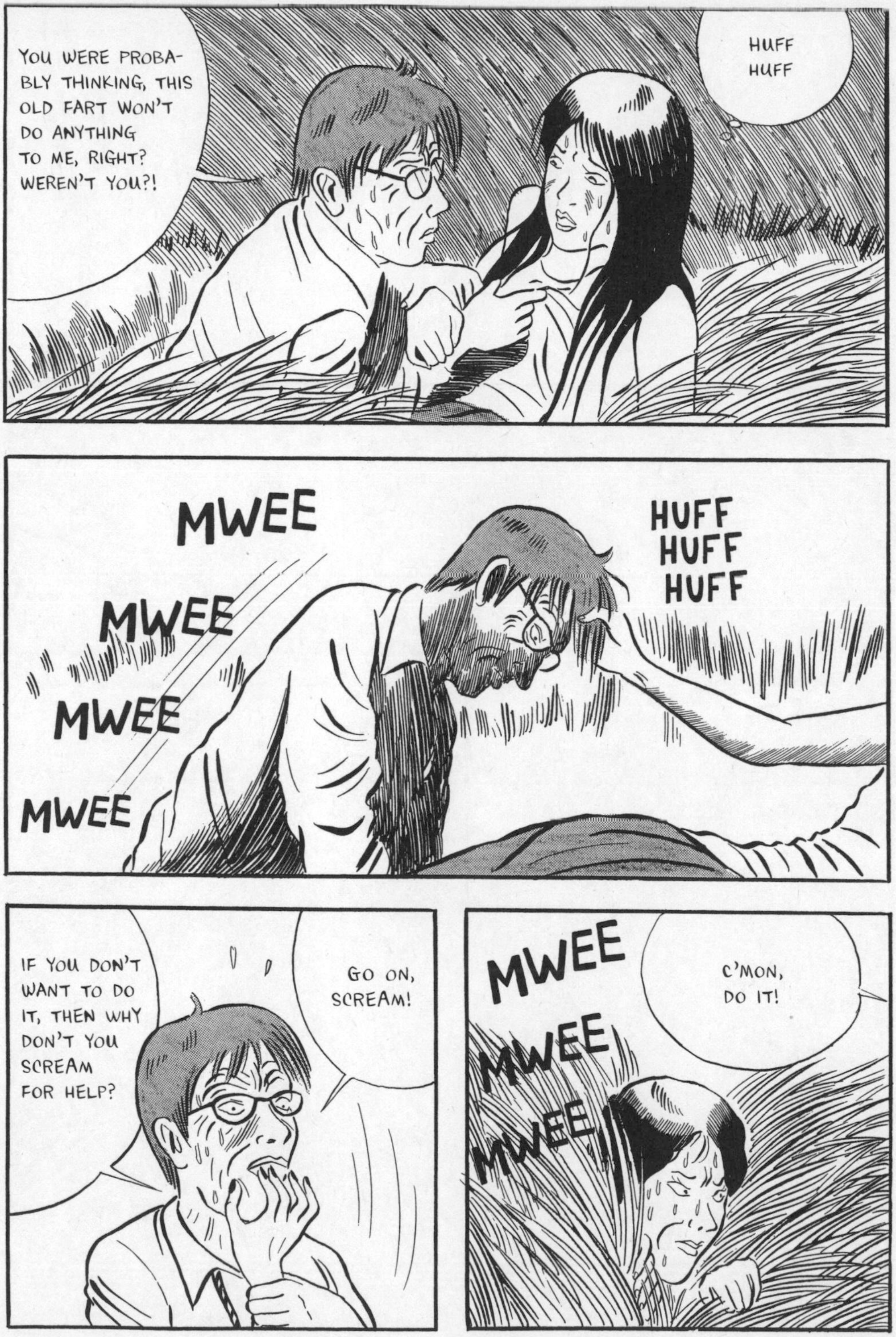
YOU WERE PROBA-BLY THINKING, THIS OLD FART WON'T DO ANYTHING TO ME, RIGHT? WEREN'T YOU?!
HUFF HUFF
MWEE
MWEE
MWEE
MWEE
HUFF HUFF HUFF
IF YOU DON'T WANT TO DO IT, THEN WHY DON'T YOU SCREAM FOR HELP?
GO ON, SCREAM!
MWEE
MWEE
MWEE
C'MON, DO IT!

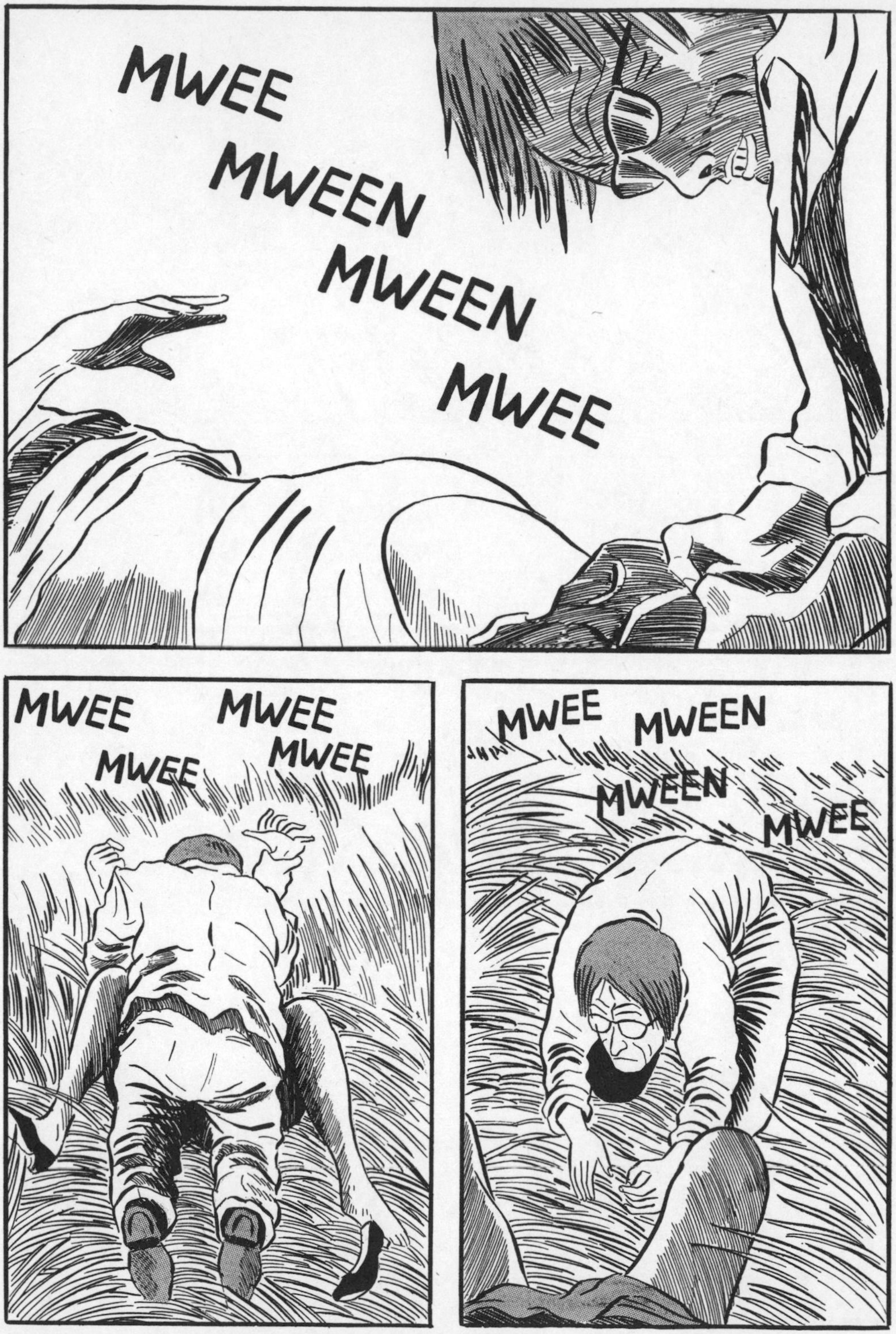
MWEE
MWEEN
MWEEN
MWEE
MWEE
MWEE
MWEE
MWEE
MWEE
MWEEN
MWEEN
MWEE

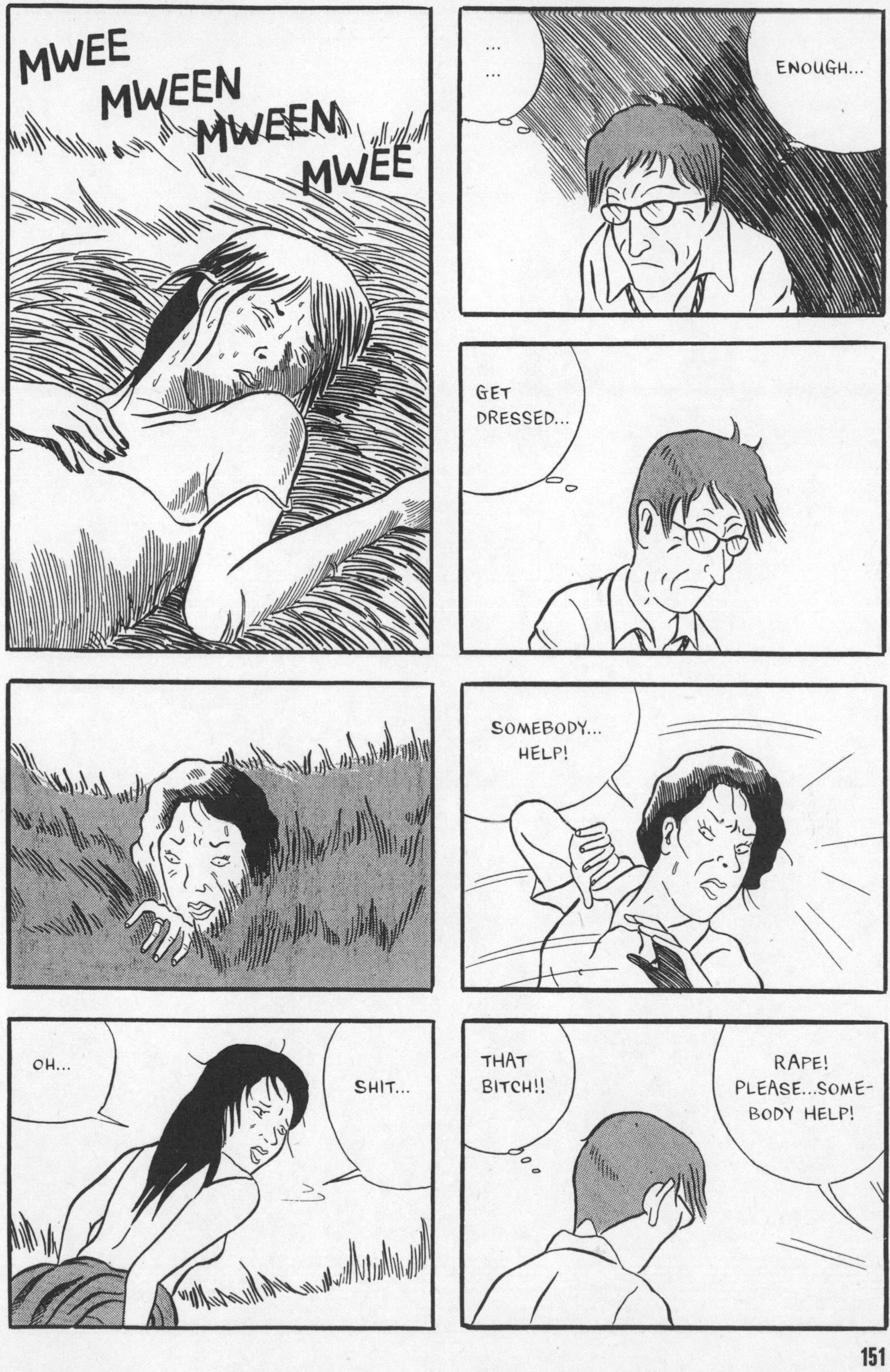
MWEE
MWEEN
MWEEN
MWEE
...
...
ENOUGH...
GET DRESSED...
SOMEBODY... HELP!
OH...
SHIT...
THAT BITCH!!
RAPE! PLEASE...SOME-BODY HELP!

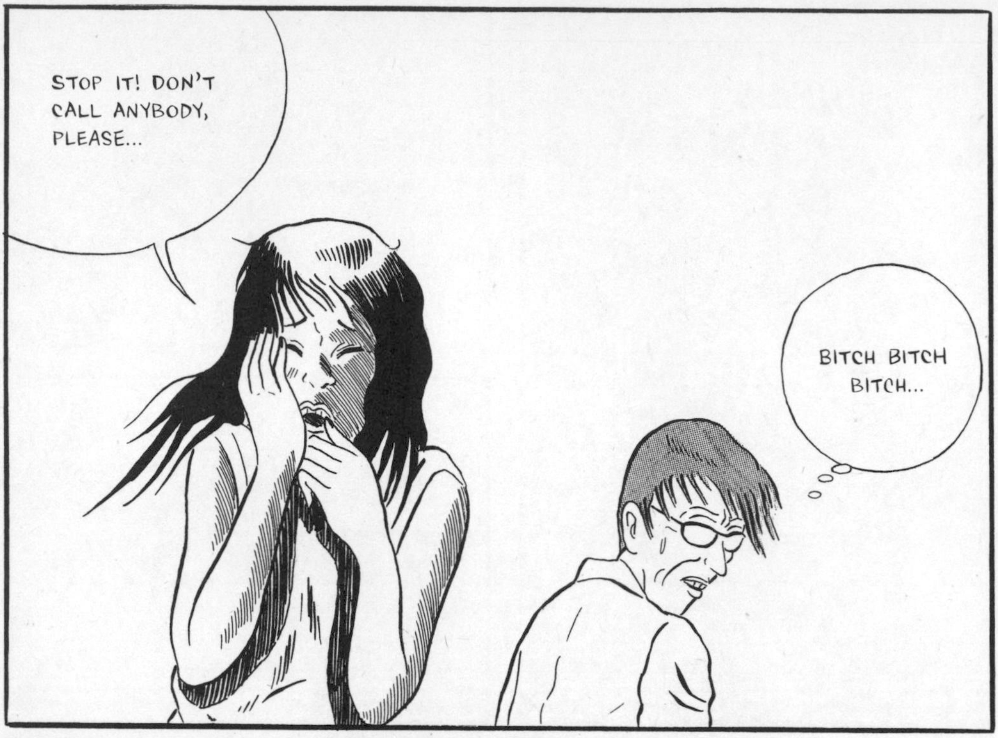
STOP IT! DON'T CALL ANYBODY, PLEASE...
BITCH BITCH BITCH...

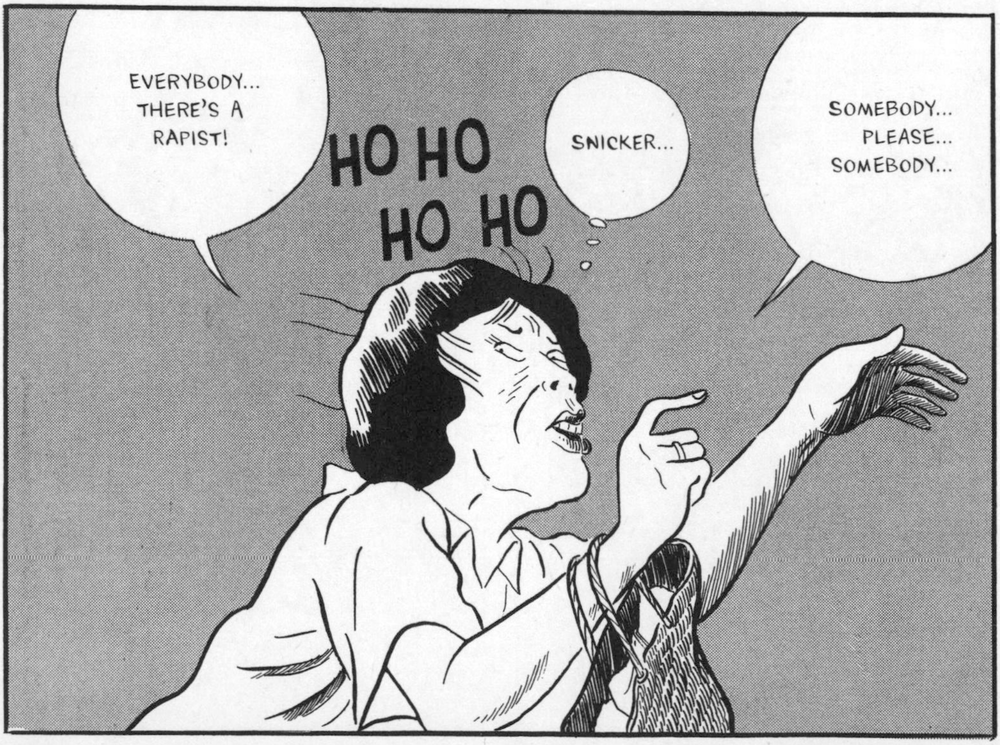
EVERYBODY... THERE'S A RAPIST!
HO HO HO HO
SNICKER...
SOMEBODY... PLEASE... SOMEBODY...

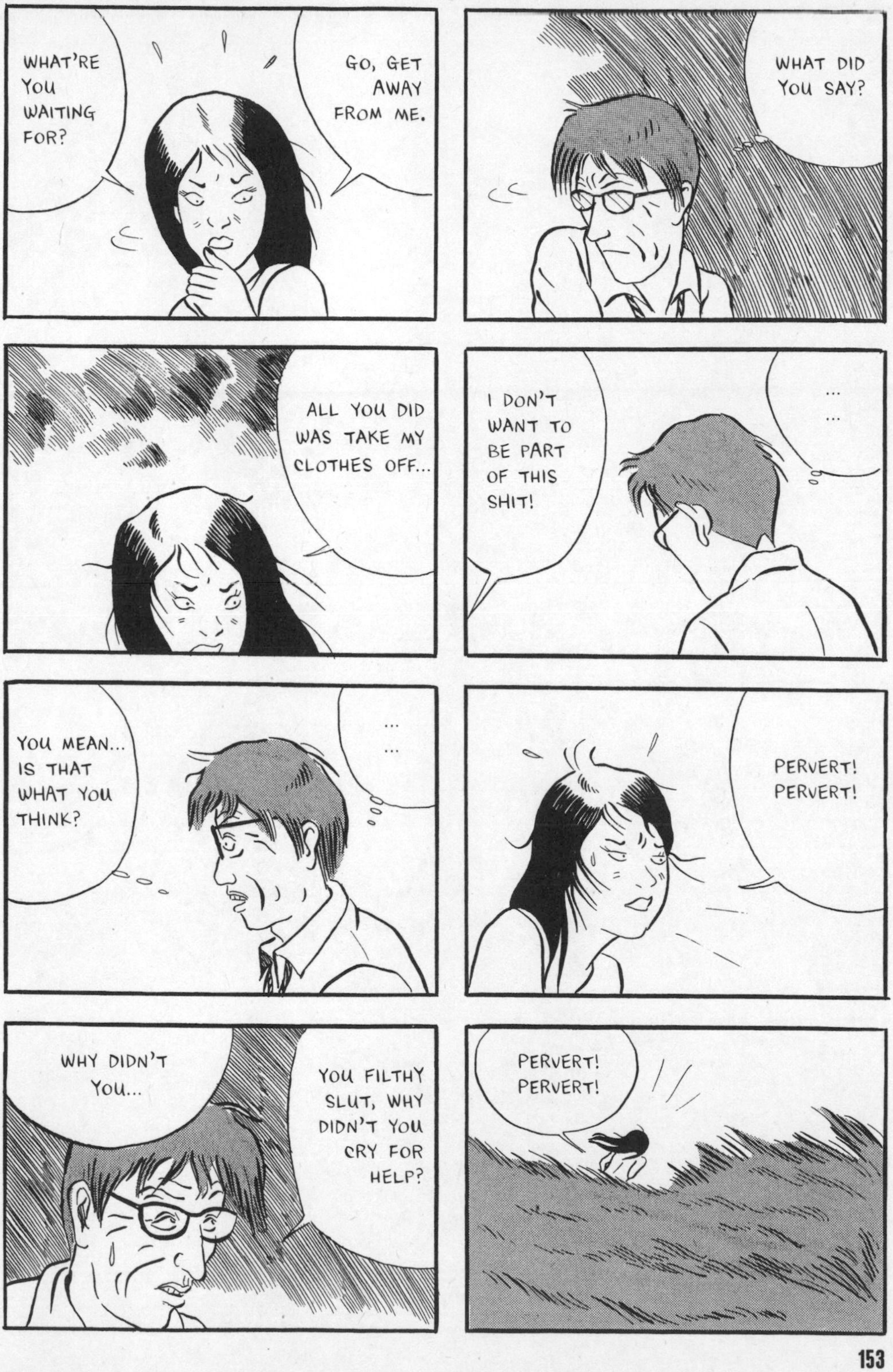
WHAT'RE YOU WAITING FOR?
GO, GET AWAY FROM ME.
WHAT DID YOU SAY?
ALL YOU DID WAS TAKE MY CLOTHES OFF...
I DON'T WANT TO BE PART OF THIS SHIT!
... ...
YOU MEAN... IS THAT WHAT YOU THINK?
... ...
PERVERT! PERVERT!
WHY DIDN'T YOU...
YOU FILTHY SLUT, WHY DIDN'T YOU CRY FOR HELP?
PERVERT! PERVERT!

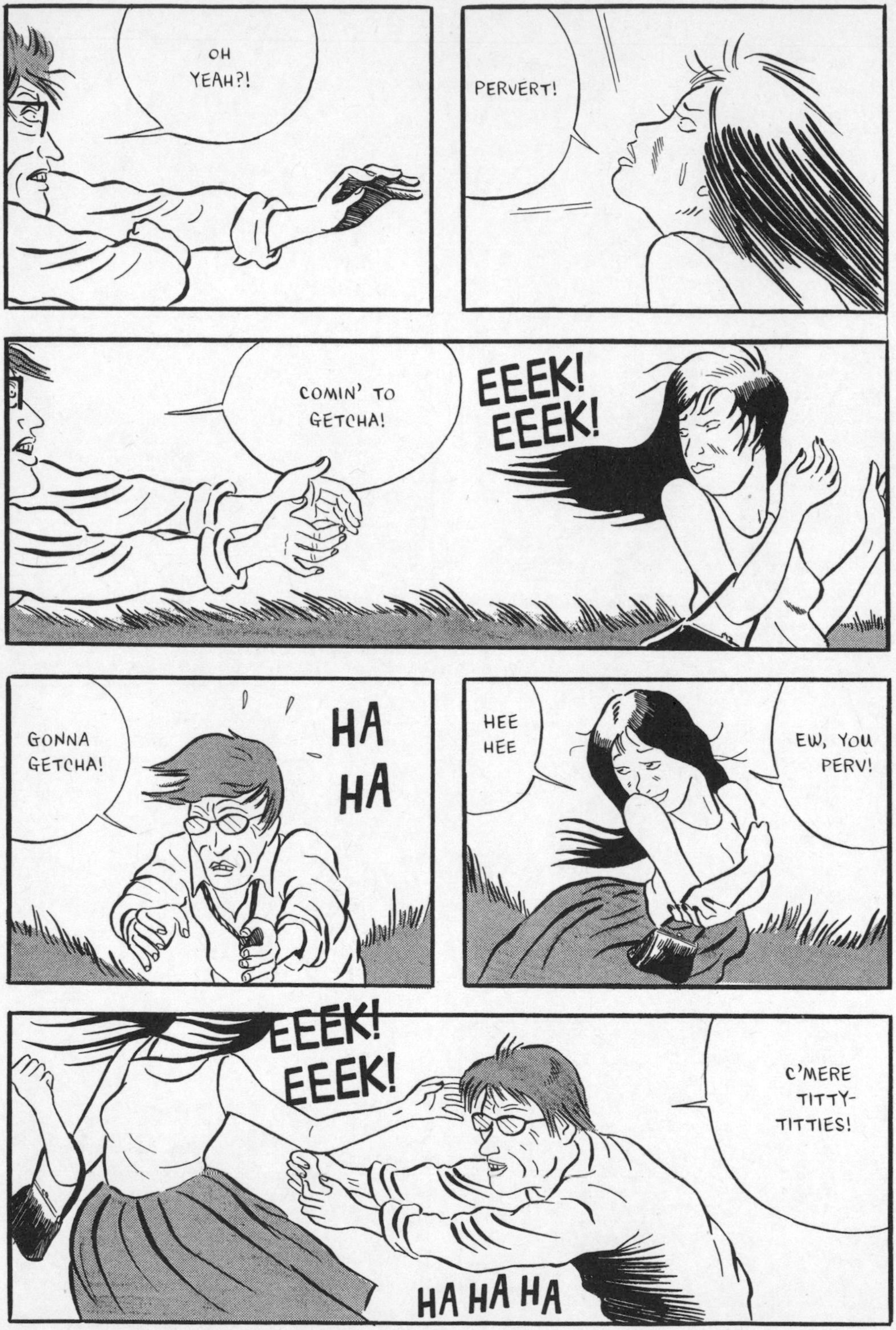
OH YEAH?!
PERVERT!
COMIN' TO GETCHA!
EEEK! EEEK!
GONNA GETCHA!
HA HA
HEE HEE
EW, YOU PERV!
EEEK! EEEK!
C'MERE TITTY-TITTIES!
HA HA HA

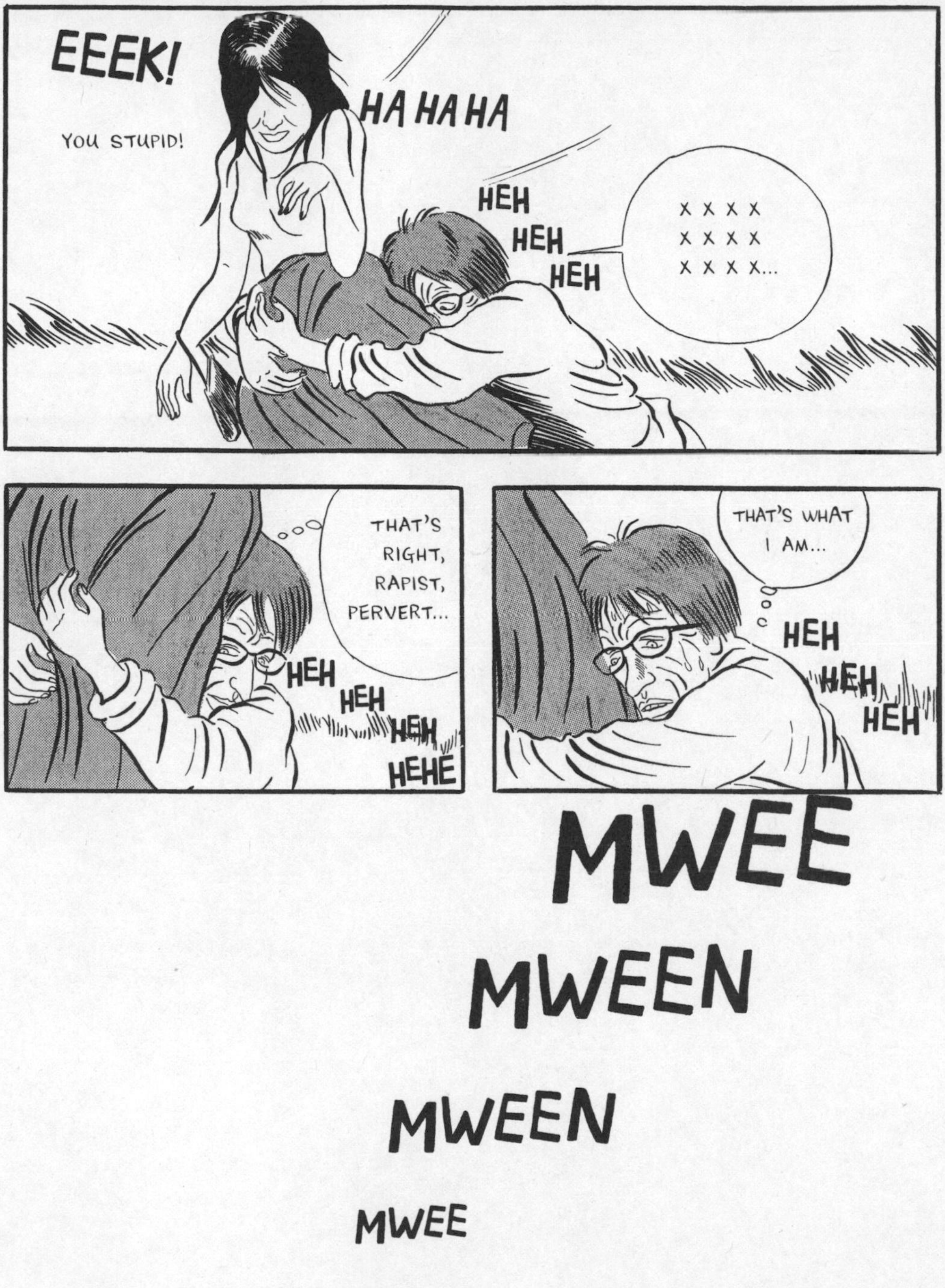
EEEK!
YOU STUPID!
HA HA HA
HEH
HEH
HEH
X X X X
X X X X
X X X X...
THAT'S RIGHT, RAPIST, PERVERT...
HEH
HEH
HEH
HEHE
THAT'S WHAT I AM...
HEH
HEH
HEH
MWEE
MWEEN
MWEEN
MWEE
MWEE

A TALE OF ABSOLUTE AND UTTER NONSENSE

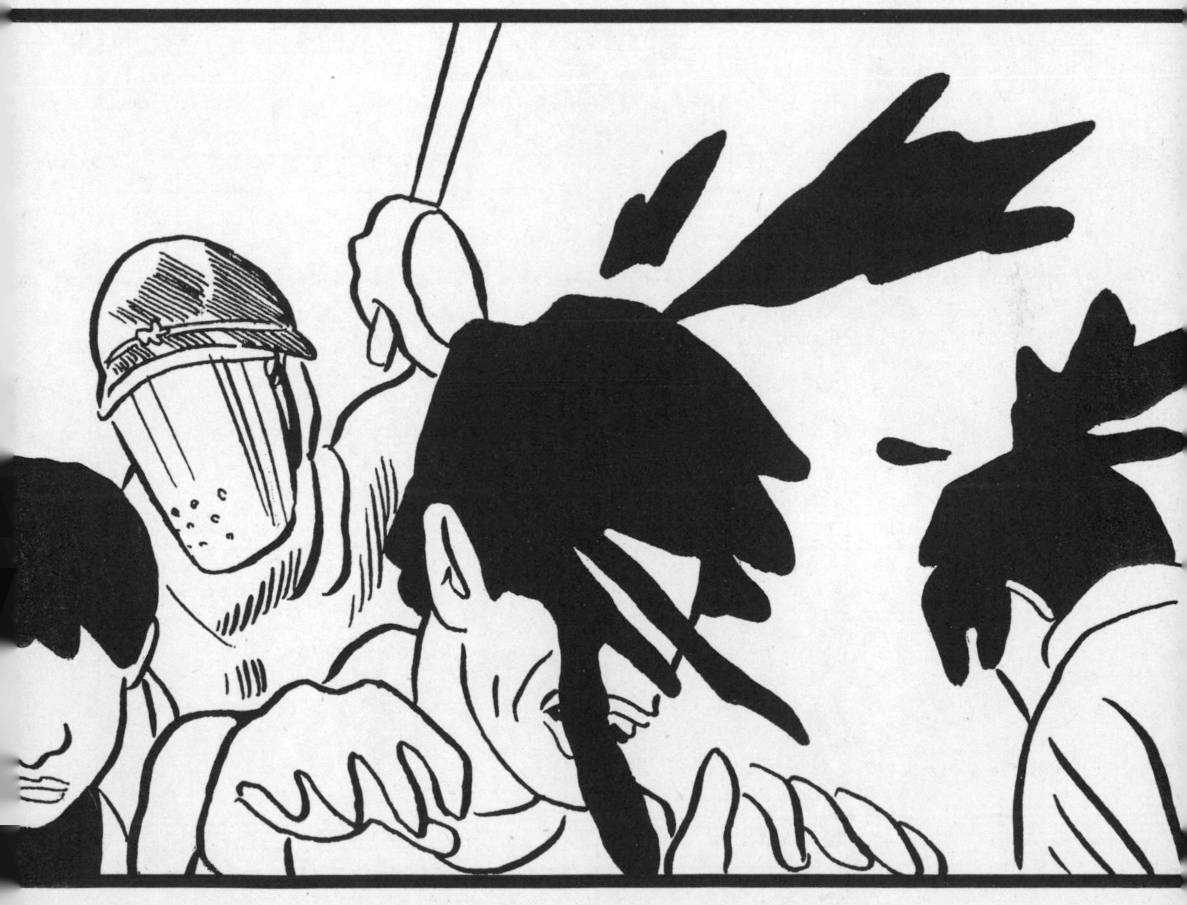

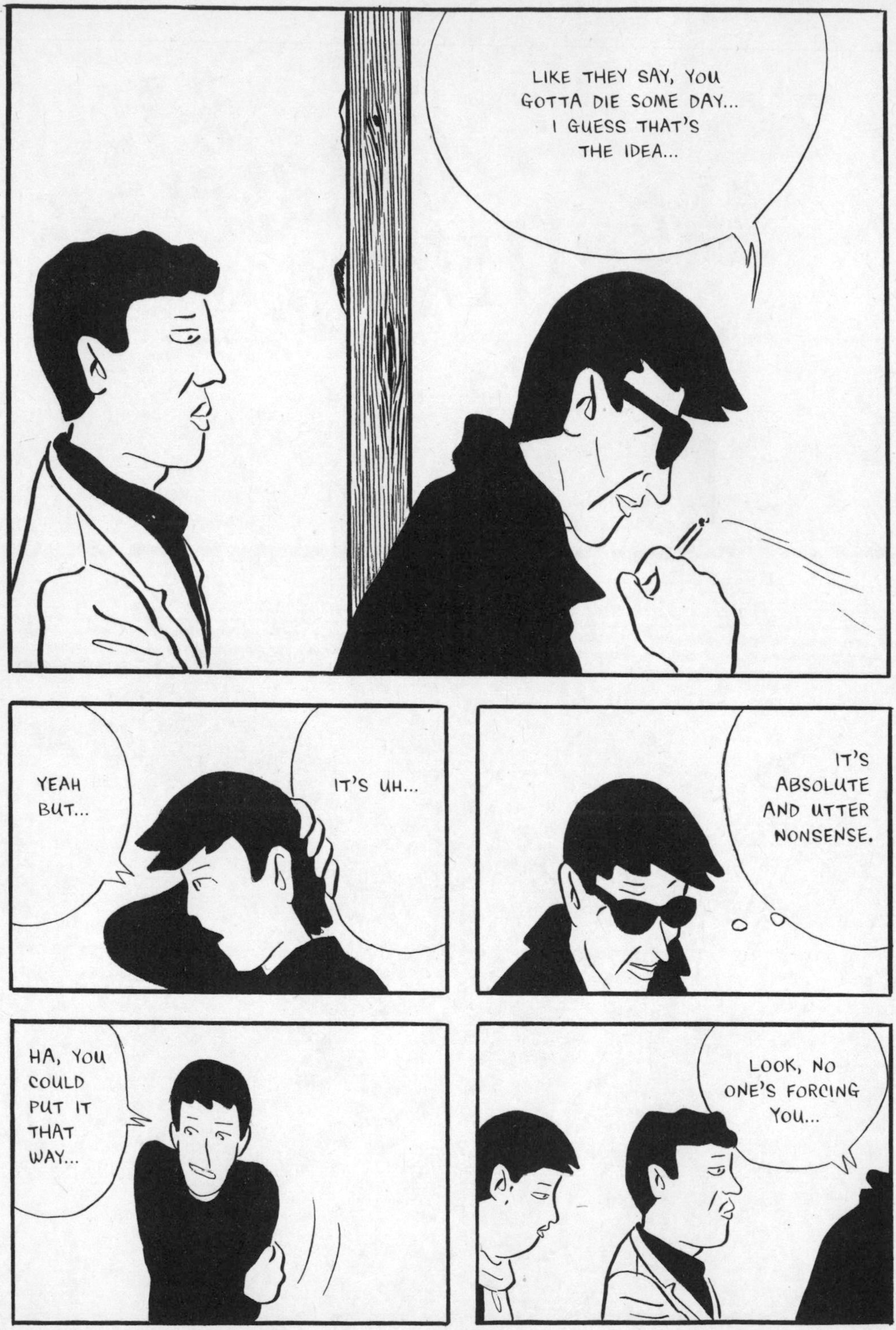
LIKE THEY SAY, YOU GOTTA DIE SOME DAY... I GUESS THAT'S THE IDEA...
YEAH BUT...
IT'S UH...
IT'S ABSOLUTE AND UTTER NONSENSE.
HA, YOU COULD PUT IT THAT WAY...
LOOK, NO ONE'S FORCING YOU...

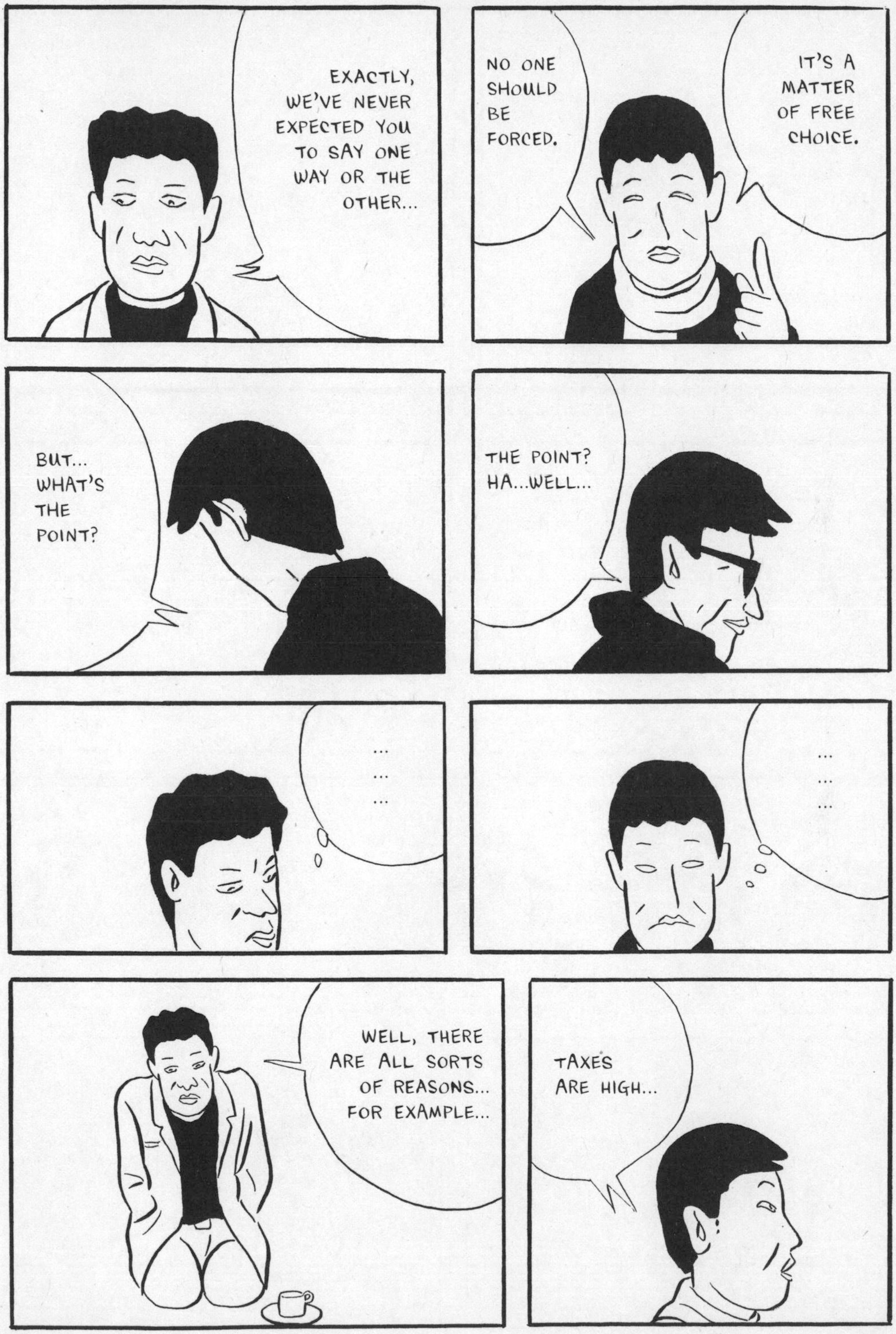
EXACTLY, WE'VE NEVER EXPECTED YOU TO SAY ONE WAY OR THE OTHER...
NO ONE SHOULD BE FORCED.
IT'S A MATTER OF FREE CHOICE.
BUT... WHAT'S THE POINT?
THE POINT? HA...WELL...
...
...
...
...
...
...
WELL, THERE ARE ALL SORTS OF REASONS... FOR EXAMPLE...
TAXES ARE HIGH...

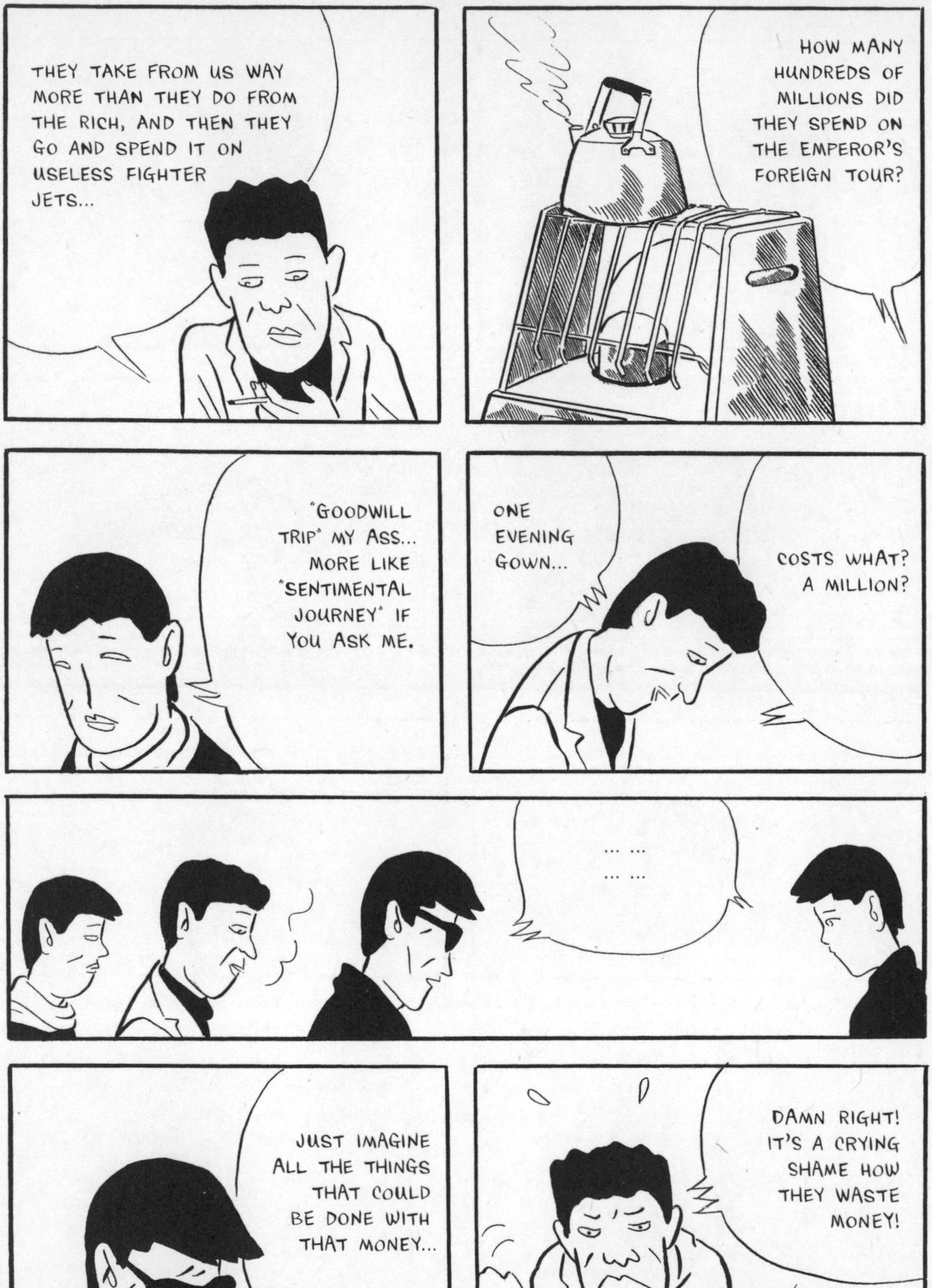
THEY TAKE FROM US WAY MORE THAN THEY DO FROM THE RICH, AND THEN THEY GO AND SPEND IT ON USELESS FIGHTER JETS...
HOW MANY HUNDREDS OF MILLIONS DID THEY SPEND ON THE EMPEROR'S FOREIGN TOUR?
"GOODWILL TRIP" MY ASS... MORE LIKE "SENTIMENTAL JOURNEY" IF YOU ASK ME.
ONE EVENING GOWN...
COSTS WHAT? A MILLION?
... ...
... ...
JUST IMAGINE ALL THE THINGS THAT COULD BE DONE WITH THAT MONEY...
DAMN RIGHT! IT'S A CRYING SHAME HOW THEY WASTE MONEY!

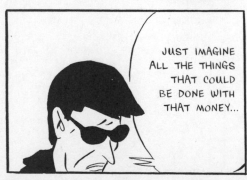

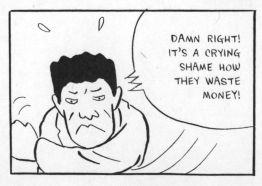

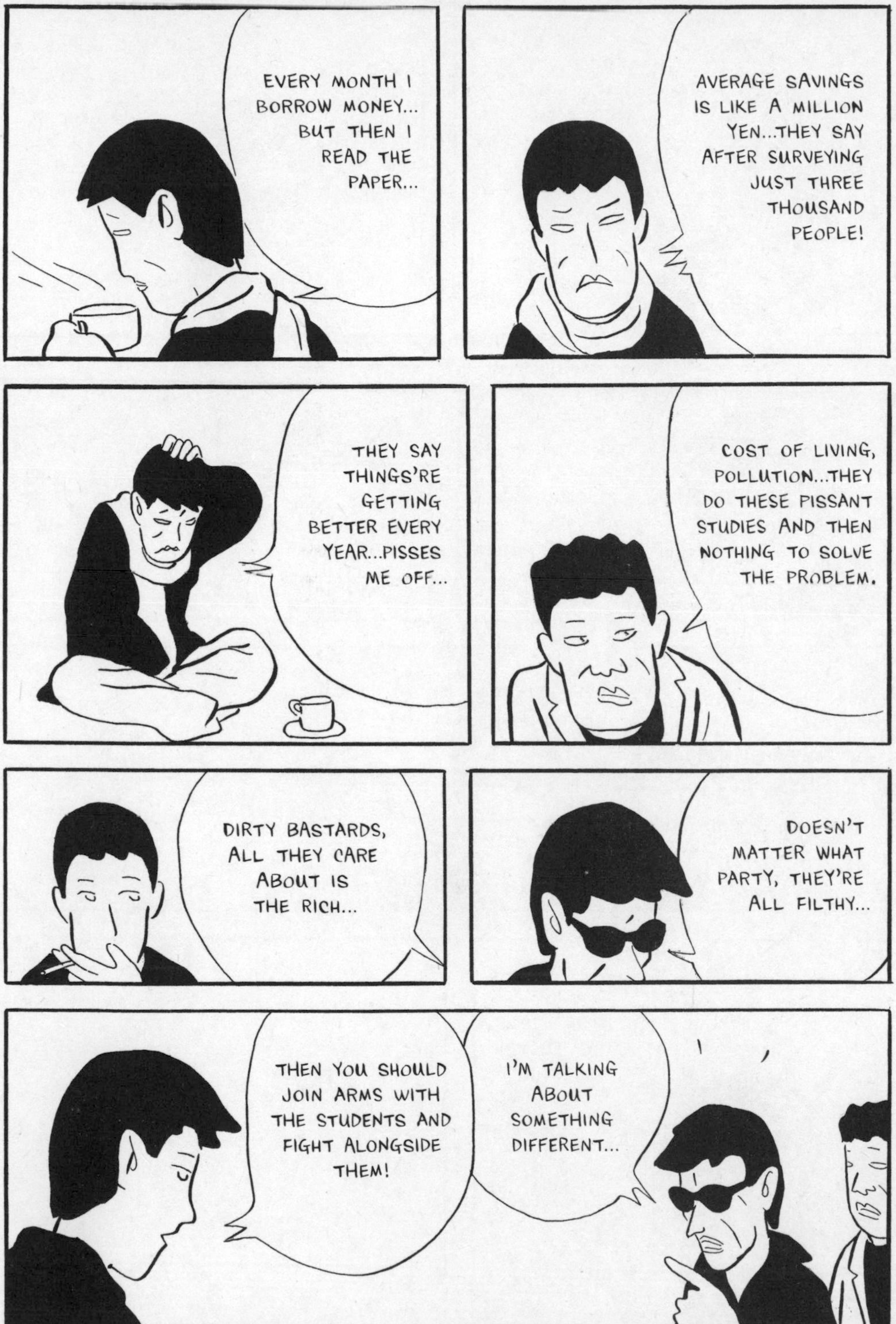
EVERY MONTH I BORROW MONEY... BUT THEN I READ THE PAPER...
AVERAGE SAVINGS IS LIKE A MILLION YEN...THEY SAY AFTER SURVEYING JUST THREE THOUSAND PEOPLE!
THEY SAY THING'S'RE GETTING BETTER EVERY YEAR...PISSES ME OFF...
COST OF LIVING, POLLUTION...THEY DO THESE PISSANT STUDIES AND THEN NOTHING TO SOLVE THE PROBLEM.
DIRTY BASTARDS, ALL THEY CARE ABOUT IS THE RICH...
DOESN'T MATTER WHAT PARTY, THEY'RE ALL FILTHY...
THEN YOU SHOULD JOIN ARMS WITH THE STUDENTS AND FIGHT ALONGSIDE THEM!
I'M TALKING ABOUT SOMETHING DIFFERENT...

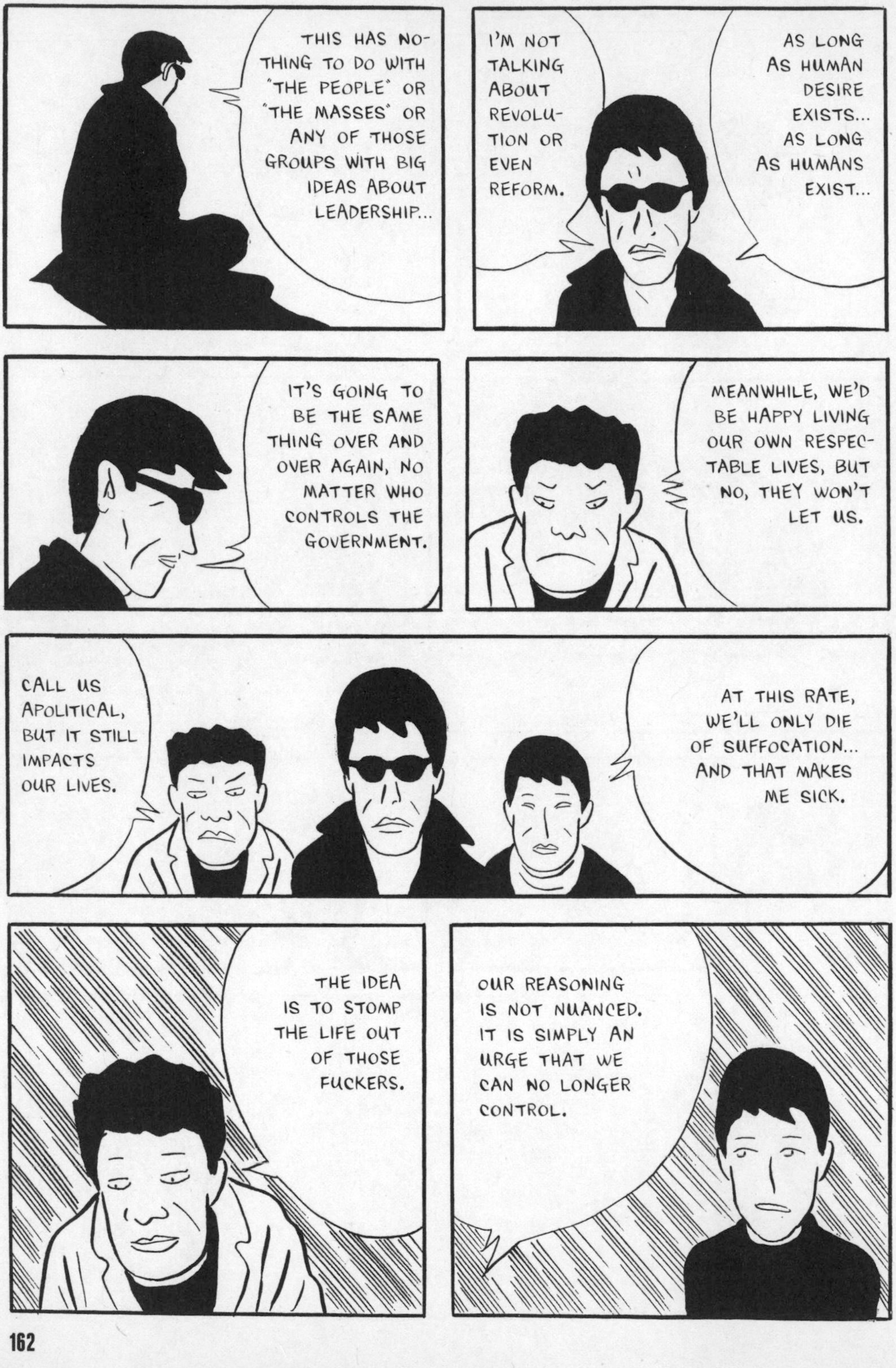
THIS HAS NOTHING TO DO WITH "THE PEOPLE" OR "THE MASSES" OR ANY OF THOSE GROUPS WITH BIG IDEAS ABOUT LEADERSHIP...
I'M NOT TALKING ABOUT REVOLUTION OR EVEN REFORM.
AS LONG AS HUMAN DESIRE EXISTS... AS LONG AS HUMANS EXIST...
IT'S GOING TO BE THE SAME THING OVER AND OVER AGAIN, NO MATTER WHO CONTROLS THE GOVERNMENT.
MEANWHILE, WE'D BE HAPPY LIVING OUR OWN RESPECTABLE LIVES, BUT NO, THEY WON'T LET US.
CALL US APOLITICAL, BUT IT STILL IMPACTS OUR LIVES.
AT THIS RATE, WE'LL ONLY DIE OF SUFFOCATION... AND THAT MAKES ME SICK.
THE IDEA IS TO STOMP THE LIFE OUT OF THOSE FUCKERS.
OUR REASONING IS NOT NUANCED. IT IS SIMPLY AN URGE THAT WE CAN NO LONGER CONTROL.

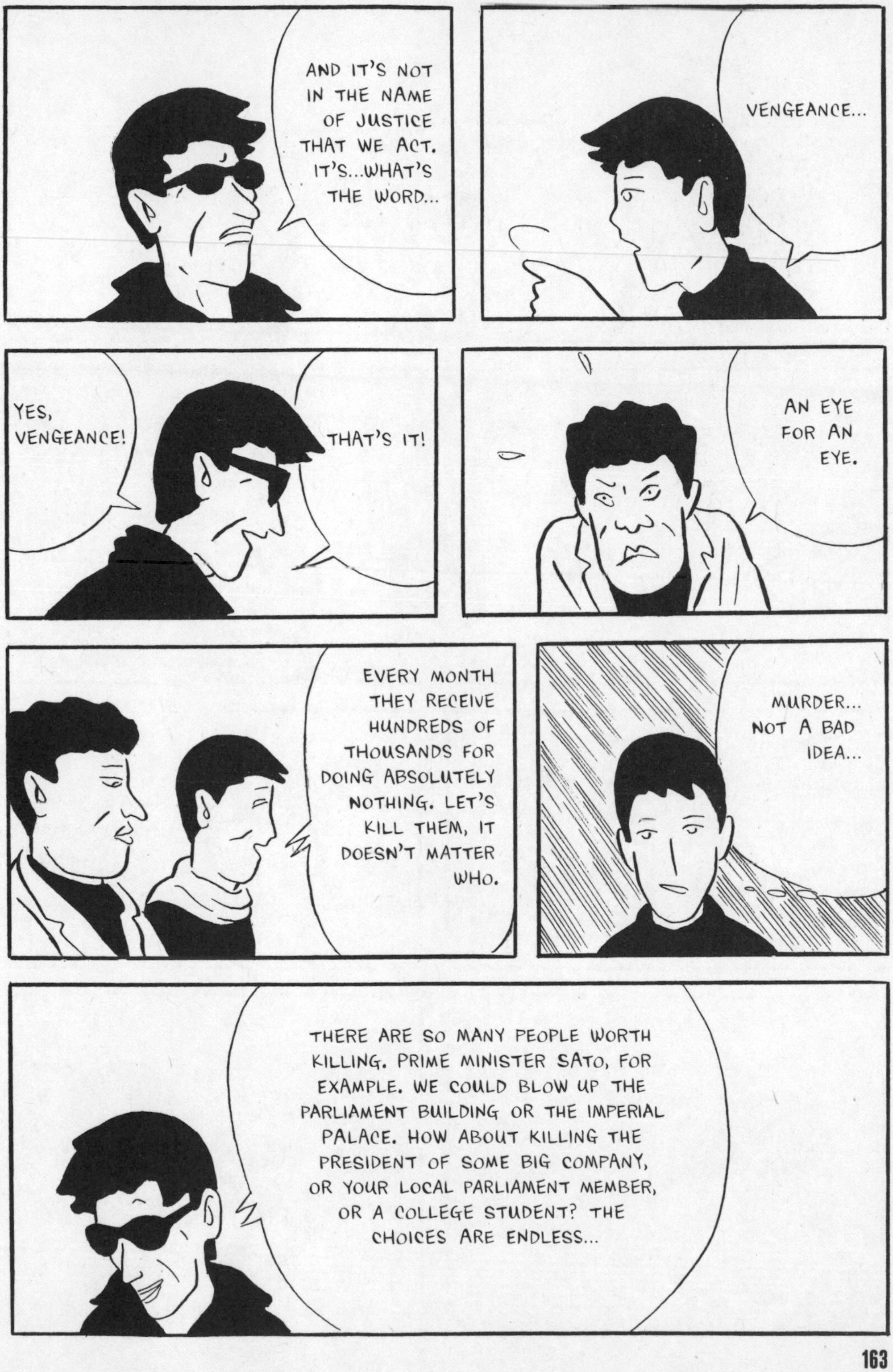
AND IT'S NOT IN THE NAME OF JUSTICE THAT WE ACT. IT'S...WHAT'S THE WORD...
VENGEANCE...
YES, VENGEANCE!
THAT'S IT!
AN EYE FOR AN EYE.
EVERY MONTH THEY RECEIVE HUNDREDS OF THOUSANDS FOR DOING ABSOLUTELY NOTHING. LET'S KILL THEM, IT DOESN'T MATTER WHO.
MURDER... NOT A BAD IDEA...
THERE ARE SO MANY PEOPLE WORTH KILLING. PRIME MINISTER SATO, FOR EXAMPLE. WE COULD BLOW UP THE PARLIAMENT BUILDING OR THE IMPERIAL PALACE. HOW ABOUT KILLING THE PRESIDENT OF SOME BIG COMPANY, OR YOUR LOCAL PARLIAMENT MEMBER, OR A COLLEGE STUDENT? THE CHOICES ARE ENDLESS...

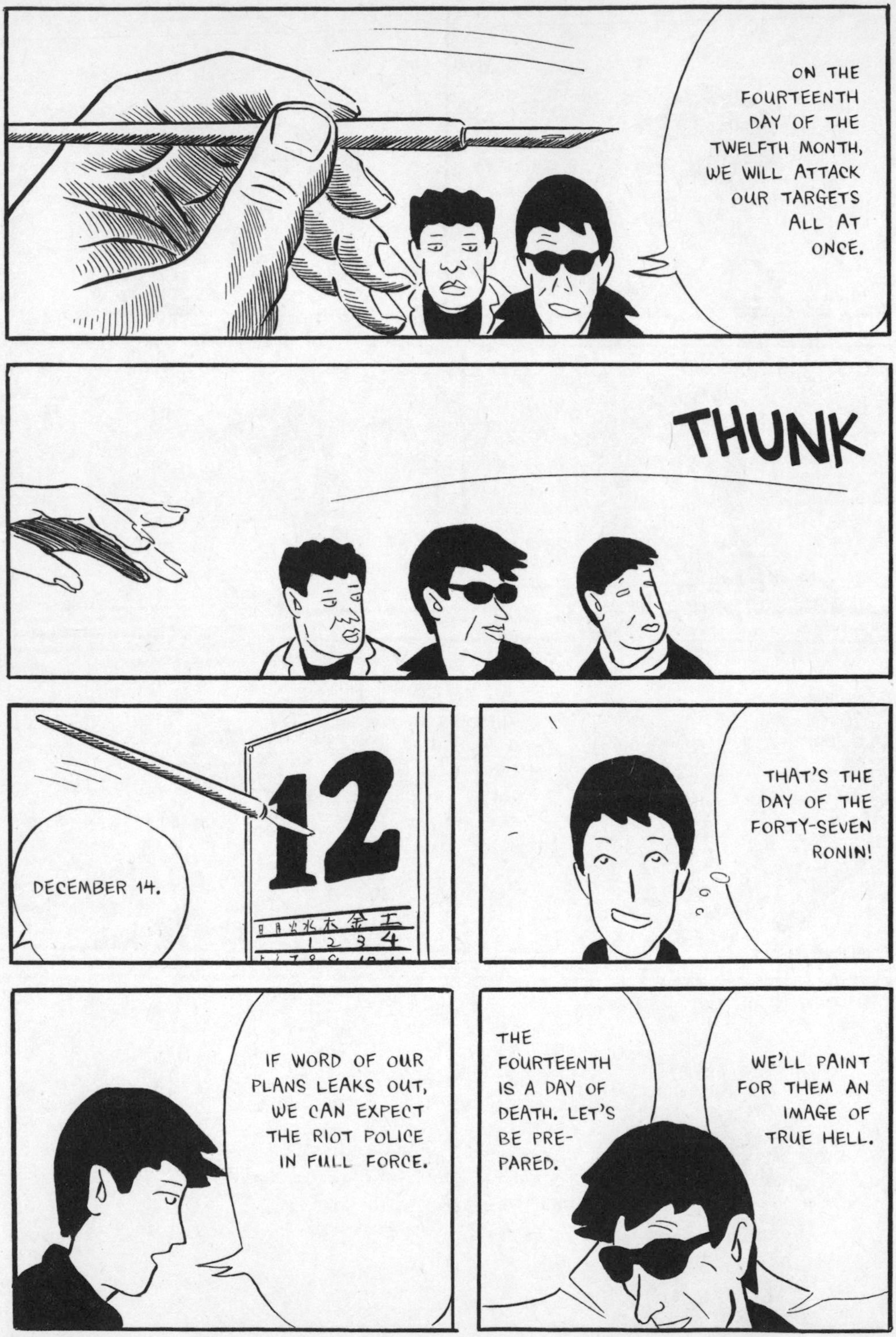
ON THE FOURTEENTH DAY OF THE TWELFTH MONTH, WE WILL ATTACK OUR TARGETS ALL AT ONCE.
THUNK
DECEMBER 14.
12
THAT'S THE DAY OF THE FORTY-SEVEN RONIN!
IF WORD OF OUR PLANS LEAKS OUT, WE CAN EXPECT THE RIOT POLICE IN FULL FORCE.
THE FOURTEENTH IS A DAY OF DEATH. LET'S BE PRE-PARED.
WE'LL PAINT FOR THEM AN IMAGE OF TRUE HELL.

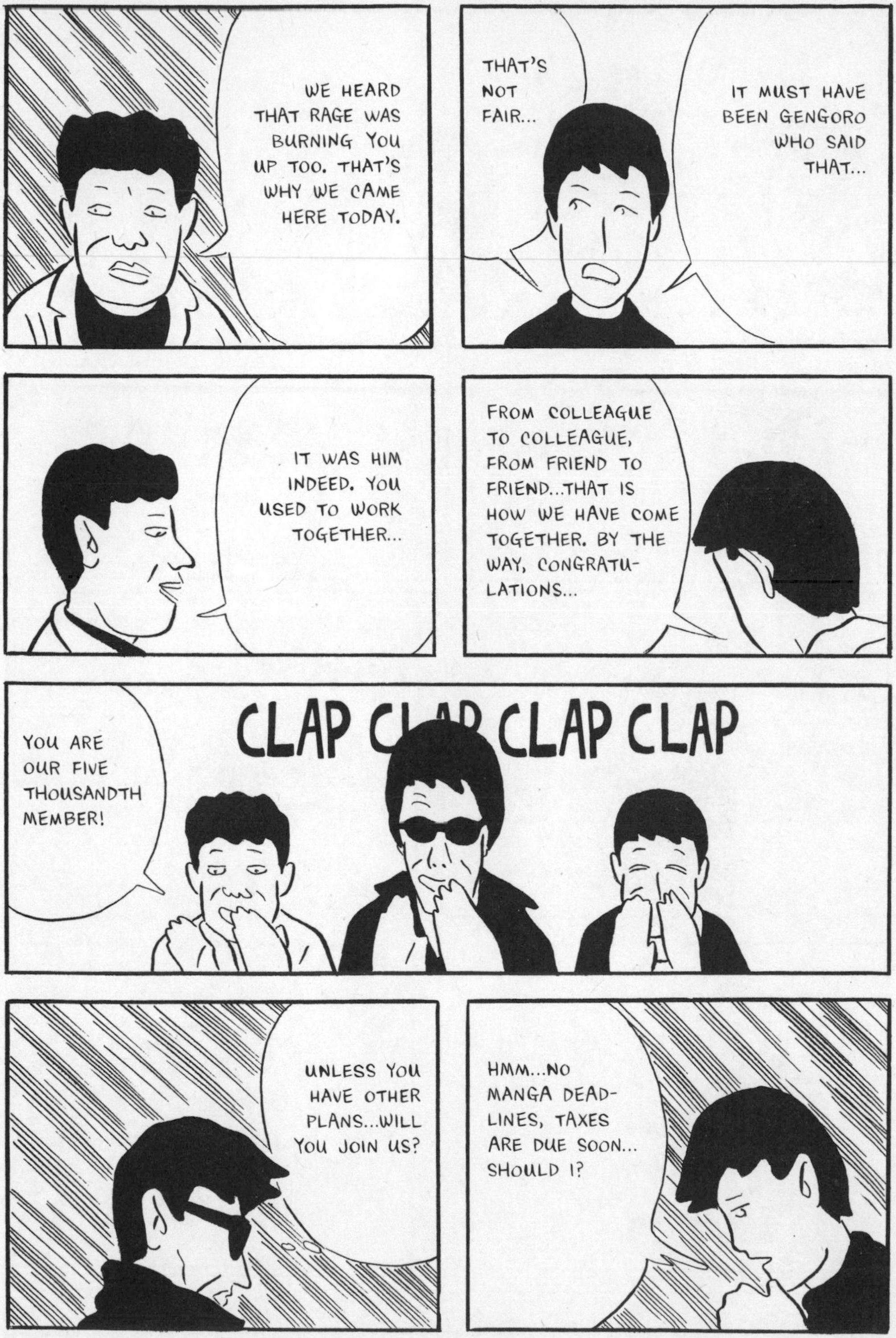
WE HEARD THAT RAGE WAS BURNING YOU UP TOO. THAT'S WHY WE CAME HERE TODAY.
THAT'S NOT FAIR...
IT MUST HAVE BEEN GENGORO WHO SAID THAT...
IT WAS HIM INDEED. YOU USED TO WORK TOGETHER...
FROM COLLEAGUE TO COLLEAGUE, FROM FRIEND TO FRIEND...THAT IS HOW WE HAVE COME TOGETHER. BY THE WAY, CONGRATU-LATIONS...
YOU ARE OUR FIVE THOUSANDTH MEMBER!
CLAP CLAP CLAP CLAP
UNLESS YOU HAVE OTHER PLANS...WILL YOU JOIN US?
HMM...NO MANGA DEAD-LINES, TAXES ARE DUE SOON... SHOULD I?

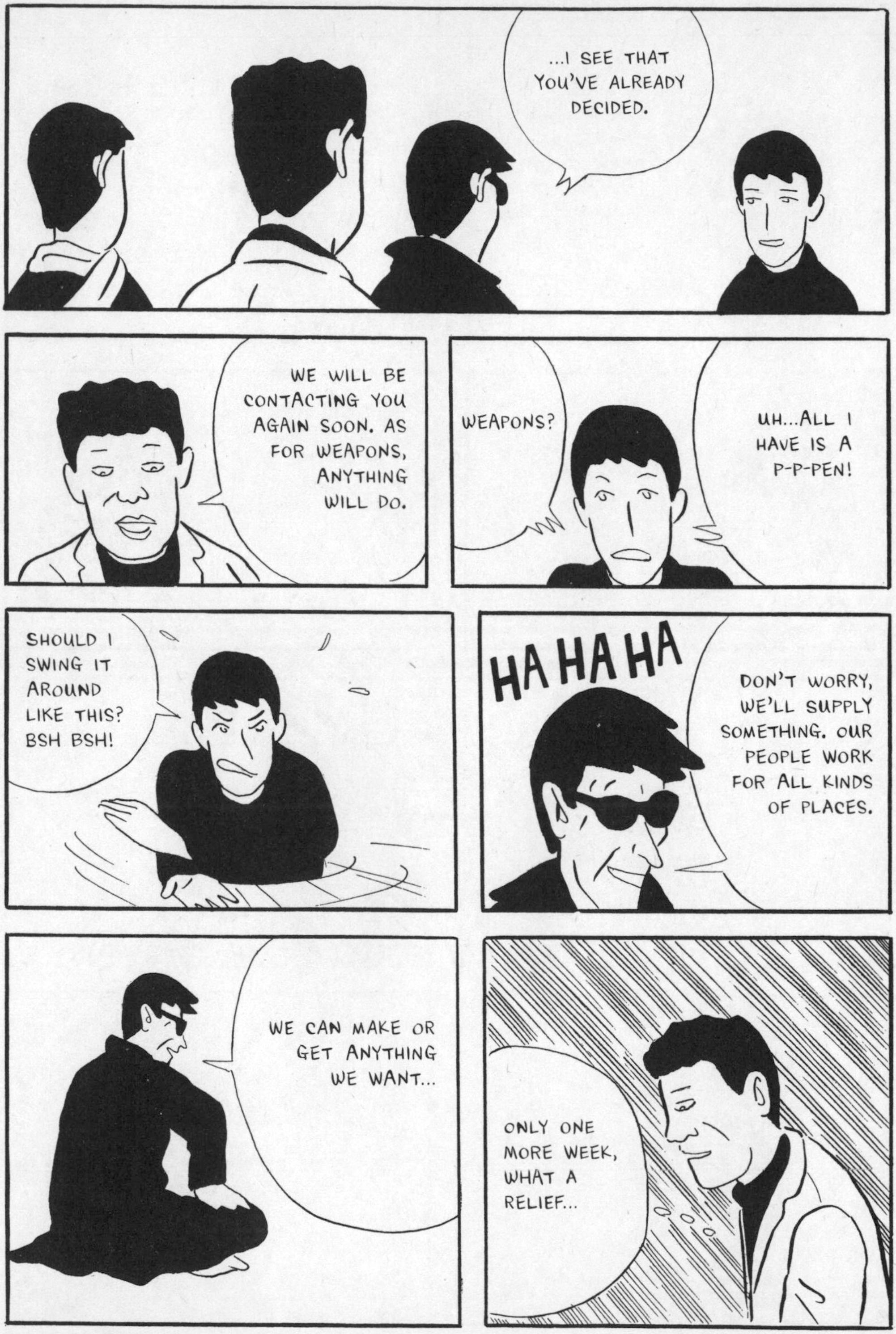
...I SEE THAT YOU'VE ALREADY DECIDED.
WE WILL BE CONTACTING YOU AGAIN SOON. AS FOR WEAPONS, ANYTHING WILL DO.
WEAPONS?
UH...ALL I HAVE IS A P-P-PEN!
SHOULD I SWING IT AROUND LIKE THIS? BSH BSH!
HA HA HA
DON'T WORRY, WE'LL SUPPLY SOMETHING. OUR PEOPLE WORK FOR ALL KINDS OF PLACES.
WE CAN MAKE OR GET ANYTHING WE WANT...
ONLY ONE MORE WEEK, WHAT A RELIEF...

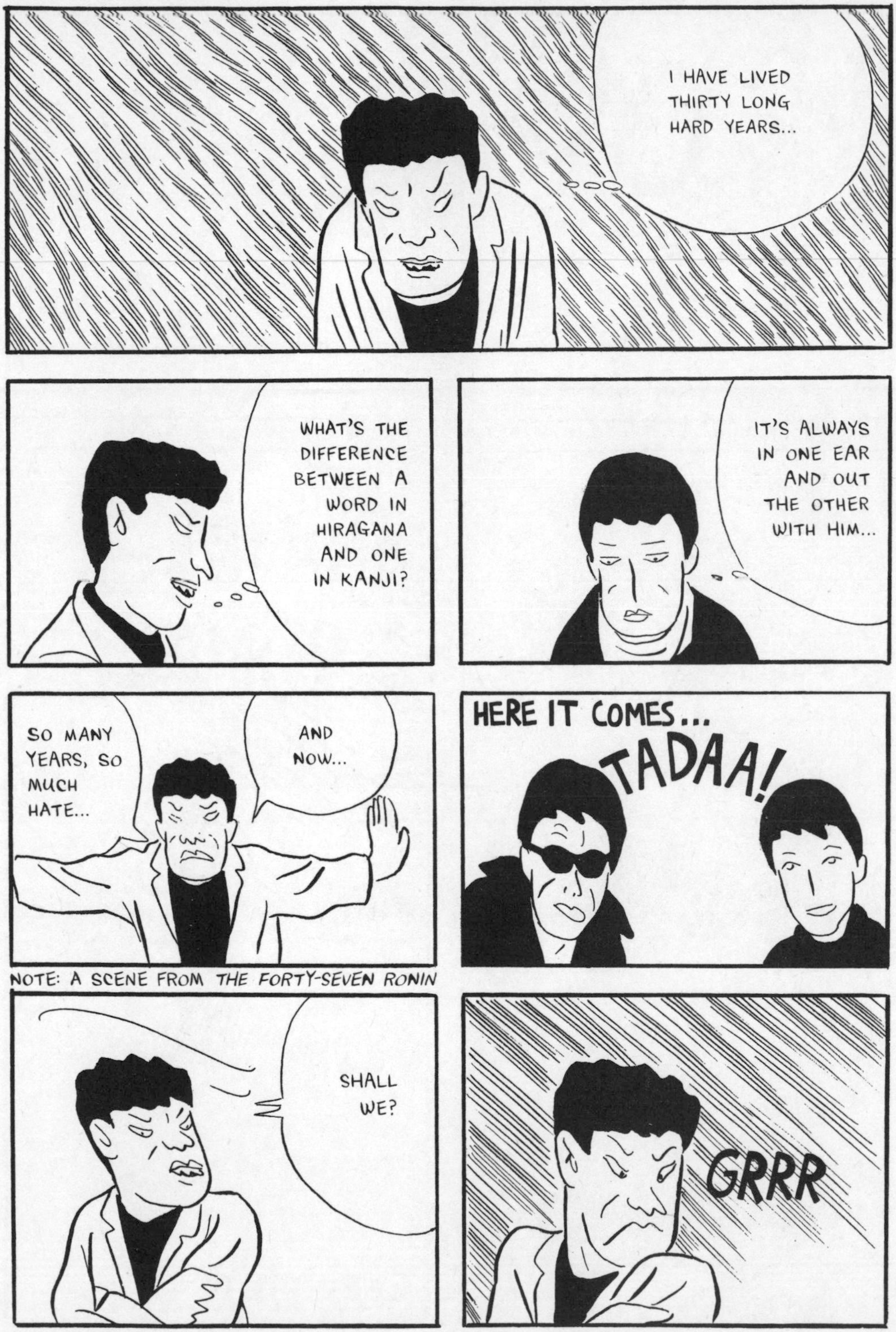
I HAVE LIVED THIRTY LONG HARD YEARS...
WHAT'S THE DIFFERENCE BETWEEN A WORD IN HIRAGANA AND ONE IN KANJI?
IT'S ALWAYS IN ONE EAR AND OUT THE OTHER WITH HIM...
SO MANY YEARS, SO MUCH HATE...
AND NOW...
NOTE: A SCENE FROM *THE FORTY-SEVEN RONIN*
HERE IT COMES...
TADAA!
SHALL WE?
GRRR

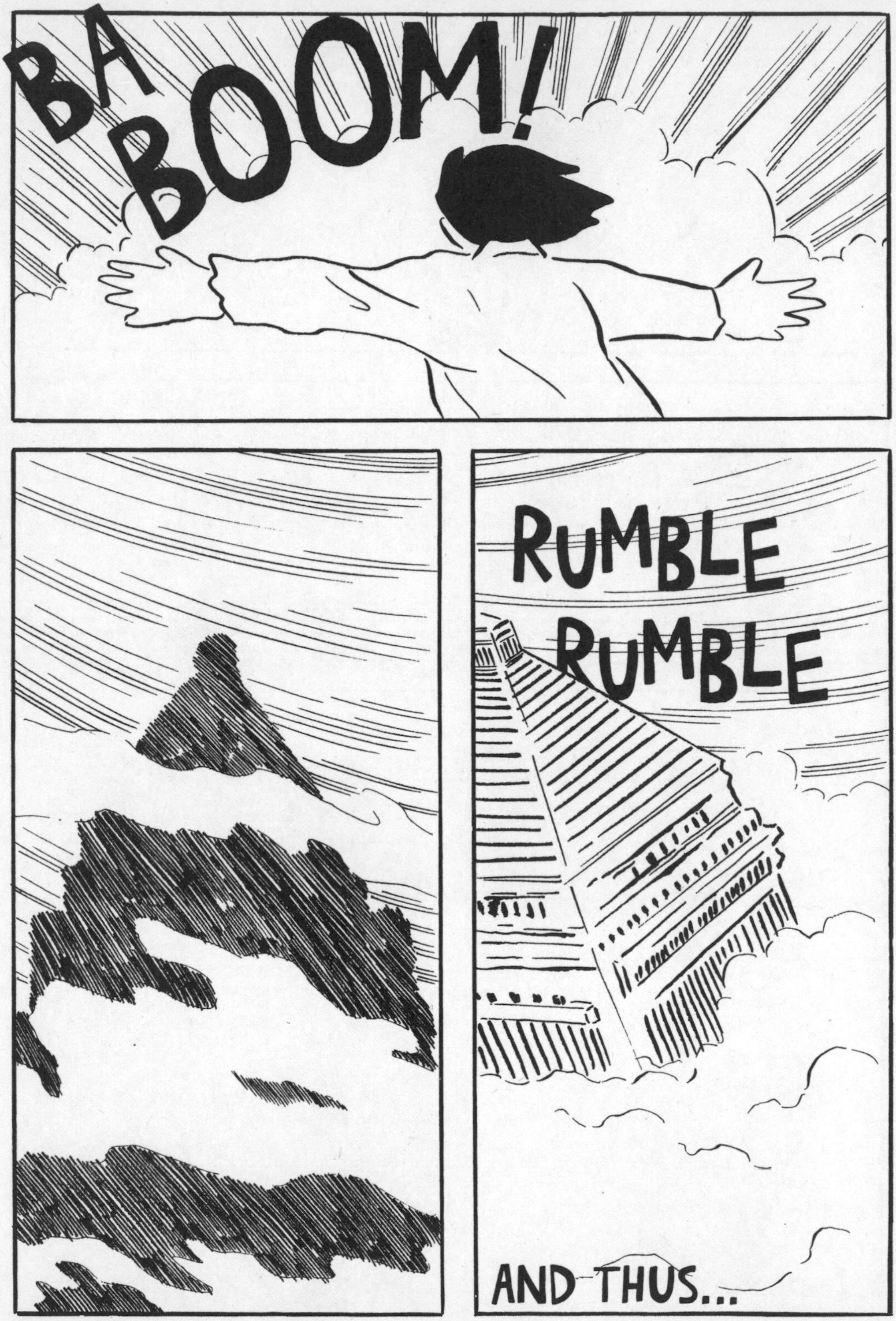
BA BOOM!
RUMBLE RUMBLE
AND THUS...

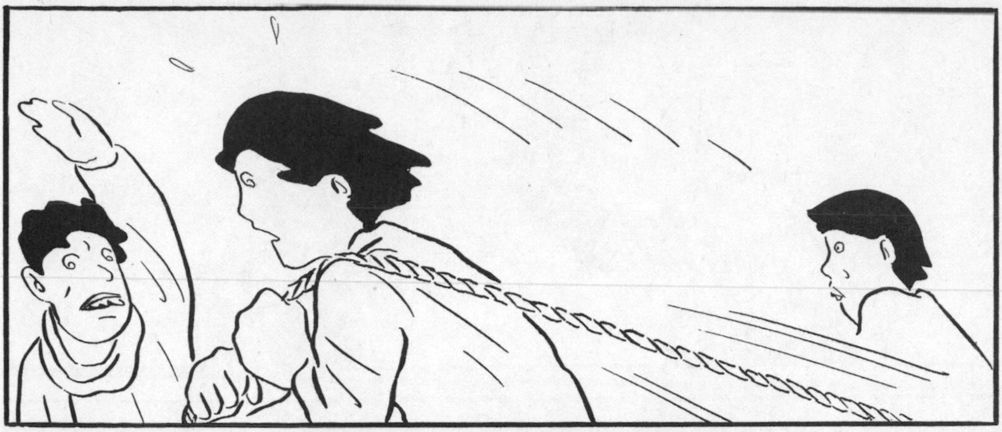

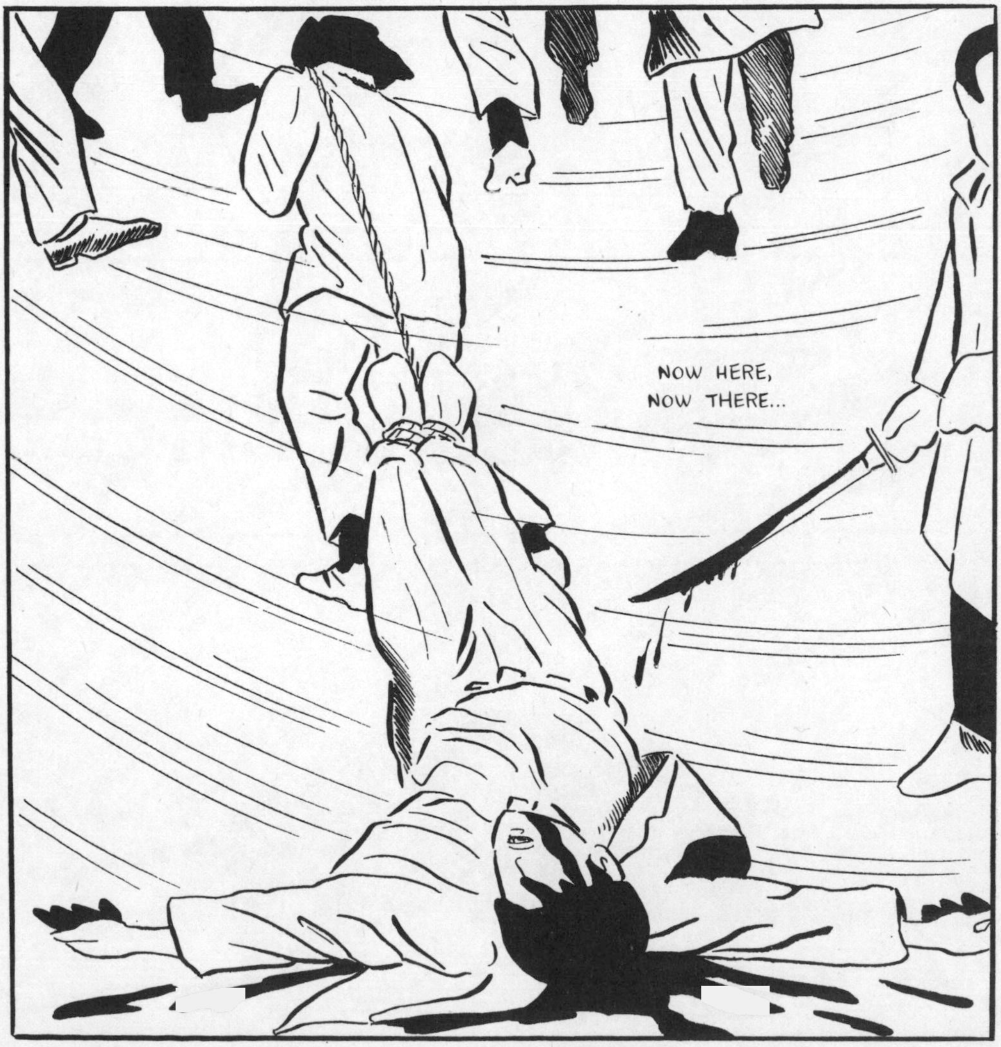
NOW HERE,
NOW THERE...

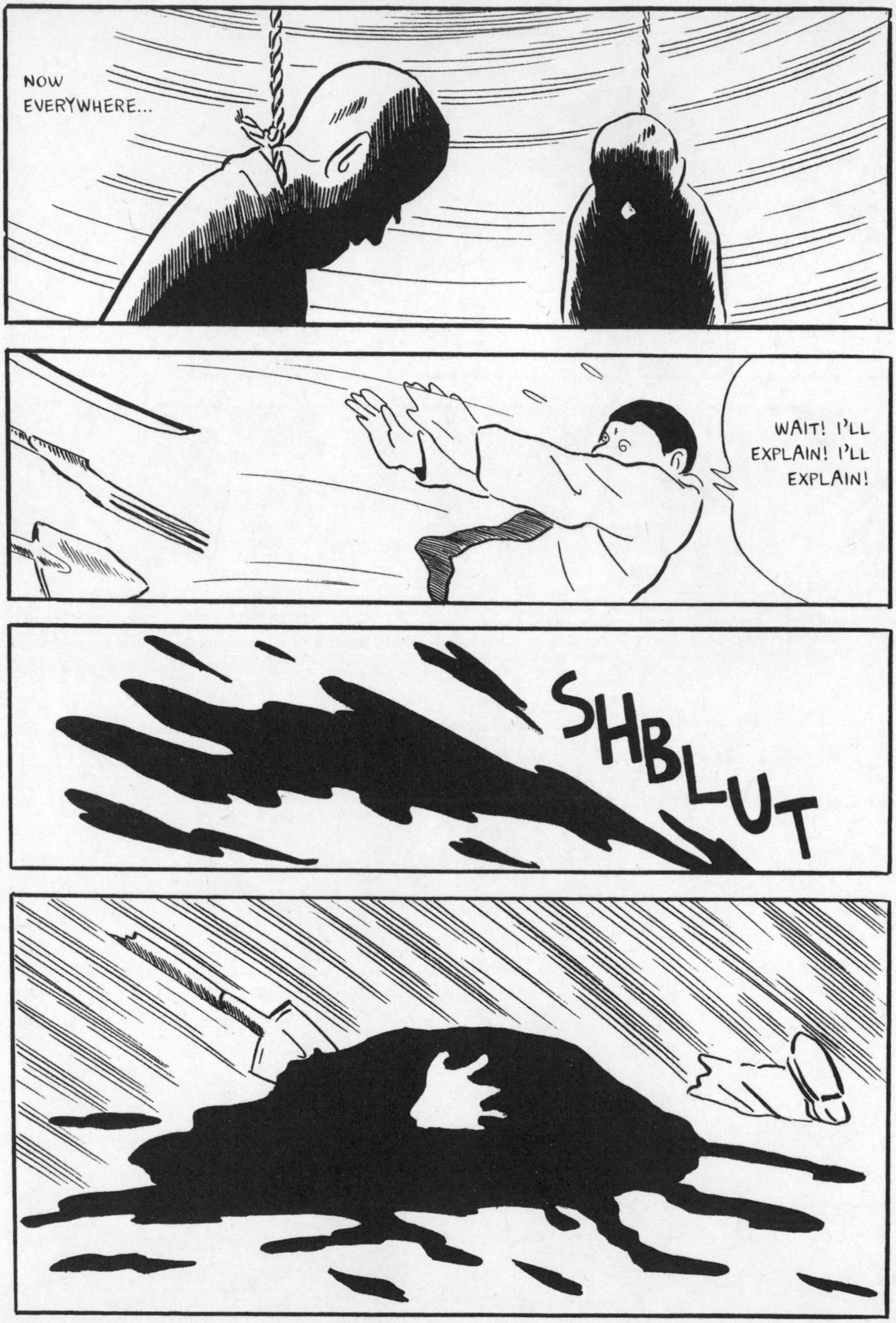
NOW EVERYWHERE...
WAIT! I'LL EXPLAIN! I'LL EXPLAIN!
SHBLUT

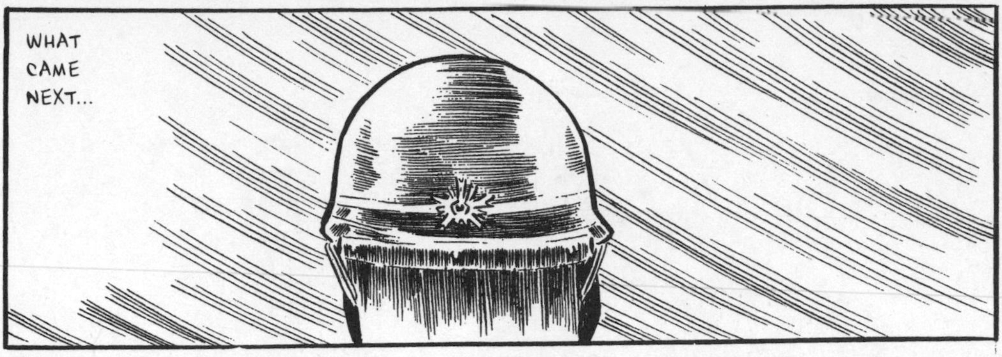
WHAT CAME NEXT...
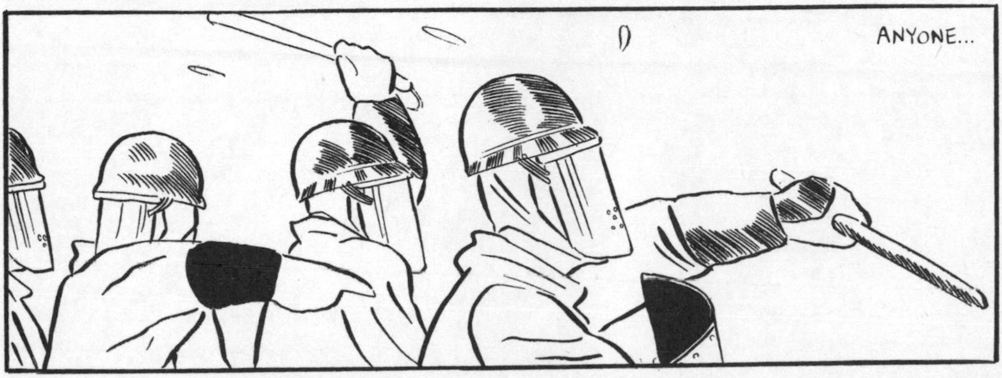
ANYONE...
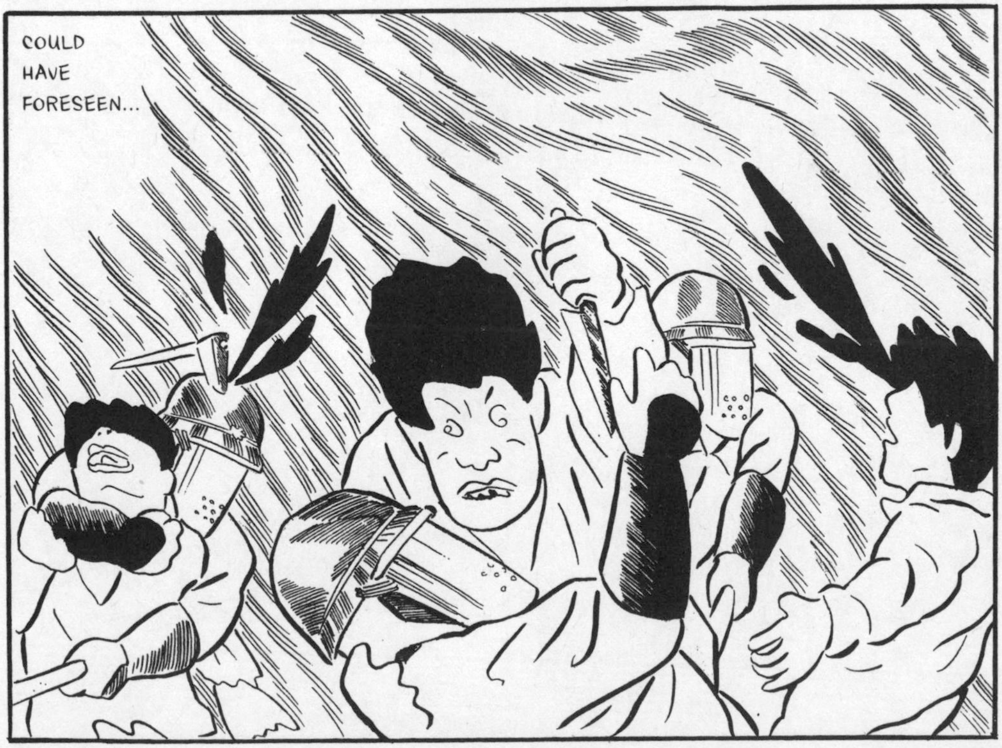
COULD HAVE FORESEEN...

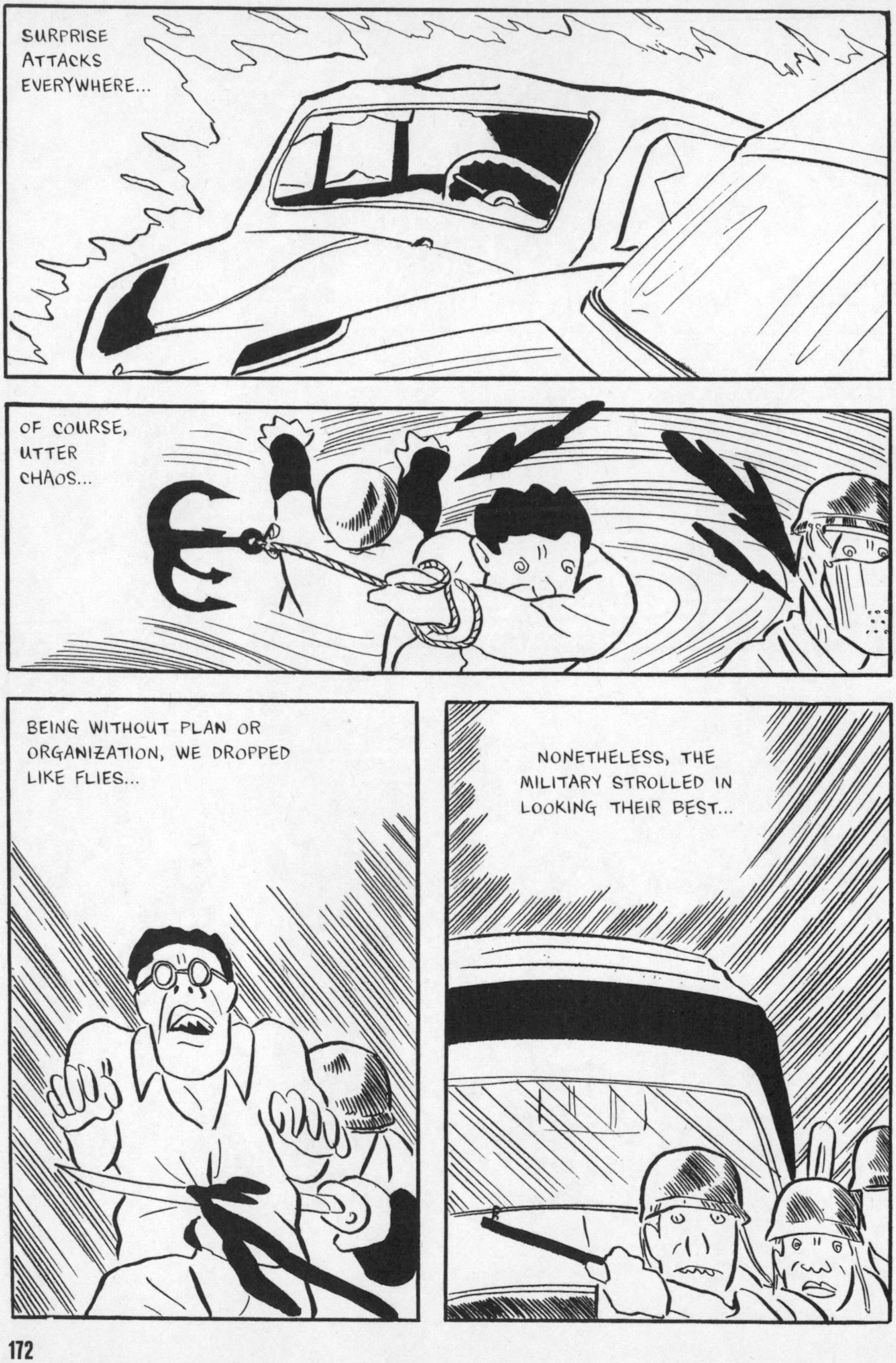
SURPRISE ATTACKS EVERYWHERE...
OF COURSE, UTTER CHAOS...
BEING WITHOUT PLAN OR ORGANIZATION, WE DROPPED LIKE FLIES...
NONETHELESS, THE MILITARY STROLLED IN LOOKING THEIR BEST...

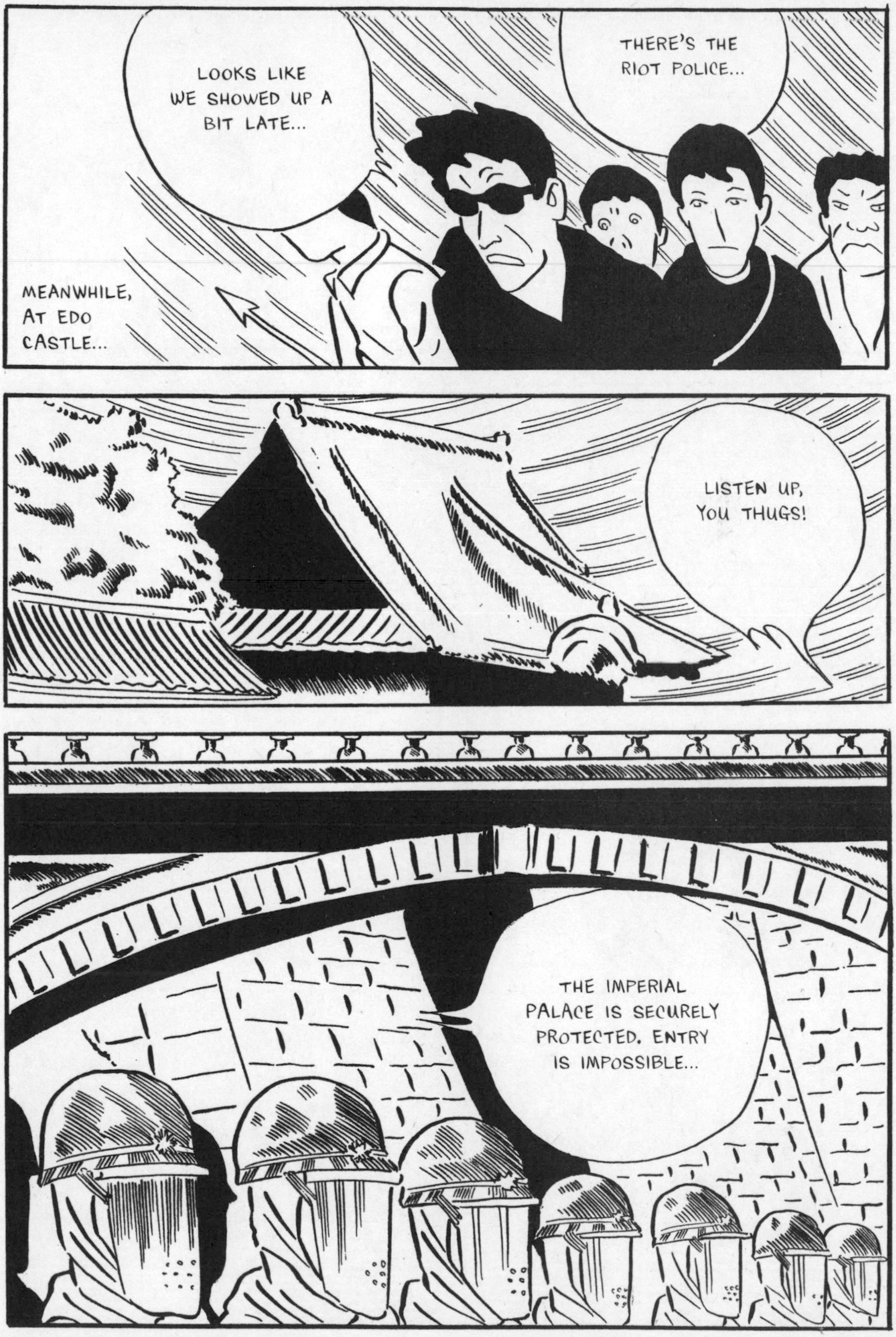
MEANWHILE, AT EDO CASTLE...
LOOKS LIKE WE SHOWED UP A BIT LATE...
THERE'S THE RIOT POLICE...
LISTEN UP, YOU THUGS!
THE IMPERIAL PALACE IS SECURELY PROTECTED. ENTRY IS IMPOSSIBLE...

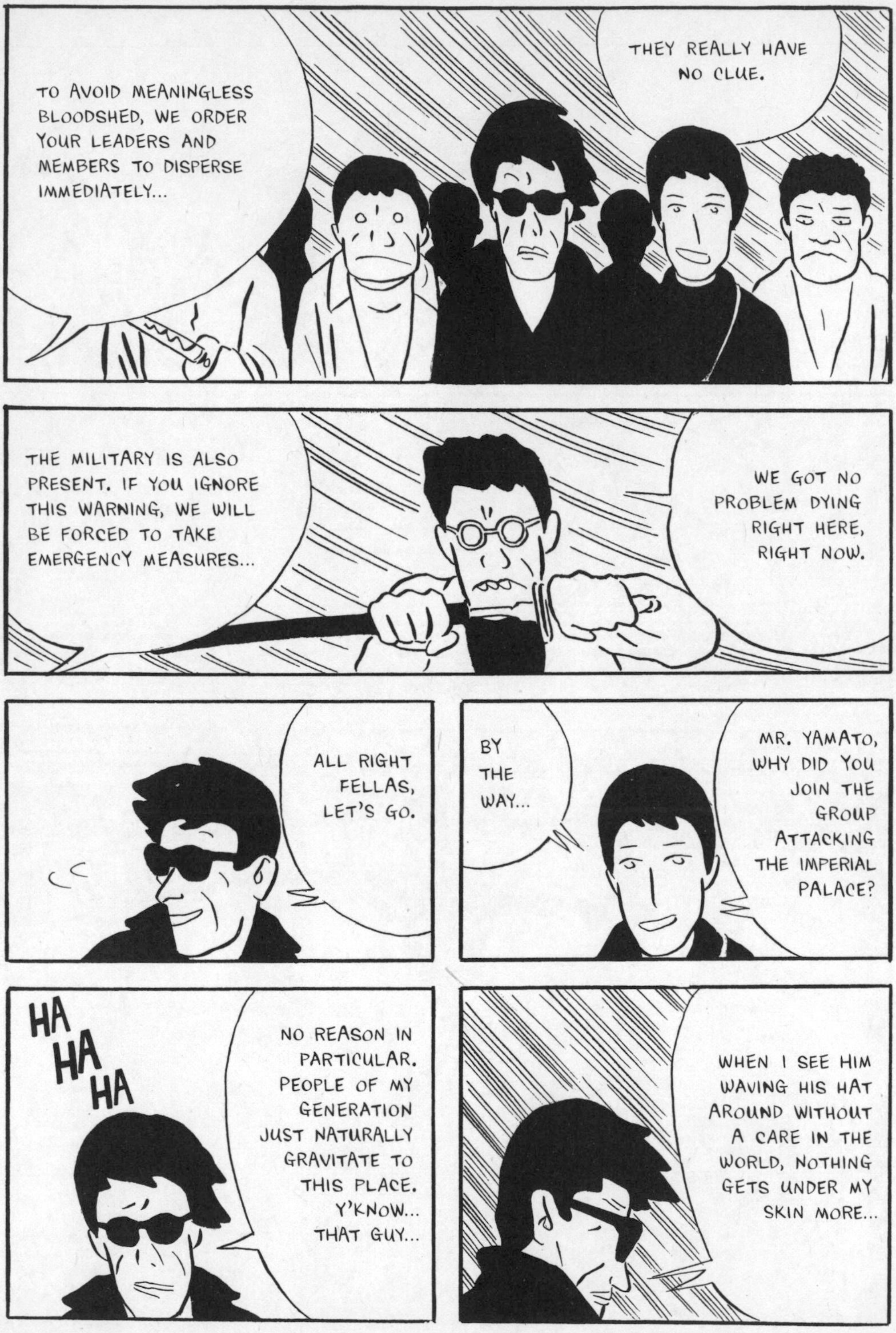
TO AVOID MEANINGLESS BLOODSHED, WE ORDER YOUR LEADERS AND MEMBERS TO DISPERSE IMMEDIATELY...
THEY REALLY HAVE NO CLUE.
THE MILITARY IS ALSO PRESENT. IF YOU IGNORE THIS WARNING, WE WILL BE FORCED TO TAKE EMERGENCY MEASURES...
WE GOT NO PROBLEM DYING RIGHT HERE, RIGHT NOW.
ALL RIGHT FELLAS, LET'S GO.
BY THE WAY...
MR. YAMATO, WHY DID YOU JOIN THE GROUP ATTACKING THE IMPERIAL PALACE?
HA HA HA
NO REASON IN PARTICULAR. PEOPLE OF MY GENERATION JUST NATURALLY GRAVITATE TO THIS PLACE. Y'KNOW... THAT GUY...
WHEN I SEE HIM WAVING HIS HAT AROUND WITHOUT A CARE IN THE WORLD, NOTHING GETS UNDER MY SKIN MORE...

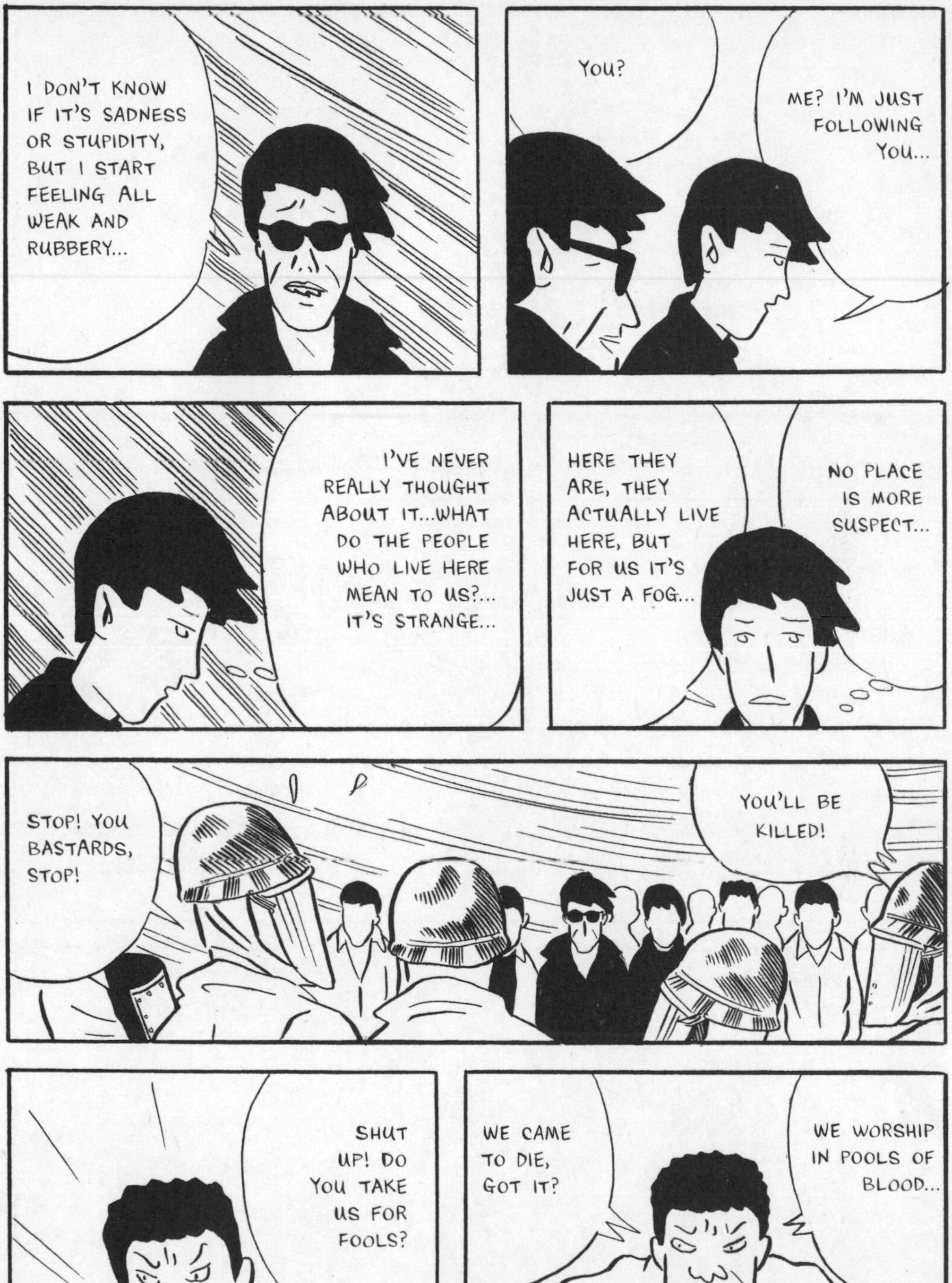
I DON'T KNOW IF IT'S SADNESS OR STUPIDITY, BUT I START FEELING ALL WEAK AND RUBBERY...
YOU?
ME? I'M JUST FOLLOWING YOU...
I'VE NEVER REALLY THOUGHT ABOUT IT...WHAT DO THE PEOPLE WHO LIVE HERE MEAN TO US?... IT'S STRANGE...
HERE THEY ARE, THEY ACTUALLY LIVE HERE, BUT FOR US IT'S JUST A FOG...
NO PLACE IS MORE SUSPECT...
STOP! YOU BASTARDS, STOP!
YOU'LL BE KILLED!
SHUT UP! DO YOU TAKE US FOR FOOLS?
WE CAME TO DIE, GOT IT?
WE WORSHIP IN POOLS OF BLOOD...

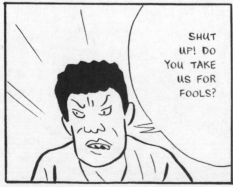

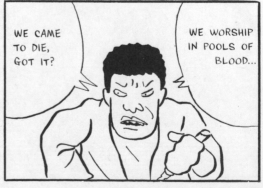

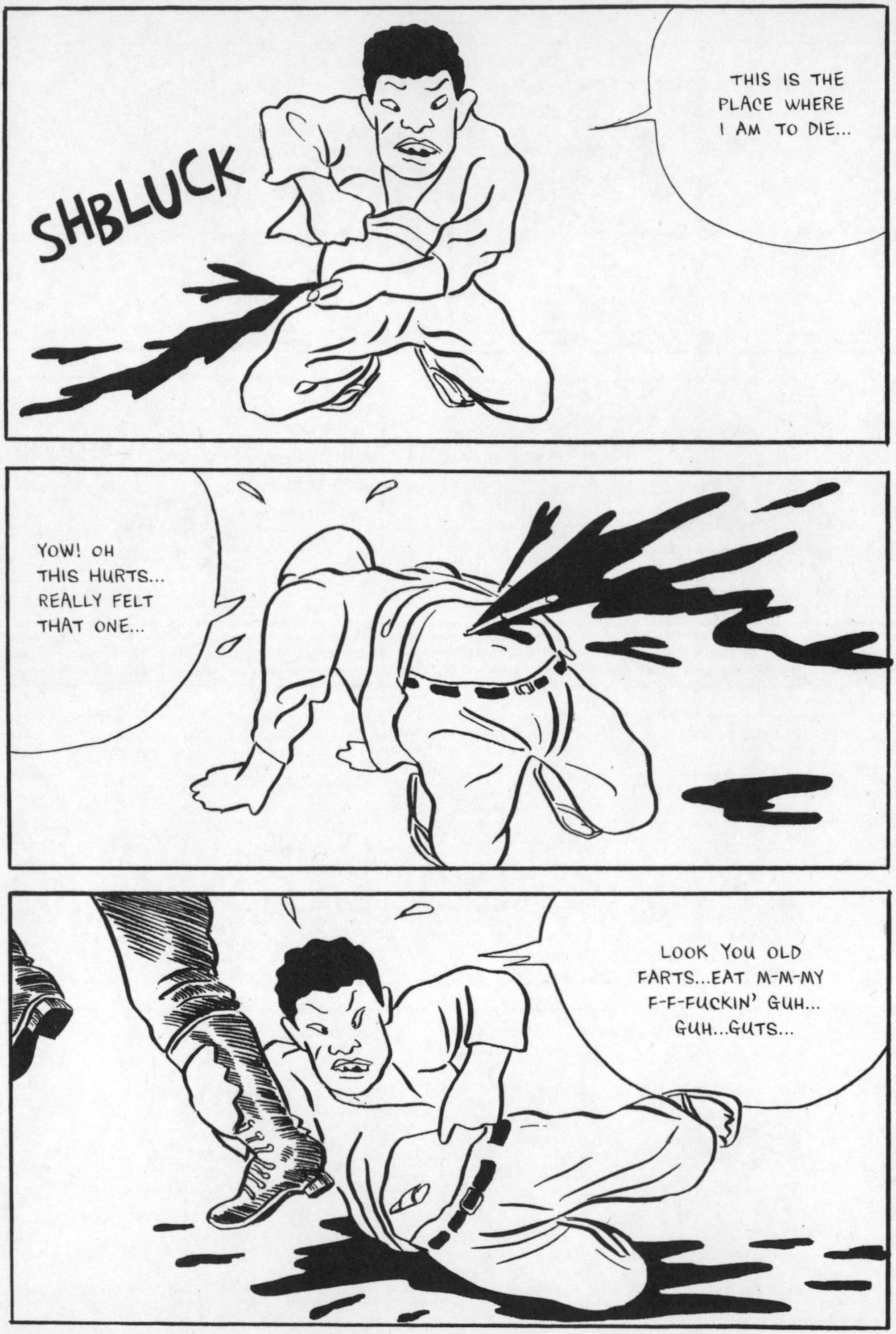
SHBLUCK
THIS IS THE PLACE WHERE I AM TO DIE...
YOW! OH THIS HURTS... REALLY FELT THAT ONE...
LOOK YOU OLD FARTS...EAT M-M-MY F-F-FUCKIN' GUH... GUH...GUTS...

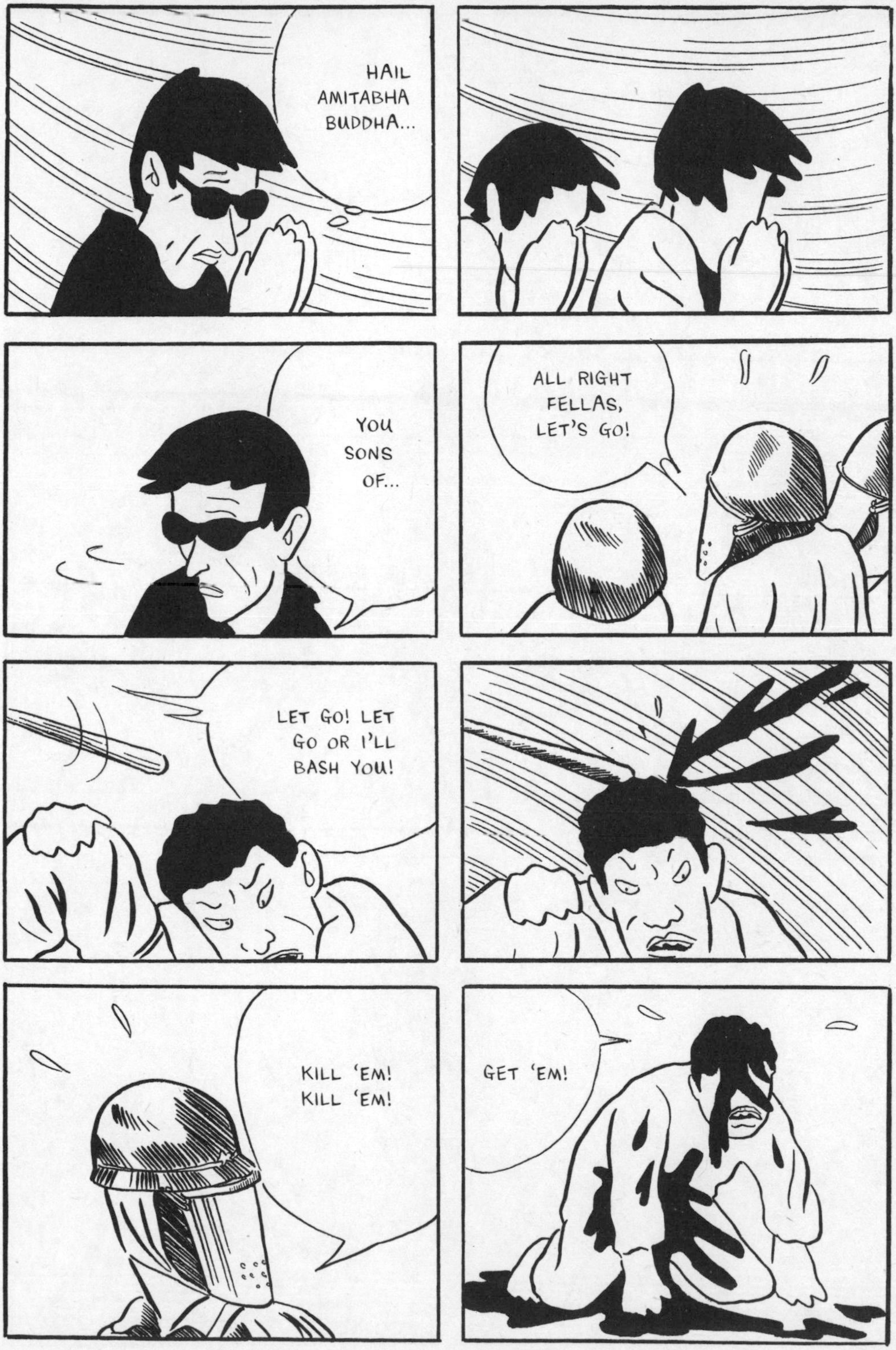
HAIL AMITABHA BUDDHA...
YOU SONS OF...
ALL RIGHT FELLAS, LET'S GO!
LET GO! LET GO OR I'LL BASH YOU!
KILL 'EM! KILL 'EM!
GET 'EM!

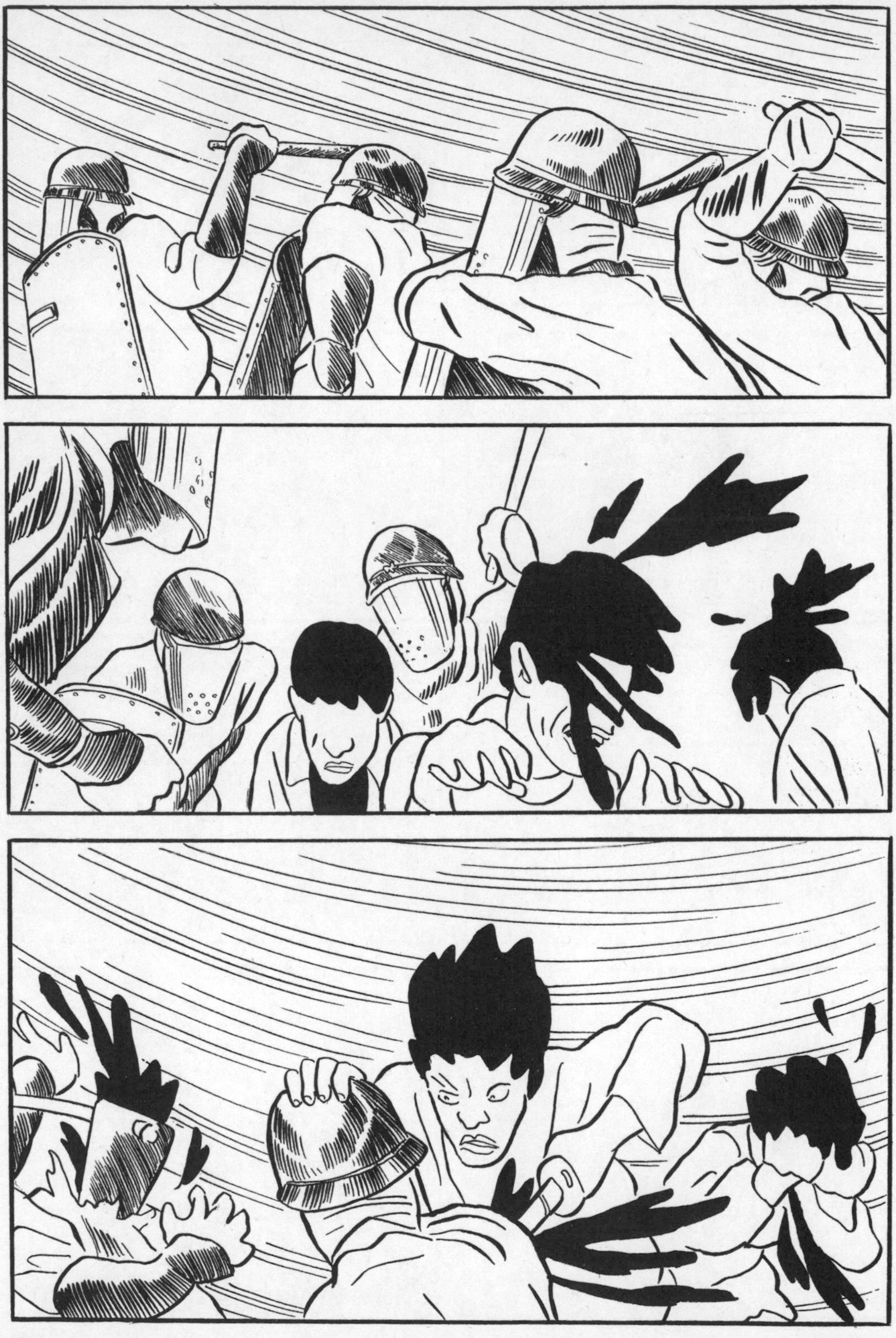

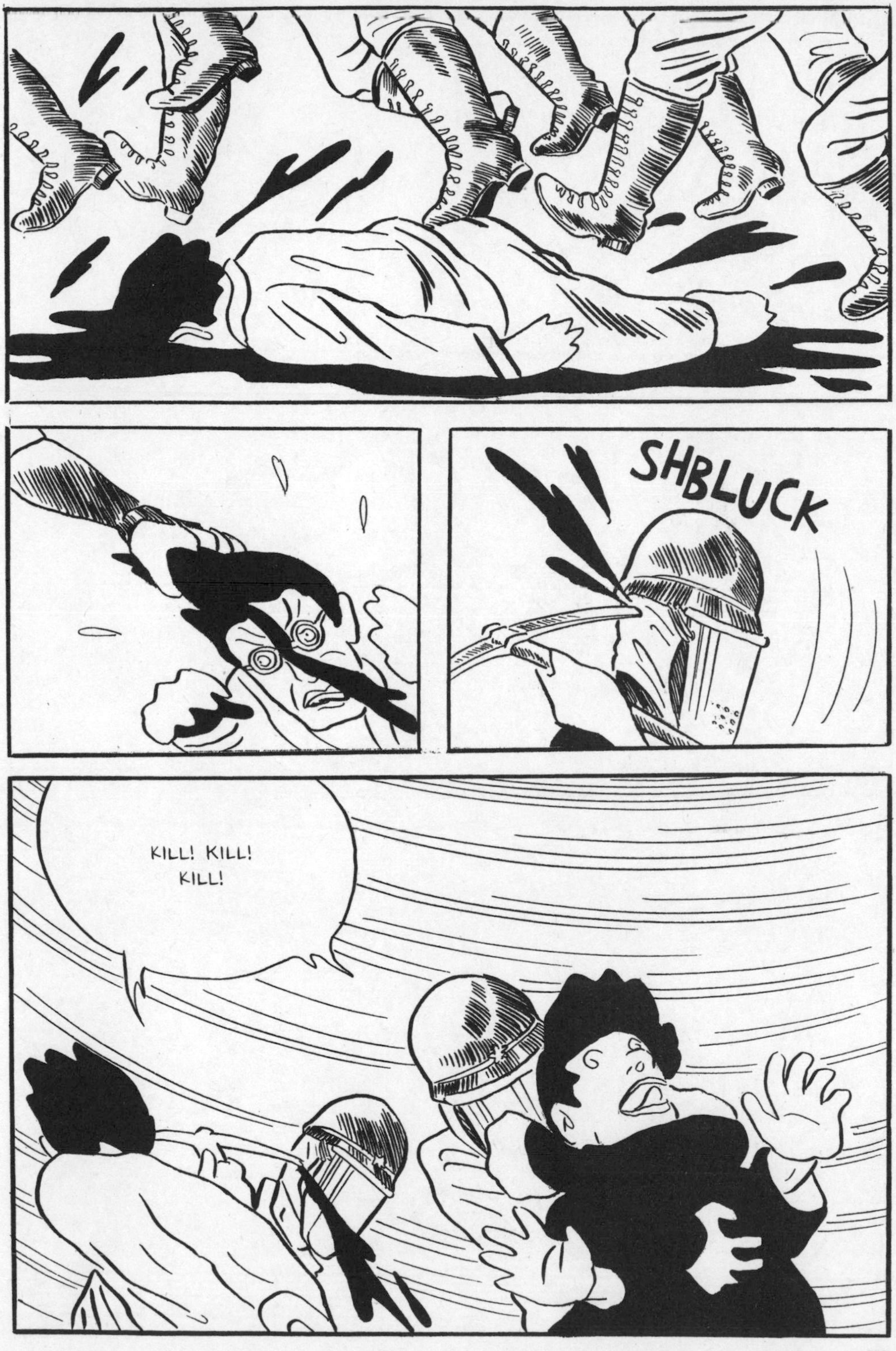
SHBLUCK
KILL! KILL! KILL!

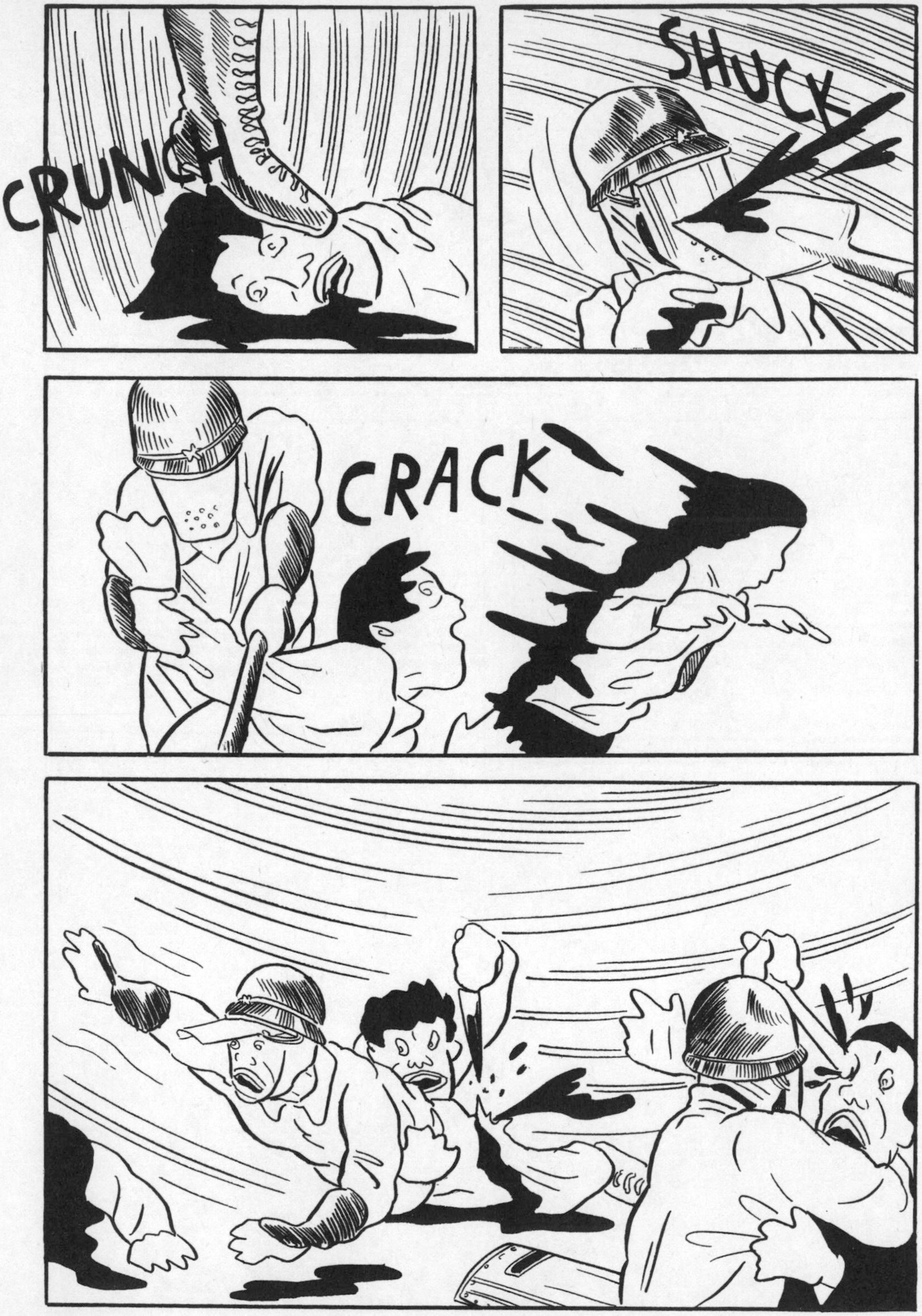
CRUNCH
SHUCK
CRACK

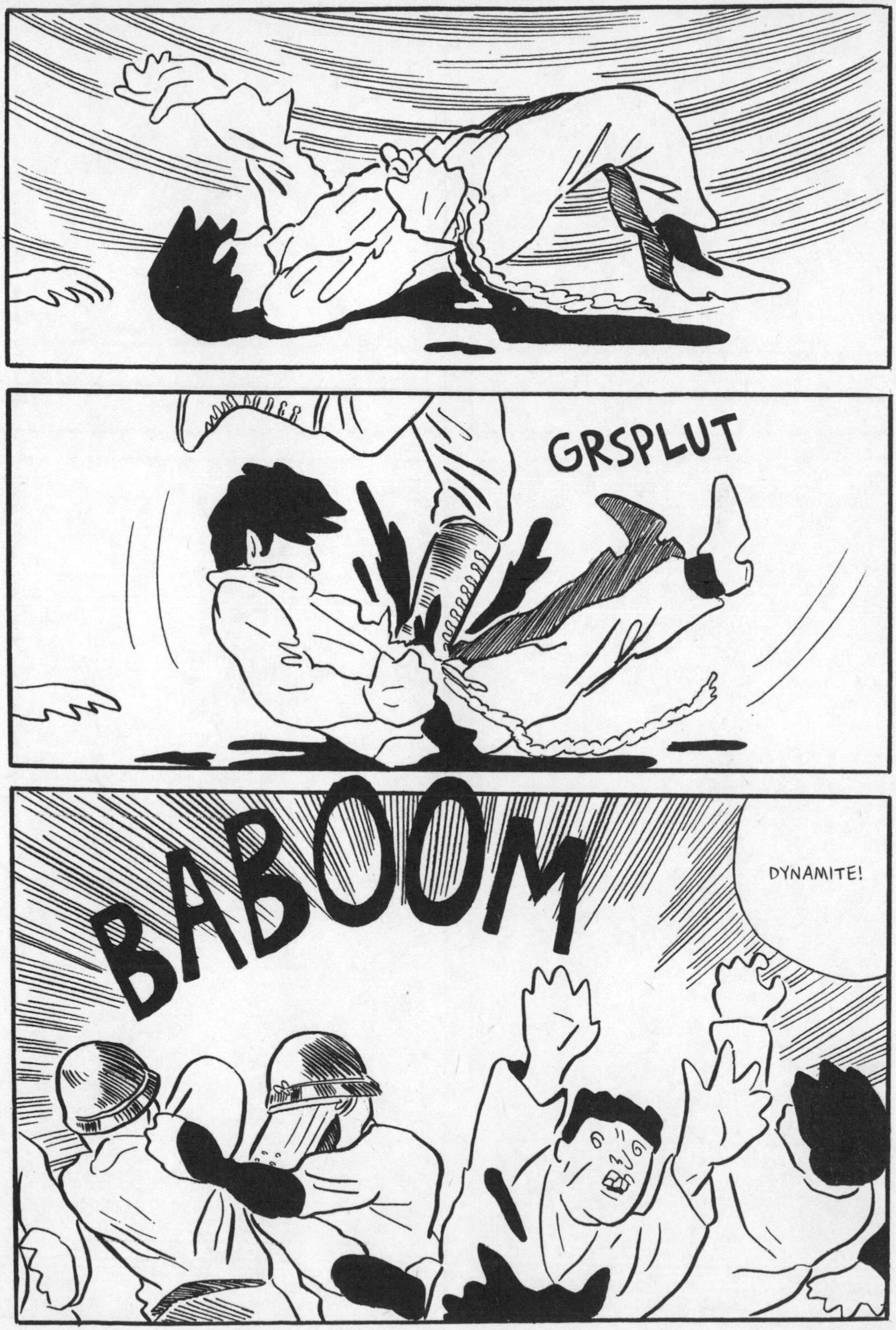
GRSPLUT
BABOOM
DYNAMITE!

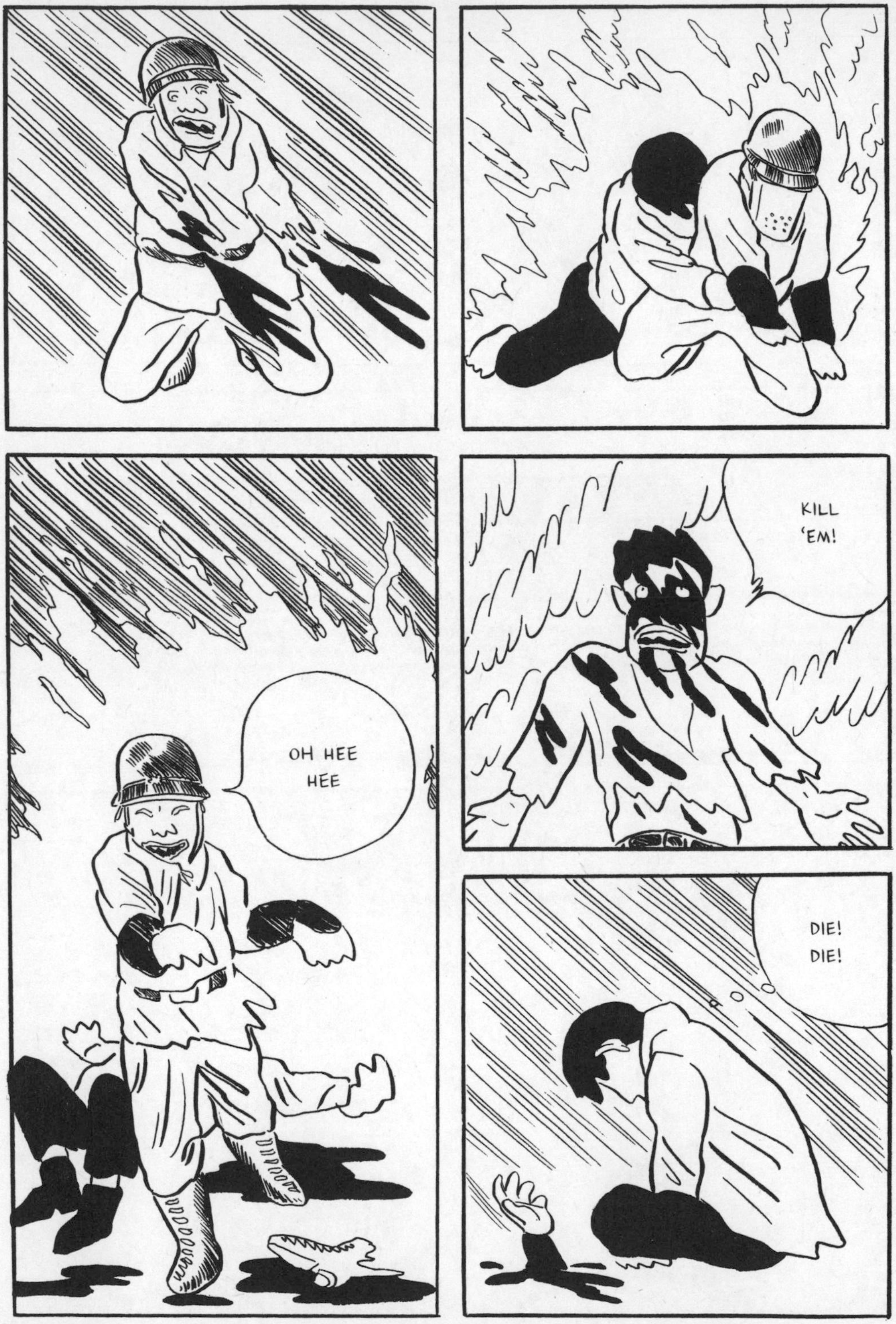
OH HEE
HEE
KILL
'EM!
DIE!
DIE!

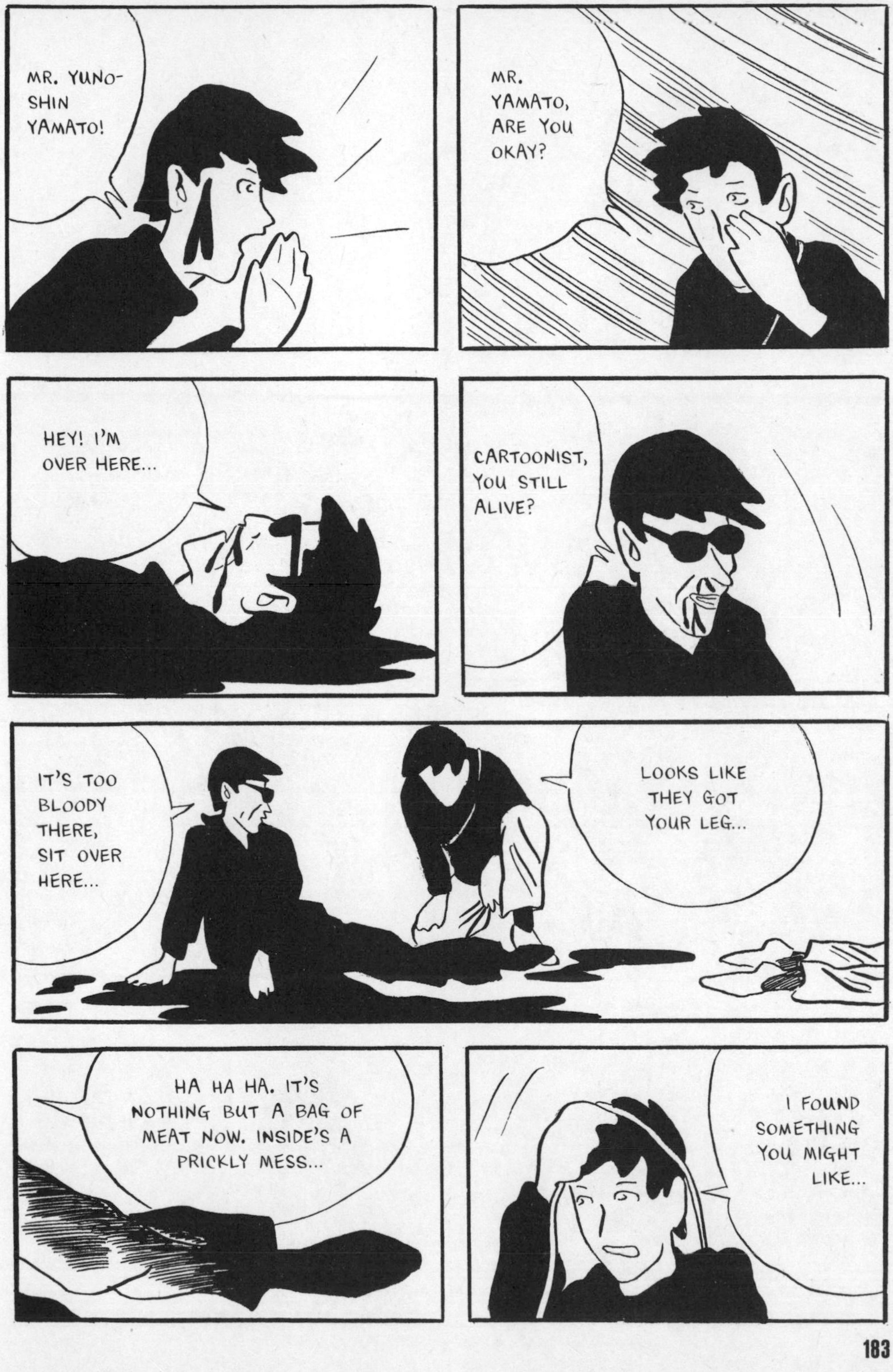
MR. YUNO-SHIN YAMATO!
MR. YAMATO, ARE YOU OKAY?
HEY! I'M OVER HERE...
CARTOONIST, YOU STILL ALIVE?
IT'S TOO BLOODY THERE, SIT OVER HERE...
LOOKS LIKE THEY GOT YOUR LEG...
HA HA HA. IT'S NOTHING BUT A BAG OF MEAT NOW. INSIDE'S A PRICKLY MESS...
I FOUND SOMETHING YOU MIGHT LIKE...

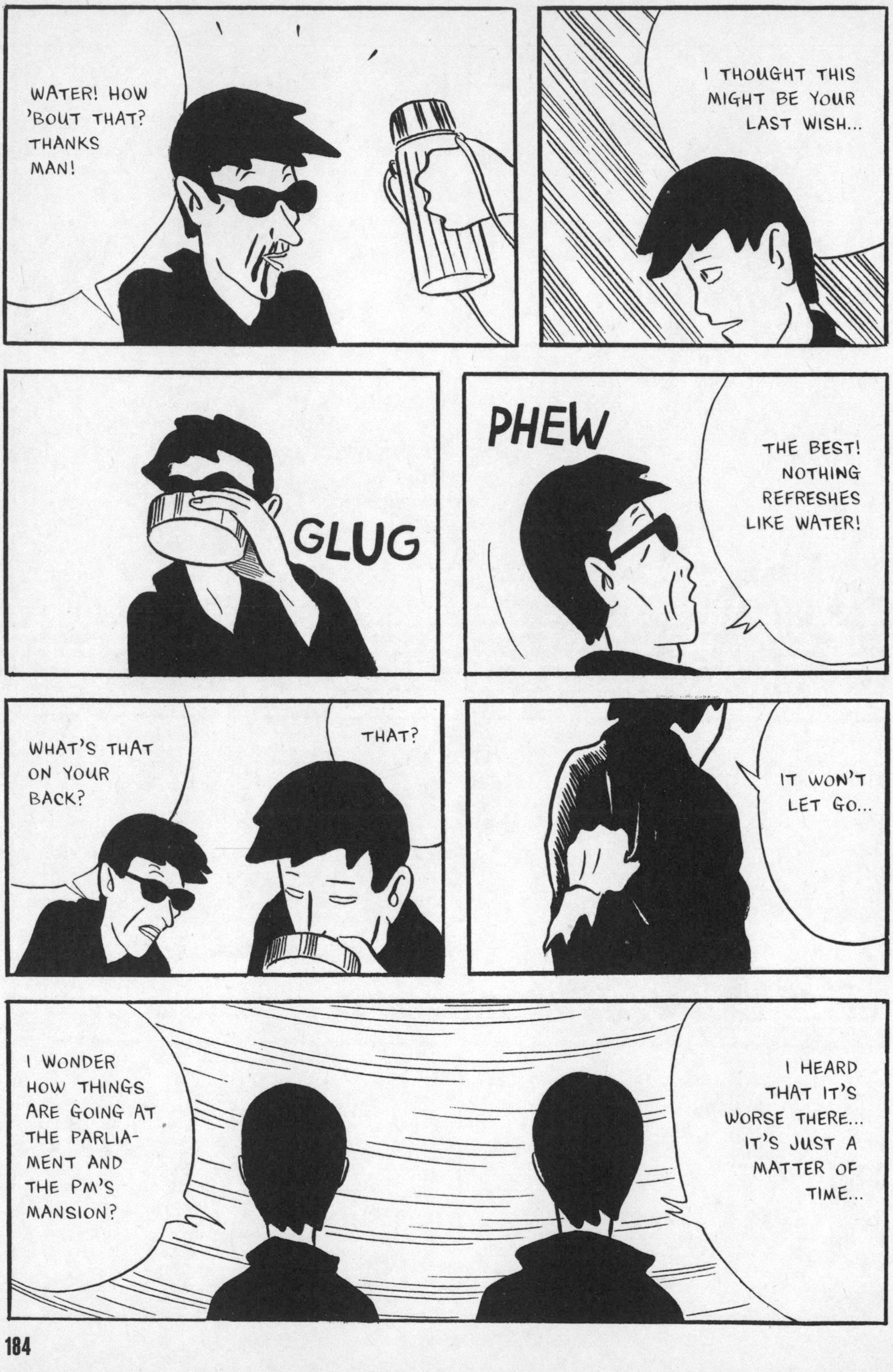
WATER! HOW 'BOUT THAT? THANKS MAN!
I THOUGHT THIS MIGHT BE YOUR LAST WISH...
GLUG
PHEW
THE BEST! NOTHING REFRESHES LIKE WATER!
WHAT'S THAT ON YOUR BACK?
THAT?
IT WON'T LET GO...
I WONDER HOW THINGS ARE GOING AT THE PARLIAMENT AND THE PM'S MANSION?
I HEARD THAT IT'S WORSE THERE... IT'S JUST A MATTER OF TIME...

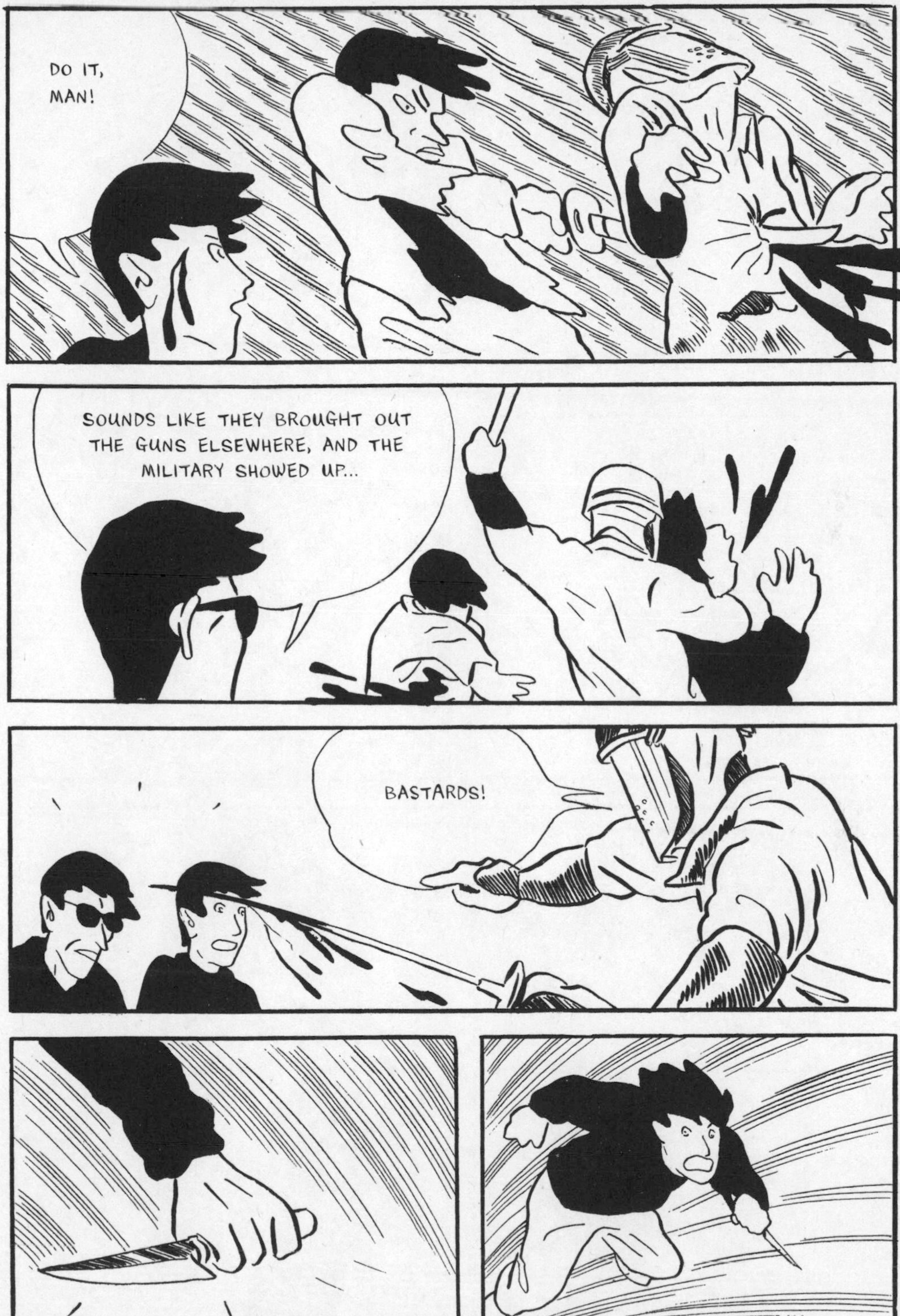
DO IT, MAN!
SOUNDS LIKE THEY BROUGHT OUT THE GUNS ELSEWHERE, AND THE MILITARY SHOWED UP...
BASTARDS!

KEEP YOUR GUARD UP!

CRACK

AMEN

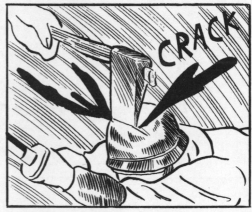

I COULD GET USED TO THIS...

I DIDN'T REALIZE HOW VIOLENT I REALLY AM...

WHAT DIFFERENCE DOES IT MAKE?

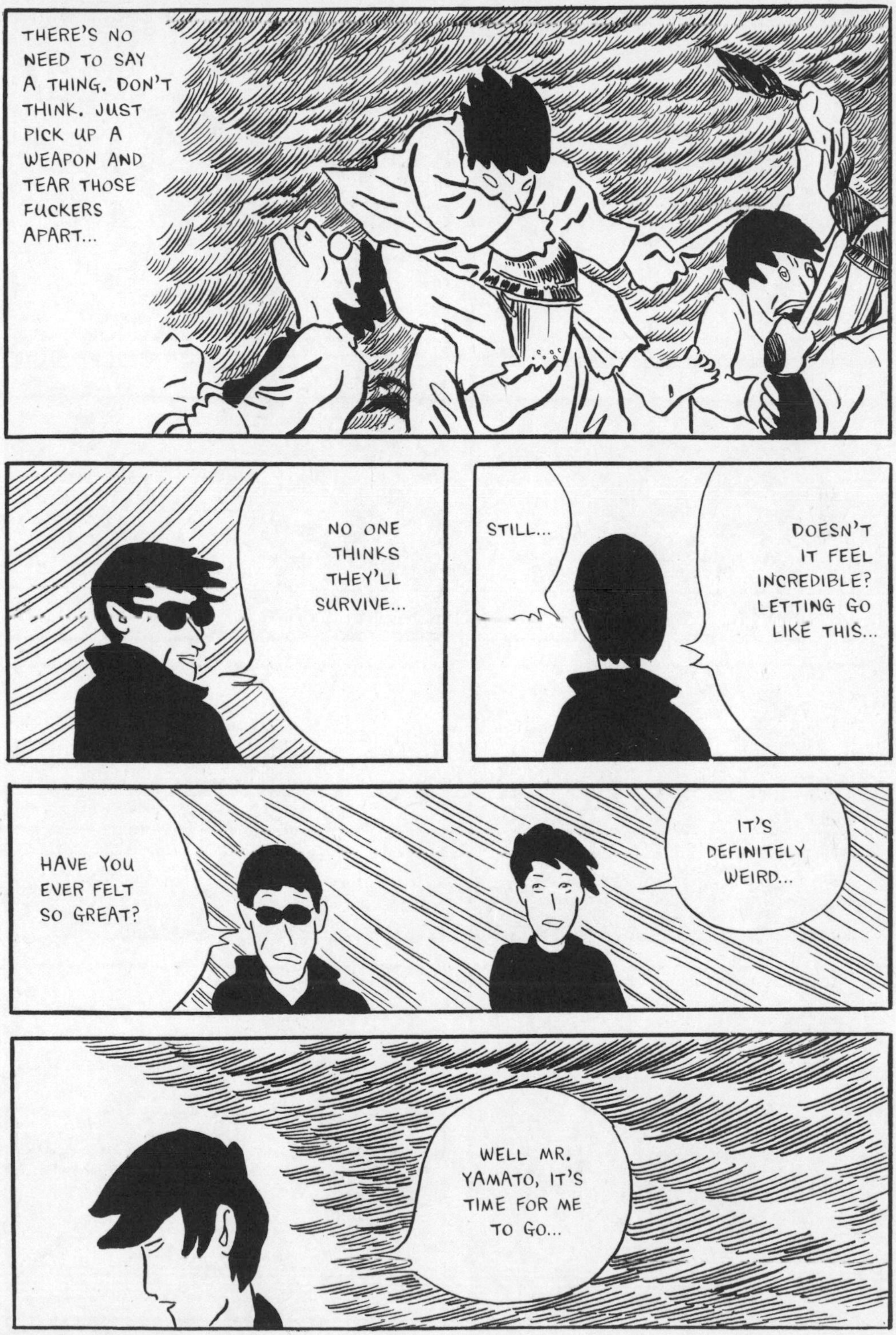
THERE'S NO NEED TO SAY A THING. DON'T THINK. JUST PICK UP A WEAPON AND TEAR THOSE FUCKERS APART...
NO ONE THINKS THEY'LL SURVIVE...
STILL...
DOESN'T IT FEEL INCREDIBLE? LETTING GO LIKE THIS...
HAVE YOU EVER FELT SO GREAT?
IT'S DEFINITELY WEIRD...
WELL MR. YAMATO, IT'S TIME FOR ME TO GO...

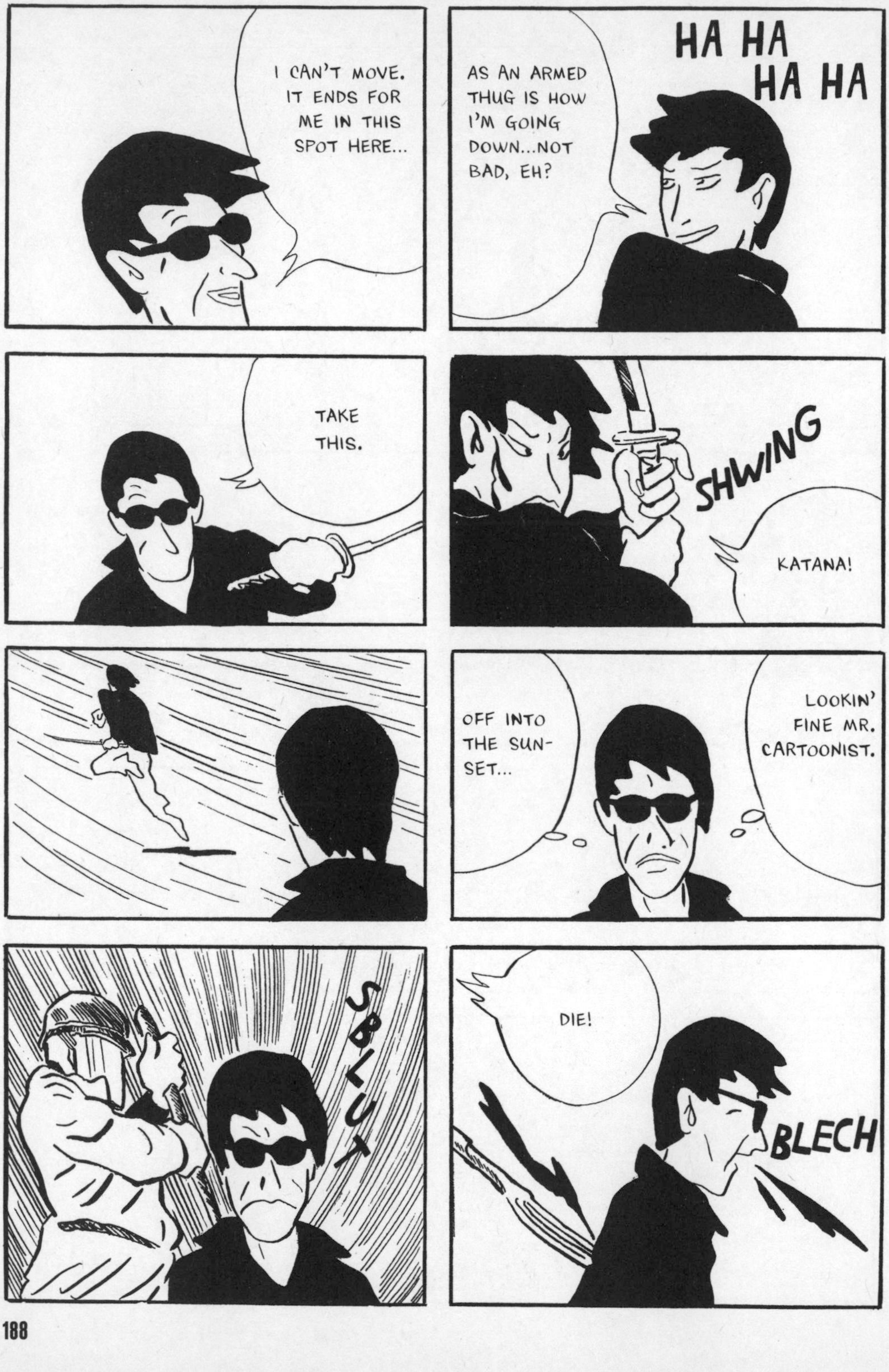
I CAN'T MOVE. IT ENDS FOR ME IN THIS SPOT HERE...
AS AN ARMED THUG IS HOW I'M GOING DOWN...NOT BAD, EH?
HA HA HA HA
TAKE THIS.
SHWING
KATANA!
OFF INTO THE SUN-SET...
LOOKIN' FINE MR. CARTOONIST.
SBLUT
DIE!
BLECH

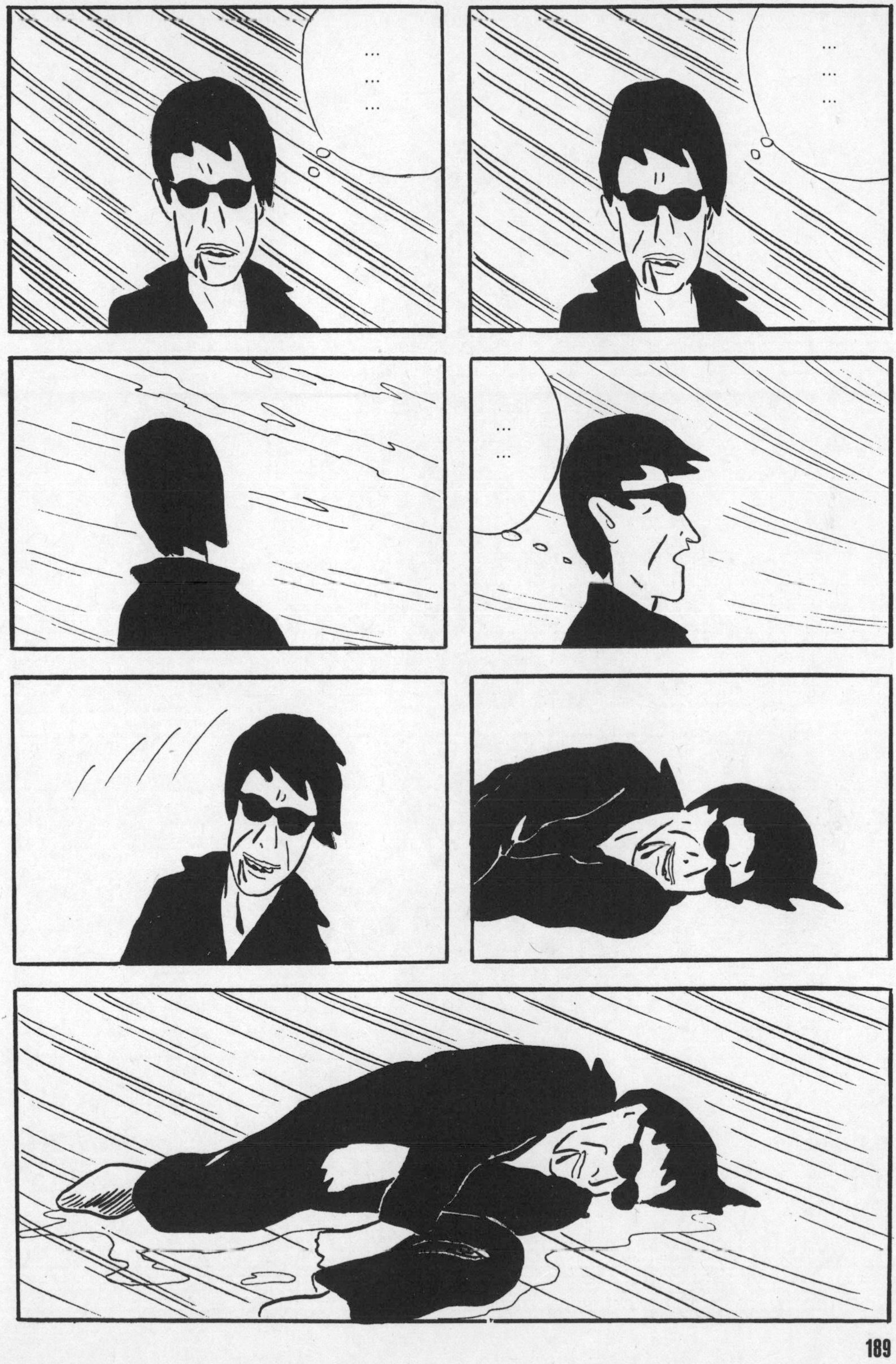

... ...
... ...
... ...

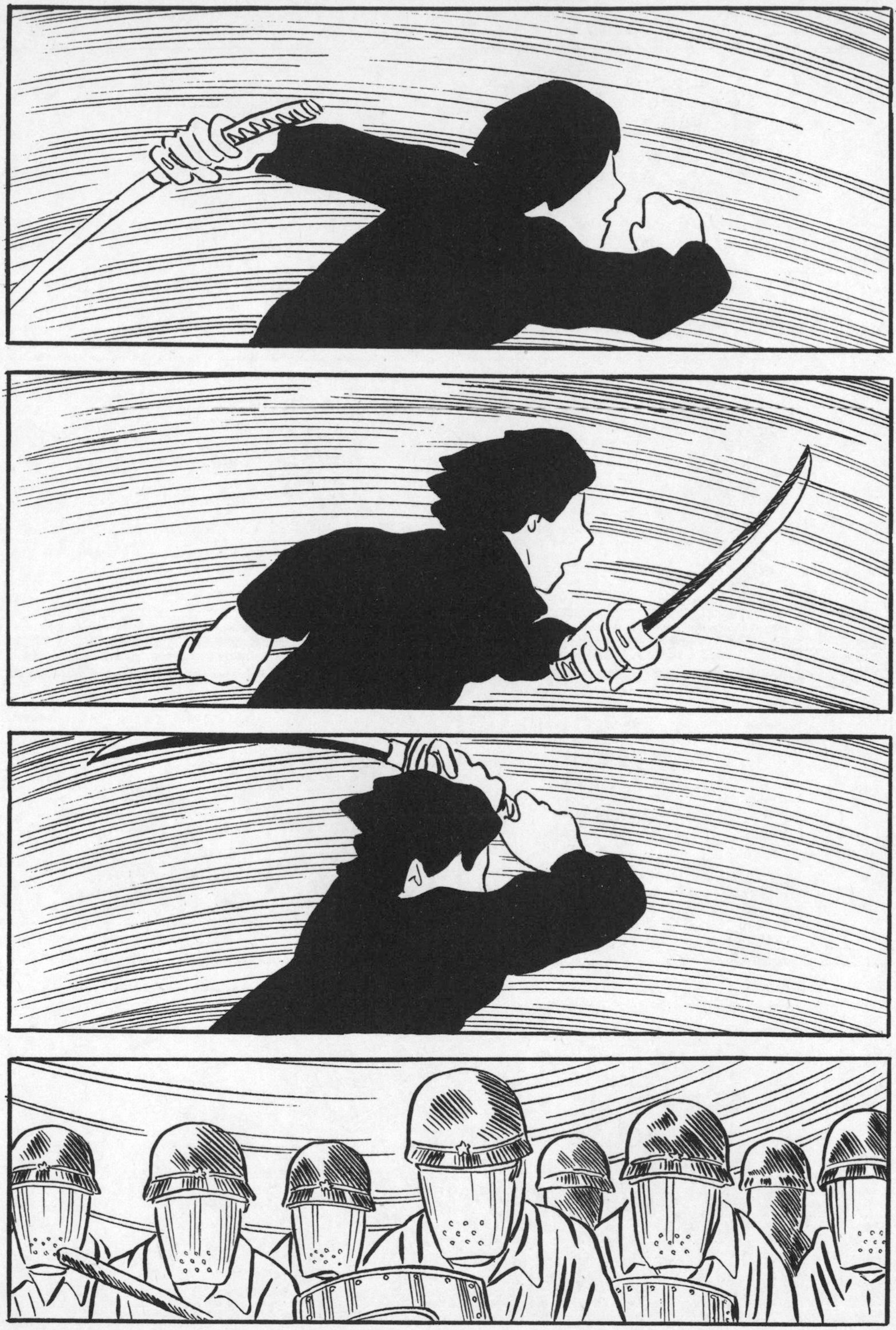

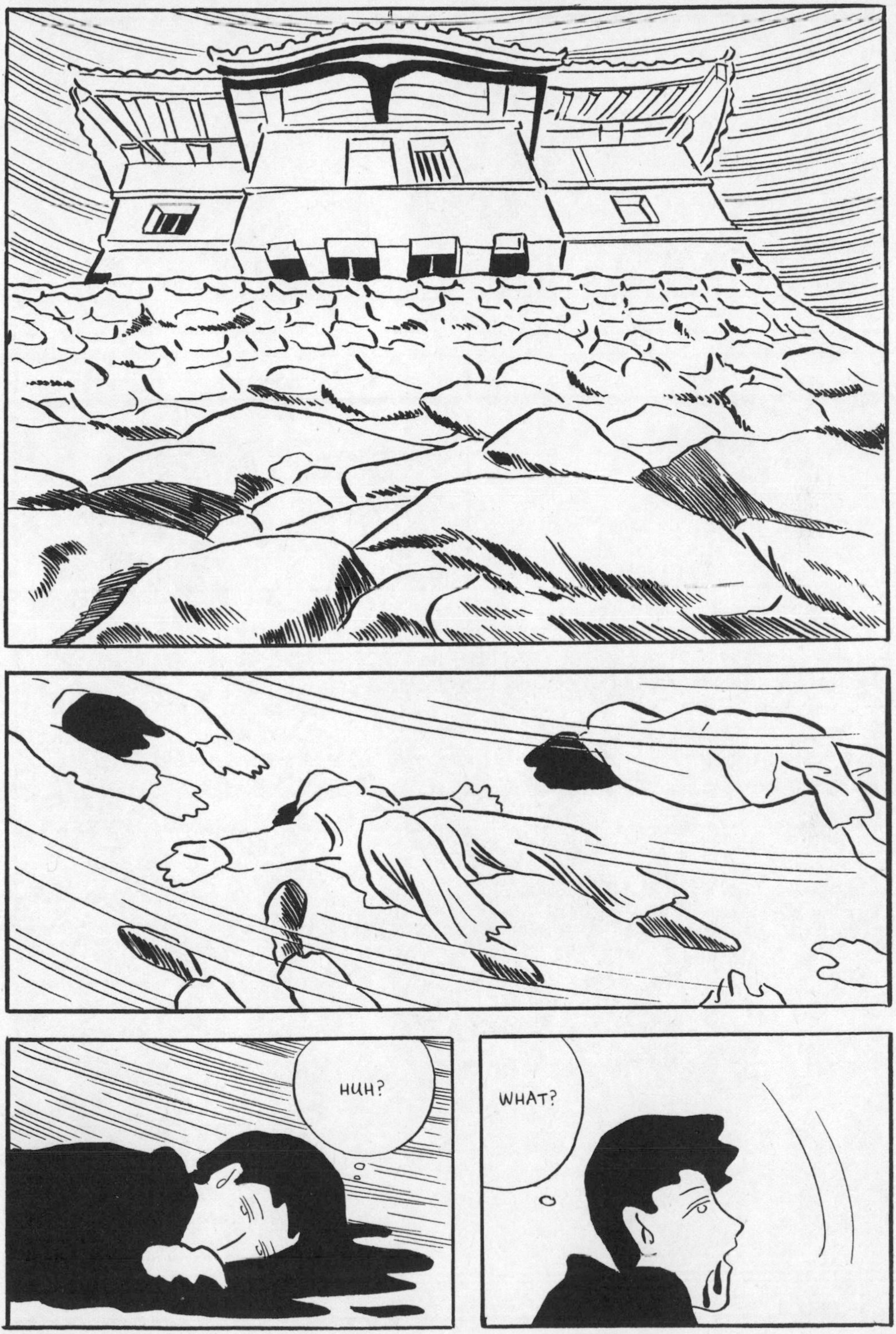
HUH?
WHAT?

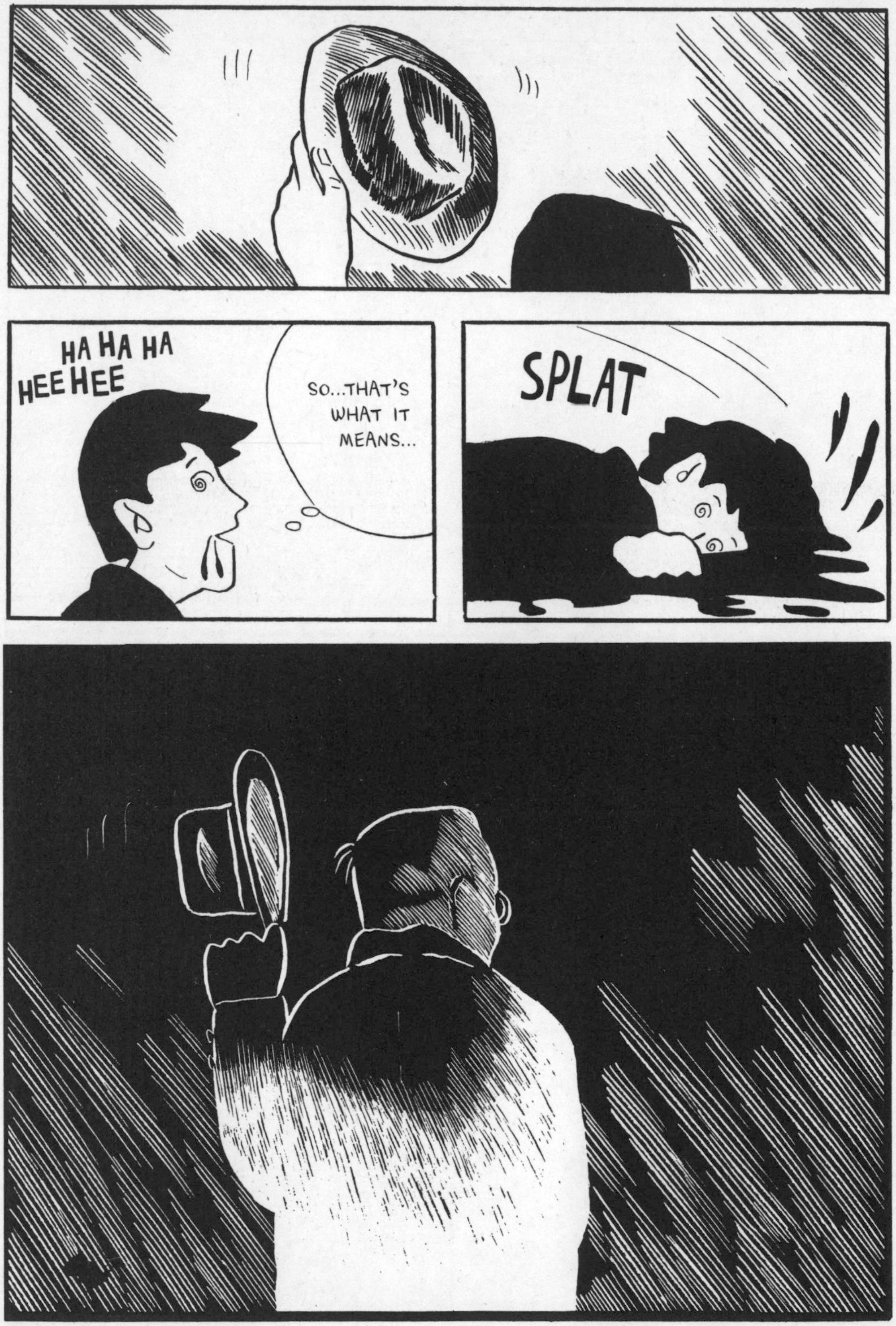
HA HA HA
HEE HEE
SO...THAT'S WHAT IT MEANS...
SPLAT

TRASH MARKET

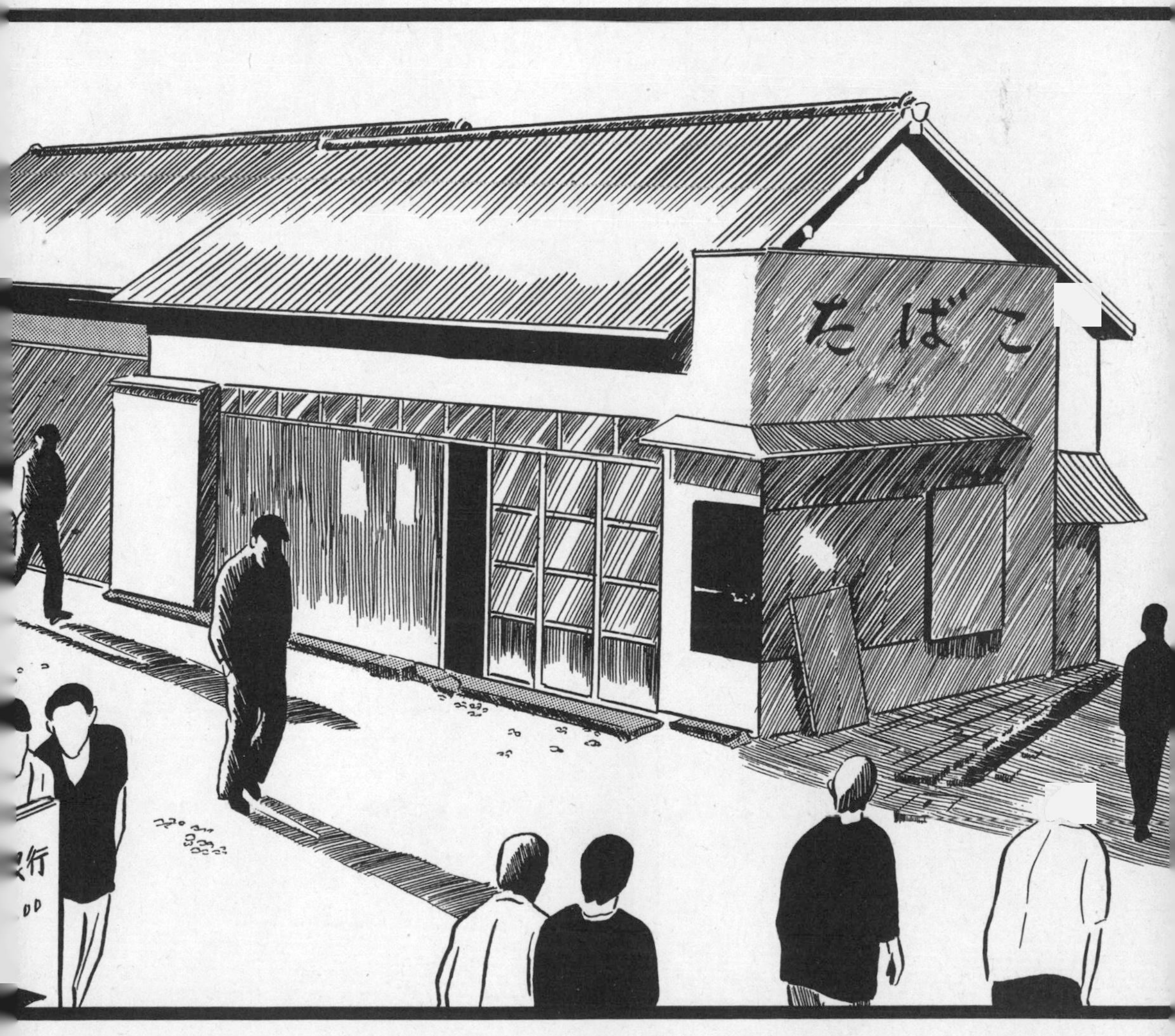
たばこ

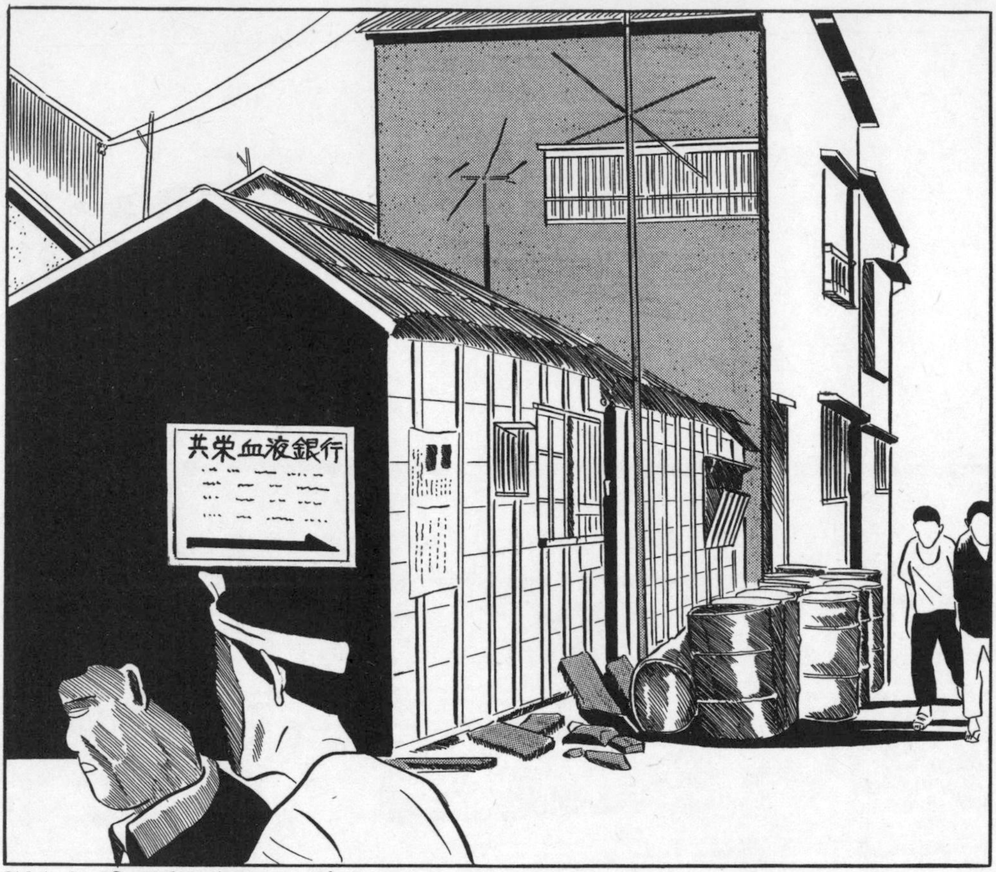
共栄血液銀行

SIGN: CO-PROSPERITY BLOOD BANK

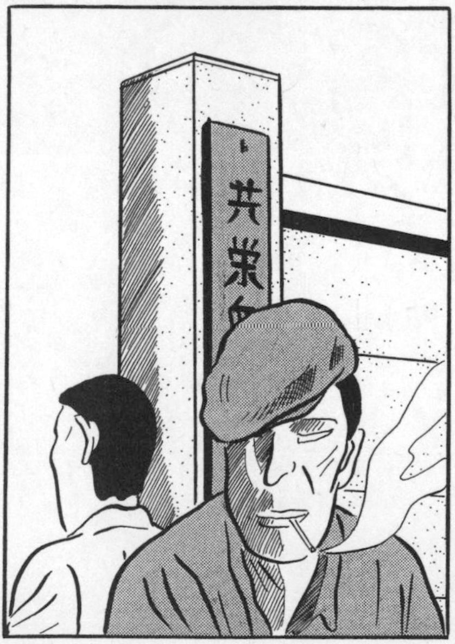
共栄

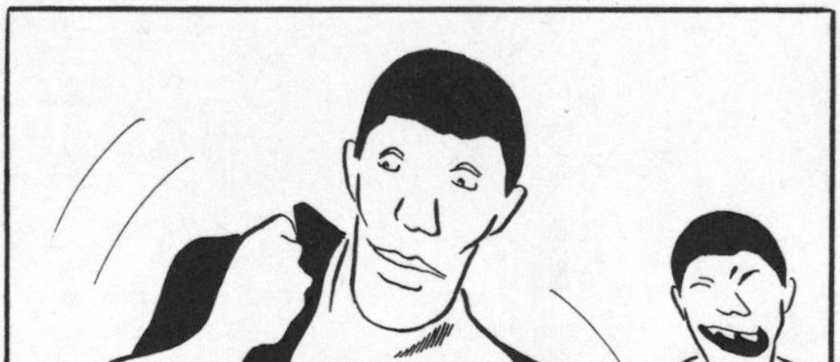

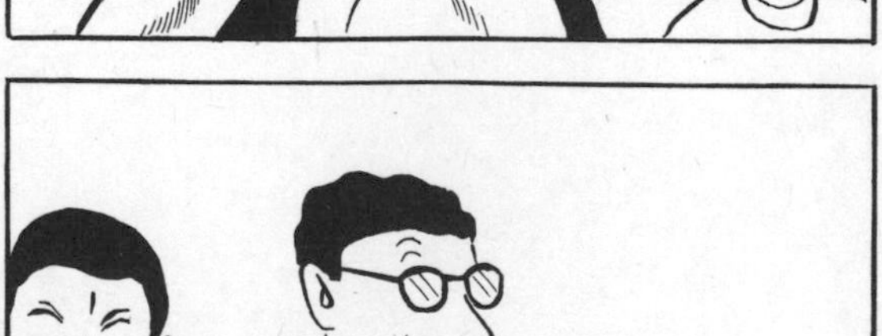

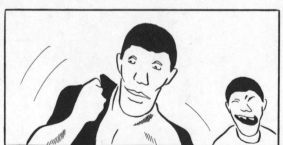

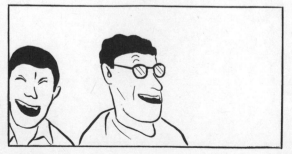

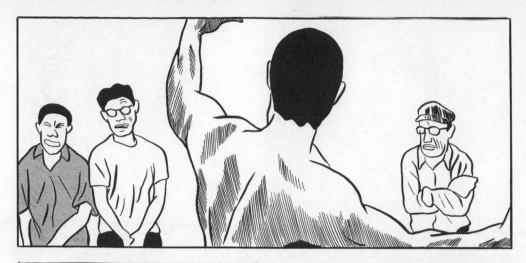

PUK
PUK

PUK

... ...
... ...

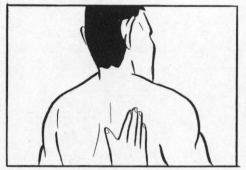

OWW!

GROSS, DUDE...

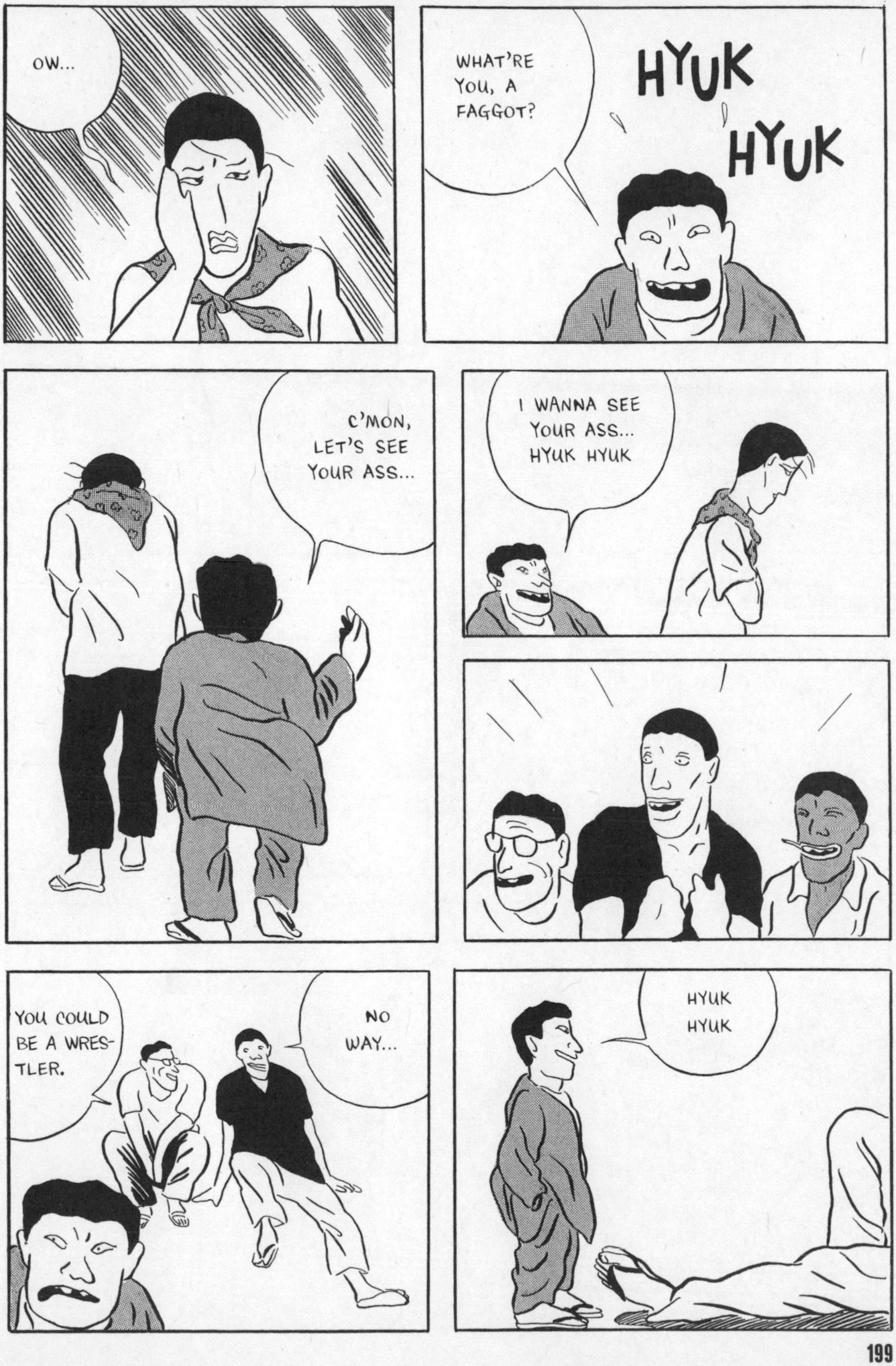
OW...
WHAT'RE YOU, A FAGGOT?
HYUK HYUK
C'MON, LET'S SEE YOUR ASS...
I WANNA SEE YOUR ASS... HYUK HYUK
YOU COULD BE A WRES-TLER.
NO WAY...
HYUK HYUK

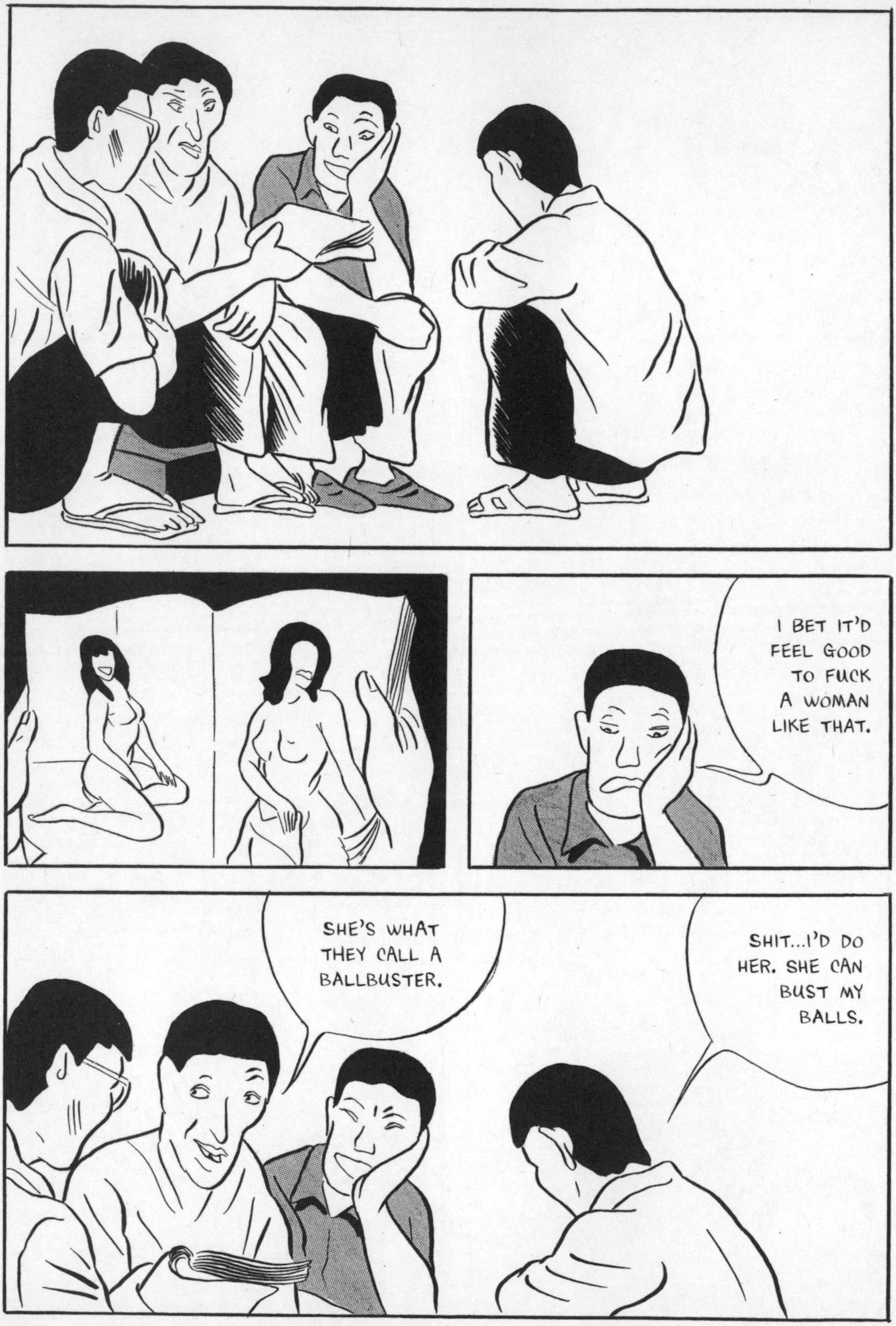

I BET IT'D FEEL GOOD TO FUCK A WOMAN LIKE THAT.
SHE'S WHAT THEY CALL A BALLBUSTER.
SHIT...I'D DO HER. SHE CAN BUST MY BALLS.

TADAAA!

YO! TALKING ABOUT XXX AGAIN? AHA HA HA...

HEY MAN, YOU'RE LATE.

YEAH A BIT. LOOKS CROWDED TODAY...

WE'RE NOT GETTIN' SEEN TILL THE AFTERNOON...

SKIPPIN' LUNCH?

WE LOOKED IN THE CAFETERIA AND IT'S ALL FRIED STUFF TODAY. THEY WON'T TAKE YOUR BLOOD IF YOU EAT ANYTHING GREASY.

YEAH WHATEVER... SHIT IT'S HOT.

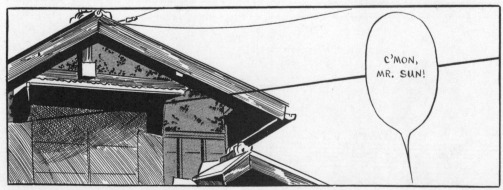

C'MON, MR. SUN!

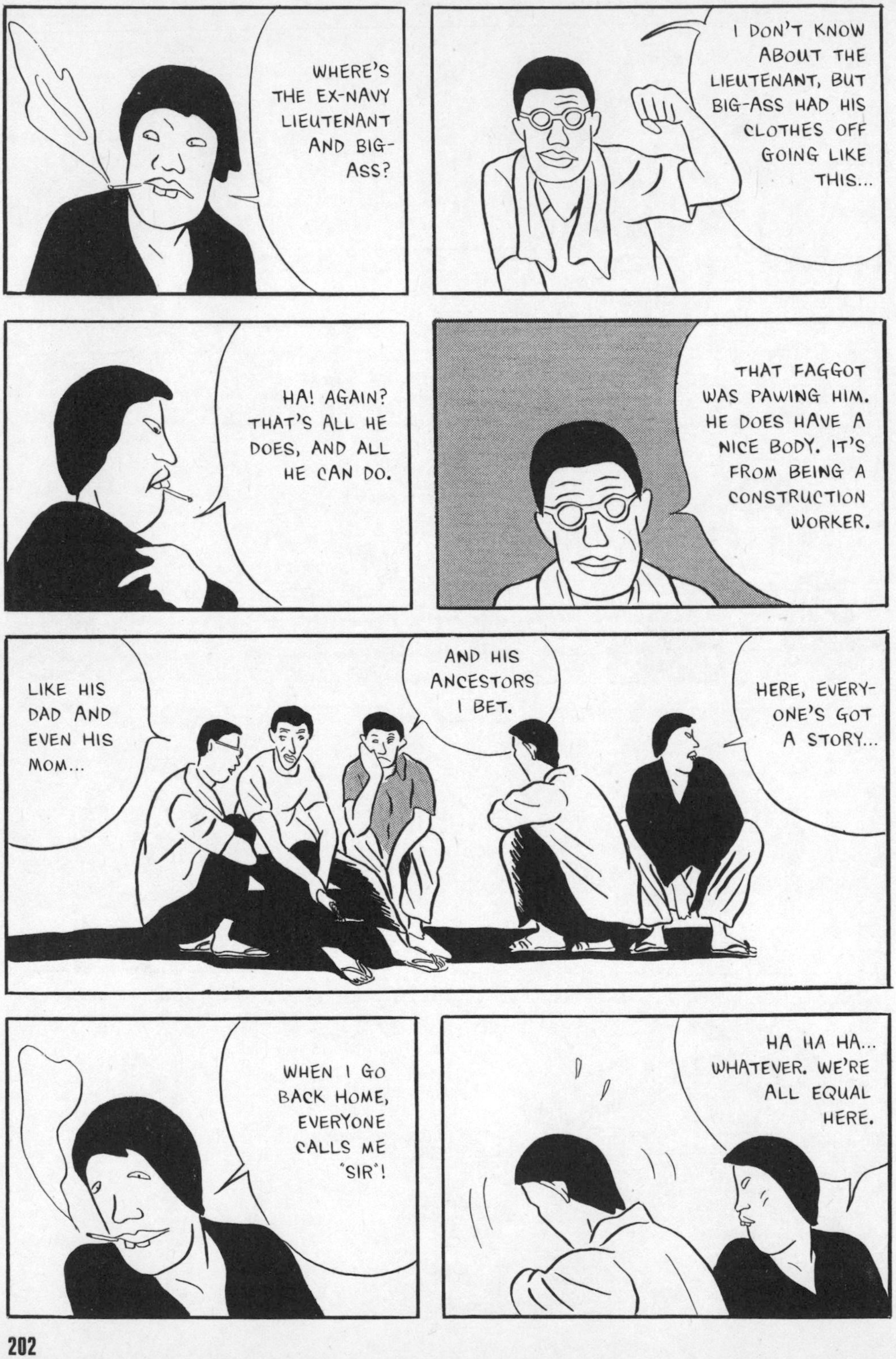
WHERE'S THE EX-NAVY LIEUTENANT AND BIG-ASS?
I DON'T KNOW ABOUT THE LIEUTENANT, BUT BIG-ASS HAD HIS CLOTHES OFF GOING LIKE THIS...
HA! AGAIN? THAT'S ALL HE DOES, AND ALL HE CAN DO.
THAT FAGGOT WAS PAWING HIM. HE DOES HAVE A NICE BODY. IT'S FROM BEING A CONSTRUCTION WORKER.
LIKE HIS DAD AND EVEN HIS MOM...
AND HIS ANCESTORS I BET.
HERE, EVERY-ONE'S GOT A STORY...
WHEN I GO BACK HOME, EVERYONE CALLS ME "SIR"!
HA HA HA... WHATEVER. WE'RE ALL EQUAL HERE.

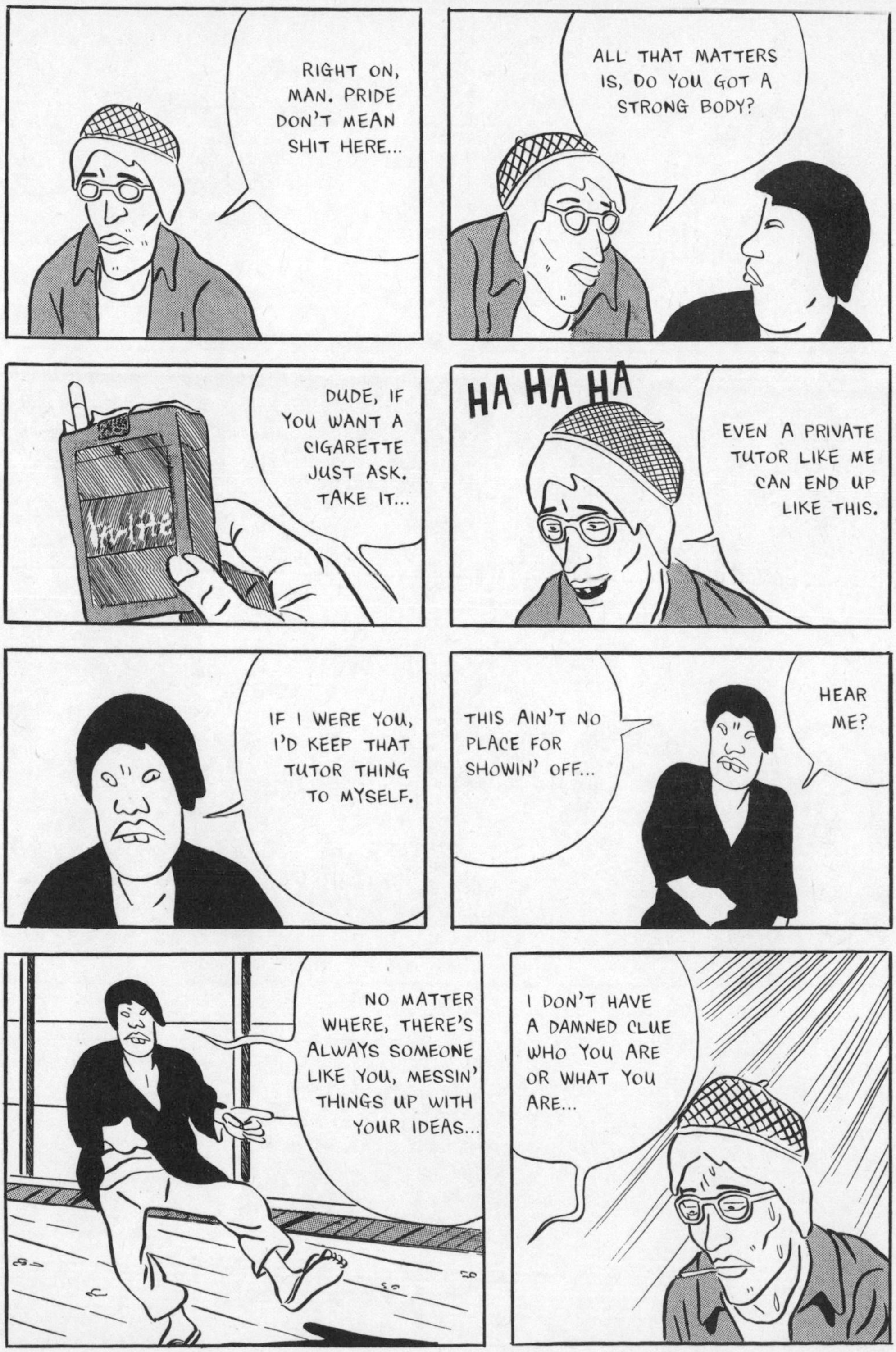
RIGHT ON, MAN. PRIDE DON'T MEAN SHIT HERE...
ALL THAT MATTERS IS, DO YOU GOT A STRONG BODY?
DUDE, IF YOU WANT A CIGARETTE JUST ASK. TAKE IT...
HA HA HA
EVEN A PRIVATE TUTOR LIKE ME CAN END UP LIKE THIS.
IF I WERE YOU, I'D KEEP THAT TUTOR THING TO MYSELF.
THIS AIN'T NO PLACE FOR SHOWIN' OFF...
HEAR ME?
NO MATTER WHERE, THERE'S ALWAYS SOMEONE LIKE YOU, MESSIN' THINGS UP WITH YOUR IDEAS...
I DON'T HAVE A DAMNED CLUE WHO YOU ARE OR WHAT YOU ARE...

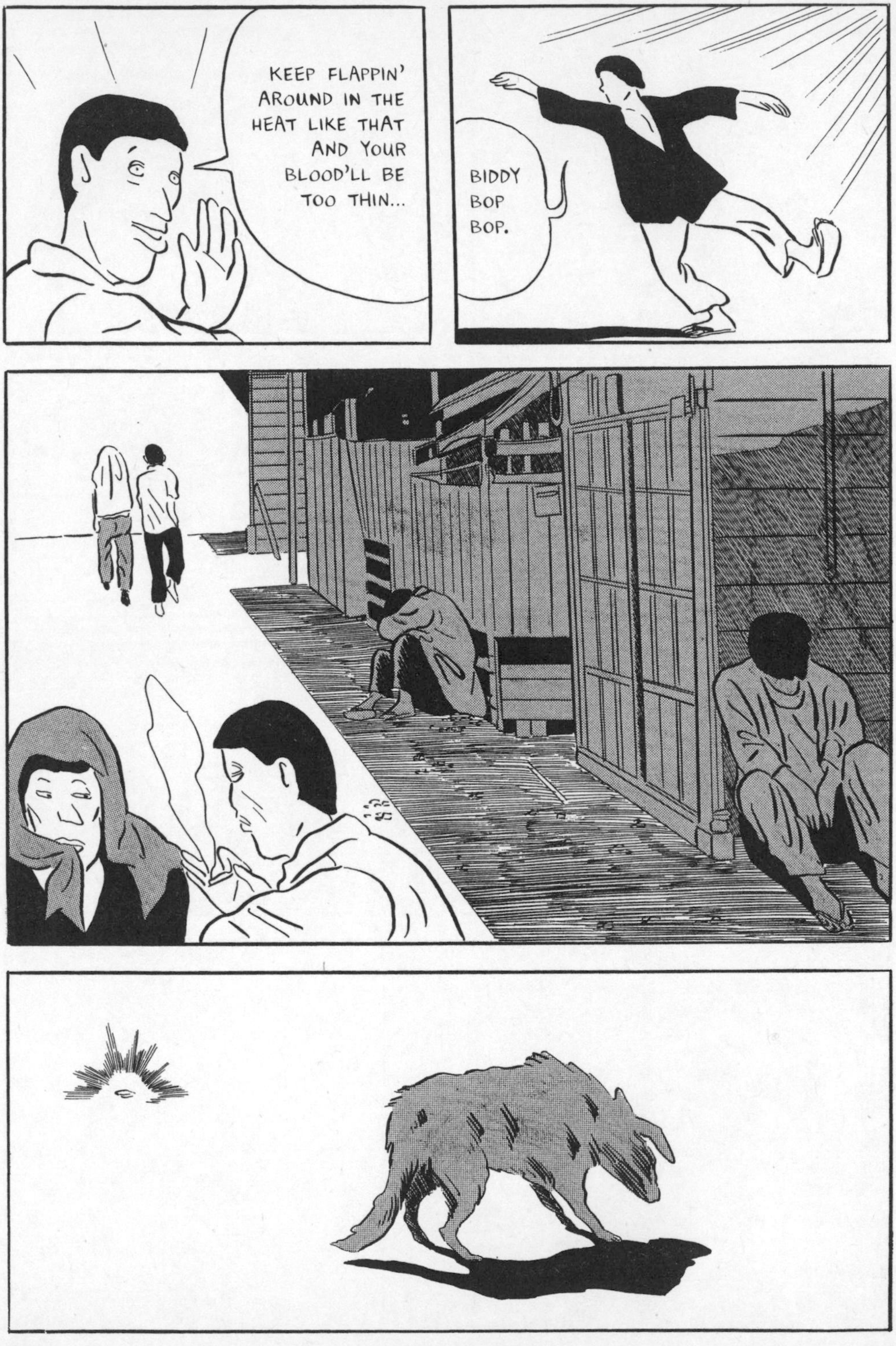
KEEP FLAPPIN' AROUND IN THE HEAT LIKE THAT AND YOUR BLOOD'LL BE TOO THIN...
BIDDY BOP BOP.

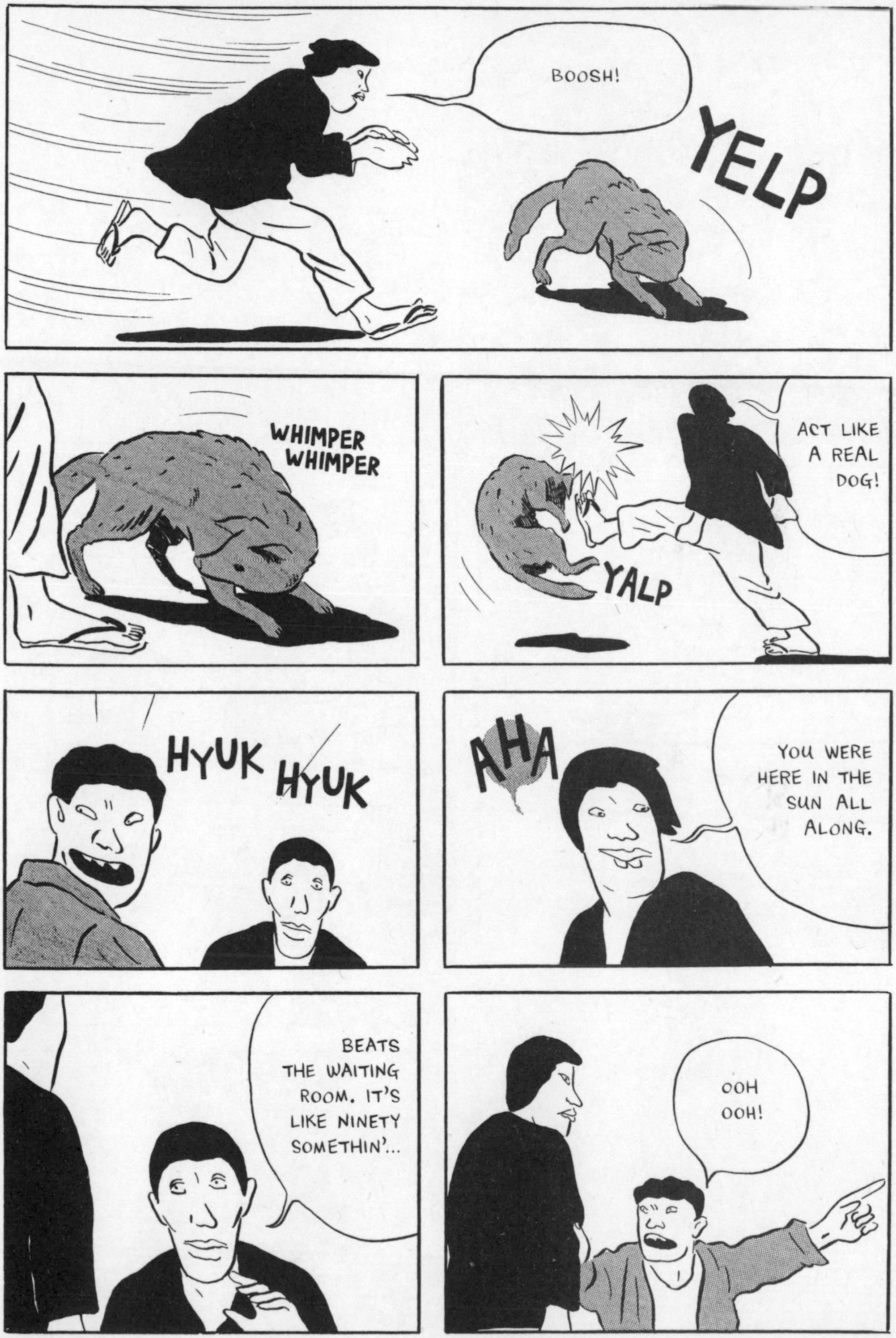
BOOSH!
YELP
WHIMPER WHIMPER
ACT LIKE A REAL DOG!
YALP
HYUK HYUK
AHA
YOU WERE HERE IN THE SUN ALL ALONG.
BEATS THE WAITING ROOM. IT'S LIKE NINETY SOMETHIN'...
OOH OOH!

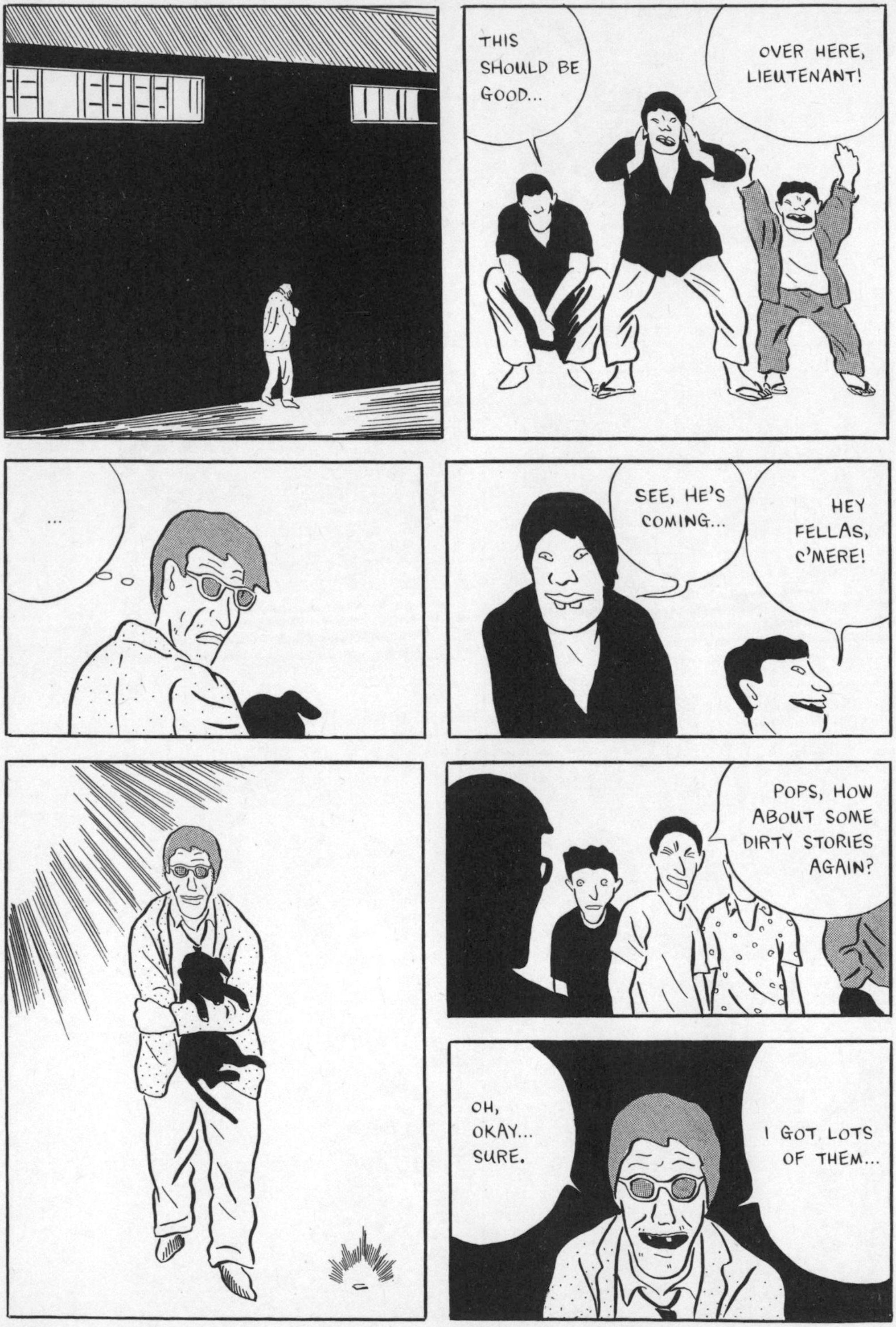
THIS SHOULD BE GOOD...
OVER HERE, LIEUTENANT!
...
SEE, HE'S COMING...
HEY FELLAS, C'MERE!
POPS, HOW ABOUT SOME DIRTY STORIES AGAIN?
OH, OKAY... SURE.
I GOT LOTS OF THEM...

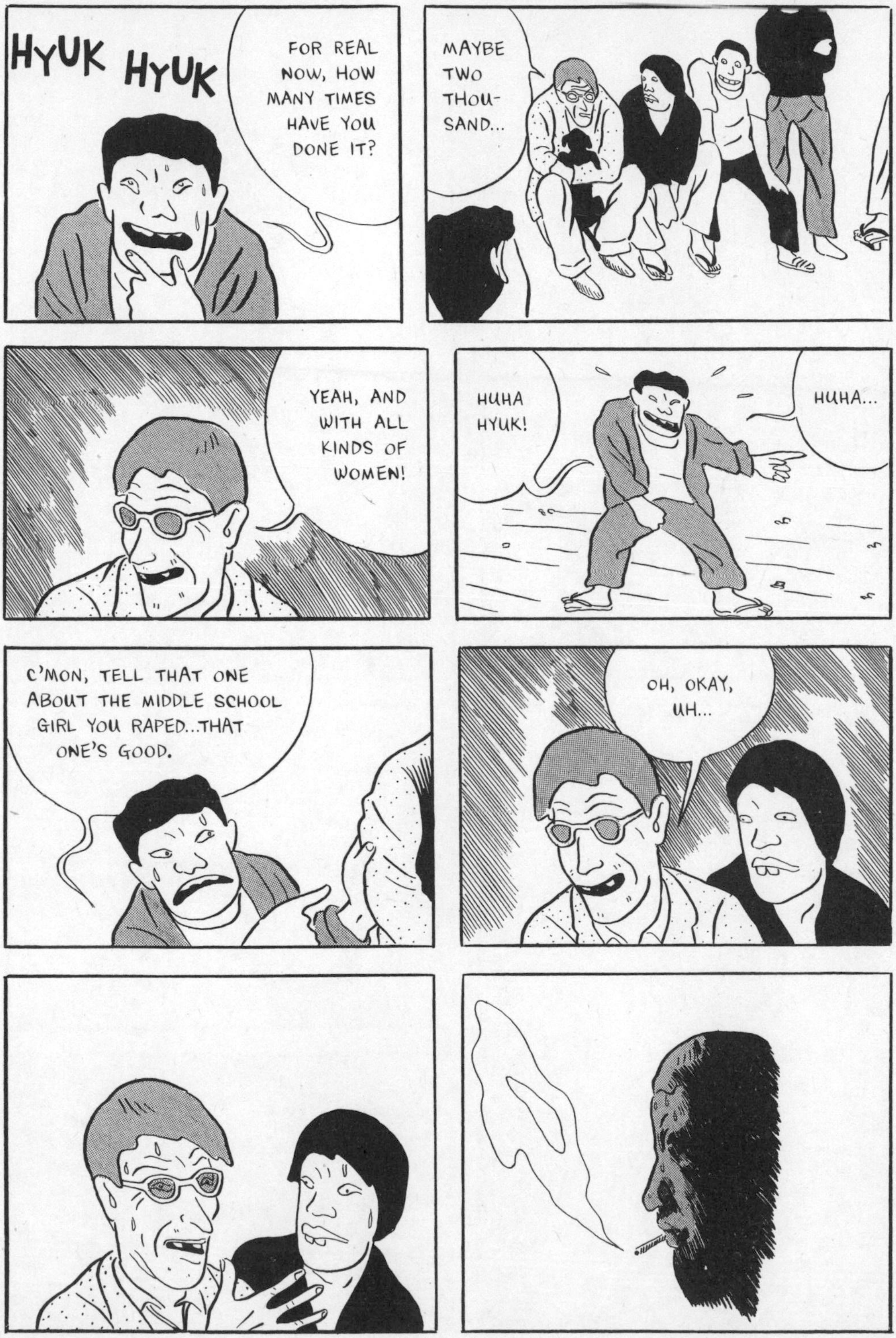
HYUK HYUK
FOR REAL NOW, HOW MANY TIMES HAVE YOU DONE IT?
MAYBE TWO THOU- SAND...
YEAH, AND WITH ALL KINDS OF WOMEN!
HUHA HYUK!
HUHA...
C'MON, TELL THAT ONE ABOUT THE MIDDLE SCHOOL GIRL YOU RAPED...THAT ONE'S GOOD.
OH, OKAY, UH...

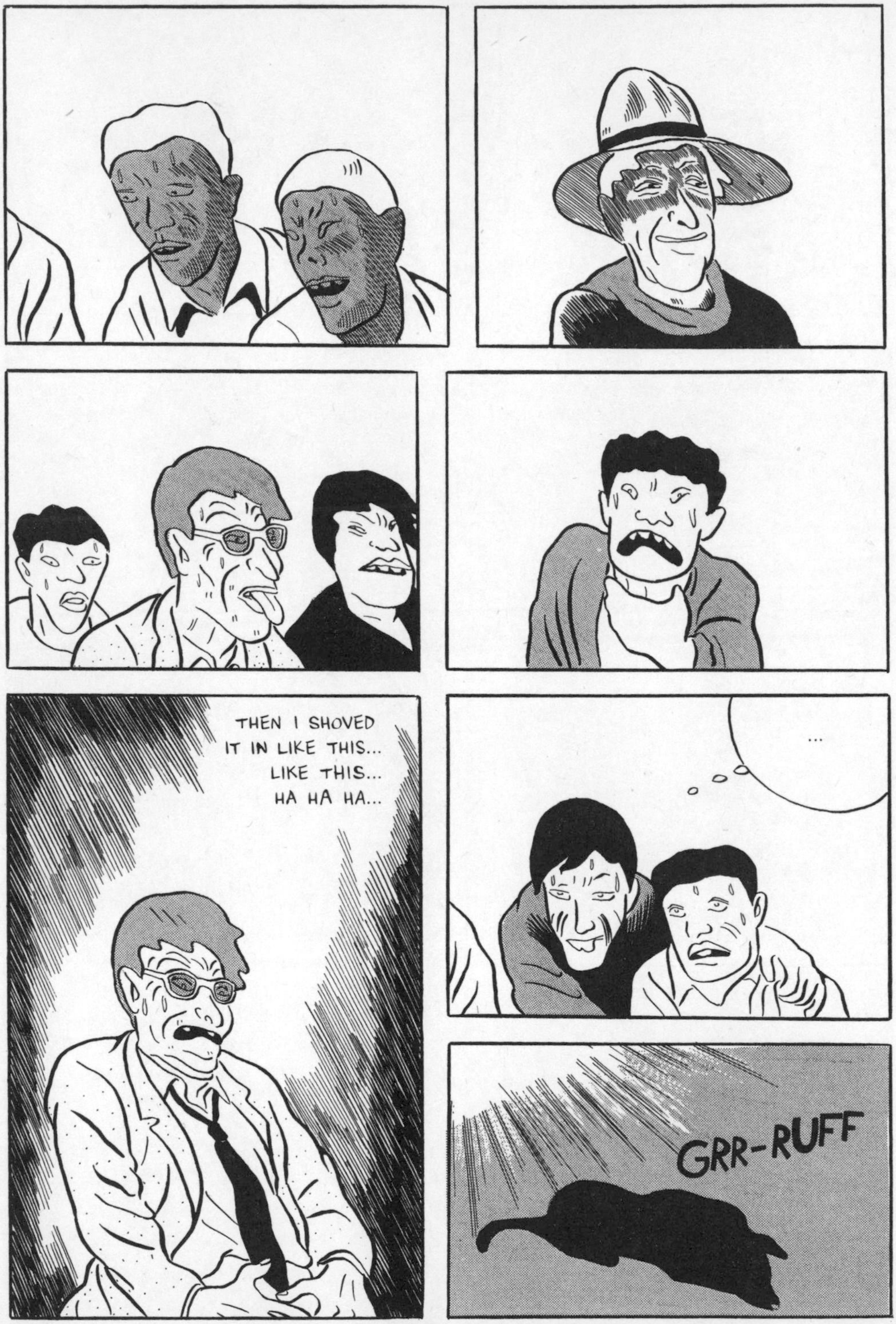
THEN I SHOVED
IT IN LIKE THIS...
LIKE THIS...
HA HA HA...
...
GRR-RUFF

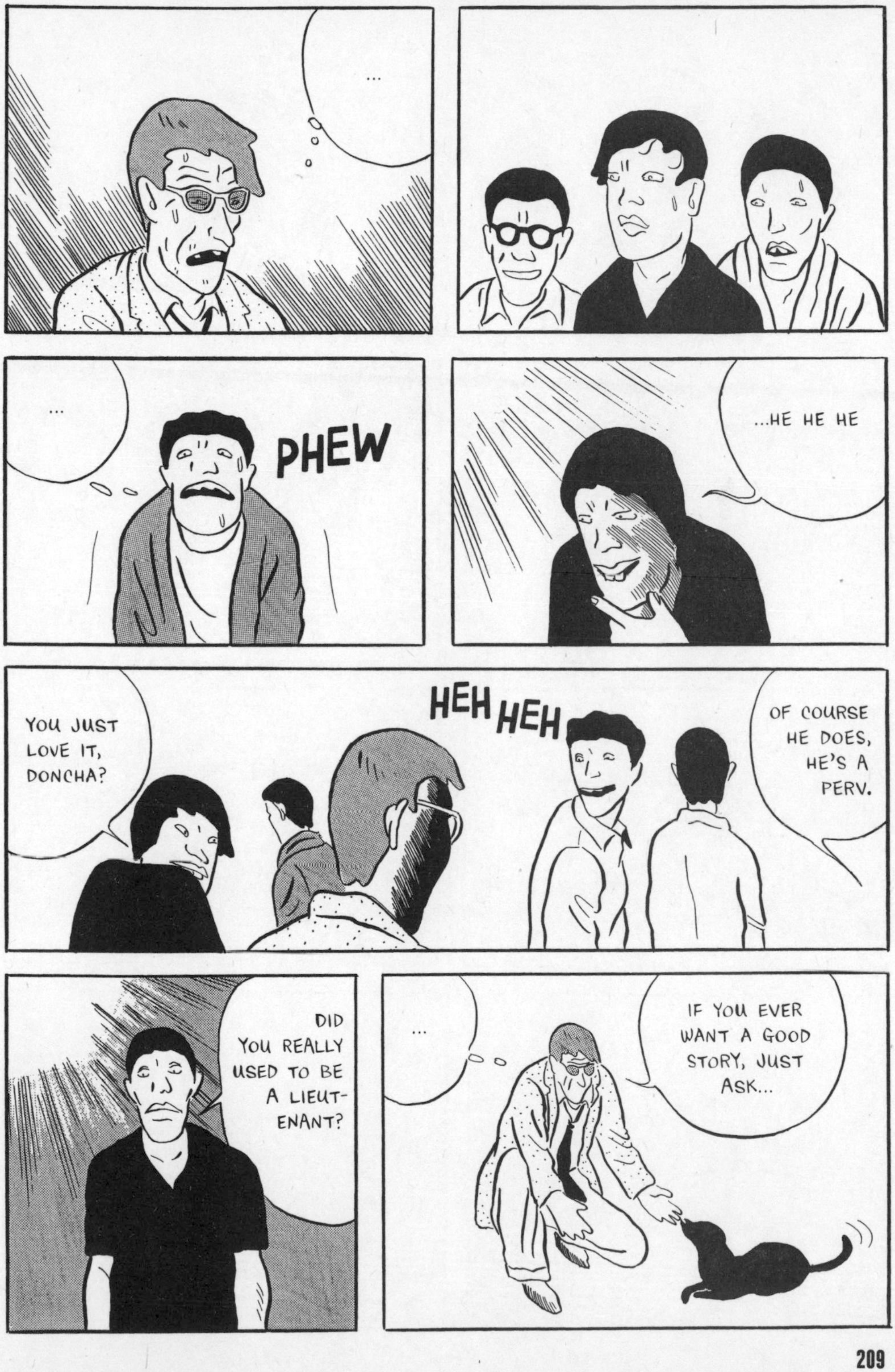
...
...
PHEW
...HE HE HE
YOU JUST LOVE IT, DONCHA?
HEH HEH
OF COURSE HE DOES, HE'S A PERV.
DID YOU REALLY USED TO BE A LIEUT-ENANT?
...
IF YOU EVER WANT A GOOD STORY, JUST ASK...

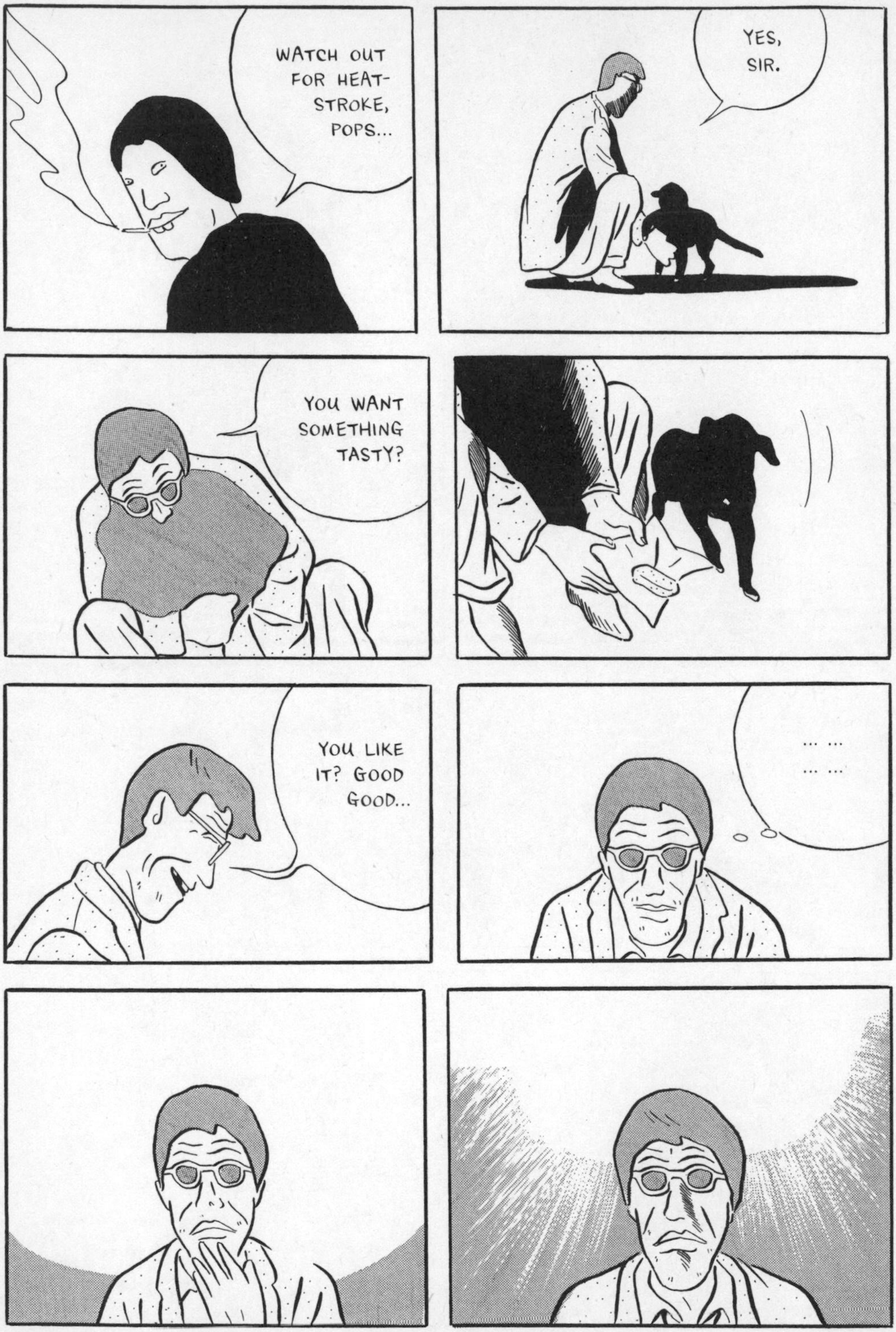
WATCH OUT FOR HEAT-STROKE, POPS...
YES, SIR.
YOU WANT SOMETHING TASTY?
YOU LIKE IT? GOOD GOOD...
... ...
... ...

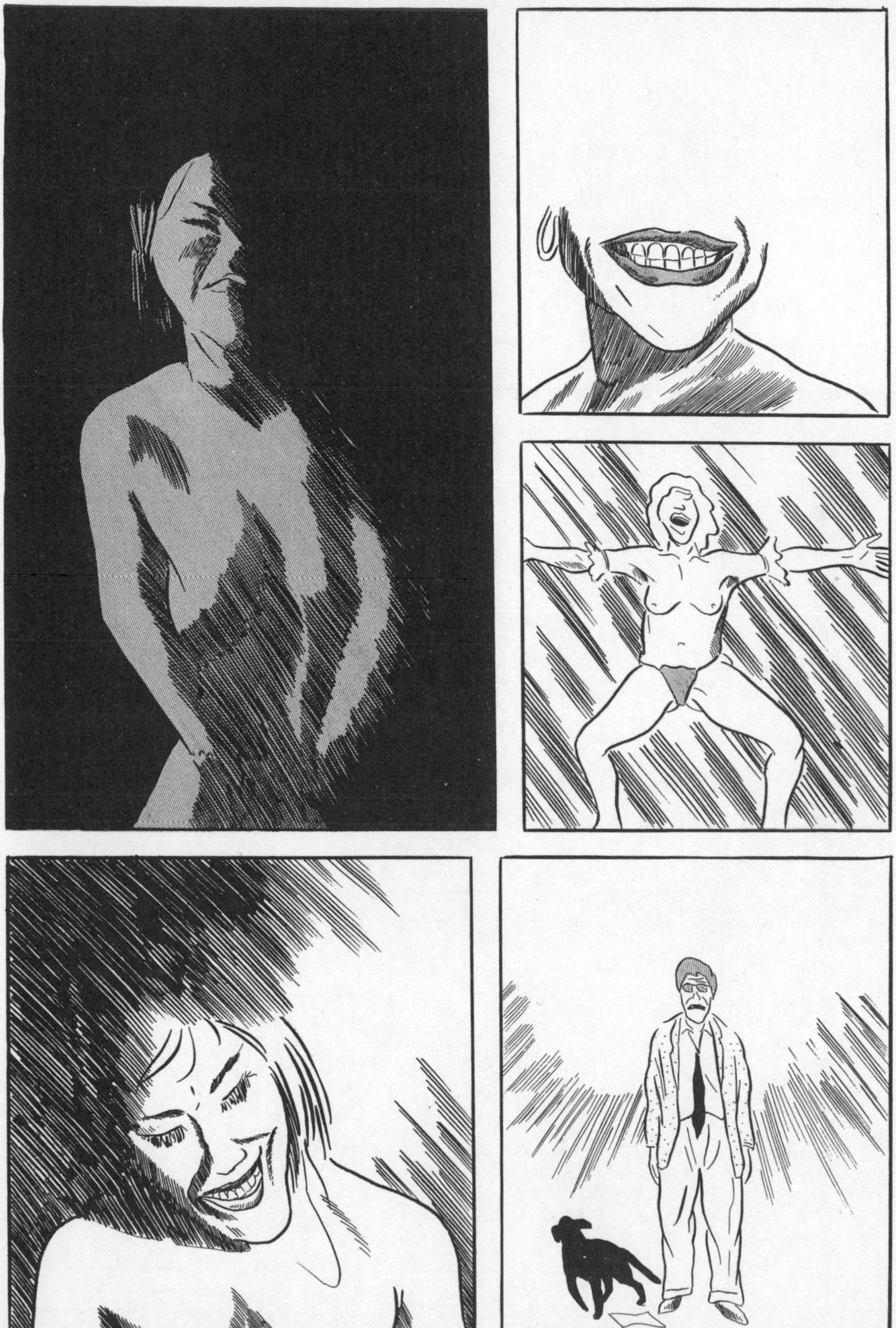

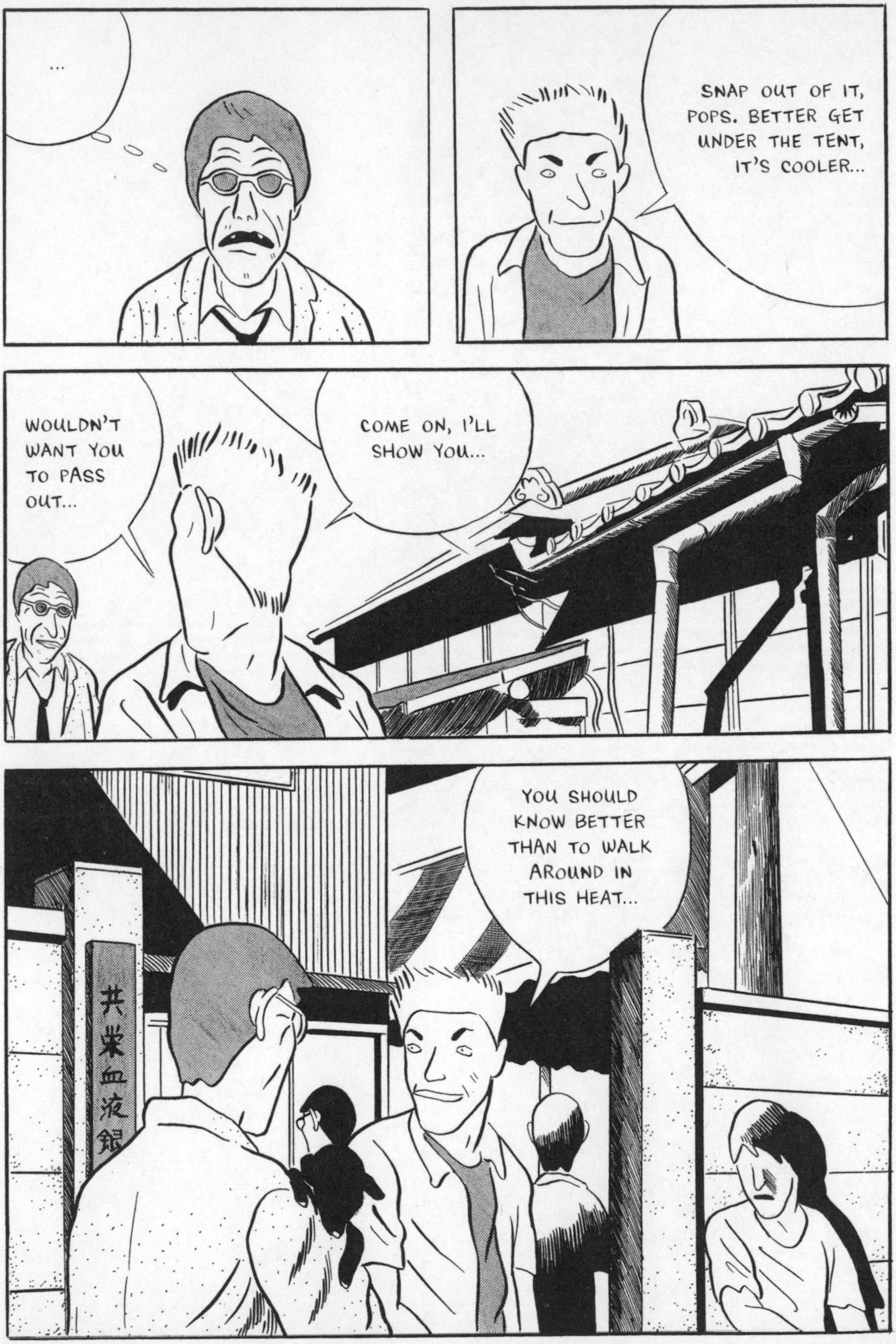
...
SNAP OUT OF IT, POPS. BETTER GET UNDER THE TENT, IT'S COOLER...
WOULDN'T WANT YOU TO PASS OUT...
COME ON, I'LL SHOW YOU...
YOU SHOULD KNOW BETTER THAN TO WALK AROUND IN THIS HEAT...
共栄血液銀

THE BENCH IS FULL...
NO PROBLEM, LET'S GO IN THE BACK.
WHAT NUMBER ARE YOU TODAY?
W. C
304... I THINK...
GOT ANY CIGARETTES?

THE CLEAR BLU-OOO SKY
THE STIR-IIING WIND

SONG: "AKOGARE NO HAWAI KORO" (1948)

THATS'S HARUKO OKA'S SONG, NOT BAD!

WHAT ELSE YOU GOT?

I DON'T LIKE THESE NEW SONGS...

SO ANOTHER OLDIE.

FROM WAVE TO WA-AVE

YEAH BABY!

SONG: YOSHIO TABATA'S "KAERI BUNE" (1946)

I MEAN, SO AM I, BUT...POPS, YOU'RE ALWAYS HERE...

SWAYING
SWAY-AY-AYING

MAYBE THREE TIMES EVERY TWO WEEKS...

THAT'S ROUGH... BUT I'VE MET GUYS THAT COME EVERY THREE DAYS.

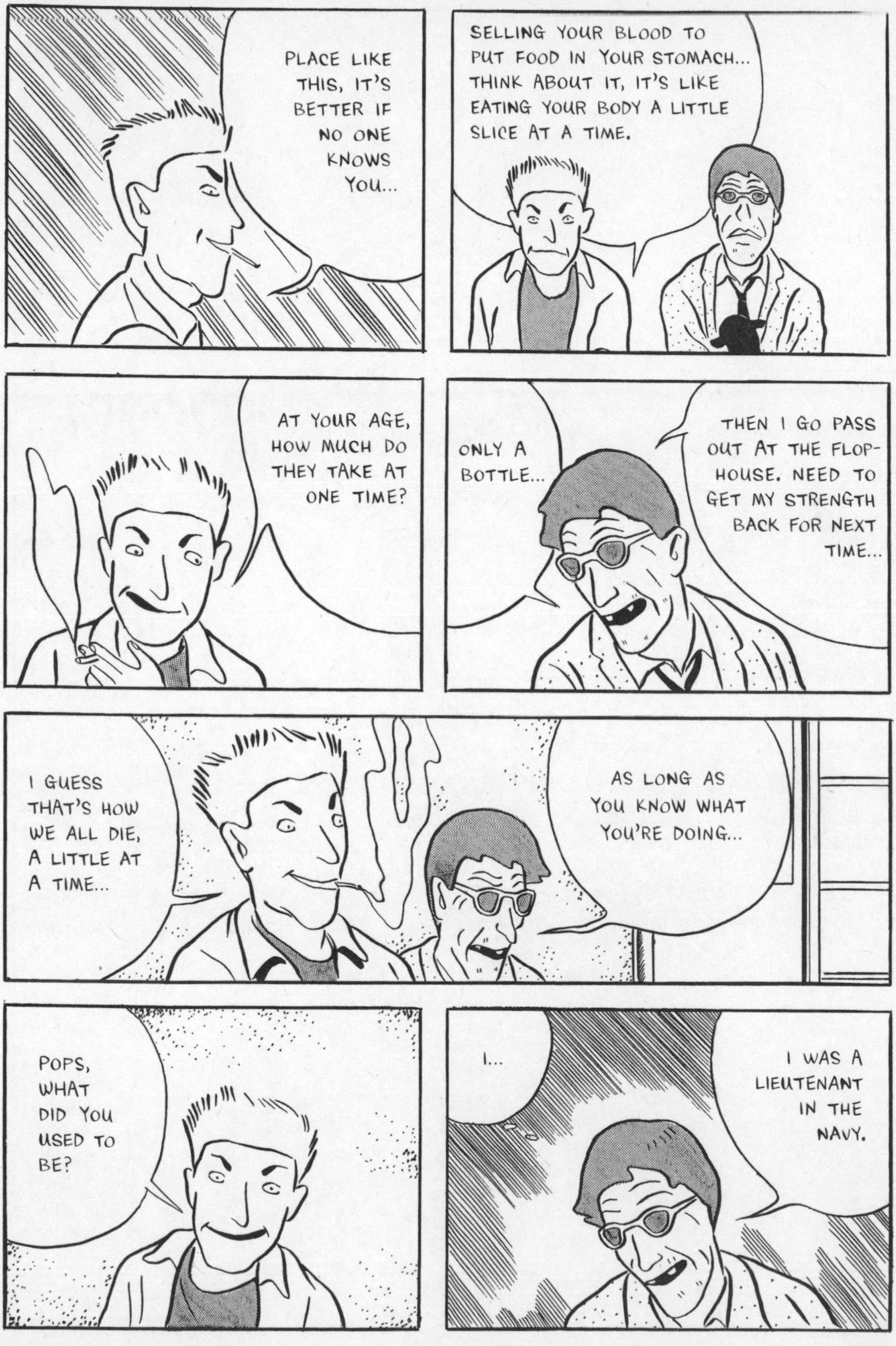
PLACE LIKE THIS, IT'S BETTER IF NO ONE KNOWS YOU...
SELLING YOUR BLOOD TO PUT FOOD IN YOUR STOMACH... THINK ABOUT IT, IT'S LIKE EATING YOUR BODY A LITTLE SLICE AT A TIME.
AT YOUR AGE, HOW MUCH DO THEY TAKE AT ONE TIME?
ONLY A BOTTLE...
THEN I GO PASS OUT AT THE FLOP-HOUSE. NEED TO GET MY STRENGTH BACK FOR NEXT TIME...
I GUESS THAT'S HOW WE ALL DIE, A LITTLE AT A TIME...
AS LONG AS YOU KNOW WHAT YOU'RE DOING...
POPS, WHAT DID YOU USED TO BE?
I...
I WAS A LIEUTENANT IN THE NAVY.

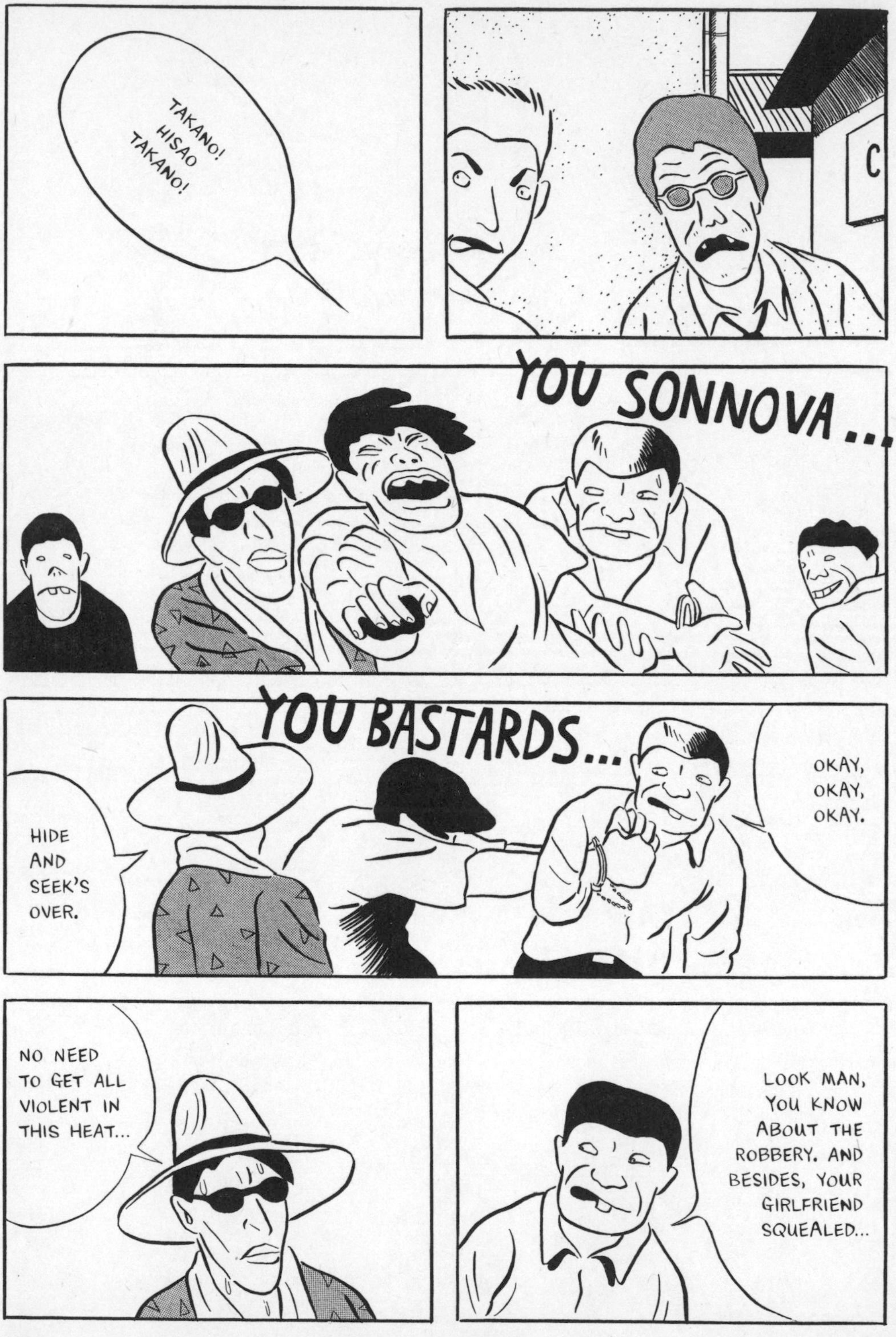
TAKANO! HISAO TAKANO!
YOU SONNOVA...
YOU BASTARDS...
HIDE AND SEEK'S OVER.
OKAY, OKAY, OKAY.
NO NEED TO GET ALL VIOLENT IN THIS HEAT...
LOOK MAN, YOU KNOW ABOUT THE ROBBERY. AND BESIDES, YOUR GIRLFRIEND SQUEALED...

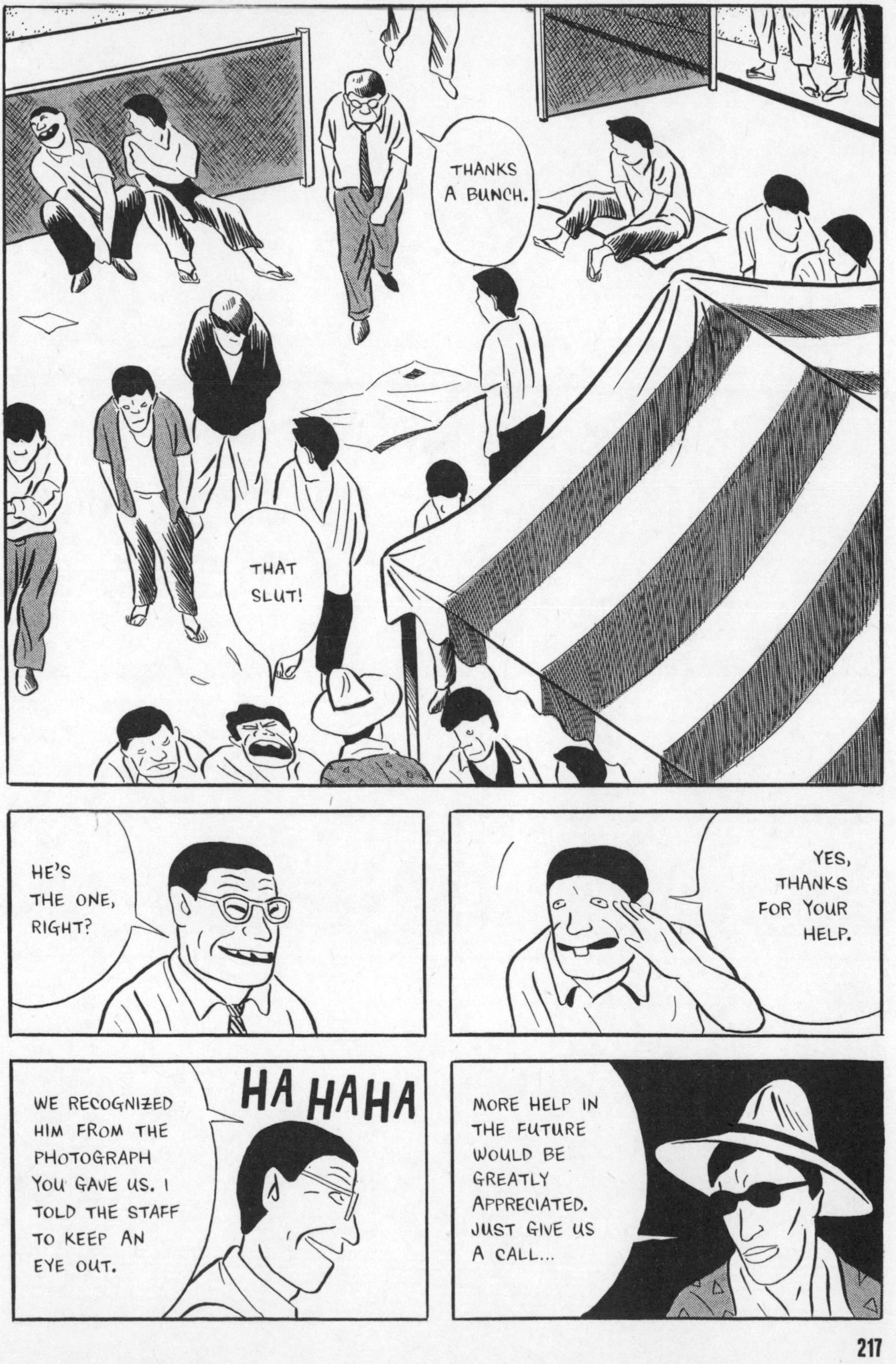
THANKS A BUNCH.
THAT SLUT!
HE'S THE ONE, RIGHT?
YES, THANKS FOR YOUR HELP.
WE RECOGNIZED HIM FROM THE PHOTOGRAPH YOU GAVE US. I TOLD THE STAFF TO KEEP AN EYE OUT.
HA HAHA
MORE HELP IN THE FUTURE WOULD BE GREATLY APPRECIATED. JUST GIVE US A CALL...

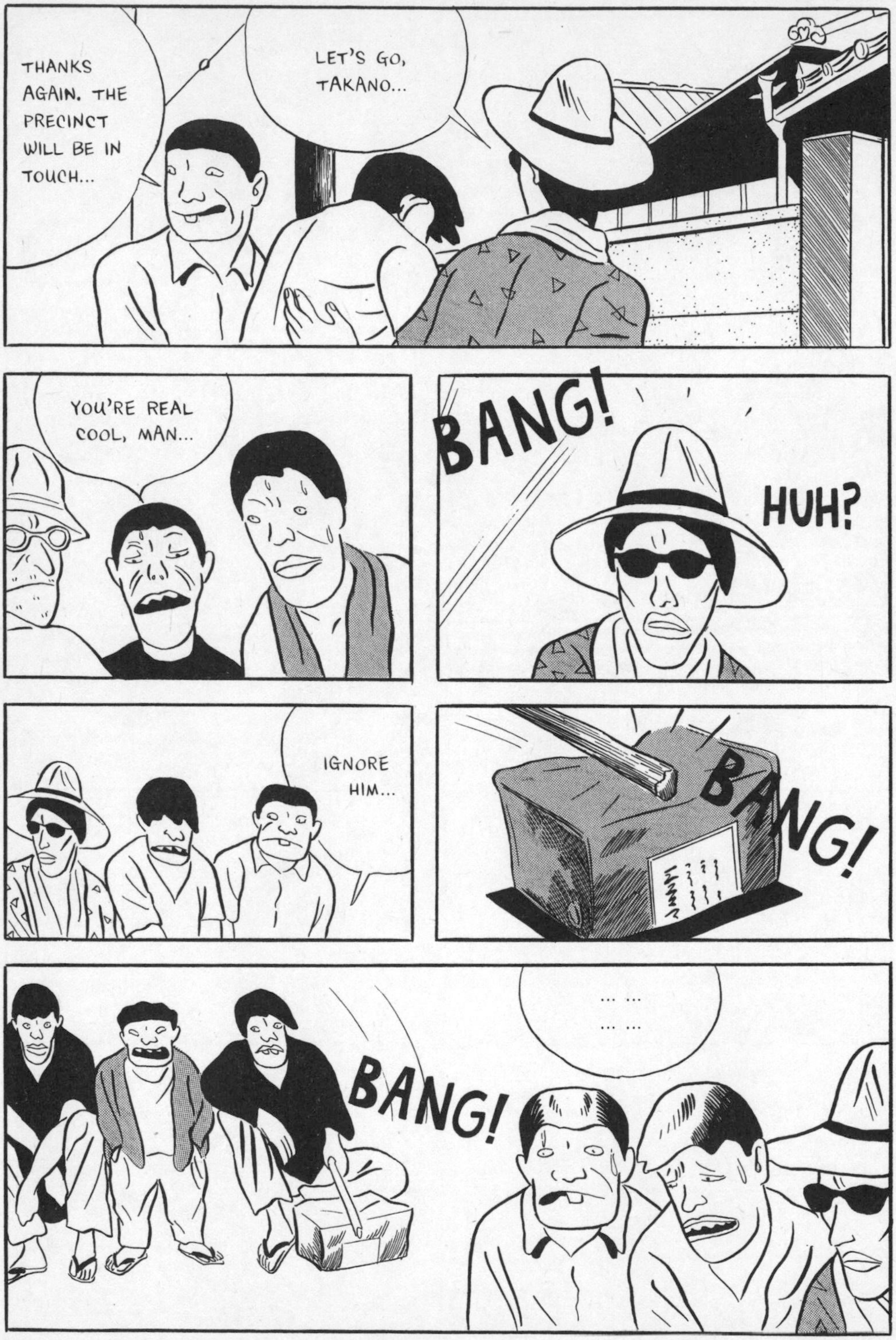
THANKS AGAIN. THE PRECINCT WILL BE IN TOUCH...
LET'S GO, TAKANO...
YOU'RE REAL COOL, MAN...
BANG!
HUH?
IGNORE HIM...
BANG!
BANG!
... ...
... ...

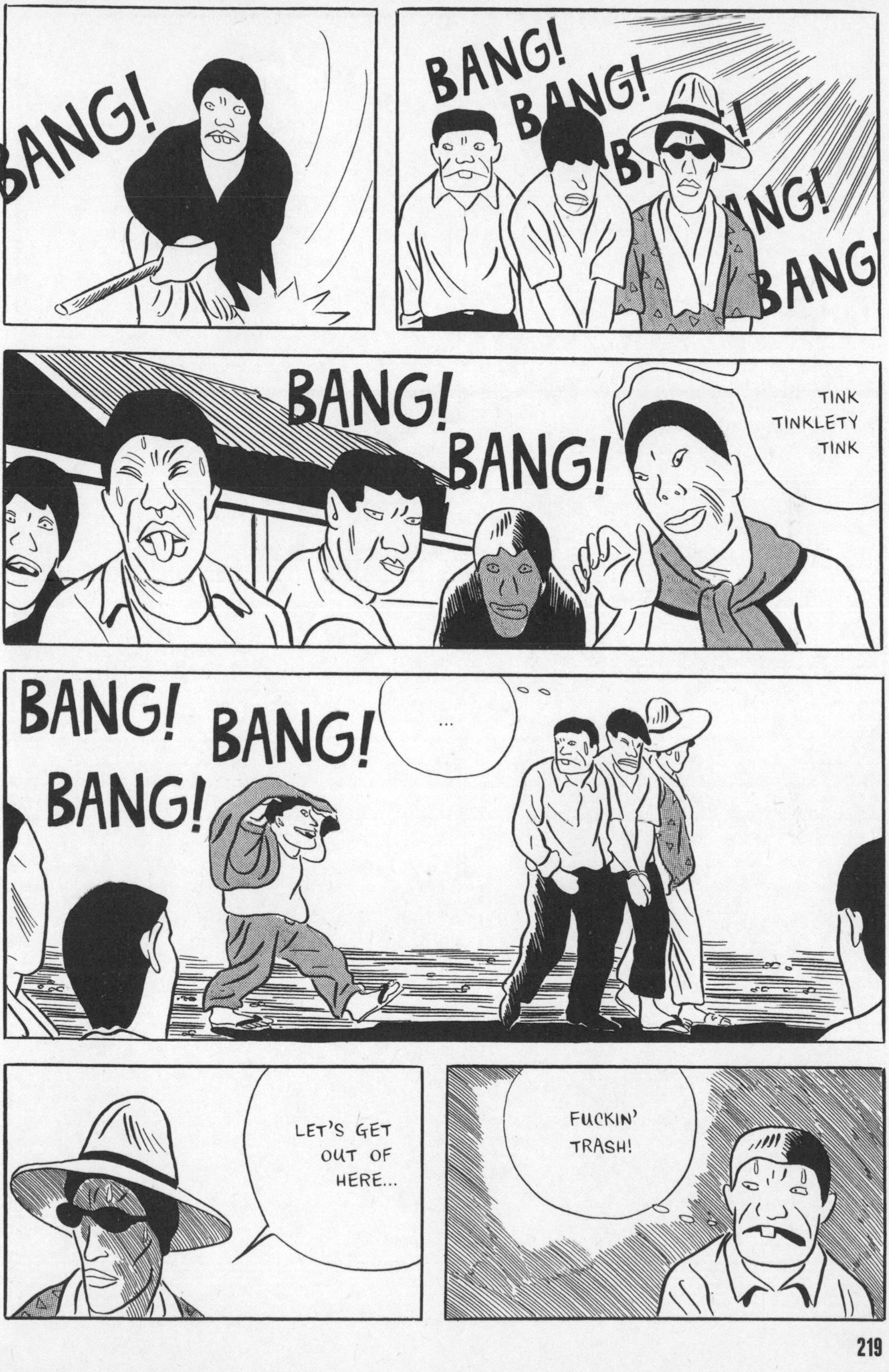
BANG!
BANG!
BANG!
BANG!
BANG!
BANG!
BANG!
TINK
TINKLETY
TINK
BANG!
BANG!
BANG!
...
LET'S GET OUT OF HERE...
FUCKIN' TRASH!

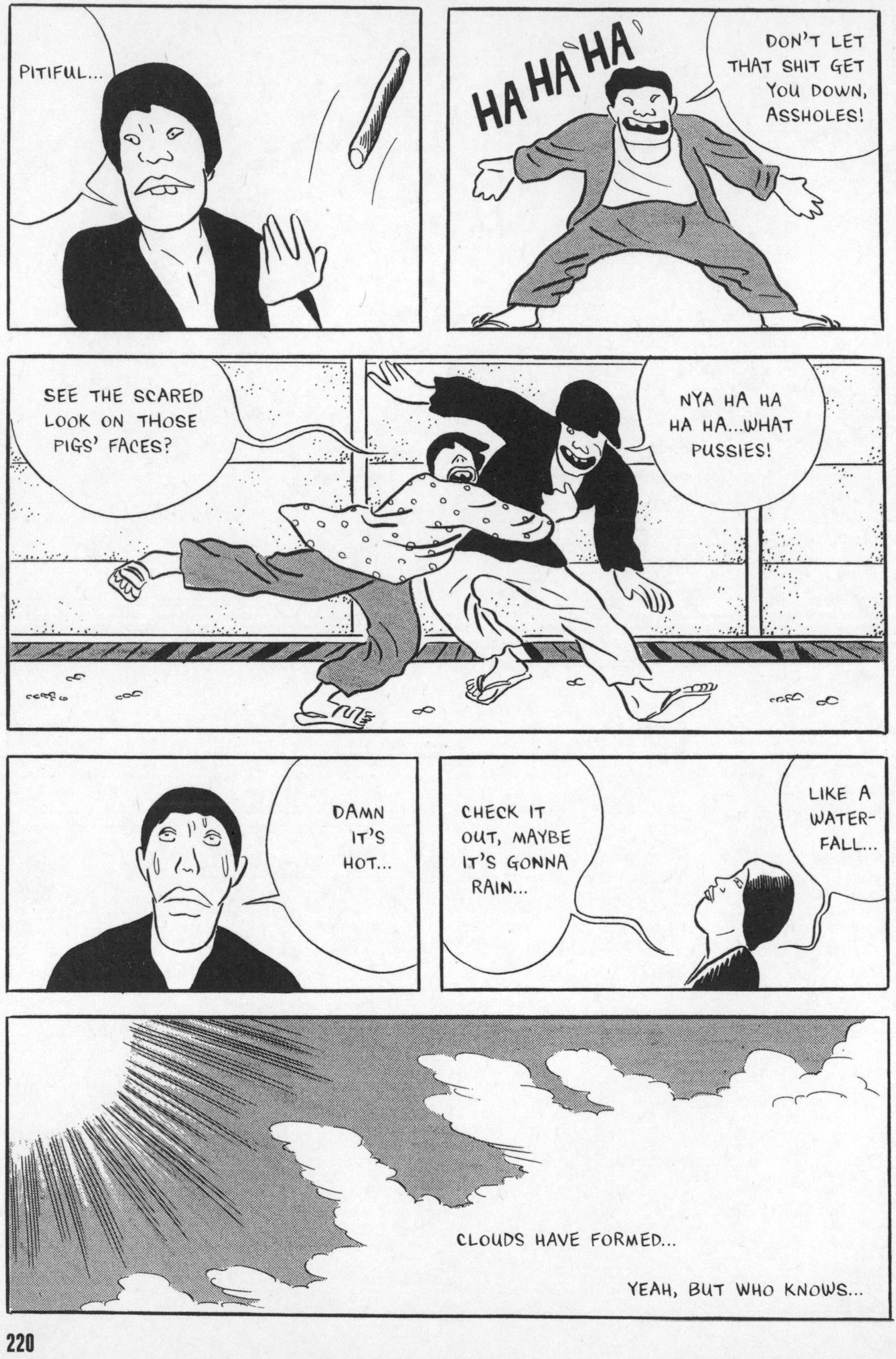
PITIFUL...
HA HA HA
DON'T LET THAT SHIT GET YOU DOWN, ASSHOLES!
SEE THE SCARED LOOK ON THOSE PIGS' FACES?
NYA HA HA HA HA...WHAT PUSSIES!
DAMN IT'S HOT...
CHECK IT OUT, MAYBE IT'S GONNA RAIN...
LIKE A WATER-FALL...
CLOUDS HAVE FORMED...
YEAH, BUT WHO KNOWS...

NUMBERS 300 TO 320. PLEASE WASH YOUR ARMS THOROUGHLY AND COME TO THE EXAMINATION ROOM.

WE'RE UP!

LET'S DO THIS THEN GET A BITE TO EAT.

OKAY.

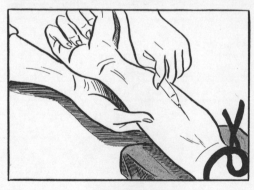

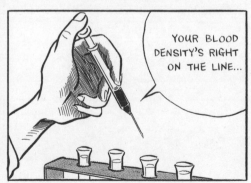

YOUR BLOOD DENSITY'S RIGHT ON THE LINE...

DON'T SAY THAT. I'VE BEEN WAITIN' ALL MORNING.

IT'S NOT LIKE I HAVE SYPHILIS...

TODAY IT'S FINE, BUT YOU TAKE IT EASY.

SAN KYUU.

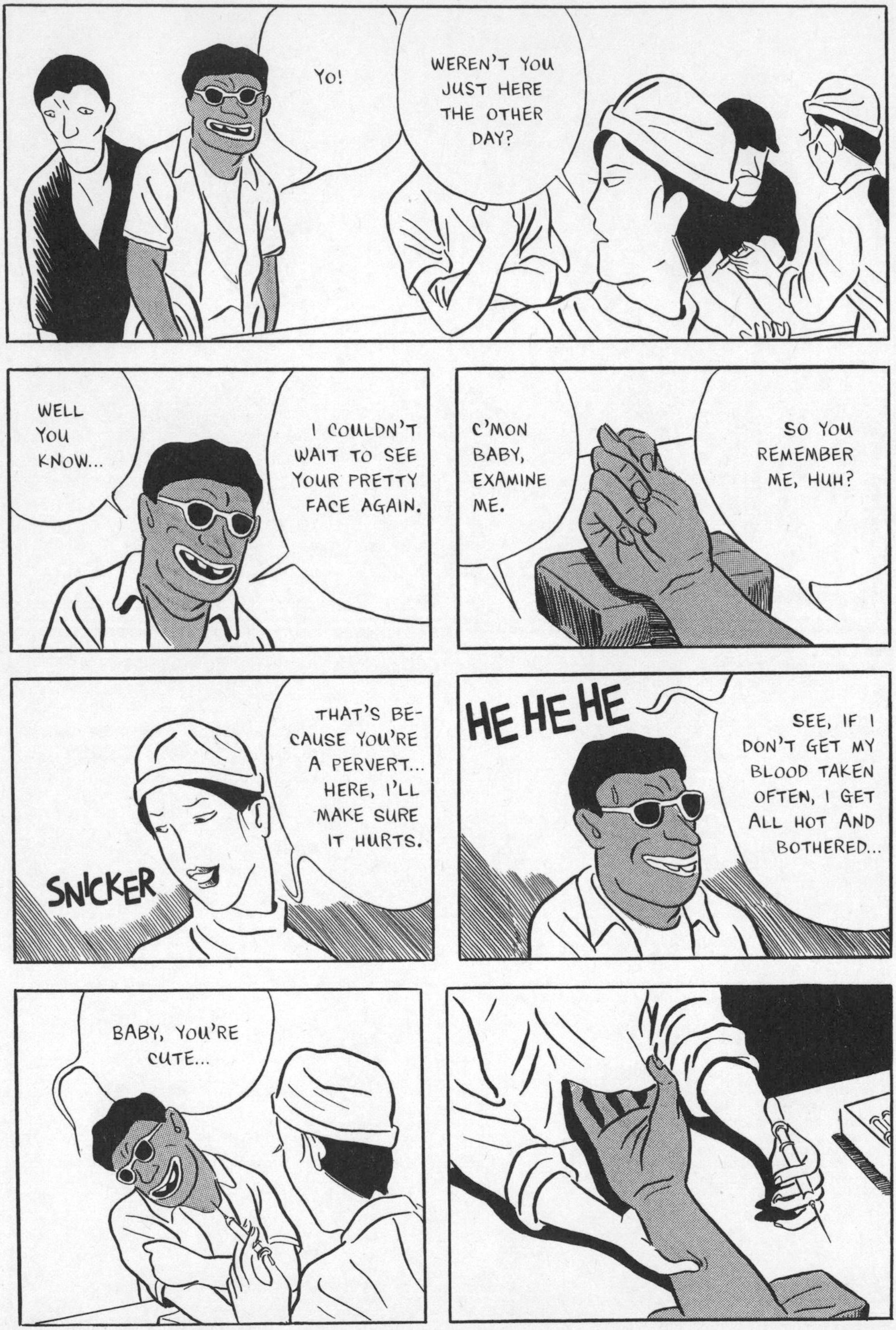
YO!
WEREN'T YOU JUST HERE THE OTHER DAY?
WELL YOU KNOW...
I COULDN'T WAIT TO SEE YOUR PRETTY FACE AGAIN.
C'MON BABY, EXAMINE ME.
SO YOU REMEMBER ME, HUH?
THAT'S BE- CAUSE YOU'RE A PERVERT... HERE, I'LL MAKE SURE IT HURTS.
SNICKER
HE HE HE
SEE, IF I DON'T GET MY BLOOD TAKEN OFTEN, I GET ALL HOT AND BOTHERED...
BABY, YOU'RE CUTE...

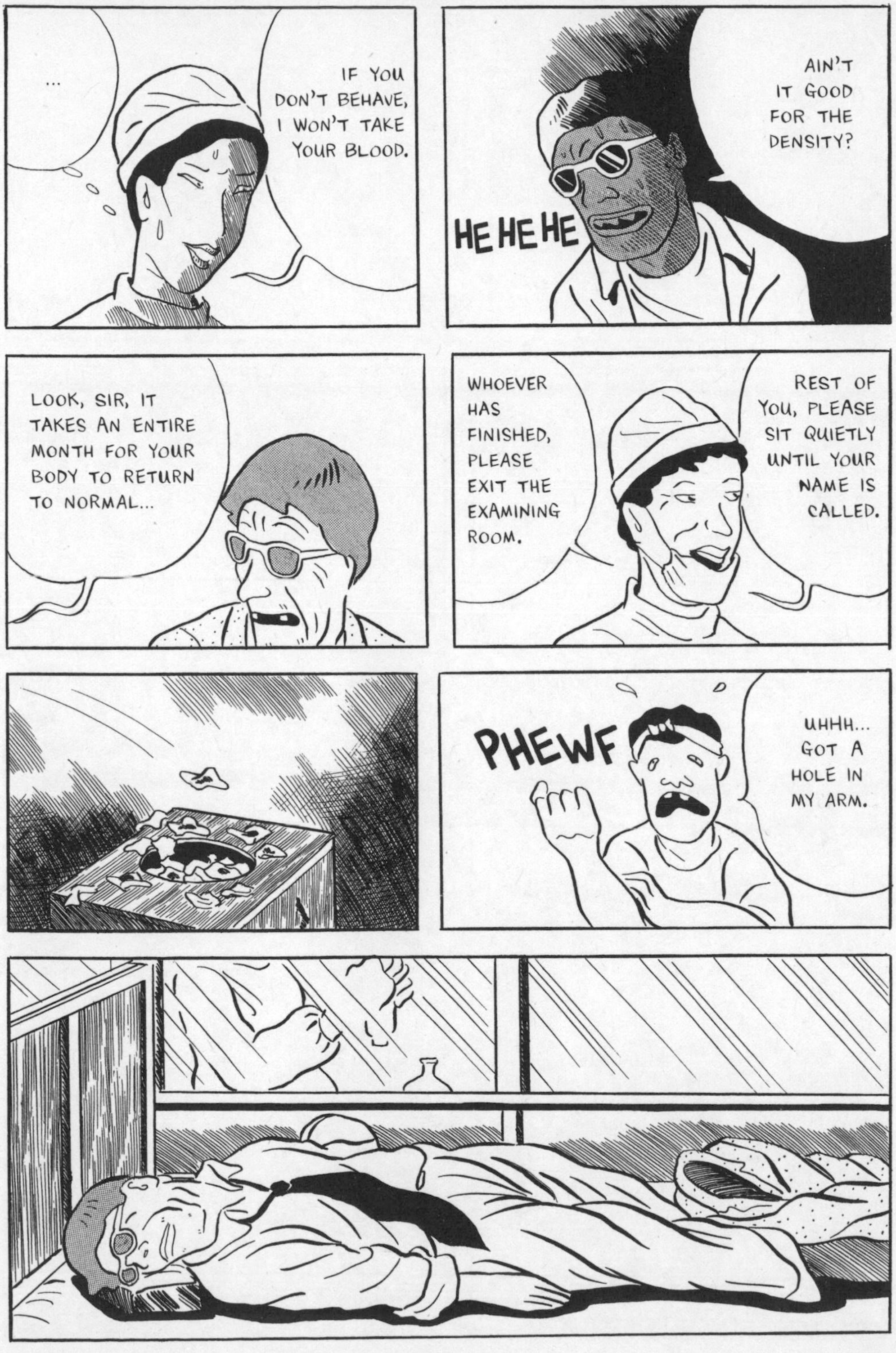
...
IF YOU DON'T BEHAVE, I WON'T TAKE YOUR BLOOD.
AIN'T IT GOOD FOR THE DENSITY?
HE HE HE
LOOK, SIR, IT TAKES AN ENTIRE MONTH FOR YOUR BODY TO RETURN TO NORMAL...
WHOEVER HAS FINISHED, PLEASE EXIT THE EXAMINING ROOM.
REST OF YOU, PLEASE SIT QUIETLY UNTIL YOUR NAME IS CALLED.
PHEWF
UHHH... GOT A HOLE IN MY ARM.

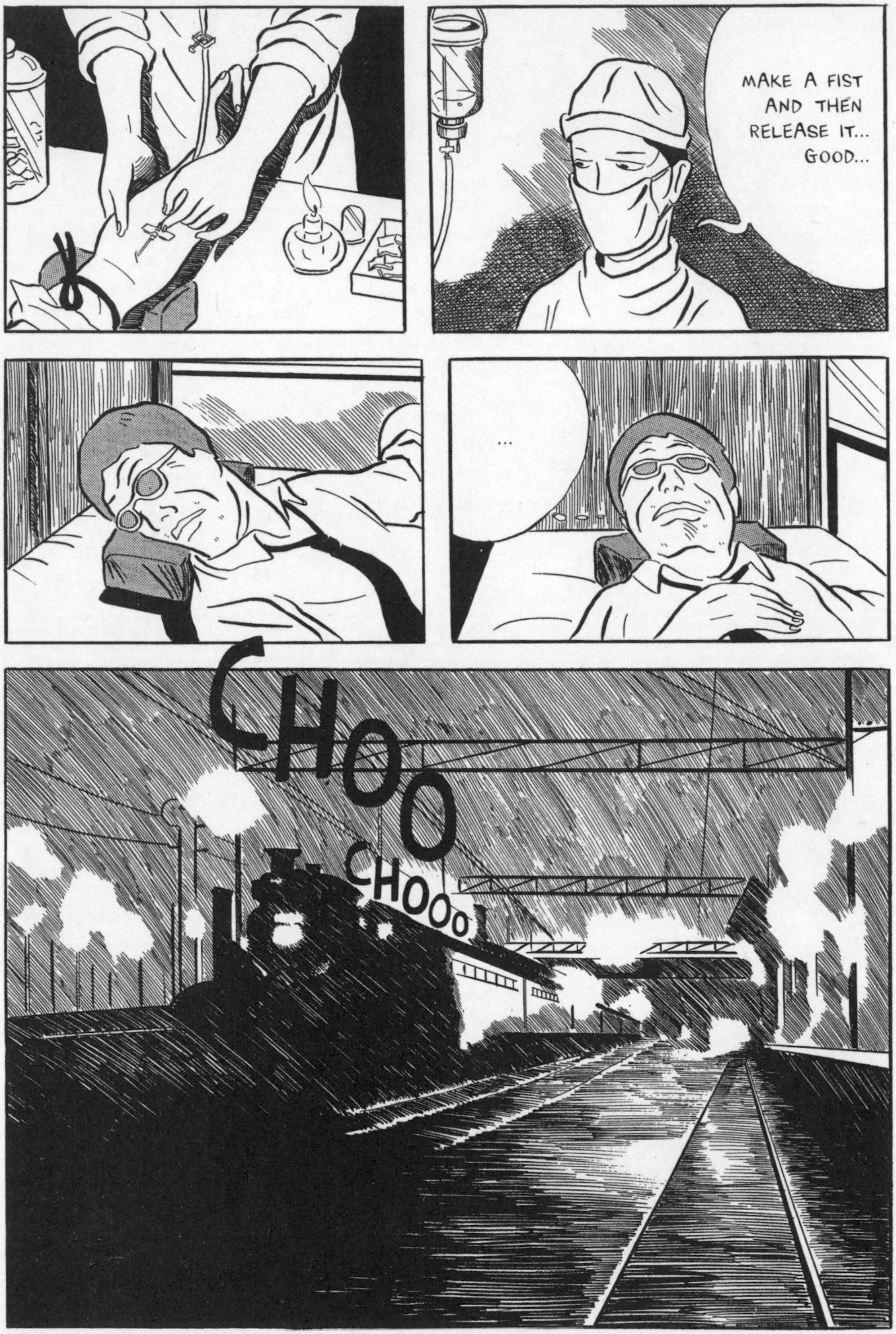
MAKE A FIST AND THEN RELEASE IT... GOOD...
...
CHOO
CHOO
CHOOo

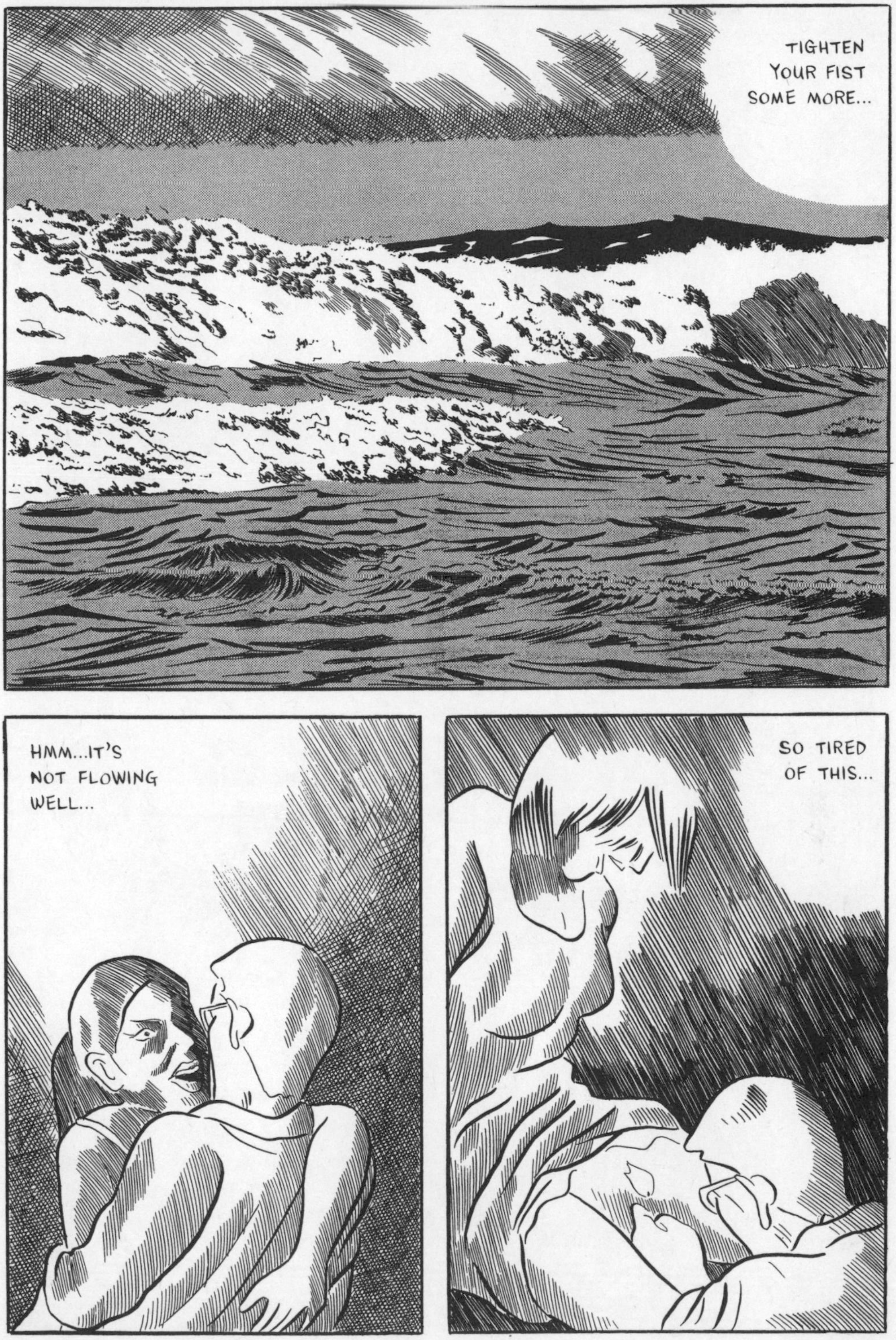
TIGHTEN YOUR FIST SOME MORE...
HMM...IT'S NOT FLOWING WELL...
SO TIRED OF THIS...

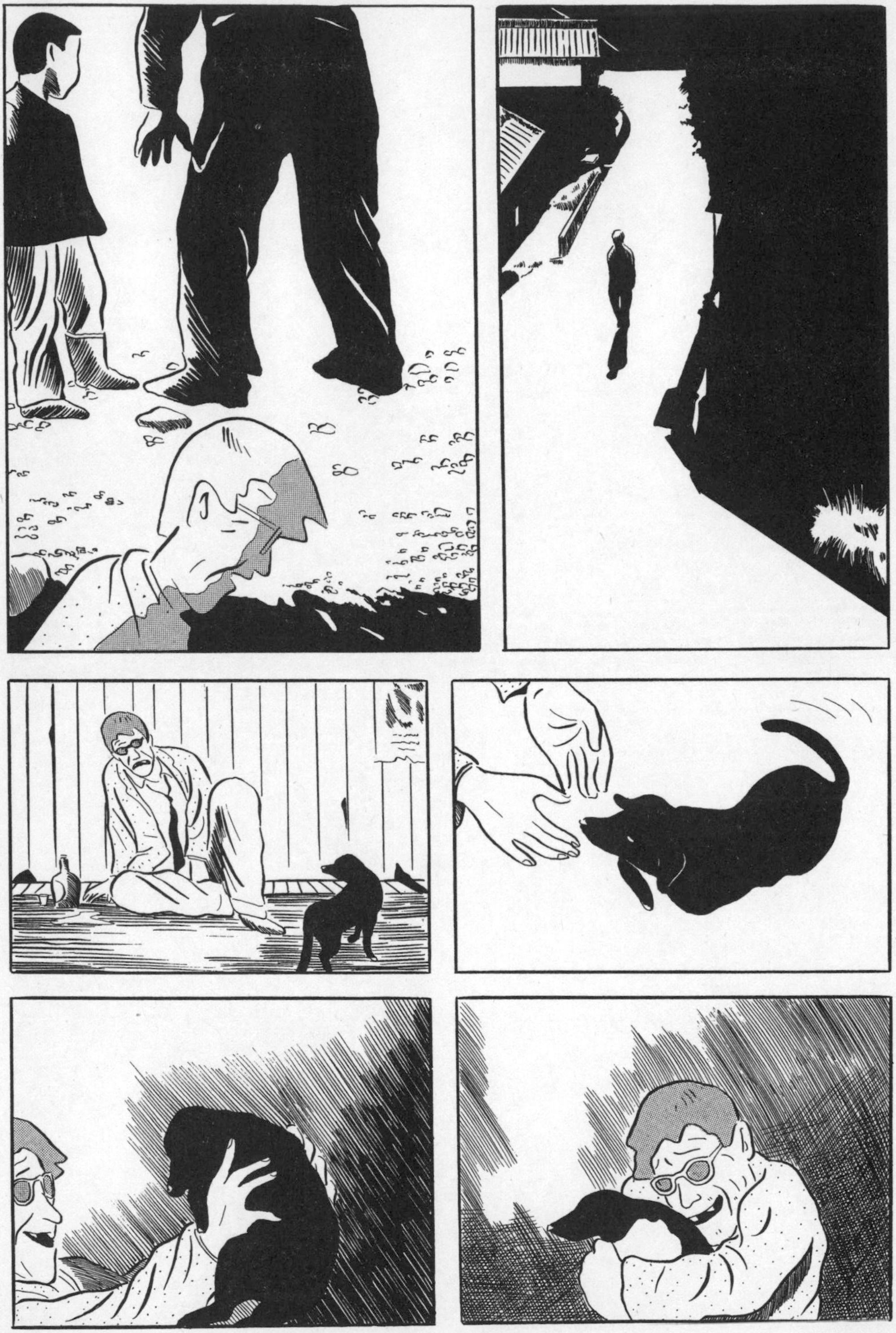

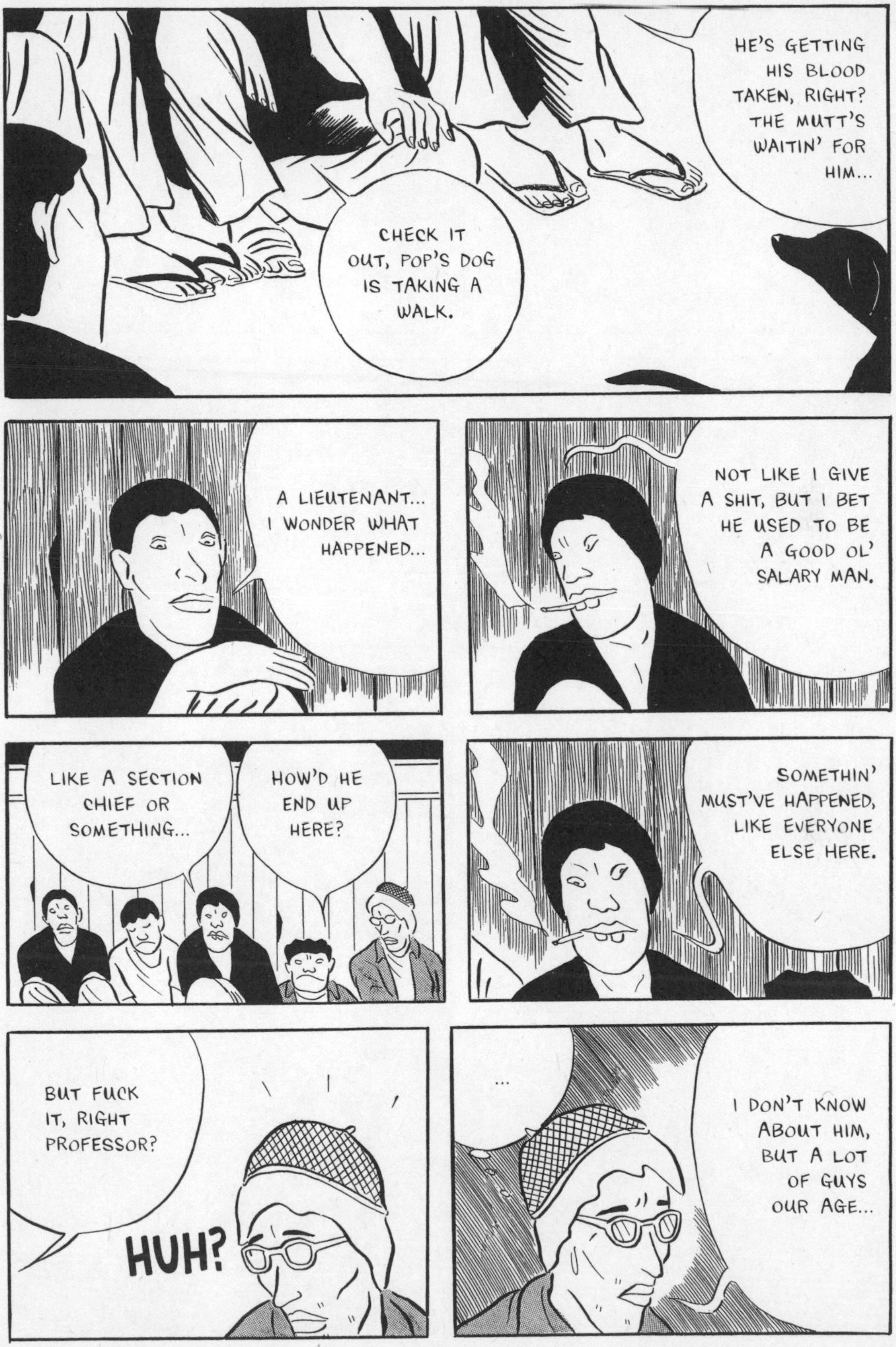
CHECK IT OUT, POP'S DOG IS TAKING A WALK.
HE'S GETTING HIS BLOOD TAKEN, RIGHT? THE MUTT'S WAITIN' FOR HIM...
A LIEUTENANT... I WONDER WHAT HAPPENED...
NOT LIKE I GIVE A SHIT, BUT I BET HE USED TO BE A GOOD OL' SALARY MAN.
LIKE A SECTION CHIEF OR SOMETHING...
HOW'D HE END UP HERE?
SOMETHIN' MUST'VE HAPPENED, LIKE EVERYONE ELSE HERE.
BUT FUCK IT, RIGHT PROFESSOR?
HUH?
...
I DON'T KNOW ABOUT HIM, BUT A LOT OF GUYS OUR AGE...

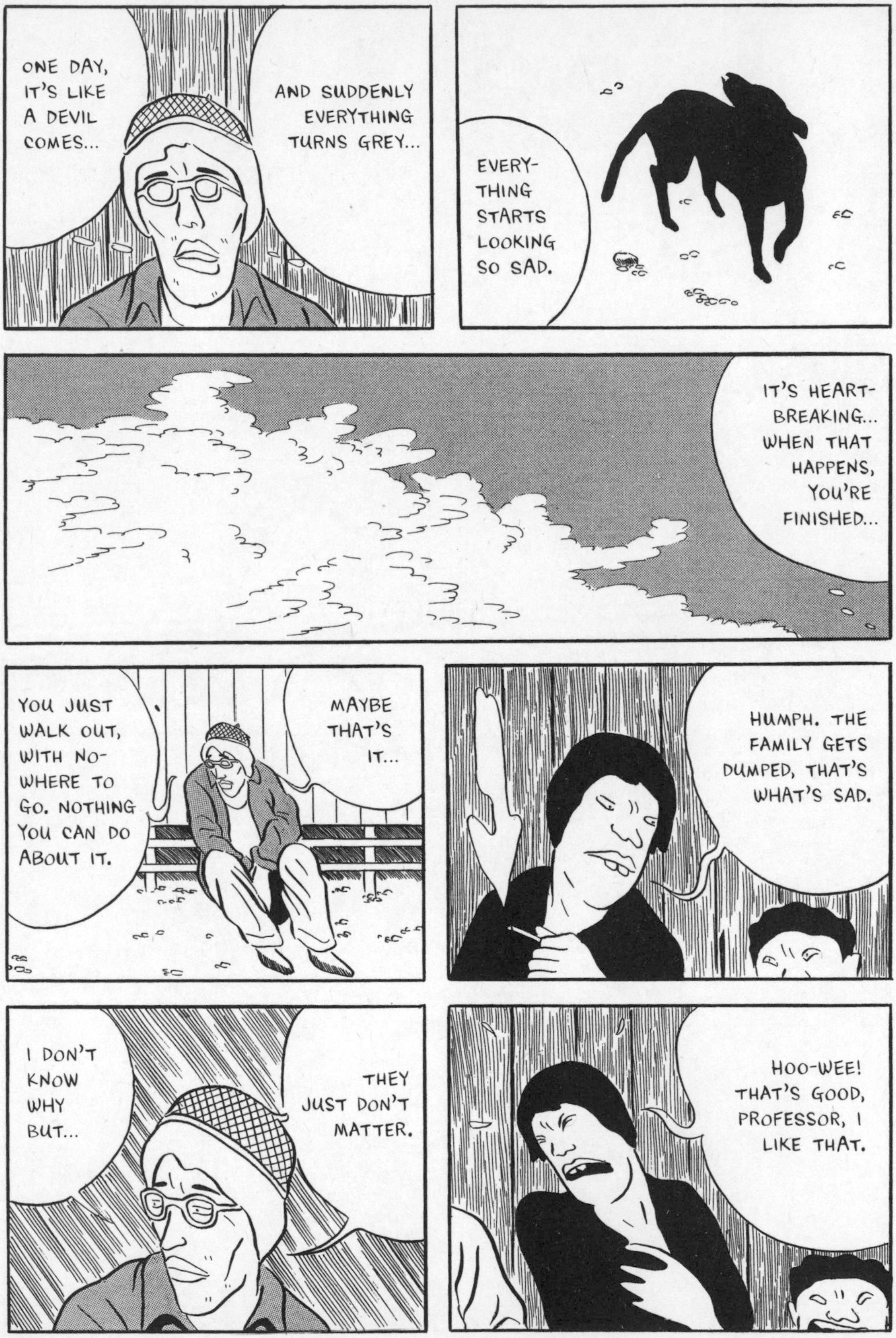
ONE DAY, IT'S LIKE A DEVIL COMES...
AND SUDDENLY EVERYTHING TURNS GREY...
EVERY-THING STARTS LOOKING SO SAD.
IT'S HEART-BREAKING... WHEN THAT HAPPENS, YOU'RE FINISHED...
YOU JUST WALK OUT, WITH NO-WHERE TO GO. NOTHING YOU CAN DO ABOUT IT.
MAYBE THAT'S IT...
HUMPH. THE FAMILY GETS DUMPED, THAT'S WHAT'S SAD.
I DON'T KNOW WHY BUT...
THEY JUST DON'T MATTER.
HOO-WEE! THAT'S GOOD, PROFESSOR, I LIKE THAT.

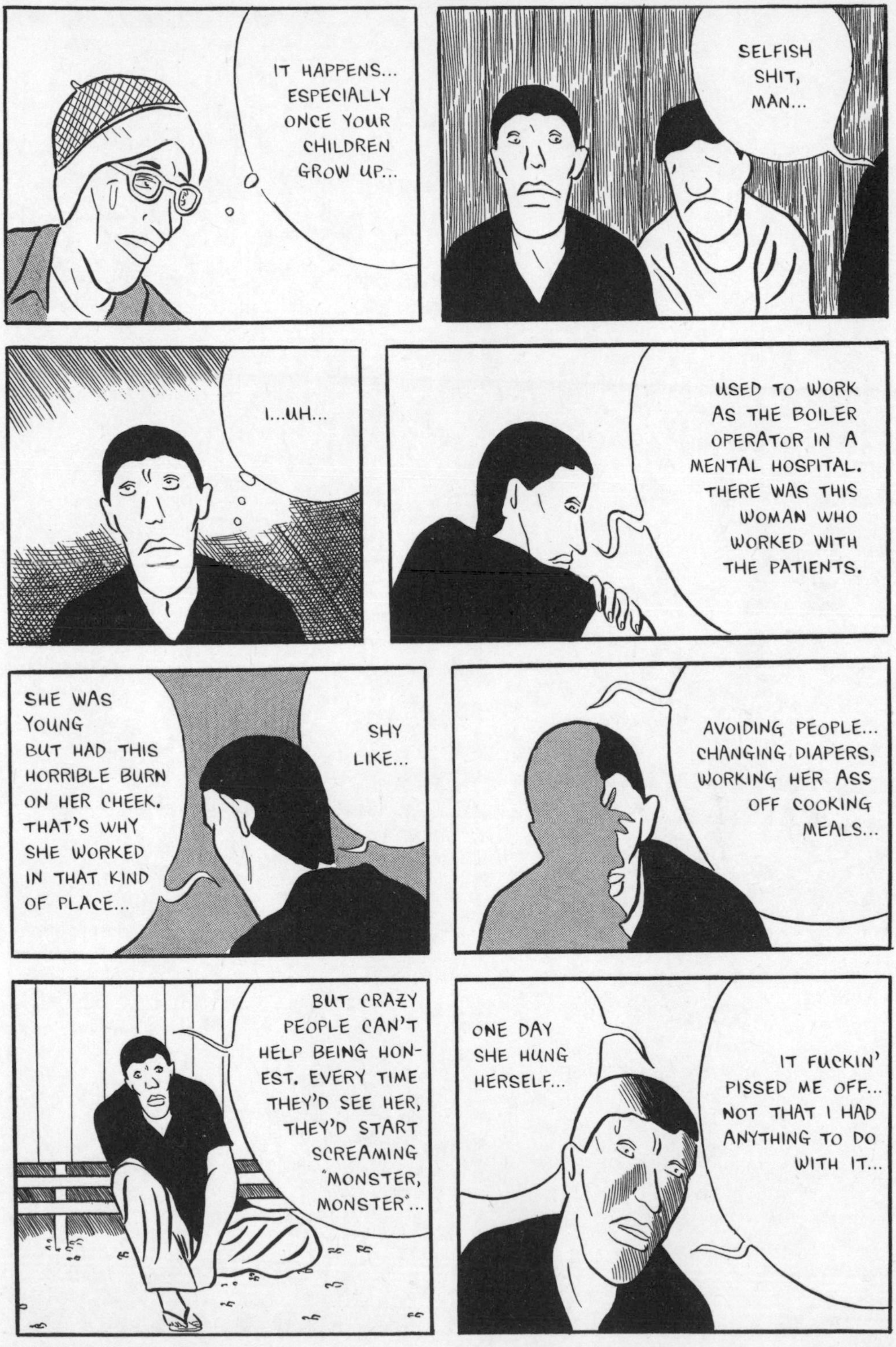
IT HAPPENS... ESPECIALLY ONCE YOUR CHILDREN GROW UP...
SELFISH SHIT, MAN...
I...UH...
USED TO WORK AS THE BOILER OPERATOR IN A MENTAL HOSPITAL. THERE WAS THIS WOMAN WHO WORKED WITH THE PATIENTS.
SHE WAS YOUNG BUT HAD THIS HORRIBLE BURN ON HER CHEEK. THAT'S WHY SHE WORKED IN THAT KIND OF PLACE...
SHY LIKE...
AVOIDING PEOPLE... CHANGING DIAPERS, WORKING HER ASS OFF COOKING MEALS...
BUT CRAZY PEOPLE CAN'T HELP BEING HON-EST. EVERY TIME THEY'D SEE HER, THEY'D START SCREAMING "MONSTER, MONSTER"...
ONE DAY SHE HUNG HERSELF...
IT FUCKIN' PISSED ME OFF... NOT THAT I HAD ANYTHING TO DO WITH IT...

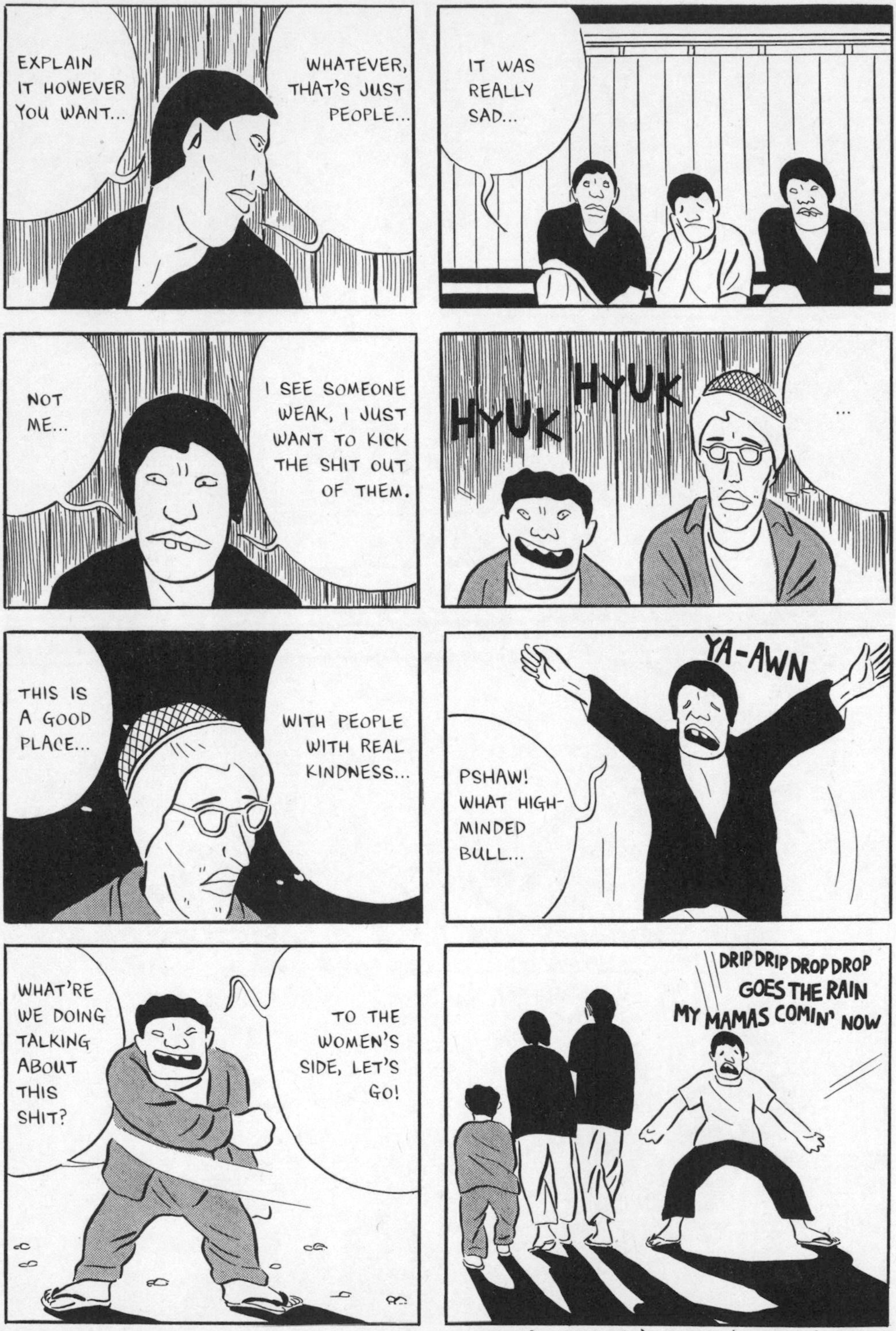
EXPLAIN IT HOWEVER YOU WANT...
WHATEVER, THAT'S JUST PEOPLE...
IT WAS REALLY SAD...
NOT ME...
I SEE SOMEONE WEAK, I JUST WANT TO KICK THE SHIT OUT OF THEM.
HYUK HYUK
...
THIS IS A GOOD PLACE...
WITH PEOPLE WITH REAL KINDNESS...
YA-AWN
PSHAW! WHAT HIGH-MINDED BULL...
WHAT'RE WE DOING TALKING ABOUT THIS SHIT?
TO THE WOMEN'S SIDE, LET'S GO!
DRIP DRIP DROP DROP
GOES THE RAIN
MY MAMAS COMIN' NOW

SONG: CHILDREN'S SONG, "AMEFURI" (1925)

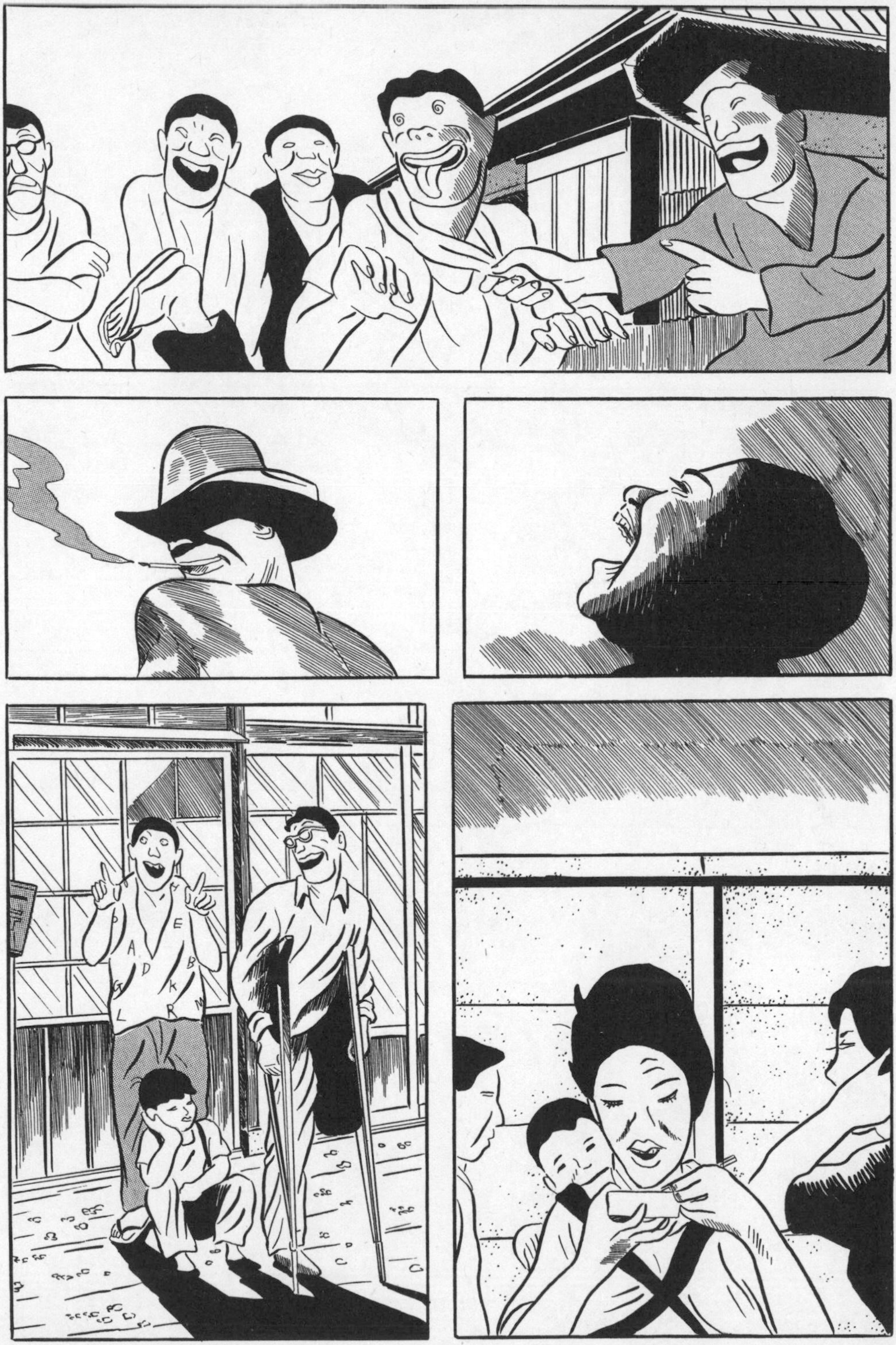

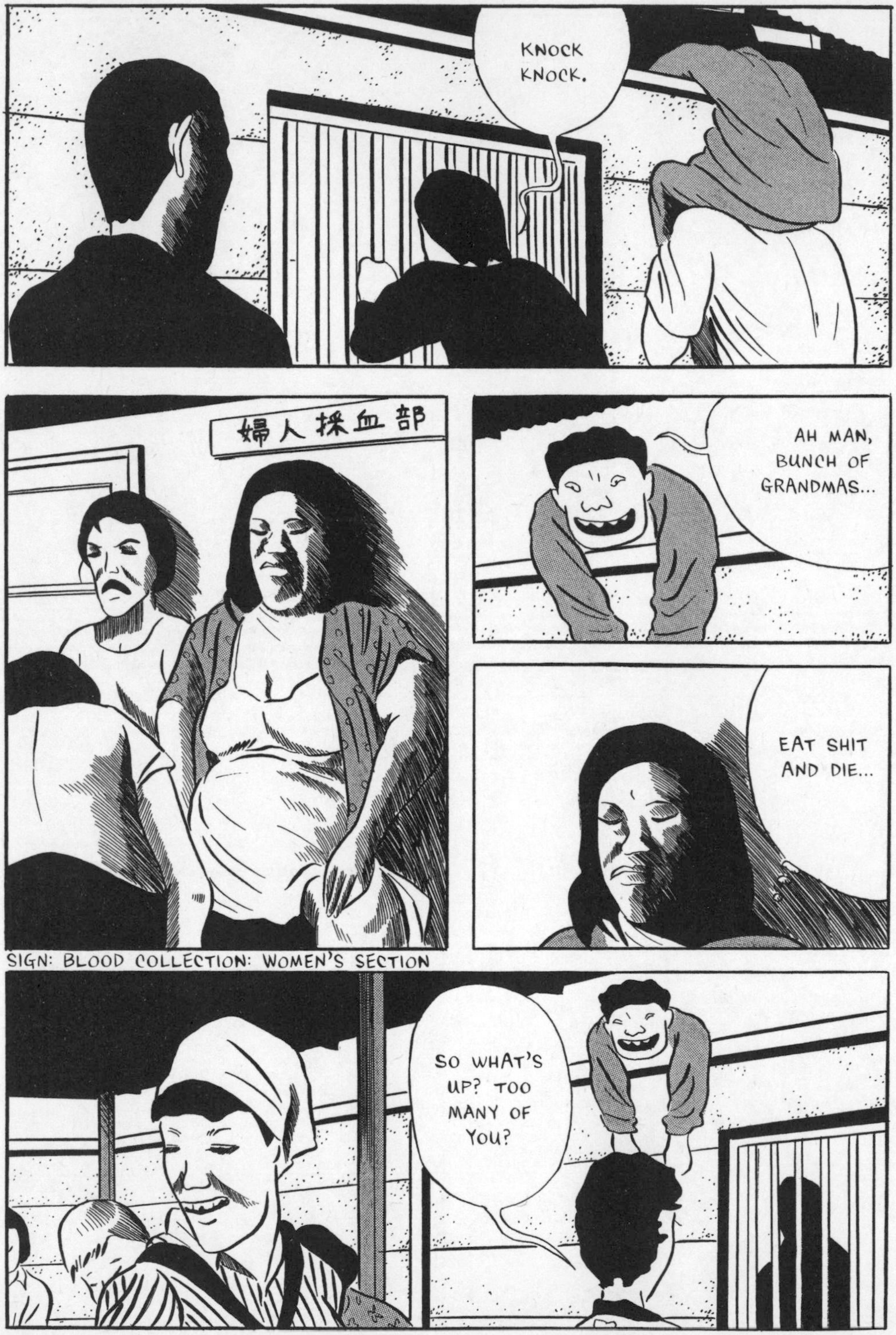
KNOCK KNOCK.
婦人採血部
SIGN: BLOOD COLLECTION: WOMEN'S SECTION
AH MAN, BUNCH OF GRANDMAS...
EAT SHIT AND DIE...
SO WHAT'S UP? TOO MANY OF YOU?

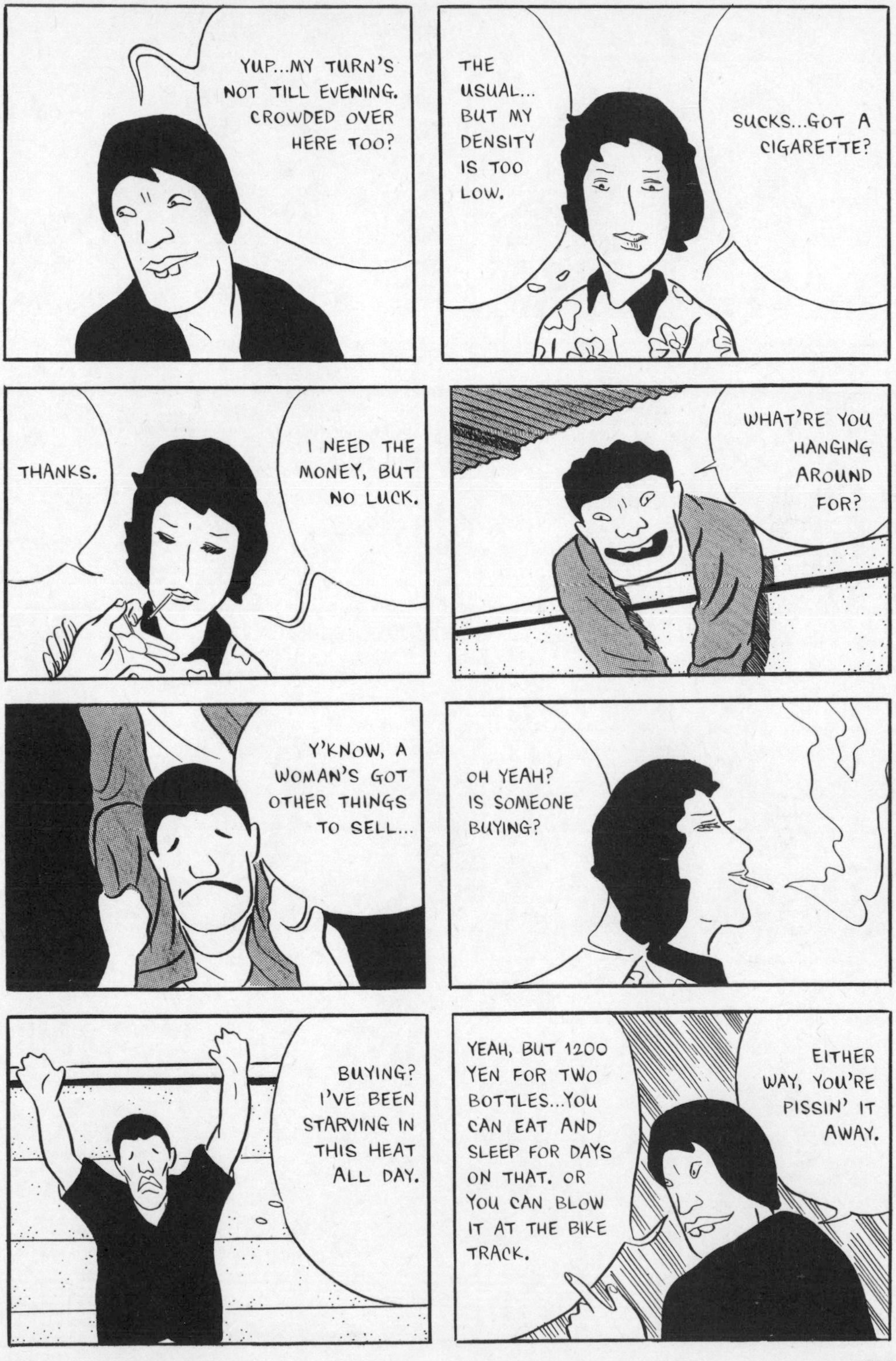
YUP...MY TURN'S NOT TILL EVENING. CROWDED OVER HERE TOO?
THE USUAL... BUT MY DENSITY IS TOO LOW.
SUCKS...GOT A CIGARETTE?
THANKS.
I NEED THE MONEY, BUT NO LUCK.
WHAT'RE YOU HANGING AROUND FOR?
Y'KNOW, A WOMAN'S GOT OTHER THINGS TO SELL...
OH YEAH? IS SOMEONE BUYING?
BUYING? I'VE BEEN STARVING IN THIS HEAT ALL DAY.
YEAH, BUT 1200 YEN FOR TWO BOTTLES...YOU CAN EAT AND SLEEP FOR DAYS ON THAT. OR YOU CAN BLOW IT AT THE BIKE TRACK.
EITHER WAY, YOU'RE PISSIN' IT AWAY.

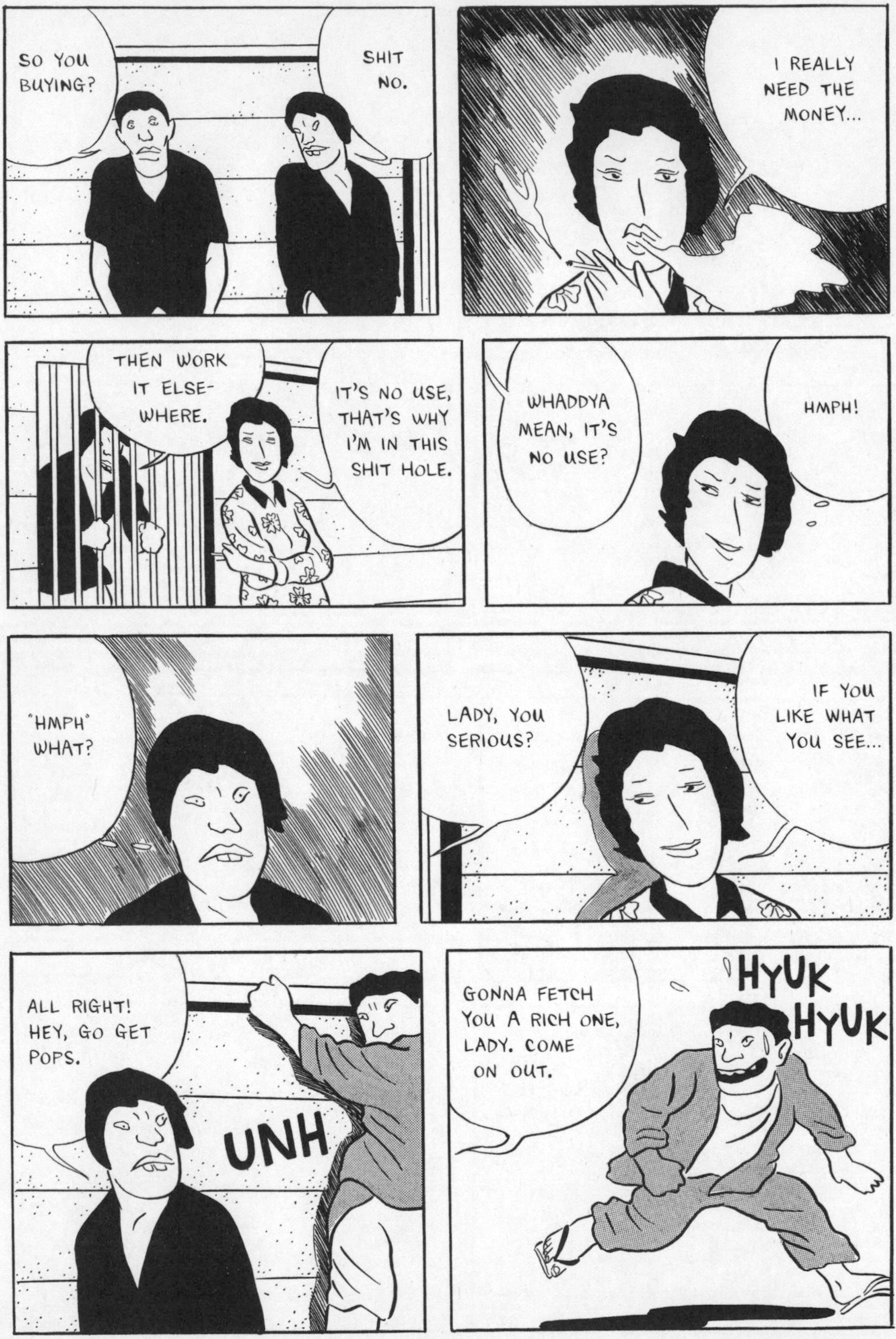
SO YOU BUYING?
SHIT NO.
I REALLY NEED THE MONEY...
THEN WORK IT ELSE-WHERE.
IT'S NO USE, THAT'S WHY I'M IN THIS SHIT HOLE.
WHADDYA MEAN, IT'S NO USE?
HMPH!
"HMPH" WHAT?
LADY, YOU SERIOUS?
IF YOU LIKE WHAT YOU SEE...
ALL RIGHT! HEY, GO GET POPS.
UNH
GONNA FETCH YOU A RICH ONE, LADY. COME ON OUT.
HYUK HYUK

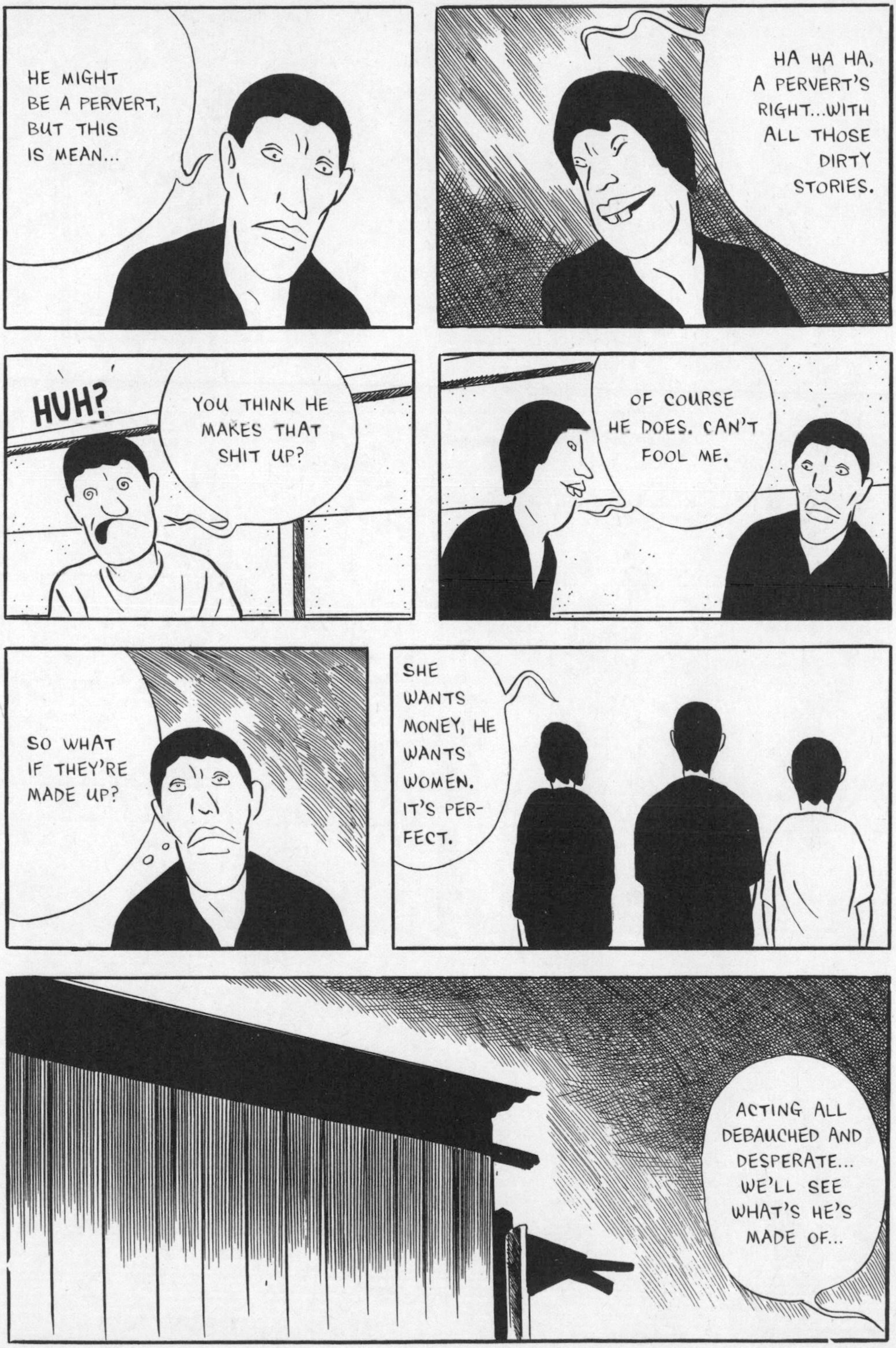
HE MIGHT BE A PERVERT, BUT THIS IS MEAN...
HA HA HA, A PERVERT'S RIGHT...WITH ALL THOSE DIRTY STORIES.
HUH?
YOU THINK HE MAKES THAT SHIT UP?
OF COURSE HE DOES. CAN'T FOOL ME.
SO WHAT IF THEY'RE MADE UP?
SHE WANTS MONEY, HE WANTS WOMEN. IT'S PER-FECT.
ACTING ALL DEBAUCHED AND DESPERATE... WE'LL SEE WHAT'S HE'S MADE OF...

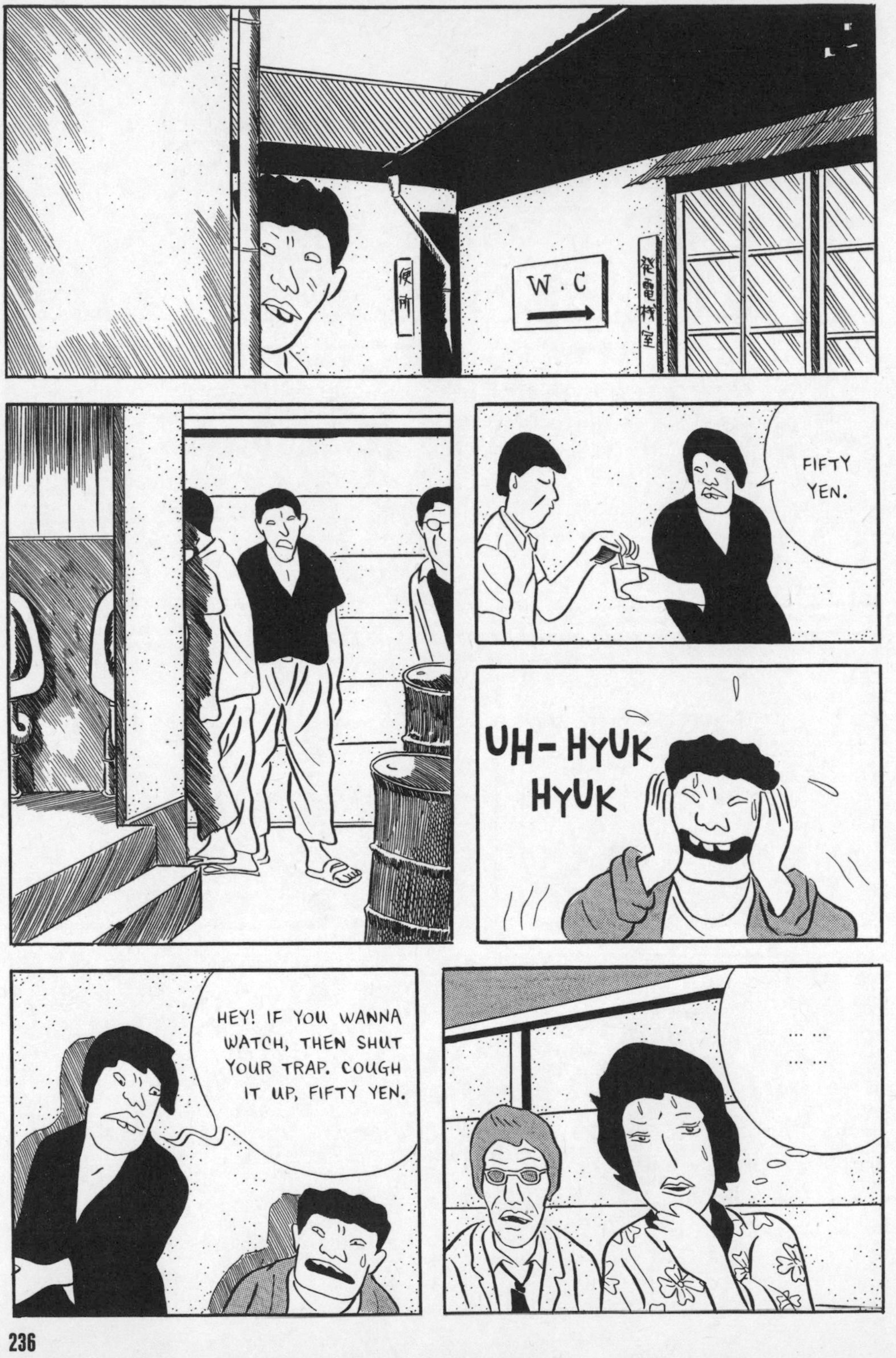
便所
W.C
FIFTY YEN.
UH-HYUK HYUK
HEY! IF YOU WANNA WATCH, THEN SHUT YOUR TRAP. COUGH IT UP, FIFTY YEN.
... ...
... ...

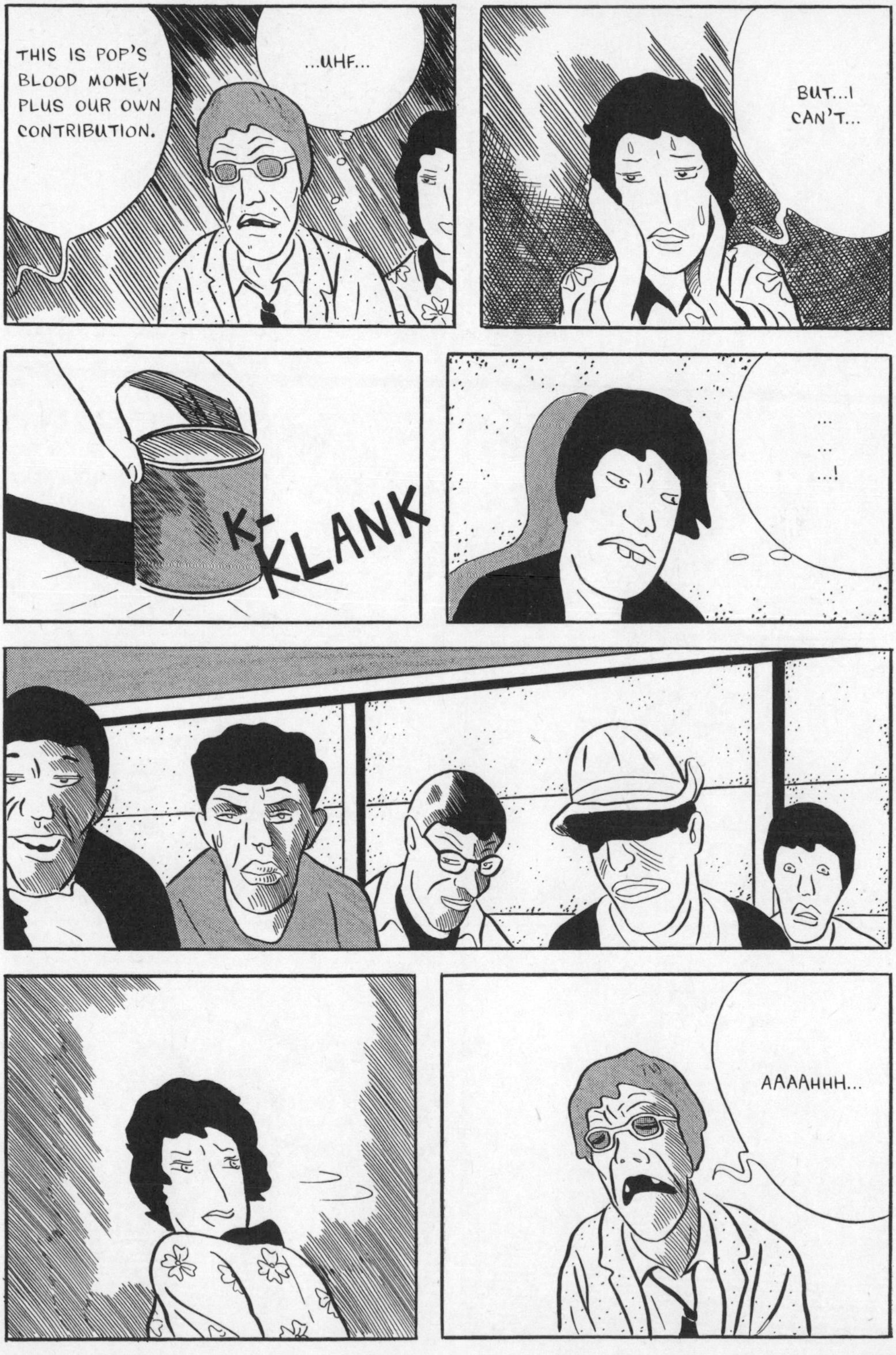
THIS IS POP'S BLOOD MONEY PLUS OUR OWN CONTRIBUTION.
...UHF...
BUT...I CAN'T...
K-KLANK
...
...
...!
AAAAHHH...

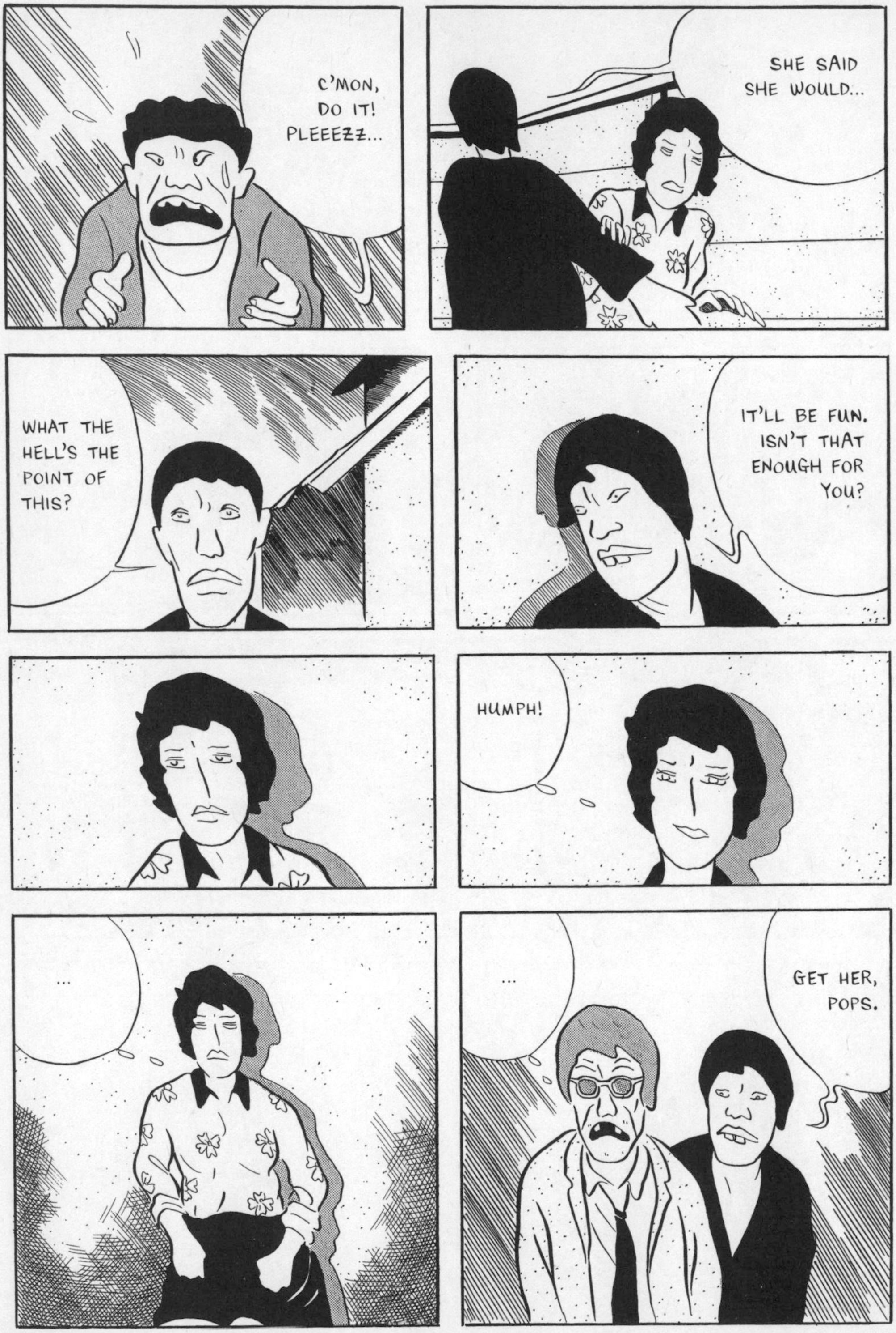
C'MON, DO IT! PLEEEZZ...
SHE SAID SHE WOULD...
WHAT THE HELL'S THE POINT OF THIS?
IT'LL BE FUN. ISN'T THAT ENOUGH FOR YOU?
HUMPH!
...
...
GET HER, POPS.

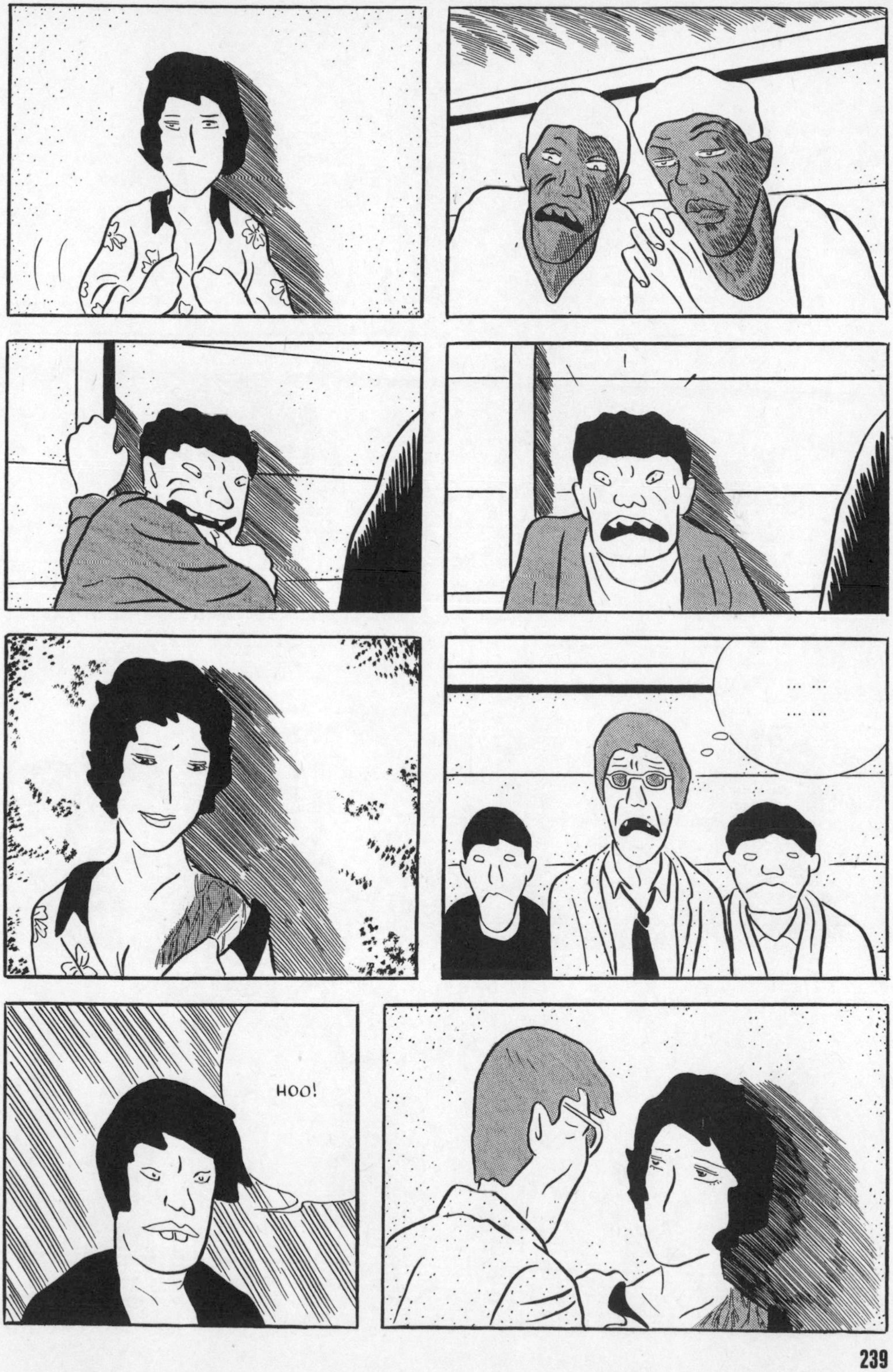

... ...
... ...
HOO!

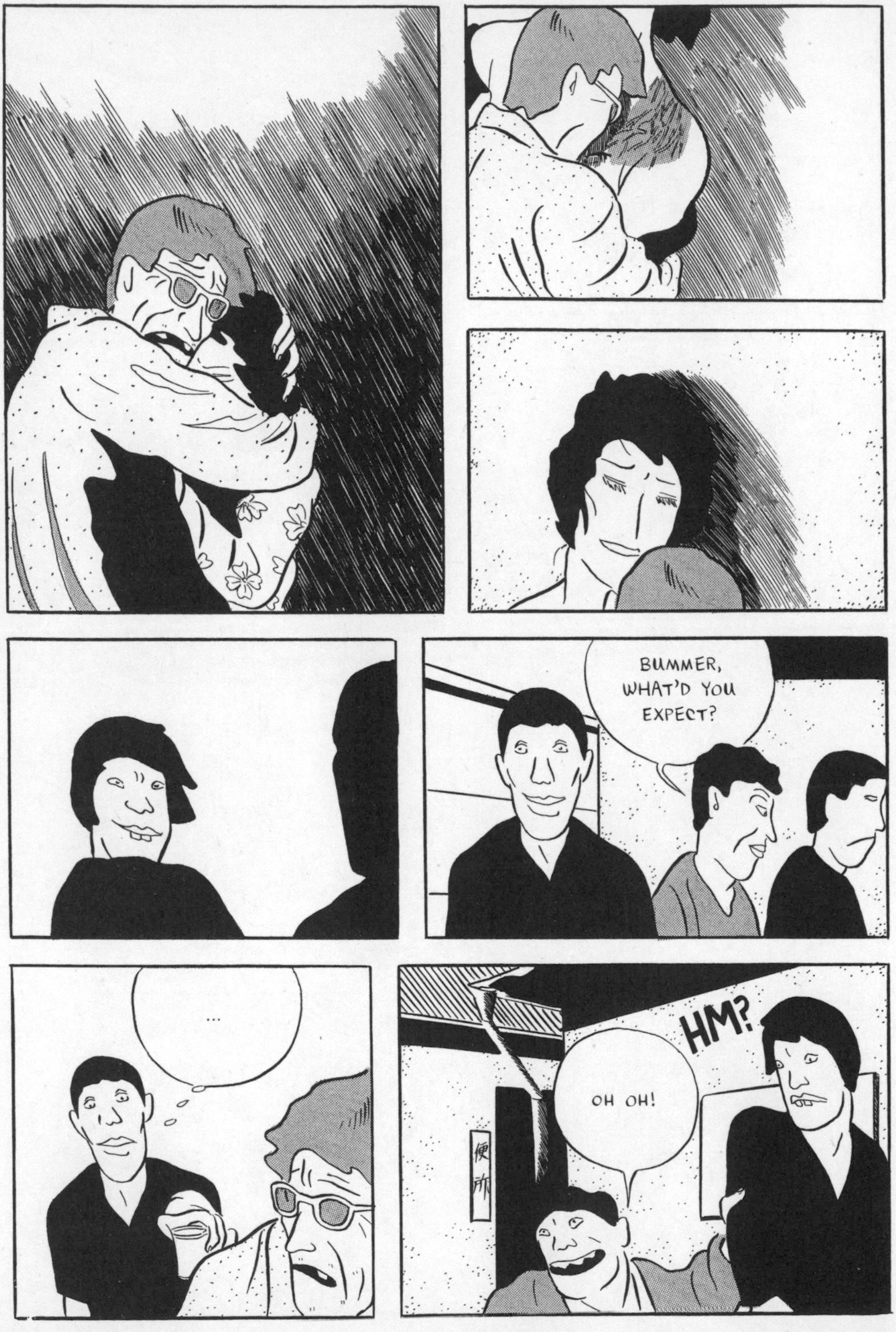

BUMMER, WHAT'D YOU EXPECT?
...
HM?
OH OH!
便所

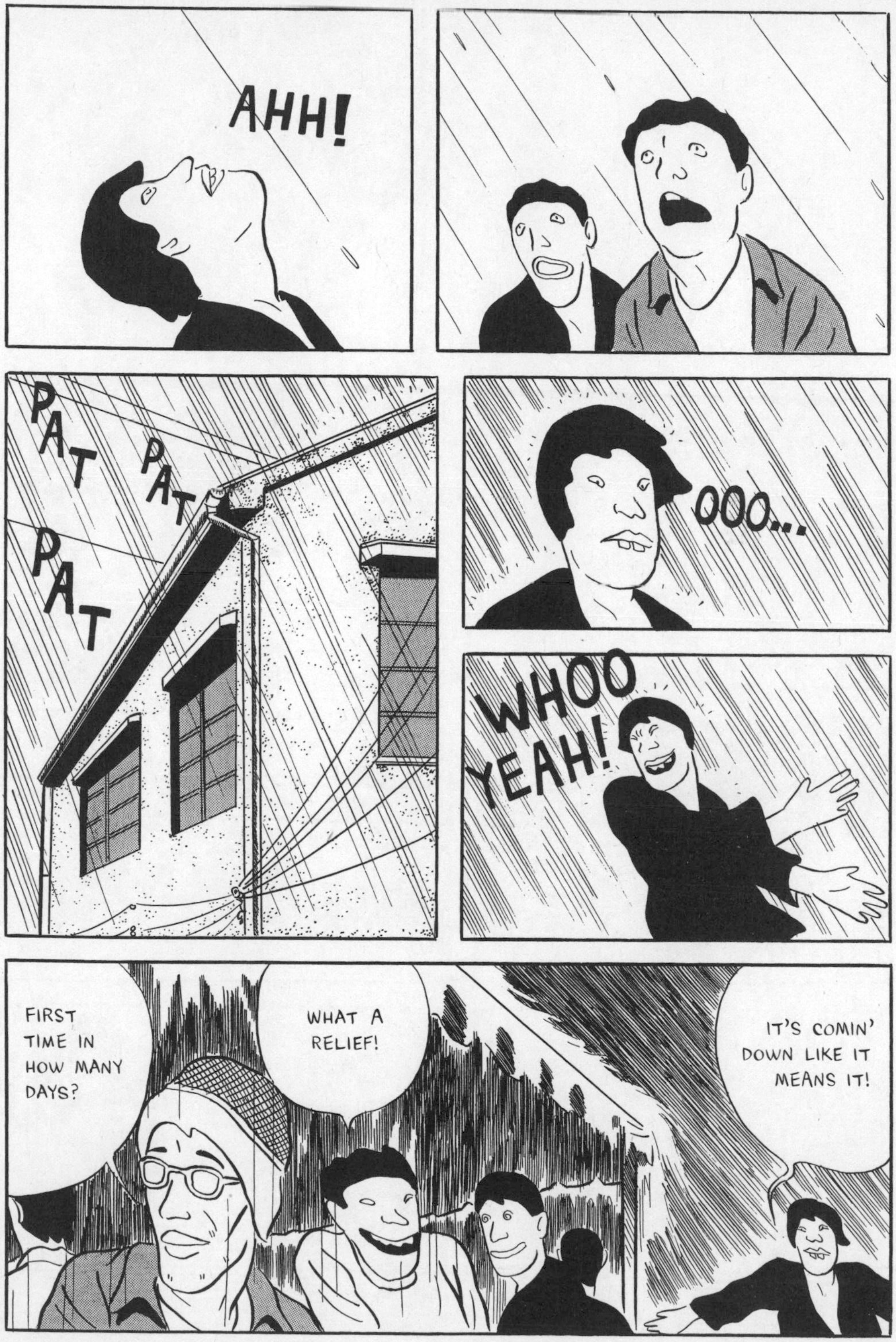
AHH!
PAT PAT
PAT PAT
OOO...
WHOO YEAH!
FIRST TIME IN HOW MANY DAYS?
WHAT A RELIEF!
IT'S COMIN' DOWN LIKE IT MEANS IT!

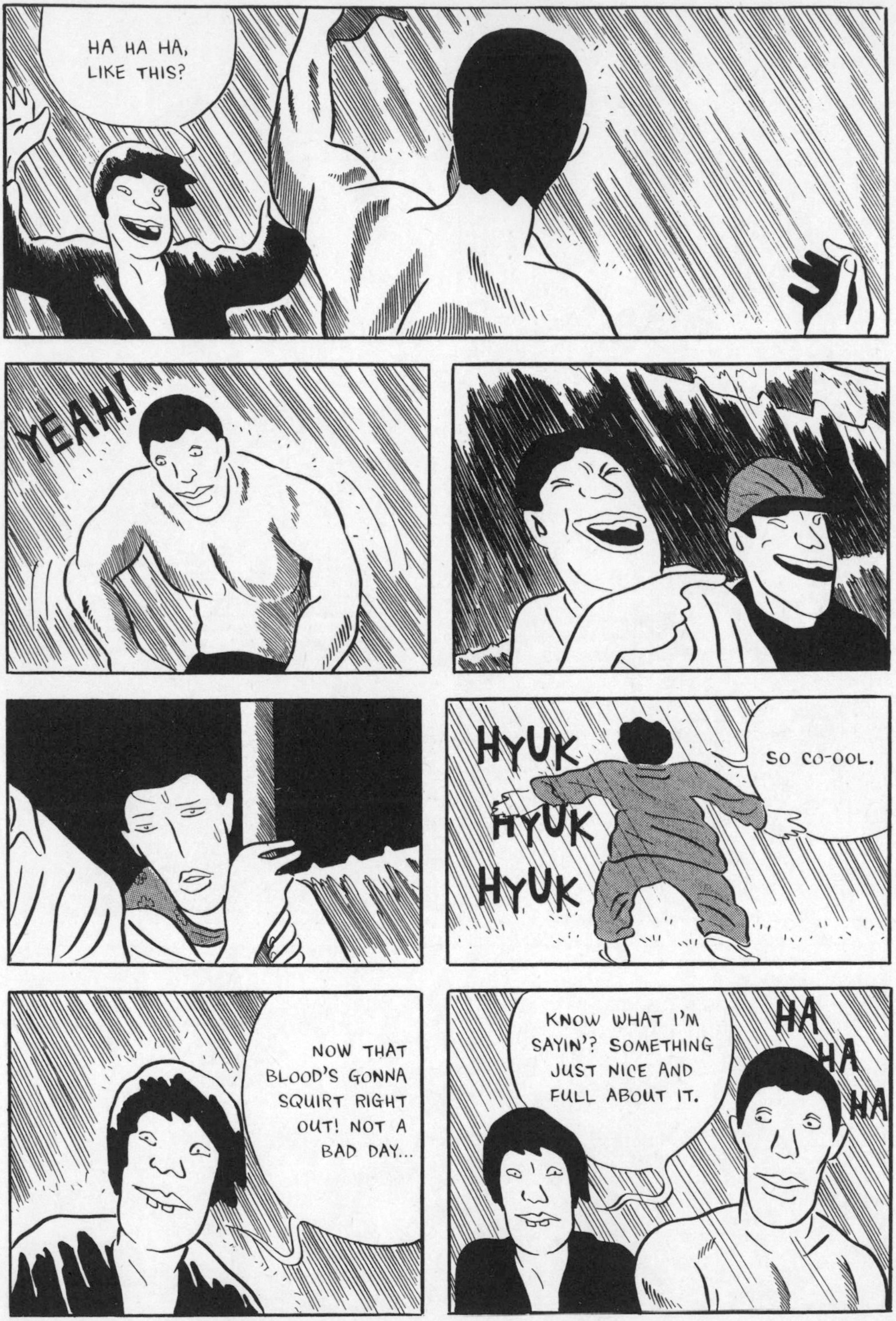
HA HA HA,
LIKE THIS?
YEAH!
HYUK
HYUK
HYUK
SO CO-OOL.
NOW THAT BLOOD'S GONNA SQUIRT RIGHT OUT! NOT A BAD DAY...
KNOW WHAT I'M SAYIN'? SOMETHING JUST NICE AND FULL ABOUT IT.
HA
HA
HA

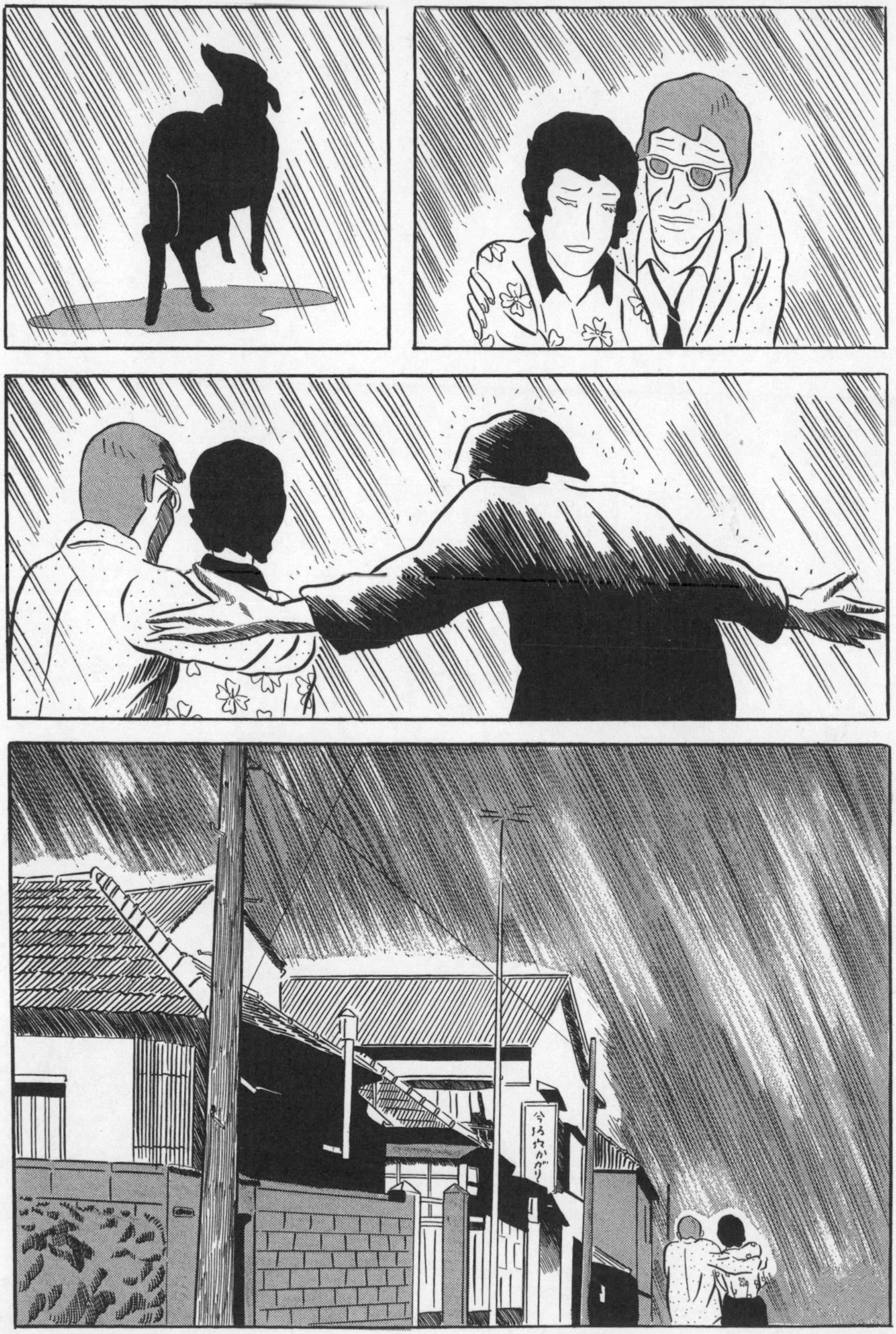

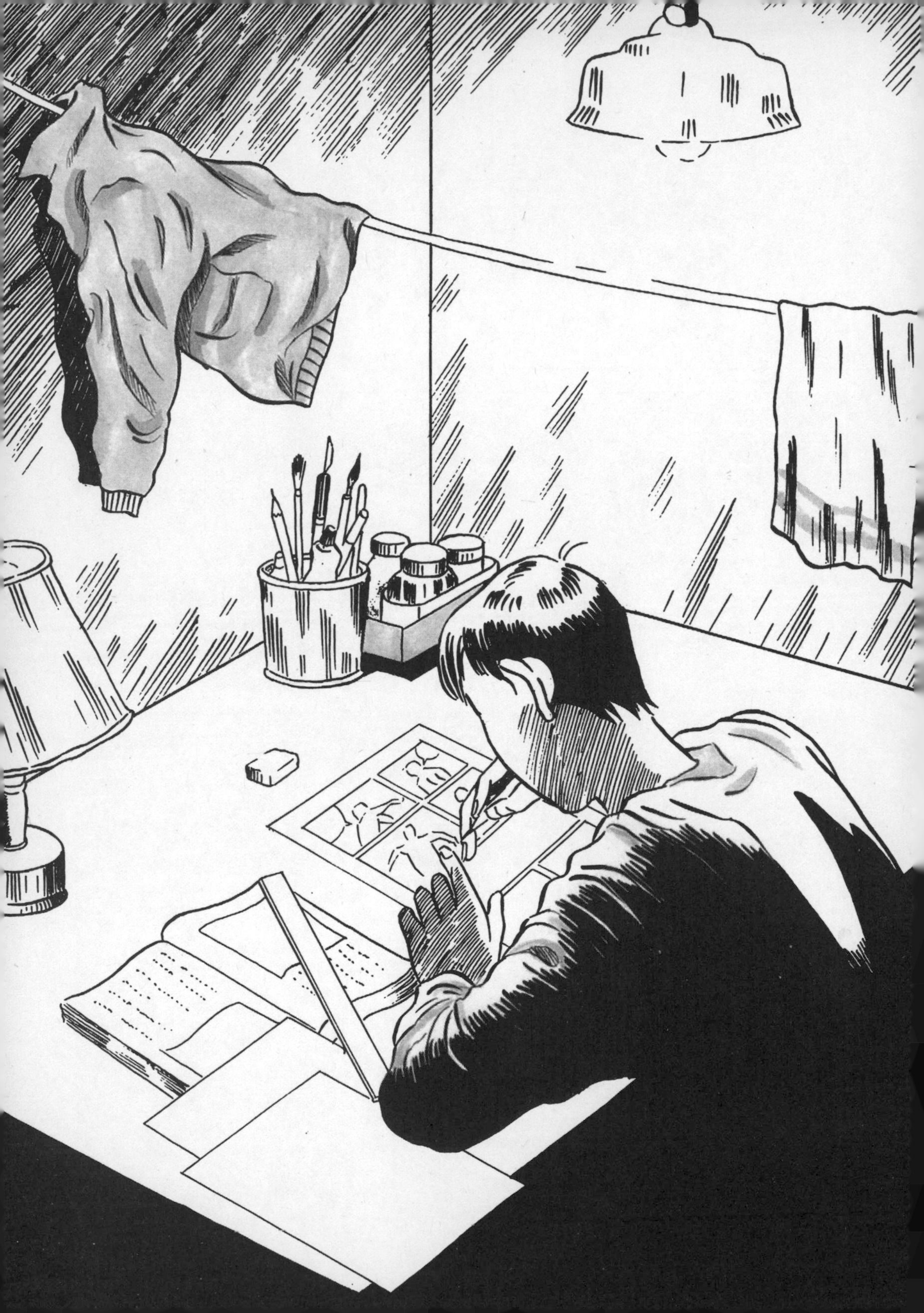

THE TADAO TSUGE REVUE (1994–97)
TADAO TSUGE

Between 1994 and 1997, Tadao wrote a series of autobiographical articles under the collective title *The Tadao Tsuge Revue* (*Tsuge Tadao gekijō*) for *And Flowers And Storms* (*Arashi mo hana mo*), a nostalgic youth culture magazine whose historical coverage stretched back to the prewar period and across *shōjo* and *shōnen*. Translated here are a few of the more colorful and relevant installments of that series, with a handful of the original illustrations.

Katsushika, the easternmost of Tokyo's twenty-three wards, a portion of which borders the northern part of Chiba Prefecture, belongs to what they call shitamachi, the "low city." I spent the bulk of my childhood in that ward's Tateishi-chō. That would probably be from soon after the war, from around 1947, for ten years. In terms of age, from when I was about six until I was fifteen or sixteen.

The reason I say "probably" regarding when I moved there is that my memory of that period is obscured with dust. What do you expect? We're talking about something that happened forty-five, forty-six years ago. I could brush the dust off if I wanted to, but I detest tedium.

Moving ahead a few years though, I can remember things from about fourth grade onward without too much effort. I imagine that's because the impressions of everyday life grow stronger as one, by watching and copying, and despite frustration and setbacks, borrows from adult wisdom and becomes capable of judging and acting on one's own. Adult protection can be like shackles. I began wriggling out of that little by little.

I don't know if I was an early or late bloomer, but in those years no one raised their eyebrows at kids suddenly acting like adults. By the time you reached fourth grade, the majority of adults expected you to do most things yourself, and that was probably for the best. After all, who had the time to worry year-round about every little this and that child's problem?

Around 1951–52, the gap between haves and have-nots was gradually widening. Not being able to obtain certain things remained a dire problem. Most people continued to run around frantically trying to get hold of what they needed. Or so I think. At any rate, that's how it was at my house.

I was constantly hungry. Still, I played a lot. When I got home from school, I would put my bag down and, in the blink of an eye, escape back outside. And "escape" is definitely what it was. Home was a dangerous place for me. I might be hit at any moment, for any little reason.

There was my stepfather—too sick to work and with an awful temper. There was my hot-blooded mother. And there was my mother's foster father, a rowdy old fisherman. They all lived under the same roof and, who knows why, were constantly at each other's throats. I was dragged into the middle of that mess. I could go into detail, but it's pointless and would be a pain, so let's forget about it. Anyway, the never-ending bickering and fighting I could only attribute to the presence of a demon lying sprawled out somewhere in the house with an evil smirk on its face.

My two older brothers offered some protection, but since they had started working before finishing middle school, they weren't at home during the day. So it was imperative that, no matter what, I not be in the house.

There were many places to play, and I had lots of friends. My neighborhood, which was not large, was divided into north and south by the Keisei Railway tracks. In the north was the red-light district. To the south was a shopping area at the center of which was a plywood market. Around that were low-eaved *nagaya* row houses sitting squat on the ground. There were countless alleyways. This is where children socialized.

Below the bright sun in the alleyways, there was always cries and shouts of joy. Sometimes you heard a mother's angry voice. My friends, scattering instantly like baby spiders, ran for the main road and then loitered about on the shopping street with no real purpose. Upon this picture of prosperity, once in a while there appeared an injured war veteran. Adults tended to look

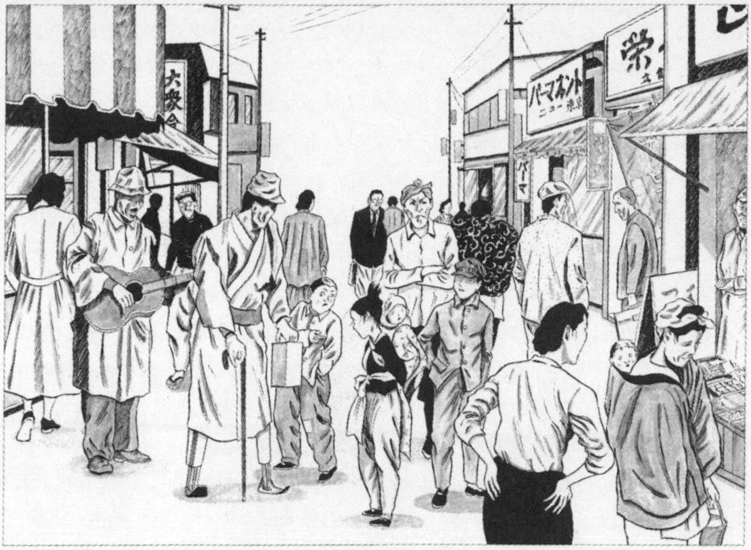
パーマネント
ニュー東京
パーマ

down or away from the man, while we surrounded him and stared, with held breath, at his prosthetic leg. One time we did so for too long and he yelled at us. “Get away,” he said in a deep growl. His eyes burned with a color fierce beyond hatred or anger. Even today, considering that we were only children, I still think the look he gave us was overly harsh.

The sun set. My friends dispersed one by one. But I stayed outside. I waited for my brothers to come home. The sky got darker and the bats began flying around madly. Presumably that other, “red” world on the north side of town came to life. But as a kid, what did I know about that?

I got a job immediately after graduating from middle school. It was at a pharmaceuticals company about a ten-minute walk from my home.

“Pharmaceuticals, that sounds cool. And you can go to work in sandals or wooden *geta*.” Those were the sole reasons I chose that company from the mimeographed job listings given to me by one of my teachers, whose responsibility it was to find jobs for students.

If I had to commute by train or bus, it would mean worrying about what I wore. For what they call “dressing up,” I didn’t own a shred. Had I been left no choice but to ride public transportation, I suspect my mother would have found a way to get some money together to buy me something spiffy without my stepfather knowing. But there was no way I could ask that of her myself. It’s not that I was overly concerned with our family finances. I just didn’t have the guts to ask.

At all times, remain silent. The last thing I wanted to be was the spark setting off a household riot. I worried about that all the time. My mother and stepfather had rows at the drop of a hair. By that time, around 1956, my older brothers were already capable of taking care of themselves and spent little time at home. There was no way I was going to mediate those husband and wife fights. As soon as their moods darkened, I got the hell out of there. It was a rare moment when I could sit at home peacefully.

I think it was around the time I entered my third year of middle school. I started actively hanging out with a group of delinquents. Every night I followed them as they wandered the streets and back alleyways. Apparently they didn't really think of me as one of them. They let me participate in small mousey crimes, like picking fights with passersby in the street or swiping scrap iron from factories. But when it came to something more involved, they always left me behind. "You, stay out of this," the group leader would say, and the rest would silently nod.

Thing was, I had a certain talent. It's a bit disingenuous to call it a talent, but I was good at drawing comics. All I did was copy the works of famous authors, but even just that made everyone cheer. I think that was the only reason people saw me as special. It's not uncommon for a child who excels simply at one thing to end up receiving preferential treatment for everything, and my case was no exception. Everyone expected me to become a cartoonist. Ultimately, they got it half right.

Gradually I grew distant from that group. I became resentful of their protectiveness and began wandering the neighborhood on my own. What happened to those friends? After I got a job, I completely lost touch with them, even with those whose family situations were similar to my own.

The pharmaceutical company I worked for was involved in the buying and selling of blood. In other words, it was a blood bank. At first I thought I had gotten myself mixed up in some kind of racket. I stopped caring quickly enough. I was a bit young to have such an attitude of resignation.

The first two years of my job went by without incident. Almost a thousand people a day came to sell their blood. Unemployed day laborers, the physically handicapped, hoodlums, thugs—all sorts of people gathered in the waiting room and outside in the yard.

"Hey man, long time no see!" someone called out as I was crossing the yard one day during work. When I turned around, there standing coolly was the leader of that gang I used to hang out with. "What are you doing working here?" he said to me, looking me up and down in my work clothes, before I

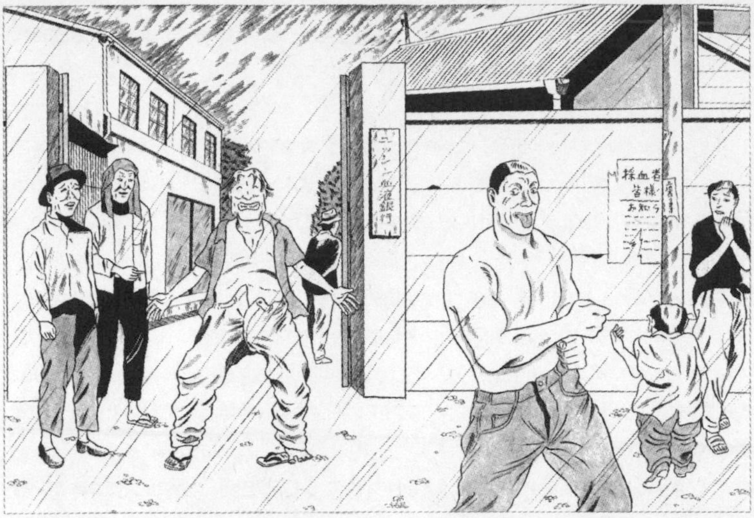
血液銀行
採血者
皆様
お知ら

could get out a hello. "I thought you were gonna be a cartoonist." His eyes, once so sharp, were entirely bloodshot. He looked every inch the image of a good-for-nothing. Clearly he had come to sell his blood. The company had a policy of refusing minors, but from his face and body no one would have guessed he was under twenty. No doubt he had lied to the receptionist.

"Well, I guess you're just like everybody else after all." That's what he said to me disappointedly after bumming a cigarette. He spun and turned his back on me and sauntered into the waiting room. Whatever interest he once had in me was entirely gone.

As I said, right after graduating from middle school, I began working for a blood bank. This was in 1957.

Since some years earlier, a series of new developments had given society a feeling of disorderly hustle and bustle. Japan's economy witnessed drastic growth. I imagine adults frantically crying "forward, march, now's the chance" in the name of postwar recovery. In 1956, amid the Emperor Jinmu Economy (the peak of this blessed period), the government's economic planning bureau issued a manifesto declaring that the postwar era was now over. At least that's how the year is memorialized in most books interpreting Shōwa history. Apparently that was the state of things.

"Apparently," I say, because my own family knew nothing about these changes. We did not benefit from them at all. It is true, looking back on things more closely, that we no longer worried about whether or not we could eat, so I really can't say that we were entirely unaffected. Still, at the level of lived experience, the influence of the recovery felt altogether too light. It actually just makes me more irritated to learn after the fact how things had been changing.

It was in the same year that Shintarō Ishihara's Akutagawa Prize-winning novel *Season of the Sun* (*Taiyō no kisetsu*) inspired the "sun-tribe" boom. The novel was made into a movie, debuting his younger brother Yūjirō. I didn't read the novel at that time. Nonetheless, I heard people whispering and sniggering about it here and there, so I knew about that "certain passage." Sure, the novel had been awarded the Akutagawa Prize, but more than its literary reputation, it was that "certain passage" that established the book's fame. It made a strange impression even on middle-schoolers like me.[I]

The novel and the movie gave birth to the buzzword "dry," meaning detached and cool, as well as to the sun-tribe youth-culture style, which inspired all sorts of public debates. Nevertheless, the boom faded after about a year. In retrospect, it gave us Yūjirō Ishihara, who after the following year's *Man Who Causes a Storm* (*Arashi o yobu otoko*) was suddenly a big star. It's ironic what happened to his career after that.[II]

The Jinmu Economy also raced toward an early end. From late 1957, the deflationary tide of the so-called "bottom of the pot" (*nabe soko*) began to slowly wash over our feet. This too is recorded in various books about postwar history. Again, from personal experience, I can only speak about this as "apparently." It didn't matter whether the economy was up or down: my family always suffered regardless of how the dice fell.

Every day I went pitter-pattering in my sandals to the plant. The rockabilly whirlwind and the superhero Gekkō Kamen tore wildly past, disappearing quickly after a year or two. I had become fully accustomed to my job. The cleaning and reassembling of used blood-collecting equipment was largely a matter of water. About 600–800 people came to the blood bank each day. Sometimes there were more than a thousand, which meant that every day we had to assemble and clean that many equipment sets.

After collecting the equipment from the examination rooms, we disassembled them in an aluminum tub filled with water, and cleaned out the

---

I Tadao is referring here to the passage in Ishihara's novel in which the main character seduces a girl by punching a hole in a panel of a sliding paper door with his erect penis. This scene does not appear in the movie adaptation.

II Yūjirō Ishihara sustained a number of sporting injuries in the 1960s, was arrested in 1965 for possession of a handgun, quickly gained weight from heavy drinking in the late '60s and '70s, suffered from oral cancer in the '70s, and died from liver cancer in 1987.

needles and rubber tubes with a brush and water. It was literally "bloody work," and there was nothing glamorous about it. When you scrubbed out the blood that had coagulated and stuck to the rubber tubing, it would break up into specks inside the water and creep beneath your fingernails and into your hair follicles.

The faucet was just left running. Dirty water was sent straight down the drain and out into the gutter, which made it necessary to dilute it heavily so that it was less the color of blood. An old janitor was appointed to faithfully clean out the sludge in the gutter. When it got backed up, the rotting smell was awful. Neighborhood residents, looking at the color of the sewage, would put one and one together and come to complain. Still, that was relatively easy to take care of. It was an entirely different matter when it came to stored blood that had passed its expiration date, or other sorts of unusable blood that we had to dispose of, and that's because the volume was so much greater.

It was first dumped into a drum can outside the workroom's window. Then someone on the night shift would go in the dead of night, when no one would notice, and thin it with water while letting it out into the gutter. I had to do that job some years later, after I was put on the night shift. You opened the spigot at the bottom of the can, and the thinned blood exited making this tiny blub blub sound, flowing out into the darkness.

Most of us responsible for the water-related jobs were called "preparatory staff." There were about fourteen or fifteen of us.

We were responsible for many cleaning tasks, particularly for the sanitation of used blood-collecting equipment like bottles, needles, and examination tubing of various sizes. After disposing of whatever was leftover in the vessels and washing them out, we had to sterilize them with dry heat and ready them for reuse. Where we worked was essentially the plant's kitchen. Any new employee with only a middle school degree was first sent here.

Out of the fourteen or fifteen people in our group, there were only five men. Maybe that was because cleaning and assembling equipment demanded a special knack for detail. Still, some heavy lifting was required, so that probably explains the ratio. It was enjoyable work, but as a trade-off you had to handle blood, and that kind of cleaning job ended up being handed over to the men.

One time I was ordered to clean the blood-sellers' bathroom. Nothing rare about that. The task was passed on to the preparatory staff whenever the old guy who was the janitor didn't come in. Inevitably, youngsters with the fewest years under their belts were made to fill in. The bathroom, its walls colorfully decorated with obscene graffiti, was truly overwhelming. You wanted to finish and get out of there as fast as possible, but you also knew that waiting for you were jobs that were really not so different from cleaning the stall.

Carefully inspecting the graffiti, I was caught off guard by the following line in pencil: "Even I, a former lieutenant in the navy, have been reduced to selling my blood." I was only seventeen or eighteen, so anything too nuanced went over my head. But at that moment, as if peeping through a crack, I caught my first glimpse of the true meaning of what they called "the postwar." After that, I kept looking, among the clients hanging out in the waiting room and in the yard, for that "somebody" who had written those words. Of course I never

did figure out who that somebody was. But the shadow of that former navy lieutenant turned blood seller still weighs heavily on my heart.

One other seller made an indelible impression. He was about six feet tall and had the brawny physique of a pro wrestler. This man did not have a normal face. The only way to describe this tragedy is to say that, from his mouth up, it looked like a volcano had exploded. All you could roughly make out in that red-black mass of flesh were eyes and a nose, more or less where you would expect them to be. He came to sell blood two or three times a month. The nurses often talked about him. Which is to say, he gave them the creeps.

One day they were gossiping about him at work. Through the glass wall that separated them from the waiting room, you could hear everything they said. I guess they didn't notice him, probably because of the number of

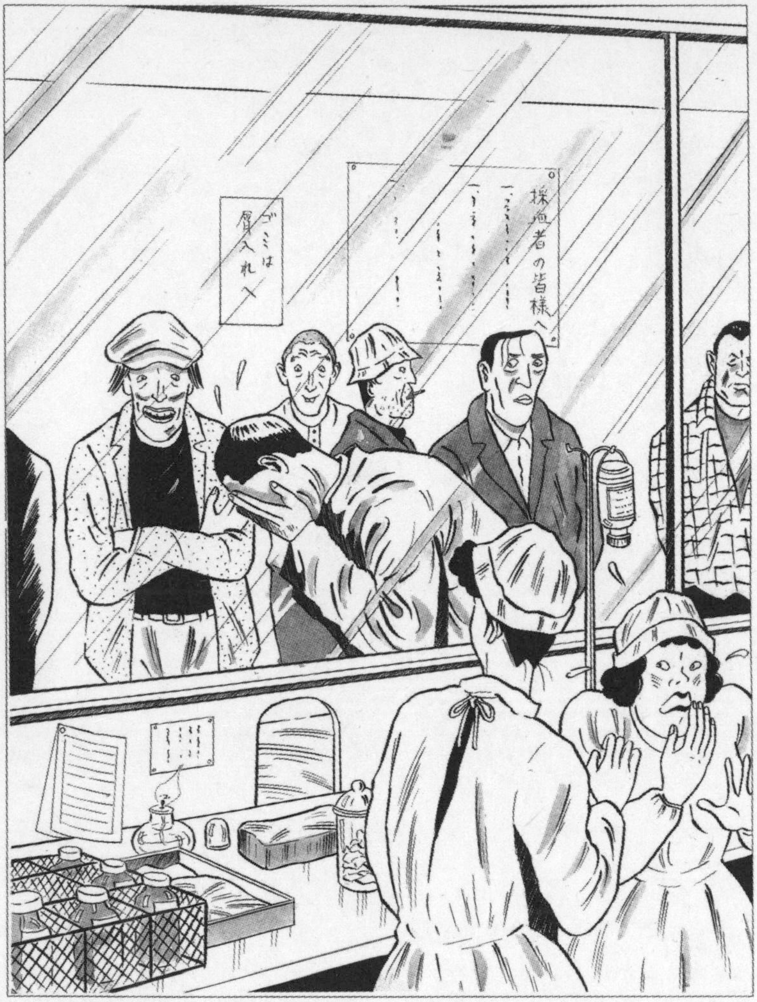
ゴミは屑入れへ
採血者の皆様へ

people coming and going. Suddenly he stood up, covered his face with his hands, and began wailing at the top of his lungs.

What happened then, I don't know. I didn't witness this myself. I only heard about it from others. I can only imagine it was a painful scene. It might have been easy to handle the situation had the guy lost it and gone berserk. But how difficult it must have been to deal with the sorrow behind those gentle tears.

All this senselessness and powerlessness cut up my heart. As my time as preparatory staff grew longer, I started to give off an odd odor. After washing objects of blood, I always submerged my hands in disinfectant. I did that multiple times a day. Eventually, my skin got stained with a mix of blood and cresol fluid, though having gotten used to it I couldn't smell it myself.

However, my stepfather couldn't stand it and was constantly grumbling under his breath during dinner about how I stunk. So I started eating alone. We had never gotten along anyway, so the arrangement was a relief.

After eating, I'd immediately head outside. As my salary went directly to household expenses, I didn't have money to play with. Simply wandering around at night in the city's back streets and alleyways was entertaining enough. I'm sure it would have been more fun with a girl, but smelly and penniless as I was, there was no chance of that.

It was not long until I got back at the world by disappearing into the land of literature.

My older brother, the cartoonist Yoshiharu Tsuge, has a story called "The Woman Next Door" ("Tonari no onna," 1984).

The story is told by a *watakushi* (a first-person I), a destitute cartoonist who lives in a boarding house and draws badly-selling rental *kashihon* comics. He is surrounded by people whose lives are unimaginably reckless, haphazard, and lawless, though they believe that's the best way to be. The story is long, so I won't go into detail.

The watakushi protagonist is of course my brother himself, appearing not as Tsuge but as Tsube. The setting seems to be 1959–60. That's not explicitly noted anywhere, but it's easy to tell from the conversation and monologue on the last page. I will address that later. If that is indeed the setting, this was presumably the period when my brother was suffering extreme poverty while living as a poor cartoonist in a boarding house in Taihei-chō, in the Sumida ward of Tokyo.

One is disgusted and then filled with wonder by the reckless, lawless, but ultimately openhearted lives of the supporting characters. All the troubles they get into make "The Woman Next Door" strongly I-Novel-like in flavor. But it's hard to tell how much of the story is actually veiled in fiction.

Unable to make a living on comics alone, the cartoonist works part time hauling things. Certain circumstances result in him losing that job. Next he helps out reprocessing gunnysacks for grain. On the last page, the cartoonist and his boss have a conversation while working: "Mr. Tsube, you know about Anpo?" he asks. "Anpo? What's that?" Tsube replies. "I was hoping you could tell me." And then, in the last panel, you see the cartoonist from behind as he silently pulls along a loaded wagon. The story wraps up with the following monologue: "They say that the demonstrations against the Anpo Security Treaty were intense in those days, but not even a murmur reached my ears."

I've gone on a little too long. Interpreting my brother's work is not my intention. I simply wanted to draw attention to a particular mentality regarding the renewal of the Security Treaty and the demonstrations opposing it. After reading this story, I chuckled and thought to myself, yes, that's exactly how things were. If you had stopped people who had their hands full getting through each day and asked them, "What is Anpo?" I am sure most of them wouldn't have had a clue.

Not only me and my cartoonist brother, but also our eldest brother, who was working at the time in some factory—we all trod silently with our heads hung along a horizon that had no connection to politics, society, or ideology.

That said, at the blood bank where I worked there were about a hundred employees, and because there was a union we were forcibly dispatched to the demos at the Diet. Being under the umbrella of Sōhyō (the General Council of Trade Unions of Japan), we had no choice in the matter.

As the anti-Anpo demonstrations intensified, organizational meetings increased. A number of people from each workplace were assigned to participate. Who went from my work group was more or less decided by drawing lots. That's because no one would volunteer to participate in the demos. Unfortunately I have bad luck with drawing lots, and so ended up having to go multiple days in a row. I imagine the process was similar at other companies. We thirty or so unlucky ones were organized into a demo group headed by one of the union activists. It was under a thick cloud of ill will that we headed toward the Diet building in the evening after our shift was over.

If you didn't show up, or if you skipped out midway, you were forced to pay many months' worth of union dues as penalty. Despite participating many times in those historical demonstrations, I can hardly remember what I heard, what I saw, or what I was thinking.

Cries of rage, jeers, shouts, cries of lament, voices in song…students, workers, police, members of parliament, brawls, zigzag marching, countless different union flags. And then the Diet building sitting there still and quiet amid the darkness. All I have are these fragmentary images crisscrossing the back of my brain.

There's just one thing I find really strange: why, while out there at the time, was I constantly on edge, feeling irritable for no good reason like a punk loitering on the streets?

At midnight, June 19, 1960, the new treaty was "automatically ratified." It was a while after this that I first started drawing comics seriously, where

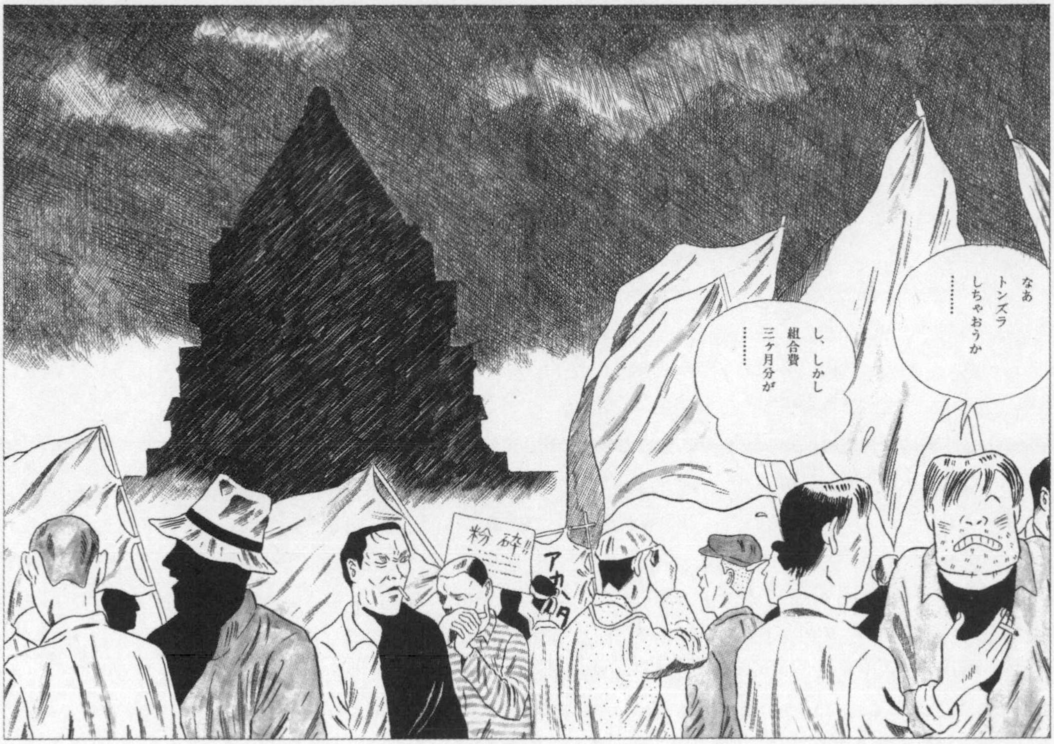
粉砕!!
なあ トンズラ しちゃおうか ……
し、しかし 組合費 三ヶ月分が ……

I had previously only done so as a hobby. There was no real reason for this shift.

My horse betting career goes back quite a way.

It probably started around thirty years ago. I haven't made that many actual bets. It's been mainly just guessing who would win. There was a time I actually gave serious consideration to becoming a professional tipster. I still feel that way a little. This pastime is something I picked up from senior cooks during a short stint I worked as an apprentice at a restaurant in Asakusa.

I worked at the blood bank for a total of about ten years. But actually I quit for a time around the third year in. The reason was to draw comics. This was around 1960–61, when my brother Yoshiharu, who was already supporting himself as a cartoonist, was asked to be the editor of a monthly comics magazine and invited me to contribute.[1] Though the page

1 The "monthly comics magazine" in question was *The Labyrinth* (*Meiro*), a rental kashihon detective and thriller anthology published by Wakaki Shobō. Tadao either has the date wrong here (he first drew for *Meiro* in 1959) or he is thinking of the second time he worked for his brother, as an assistant drawing *jidaigeki* manga (not for *Meiro*), beginning in late 1960.

count he allowed me was small, the pay was better than what I took home from the blood bank. I jumped at the opportunity to become a cartoonist. Who wouldn't?

Alas, sales were poor. After I had drawn just a few stories, the magazine ceased publication. There was nothing my brother could do about it. The manga boom was still raging like mad, but the gekiga boom had reached a stage of decline. No publisher was going to suddenly take on an unseasoned cartoonist like myself. I was unemployed before I knew it. Thankfully, I'm generally a lucky guy.

A friend of mine from middle school who I still hung out with told me that they were looking for people at his work and he'd see if they could hire me. This was the restaurant apprenticeship. I was already nineteen at this point, but the thought of what I wanted to be in the future was a luxury I could not afford. Any job was fine with me. This wasn't nihilism and resignation—I was simply optimistic.

The place where I trained was not some small shop specializing in single dishes. I worked in the trainees section of a multistoried entertainment center serving Western, Japanese, and Chinese food in different eateries and restaurants, as well as in a music club, a jazz café, an events hall, and a bathhouse. The trainees section received the ingredient orders for the entire building, prepping them so that each department just had to do the final cooking.

For some reason, only our section was independently located in a building slightly away from the main one. The off-track betting outlet was right under our nose. That's probably why a group of seven or eight of the staff got into horse racing. One of my jobs was running over and placing bets every Saturday and Sunday. It was a lot more fun than chopping up chicken and peeling yams.

It was interesting to listen to what the various tipsters had to say. They were cheerful, they were brash, sometimes they were even sincere. I was truly envious of their outrageous, devil-may-care ways. Everyone knew how crowded the off-track betting could be, so no one complained if I took my time. I simply wasn't satisfied unless I wandered about a bit to peer at these scoundrels.

Speaking of scoundrels (*burai*), I just remembered something else. There was a suspicious-looking freak show next to the trainees' building. It was one of those small structures with a spooky sign outside advertising a spider man or a woman covered from head to toe in snake scales. I don't know

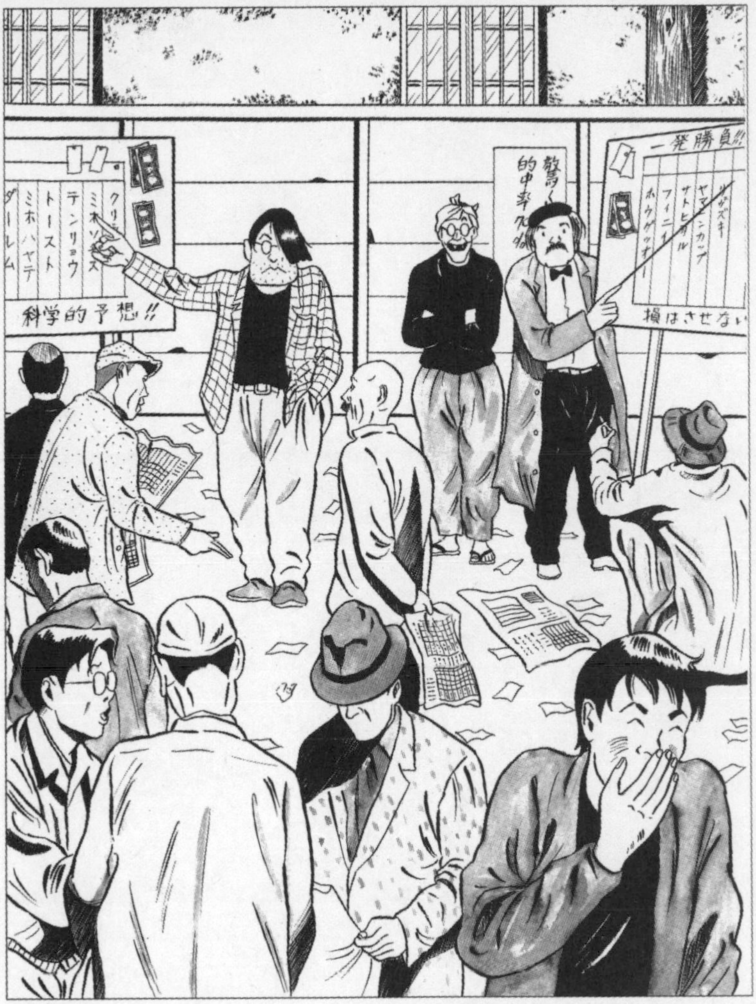
テンリュウ
トースト
ミホハヤテ
ダーレム
科学的予想!!
一発勝負!!
損はさせない

if you would call him the manager, but the man in charge had this aura that immediately said "scoundrel." Thinking about it now, for him to achieve that kind of overbearing presence, even though the job might have required it, must have involved no ordinary training.

There was a man who often showed up in the kitchen around midday. The trainees who were familiar with him knew exactly what to do. They chose some items from the ingredients lying everywhere and made him lunch. He came almost every day. Then suddenly he disappeared. A week or so later he showed up again for lunch, now with a bright white bandage wrapped thickly around the pinky finger of his left hand. No one said a thing. He took up his chopsticks like it was any other day.

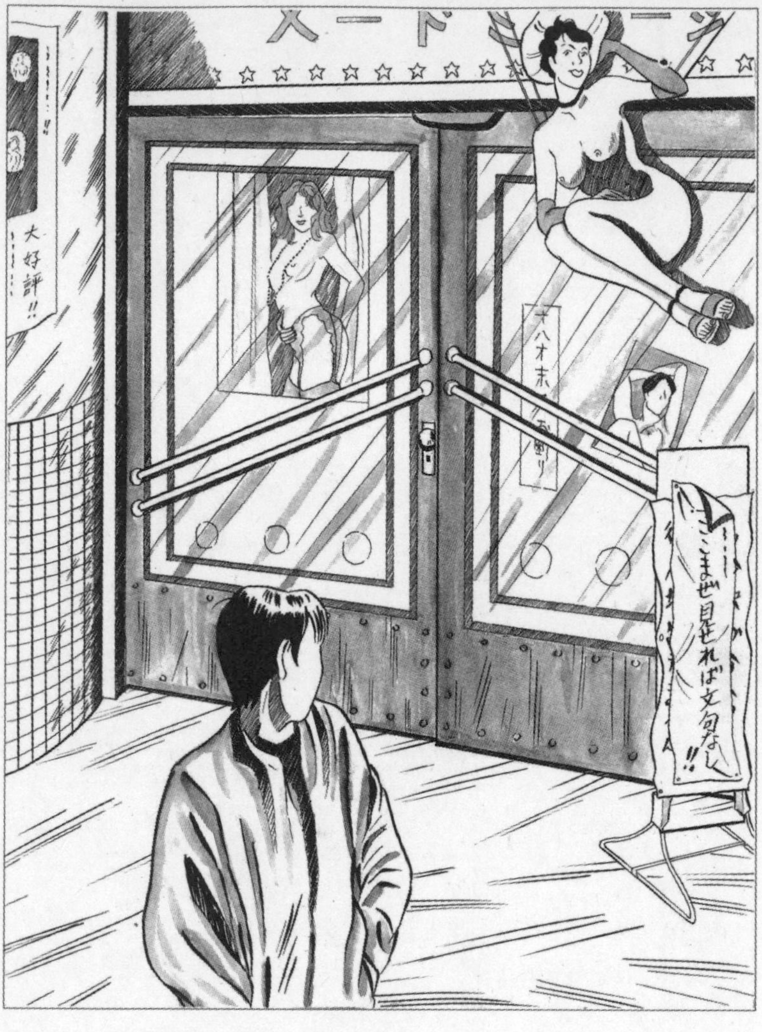
大好評!!
ここまぜ見せれば文句なし!!

As a callow nineteen-year-old, Asakusa seemed an amusing and stimulating neighborhood. On the way home from work, I'd sneak a peek at the nude photos on the strip clubs' signboards. I'd watch the hooligans fight among themselves. The queens beckoned to me...but eventually I quit. I felt bad for my friend who had gotten me the job, but I simply couldn't stand having to pay train fare.

So I returned once again to the blood bank. I learned much later that my friend quit soon after me, choosing to apprentice instead as a bartender. He and I might have drifted apart, but the racehorses I first got to know back then remain my good friends.

PORTRAIT OF THE ARTIST AS A WORKING MAN
RYAN HOLMBERG

Once a month for the past twenty-plus years, Tadao Tsuge (b. 1941) has had to visit the hospital for treatment for chronic hepatitis C.

Though lacking solid proof, he is sure that he contracted the disease while working for one of Nihon Pharmaceuticals' (Nihon seiyaku) ooze-for-booze blood banks as a young man. "At the time no one gave a thought to hygiene," he tells me. "So if you got a small cut on your hand, you just put on a band-aid and stuck your hands back in the blood. A huge number of people destroyed their livers that way. I got acute hepatitis about a year after I started working there. I had jaundice, my skin and eyes turned yellow. I had to take off two or three weeks of work." Did the company provide any care or compensation? "Nothing," he says. "They took no responsibility whatsoever, though thinking back now I suspect they knew the cause. Hepatitis C can take thirty years before it fully develops. I learned I had it about twenty years ago, when I was in my fifties, which was twenty-some years after I stopped working at the blood bank. I only learned later that quite a few blood-bank workers have died from the virus."[1]

Tadao tells me this over coffee a few train stations from his house in Chiba Prefecture, thirty miles north of Tokyo. We have arranged to meet in the morning before his monthly checkup, which is next door. "It seems that

---

[1] Unless otherwise noted, information pertaining to Tadao Tsuge's life and career stems from personal communications with the artist between 2012 and 2014.

Tadao Tsuge (c. 1971), photograph taken at Seirindō.

my work is too dark," he says as the conversation moves to comics. Dark is indeed his art's reputation.

The main reason is subject matter. Many of his comics are set in the once slummy neighborhoods of Tokyo's east side, the so-called "low city" (shitamachi) that was almost entirely flattened during the war. "Song of Shōwa" ("Shōwa go'eika"), for example, relates his painful childhood in Katsushika ward, in the former red-light district of Tateishi-chō. There are also the many depictions of the "human trash" (his words) who depended on the blood banks for a living, and the shit work that went on in the back rooms of that gristly industry. "Trash Market" ("Kuzu no ichi"), despite its unsavory cast, is actually one of the sunnier of such stories. Even when his comics are set in cheery bars or the settled homes of salaried life, as in "Gently Goes the Night" ("Yoru yo yuruyaka ni"), one finds male characters beset by anomie, festering resentment, traumatic memories, and unspeakable guilt from the war.

Tadao also attributes his comics' reputation for bleakness to a lack of outright gags, as well as a lack of plotted stories. He begins drawing with only a rough beginning, middle, and end in mind, with no script or breakdowns. "Part of the excitement of making comics," he says, "is seeing how things will turn out." He also thinks that his drawing stinks. "Women I am especially incapable of drawing." That might seem like feigned humility coming from a veteran cartoonist of fifty-plus years who has regularly created gripping images. But I have heard him say it enough times to be persuaded that he really believes it to be true. "No one's work sells worse than mine," he adds—but with a laugh. In fact, the entire conversation, despite the self-deprecations and recounted hardships, is surprisingly warm and bright. What Tadao shares with his characters is a potent lust for life despite a personal history of poverty, dead-end jobs, environmental violence, and illness.

If Tadao's readers are few by Japanese standards, his supporters are wholly committed. Probably no manga author outside the *otaku* community has as many books to their name with print runs under the usual cutoff of three thousand, with some just in the few hundreds. Most collections of his work have been published by either Hokutō Shobō, founded in 1972 by ex-*Garo* editor Shinzō Takano, or Waizu Shuppan, known for its behind-the-scenes books on Japanese pop music and cinema. Waizu also produces films, among them a handful of alternative manga adaptations, including cult director Teruo Ishii's melding of a few of Tadao's comics (including "Song of Shōwa") into the movie *Burai heiya* (1995). The artist recently acted in another Waizu-produced film, *Sturm und drang* (2013), where he plays the famed Taishō era illustrator and womanizer Yumeji Takehisa.

How Tadao describes his work to me is not new. "Too dark, won't sell, no commissions: one can't support a family on that pattern," he wrote in 1994. "So, for the past twenty years, I have pursued a living down one path and drawn comics on the side."[1] That "living" has been decidedly unglamorous. For ten years, Tadao worked at Nihon Pharmaceuticals, where he washed blood-collecting equipment, swabbed toilets, secretly dumped waste blood into city sewers, and (later, after pro-donation campaigns forced the industry to find new sources of blood) chopped and pressed human placentas. An interim was spent doing odd jobs, including the restaurant work recounted in "The Tadao Tsuge Revue." He has worked in a hardware store and delivered propane tanks nearly two times his body weight. Since the 1970s until recently, he ran the family jeans shop in the suburbs of Chiba.

However, there were times when Tadao supported himself solely on comics. The first was for about half a year beginning in late 1959. His elder brother, the legendary Yoshiharu Tsuge (b. 1937), had been asked by the publisher Wakaki Shobō to edit *The Labyrinth* (*Meiro*), a crime and thriller monthly for the kashihon market modeled on *The Shadow* (*Kage*) and *The City* (*Machi*), the mystery anthologies that launched the gekiga boom. Tadao was initially allowed a series of half-page comics (*hansai* manga)—short multi-page stories printed on half-size sheets of paper used by publishers since before the war to fatten volumes without the production costs of insert premiums. At this rookie stage, Tadao's drawing is primitive: a simplified version of the heavy outline-and-fill style that Yoshiharu was using, which in turn was partially derived from gekiga pioneer Yoshihiro Tatsumi's work,

---

1 Tsuge Tadao, afterword, *Burai heiya* (Tokyo: Waizu Shuppan, 1994), p. 269.

partially from the urbane coffeehouse cartooning style of Shinji Nagashima, and partially from the jazzy Ben Shahn and David Stone Martin-inspired spot illustrations in mystery magazines. The plots are familiar: revenge stories with a twist, mistaken identities, accidental witnesses who are hunted by the murderer. Tadao's knack for irony and mystery imparted a uniquely creepy quality to this genre material.

He doesn't mention it in "The Tadao Tsuge Revue," but Tadao began working a second time with his brother in late 1960. After the collapse of *The Labyrinth*, Yoshiharu shifted to samurai and ninja stories. Looking for a cheap assistant to help mass-produce knockoffs of Sanpei Shirato's *The Legend of Kagemaru* (*Ninja bugeichō: Kagemaru-den*, 1959–1962), Yoshiharu turned again to his younger brother. Tadao was assigned to draw figures and backgrounds, a fairly simple task given the style: sheaths of scratchy speed lines and inky spurts of blood, as ninja and samurai slash and blow each other apart. The primary fruit of the Tsuge brothers' collaboration was *Secret Scrolls of the Ninja* (*Ninja hichō*, 1960–1961), from the same Wakaki Shobō that had published *The Labyrinth*. Twelve or thirteen volumes were planned. The publisher pulled the plug at the fourth. Even before the final volume was published in May 1961, Tadao received fewer and fewer calls from Yoshiharu to come over and help. Soon he was out of a job entirely and forced to rely on his own artistic resources.[1] He succeeded in getting a few stories printed in mystery and *jidaigeki* (period drama) anthologies from Sanyōsha, a new kashihon publisher headed by Katsuichi Nagai, who a couple of years later would establish Seirindō, the future publisher of *Garo*. But the work was too little, and Tadao was forced to return to Nihon Pharmaceuticals, where he stayed until the end of 1968.

Garo provided the longest stretch of independence for Tadao: about three years between 1969 and 1971. The celebrated alternative comics magazine was

"A Black Memory," *The Labyrinth, vol. 14* (December 1959).

---

1 Tsuge Yoshiharu, "Tsuge Tadao no kurasa," in Tsuge Tadao, *Kinakoya no baasan* (Tokyo: Shōbunsha, 1985), pp. 228–29.

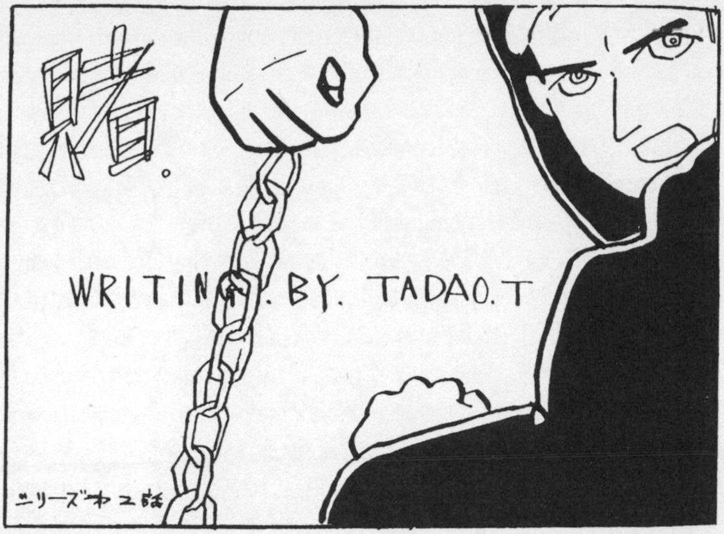
賭。
WRITING. BY. TADAO.T
"The Bet," The Labyrinth *[series 2], vol. 4 (April 1960).*

then at its peak, selling over 80,000 copies per month and able to pay its authors a living wage.[I] Thanks to their work for *Garo*, artists like Seiichi Hayashi, Maki Sasaki, and the elder Tsuge became darlings of the counterculture, which in turn opened the door to artistic careers beyond the touch-and-go market of alternative comics. But Tadao, who rarely even made the trip into Tokyo and was never part of any artistic social scene, hardly ever received external commissions. By the time *Garo*'s print run started plummeting in 1971 after the conclusion of magazine co-founder Sanpei Shirato's epic *The Legend of Kamuy* (*Kamui den*), the window of opportunity for Tadao had more or less closed. He was invited by the magazine *Housewives' Review* (*Fujin kōron*) to write an illustrated reportage piece on rural depopulation, only to have his submission rejected. It was later adapted for *Garo* as the manga "Uranishi Village" ("Uranishi no sato," March 1971), one of the world's earliest examples of extended comics journalism. For two years beginning in 1972, he penned an illustrated series on his favorite pastime, fishing, for *Monthly Hera* (*Gekkan hera*), named after a popular Japanese freshwater fish.[II] And that was pretty much it. It was back to a job.

Working—or, more generally, "doing something to get paid"—underwrites most of Tadao's early stories. Yet one cannot describe him as an artist interested in labor per se. In the 1960s and early '70s, there were many Japanese cartoonists and comics writers, in both the mainstream and alternative circuits,

I On this era of *Garo*, see Ryan Holmberg, *Garo Manga: The First Decade, 1964–1973* (New York: The Center for Book Arts, 2010).

II These articles are collected in Tsuge Tadao, *Tsuri tanoshi, bentō umashi* (Tokyo: Waizu Shuppan, 2010).

who feigned understanding of the Japanese working class. There were writer Ikki Kajiwara's sports melodramas for the best-selling *Shōnen Magazine*—*Star of the Giants* (*Kyojin no hoshi*, 1966–1971) and *Tomorrow's Joe* (*Ashita no jō*, 1967–1971)—about preternatural athletes from Tokyo's slums who become heroes of the underclass by achieving superstardom. There was Shirato's solidarity of the socially and economically oppressed in the *The Legend of Kamuy* (1964–1971). There were the hyperbolic symbols of alienation and castration in Yoshihiro Tatsumi's neo-gekiga stories (the ones that Drawn & Quarterly has translated), a few of which originally appeared in *Garo*. Though these artists were extremely hardworking, none of them had any experience of the shop floor, and I think it shows in their handling of the working poor. Shirato experienced poverty during and after the war, but after his first manga in 1957, at the age of twenty-five, he never again worked as anything but a cartoonist. Tatsumi published his first book in 1954, at the age of nineteen, and immediately found himself busy as a full-time artist. He ran his own small publishing house in the '60s, and opened a vintage manga store in 1986. Outside of that, Tatsumi did nothing but cartoon. Kajiwara dropped out of high school in the early '50s and worked only for a few years as an editor before ascending rapidly as a writer of stories and manga scripts for major boys' magazines.

Tadao, on the other hand, held blue-collar jobs almost continuously after graduating from middle school at the age of fifteen. By no means can one call his work "proletarian art," not least considering the artist's patent disinterest in heroic depictions of labor and the politics of class struggle. Tadao admits to a fair quotient of self-portraiture in the character of the apolitical copyist painter in "Up on the Hilltop, Vincent van Gogh…" ("Oka no ue de, Vinsento van Gohho wa…"). In describing Tadao's characters, writers associated with *Manga-ism* (*Manga shugi*, 1967–1974), Japan's first journal dedicated to comics criticism, insisted on using the name "people who work for a living" (*seikatsusha*), avoiding the politically laden term "laborer" (*rōdōsha*) and emphasizing the fact that the struggles Tadao depicts are typically rooted in his characters' home and private psychic lives.[1] Work is never uplifting in Tadao's comics, but the idea of organizing against exploitation is treated by his characters as a joke. On the one occasion when rebellion is seriously entertained, in "A Tale of Absolute and Utter Nonsense" ("Kōtō mukei dan"), it results in a self-annihilating outburst of resentment by the lumpen horde.

---

[1] See for example Kikuchi Asajirō, "Uragirareyuku chinmoku," *Garo* no. 93, Tsuge Tadao special supplementary issue (May 1971), p. 227. From a later era, see Miyaoka Renji, "Seikatsusha no kutsū to jiko hakai," in *Tsuge Tadao dokuhon* (Tokyo: Hokutō shobō, 1988), pp. 245–63.

His comics are still a worker's art of a literal sort. Most of them were made while Tadao was working full-time doing unskilled manual jobs, though in the present collection this only applies to the first and last two stories. His representations of blue- and white-collar workers at small and medium-sized firms are, though fictionalized, based on intimate insider experience. "What is most important to me," he said in an interview in *Garo* in 1970, "is depicting people as they are. I do it very carefully. I want to continue observing and drawing different types of people...It doesn't matter to me that I know so little about society in general. There really is too much I don't know. On the other hand, I truly understand the kind of people I used to work with. They don't have to say a thing, and still I understand them. I'm interested in the things the kind of factory workers I used to work with say on a daily basis."[I] Even Tadao's principal romantic type, the cool middle-aged vagabond—who, significantly, appears with greater frequency after the artist rejoined the workforce in the early '70s—was inspired by the men who frequented the blood banks and by the small-time gangsters from the black markets of his Occupation-era youth.

In general, then, Tadao is an artist for whom life experiences, especially those as a child growing up poor in Tokyo during the Occupation and those as a working teen and man, have meant far more to his practice than postwar Japan's iconic social and political currents. Still, he rarely did straight reportage or naked character sketches. In the early stories collected here, the shaping power of genre, particularly the detective material he had read and emulated in his youth, remained great. "Manhunt" ("Sōsaku"), for example, turns the police procedural inside out, such that the investigative journalists' own speculative interpretation of events gets forced upon the interrogated subject (the prodigal husband) as scripted memory. One might cite Kōbō Abe's novel *The Ruined Map* (*Moetsukita chizu*, 1967) or Shōhei Imamura's film *A Man Vanishes* (*Ningen jōhatsu*, 1967) as precedents for Tadao's manipulation of detective-genre codes around the social phenomenon of so-called "evaporating people" (*jōhatsu ningen*). One should also recognize the influence of the gothic travel fiction that his brother was publishing in *Garo*. Yoshiharu's wanderers probably inspired Tadao's characters to head out beyond the undeveloped fringes of Tokyo, where they often find themselves pulling up on the brink of an existential sublime. There is also the surrealistic deployment of photographic sources, which Yoshiharu used to powerful effect in works like "Nejishiki" (*Garo*, June 1968) following contact with the method as an assistant at Shigeru Mizuki's studio.

I Tsuge Tadao and Gondō Susumu, "Sengo ni mukete" (1970), rpt. in *Tsuge Tadao dokuhon*, pp. 88, 90.

月刊漫画 ガロ

NO.117

5

Garo, no. 117 (May 1973), cover art by Tadao Tsuge.

Engagement with photography led to fundamental changes in Tadao's artwork. Abandoning the rubbery contour-based mode of his kashihon comics, he began experimenting with texture and tone, resulting in a crosshatch-heavy style in which characters are sometimes obscured or disfigured by fields of splintery lines and stark tonal contrasts. Like many other cartoonists in the '60s, Tadao was particularly attracted to Ken Domon's so-called "beggar photographs" (*kojiki shashin*) of slums and the poor. Tadao copied a number of Domon's photographs into his stories by hand in order to infuse his settings with a heightened sense of realism and palpable everyday poverty. Images by other photographers were similarly adopted in "Song of Shōwa" to approximate the actual feel of the underclass city in the immediate postwar period. (When Yoshiharu began publishing stories about his own impoverished youth in the early '70s, the themes and graphics indicate that he had been inspired by Tadao's previous work in this vein.) Meanwhile, in "Manhunt," the use of photographs is both more literal and more metaphorical. The magic allure of a photograph of a train in a magazine becomes the impetus for the man's vanishing, while the journalists' account of his wanderings is rendered visually in a style in which the man literally disappears into the shadows and ghostly imprints of appropriated photographs.

Tadao was also an avid reader of literary fiction. Kenzaburō Oe and Takeshi Kaikō topped his list in the '60s. Before Tadao was recruited for *Garo* in 1968, he and two blood bank coworkers created their own mimeographed literary magazine. It lasted only two issues.[I] "I had dreams of publishing in one of the many literary magazines out there," he told me, "but I never took it very seriously. It didn't go anywhere." Nor was the effort wasted. His first work for *Garo*, "Vincent van Gogh," actually originated as a story in prose. It was remade as a comic when Shinzō Takano, who was essentially running *Garo* in the late '60s and early '70s, asked Tadao if he had something to submit to the magazine.

Ironically, it seems that Takano later left *Garo* because of one of Tadao's works. According to Tadao, *Garo*'s editors were purportedly of two minds about the last panel of "A Tale of Absolute and Utter Nonsense," which shows Hirohito in his postwar "human emperor" guise waving his homburg at the crowd. Takano supported the work's unedited publication. Katsuichi Nagai, owner of Seirindō, knowing the violence right-wing groups had inflicted on publishers in the past for acts of perceived *lèse-majesté*, erred on the side of caution. As a result, the last panel was left blank, making the referent of the protagonist's dying gasp ambiguous, but still guessable given its setting in the plaza in front of the Imperial Palace. Tadao, who did not learn about the censorship until after the issue was published, claims to have not been particularly troubled by the decision. But Takano apparently was, enough so to quit Seirindō and found his own publishing house, Hokutō Shobō, which became Tadao's greatest supporter in the '70s.[II] It also became the torchbearer of the original *Garo* spirit, recruiting many of the magazine's harder-edged contributors while *Garo* itself, after its flirtation with the "chrysanthemum taboo," veered increasingly toward the crass frivolousness of its next, *omoshiroshugi* (fun-ism) phase.

So, maybe Tadao's books haven't sold particularly well. Since the late '60s, even the artist's advocates have found his drawings a bit stiff. The average

---

I   Tsuge and Gondō, p. 80.

II   The above is hearsay. The censorship of the last panel of "A Tale of Absolute and Utter Nonsense" is a fact, but Tadao has never confirmed the behind-the-scenes story with the editors directly involved.

comics reader, expecting speedy narrative action from the medium, might get frustrated with Tadao's long tracts of dialogue. The settings might depress. Yet the sum total is as compelling as it is original. His stories cross and invert genres in ways not found anywhere else within international comics history. His experiments with photographic imagery, which generated stunning graphic effects, were part of a wider exploration of the boundary between fiction and documentary. And, as the creations of an artist who had the luxury of only momentary respites from the blue-collar grind, Tadao's comics offer an opportunity to imagine what it was actually like to live as a man inside the human trash market of postwar Japan.

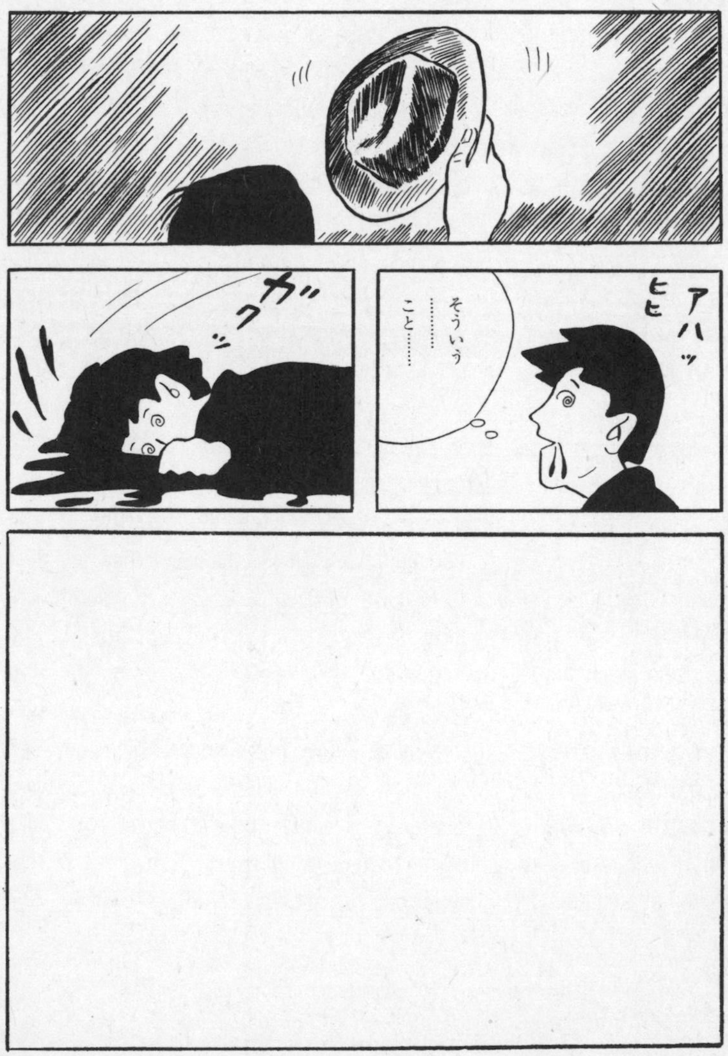
ガクッ
そういう……
こと……
アハッ
ヒヒ

"A Tale of Absolute and Utter Nonsense," Garo, no. 102 (February 1972).